ENVIRONMENTAL CRIME

Enforcement, Policy, and Social Responsibility

Mary Clifford, PhD
Department of Criminal Justice
St. Cloud State University
St. Cloud, Minnesota

AN ASPEN PUBLICATION®
Aspen Publishers, Inc.
Gaithersburg, Maryland
1998

Library of Congress Cataloging-in-Publication Data

Environmental crime: enforcement, policy, and social responsibility/
edited by Mary Clifford
p. cm.
Includes bibliographical references and index.
ISBN 0-8342-1009-6 (paper)
1. Offenses against the environment—United States.
2. Environmental policy—United States. 3. Environmental justice—United States.
4. Social responsibility of business—United States. I. Clifford, Mary, 1964–xxx.
HV6403.E595 1998
364.16'8—dc21
97-37192
CIP

Orders: (800) 638-8437
Customer Service: (800) 234-1660

About Aspen Publishers • For more than 35 years, Aspen has been a leading professional publisher in a variety of disciplines. Aspen's vast information resources are available in both print and electronic formats. We are committed to providing the highest quality information available in the most appropriate format for our customers. Visit Aspen's Internet site for more information resources, directories, articles, and a searchable version of Aspen's full catalog, including the most recent publications:
http://www.aspenpub.com
Aspen Publishers, Inc. • The hallmark of quality in publishing
Member of the worldwide Wolters Kluwer group.

Editorial Resources: Ruth Bloom
Library of Congress Catalog Card Number: 97-37192
ISBN: 0-8342-1009-6

Printed in the United States of America

1 2 3 4 5

For my grandmothers,
Frances Delaney Clifford,
Virginia Sanders Russell,
Marion Riker VanGelder, and
Betty Osborn VanValkenburgh,
and
in loving memory of their spouses,
William J. Clifford, Sr.,
David Russell,
George VanGelder, Sr.,
Richard VanValkenburgh;
Remembering kind actions taken on behalf of others.

Calvin and Hobbes

by Bill Watterson

Table of Contents

List of Contributors

Harold Barnett, PhD
Professor
Department of Economics
University of Rhode Island
Kingston, Rhode Island

Tim Carter, PhD
Assistant Professor of Criminal Justice
University of Houston—Downtown
Houston, Texas

Mary Clifford, PhD
Assistant Professor of Criminal Justice
Director of Private Security Minor
St. Cloud State University
St. Cloud, Minnesota

Mark A. Cohen, PhD
Director
Vanderbilt Center for Environmental
    Management Studies
Associate Professor of Management
Owen Graduate School of Management
Vanderbilt University
Nashville, Tennessee

Dion Dennis, PhD
Assistant Professor
Department of Criminal Justice, History,
    and Political Science
Texas A&M International University
Laredo, Texas

Sally M. Edwards, PhD
Assistant Professor
Department of Political Science
University of Louisville
Louisville, Kentucky

Terry D. Edwards, JD
Associate Professor
Administration of Justice Program
University of Louisville
Louisville, Kentucky

Joel Epstein, JD
Senior Associate and Consulting Attorney
Education Development Center, Inc.
Newton, Massachusetts

Bill Hyatt, JD
Professor of Criminal Justice
Western Carolina University
Cullowhee, North Carolina

Brian Lipsett, ABD
Doctoral Candidate
Administration of Justice Program
Executive Director of a Private Nonprofit
  Environmental Organization
Pennsylvania State University
State College, Pennsylvania

Ray Michalowski, PhD
Professor
Department of Criminal Justice
Northern Arizona University
Flagstaff, Arizona

Richard G. Opper, MPA, JD
Partner
Environmental Department
McKenna and Cuneo, LLP
San Diego, California

Donald J. Rebovich, PhD
Associate Professor
School of Public Administration and
  Urban Studies
Department of Criminal Justice
  Administration
San Diego State University
Calexico, California

Mark Seis, PhD
Assistant Professor
Department of Sociology
Ft. Lewis College
Durango, Colorado

Mark J. Spalding, JD, MPIA
Guest Scholar
Center for U.S.-Mexican Studies
University of California—San Diego
Consultant
International Environmental Policy and
  Law
Del Mar, California

Gary Walker, PhD
Associate Professor of Biology
Appalachian State University
Boone, North Carolina

Nanci Koser Wilson, PhD
Associate Professor
Criminology and Women's Studies
Indiana University of Pennsylvania
Indiana, Pennsylvania

Preface

Humans have always interacted with the natural environment. In the United States since the turn of the century, various groups interested in environmental issues have called attention to "questionable" environmental practices. The categorization of certain actions as questionable, however, has resulted in a seemingly endless series of debates about what constitutes "acceptable" environmental practices. Some groups seek potential economic gain by extracting natural resources from the Earth, while other groups fight to make sure old growth and wild areas are protected for future generations.

Beginning in the 1970s, environmental legislation was passed at an unprecedented rate. Throughout the 1980s and 1990s, legislative action expanded enforcement provisions, identifying criminal sanctions for environmental violations. Efforts by legislators to retract elements of environmental protection statutes in the mid-1990s were met with stiff opposition. Collectively, these actions continue to suggest a heightened interest in protecting the natural environment against the potentially negative effects of human enterprises. In spite of popular concerns, congressional action, and expanded enforcement provisions, the history of environmental enforcement efforts shows us that the application of these sanctions is the exception rather than the rule. Popular sentiment suggests people in the United States want to "get tough" on environmental crime.

At this point in the study of environmental crime, researchers and practitioners have uncovered more questions than answers. This primer on environmental crime is a compilation of relevant interdisciplinary research on the natural environment, social action, politics, economics, the legislative process, law enforcement, and the application of penalties. It reviews the history of environmental protection efforts and contains one of the first comprehensive discussions on the role of the criminal justice system in determining the social response to environmental crime. Selected case studies highlight some of the most controversial environmental enforcement issues, both in the United States and beyond its border.

While the central purpose of the book is to explore the enforcement of environmental protection legislation, the book ranges over many other topics. The contributing authors include several highly regarded individuals who are exploring the emerging field of environmental crime. Collectively they have brought this area of study to national and international arenas. They are writers, lawyers, academics, consultants, and researchers, and they represent the disciplines of biology, criminal justice, ecology, economics, law, political science, and sociology.

The diversity in the backgrounds of the contributors reflects the interdisciplinary nature of the subject matter. Although the authors represent various disciplines, they have a simple objective for the book: to expand the limits of discussion among solicitous individuals interested in environmental protection and enforcement issues.

The book is divided into four parts. Part I provides a discussion of background issues related to environmental crime as a subject of study. Chapter 1 introduces the readers to the difficulties and controversies associated with developing a definition of environmental crime. Chapter 2 reviews the history of the environmental movement in the United States. Chapter 3 discusses the intricate relationship between economics and politics, especially as it affects environmental issues. Chapter 4 provides a brief review of several scientific principles to be considered throughout the reading of this text. Finally, Chapter 5 outlines eight significant federal environmental statutes for which criminal penalties apply. In sum, the introductory section exposes the reader to a breadth of research issues related to understanding environmental crimes and subsequent enforcement efforts.

Part II introduces the enforcement options available to regulatory and police agencies pursuing environmental criminals. Chapter 6 discusses the federal structure for environmental protection. Using this federal structure as a model, many state environmental protection agencies have developed their own regulatory structures. Chapter 7 focuses on environmental enforcement efforts at the state and local level and discusses some of the environmental issues specific to local communities and enforcement agencies.

Once presented with information about the diverse types of environmental crimes, it becomes easier to understand the variety of tactics being used by police to enforce environmental statutes and apprehend environmental offenders. Chapter 8 identifies specific tactics used by police departments to investigate and arrest environmental offenders. Even when working closely with the police during the investigation and arrest stages, to achieve a conviction the prosecutor faces a formidable task. Chapter 9 looks at the legal requirements and the specific elements that make environmental crime cases unique. Addressing the controversies associated with environmental enforcement, Chapter 10 considers the record of sentences handed down in cases involving violations of environmental regulations. The central focus is on the effect of "overcriminalizing" environmental crimes.

Part III consists of chapters that present the practical and theoretical issues in environmental crime research that have thus far emerged as especially important. Introducing the section, Chapter 11 discusses the diverse types of environmental offenders, including federal and state governments and municipalities as well as private corporations and individuals. Chapter 12 challenges the present ethical foundations for human attitudes toward the natural environment by exploring the question, "Is there a place for environmental ethics?"

Building on the interdisciplinary foundation of environmental studies, Chapter 13 invites the reader to explore the social context of the current environmental debate. Images of the "natural environment" have been used to endorse products that are arguably harmful to the natural environment. Separating the message from the messenger can prove quite instructive. The construction and presentation of media images of the natural environment raise questions for even the most sincere environmentalist.

In Chapter 14, attention is given to the "global village." The environmental law issues being debated in the United States are also confronting other countries. Further, as indicated in this chapter, laws and/or enforcement agents responsible for addressing international environmental issues, such as water rights, air pollution, and toxic waste disposal, have not yet been adequately identified or implemented. Chapter 15 takes a look at the most prominent research on environmental crime to date. Continued research focused on both traditional and newly arising issues is essential.

The last section in the book, Part IV, is a collection of five case studies. The case studies were selected because they exemplify many of the issues and themes presented earlier in the text—activism, politics, economics, legislation, hazardous waste, government involvement, and international issues. For ease of both instructor and reader, Part IV was ordered to generally reflect the presentation of ideas in the book. Case Study 1 describes a community conflict over a hazardous waste incinerator project. Case Study 2 considers the statutory and regulatory provisions outlined for addressing one of the most contentious environmental problems in the United States, the hazardous waste problem.

Case Study 3 involves identification of the government as a possible environmental criminal. The case study concerns the Rocky Flats weapons manufacturing plant about 15 miles outside of Denver, Colorado. Although unique in certain aspects, it raises typical questions about the search for "environmental justice."

The issue presented in Case Study 4 became a matter for the courts. Controversy resulting from the Endangered Species Act (ESA) resulted in a Supreme Court decision to determine what Congress intended by the language used in the ESA. As with many cases of environmental conflict, a court was the ultimate arbitrator when the parties could not reach a resolution. Finally, Case Study 5 considers the "crimes" being committed at the U.S.-Mexican border. This case study centers on the role economics plays in establishing responsible international relations and environmental practices.

For reference purposes, several appendixes have been included at the back of the book. Appendix A is a glossary of terms that appear throughout the text. In addition, the student will notice several of the most important terms are identified at the beginning of each chapter. Appendix B includes a timeline of various important issues affecting the environmental attitudes in the United States. Appendix C provides an overview of the criminal provisions contained in existing environmental legislation. Appendix D is a list of precedent-setting environmental cases. Appendix E provides an example of one county's guidelines for environmental crimes investigations for law enforcement officers.

This text is one of the first books on environmental issues to integrate the social justice questions with an introduction and assessment of enforcement options. Decisions must be made about the role the criminal justice system will play in the future of environmental crime enforcement. Looking ahead to the criminal justice reaction is essential if communities, states, and the nation intend to produce a thoughtful, well-considered response to the growing number of environmental controversies.

The book is intended to be an introductory text. The topics covered here will introduce the reader to the complexities associated with the decisions that will ultimately determine the nature of human-environmental interactions. The history of the environmental movement, the environmental regulatory and enforcement structure, and predictions about the role of local law enforcement in environmental enforcement are only a few of the large number of topics that environmental studies must deal with. Citizens' groups, politicians, regulatory officials, corporate officials, and any individual or group interested in the ongoing environmental debates will benefit from having considered the questions raised by the authors in the following pages.

The future course of environmental protection legislation and its enforcement is uncertain. At present, citizens are frustrated. If little or no enforcement takes place, they will protest. But they also will protest if "overzealous" enforcement takes place. A resolution to the conflict must come through thoughtful, well-informed analysis and deliberation. Environmental crime research must acknowledge its dependence on diverse academic disciplines and its seemingly unavoidable placement within the criminal justice system. Future actions, be they legislative, administrative, judicial, social, cultural, or other, must be carefully considered. Significant weight should be given to determining the impact those actions will have on the criminal justice system's ability to effectively enforce pertinent legislation. Contributions to the achievement of this objective will need to come from practitioners in the field as well as academicians and researchers.

Environmental crime will continue to be a source of immense social, political, and economic conflict. My goal in editing this book was to inform, educate, frustrate, and provoke readers and inspire them to think critically about every environmental question. Critical commentary, by its essence, sparks controversy. Perhaps it will be, as Rachel Carson suggested in her introduction to *Silent Spring*, "the thousands of small battles that in the end will bring victory for sanity and common sense in our accommodation to the world that surrounds us."

Mary Clifford

Acknowledgments

A great round of applause is due to the individuals who contributed to this book. The project simply would not have been as comprehensive without their expertise. For their dedication to the project and their willingness to participate in this rather nontraditional endeavor, a heartfelt thanks to everyone.

Thanks to the many students who assisted us with our work. Bill Hyatt would like to recognize Kristen Hebert, a criminal justice major at Western Carolina, for all her hard work. I extend heaps of thanks to Shari McLean, Steve Cobel, and Dana Pope, students in the Masters in Public Administration program at Appalachian State University. Thanks also to the office staff, Sherrye Perry and Kathy Locke, at ASU for their help while I was there and for their diligence in forwarding mail since my departure. A special thanks to the office coordinator at St. Cloud State University in the department of criminal justice, Deb Yorek, and the work-study students, Jeanie Hoium, Julie Willy, Kim Behnen, and Tenile Gaslin. Thanks for doing so well the job that you do. Thanks to Rick, Jessica, and Susan at Aspen Publishers. Susan, I am particularly grateful to you for your infinite patience with me throughout this process. I hope that headache you got about the time this project started is finally gone.

On a personal note, I would like to recognize two groups of colleagues. I was fortunate to have spent time at Appalachian State; never has a group of people worked and played so well together. Thanks for the fond memories. To Dick Andzenge, Rich Lawrence, Kathleen Maloney, Bob Prout, Barry Schreiber, and Chuck Seefeldt at St. Cloud State I offer my gratitude. You helped me feel very welcome very quickly. I would also like to publicly thank Dean Ray Merritt, at St. Cloud State, for the reassign time he made available to me while I was finishing this book. The only reason I am not still revising and editing chapters is because of his willingness to accommodate the publication process. Along the same lines, thanks to Zane Dodds, a graduate student in the criminal justice graduate program, for his efforts with the security concentration. Your excellent work allowed me to have several worry-free hours when I needed them most.

Several students in the criminal justice program at St. Cloud State provided critical commentary about the first draft of the text. They are:

Heide Arbuckle	Scott McCarty
Kyle Bertelsen	Gary Menke
Anthony Bidwell	Tony Morrow
Brian Boll	Dan Mott
Scott Branson	Jacky Niska
Andy Claypool	Matt Schwartz
Jon Dahlvang	Stephanie Shaler
Tanya Dierkhising	Michael Snicker
Robin Dingmann	Chad Staul
Jesse Douvier	Tamara Stratton
Brent Foss	Chad Sylvester
Lynn Frasl	Jennifer Thomas
David Gerhardson	Josh Thompson
Ana Gorman	Mike Whisler
Amy Johnson	Sean Whitlock
Amy Kantorowicz	Kate Winkleman
John Kresl	Amy Woods

Their contributions helped to make this a better book for other students. I would like to thank them.

As always, thanks to my family for their constant support: to Julie, the "Clifford" responsible for the artwork on the back book cover, a woman as intellectually impressive as her art; to Dave, Deb, Steve, and Tami, for your love, the laughs, and the encouragement. To the VanGelder family, thanks for putting up with me. Gratitude extends beyond words to my parents Sue Russell Clifford and Bill Clifford. I am extremely fortunate to have parents who continue to inspire me. They continue to teach me; suggest the lessons in life are what life is all about; and remind me often to play more. When I grow up, I want to be just like them. Finally, a world of thanks to the love of my life, Mark VanGelder, for putting up with all the long hours, for doing all of the cooking and most of the laundry, and especially for smiling politely when I brought up the subject of doing a second book.

An Introduction to the Study of Environmental Crime

Numerous social science disciplines have directed specific research efforts toward increasing human understanding of environmental conditions throughout the world. "Environmental" research, however, has traditionally focused almost exclusively on social, cultural, political, and/or economic environments, rather than the natural environment. Biological or ecological systems and related components have been mainly the concern of the natural sciences, especially biology, ecology, chemistry, and physics.

Clearly, the full significance of the information collected about the natural environment is difficult to fathom. And of course a large number of questions remain unanswered. While the objectives in the natural sciences are, arguably, different from the objectives for research in the social sciences, the natural science community does not hold a corner on the market of unknowns. Questions about the social conditions are equally intriguing, and more remain than have been answered. Relatively recently, sociologists and other social scientists have begun to view environmental problems as "social in nature by virtue of both their origins and their consequences."[1] Consequently, efforts to understand the impact of human actions on the natural environment are becoming more commonplace, including studies intended to assess the long-term effects of human intervention on natural systems. This means that students interested in developing a comprehensive understanding of both human and natural environments must become comfortable with various types of scientific research.

In order to meet the needs of these students, universities across the country are creating interdisciplinary "environmental studies" programs. These programs are usually structured to be easily attached to any existing degree program. For example, a student majoring in business and a student majoring in chemistry could both minor in environmental studies.

1

An understanding of concepts common to both the natural and social sciences will be important for any student interested in environmental studies. It is for this reason Part I includes contributions from a variety of disciplines. Clearly both natural and social sciences have made and will continue to make contributions to the study of the interaction between social and natural environments.

More important, parties on either side of the ongoing environmental conflict have offered academic research in the hopes of substantiating their claims. In some cases, the results are not easily accessible to all parties with an expressed interest in a specific conflict. In some cases, research findings are presented in such a way that only someone with detailed disciplinary knowledge would be able to interpret the method used for analyzing the data being considered or identify the implications of the study's conclusions. Students interested in environmental studies must become familiar with the idiosyncrasies associated with various disciplines. This multiplicity of understanding will make it possible to better understand the data being collected to explain the natural environment and the human impact.

The first chapter in Part I describes the difficulties associated with defining the term *environmental crime*. Several of the current controversies being debated among academics and practitioners are presented for the reader's consideration. While a definition of *environmental crime* is necessary for comparative and descriptive analysis, it quickly becomes apparent that various activities commonly referred to as environmental crimes do not lend themselves easily to such a specific classification. Therefore, the authors emphasize two definitions for consideration: a philosophical definition and a legal definition.

Once the definitional issues have been discussed, several contributions from the social sciences are presented. Chapter 2 provides a history of the environmental movement in the United States. It first describes the roots of the modern environmental movement and then portrays the "conservation" and "preservation" ideologies from their beginnings through their evolution up to the present. Chapter 3 discusses the economic and political elements associated with the ongoing environmental conflict. Several recent environmental conflicts pit "jobs" against "the environment." Some of the themes of this controversy are explored, and attention is given to the possibility of jobs *and* the environment.

Chapter 4, which is written by a biologist, reviews crucial scientific principles relevant for studying environmental issues. It is important to remember that the issues discussed in this book are linked to natural science principles as well as social science interpretations.

To understand the environment as a living system, it is important to remember the scientific principles used to explain the Earth's life-generating systems. Of course, it is also important to remember that the analyses of the Earth's systems offered by biology, ecology, chemistry, and physics are outlined within a social context. Galileo and Darwin are two good reminders of this. Therefore, to understand the objectives, motivations, and ultimate consequences stemming from human interaction with the natural environment, one must develop an ability to critically evaluate social and scientific analyses.

In the social sciences, answering environmental questions involves the assessment of social policies, economic decisions, legal protections, and perceptions of risk or harm, for example. Clearly, a natural science explanation would be sought if, for example, someone had a question about the molecular breakdown of the organic and inorganic materials processed through a hazardous waste incinerator. But this is not the only issue of concern associated with hazardous waste incineration. Someone else might wonder why people across the country are rejecting proposals to site hazardous waste incinerators in their communities. The social sciences are better equipped to address this specific issue.

Chapter 5, the final chapter in Part I, integrates science and social analysis. Eight pieces of environmental protection legislation are presented for consideration. Legal scholars may argue about the social influences most directly relevant to understanding existing environmental protection legislation, but a discussion of this topic would not be complete without a consideration of the influence of science. Scientific information is integrated throughout legislative and regulatory decision-making processes to help determine acceptable limits for pollution. Although not a pure process (some contend that "scientific findings" can easily be manipulated to serve politics or economic ends), the laws established to provide environmental protection result from the reconciliation of the best *scientific* understandings within an explicitly *social* process.

The chapters in Part I provide a solid foundation for the remainder of the book. The natural and social science information related to environmental studies contained therein provides readers with a foundation upon which to build their own understanding of environmental crimes. More important, perhaps, the readers are reminded of the role natural science and social science inquiry plays in all environmental research.

REFERENCE

1. S. Cable and C. Cable, *Environmental Problems, Grassroots Solutions: The Politics of Grassroots Environmental Conflict* (New York: St. Martin's Press, 1995), 4.

CHAPTER 1

Defining "Environmental Crime"

Mary Clifford and Terry D. Edwards

TERMS		
Chicago School of Human Ecology	mala in se	
civil enforcement	mala prohibita	
common law	manifest	
compliance	midnight dumping	
crimes against nature	natural law	
criminal enforcement	natural order	
criminaloid	noncompliance	
environmental criminology	regulatory enforcement	
green crime	Ross, E.A.	
invasion, dominance, and succession	strict liability	
	Sutherland, Edwin	
	symbiosis	
legal standard	wildlife crimes	

Many of us have heard the term *environmental crime* in national news stories or in local newspaper articles. It typically refers to crimes involving hazardous wastes, irresponsible corporate activities, water contamination, or other violations of environmental law. While our collective understanding of the term is useful for contextualizing media information, news stories do not explicitly identify the kinds of activities that constitute environmental crime.

As students of the subject themselves, researchers must establish specific parameters from which to begin a more detailed analysis of the topic of environmental crime. The topic is so new that definitional clarity has not yet been developed. One objective is to determine whether an action is appropriately—or at least consistently—identified as an environmental crime. This chapter is structured to make progress toward that goal.

This chapter will explore the difficulties associated with developing a definition for a term that has been extensively used in popular culture. A second issue to be explored is the use of natural science terms in social science research. The closely related histories of criminology and sociology provide insight into some of the definitional difficulties. Attention is given to the trend in academic research to categorize environmental crime as a subdivision of white-collar crime. Finally, two definitions of environmental crime are offered—a philosophical definition and a legal definition.

5

ENVIRONMENTAL CRIME, CRIMINOLOGY, AND WHITE-COLLAR CRIME

The term *environmental crime* has been used in popular journals, magazines, and newspapers to describe acts that cause harm to the natural environment. *Offenses against the environment* is another phrase offered to clarify the concept. Yet at the current time, both terms continue to be used without a specific definition or identification of the activities to which the terms are referring. What does it mean to refer to something as an environmental crime, or to commit an offense against the environment? Neither scholars nor practitioners offer much to help develop an understanding of how the terms are used. We argue that the terms presently exist without real meaning.[1]

As discussed above, the term environmental crime has been used extensively over the last several years, although no common boundaries for the term have been identified. Several of the examples of their use are offered for the reader's consideration. But we still have a way to go before we reach our goal—to establish a definition for environmental crime. To some degree, the collective history of sociology and criminology complicates the current issue. Both disciplines have used natural science terms to describe social phenomena. Some traditional and contemporary criminal justice terms are used to illustrate the related linguistic complexities. And finally, attention will be given to the preliminary efforts by academics to classify environmental crime as a subcategory of white-collar and organized crime.

Contemporary Uses

The term environmental crime has been used almost indiscriminately and without any universally accepted definition. Laws, organizations, government agencies, academics, lawyers, and others have added to the confusion by using the term without specifying what they mean. A review of contemporary uses may prove instructive.

A variety of laws have been enacted that include the use of the term environmental crime. In 1992, a federal Environmental Crimes Act (H.R. 5305) was passed. Although no analysis has been done to determine specific numbers, several states have enacted "environmental crime statutes."[2] The U.S. Department of Justice maintains an Environmental Crimes Unit,[3] and at least one U.S. attorney's office has an environmental crime coordinator.[4] The Federal Bureau of Investigation dedicated an entire issue of its *Law Enforcement Bulletin* to environmental crimes.[5]

Along the same lines, the U.S. Environmental Protection Agency maintains an Office of Criminal Enforcement and publishes a brochure to assist the law enforcement community. At the state level, Massachusetts has formed an Environmental Crimes Strike Force[6] as has Los Angeles County,[7] and the Sheriff's Office in Palm Beach County, Florida, has an Environmental Crimes Unit.[8] The International Association of Chiefs of Police (IACP) has an Environmental Crime Committee[9] and has published a model training introduction entitled *Environmental Crime Enforcement.*[10] The American Bar Association (ABA) has two committees whose focus is environmental crime: the Environmental Crimes and Enforcement Committee is part of the Section of Natural Resources, Environmental, and Energy Law, and the Subcommittee on Environmental Crimes is part of the Business Law Section.[11]

Many conferences and seminars have also adopted the term. In October 1989, the ABA sponsored the Environmental Crimes Conference in Buffalo, New York, which drew over 300 prosecutors and investigators.[12] In April 1994, the Southern Environmental Enforcement Network (SEEN) sponsored a nationally broadcast training seminar entitled "Introduction to Environmental Crime Enforcement," which drew over 1,000 attendees.[13] The American Prosecutors Research Institute (APRI), the research affiliate of the National District Attorneys Association (NDAA), sponsored the National Conference on the Prosecution of Environmental Crime in May 1994, attracting over 125 attendees.[14] With the increased attention being given to environmental crime, even researchers and academics, perhaps the most likely to be interested in definitional clarity, have yet to develop a clear definition for the concept. Further research is essential if an accurate and useful definition is to be developed.

Frequently environmental crime is characterized in very broad terms. Consider examples from some of the following academic efforts. For in-

Calvin and Hobbes   by Bill Watterson

Source: CALVIN AND HOBBES © 1989 Watterson. Dist. by UNIVERSAL PRESS SYNDICATE. Reprinted with permission. All rights reserved.

stance, one author asserted that society increasingly recognizes the threat of environmental crimes, but he does not offer any guidance as to what the term means or what the threat might be.[15] Another author claimed that the "increased willingness of courts to view environmental crime for what it really is—an egregious departure from responsible citizenship—is an equally important factor in explaining 'the rise in the number of environmental crimes.'"[16(p.919)] Again, without offering any definitional structure, another article concludes, "The prosecution of individuals and corporations for environmental crimes has been increasing steadily in recent years."[17(p.1123)]

In addition to characterizations and categorizations of environmental crime, authors draw conclusions about environmental crime, without offering any concrete definition of the term. Typical of these statements was an article that asserted "Environmental crimes pose serious risks to the public and the environment."[18(p.1179)] The question is, can a reasonable person assume then, any act that poses "serious risk to the public and the environment" is an environmental crime? Such a broad application brings with it some serious questions. Could war, for example, be classified as an environmental crime?

Finally, public opinion polls sometimes probe the public's view of environmental crime, usually without providing an adequate definition. For example, a 1984 poll attempted to measure public perceptions of the seriousness of specific criminal activities. The researchers specifically noted that environmental crime ranked seventh in the poll, ahead of heroin smuggling, skyjacking, and armed robbery.[19,20] The poll, however, illustrated environmental crime by using three classic water and air pollution cases,[21] each of which involved the introduction of a harmful chemical agent into the air or water. In other words, the respondents were led to consider "worst-case scenarios." Had the examples involved littering, threats against spotted owls, or fishing without dolphin-free tuna nets, it is unclear whether the general public would have classified these acts as environmental crimes. Certainly, with a broader definition, it is unclear if environmental crimes would have ranked as high in the survey.

Natural Law and Environmental Criminology

Mainstream perceptions of crime and criminals may vary dramatically from the ideas held by academics and criminal justice practitioners. An outsider interested in environmental issues coming into the field of criminal justice for the first time might initially be confused by references to natural law and social ecology. These terms have been used in the social science and legal disciplines to describe social factors. Rather than referring to natural ecosystems, **natural law** refers to the "immutable moral principles" associated with the natural order, including principles that were promoted by the Church and that later directed the development of English **common law**,[22] the legal system from which the U.S. court system derived. The term **natural order** indicates a moral assessment of the natural *social* order. Throughout the history of criminal justice, the concept of natural law has been associated with the view that certain actions are **mala in se** (i.e., evil in themselves). Certain actions, in other words, are so heinous, they go against the moral order of society and are considered violations of the natural order. Murder, rape, and robbery are good examples, and they are all thought to be deserving of harsh punishment. These are contrasted with **mala prohibita** acts, or acts considered evil because they have been prohibited by law, such as drug use, prostitution, and traffic violations. The assumption of English common law is that law aids in ensuring preservation of the natural order. But this natural order does not refer to the natural environment.

Crimes against nature is another traditional concept established under the common law. The term typically refers to acts that offend the moral sensibilities of society. Examples include homosexuality, oral copulation, and child molestation.[23] Again, while these acts are argued to go against the natural order, they are not crimes involving the natural environment or ecosystems.

One last example. Criminologists and sociologists have traditionally referred to social ecology and the social environment and have established a school of thought under the categorical heading **environmental criminology**. The theories included within the field of environmental criminology have proven extremely interesting yet tell us little about "environmental crime."

In developing the "theory of human ecology" in 1936, Robert Park used terms that until that time had been reserved for describing the natural environment.[24] Consider the following description:

> Plant life and animal life are seen as an intricately complicated whole, a web of life in which each part depends on almost every other part for some aspect of its existence. Organisms in their natural habitat exist in an on-going balance of nature, a dynamic equilibrium in which each individual must struggle to survive. Ecologists study this web of interrelationships and interdependencies in an attempt to discover the forces that define the activities of each part. . . . From the study of plant and animal ecology [Robert Park] derived two key concepts that formed the basis of what he called the "theory of human ecology."[25(p.118)]

For example, **symbiosis** refers to relationships between species that offer benefits to each, and **invasion, dominance, and succession** refers to a process in which a new species invades an area, comes to dominate it, and then drives out other life forms. Although Park used these terms to elucidate the emergence of certain social conditions, it was not long before others were using them to explain the occurrence of criminal activity.

The **Chicago School of Human Ecology** was one result of Park's effort. Delinquent activities were associated with the individuals' environment— their social environment. In the early 1970s, the school flourished. Efforts were focused on providing theoretical explanations for the relationship between crime and environmental factors (e.g., urbanization, social conditions, and family structure). As the area of study emerged, a debate arose over what term would best indicate its essence, and some argued that *environmental studies* more accurately reflected spatial aspects of crime and justice than did the term *ecological studies*.

> In the United States ecological research has become largely divorced from theory and focuses instead on the description of spatial aspects of crime and justice. . . . Spatial distributions of various aspects of the criminal justice system have also been examined. These are more accurately described as "geographical" or "environmental" studies of crime and justice rather than ecological studies.[26] (pp.178–179)

Brantingham and Brantingham provide one of the most comprehensive explanations of what has developed into the criminological discipline referred to as environmental criminology. Their 1991 edited collection of articles, entitled *Environmental Criminology*, brings together scholars whose works are centered around the idea "that criminal events must be understood as [unions] of offenders, victims or criminal targets, and laws in specific settings at particular times and places."[27](p.2) The emphasis in this branch of criminology is on spatial and locational patterns of behaviors by both offenders and victims of criminal acts.

> The studies that could most clearly be classified as environmental criminology during the 1970s and early 1980s tended to explore patterns of property offenders and to analyze the range of social, geographic, and perceptual/cognitive factors influencing the situations and settings in which crimes are likely to occur.[28](p.239)

Environmental criminology has emerged as an established discipline, focusing on social ecology or structural (environmental) factors and their relationship to criminal activity. Crime and victimization are thought to be related to community design or the structural manifestations of poverty, for example. The work being done in this area is well respected, and continues today; however, it does not address—or really even relate to—environmental crime.

Environmental crime is a relatively new area of study within criminology, and just as academics argued in the 1970s about the best term for describing the emerging field of human ecology, researchers studying environmental crime confront the problem of what to call it. Some believe the term environmental crime, because of its close association to the field environmental criminology, is limiting or inadequate and potentially confusing. Further, the term implies some type of crime has been committed, yet it is commonly applied in cases involving accidents or incidents where no criminal charges are being considered. Perhaps for this reason it is more appropriate to use the phrase *offense against the environment*. Other terms and phrases have also been suggested. The term *environmental deviance*, for example, has been argued to be a better indicator of the concept at issue,[29] because it would not be as easily confused with the concept of environmental criminology, nor would it imply criminal behavior prior to a finding of guilt. While the suggestions are intriguing, the fact is that the term *environmental crime* continues to be so pervasive in the literature that trying to replace it with another term would probably complicate matters further.

Linkages to Existing Crime Classifications

Despite its widespread use, not a single article or author has provided a theoretically useful definition of the term *environmental crime*. Without offering even a hint of a definition, researchers and practitioners working in the area of criminal justice have begun to identify environmental crime as a subset or category of more well-established criminological theories. One article, for example, asserts that "over the last few years, as a result of legislative and administrative reforms and a change in emphasis by law enforcement entities, environmental crimes have attained parity with other so-called white collar or managerial crimes."[30(p.161)] Another states that "no longer are environmental crimes to be considered lesser offenses than other white collar crimes."[31(p.407)] The tendency has been to focus environmental crime studies on crimes committed by corporations or businesses and by organized crime syndicates.[32–35] As a consequence, environmental crime theory is linked to white-collar crime and organized crime theory.[36]

We argue here and elsewhere[37] that environmental crime as a subject of study is not easily contained within existing theoretical frameworks. Too many types of environmental crimes are omitted if white-collar and organized crime theory is used as the baseline for studying environmental crime.

In light of the lack of definitional clarity, outlining the specific attributes cited when environmental crime is discussed may be the most responsible approach to constructing a useful definition.

ON DEVELOPING A THEORY OF ENVIRONMENTAL CRIME

Although a potentially limiting strategy, environmental crime has been discussed as a subset of white-collar crime for good reason. The student engaged in a dedicated quest for a better understanding of environmental crime will eventually be struck by the similarities between the current discussion of environmental crime and **Edwin Sutherland**'s earlier discussion of white-collar crime.[38] Beginning in the 1940s, Sutherland offered a dramatic shift in focus from traditional notions of crime. His pioneering discussions of the white-collar criminal called into question traditional understandings of criminological theory. Sutherland referenced the term **criminaloid**, presented in the work by **E.A. Ross**, as the first significant sociological statement about white-collar crime.[39] Sutherland wanted the disciplines of sociology and criminology to focus on the overlap between immoral and illegal behavior. Using Ross's term as a centerpoint, Sutherland argued that the powerful in society determined what was to be acceptable, and therefore what would constitute legal (and illegal) behavior. Sutherland's interest was in focusing studies on the relationship between law construction and the benefits people in power received from creating such laws. Ross defined criminaloids as being "the powerful and wealthy corporate and business leaders who victimized an unsuspecting public—enjoyed immunity from the law, exhibited 'moral insensibility,' and preferred to prey on the anonymous public."[40(p.14)] Ross predicted they would continue to flourish until the "growth of morality overtakes the growth of opportunity to prey."[41(p.14)] In short, Sutherland believed people in power made laws to suit their needs. Therefore, when questionable actions were taken, they had the law on their side. It could be argued, however, that many of their actions constituted questionable or immoral activities. With the reintroduction of Ross's concept, criminological research efforts were expanded to include (among other things) the study of law, the legislative process, and the impact of the powerful on the study of crime and criminals. Society, including sociologists and criminologists, was warned against the excesses of the powerful, hoping to raise public consciousness and curb the potentially harmful behavior of the powerful.

A clear parallel exists between the actions taken by what Ross called the criminaloid and the commission of environmental crimes. Although many argue actions such as dumping toxic waste into a local stream or emitting

INSIGHT

Love Canal

Before the turn of the century, William T. Love planned to dig a canal to reroute water from the Niagara River around Niagara Falls. The project was intended to generate electricity, but with construction under way, investors withdrew money and the canal was left abandoned. Known since that time as Love Canal, a 3,000-foot-long, 60-foot-wide, and 10-foot-deep trench remained within the city limits of Niagara Falls, New York.[1]

In 1942 Hooker Electrochemical Company bought the canal for chemical waste disposal. In a 10-year period, more than 21,000 tons of chemical waste were disposed of in Love Canal.[2] Only a few months after dumping began, Hooker's operation violated most of the disposal practices recommended at the time of purchase.[3] By 1953 the canal was covered over with earth and clay and sold to the school board of Niagara Falls for the token sum of one dollar. Construction of an elementary school began in 1954, and the school was opened to students in 1955. Eventually a residential community of roughly 1,000 families was built on land adjacent to the school.

As early as 1950, chemical odors were noted. Children playing barefoot near the school developed skin problems on their feet. Holes would spontaneously appear in playing fields when rusty 55-gallon drums collapsed. Spontaneous chemical fires and small explosions were reported.

Beginning in 1976 a series of events brought attention to the health risks at the canal. Environmental monitoring, health surveys, and media coverage indicated that something might be horribly wrong. In 1978 government officials began to hold public meetings to discuss the problems. Local citizens became frustrated with the lack of information concerning the dangers this area posed to them.

In August 1978, the area was declared a "serious threat" to the health, safety, and welfare of those using it.[4] The governor announced the state would buy all of the approximately 300 homes adjacent to the canal. Families in rings I and II (i.e., those closest to the canal) were permanently relocated. The families in ring III wanted to know why the state did not move them. They wondered why people living across the street had been evacuated but they were told their homes were safe.

After two years marked by several noteworthy events, the citizens living in ring III were relocated. The final straw was the publication of an Environmental Protection Agency (EPA) chromosome study that showed an elevation in chromosome damage among Love Canal residents. EPA officials were held hostage for six hours in the office of the Love Canal Homeowners Association. The remaining Love Canal homes were purchased in August 1980. On April 1, 1981, proposed studies of the health effects of Love Canal were cancelled by the Reagan administration.[5]

Although many remain skeptical, studies suggest the contamination at Love Canal has been cleaned up, and people began moving back into the area in 1993.

1. H.M. Vyner, *Invisible Trauma: The Psychosocial Effects of the Invisible Environmental Contaminants* (Lexington, MA: Lexington Books, 1988), 41.
2. Vyner, *Invisible Trauma*, 41.
3. C.E. Colten, and P.N. Skinner, *The Road to Love Canal: Managing Industrial Waste before EPA* (Austin, TX: University of Texas Press, 1996), 153.
4. Vyner, *Invisible Trauma*, 42.
5. Vyner, *Invisible Trauma*, 48.

poisonous gases into the air are unconscionable or immoral, with economic growth and industrialization *en vogue*, the morality of these actions has not been questioned until recently.[42] Several disasters linked to abuses of power from corporate officials and legislators have reinvigorated the works of Ross and Sutherland. Almost a century after Ross's work, and 50 years after Sutherland's plea to revisit the construction of crime and criminals, their work is being used to explain both the justification for environmental damage, and the social reaction to environmental crimes.

Criminologists agree that environmental crime is only one type of white-collar crime. But it is important to note that not all "environmental crime" is white collar.[43] Consider, for example, the sale of exotic animals or animal skins. If such black market operations involve organized crime figures, would it then be best to classify them as white-collar crime or organized crime? If those trafficking in rare and exotic animals work in state-owned zoos or private animal refuges, would it be best to identify their actions as crimes against the state, organizational crime, or corporate crime? Should all of these activities be classified as environmental crimes? The need for further definitional clarity quickly becomes apparent. Certainly, these acts are not necessarily best classified as white-collar crimes. But at this point, when a definition of environmental crime has not been established, one must wonder whether treating environmental crimes as separate category will prove to be useful. This crucial question is currently being debated by criminologists, and the answer is not certain.

There are other examples where environmental crimes do not fit the white-collar crime model. Take Benjamin's Autobody Shop or Chase's Dry Cleaners. These two small businesses depend on the use of hazardous chemicals and the subsequent disposal of hazardous wastes. Many would agree that individual business owners who do not comply with the law in their use of these chemicals are committing an environmental crime. But are such offenses white-collar crimes? Or are they best classified as blue-collar or occupational crimes? Is the inappropriate use of the chemicals a white-collar crime and the inappropriate disposal of the chemicals an environmental crime? Does classifying them as environmental crimes provide a better picture of the activities researchers are interested in studying?

Environmental crime, as a field of study, is new. The absence of a theoretical framework for studying the types of acts classified as environmental crime slows efforts to develop a comprehensive understanding of the phenomenon, and this in turn delays enactment of preventive measures and enforcement provisions. Reviewing Ross's and Sutherland's work can provide an opportunity for researchers and students interested in developing theories to sharpen their understanding of environmental crime. Students should be cautioned, however, against using white-collar crime theory exclusively. They may overlook important elements as a result.

Students must also remember that, as the field of criminology developed, little, if any, attention was given to environmental issues. Only recently has the topic of environmental crime emerged. Thus, criminologists are just beginning the lengthy process of integrating explanations for the commitment of environmental crimes with existing theories about crime and justice. As the process of theory development continues, gaps and limitations will undoubtedly be revealed. These must be acknowledged. Given time, findings from academic research will be combined with practitioner experiences in the field to provide a more refined understanding.

ENVIRONMENTAL CRIME AS A PHILOSOPHICAL CONCEPT

Before discussing environmental crime as a legal concept, we need to consider several issues from a more philosophical perspective. For example, what environmental damage is occurring but is not covered under the existing environmental protection statutes? Should criminal provisions be attached as sanctions for less serious environmental violations? Is more environmental legislation needed? Is there already too much environmental protection legislation? When establishing philosophical definitional criteria, at least five different elements may be considered: (1) the type of activity, (2) the specific act(s), (3) the actor(s), (4) the social status of the actor(s), and (5) the sanction applied.[44]

First, consider the type of activity. There are a wide variety of activities casually referred to in the popular media and the academic literature as environmental crimes.[45] It is unclear, however, whether environmental crimes include only those actions that directly diminish the quality of the environment (e.g., pollution) or whether they include actions that have the potential to do harm to the environment. Or, posed another way, to what degree does the environment have to be involved before a "regular" crime becomes converted into an environmental one?

For example, it can be argued that a simple murder (if there is such a thing) adversely affects a biological system. If someone shoots John, killing him, a biological system has been altered—John's. Most people would agree the act of murder is appropriately labeled a crime against a person. But would labeling it an environmental crime be appropriate? Consider the practice of ethnic cleansing, where an entire culture is placed in danger of extinction. Could or should this be classified as an environmental crime?

INSIGHT

Bug Smuggling: An Environmental Crime?[1]

Welcome to the world of exotic insect contraband, where sellers have PhDs and buyers have names like Smithsonian.[2]

Since 1991, U.S. Fish and Wildlife Service agents have seized 40,000 butterflies, moths, and beetles from collectors from all over the United States. At least five collectors have pleaded guilty to violations of federal laws, including the Endangered Species Act and the Lacey Act.

Many entomologists and other collectors argue the government has spent money protecting species that do not need protection. Much of the government action is directly linked to the Lacey Act. Almost 100 years old, the Lacey Act identifies federal penalties for anyone who poaches a plant or animal protected in another country and then brings it into the United States. Penalties can include up to five years in jail and a $250,000 fine. The law was revised in 1981 to include insects.

A significant portion of the conflict concerns the issue of scale. Entomologists and lepidopterists who collect insects and butterflies for study argue that their impact is minimal when compared to habitat destruction. Others disagree, arguing the removal of any amount of butterflies can impact the overall butterfly population.

In June 1996, after a one-year investigation, special agents with the U.S. Fish and Wildlife Service raided a Fort Davis, Texas, smuggling operation. Believed to be the largest importer and exporter of insect specimens in the United States, the individual in charge of the operation handles about 10,000 different species, and his collection is estimated to contain more than 5 million individual specimens. Although most species sell for a few dollars, a tiger beetle from Nambia sells for $1,300, and a pair of alpine silks can sell for more than $30,000. Prices on the black market are especially high.

1. R. Bryce, "Federal Crackdown on Bug Smuggling," *Christian Science Monitor,* 9 July 1996, 1, 4.
2. Bryce, "Federal Crackdown," 1.

As another example, consider poaching. Poaching is defined as the taking of a game animal out of season or through illegal means. Certainly the law allows hunters to kill animals, but hunting is closely regulated. If an animal is killed out of season, would this be an environmental crime? If only one animal was taken, rather than, say, 20 animals, would that be an environmental crime?

The taking of single nonhuman animals happens all of the time in the wild, regardless of designated hunting seasons. So the assumption is, then, that such a taking is an environmental crime only when the taking is done by a human—out of season. What if the animal taken is a member of an endangered species for which no season is ever designated? Here we see a difference between the type of crime (poaching) and the act (killing an animal).

In criminal justice, a person accused of a serious crime is fully responsible for that crime only if that individual intended to commit the act. Apply the intent criterion to an alleged environmental crime. Consider the case where a hunter takes a deer out of season. Many would agree an environmental crime had been committed. If the deer were killed as the result of a collision with a car, however, would this act be considered an environmental crime? Would it matter if the accident happened outside of the dates designated for hunting season or do different standards apply, based on the absence of intent to kill this deer? The hunter who shot the deer out of season may in fact eat the deer, but hitting a deer with a car is not serving any purpose. Must additional considerations be factored in before either act (shooting the deer or hitting the deer with a car) could be classified as an environmental crime?

Finally, consider the simple act of throwing a chewing gum wrapper out of a car window. While defined as a crime in some states—the crime of littering—is this act an environmental crime? Should a seemingly minor violation, such as littering, qualify as an environmental crime? Littering would not compare to the Exxon Valdez oil spill, for example. Should they both be classified as environmental crimes?

Overall, the nature of the act remains an essential element in environmental crime classification. Perhaps environmental crimes should be graduated, like other types of crime in the criminal justice system. Various acts are crimes, but the social response to the act (the punishment) is consonant with the severity of the crime. The Exxon Valdez and littering might both be environmental crimes, since they both involve disregard for the environmental consequences of one's actions. The difference would be noted in the punishment. If the severity of the crime is used to determine the punishment, who decides—and how is it decided—that one action is more severe than another?

The third definitional element is the actor. Is the actor a corporation or an individual? In many cases, it is unclear who, in fact, is the person responsible for committing the act. Consider an instance of knowingly disposing of hazardous waste. To what degree should a business or corporation be held liable for this crime when the relevant actions were accomplished by relatively few—or, in some instances, by only one—employee?

When an individual responsible for the disposal of hazardous wastes intentionally and knowingly dumps the waste in a river, quite clearly this is an environmental crime. But who is the actor? The individual yes, the corporation maybe. Should environmental crimes be classified differently depending on whether the actor was an individual or a corporation?

Nancy Frank and Michael Lynch[46] propose that the term **green crime** be specifically applied to wrongful corporate activities. They argue the goal of green criminology is to "analyze how political and economic factors are tied to the occurrence of corporate violence against the environment, animals, plants, etc."[47(p.82)] They offer a further distinction between environmental crimes by identifying **wildlife crimes** as "violations of criminal law designed to protect wildlife."[48(p.80)]

While the majority of environmental crime research has focused on corporate activity, some researchers do focus on the individual offender. Rebovich, for example, reminds us that the generators of hazardous waste "also include the end-user, private homeowners who improperly dispose of household chemical cleaners and disinfectants every day."[49(p.2)] Clearly, the actors referred to here are individuals, not corporations.

Strict liability, discussed in more detail in Chapter 5 and Case Study 2, has been the legal standard used to assign culpability in Superfund cases involving hazardous waste disposal. Under the strict liability standard, a person who commits an act is responsible for that act whether he or she intended to cause harm or whether the act was legal at the time it was committed. In the case of Superfund, anyone identified as being responsible for contamination can be held liable for cleanup of the site and for any damages resulting from the dumping. To what degree should strict liability be used for the type of activity, the act, or the actor associated with an alleged environmental crime? Should two people who killed deer out of season, one with a gun and the other with a car, both be held responsible for the death of the deer under a strict liability standard? Few would agree that strict liability is an acceptable standard for all environmental crimes. What role, then, should intent play in classifying a given act as an environmental crime? And how do we define the actor when the "person" involved is a corporation?

The fourth element is the status of the offender. Should attention be given to the status of the offender? Can only individuals holding authority in a company commit an environmental offense? Or can anyone commit the offense, regardless of rank, title, position, or status within the company? Does one have to be working in a position with an attached responsibility for preventing chemical spills in order to be responsible or liable if a spill occurs? Or can anyone who is employed by the company and who violates an environmental statute be held responsible?

Many discussions about environmental crime have placed the responsibility for environmental crimes at the door of large corporations. If this attribution is correct, who in the corporate structure of a company should be held responsible for the actions taken by the company? In short, does the position someone holds in the company have a direct or indirect connection to culpability for environmental violations?

The fifth and final element is the sanction. The federal legislation being discussed has focused on environmental statutes for which criminal penalties exist. Criminal penalties are only one form of sanction identified for ensuring environmental protection. Using a legal standard, both the definition of and penalty for an environmental crime is provided by the statute. Environmental enforcement strategy involves a three-pronged approach, based on **regulatory, civil,** and **criminal enforcement**.[50] Although criminal sanctions are outlined, the more severe criminal sanctions are rarely used, and the majority of environmental violations are addressed through regulatory or civil remedies. It is undetermined whether all environmental violations should be considered environmental crimes or whether environmental crimes are restricted to activities for which criminal remedies are sought. Again, classification of environmental violations has proven extremely difficult.

A 1993 National Institute of Justice publication focused on efforts being taken at the local prosecutor's office to address the problem of environmental crime in Los Angeles County.[51] The publication used the term *environmental crime* in the context of federal environmental statutes and regulations. "Each of these statutory schemes criminalizes certain acts as well as the falsification and in some instances the omission of information required to be provided to the government."[52(p.5)]

Environmental crime was divided into three basic categories:

1. violations of a permit condition,
2. violations committed outside the regulatory scheme, and
3. acts that would be illegal regardless of the regulatory provisions.[53]

Consider each of these categories. An example of a violation of a permit condition would be the dumping of waste in excess of allowed amounts.

(For a more thorough discussion of permit applications and violations, see Chapter 5.) The release of any waste or effluent into certain bodies of water requires a permit. If a company is granted a permit but releases an amount that exceeds the permit guidelines, it would be committing an environmental crime. (It is interesting that the authors of this report did not argue the offender was found guilty of an environmental violation; rather, they used the term *crime*.) In this example, as discussed earlier, the standards refer to actions as environmental crimes when no finding of guilt has been determined.

An example of a violation committed outside the regulatory scheme would be the lack of proper regulatory authority for a given task. For example, under the Resource Conservation and Recovery Act, transporters of hazardous wastes are required to carry a record (**manifest**) of the materials they are hauling. If a tanker truck is hauling a load of hazardous waste and the driver does not have a record of the waste, the driver is in violation of the act. Further, if the company who hired the driver to haul the waste away did not provide a record of the waste, it too is in violation of the act and is, according to the Los Angeles County standards, committing an environmental crime.

The third category encompasses acts that would be illegal regardless of the regulatory provisions. An example would be the opening of a tanker truck valve to get rid of hazardous waste while the truck was on the highway. No permit would be given to allow disposal of hazardous waste along a highway in such a fashion. Other examples include **midnight dumping**—emptying chemicals on the side of a road, in a riverbed, or in another unauthorized area. No permit would ever be given for midnight dumping.

One could easily argue the actions described above could more accurately be defined as alleged violations rather than crimes, particularly in light of the fact that no violation of law has been proven. Using the provisions outlined in the regulatory structure, it becomes easier to determine when a violation occurs. Classifying environmental crime based on specific references to sections of environmental statutes (and related regulatory provisions) seems to provide a viable solution to determining what can be classified as environmental crime. Yet, as we discussed above, using a legal (in this case, regulatory) standard comes at a cost. For those interested in a more philosophical or theoretical discussion, this might prove problematic. The legal/ illegal distinction is extremely useful, however, for practitioners in the field as they attempt to pursue and enforce violations of environmental crime.

We have discussed some of the difficulties associated with developing a philosophical definition of environmental crime. Deeper theoretical questions deserve further exploration. Given the introductory level of this text, a continuation of the philosophical definitional debate will be left for subsequent researchers. The three enforcement mechanisms available for enforcing environmental crimes (regulatory, civil, and criminal) may be overly simplistic for theoretical purposes. Identifying the laws, and distinguishing **compliance** from **noncompliance**, allow practitioners a means to distinguish legal from illegal activity. While not perfect for theory construction, the legal statutes provide clear boundaries for enforcement purposes.

ENVIRONMENTAL CRIME AS A LEGAL CONCEPT

The classification of crime is a professional and sometimes a social activity. Certain actions, although they may be considered immoral, are not illegal unless they infringe on a provision of a law or regulation. Crime classification, in other words, is restricted by the development and structure of the legal process. Most lawyers would agree that if there is no law, there can be no crime. Make a law, however, and if a violation of the law has occurred, then a crime has been committed. Perhaps one does not get caught, or perhaps one will eventually be convicted. In either case, a violation of law suggests a crime has been committed. Therefore, a violation of environmental law would be an environmental crime.

So, it is clear that one simple way to identify environmental crime would be to look at the environmental laws. Any violation of an environmental statute could be classified as an environmental crime. But, as in the case of white-collar crime theory and environmental crime theory, limitations exist. Chapter 5 discusses eight principal federal statutes under which criminal prosecution of environmental offenses can occur. Keep in mind, however, as Ross and Sutherland suggested when they first began looking at crimes committed by the powerful, use of a strictly **legal standard** limits criminologists when they consider immoral actions some would view as crimes. Abiding rigidly to the use of a legal standard could be restrictive if one were interested in taking a more philosophical point of view. Ross created the term criminaloid to discuss actions not currently illegal but arguably immoral. Should a distinction be made between an environmental criminal and an environmental criminaloid?

CAN A DEFINITION OF ENVIRONMENTAL CRIME BE ACHIEVED?

Bringing to a close the discussion of the definitional questions surrounding the use of the term *environmental crime*, we offer a few suggestions for those interested in either the legal or theoretical dimensions of this term.

INSIGHT

Can Corporations Be Environmental Criminals?[1]

The Michigan Chemical Company produced a number of chemicals for commercial purposes. One of those products was Firemaster BP-6, a polybrominated biphenyl (PBB). At approximately the same time, in the early 1970s, Dow and DuPont, two nationally known chemical manufacturers, evaluated the toxicity of the compound and decided not to produce a PBB product. Although the chemical was controversial, the Michigan Chemical Company continued to produce Firemaster BP-6.

At the same time, the Michigan Chemical Company produced a magnesium oxide product used to sweeten dairy cattle feed, called Nutrimaster. Michigan used color-coded bags to package its products. Each color represented a different product so company workers would not get the various chemical products confused. In the spring of 1973, the company ran out of its colored bags and began putting the products in plain brown 50-pound bags. On April 30, 1974, the Food and Drug Administration sent an inspector to determine the cause of an epidemic of cattle illness. He found a half-used bag of the Michigan "feed additive" in a brown bag. Its contents were not clearly marked. Testing showed it was Firemaster FF-1, an experimental batch of PBB. Normally the products were markedly different, but due to the experiment the products were similar in both consistency and color.

Lab tests revealed the existence of bromine in the feed. A chemist at the U.S. Department of Agriculture identified the contaminant as PBB—a flame retardant manufactured by Michigan. The connection was made when the farmer recognized Michigan Chemical as the name of the company that produced the feed additive.

The discovery of the contamination resulted in findings that hundreds of Michigan farmers were having the same livestock problems. Within three weeks, an additional 30 farms had been quarantined by the state. The U.S. Food and Drug Administration (FDA) said the milk and milk products from these farms should not be sold or consumed. At the time of the quarantine, the farmers could not sell their cows or the milk, but they also could not kill the animals because no burial site existed that was permitted to accept PBB-contaminated waste. The animals' carcasses would be considered waste, and therefore the farmers continued feeding the cows, dumping the milk, and losing hundreds of dollars a day.

By October 1974, 151 farms had been quarantined, including a total of 6,700 cattle, 341 sheep, and 850,000 chickens. Questions were raised about the level of PBB viewed as acceptable. Farmers were reporting problems with cattle whose PBB levels were lower than FDA's standard. Thus, the level considered acceptable was lowered, although many argued it was still not low enough to include all of the cows with symptoms of contamination.

By 1976, unexpected health problems were being reported among farm families, and a succession of studies indicated that PBB contamination might be the main cause. The undiagnosable symptoms that were discovered included dizziness, fatigue, joint problems, memory problems, excessive sweating, wounds that would not heal, darkening of the skin, and hypersensitivity to sunlight, but the symptoms were never linked to PBB exposure. In 1977, nervous disorders and musculoskeletal and gastrointestinal abnormalities were identified. Gradually the scare grew less intense, and the issue of PBB contamination disappeared without resolution of the questions it had raised.

---

1. H.M. Vyner, *Invisible Trauma: The Psychosocial Effects of the Invisible Environmental Contaminants* (Lexington Books: Lexington, MA, 1988), chap. 6.

The complexity of the issues associated with environmental crime makes identifying one definition quite difficult. Attempting to cover all types of criminal offenses with one definition is awkward and complicated, just as intending to cover all types of crime with one theory is awkward and not very helpful. Thus, while a legal definition of environmental crime can be used to provide a framework for most of the issues discussed throughout this text, for purposes of theory development the definition needs to be broader. Consider the following definition:

> An environmental crime is an act committed with the intent to harm the natural environment.

Limiting the definition of environmental crime to some form of environmental "harm" means that a legal definition and an assessment of harm is needed before the term is useful. Further, attention must be given to the issues of determining "intent" and defining "natural environment." Without some objective scale and universally accepted criteria to measure or assess the degree of harm, all actions resulting in harm would become environmental crimes. Minus an ability to limit or objectively quantify harm, the killing of a single deer or the cutting of one protected tree would fall into the same category as the intentional extinction of a species or the clear-cutting of an entire rain forest—they all would be environmental crimes.

Furthermore, making distinctions surrounding the issue of intent or defining the natural environment would not be easy undertakings. For example, spray painting graffiti on a rock wall in the Grand Canyon would likely be classified as an environmental crime. But would spray painting graffiti on a city park sign in Miami, Florida, also be an environmental crime? The act is the same, the actor could be the same, but the place where the action occurred is different. Certainly, although the areas are dramatically different, it would be hard to argue that a park in Miami is less a part of the natural environment than the Grand Canyon.

Another problem with the definition above arises from the distinction between actual harm and potential harm. In other words, must the harm to the environment currently be manifest or can the harm be to future generations? Consider amending the statement above to read thus:

> An environmental crime is an act committed with the intent to harm or with the potential to cause harm to ecological and/or biological systems.

Have we resolved the problems associated with the phrase "the natural environment" by substituting "ecological and/or biological systems"? Also, how is potential harm objectively measured or quantitatively assessed? If actual harm is required for classifying an action as an environmental crime, how then could the burial of drums containing hazardous waste that are not now leaking qualify as an environmental crime now? Must actions that result in future harm be evaluated in terms of "proximate cause"? If so, will every situation become a legalistic nightmare in terms of sorting out both actual and proximate harm to the environment? How can the law reflect the different levels of proximate danger?

Attention must be given to the way in which damage or harm will be assessed. Returning to a point made earlier, does a decision to require "scientific proof" of damage or harm provide an acceptable solution? It is interesting to note that in many cases the application of a scientific standard has further polarized groups of "scientific experts" and "community activists." Some examples of this are discussed in the ENSCO case study (Case Study 1), and in Chapter 2, which contains a history of the environmental movement.

In an effort to integrate the issue of intent, we might alter the definition of environmental crime as follows:

> An environmental crime is an act committed with the intent to harm or with the potential to cause harm to ecological and/or biological systems, for the purpose of securing business or personal advantage.

Identifying intent as a determining factor for assigning culpability, attention in the definition refers to acts committed for personal or business advantage. This separates those who intend to commit harm from cases where no intent to commit harm is present. Or we might want to restrict environmental crimes to the breaking of laws that outline sanctions as an appropriate punishment for specific violations, as in this definition:

> An environmental crime is an act committed with the intent to harm or with the potential to cause harm to ecological and/or biological systems, for the purpose of securing business or personal advantage, and in violation of state or federal statutes for which criminal sanctions apply.

This definition, while more inclusive than the first, restricts the application of the term beyond the legal definition of criminal sanctions. The key phrase in this definition is "for which criminal sanctions apply." Suppose a group of farmers were applying the maximum amounts of herbicides and pesticides allowed under state and federal regulations. The farmers were acting within application limits, but suppose they knew the chemicals were increasingly being detected in the local groundwater and thus were creating a potential threat to the surrounding community. Some scholars and a significant portion of the general public would want to characterize their continued use of the chemicals as an environmental crime even though no violation of the law occurred. Furthermore, the definition excludes many environmental actions covered by administrative and civil regulations. For example, municipalities sometimes establish local ordinances intended to address community environmental concerns, and the infringement of these ordinances is excluded.

As Sutherland argued, and Ross before him, when critically evaluating the concept of white-collar crime, while the actions taken by the farmers described above might be offensive, or morally wrong, they are not illegal. Therefore, they should not be viewed as criminal. The farmers, regardless of their knowledge of the harm they were causing, did not violate any laws. The element of intent is difficult to evaluate, because while the farmers knew of the possible connection to public harm, they did not intend to harm anyone; they simply wanted the biggest crop yield possible. So, as the definition becomes more specific, our ability to discuss the intricacies of the concept is reduced.

One point to keep in mind is that for some purposes we would like a definition of environmental crime to be useful for police officers and regulatory officials. Consider the objectives of a local law enforcement agency charged with the task of investigating an alleged environmental crime. How useful would the last definition be in this instance? Could a law enforcement officer decide whether it was appropriate to arrest someone who had, say, dumped toxic materials in a wilderness area?

In this instance, the following type of definition is more appropriate:

> An environmental crime is an act in violation of an environmental protection statute that applies to the area in which the act occurred and that has clearly identified criminal sanctions for purposes of police enforcement.

As discussed earlier, it is much more practical to identify environmental crimes as violations of existing environmental protection statutes. For one thing, police officers are intimately familiar with how to deal with violations of law. We are reminded once again, for the purposes of environmental enforcement, a legal definition serves the greatest purpose.

CONCLUSION

Over the last 20 years criminologists and other social scientists have focused increased attention on the emerging field of environmental crime.

Researchers, politicians, environmentalists, and community groups have expressed concern about activities that cause substantial harm to the natural environment. When asked about environmental hazards, people want more protection—which means they want laws and they want those laws enforced.

This chapter is intended to provide an overview of various important but unexplored aspects of the concept of environmental crime. Its ultimate objective is to provide students a viable definition. In fact, it offers two. For those interested in the broader philosophical issues, we propose the following definition:

> An environmental crime is an act committed with the intent to harm or with a potential to cause harm to ecological and/or biological systems and for the purpose of securing business or personal advantage.

The second definition is for those practitioners who need a legal framework:

> An environmental crime is any act that violates an environmental protection statute.

Establishing an adequate definition of environmental crime has proven to be extremely difficult. Research on environmental crime will only benefit from the resolution of the remaining theoretical conflicts. Perhaps the solutions are not as unattainable as it might at first appear. A workable definition could easily incorporate "classes" of violations based on the degree of harm and the determination of intent. It is true that the difficulties associated with intent and the assessment of harm might be intimidating, but the process would be no different than the process police and prosecutors use in pursuing other criminal charges. The criminal justice system is already required to make these distinctions. Consider crimes such as assault and murder, for example.

To date, criminologists and others studying environmental issues have focused on activities that may not be defined as criminal. While a philosophical discussion about moral responsibility for environmental harm is perhaps a better mechanism for developing a comprehensive definition of environmental crime, it is not very useful for practitioners in the field trying to determine whether to make an arrest.

Also, an extremely broad definition is not particularly useful for purposes of analysis because everything can be included in the definition. As regards future research, one of the objectives of defining environmental crime is to make reasonable comparisons possible; this could not be done if the definition was so broad as to preclude meaningful distinctions. As more research is conducted, researchers and practitioners will know more about how to best address the concept of environmental crimes both in the community and in the classroom. The remainder of the text is devoted to explaining the initial efforts being undertaken to better understand environmental crime and its enforcement.

REVIEW QUESTIONS

1. Identify several of the issues that make finding a definition of environmental crime difficult.
2. What are the differences between green crime, wildlife crime, and environmental crime?
3. Does the theory of natural law provide any insight into the nature of environmental crime? Explain.
4. How have theories of human ecology been used to explain social behavior? Can they help in the search for a definition of environmental crime? Explain.
5. How is the discipline of environmental criminology related to environmental crime?

DISCUSSION QUESTIONS

1. How would the study of environmental crime benefit from a theoretically useful definition?
2. What is the difference between a theoretically useful definition and a legal definition?
3. What are the restrictions imposed on researchers when using a definition of environmental crime based on the law? Is it possible to get around some of these restrictions?
4. Consider the definitions of environmental crime discussed in the chapter. How would you evaluate each of them? What considerations would you add?

REFERENCES

1. M. Clifford et al., "Defining Environmental Crime: Is the Genie out of the Bottle?" Submitted for publication.
2. S. Edwards, "Environmental Criminal Enforcement: Efforts by the States," in *Environmental Crime and Criminality: Theoretical and Practical Issues*, eds. S. Edwards, T. Edwards, and C.B. Fields. (New York: Garland Pub., 1996), 205–244.

3. J. Starr, "Turbulent Times at Justice and EPA: The Origins of Environmental Criminal Prosecutions and the Work That Remains," *George Washington Law Review* 59 (1991): 900–915.

4. P.G. Nittoly, "Environmental Criminal Cases: The Dawn of a New Era," *Seton Hall Law Review* 21 (1991): 1125–1152.

5. U.S. Department of Justice, "Environmental Crimes," *FBI Law Enforcement Bulletin* 60, no. 4 (1991).

6. W.S. Hood, Jr., "Environmental Crimes: Willful vs. Unwitting Conduct: Focusing on the Little Guy," in *Minimizing Liability for Hazardous Waste Management Symposium*, C506 ALI-ABA 29 (Chicago: American Bar Association, 1990), 29–42.

7. U.S. Department of Justice, *Prosecuting Environmental Crime: Los Angeles County* (Washington, DC: National Institute of Justice, 1993).

8. J.D. Pearsall, *Local Agency Criminal Enforcement Investigation: A Place To Start* (West Palm Beach, FL: Palm Beach County Sheriff's Office Environmental Crimes Unit, 1993).

9. R.C. Vaughn, "IACP's Environmental Crimes Committee," *The Police Chief* 4, no. 2 (1992): 6.

10. International Association of Chiefs of Police, *Environmental Crime Enforcement*, Training Key #436 (Alexandria, VA: International Association of Chiefs of Police, 1993).

11. American Bar Association, *Environmental Law Newsletter* 14, no. 1 (1994).

12. D.C. Vacco, "Government's Response to Compliance in Environmental Matters in the Western District of New York," in *Theoretical Criminology*, 3d ed. (New York: Oxford University Press, 1990).

13. "Introduction to Environmental Crime Enforcement," seminar materials, Southern Environmental Enforcement Network, Montgomery, AL, 1994.

14. National College of District Attorneys, conference materials for National Conference on the Prosecution of Environmental Crime, San Francisco, CA, May 19–22, 1994.

15. J.P. Calve, "Environmental Crimes: Upping the Ante for Non-compliance with Environmental Laws," *Military Law Review* 133 (1991): 279–348.

16. J.M. Strock, "Environmental Criminal Enforcement Priorities for the 1990s," *George Washington Law Review* 59 (1991): 916–937.

17. J.R. Mayo, and F.M. Zachara, "The Erosion of Mens Reas in Environmental Criminal Prosecutions," *Environmental Law Symposium, Seton Hall Law Review* 21 (1991): 1100–1123.

18. I.L. Dotterrer, "Attorney-Client Confidentiality: The Ethics of Toxic Dumping Disclosure," *Wayne Law Review* 35 (1989): 1157–1179.

19. S. Bernstein, "Environmental Criminal Law: The Use of Confinement for Criminal Violators of the Federal Clean Water Act," *New England Journal of Criminal and Civil Confinement* 17 (1991): 107–132.

20. R. Milne, "The Mens Rea Requirement of the Federal Environmental Statutes: Strict Criminal Liability in Substance but Not Form," *Buffalo Law Review* 37 (1988): 307.

21. E.D. Muchnicki, "Criminal Enforcement of State Environmental Laws: The Ohio Solution," *Harvard Environmental Law Review* 14 (1990): 217–251.

22. F. Schmalleger, *Criminal Justice Today: An Introductory Text for the Twenty-first Century* (Upper Saddle River, NJ: Prentice Hall, 1997), 116.

23. Schmalleger, *Criminal Justice Today*, 118.

24. E. Warming, "Plant Communities," in *Introduction to the Science of Sociology*, eds. R.E. Park and E.W. Burgess (Chicago: University of Chicago Press, 1969), 175–182.

25. G.B. Vold and T.J. Bernard, *Theoretical Criminology*, 3d ed. (New York: Oxford University Press, 1986), 161.

26. Vold and Bernard, *Theoretical Criminology*, 178–179.

27. P. Brantingham and P. Brantingham, *Environmental Criminology* (Prospect Heights, IL: Waveland Press, 1991).

28. Brantingham and Brantingham, *Environmental Criminology*, 239.

29. "Defining Environmental Crime," panel presented at the Academy of Criminal Justice Sciences, Boston, 1995.

30. J.A. Brozost, "The Corporate Counsel's Response to the Knock on the Door," in *Criminal Enforcement of Environmental Laws*, C496 ALI-ABA 159 (Chicago: American Bar Association, 1990), 159–180.

31. J.M. Nolan, Jr., and S.K. Stahl, "The Rules Have Changed, but the Game Remains the Same: Why the Government Has Turned to Criminal Prosecution as a Means of Enforcing Environmental Laws," *Cooley Law Review* 7 (1990): 407–428.

32. N. Frank and M. Lynch, *Corporate Crime, Corporate Violence: A Primer* (New York: Harrow and Heston, 1992).

33. D. Simon and D.S. Eitzen, *Elite Deviance*, 4th ed. (Needham Heights, MA: Allyn & Bacon, 1993).

34. A. Block and F. Scarpitti, *Poisoning for Profit: The Mafia and Toxic Waste in America* (New York: Morrow, 1985).

35. D. Rebovich, *Dangerous Ground: The World of Hazardous Waste Crime* (New Brunswick, NJ: Transaction Publishers, 1992).

36. Block and Scarpitti, *Poisoning for Profit*.

37. Clifford et al., "Defining Environmental Crime."

38. Several of E.H. Sutherland's important early contributions on the study of white-collar crime include the following: *White Collar Crime: The Uncut Version* (New Haven, CT: Yale University Press, 1983); *White-Collar Crime* (New York: Holt, Reinhart and Winston, 1949); "Is 'White-Collar Crime' Crime?" *American Sociological Review* 10 (1945): 132–139; "Crime and Business," *Annals of the American Society of Political and Social Science* 217 (1941); "White-Collar Criminality," *American Sociological Review* 5 (1940): 1–12.

39. E.A. Ross, "The Criminaloid," in *White-Collar Crime: Offenses in Business, Politics and the Professions* (New York: The Free Press, 1977; original work published 1907).

40. Frank and Lynch, *Corporate Crime, Corporate Violence*, 14.

41. Frank and Lynch, *Corporate Crime, Corporate Violence*, 14.

42. G. Mueller, "An Essay on Environmental Crime," in *Environmental Crime and Criminality: Theoretical and Practical Issues* (New York: Garland Pub., 1996), 3–33.

43. Clifford et al., "Defining Environmental Crime."

44. Clifford et al., "Defining Environmental Crime."

45. Clifford et al., "Defining Environmental Crime."

46. Frank and Lynch, *Corporate Crime, Corporate Violence*, 81–84.

47. Frank and Lynch, *Corporate Crime, Corporate Violence*, 82.

48. Frank and Lynch, *Corporate Crime, Corporate Violence*, 80.

49. Rebovich, *Dangerous Ground*, 2.

50. U.S. Department of Justice, *Law Enforcement Response to Environmental Crime* (Washington, DC: National Institute of Justice, 1995).

51. U.S. Department of Justice, *Prosecuting Environmental Crime*.

52. U.S. Department of Justice, *Prosecuting Environmental Crime*, 5.

53. U.S. Department of Justice, *Issues and Practices* (Washington, DC: National Institute of Justice, 1993), 8.

CHAPTER 2

A History of the U.S. Environmental Movement

Sally M. Edwards

TERMS	carcinogens	human centered
	classical liberalism	individual rights
	conservation	preservationism
	Delaney Amendment	Progressive Conservation Movement
	environmental justice	Sagebrush Rebellion
	environmental racism	synthetic chemicals
	grassroots groups	Wise Use Movement

The roots of the modern environmental movement are as deeply fractured as environmental activism is today. The environmental groups discussed in this chapter have clearly defined differences and varying goals. The diversity of goals leads to as much political conflict among environmentalists as exists between environmentalists and nonenvironmentalists. The story of the environmental movement in the United States includes, at a minimum, these elements: citizen action, public opinion, law, culture, economics, and political ideology. Portraying the environmental movement as monolithic in purpose or structure would be misleading. With so many elements to be considered, the resulting conflict is not surprising.

This chapter starts with a historical analysis of the social, economic, and cultural conditions that existed during the Progressive Conservation Movement. Then it discusses preservationist and conservationist ideologies. Some of the differences between current environmental groups can be traced to the philosophical writings of their predecessors and the environmental and social conditions and public attitudes of the nineteenth and early twentieth centuries. These writings, conditions, and attitudes have profoundly influenced the modern environmental movement and related politics and policies, and knowing something about them can help one develop a better understanding of the environmental attitudes seen today. Although the number of individual and collective rationales for establishing environmental groups has expanded, the tenets of the conservation and preservation ideologies remain essentially the same. After reviewing the history of the environmental movement in the United States, the chapter closes with a brief introduction to several groupings in the modern environmental movement and identifies certain prominent environmental groups.

EARLY ENVIRONMENTAL ACTIONS

The first recorded "environmental" action in what was to eventually become the United States occurred in 1626, when Plymouth Colony enacted ordinances concerning the harvesting of timber on colony lands.[1] This action, like others adopted during the seventeenth century,[2] was designed to conserve vital economic resources for future use. **Conservation** was identified as a means to an end—a maintenance of natural resources to safeguard their economic benefits for the long term. The conservation ideology suggested that **natural resources**, or natural commodities with economic value, must be protected to ensure the quality of life for future generations. The conservation philosophy later became formally embodied in the **Progressive Conservation Movement** of the 1890s and 1900s. Early conservation laws and regulations of the era defined nature in terms of human values and human needs. When dealing with natural resources, the conservationist ideology was and remains **human centered**.

A related but distinctly different set of ideas concerning early management of natural resources is represented by the ideology, **preservationism**. Preservationists were much more interested in "preserving" nature for its intrinsic value. Basically nature centered, preservationists wanted to see wilderness preserved regardless of human consumption and human needs.[3]

The Progressive Conservation Movement eventually splintered into two factions. Disagreement between environmentalists about how to best protect the natural environment was a primary reason for the split. The terms *preservation* and *conservation* came to reflect differences in the two emerging ideologies.[4] Beginning at the turn of the twentieth century, disputes about economic growth, development, and environmental protection led to political battles between environmental groups—battles that continue to the present day.[5]

The conservationist ideology has prevailed most often in the ongoing struggle between the two factions.[6] To date, acts of preservation have been rare. The establishment of Yellowstone in 1872 as the first national park is one example. The preservationist viewpoint established a toehold in American thought at around that time and later reappears as a prevalent theme, influencing certain groups in the modern environmental movement.

The Progressive Conservation Movement

In 1890, the U.S. Census Bureau announced "the frontier" was closed. This announcement had a major impact on public attitudes concerning natural resources and the environment.[7] The closing of the frontier required significant adjustments in the way Americans viewed opportunity and prosperity. The reason for this was twofold. First, the tenets of classical liberalism,[8] the national political ideology, were called into question. Second, the economic and social conditions of the time were in transition.

The term **classical liberalism** embodies several themes central to the U.S. Constitution and the democratic form of governance. The individual is at the heart of the classical liberalism ideology. Accordingly, the protection of **individual rights** is identified as a primary purpose of government.[9] As a political belief system, classical liberalism found a receptive audience in America.

A second idea shaping American political attitudes of that time was the principle of equal opportunity. All citizens in the United States could feel secure that their rights and their opportunities to succeed would not be impeded. The U.S. government was designed to ensure the protection of these rights and opportunities. While not all Americans accepted the tenets of classical liberalism, consideration of this ideology helps in understanding why the closing of the frontier had such a significant impact on many Americans at that time.

When the Constitution was written, prosperity was often linked to property ownership. Furthermore, the natural resources in the United States, including land, were believed to be virtually unlimited. This meant that for the industrious the future was wide open. If you could not find economic prosperity where you were, there was always land over the horizon. Although the reality did not always live up to its billing, Americans generally believed everyone had a chance to achieve prosperity. Move west, stake out your claim, work hard, and you too could become prosperous on the American frontier.

According to the classical liberalism ideology, if the government protected individual rights and freedoms, unending economic opportunity was available to anyone regardless of inheritance or class. This belief was largely supported by the endless resources provided on the North American continent. The announcement that the frontier was closed shocked this early American belief system. Prosperity was no longer just over the horizon. Economic security, at the very least, was precarious because the land and resources in the West had all been occupied or claimed. You needed to succeed where you were, since there was nowhere else for you to go.

The frontier closing had a considerable impact on popular attitudes because this happened in a time of dramatic **social transformation**. The country was rapidly moving from an agrarian-based economy to an industrial economy, and this transformation had profound effects on the daily lives of almost all Americans. The changes set off a profound reaction, and the Progressive Conservation Movement became part of a broader movement to preserve and protect traditional values and traditional American lifestyles.

Securing economic benefits from natural resources was a major focus of federal laws enacted during this period in history. The conservation of natural resources for future generations was one of the most significant priorities. When referencing the Progressive Conservation Movement, three things should be remembered. First, as the frontier closed, an overriding concern surfaced about limited resources. Second, the U.S. economic base was in transition, moving away from agriculture, toward industry. Finally, as the country moved through this transitional period, a struggle was developing over the emerging social values. The ideas associated with conservation came to reflect a broader need to protect traditional values.

One of the liveliest controversies concerned the management of these resources. Whether to protect natural resources and how best to protect them were among the issues debated by writers, politicians, and local citizens.

Preservationist Writings and Social Actions

Although **Henry David Thoreau** is widely regarded as the first advocate of environmental preservation, others came before him. For example, **George Catlin**, whose writings preceded Thoreau's by approximately 20 years, was a famous artist who traveled extensively in the western part of the United States territory, painting pictures depicting Native American life. From 1832 to 1839, Catlin kept a journal of his thoughts and ideas concerning the American West. In 1832, a New York newspaper published some articles by him, one of which included a call for a national park to preserve a part of the American wilderness before the wilderness vanished.[10]

Although Catlin's essays contained spiritual overtones, Henry David Thoreau's writings are renowned for establishing the "spiritual" need for an unspoiled environment. In Thoreau's view, humans required wilderness in order to remain civilized. By communing with nature, humans could stay in touch with their spiritual self. For this to happen, though, nature needed to remain undisturbed by human activity.

Thoreau's idea that human spirituality could be fostered by contact with unspoiled nature was echoed by **John Muir**. Muir was the first president of the Sierra Club, founded in 1892. For Muir, undisturbed wilderness led to the best communion with God. Humans could only sustain their spirituality through exposure to God's undisturbed creations. This communion with God could only be found in the wilderness, away from the chaos and conditions associated with urban life. For this reason, wilderness needed to be protected.[11]

Although associated with modern preservationist ideologies, Thoreau's and Muir's writings, actions, and calls for wilderness protection were centered on human needs. Whether considered necessary for economic or spiritual reasons, or for democracy's survival, their writings were clearly human centered. Wilderness was needed to preserve human civilization and civilized people. It was only later that their writings, along with those of **Aldo Leopold**,[12] were interpreted as nature centered. As differences emerged from within the Progressive Conservation Movement, these works became linked to the preservation ideology. Today the deep ecology movement and other radical environmental groups find their roots deeply embedded in the preservation ideology.*

Groups affiliated with radical environmentalism, discussed later in the chapter, argue that nonhuman animals and plants deserve the same respect and survival opportunities afforded to humans. Aldo Leopold is considered the father of the modern preservation ideology. Dave Foreman, cofounder of the radical environmental group Earth First!, called Leopold's *A Sand County Almanac* "the century's most important book, period."[13(p.28)]

Leopold argued that each individual needed to be recognized as "a member of a community of interdependent parts" and that it was essential to "preserve all the parts of the land mechanism."[14(p.143)] To make a wild area accessible to public use, through roads and mechanical transportation, is to destroy the wilderness.[15] Expressing his disenchantment with existing conservation practices, Leopold wrote, "The practices we now call conservation are, to a large extent, local alleviations of biotic pain. They are necessary, but they must not be confused with cures. The art of land doctoring is being practiced with vigor, but the science of land health is yet to be born."[16(pp.195–196)]

In the forward to *A Sand County Almanac*, Leopold wrote,

> Like winds and sunsets, wild things were taken for granted until progress began to do away with them. Now we face the question whether a still higher "standard of living" is worth its cost in things natural, wild, and free. For us of the minority, the opportunity to see geese is more important than television, and the chance to find a pasque-flower is a right as inalienable as free speech. These wild things, I admit, had little human value until mechanization assured us of a good breakfast, and until science disclosed the drama of

---

*See, for example, literature in deep ecology, such as Duvall and Sessions (1985), *Deep Ecology: Living As If Nature Mattered*. Layton, Utah: Gibbs Smith; or books on radical environmentalism, such as Manes (1990), *Green Rage: Radical Environmentalism and the Unmaking of Civilization*. Boston: Little, Brown and Co.; or Foreman (1991), *Confessions of an Eco-Warrior*. New York: Harmony Books.

where they come from and how they live. The whole conflict thus boils down to a question of degree. We of the minority see a law of diminishing returns in progress; our opponents do not.[17(p.vii)]

Leopold's book, published in 1949, became the bible of the environmental movement of the 1960s and 1970s. Despite inroads by the preservationists, however, conservationism remains the ideology governing environmental policy.

Conservationist Writings and Social Actions

The preceding discussion highlights the roots of the preservationist ideology as it emerged during the early environmental movement in the United States. The themes of the conservationist ideology can be found in political and social writings from the same historical era, the late 1800s and early 1900s. In these writings are the ideas that prevailed in environmental politics and policy until the 1960s and 1970s.

George Perkins Marsh wrote *Man and Nature; or Physical Geography As Modified by Human Action*, published in 1864. In this work, Marsh identified the importance of human responsibility for protecting the land. In destroying the land, Marsh argued, humans destroy themselves. He suggested the demise of earlier civilizations occurred because they had destroyed their environment. Wanton destruction of our environment would lead to the destruction of our society. Thus, Marsh argued, humans needed to care for the land and utilize its resources in a sustainable way. His was very much a conservationist, or human-centered, concern for the environment. For Marsh, humans had a responsibility to conserve and use resources wisely by adopting policies that protected the environment.[18]

Frederick Law Olmsted, Marsh's contemporary, was very active in the establishment of urban parks, the most famous of which is Central Park in New York City. Similar to Thoreau, Olmsted believed the natural environment met an intrinsic human need. But whereas Thoreau advocated the preservation of wilderness, Olmsted was interested in land management for public use and recreation. The preservationists and the conservationists, however, could work together. For example, actions taken by John Muir, a preservationist, and Olmsted, a conservationist, led to the establishment of Yosemite National Park in 1891.

Another influential conservationist was **John Wesley Powell**, hired by the U.S. government to explore the American West. He and a team of men were the first known nonindigenous people to explore the Colorado River through the Grand Canyon. For several years he explored the Rocky Mountain Ranges and areas of the arid West.[19] His *Report on the Lands of the Arid Region of the United States*, presented to the United States Congress in 1878, advocated a system of water reclamation (e.g., dams and canals) to turn desert into productive agricultural lands. His work at the United States Geological Survey culminated in the adoption of the **Reclamation Act of 1902.**[20] This act created the federal water storage and irrigation policies still in effect today. Much of California's current agricultural industry, for example, exists because of the system of dams and canals that provide water to its arid lands at low prices subsidized by the federal government.[21]

These are only a few of the people commonly associated with the preservation and conservation ideologies. The line separating conservationism from preservationism is very thin indeed. To place a person (or group) in either camp is difficult unless that person's philosophical justifications for protecting the environment are clearly nature centered or human centered. These two ideologies, reflecting the split in the Progressive Conservation Movement, provide the cornerstone for most of the discourse on environmental protection today. Throughout the 1890s and early 1900s, the public demand for conservation to prolong the "lifespan" of the nation's resources increased. The fears of a changing society and the official closing of the frontier fueled the politics of the day.

TEDDY ROOSEVELT AND THE PROGRESSIVE CONSERVATION MOVEMENT

The undisputed political leader of the Progressive Conservation Movement was Theodore Roosevelt, and he took the conservation viewpoint with him to the White House. During Roosevelt's tenure as president, a few crucial pieces of legislation were enacted.[22] Roosevelt advocated the use of good scientific management of natural resources. To that end, he established the Inland Waterways Commission in 1907 to develop a comprehensive, multipurpose river development plan. In 1908, Roosevelt held a governor's conference to discuss conservation, and he appointed a National Conservation Commission to inventory natural resources.[23] Under Roosevelt's guidance, the Progressive Conservation Movement reached its zenith. Yet, scientific management of natural resources meant the end of business as usual, and a backlash against the conservation movement had already begun.

East versus West

Private interest groups had traditionally had access to public resources at bargain basement prices. In many ways, the opposition to conservation was

Our National Parks[1]

Among our country's most prized posses-sions are our national parks. Every year millions of people visit them, and their splendor has been captured in books, paintings, and film. Yellowstone, America's first national park, was established in 1872. President Grant signed the act at the urging of a small group of men who had traveled through Yellowstone and believed that its wonders should be open to everyone forever.

Since then 365 other areas have joined Yellowstone to make up the national park sys-tem. The system contains a wide variety of sites and areas throughout the United States, includ-ing national parks, national forests, and wilder-ness areas. A *national park* is an area of special scenic, historical, or scientific importance set aside and maintained by the national govern-ment specifically for recreation or study. A *na-tional forest* is an unused forested area of consid-erable size that is preserved by government decree from private exploitation and is har-vested only under supervision. It is often used for the practice and demonstration of proper forestry methods. A *wilderness area* is an area set aside by the government for the preservation of natural conditions for scientific or recreational purposes; no roads are permitted. In spite of the sheer numbers of these federally owned lands, Congress did not officially recognize the con-cept of a national park system until 1970.

The National Park Service, created in 1916, administers the national park system. It trains park rangers, who oversee monuments, battle-fields, cemeteries, parks, houses, and numer-ous other sites. They give tours of these sites, patrol them to prevent damage, and supervise the opening of new parks. During the Great Depression the National Park Service provided employment for over 100,000 men. These men built roads, bridges, buildings, and hun-dreds of recreation facilities—some of which are still in use today. The National Park Service also helped develop the state park systems during the 1930s. It developed many areas that were later turned over to the states. State parks are quite similar to national parks. Na-tional parks are usually larger but also include smaller sites deemed to be of national histori-cal value.

Since the end of World War II, the national park system has more than doubled in the number of sites and in acreage. The number of yearly visitors to the park sites has reached 364 million. The budget to keep the park system running has passed $1 billion dollars per year. The national park system has become increas-ingly complex, and recently several controver-sies over the use of the parks have emerged. The largest controversy is over whether to charge admission fees to visit the parks. At present, admission charges vary, and some parks have no fee at all. Many feel the fees charged are unfair because it is taxpayer money that provides for the upkeep of the parks. Therefore, they feel all taxpayers should have free and equal access to all the parks. Others claim that the income from the fees is needed to keep the parks running. They argue the fees are low and represent a reasonable contribution to park upkeep. Further, the fees heighten the awareness that littering and van-dalism hurt the parks.

Another controversy concerns the use of waiting lists to reserve access to the most popular parks, such as Yellowstone and the Grand Canyon. These lists, mainly for camping permits, fill up years in advance. Many people feel it is unfair to deny any citizens the right to use the parks they help support. The park ser-vice points out that severe damage could be done to especially popular parks if masses of

Note: A special thanks to **Shari McLean** for her work on this insight.

people were to roam throughout them unchecked. Such damage could permanently alter the parks, or take years to repair.

Other national park controversies remain somewhat constant. Some recommend an increase in tourism at the parks to generate money. To attract more visitors, they believe the parks should build hotels and restaurants on or near park property.[2] Others suggest opening trails to motorized vehicles. Commercial development in the parks is opposed by many environmental groups, who argue such development would spoil the natural condition of the land.

Using a "money generation model," the National Park Service has calculated that the parks bring in about $10 billion annually to the economies of the surrounding regions.[3] A bill introduced into the 1995 federal budget reconciliation package, the "park closure" bill (H.R. 260), called for the creation of a commission to determine which units of the national park system should be closed.[4] James V. Hansen, chair of the House Parks Subcommittee, wanted the commission to remove 150 parks from the park service's control.[5] The public outcry resulted in the legislation being removed from consideration. Many remain concerned, however, about the fate that awaits our national parks. Are they a commodity to be bought and sold or a treasure to be safeguarded for future generations?

1. D.F. Rettie, *Our National Park System* (Chicago: University of Illinois Press, 1995).
2. "Development Opportunity? The Grand Canyon," *The Economist*, 31 August 1996, 29.
3. V. Rose, "What's a Park Worth? Last Year's Shutdown Focused Attention on Both the Economic and Intrinsic Value of Parks," *National Parks* 70, no. 5-6 (1996): 51–52.
4. K.A. O'Connel, "Concessions Battle Part of Budget War: 'Reform' Language Perpetuates Monopolies in Parks," *National Parks* 70, no. 1 (1996): 12–13.
5. M. Kriz, "Land Wars," *National Journal* 27 (1995): 2146–2151.

a matter of East versus West. Groups in different parts of the country had different stakes in the government's development of plans to use the natural resources on **public land**,[24] or land held by the government for public use.

The backlash against conservation created a schism in the Republican Party, which had dominated national politics since the Civil War. This schism is represented by the 1909 battle between Secretary of the Interior **Richard A. Ballinger** and Chief Forester **Gifford Pinchot**.[25] Because of the geology, geography, and historical settlement of the West, the federal government held large land holdings.[26] Westerners argued the Eastern bureaucrats and wealthy East Coast urban residents were making policies that would affect Westerners but not them. In fact, people in the West saw the Progressive Conservation Movement as a threat to their livelihoods. At the heart of the debate were money and lifestyle.

This was an example of the classic "haves versus have nots" debate that plagues environmentalism today. The economic sacrifices expected from one group (the Westerners) were the result of policies that would not adversely impact the groups pushing for the policies (the East Coast bureaucrats). The opposition to these policies was a precursor of the Sagebrush Rebellion of the late 1970s and 1980s and the Wise Use Movement of the late 1980s and 1990s.

Although controversial, the early land management practices resulted from the placement of Gifford Pinchot in the Division of Forestry in 1898.[27] Pinchot had been trained as a forester and outlined a plan to scientifically manage forests as a crop for the use of future generations. Richard Ballinger, then Secretary of the Interior, was believed to represent corporate interests.[28] Ballinger, it was alleged, intended to extract natural resources from public lands at the public's expense. Conservationists saw Pinchot as the only hope for preventing the Taft administration (and Ballinger) from turning over the public lands to corporate monopolies and other private interests.

The Pinchot-Ballinger struggle came under public view in 1909, when Pinchot accused Ballinger of selling out the public trust. In 1910, President Taft fired Pinchot for insubordination because Pinchot openly challenged Ballinger's environmental policies.[29] The rift in the Republican party became complete when Teddy Roosevelt ran on the Bull Moose ticket in the 1912 presidential election. Roosevelt represented the conservation side of the Republican party and Taft the business side. The rift led to the election of Woodrow Wilson, only the second Democratic president to be elected since the Civil War. Wilson's conservation principles were virtually indistinguishable from Taft's.[30] The conservation impulse did not totally die with the election of Taft and later Wilson, but its influence on national public policy decreased. It would reappear only after the election of another Roosevelt, Franklin D. Roosevelt, and a national economic crisis.

Conservation in the Period between the Roosevelts

Even though the Progressive Conservation Movement went into dormancy after the conflict in the Republican party, ideas associated with the movement were not dead. The Save-the-Redwoods League was established in 1918, the National Parks and Conservation Association was established in 1919, and the Izaak Walton League was founded in 1922. Federal environmental laws continued to be enacted,[31] and segments of the public were still responding to the conservationist ideology. For the most part, however, conservation advocates were perceived as elitists, and the opposition between Eastern and Western attitudes resulted in significant fractures between environmental groups. Individuals began to form groups to address environmental concerns in their communities. Two themes emerged that would influence the agendas of the modern environmental groups. First, environmental groups became more oriented toward local issues. Second, the ideological differences between groups increased.

THE APEX OF THE CONSERVATION MOVEMENT

The election of Franklin D. Roosevelt in 1932, in the wake of the 1929 stock market crash, ushered in a new conservation era at the federal level. Americans attributed their deteriorating economic conditions to a devastated environment.[32,33] Farmers in the plains states suffered drought and dust bowl conditions created by environmentally destructive farming practices. Southern farmers were also plagued by erosion; they unwisely planted crops on steep hillsides, and the soil was washed away during the hard rains typical of the region. A further compounding burden was the 1927 Mississippi River flood, which left tens of thousands of people temporarily homeless.[34]

All of these problems added to the economic chaos of the Great Depression and created an impetus to enact several pieces of federal legislation that conservation groups had been working on for years.[35] The **Taylor Grazing Act** of 1934 established federal regulatory control of public lands in the West.[36] Ranchers would have to buy permits to graze cattle on public lands. The fee system established at that time may have been economically beneficial, but today cattle grazing on public lands has become controversial. Critics of the policy argue the government subsidy for Western ranchers comes at the cost of deteriorating conditions on public lands.[37-39]

The present controversy over the Taylor Grazing Act indicates that the preservation ideology is gaining added favor. People are interested in preserving the public lands, not in determining how to make the public lands serve human objectives. In fact, many of the federal laws and regulations enacted during the Progressive Conservation period are under attack today as harmful to the environment. For example, human efforts to control flooding along the Mississippi River are argued to have indirectly led to the massive flooding along that river in the summer of 1993.[40]

The environmental policies of the 1930s were human centered and intended to serve economic needs. The laws were enacted, for the most part, to conserve, protect, reconstruct, or prolong natural resources in order to support their use for economic purposes. Some people, however, were moving toward preservationism. Indeed, two important preservationist groups were founded in the 1930s, the Wilderness Society in 1935 and the National Wildlife Federation in 1936.[41] The slow but steady transformation of activism and legislation in the direction of preservationism, however, occurred after World War II.[42] It was also during this time the hazards associated with pollution became a popular concern.

THE POSTWAR ERA: THE RISE OF THE MODERN
ENVIRONMENTAL MOVEMENT

World War II and the postwar era of American economic dominance led to a rapid increase in American industrialization and industrial inventiveness. Innovations included nuclear power and many new **synthetic chemicals**, and the effects of the toxic pollutants became a matter of grave concern. Concern about environmental protection became entangled with the fallout from detonation of the first atomic bomb on Hiroshima, Japan, in 1945.

In 1959, for example, the "great cranberry scare" alerted the public to the potential health hazards associated with the increasing use of chemicals, especially pesticides.[43] In 1958, Representative James Delaney of New York succeeded in adding one simple sentence to the Food Additives Amendment: "no additive shall be deemed safe if it is found to induce cancer when ingested by man or animal."[44] Known as the **Delaney Amendment**, this simple sentence allowed the federal Food and Drug Administration (FDA) "to ban any suspected carcinogen."[45] **Carcinogens** are chemical substances that can cause cancer in exposed animals. Since the Delaney Amendment became law, several food products and chemicals used on food products have been identified as carcinogenic. Some scares, however, have later been determined to be false alarms.[46]

Just as Aldo Leopold's *A Sand County Almanac* put into words the preservation ideology, Rachel Carson's 1962 book *Silent Spring* articulated public concern about the effect of synthetic chemicals on humans and nonhuman animals. Carson warned that contamination of the earth, along with nuclear war, constituted the most serious threat to life.[47] She cautioned against synthetic chemicals "created in man's inventive mind, brewed in his laboratories, and having no counterparts in nature."[48(p.7)] About synthetic insecticides she wrote,

> They have immense power not merely to poison but to enter into the most vital processes of the body and change them in sinister and often deadly ways. Thus, as we shall see, they destroy the very enzymes whose function is to protect the body from harm, they block the oxidation processes from which the body receives its energy, they prevent the normal functioning of various organs, and they may initiate in certain cells the slow and irreversible change that leads to malignancy.[49(pp.16–17)]

The publication of Carson's book was only one of several events in the 1960s that raised public consciousness about environmental degradation. In 1969 Lake Erie was declared "dead" due to industrial pollution.[50–53] The Cuyahoga River in Cleveland spontaneously burst into flames.[54] In 1969 a huge oil spill off the coast of Santa Barbara seemed to presage an environmental crisis. Media coverage of the event was extensive, and the dramatic pictures of the disastrous effects on wildlife deeply penetrated the American psyche.[55]

The swell of public demand for environmental protection culminated in the first Earth Day, celebrated on April 22, 1970. The event was organized by Senator Gaylord Nelson of Wisconsin, but the turnout exceeded all expectations.[56] It solidified popular demand for an increase in environmental protection efforts. Mainstream environmental organizations such as the Sierra Club and the Audubon Society began changing their strategy and priorities as more politically active groups emerged.[57]

The "Washingtonization" of Traditional Environmental Groups

Although some major federal actions to protect the environment had occurred during the 1960s,[58] the federalization of environmental laws did not occur until the following decade. Laws such as the Clean Air Act and Clean Water Act were driven by public demand (see Chapter 5). At the same time, membership of mainstream environmental groups expanded enormously, and these groups soon became major players on the national scene. Many groups moved their headquarters to Washington, D.C., and became professional lobbying organizations. They focused on influencing the environmental policies of Congress and other Washington institutions.

In a sense, the mainstream groups became the official voice of the environmental movement within the halls of Capitol Hill, and some of the top-level administrators attained six-figure incomes and were accorded many of the perks CEOs of major corporations received: limo service, club memberships, furnished apartments, and so on.[59] Eventually, the Washingtonization of these groups had a profound impact on the environmental movement itself, both in Washington and in the rest of the country. The dynamics of the movement changed again and produced new environmental groups with different agendas. In many ways these groups would refocus attention onto controversial environmental issues, and bring attention back to the agenda of the environmental movement.

Environmental Group Membership

Membership in the mainstream environmental organizations continued to grow at a steady pace throughout the 1970s and then exploded in the 1980s in response to President Reagan's attempt to administratively weaken environmental enforcement by decreasing budgetary support.[60] Reagan reduced the Environmental Protection Agency (EPA) budget and the environmental budgets in other agencies, and he appointed people to key positions who tried to administratively alter legislative intent.[61,62] For example, Anne Gorsuch Burford, appointed as head of the EPA, constantly reorganized the agency in an effort to curtail enforcement of EPA regulations.[63] She was eventually cited in contempt of Congress for refusing to hand over documents concerning Superfund.[64,65] Rita Lavelle, a public relations specialist who had worked in the California state government during the Reagan governorship, was charged with and later convicted of perjury when testifying before Congress while assistant administrator for solid waste and emergency response and head of the Superfund program.[66]

James Watt, as secretary of the interior, created public controversy almost from his first day in office. Watt was prodevelopment and wanted to open up public lands for oil exploration and mining. He was publicly hostile to environmentalists.[67,68] By the time of his forced resignation in 1983, Watt was seen as a liability hurting Reagan's reelection campaign.[69] Watt's actions had helped to increase membership in mainstream environmental groups, and the Reagan administration was forced to acknowledge it had misread public opinion regarding environmental issues.

INSIGHT

Greenpeace International Strikes Again

In the summer of 1995, Greenpeace found itself in a familiar place: the international headlines.[1] From atop the Brent Spar oil platform off the coast of Scotland, Greenpeace activists were protesting the sinking of an old oil rig. They argued the Brent Spar oil rig contained 100 tons of poisonous sludge, and Shell's plan to sink the 65,000-ton storage platform to the ocean floor about one and a half miles below constituted an unacceptable use of the ocean as a dumping ground. Company officials were faced with a bill of approximately $80 million to dispose of the rig on dry land, compared with the $16 million it would have cost to sink the rig. Shell UK (a subsidiary of Royal Dutch Shell) gave in to international pressure—applied largely by Greenpeace—and dropped the proposed offshore disposal plan.

While officials in the UK were said to be furious at the company's willingness to submit to blackmail, members from the Offshore Operators Association argued that the Shell decision would have "enormous implications" for the oil industry because there were about 50 rigs due to be disposed of in the next 10 years. Some of the rigs waiting to be disposed of weighed up to 500,000 tons.

Perhaps the biggest victory in its history, Greenpeace took advantage of the fact that it has offices in 30 countries. In April, as Shell began fitting explosives to the rig, Greenpeace sent alpine climbers to occupy the rig. In Germany, Sweden, Norway, and other European countries, motorists began boycotting Shell filling stations, and the company's gasoline sales were reported to have dropped by 30 percent. Shell attempted to force Greenpeace protesters to leave the rig by using high-pressure hoses. Those attempts failed.

Ultimately, the taxpayers may have received the biggest hit, because existing tax rules permit governments to allow companies to write off up to 70 percent of decommissioning costs. Higher costs to the companies mean higher costs to the taxpayers.

---

1. A. MacLeod, "'Land Ho' for Sludge-filled Oil Rig in the North Sea," *Christian Science Monitor*, 22 June 1995, 6.

FISSURES IN THE ENVIRONMENTAL MOVEMENT: 1970s AND 1980s

The success of the mainstream environmental groups on Capitol Hill led to splits in the environmental community, especially at the grassroots level. As Washington insiders, the mainstream groups had to play by Washington rules. Policy making in the United States means bargaining and compromising, and the mainstream groups began giving priority to national issues over important local issues. Local protests to protect community interests became more common,[70] and grassroots environmental groups quickly identified the mainstream groups as a part of the problem. These grassroots groups felt sold out by the mainstream environmental groups.[71] Individuals fighting environmental crises at the local level received little or no support from them and consequently felt distrust of them.

By the early 1990s the membership rolls of the mainstream groups had stagnated if not declined.[72] The groups also experienced budgetary problems, which were pointed to as an indication of the weakening of the environmental movement. The surface appearance, however, disguised the truth: people had merely shifted their energies from national issues to local issues, and they had moved their money and membership from national environmental organizations to local ones. But the shift in national numbers and budgetary retrenchment by Washington environmental groups had an impact on national policy making. Declining national membership levels left the impression that support for environmental programs was declining among the American public in general. The increased numbers of grassroots organizations were overlooked by politicians at the national level, including the Reagan administration.

THE MODERN ENVIRONMENTAL MOVEMENT

The increasing emphasis on local environmental issues underscored another problem emerging between local grassroots groups and Washington-based environmental groups. The latter have often been accused of being elitist, upper-middle class organizations, more concerned about recreational issues than serious environmental hazards in the workplace or poor neighborhoods.[73] Today the environmental movement has seen an expanding range of environmental issues come under its umbrella. This expansion of issues has resulted in an increase in competing ideologies. In particular, conflict in the modern environmental movement has erupted over the best means to confront alleged offenses against the environment. Consider the following brief descriptions of groups representing the modern environmental movement.

NIMBY Groups

While the Washington-based environmental groups typically concentrate on wilderness protection, **grassroots groups**, often referred to as **NIMBY** (not in my backyard) groups, organize at the local level to halt environmental degradation in their own neighborhoods. The organizational structure and membership of the Washington-based groups is markedly different from those of the grassroots groups. NIMBY groups would organize around a specific local issue. In many cases, a group would disband when the local issue had been resolved, or its focus would shift to a different concern. The leader and group members typically come from the community. Members engage in letter-writing campaigns, meet with government or industry officials, wage media campaigns, and do anything they can to help their cause. Group formation is spontaneous and typically in response to unwanted actions or perceived threats in the community. Some of the most highly publicized incidents involving NIMBY activism in recent years were in response to efforts by government and industry to place hazardous waste incinerators near populated areas (see Case Study 1).[74]

Environmental Justice

Attention has recently been focused on the idea of **environmental justice**. It is argued that wealthier communities have the money, education, and political clout needed to prevent locally unwanted land uses (LULUs), whereas poorer communities lack these resources. As a result, unwanted facilities are disproportionately located in low-income, minority communities,[75–76] which is claimed to constitute a form of so-called **environmental racism**.[77–80] One example is found in Washington, D.C. The Potomac River, which flows next to the Jefferson Monument, was cleaned up; the Anacostia River, running through mostly poor African-American communities, remains untouched.

Individuals and groups concerned with the question of environmental justice argue that the willingness to clean wealthy areas but not to address the needs of poor areas is blatantly racist. Because race and class issues are intricately woven together in U.S. society, making distinctions between these issues can be difficult. Fuel was added to the fire when in 1984 a study commissioned by the California Waste Management Board (prepared by Cerrell and Associates and therefore known as the **Cerrell Report**) identified the demographic characteristics of neighborhoods most likely and least likely to oppose the local placement of a hazardous waste facility. The report was used by businesses to target communities that would be less likely to oppose the placement of such facilities. As a result, working class and minority communities were overwhelmingly selected. The environmental justice movement has mobilized to protect people of color and the poor from an increased risk of environmental hazards.[81]

Mainstream Environmental Groups

The environmental movement became institutionalized in the late 1960s and early 1970s. The Environmental Defense Fund was formed in 1967, Friends of Earth was organized in 1969, the Natural Resource Defense Council and Environmental Action were established in 1970, and the Environmental Policy Institute was founded in 1972. With all of the groups evolving, the environmental movement vastly increased in diversity.[82] Environmentalism came to mean many different things to different people.[83] Some groups spend a considerable amount of time lobbying for environmental policies. Other groups pursue dramatically different activities, such as conducting research, litigating, developing education programs, purchasing land, and developing maintenance programs for the land.[84] In general, the primary focus of mainstream environmental groups is education and aggressive lobbying.[85]

Radical Environmental Groups

Direct action can be used to draw attention to an environmental controversy. Groups known for using direct action tactics, such as Greenpeace and

Calvin and Hobbes   by Bill Watterson

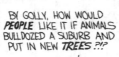

Source: CALVIN AND HOBBES © 1987 Watterson. Dist. by UNIVERSAL PRESS SYNDICATE. Reprinted with permission. All rights reserved.

Earth First!, are classified as **radical environmental groups**. These groups developed in response to the "selling out" of the national environmental groups.

Members of radical environmental groups call for the preservation and restoration of wilderness areas and environment. Referred to by some conservative groups as eco-terrorists, Earth First! adopted extreme tactics to combat environmental degradation.

One of the most famous tactics used by Earth First! was tree spiking. Earth First!ers would place a specific number of metal spikes into a stand of timber. Hoping to slow the logging process down, the group knew that the timber company had to find the spikes before the timber was processed or else they would damage equipment and personnel. Still at issue is whether this activity is terrorism. The timber companies accused Earth First! of intending to hurt people who make their living in the logging industry. Articles about Earth First! suggest the group always notified the relevant timber company prior to the spiking of any trees. While the organization's intent may be debated, its slogan, "No Compromise in Defense of Mother Earth," clearly reflects its agenda.

Another group linked to radical environmentalism is Greenpeace. Established in 1969, Greenpeace gained notoriety in 1975 when some of the members confronted whaling ships, putting themselves between the vessels' harpoons and the whales. Greenpeace has since developed into an international environmental action group. In addition to its efforts to protect the whales, Greenpeace has been active in efforts to stop hazardous waste incinerator placement, has protested nuclear testing, and has effectively stopped harp seal hunting.[86] Its tactics too have been called into question. For example, when Greenpeace spray painted seals in an effort to protect them from hunters (who were collecting the skins for sale), critics argued the only effect of this tactic was to make the seals more vulnerable to natural predators. Dismissing the controversy their activities generate, members of radical environmental groups argue that too little is happening in boardrooms and legislatures. They support going directly to the source of the problem and taking direct action.

The Sagebrush Rebellion and the Wise Use Movement

During the late 1970s, an environmental backlash developed in the American West—the **Sagebrush Rebellion**. After becoming frustrated over the federal management of lands within their borders, several states passed legislation that assumed ownership of all federal lands held within their boundaries. Other states enacted less drastic resolutions that merely asserted control over federal lands.[87]

In the wake of the Sagebrush Rebellion, grassroots groups made up of land owners who felt threatened by federal land management practices began an active campaign opposing the federal environmental management policies. These individual acts are attributed to groups comprising the **Wise Use Movement**. These groups argue the federal government is trying to steal their land, and environmentalists are thought to be conspiring with the government in the theft.[88] In 1988, several hundred grassroots organizations funded primarily by corporate donors affiliated with the mineral extraction industry, spoke out in opposition to environmental policies and practices. Small land owners in the West felt threatened by federal and state actions taken on public lands. As part of their response, offices and vans belonging to the Bureau of Land Management have been bombed, guns have been drawn on park rangers and agents of the Fish and Wildlife Service, and multiple direct threats of bloodshed have been made against other officers.[89,90]

Wise Use groups have followed the same organizational and procedural tactics common in mainstream environmental groups. These groups, however, have an antienvironment message mixed with their antigovernment attitudes. The groups advocate violence against environmentalists and are claimed to be "much more militant than even the most radical environmental group."[91,92]

THE FUTURE OF THE ENVIRONMENTAL MOVEMENT IN THE UNITED STATES

The future of environmental protection in the United States is uncertain. The preservation and conservation themes originating with the Progressive Conservation Movement are easily identified in the modern environmental movement. Public support for environmental protection remains stable but has shifted from the national level to the local level. Tired of having their wells poisoned by unregulated and irresponsible chemical handlers, members of local communities have become active in demanding action from the government. While actions have been taken to implement environmental protection laws and regulations, some are eventually called into question as knowledge about the environment increases. The question of the past was, "Should efforts be directed toward protecting the natural environment?" The question for today seems to be *"How* can the natural environment best be protected?"

Direct Action Can Be Deadly

Controversy in southern California over the Torres-Martinez dump site resulted in gunfire and death. Several activists openly protesting the ongoing dumping of sludge on land owned by the Torres-Martinez Desert Cahuilla Indians have reported receiving death threats. On August 6, 1994, a 14-year-old youth was found dead, shot twice in the head. His aunt, an outspoken opponent of the dumping, believes his death is related to the ongoing community opposition to the dumping.

On August 4, 40 Indians and environmentalists formed a human blockade, preventing at least a dozen trucks from dumping their load of sewage sludge laced with toxic metals and organic compounds. Concerned about family members who had become sick and believing the illnesses to be related to the dump, the activists stood vigil all day in triple-digit heat to prevent the trucks from passing.[1]

Many Indian communities in southern California find themselves in conflict over proposed or existing waste operations on Indian land.

---

1. "Violence in Indian Country over Wastes," *Rachel's Environment and Health Weekly* (Formerly *Rachel's Hazardous Waste News*), 25 August 1994. (Internet address: erf@igc.apc.org.) For further information on the waste wars in southern California, contact California Indians for Cultural and Environmental Protection (CICEP), Star Route Mesa Grande, San Ysabel, CA 92070; or The Indigenous Environmental Network (IEN), P.O. Box 485, Bemidji, MN 56619.

REVIEW QUESTIONS

1. What is the Delaney Amendment?
2. What is the critical difference between preservationism and conservationism?
3. How are the Sagebrush Rebellion and the Wise Use Movement related?
4. What is a grassroots environmental group? Provide several examples.
5. Identify the elements of classical liberalism that affect the environmental attitudes of Americans. How have these concepts affected the environmental movement in the United States?
6. Identify examples of "public lands" in the United States.

DISCUSSION QUESTIONS

1. How would you describe the ideals of the Progressive Conservation Movement? How are preservationism and conservationism related to these ideals?
2. Considering the history of the environmental movement in the United States, what environmental activities might be expected on a global level?
3. If you were to draw a continuum with preservationism on one end and conservationism on the other end, where would you place the following people discussed in the chapter and why? John Muir, H.D. Thoreau, Aldo Leopold, members of the Wise Use Movement, members of Earth First!, Gifford Pinchot, and George Catlin.
4. Can a grassroots group be a national group? Justify your response.
5. Environmental groups are divided partly because of their different ideologies. What other causes might play a role in explaining the continued splintering of modern environmental groups?

REFERENCES

1. R. Nash, *The American Environment: Readings in the History of Conservation*, 2d ed. (Reading, MA: Addison-Wesley, 1976).
2. For example, deer hunting restrictions in Rhode Island and forest protection policies in Pennsylvania (see Nash, *The American Environment*).
3. D.H. Strong, *Dreamers and Defenders: American Conservationists* (Lincoln, NE: University of Nebraska Press, 1988).
4. Strong, *Dreamers and Defenders*, 66.

5. S. Cable and C. Cable, *Environmental Problems, Grassroots Solutions: The Politics of Grassroots Environmental Conflict* (New York: St. Martin's Press, 1995), especially chaps. 3, 4, 5.

6. J.V. Switzer, *Environmental Politics: Domestic and Global Dimensions* (New York: St. Martin's Press, 1994), 7.

7. Cable and Cable, *Environmental Problems, Grassroots Solutions*, 55.

8. Classical liberalism is an area of study in its own right. The premise is that the individual is of primary importance, not the community. The state (community) is organized to solve a particular set of problems and essentially exists as a means for people to pursue their private ends.

9. The basic texts of classical liberalism include John Locke's *Second Treatise of Civil Government*, Thomas Jefferson's *Democracy*, Immanuel Kant's *Critique of Pure Reason*, and John Rawls's *Political Liberalism*.

10. G. Catlin, *Letters and Notes on the Manners, Customs, and Conditions of the North American Indians* (London: H.G. Bohn, 1844).

11. Nash, *The American Environment*.

12. For example, A. Leopold, *A Sand County Almanac* (New York, Ballantine Books, 1966; originally published in 1949).

13. S. Zakin, *Coyotes and Town Dogs: Earth First! and the Environmental Movement* (New York: Penguin, 1993), 28.

14. Strong, *Dreamers and Defenders*, 143.

15. Strong, *Dreamers and Defenders*, 146.

16. Strong, *Dreamers and Defenders*, 195–196.

17. Leopold, *A Sand County Almanac*, vii.

18. Nash, *The American Environment*.

19. Strong, *Dreamers and Defenders*, 41–58.

20. Nash, *The American Environment*.

21. Switzer, *Environmental Politics*, 157.

22. Specifically worthy of note are the 1902 Reclamation Act and the 1906 Antiquities Act.

23. Nash, *The American Environment*.

24. Switzer, *Environmental Politics*, chap. 4.

25. Strong, *Dreamers and Defenders*, 80–84.

26. Switzer, *Environmental Politics*, 75.

27. Strong, *Dreamers and Defenders*, 66.

28. Strong, *Dreamers and Defenders*, 80–84.

29. Strong, *Dreamers and Defenders*.

30. Strong, *Dreamers and Defenders*.

31. For example, in 1911 the Weeks Act was signed into law. This act allowed the federal government to establish national forests in the East. In 1916 the National Park Service Act was signed into law, and in 1920 the Mineral Leasing Act allowed for the regulation of mining on public lands.

32. R. Dunlap and A. Mertig, *American Environmentalism: The U.S. Environmental Movement, 1970–1990* (Washington, DC: Taylor and Francis, 1992), 2.

33. J.P. Lester, *Environmental Politics and Policy: Theories and Evidence* (Durham, NC: Duke University Press, 1989), 26.

34. C. Clark, "Taming the Mississippi," in *Floods* (Alexandria, VA: Time Life Books, 1982), 65–95. Also worthy of note is the federal response to the 1927 Mississippi flood. The Flood Control Act of 1928 was the first in a long line of federally funded statutes attempting to control flooding in the United States.

35. In 1933, for example, the Civilian Conservation Corps and the Soil Erosion Service were established. The Tennessee Valley Authority finally gained approval after a 15-year struggle.

36. Nash, *The American Environment*.

37. B. Knickerbocker, "Ranchers Clash with Rangers in Wild West," *The Christian Science Monitor*, 13 July 1995, 1.

38. B. Knickerbocker, "Ranchers Chafe at New Rules on Range," *The Christian Science Monitor*, 16 August 1995, 4.

39. L. Drew, "Whose Home *Is* the Range, Anyway?" *National Wildlife*, December–January 1994, 12–18.

40. J. Abramovitz, *Imperiled Waters, Impoverished Future: The Decline of Freshwater Ecosystems*, Worldwatch Paper 128 (Washington, DC: Worldwatch Institute, 1996), 16–22.

41. Dunlap and Mertig, *American Environmentalism*, 12.

42. Dunlap and Mertig, *American Environmentalism*, 2.

43. The controversy surrounding such claims is discussed in A. Wildavsky, *But Is It True? A Citizen's Guide to Environmental Health and Safety Issues* (Cambridge, MA: Harvard University Press, 1995), 11–19.

44. Delaney was passed in 1958 as a title of the Food, Drug and Cosmetics Act. See the current debate about the present usefulness of the Delaney Clause in G. Easterbrook, *A Moment on the Earth: The Coming of Environmental Realism* (New York: Viking Penguin, 1995), 447–449.

45. It did not take long for the Delaney Amendment to have an impact. Health Education and Welfare Secretary Arthur S. Flemming declared in November 1959 "that some cranberry products currently on the market were contaminated by residues of aminotriazole, which the FDA claimed caused cancer in laboratory rats." Flemming went on to warn consumers not to buy cranberries in any form until they could ascertain the cranberry's purity. This, of course, was an impossible task. The result was mass hysteria among the public concerning the safety of the food supply, particularly cranberries, and the bottom fell out of the cranberry market. This public scare laid the foundations for the renewed strength of the environmental movement in the 1960s and 1970s. See C.J. Bosso, *Pesticides and Politics: The Life Cycle of a Public Issue* (Pittsburgh, PA: University of Pittsburgh Press, 1987), 97.

46. See Wildavsky, *But Is It True?* Wildavsky critically reviews a variety of environmental policy decisions that are essentially "reactive" responses rather than responses based on justified concerns. The topics discussed include DDT, Agent Orange, hazardous waste sites, asbestos, alar, acid rain, and ozone depletion.

47. Strong, *Dreamers and Defenders*, 189.

48. R. Carson, *Silent Spring* (Boston: Houghton Mifflin, 1962), 7.

49. Carson, *Silent Spring*, 16–17.

50. Easterbrook, *A Moment on the Earth*, 629–630.

51. T. Colborn et al., *Great Lakes: Great Legacy?* (Washington, DC: The Conservation Foundation, 1990).

52. A. Markham, *A Brief History of Pollution* (New York: St. Martin's Press, 1994), 61–63.

53. Switzer, *Environmental Politics*, 74–175.

54. For an extensive history of what is now the Cuyahoga Valley National Recreation Area, see R. Cockrell, *A Green Shrouded Miracle: The Administrative History of the Cuyahoga Valley National Recreation Area* (Omaha, NE: U.S. Department of the Interior, National Park Service, 1992).

55. P.C. Yeager, *The Limits of Law: The Public Regulation of Private Pollution* (New York: Cambridge University Press, 1992), 104.

56. Dunlap and Mertig, *American Environmentalism*, 2.

57. In 1967 the Environmental Defense Fund was established, and Friends of the Earth came into existence in 1969. The League of Conservation Voters was founded in 1970, as was the National Resources Defense Council and Environmental Action. The more radical environmental group Greenpeace was established in 1971.

58. For example, the Wilderness Act of 1964, the National Wild and Scenic Rivers Act of 1968, and the National Trails System Act of 1968.

59. C. Manes, *Green Rage: Radical Environmentalism and the Unmaking of Civilization* (Boston: Little, Brown, 1990), 66–83.

60. Dunlap and Mertig, *American Environmentalism*, 102–106.

61. Switzer, *Environmental Politics*, 59–62.

62. Lester, *Environmental Politics and Policy*, 200–201.

63. Switzer, *Environmental Politics*, 61–62.

64. Switzer, *Environmental Politics*, 61.

65. N.J. Vig, "Presidential Leadership: From Reagan to the Bush Administration," in *Environmental Policy in the 1990s*, eds. N.J. Vig and M.E. Draft (Washington, DC: CQ Press, 1990).

66. H. Barnett, *Toxic Debts and the Superfund Dilemma* (Chapel Hill, NC: University of North Carolina Press, 1994), 76.

67. Switzer, *Environmental Politics*, 59–60.

68. Lester, *Environmental Politics and Policy*, 113–114, 131–132.

69. Switzer, *Environmental Politics*, 60.

70. C. Piller, *The Fail-Safe Society: Community Defiance and the End of American Technological Optimism* (New York: Basic Books, 1991).

71. Manes, *Green Rage*.

72. A. Szasz, *EcoPopulism: Toxic Waste and the Movement for Environmental Justice* (Minneapolis, MN: University of Minnesota Press, 1994).

73. For a more comprehensive discussion of these issues, see R. Gottlieb, *Forcing the Spring: The Transformation of the American Environmental Movement* (Washington, DC: Island Press, 1993).

74. Piller, *The Fail-Safe Society*.

75. R. Bullard, *Confronting Environmental Racism: Voices from the Grassroots* (Boston: Southend Press, 1993).

76. R. Bullard, *Dumping in Dixie* (Boulder, CO: Westview Press, 1990).

77. Bullard, *Confronting Environmental Racism.*

78. Bullard, *Dumping in Dixie.*

79. C. Lee, *Toxic Wastes and Race in the United States: A National Report on the Racial and Socio-economic Characteristics of Communities with Hazardous Waste Sites* (New York: United Church of Christ, Commission for Racial Justice, 1987).

80. R. Bush, *Hazardous Waste Facilities: Race as a Siting Factor* (Arlington, VA: Citizen's Clearinghouse for Hazardous Wastes, 1988).

81. J. Petrikin, *Environmental Justice* (San Diego, CA: Greenhaven Press, 1995).

82. Dunlap and Mertig, *American Environmentalism*, 5.

83. R. Gottlieb, "An Odd Assortment of Allies: American Environmentalism in the 1990s," *Gannett Center Journal* 4 (1990): 42.

84. Dunlap and Mertig, *American Environmentalism*, 17.

85. Dunlap and Mertig, *American Environmentalism*, 19.

86. P. List, *Radical Environmentalism: Philosophy and Tactics* (Belmont, CA: Wadsworth, 1993), chap. 4.

87. The region in which the Sagebrush Rebellion occurred comprised the states of Alaska, Arizona, California, Colorado, Idaho, Montana, Nevada, New Mexico, North Dakota, Oregon, Utah, Washington, and Wyoming. In some of these the "rebellion" was more intense than in others.

88. M. Dowie, *Losing Ground: American Environmentalism at the Close of the Twentieth Century* (Cambridge, MA: MIT Press, 1995).

89. Knickerbocker, "Ranchers Clash with Rangers in Wild West," 1.

90. E. Larson, "Unrest in the West: Welcome to Nevada's Nye County, Whose Angry Residents Are Spearheading the Region's Charge against Washington," *Time*, 23 October 1995, 52–60.

91. Knickerbocker, "Ranchers Clash with Rangers in Wild West."

92. Larson, "Unrest in the West."

CHAPTER 3

Economics, Politics, and Environmental Protection

Mary Clifford

TERMS		
	abatement	environmental impact
	accumulation	statement
	capital	externalities
	capitalism	legitimization
	commodities	natural resources
	consumer satisfaction	public goods
	cost-benefit analysis	Reclamation Act of 1902
	economic growth	sustainable development
	economics	U.S. Bureau of Reclamation
	efficiency	wetlands

Throughout the history of the environmental movement, the relationships between politics, economics, and given environmental issues have occasionally taken center stage. Environmental issues are, or quickly become, political and economic issues. The controversy over the spotted owl is an excellent example (see Case Study 4). People tended to support either the timber industry or the environmental groups, and the controversy became a battle over preserving jobs or protecting the environment. At the center of the controversy, a critical question remains unanswered: How should the United States manage natural resources both in the short term and over the long term?

Early product development relied on the extraction of natural resources from the earth. Examples include fishing, harvesting timber, drilling for petroleum, and mining for metals (e.g., gold, silver, copper, etc.) and energy sources (e.g., coal and uranium). In the emerging computer age, product development also requires use of synthetic materials (e.g., materials developed in a lab). As illustrated in the history of the environmental movement, people increasingly express concern about the risk posed by new technologies. Today, markets increasingly include products with untested or unknown safety results.[1] As much as people desire the government to provide a stable economic climate, they also expect the government to protect them from unnecessary harm.

The question cited at the close of Chapter 2 was, How can the natural environment best be protected? When politics and economics are introduced, the question must be expanded: How can the United States best manage its remaining natural resources, allow for economic expansion through technological development, and protect citizens from untested, potentially damaging processes in the short term and over the long term? An understanding of how economic and political forces impact the modern environmental movement will better prepare students to address this question.

In this chapter, fundamental concepts from the field of economics are reviewed. The economic and political dimensions of the production process are used to explain aspects of current environmental controversies. Will the push to protect the natural environment result in job losses and future economic insecurity for citizens in the United States? Several examples of current environmental conflicts are used to illustrate the problems associated with changes in economic and political agendas. As we will see, solutions provided in one era may return as environmental problems in the future. The chapter closes with some final reflections on the relationship between politics and economics.

THE PRODUCTION PROCESS

The production process begins with the extraction of raw materials or **natural resources**. Once the raw materials have been mined or harvested, they are transported to a factory where workers transform the raw materials into manufactured products. The final products are transported to a marketplace where they can be sold to the public.

Calvin and Hobbes   by Bill Watterson

Source: CALVIN AND HOBBES © 1995 Watterson. Dist. by UNIVERSAL PRESS SYNDICATE. Reprinted with permission. All rights reserved.

The production process, outlined in simple terms above, refers to only one of an infinite number of production processes making up the economic system of a country. A country establishes an economic system to answer basic questions about how people's needs and wants will be satisfied. The economic base of a country is fluid, meaning it can change. In the early 1900s, the U.S. economy changed from having an agricultural base to having an industrial base. At present, some believe the U.S. economy is changing again, this time into a computer-based economy.

People who participate in the economic system benefit by being paid to provide labor in the production process and by having access to the merchandise the production process creates. The economic system in the United States is capitalism. **Capitalism** is characterized by freedom of the marketplace. The idea is to establish private ownership of product development and distribution. Ownership increases proportionately with increases in accumulation and reinvestment of profits.[2] Let's say Meredith decides to start her own business. Once her corporation begins to make a profit, she will begin to accumulate wealth. If she reinvests her wealth, she further increases her potential for profit. The more she invests, the more profit she stands to make. The greater her profits, the greater her opportunities to invest. Investment, however, also involves risk. Not all investments result in profit. Many business opportunities are built on a series of assumptions. If Meredith allots her money to a risky venture and the assumptions she makes are incorrect, she could lose all of her investment.

Over time, individuals hope to increase their capital, and the country hopes to increase its economic growth. **Capital** includes property, machines, buildings, tools, and money used to produce goods and services. A country's **economic growth** reflects the increase in the capacity of the economy to provide goods and services for final use. All parties in a capitalist economic system benefit from and therefore pursue growth.

The "free market" in the United States under capitalism is not as free as some would like.[3] A variety of restrictions or regulations dictate how businesses can be run. Regulations for environmental protection are one example. People argue that the regulations fall unfairly on the shoulder of midsized firms because large corporations can absorb the enormous costs of environmental regulatory compliance.[4,5]

Other environmental actions affect businesses more directly. Consider the Everglades restoration project in Florida. After a disastrous effort to gain control over the **wetlands** of Florida through the construction of a mammoth canal system, all levels of government are cooperating to return the wetlands back to their natural state.[6–8] The canal system was developed to drain the land for farming, but scientists say the land needs to be returned to marsh in order to restore the natural flow of cleaner water to the Atlantic. Sugar producers in Florida argue the restoration will cost over 40,000 jobs, and any more environmental cleanup costs will force their businesses under.[9] The farmers benefited from the draining of the wetlands, and the return of the wetlands could mean their economic ruin. So for many people of south Florida, the question is whether the government should restore the Everglades or protect the economic stability of businesses like the sugar cane industry.

ECONOMICS

Economics is the science that studies the production, distribution, and consumption of commodities. **Commodities** are articles of trade or commerce, traditionally agricultural and mining products. Natural resources are one type of commodity. Using economic terms, environmental problems can be analyzed in terms of consumer satisfaction, efficiency, externalities, and public goods.[10] **Consumer satisfaction** is related to the ability of a product to make buyers of the product happy with their purchase. Good sales indicate high consumer satisfaction.

Efficiency refers to a company's ability to develop and produce a high-selling product using a minimum of resources and technology. From the perspective of the industry, the objective is to develop a product people want to buy, at the lowest cost to the company. Any excess cost produces an inefficient system. **Externalities** are the effects the production process has on those not a party to the benefits of the process. A release of toxic waste into a river, for example, is an externalized cost. Instead of paying to dispose of the waste properly, the business saves disposal costs by transferring those costs to the people downstream. A cost is not necessarily monetary; it could be an adverse health effect or a mass killing of fish, for example. The resulting contamination may adversely affect a public good. **Public goods** are those goods that cannot be efficiently supplied to one person without also enabling many other persons to enjoy them.[11] The national parks are a public good.

Economics is argued to play a critical role in environmental policy decisions. Economists typically recommend a **cost-benefit analysis** as a viable solution to environmental dilemmas.[12] A cost-benefit analysis assesses the costs of a particular action and weights them against the benefits derived from that same action. In assessing pollution reduction efforts, a cost-benefit analysis would balance the costs of abatement against the benefits of pollution reduction.[13] **Abatement** is the process of reducing or eliminating pollution in a given area.[14] So if completing the abatement process created

INSIGHT

Can Computers Be Environmentally Friendly?

Computers are changing the way Americans think, the way they shop, and the way they do business. Global pressures are increasing the demand for shorter product development time frames, lower costs, and products with reduced environmental impact.[1] To achieve these objectives, manufacturers must consider, in the design phase of a product, all following phases, including manufacturing, marketing, distribution, and product recycling.[2]

The computer industry is responding to public demand that it become greener. As PC components become more integrated, the power requirements for the machine drop significantly.[3] This is particularly evident with the energy-saving processors and motherboards. Intel Corporation has machines enter "sleep" mode during inactive periods, and it no longer uses toxic nickel-based plating in its processors and motherboards.[4]

Other computer manufacturing processes are designed to eliminate the need for toxic materials. For example, use of CFCs (chlorofluorocarbons), once standard in computer manufacturing processes, has been completely eliminated by Compaq.

The Santa Clara County Manufacturing Group, with 25 member companies in Santa Clara County, reduced their collective chemical emissions by 1 million pounds in 1990 and by 4.3 million pounds (74 percent) since they began reduction efforts in 1987.[5] The companies in the group include Apple Computer, Intel, Lockheed, Digital Equipment Corporation, and the Amdahl Corporation.

Companies are finding that the costs of instituting green policies are offset by the benefits. In addition to complying with government regulations and providing positive public relations, the elimination of environmentally unfriendly practices can mean cost savings.[6] Batteries, toner cartridges, and floppy disks provide unique difficulties for cleanup and recycling efforts,[7] but, while current solutions are not perfect, the increasing efforts to deal with them suggest positive outcomes may be possible in the future.

1. S.R. Hedberg, "Design of a Lifetime," *Byte*, October 1994, 103–106.
2. Hedberg, "Design of a Lifetime."
3. K. Doyle, "PC Makers Work To Clean up Toxic Manufacturing Process: Buyers, Vendors See Green in Ecological PCs," *PC Week*, 15 November 1993, 179.
4. Doyle, "PC Makers."
5. "Santa Clara Firms Reduce Emissions," *Chilton's Electronic News*, 29 July 1991, 21.
6. M. Perenson, "Clean Machines," *PC Magazine*, 12 October 1993, 32.
7. Perenson, "Clean Machines."

financial difficulties for a company (a cost) without providing compensatory benefits, a cost-benefit analysis would not support continuing with the abatement process.

Economists argue that the "extreme environmentalist position" of prohibiting *all* pollution would generally be wasteful.[15] The benefits of driving a car, for example, far outweigh the costs of the air pollution emitted. Adherence to a "zero discharge" policy would mean banning all cars with any level of emissions. In this case, "economic efficiency calls for a compromise—a substantial but not complete reduction of emissions—balancing the value of the industry's output against the damage caused from pollution."[16(p.773)]

Economist William Baxter argues that environmental problems are economic problems: "To assert that there is a pollution problem or an environmental problem is to assert, at least implicitly, that one or more resources is not being used so as to maximize human satisfaction."[17(p.17)] Because economics is especially concerned with efficiency, it is identified as the best discipline for understanding the inefficiency associated with pollution.[18]

But while supporters claim economics is the best means for solving existing environmental problems, others argue that the use of economics alone is limiting. For example, economics does not adequately address externalities. Perhaps Joshua decides not to drive a car because he wants cleaner air and he knows car exhaust is a major source of air pollution. Even though Joshua does not purchase an automobile, the pollution from the automobile production process affects him. Among other things, he is subject to the negative effects of air pollution coming from car exhausts. No one, including the car manufacturers, pays for the auto exhaust emissions.

If people refused to buy cars that produced air pollution and they demanded the automakers develop clean-burning technologies, then perhaps Joshua's objective, cleaner air, would be met. But as it is, people who purchase cars argue that the benefits derived from driving a car far outweigh the costs of air pollution. With this as the prevailing ideology, car manufacturers can still produce cars that pollute the air, and depend on people to buy them.

Economic efficiency has traditionally meant achieving the maximum satisfaction of consumer preferences. Preferences are revealed through consumer choice or by monitoring the products people buy. Although society as a whole is affected by air pollution emitted from car exhausts, the collective consumer preference for cars remains stable. People want to buy automobiles. Because Joshua is a voice of only one, his opposition to car emissions has little effect. If he desires a better solution to the air pollution problem, he might do best to become involved in the democratic political process.

POLITICS

Politics in the United States is closely linked to economics. In an economic model, environmental policy is focused on "achieving the maximum or optimal amount of human satisfaction possible, given all the conflicting demands on the natural resources at stake."[19(p.15)] Yet, what exactly is the optimal amount of human satisfaction? Further, how does one measure human satisfaction? These questions are addressed, if not answered, in the political arena.

Typically the basis used in economics for determining consumer preferences is self-interest.[20] People buy what they want, what makes them happy, and what they think they need. Environmentalists have long resented efforts to place the environment and natural resources into a human satisfaction formula.[21] They disagree with the idea of using individual preferences for determining consumer preferences, arguing instead that economists cannot account for consumers who, rather than pursue strictly individual interests, are more interested in protecting the collective good.[22] In theory, at least, political activity is supposed to provide a vehicle for airing and criticizing opinions, then settling upon what might be called the community opinion.[23]

Clearly, not all legislation is based on the economic model and cost-benefit analysis. Congress passed the Endangered Species Act to protect threatened species even if the costs outweighed the economic benefits. The same is true of the Clean Air Act and the Clean Water Act.[24] Environmental laws constitute at least one instance where the United States is governed by legislative and political systems over economic markets.[25]

Recent reports suggest a majority of Americans strongly prefer environmental laws that are not necessarily economically efficient. In the summer of 1992, a poll taken by the Wirthlin group found that 80 percent of those questioned agreed that "protecting the environment is so important that requirements and standards cannot be made too high, and continuing environmental improvement must be made regardless of cost."[26(p.1155)] The poll also found that, if forced to choose between economic growth and a clean environment, the public favored environmental protection by a two-to-one margin.[27]

The public's current attitude is markedly different than its attitude 30 years ago. In 1965, national opinion polls found Americans typically ranked water and air pollution well below concerns such as juvenile delinquency, unemployment, and even recreation.[28] Other survey research suggested two-thirds of the American public was unwilling to pay anything in increased taxes for water purity improvement and air pollution abatement.[29]

Should Plastics Be Banned?

In 1988 Suffolk County, New York, banned plastic bags as well as plastic, foam, and other polystyrene containers used primarily in food stores and restaurants. Originally hailed as a "landmark law against our throwaway society,"[1(p.40)] it eventually generated mounting opposition. Full implementation of the law was held up by litigation from the plastics industry, and although it was never vigorously enforced, businesses and even some environmental groups opposed the law. The environmental groups were concerned such a ban would result in an increased use of paper products and an increased loss of trees. Further, many agreed that plastics, when compacted in landfills, are not much worse for the environment than paper.[2] In 1992, the law was set aside, to be reconsidered after a study was completed. Six years after the ban was proposed, the legislature adopted an amendment to eliminate the ban on plastics and push for more recycling instead.[3] The resulting legislation encourages consumers to place plastic refuse in plastic barrels for recycling. Further, it encourages towns and villages to create drop-off sites for polystyrene materials coming from homeowner garbage.

1. S. Pattison, "Banning Plastic," *Consumer's Research Magazine*, May 1992, 40.
2. J. McQuiston, "Suffolk Legislators Drop a Ban on Plastic Packaging for Foods," *New York Times*, 9 March 1994, A7.
3. McQuiston, "Suffolk Legislators."

Claims about increased support for environmental protection are contradicted to some degree by the ongoing political struggles to determine the public mood. In his 1992 election campaign, President Bush, promising to give economic costs greater weight in environmental conflicts, painted Clinton and Gore as environmental extremists.[30] In 1995, the U.S. Congress displayed a healthy distaste for environmental protection legislation in a series of heated debates on the environment.[31-33] Some members of the GOP questioned whether they "underestimated the broad public appeal of environmental safeguards."[34] Clinton denounced Republican "polluter protection" legislation,[35] a step that was argued to have given him a tremendous boost in the 1996 presidential election.

The role of government in environmental protection has been antagonistic, at best.[36,37] James O'Connor identifies two fundamental and contradictory functions of the modern advanced capitalist state.[38(p.38)] Using the terms *accumulation* and *legitimization*, O'Connor outlines two conflicting responsibilities assigned to government. First, accumulation refers to the government's obligation to create and maintain conditions under which profitable capital **accumulation** is possible. The government is charged with ensuring a climate conducive to continued economic growth. **Legitimization**, the state's second function, dictates the state's responsibility to create and maintain social harmony. This includes protecting the public from potential harms.[39] The government is legitimate if it protects the people for which it is said to operate. In the case of the environment, these two functions of government are seen to be in direct conflict with one another, as O'Connor makes clear in the following:

> The obligations of aiding economic growth while protecting the public frequently create a serious dilemma for the state: A capitalist state that openly uses its coercive forces to help one class accumulate capital at the expense of other classes loses its legitimacy and hence undermines the basis of its loyalty and support. But a state that ignores the necessity of assisting the process of capital accumulation risks drying up the source of its own power, the economy's surplus production capacity and the taxes drawn from this surplus.[40(p.6)]

Overall, economists would be correct in proclaiming the production of consumer goods under capitalism, the accumulation function, a success. The free market system has performed less well, however, when it comes to providing social benefits.[41] The success of accumulation, some argue, masks the inadequate attention given to the legitimization function. The public has not been protected from potential environmental hazards or existing environmental harm. Excessive attention has been given to the accumulation function. Resolution to the inevitable conflict can be found only in the political arena. These battles are waged over long periods of time, with different social class interests reflected on either side.[42]

It has been argued that the environmentalists that made up the Progressive Conservation Movement typically came from affluent backgrounds.[43] They were elites and acted as an interest group rather than a grassroots movement. Because participation in the political process is overwhelmingly dominated by upper-class groups, early conservationism was identified as an upper-class activity.

Beginning in 1785, the federal government sold parcels of land to the highest bidder at a minimum price of $1 per acre, with a 640-acre minimum.[44] The Taylor Grazing Act of 1934 closed remaining public land to homesteading and divided this land into grazing districts.[45] As a result of the Taylor Grazing Act, the Division of Grazing was created to establish grazing districts, set fees, and grant use permits.[46] People became concerned that the agenda at the national level was focused on elite business interests and excluded the needs of the homesteaders. The federal administration of these lands was seen as protecting the economic status of those who had already achieved wealth, while restricting opportunities for others who were less affluent. Although the government's holding of land in the public domain was arguably intended as a public benefit, it reduced the amount of overall resources available to the nation.[47] Indeed, corporate interests were generally served by the actions taken by the environmentalists in the Progressive Conservation Movement:

> Economic efficiency appealed to the federal regulatory agencies that were charged with monitoring and maintaining the "wise use" of natural resources. As a result, regulatory agency policies tended to benefit larger operators more than smaller ones. Consequently executives of the larger corporations were generally supportive of environmental progressivism as a conservative policy that protected and even enlarged their own wealth and power.[48(p.57)]

Because the government's principal concern at the time seemed to be securing stable patterns of growth, or meeting the accumulation function, the interests of the elites led the Progressive Conservation Movement. Overall, at least two important consequences resulted from the policies of the Progressive Conservation Movement. First, they contributed to the concentration of wealth. Second, they set in motion the trend of government-augmented economic growth.[49] In fact, the Progressive Conservation Movement had a symbiotic relationship with business, in marked contrast to the environmental groups of the present, which identify corporations and economic growth as enemies of the environment.

It soon became a common perception that the government could not be trusted to provide protection for "the little guy." The responsibility of government to maintain social harmony (the legitimization function) was not being met. When federal public lands, for example, were leased for grazing at fees much lower than were charged for comparable private grazing land, local landowners were outraged.[50] Low grazing fees have been identified as unfair government subsidies, biased against local ranchers who grazed their cattle on private land. Even now, this conflict is ongoing. The unfair practices associated with government subsidies for cattle grazing are only one aspect of the conflict. Many also argue the overgrazing of these public lands has devastated the natural ecosystems in those areas beyond recovery. They argue the people should be compensated for the loss of their public good.

In 1974 the Natural Resource Defense Council won a landmark suit that forced the Bureau of Land Management (BLM) to develop an **environmental impact statement** (see Chapter 5) to assess the effects of grazing on public lands, and ranchers fought back by organizing the Sagebrush Rebellion. This was the first politically viable challenge to the mainstream environmental movement since the early 1950s.[51] But legislation was passed in 1978 to require a uniform grazing fee. Additional legislation, passed in 1980, provided a formula for determining grazing fees. In 1993 the fees were changed again and set significantly lower than the amount ranchers would have to pay to graze on privately owned land.[52] At present, the controversy over grazing on public land continues.

Environmentalists want the federal government to change the grazing practices on public lands. Grazing is now permitted on 89 percent of all BLM land and 69 percent of all Forest Service lands, for a total of more than 256 million acres.[53] The same conflict is still being played out as ranchers (private landowners) clash with rangers (keepers of the public land).[54] More recently, opposition to environmental regulations has come from private landowners whose properties are affected by environmental protection legislation. They claim that they have a right to use the land they own as they choose and that environmental protection legislation has either restricted their use of their land or devalued their land completely. For example, the land is deemed economically worthless because it has been classified as protected wetlands or includes timber holdings that house endangered species. In many instances the natural resources found on a piece of property cannot be harvested or excavated. Further, a Supreme Court decision handed down in July 1995 stated that it was not enough to simply protect species; if the habitat of an endangered species was destroyed, the effect would be the destruction of the species[55] (see Case Study 4).

Citizens who have been deprived of their ability to use their own land claim that this type of restriction "violates a sacred trust."[56(p.19)] Many of them are angry and as a result they have been labeled, perhaps unfairly, anti-environment.[57] One possible solution is to widen the scope of the Fifth Amendment guarantee requiring compensation for government takings of private lands. Congress and more than 30 states are considering laws that would require taxpayers to compensate a property holder for government actions that devalue the holder's land.[58] The Endangered Species Act and wetlands declarations are two areas affected by the legislation. These actions are reflections of the Wise Use Movement, which seeks to defend property owner rights against what are considered to be intrusive government regulations.

Land management represents only one example of political battles over environmental protection efforts. In the first half of this century, the water resource development programs of the **U.S. Bureau of Reclamation** and the Army Corps of Engineers were considered conservationist.[59] The **Reclamation Act of 1902** provided for government construction of irrigation projects that would be paid for by water users.[60] Irrigation was favored as a basic means of economic development and settlement of the arid West.[61] Administered by the Bureau of Reclamation, and driven by efforts to develop hydroelectric power, 13 major storage dams were under construction by 1940.[62] The energy and water regulation from federally owned dams transformed southern California and other parts of the Southwest into industrial and agricultural centers.

Critics argue that much of this development happened too quickly and that the ecology of the region suffered.[63] In fact, many environmental groups today regret early conservation efforts conducted through the Bureau of Reclamation.[64] One of the first protests organized by the radical environmental group Earth First! was in support of *removing* the Glen Canyon Dam.[65]

Efforts to resolve differences between groups with conflicting environmental objectives resulted in an experiment conducted in 1996 at the Glen Canyon Dam.[66] Identified as a new direction in resource management policy, over 120 billion gallons of water were released, raising the Colorado River by 10 to 15 feet inside the Grand Canyon. The release was intended to mimic the annual spring floods that occurred when the river ran free. Officials hope wildlife and beaches, degraded since 1966 when the dam was built, will be restored.[67] Led by Bruce Babbitt, Secretary of the Interior, several groups were identified as "willing partners" in exploring this tactic as a way to repair damage done to the river ecosystem. Environmental groups, energy officials, and Native Americans worked together to forge a plan that would suit everyone with an interest in the project. The project does not come without a cost—an economic cost. Electric utilities say every kilowatt-hour of energy lost down river must be bought elsewhere, either through increased rates or increased taxes.[68] While the discharge was touted as an environmental victory, the economic losses may further increase the political conflict over the future of the Glen Canyon Dam.

THE RELATIONSHIP BETWEEN ECONOMICS, POLITICS, AND THE ENVIRONMENT

The popular perception about economics and the environment is that business interests are on one side and environmentalists are on the other side.[69-74] **Sustainable development,** an attempt to guide economic growth in an environmentally sound manner, is offered as a possible solution. In contrast to traditional economic growth patterns,[75] sustainable development will allow the economy to meet individual and collective needs today but provide more security for future generations.

A recent study done by the World Business Council for Sustainable Development (WBCSD) asked whether financial markets are intrinsically opposed to the goal of sustainable development.[76] Using economic models, "it almost always makes more financial sense to destroy a sustainable natural resource by overuse or overharvesting, and to put the money in the bank rather than to use the resource sustainably."[77(p.4)] This is true because a timber company would enjoy higher annual returns off of the interest on the

Calvin and Hobbes   by Bill Watterson

money in the bank, given today's interest rates, than from annual harvests of slow-growing commodities like trees.[78] The findings of the WBCSD study, however, were somewhat of a surprise: "Instead of finding gloom and doom, we found a lot of business opportunity in the slow progress toward financial markets that place value on 'sustainable' environmental practices."[79(p.19)] Without dramatic changes in the law, the researchers predict the market will begin to reward clean companies more. Their overall conclusion was that financial markets were in fact interested in sustainable development.

Leaders of Fortune 500 companies and of principal U.S. environmental groups have agreed on a general path to sustainable growth.[80] The city of San Jose, California, has developed what they call the green line.[81] To prevent urban sprawl, a perimeter for the city has been identified, and no growth is allowed to extend beyond that boundary.

Critics continue to claim that environmental regulations are bad for business, result in job losses, and have an overall negative effect on the economy. Recent studies suggest, however, that the conflict between business interests and environmentalists is being mitigated. A 1996 report concluded that environmental laws and regulations are not a big cause of job loss.[82] The report suggests these contentions are exaggerated.[83] Stephen Meyer, director of the Project on Environmental Politics and Policy at the Massachusetts Institute of Technology, has studied the relationship between strong environmental laws and economic growth in all 50 states. His research indicates that states with stronger environmental policies economically outperform states with weaker environmental policies.[84]

A variety of efforts to serve both environmental interests and business interests are being heralded as model programs. For example, Deseret Land and Livestock Corporation, a 200,000-acre Wyoming ranch, has integrated ecologically sound management practices into its ranching operations. Since the changes, the company has seen increases in both cattle and wild elk herds while earning extra money from hunting fees.[85] International Paper has set aside land for wildlife, and hunting, camping, hiking, and fishing fees have made the program profitable.[86]

Countries across the globe are confronting the economic and political issues associated with environmental protection. In New South Wales, Australia, economic interests have taken a back seat to political activities. A wood-chipping industry faces extinction in the wake of a growing environmental movement in that state. Old growth forests are being harvested, the wood chips exported to Japan, turned into paper, and then sold back to Australia at up to five times the cost. Australians see "a lot of hypocrisy in harming the environment to maintain jobs while [they] are willing to sacrifice jobs in other areas for the good of the economy."[87(p.10)] Such massive job losses (layoffs) are also common in the United States, as dictated by the economy. While the outlook for timber harvesting in the other five states of Australia is uncertain, in New South Wales it appears economics does not dictate environmental protection policy.

In the United States, many environmentalists have argued that capitalism, greed, and American consumerism are to blame for the environmental crisis. Political scientist James Q. Wilson, well known for several books on crime, identifies capitalism as the key to saving the environment: "Capitalism works to protect the environment over the long run because it is a necessary condition for democracy, which allows individuals to act politically against those who would harm air or water quality."[88] Without the prosperity that capitalism provides, people could not afford to worry about how resources are being used. Nor would the level of technological innovation needed for identifying many ongoing environmental problems have been possible.

Bruce Babbitt, the current U.S. Secretary of the Interior, favors strict regulations but fewer directives telling companies how to achieve compliance. Rather than "cookie-cutter instruction codes," Babbitt recommends "virtual regulation."[89(p.18)] Stringent objectives for environmental protection are set out by the national agency, but then local industries and communities remain free to determine what is the best strategy to meet those objectives. Allowing companies and municipalities to set their own path for compliance makes everyone feel better about the objective, and in some cases the local programs have worked better than directives from the government.[90]

Some have argued that the expanding global markets are changing the economic base of the world once again.[91] Also, computers and software have been identified as aids in the modern environmental protection efforts (e.g., they reduce the amount of trees needed to produce paper). But the manufacturing processes necessary for computer production are not universally environmentally friendly.[92-95] Industrialization and technological development are in many ways still directly linked to degradation of the environment. Yet, people quickly forget it was technological innovation that allowed scientists to detect the hole in the ozone and reduce pollution emissions from stack gases to improve air quality. Therefore, the role that economics and politics will play in protecting the environment will remain uncertain for years to come.

For the most part, individual U.S. citizens hope to achieve economic security. Home ownership and financial security in the later years in life are central elements of the modern version of the American dream. Land ownership, once a symbol of opportunity, is now restricted. Resource scarcity is a perceived threat, and the future of sustainable development is an open question. Economic and political issues, not to mention conflicts over environmental protection, will continue to take their place on center stage.

REVIEW QUESTIONS

1. What role does cost-benefit analysis play in environmental protection? What are the benefits and costs of environmental protection?
2. How do the two functions of government (creating the proper conditions for capital accumulation and maintaining social harmony) influence a government's reaction to environmental protection?
3. What are two examples of externalities?
4. Using economics as a model, would you argue the pollution policies in the United States are efficient? Explain.
5. How is the Taylor Grazing Act of 1934 related to modern environmentalism?
6. Using the Reclamation Act of 1902 and Bureau of Reclamation dam projects, explain the role of science in the political process.

DISCUSSION QUESTIONS

1. Would you argue economics or politics is more important in the controversy surrounding environmental protection? Justify your response.
2. Identify a recent news story that illustrates the relationship among economics, politics, and environmental protection.
3. What are some of the effects of computerization on the state of the environment? What information do you need to respond more completely to this question?
4. Is capitalism the major cause of the environmental problems in the United States or a major part of the solution? Explain your response.
5. Can you identify themes from the conservation and preservation movements in current economic and political discussions about the environment?

REFERENCES

1. D. Simon and D.S. Eitzen, *Elite Deviance*, 4th ed. (Boston: Allyn and Bacon, 1993), 6–12.
2. *American Heritage Dictionary of the English Language* (Boston: Houghton Mifflin, 1979), 200.

3. L.H. Rockewell, "Do Corporations Need Conscience or Freedom?" *Christian Science Monitor*, 11 March 1996, 19.

4. M. Weidenbaum, "Midsized Firms Need Regulatory Relief," *Christian Science Monitor*, 21 March 1996, 19.

5. S. Walker, "GOP Splits over How Much To Ease Regulatory 'Burden': Environmental Concerns Cause Moderates To Balk over Reform Bill," *Christian Science Monitor*, 7 March 1996, 3.

6. The sugar cane farmer controversy is covered in E. Spaid and K. Nielsen, "Florida Cane Farmers Sour on Everglades Restoration," *The Christian Science Monitor*, 21 February 1996, 3.

7. For more information on the Everglades and the restoration efforts, see A. Mairson, "The Everglades: Dying for Help," *National Geographic*, April 1994, 2–53.

8. M. Holloway, "Nurturing Nature," *Scientific American*, April 1994, 98–105.

9. E.L. Spaid, "Florida Cane Farmers Sour on Everglades Restoration: Tax on Sugar Is Part of Ambitious Effort To Revive Marshland," *Christian Science Monitor*, 21 February 1996, 3.

10. R. Percival et al., *Environmental Regulation: Law, Science and Policy* (Boston: Little, Brown, 1992), 36.

11. R. Findley and D. Farber, *Environmental Law in a Nutshell*, 3d ed. (St. Paul, MN: West Publishing Co., 1992), 87.

12. P.A. Samuelson and W.D. Nordhaus, *Economics*, 13th ed. (New York: McGraw Hill, 1989), 772–775.

13. Samuelson and Nordhaus, *Economics*, 772.

14. Percival et al., *Environmental Regulation*, 1269.

15. Samuelson and Nordhaus, *Economics*, 773.

16. Samuelson and Nordhaus, *Economics*, 773.

17. W. Baxter, *People or Penguins: The Case for Optimal Pollution* (1974), 17.

18. Baxter, *People or Penguins*, 17.

19. Percival et al., *Environmental Regulation*, 15.

20. Findley and Farber, *Environmental Law in a Nutshell*, 86–87.

21. Findley and Farber, *Environmental Law in a Nutshell*, 274–279.

22. Sagoff, "Economic Theory and Environmental Law," *Michigan Law Review* 79 (1981): 1393–1401, 1410–1417.

23. Sagoff, "Economic Theory and Environmental Law."

24. Sagoff, "Economic Theory and Environmental Law."

25. Sagoff, "Economic Theory and Environmental Law."

26. "Poll Shows Four of Five Americans Support Environment, Even over Economy," *Environmental Reporter* 23 (1992): 1155.

27. "Poll Shows Four of Five."

28. P.C. Yeager, *The Limits of Law: The Public Regulation of Private Pollution* (Boston: Cambridge University Press, 1991), 85.

29. M. Bernarde, *Our Precarious Habitat: An Integrated Approach To Understanding Man's Effect on His Environment* (New York: Norton, 1970).

30. "Bush Promised To Give Economic Costs Greater Weight in Environmental Law," *Wall Street Journal*, 15 September 1992, A18.

31. A. Kaslow, "Browner Dons Gloves for EPA: Environmental Protection Chief Battles Republican-led Effort To Shrink Agency," *Christian Science Monitor*, 8 August 1995, 1, 4.

32. J. Thompson, "Groups Say Congress Wages War on the Environment," *The Mountain Times*, 27 July 1995, 16.

33. "The GOP's Green Side," editorial, *Christian Science Monitor*, 15 August 1995, 20.

34. Walker, "GOP Splits over How Much To Ease Regulatory 'Burden.'"

35. "The GOP's Green Side."

36. Kaslow, "Browner Dons Gloves for EPA."

37. L. Bergeson, "Old Toxins in New Bottles: EPA Reinvention Falling Short," *Corporate Legal Times*, January 1996, 13.

38. S. Cable and C. Cable, *Environmental Problems, Grassroots Solutions: The Politics of Grassroots Environmental Conflict* (New York: St. Martin's Press, 1995), 38–46.

39. Cable and Cable, *Environmental Problems, Grassroots Solutions*, 38.

40. J. O'Conner, *The Fiscal Crisis of the State* (New York: St. Martin's Press, 1973), esp. chap. 4: 6.

41. Percival et al., *Environmental Regulation*, 37.

42. Cable and Cable, *Environmental Problems, Grassroots Solutions*, 38.

43. Cable and Cable, *Environmental Problems, Grassroots Solutions*, 56.

44. J.V. Switzer, *Environmental Politics: Domestic and Global Dimensions* (New York: St. Martin's Press, 1994), 75.

45. D. Strong, *Dreamers and Defenders: American Conservationists* (Lincoln, NE: University of Nebraska Press, 1988), 59.

46. The Division of Grazing merged with the General Land Office to become the Bureau of Land Management.

47. Cable and Cable, *Environmental Problems, Grassroots Solutions*, 56–57.

48. Cable and Cable, *Environmental Problems, Grassroots Solutions*, 57.

49. Cable and Cable, *Environmental Problems, Grassroots Solutions*, 57.

50. Strong, *Dreamers and Defenders*, 175.

51. Switzer, *Environmental Politics*, 78.

52. Switzer, *Environmental Politics*, 77.

53. G. Wuerthner, "How the West Was Eaten," *Wilderness* 54 (spring 1991): 28–37.

54. B. Knickerbocker, "Ranchers Clash with Rangers in Wild West," *Christian Science Monitor*, 13 July 1995, 1, 18.

55. "Supreme Court Decision: Babbitt v. Sweet Home Chapter of Communities for a Greater Oregon," *Westlaw Bulletin*, 29 June 1995.

56. T. Woods, "Newt, the Pro-Environment Zookeeper," *Christian Science Monitor*, 18 August 1995, 19.

57. W. Kaufman, "The Cost of 'Saving': You Take It, You Pay for It," *American Forests*, November–December 1993, 17–19, 58–59.

58. J.L. Tyson, "Tilling Middle Ground of Property-Rights Debate," *Christian Science Monitor*, 27 June 1995, 4.

59. H.P. Caulfield, "U.S. Water Resources Development Policy and Intergovernmental Relations," in *Western Public Lands: The Management of Natural Resources in a Time of Declining Federalism*, ed. A. Held (Totawa, NJ: Rowman, 1984).

60. Strong, *Dreamers and Defenders*, 70.

61. J.P. Lester, *Environmental Politics and Policy* (Durham, NC: Duke University Press, 1989), 22.

62. Strong, *Dreamers and Defenders*, 167.

63. Strong, *Dreamers and Defenders*, 168.

64. Lester, *Environmental Politics and Policy*, 19.

65. C. Manes, *Green Rage: Radical Environmentalism and the Unmaking of Civilization* (Boston: Little, Brown, 1990), 4.

66. B. Knickerbocker, "Artificial Deluge Used for Natural Ends," *Christian Science Monitor*, 28 March 1996, 4.

67. Knickerbocker, "Artificial Deluge Used for Natural Ends."

68. Knickerbocker, "Artificial Deluge Used for Natural Ends."

69. J. Matloff, "Poor Nations Confront Choice of Trees or Jobs," *Christian Science Monitor*, 16 August 1995, 1, 8.

70. J. Tyson, "Tilling Middle Ground of Property-Rights Debate."

71. B. Knickerbocker, "Congress Ponders Competing Proposals for Utah Wilderness," *Christian Science Monitor*, 27 June 1995, 11.

72. D. Rhode, "In Australia, Environment Wins over Jobs," *Christian Science Monitor*, 27 June 1995, 10–11.

73. J. Ross, "Unintended Enemies: Save a Rainforest, Start a Revolution," *Sierra*, July-August 1994, 45–47.

74. Kaufman, "The Cost of 'Saving.'"

75. L.H. Stevenson and B. Wyman, *The Facts on File Dictionary of Environmental Science* (New York: Facts on File, 1991), 246.

76. Knickerbocker, "Artificial Deluge Used for Natural Ends."

77. Knickerbocker, "Artificial Deluge Used for Natural Ends."

78. S. Schmidheiny, F. Zoraquin, and the World Business Council for Sustainable Development, *Financing Change: The Financial Community, Eco-efficiency and Sustainable Development* (Cambridge, MA: MIT Press, 1996).

79. S. Schmidheiny, "Greener Greenbacks: Financiers Go Eco-efficient: New Study Finds Markets, Banks, Insurers, and Accountants Discovering That Environmentally Sound Management Pays," *Christian Science Monitor*, 14 March 1996, 19.

80. "The Greening of Growth," *Christian Science Monitor*, 13 February 1996, 20.

81. D. Sneider, "To Halt Sprawl, San Jose Draws Green Line in Sand," *Christian Science Monitor*, 17 April 1996, 3.

82. "Study Says Environment Laws Aren't a Big Cause of Job Loss," *New York Times*, 18 March 1996, A10.

83. "Study Says Environment Laws Aren't a Big Cause of Job Loss."

84. "Study Says Environment Laws Aren't a Big Cause of Job Loss."

85. Kaufman, "The Cost of 'Saving,'" 59.

86. Kaufman, "The Cost of 'Saving,'" 59.

87. Rhode, "In Australia, Environment Wins over Jobs."

88. T.C. Palmer, "Capitalism Called Key to Saving Environment," *Boston Globe*, 4 June 1995.

89. B. Babbitt, "Less Regulation, More Protection: Communities Should Be Free To Meet Environmental Mandates in Their Own Way," *Christian Science Monitor*, 8 March 1996, 18.

90. Babbitt, "Less Regulation, More Protection."

91. P. Robinson, "Paul Romer. Cheap, Powerful Technology and 'Free' Information Transforms the Science of Economics. But Just How? This Young Economist Knows," *Forbes ASAP*, 5 June 1995, 67–72.

92. S.R. Hedberg, "Design of a Lifetime," *Byte*, October 1994, 103–107.

93. M. Perenson, "Clean Machines," *PC Magazine*, 12 October 1993, 32.

94. K. Doyle, "PC Buyers Work To Clean up Toxic Manufacturing Process: Buyers, Vendors See Green in Ecological PCs," *PC Week*, 15 November 1993, 179.

95. "Santa Clara Firms Reduce Emissions," *Chilton's Electronic News*, 29 July 1991, 21.

CHAPTER 4

A Social Understanding of the Natural Sciences

Gary Walker

TERMS	bioaccumulation	food web
	biosphere	indicator species
	carbon cycle	primary consumers
	ecosystem	primary producers
	ecotones	species
	entropy	

Traditional understandings of the natural environment have evolved as scientists seek to increase the collective knowledge humans have about the earth. Scientists have provided answers to many of life's questions. As a result of their ongoing investigative efforts, fewer mysteries remain. It is important to remember that a student interested in studying environmental crime must understand how scientific processes interact with social processes. When identifying and classifying environmental harms, a modicum of scientific knowledge will prove indispensable. Any attempt to regulate or control environmental conditions must heed the principles of the natural systems.

In this chapter, the scientific method and common practices used to study ecosystems are reviewed. Attention is given to fundamental biological and ecological principles used to explain the interactive processes that support life on the planet. The objective is not to provide an extensive account of biology, ecology, chemistry, or physics. Instead, the information presented here is intended to provide a brief introduction to important scientific principles relevant for discussing environmental controversies.

THE EARTH AS A LIVING SYSTEM

In simple terms, the earth can be thought of as Goldilocks' planet. This sphere upon which we ride is neither too close to nor too far from the sun.

It is neither too big, nor is it too small. It is just right. If our planet were any closer to the sun, the surface of the earth would be too hot for water to exist as a liquid. Water is an essential condition for life. If our orbit around the sun were more distant, the planet would be too cold and the water of the earth would be solid ice. Again, such a condition would not sustain life. If the size of the earth were much larger, the atmosphere would be more dense because of increased gravitational pull. Such a dense atmosphere would block the narrow spectrum of visible light that is the basis of photosynthesis.

Photosynthesis is the process in green plants in which light energy is absorbed and converted to chemical energy. During this process, carbon dioxide is combined with water to form energy-rich sugar as a byproduct, and oxygen is released. Nearly all terrestrial organisms on earth depend directly or indirectly on photosynthesis. Thus, a denser atmosphere would preclude the development of life as we now know it. On the other hand, a smaller planet would hold too thin an atmosphere, and harmful amounts of ultraviolet light would penetrate the planet's atmosphere, disrupting the molecular structure of life.

We can think of our planet as an onion with layers of gases, water, and rock. The outermost peel is the **atmosphere**, a relatively thin film of gases composed of even thinner layers. Approximately 17–48 kilometers above the earth's surface are the upper reaches of our atmosphere, collectively called the stratosphere. Even this distant stratum of gases is important for life because it contains at its lower altitudes the gas ozone (O_3), which blocks enough of the ultraviolet radiation striking our planet to allow organic molecules to remain intact. Beneath the stratosphere is the troposphere, the layer of the atmosphere that extends downward to our planet's surface. This portion contains most of the earth's air, and it is here that weather happens.

The **hydrosphere** is the part of the planetary surface where the various forms of water are found, including liquid water at the surface and underground, polar ice caps, and water vapor in the lower atmosphere. Life is intimately tied to the presence of water. Many life forms exist solely in water, and all organisms contain water in their cells. The earth's solid outer crust and upper mantle compose the lithosphere. The minerals that originate in the lithosphere include many of the nutrients that are cycled through the earth's life forms. These life forms themselves, the biota, can eventually become part of the lithosphere as fossil fuels, such as coal, oil, and natural gas.

The **biosphere** is that part of our planet where life exists. The biosphere overlays most of the other layers. Living (biotic) organisms interact with the nonliving, **abiotic** components of the environment—the water, soil, and atmosphere. It is the mission of ecologists to decipher the complex interactions of the organisms of the biosphere with each other and with the abiotic components of the planet. Therefore, ecologists study each level.

Organisms are organized into **species**, which are groups of organisms sufficiently similar genetically to potentially interbreed and produce fertile offspring. Organisms capable of reproducing without sex (asexually) are often grouped into species based on their chemical similarities. As a last resort, some especially indistinct organisms are grouped together into species based solely on their physical resemblance (morphology).

Remember, species designations are human constructs—biological pigeon holes. These designations sometimes change as we learn more about the various aspects of our fellow life forms. The concept of a species, like other classificatory concepts, is useful for communicating ideas among ourselves regarding the biota. At the level of species, scientists may conduct investigations of animal behavior or evolutionary history.

A commonly asked question in ecology is, How many species exist on the planet? In truth, scientists have no idea. Approximately 1.5 million different living species have been described and assigned scientific names thus far, and approximately 300,000 fossil species have been named based on morphological differences. Estimates of the actual number of undocumented species vary widely because the evidence is fairly sketchy. The most common estimates of species on our planet today range from 10 million to 50 million.

A group of individuals of the same species in a localized area at the same point in time is termed a **population**. Ecologists frequently study populations.[1] All of the populations in a particular place and time, including plant, animal, and microbial populations, make up a biological community. Some ecologists study the biotic interactions within communities of organisms, such as the interdependence of plants and pollinators and predator-prey relationships, for example. The change in the species composition of communities through time (often following a disturbance) is termed **succession**. An example would be the invasion of weeds into an abandoned agricultural field. The weeds, in turn, are replaced by shrubs and fast-growing trees and eventually by the species characteristic of old-growth forests.

The next level of ecological investigation is the ecosystem. An **ecosystem** includes not only the biota but also the abiotic components of the area. In some cases fire is a natural component of an ecosystem sequence. Fire suppression can alter the ecosystem and produce conditions that could result in disasters such as the Yellowstone National Park fire.[2]

Rare Plant Conservation: "Why Are We Worrying about It?"

The Center for Plant Conservation issued a report in 1988 that identified 680 species of plants in the United States that may go extinct before the year 2000. In response to the threat of extinction of many plant species, most states have their own plant conservation programs. California, which has over 5,000 native plant species, of which a third are endemic, has developed a program that has served as a model for the rest of the country. The California Fish and Game Commission designates native plants as rare, threatened, or endangered based on the potential of extinction and the need for protection and management. Land acquisition to secure the habitat of endangered or threatened species is part of the protection policy of the state. Holsinger and Gottlieb,[1] scientists interested in rare plant conservation, have found that petitions and reports submitted to the commission often offer little or no information about the biological attributes of the species. Information on the levels of genetic variability, interesting physiological capabilities, taxonomic distinctiveness, and possible relationships to agronomically or medicinally important plants is often omitted.

An example of why consideration of biological characteristics should play a role when ranking species that are threatened or endangered is found in the case of the plant *Oryctes nevadensis*. This plant is the only member of its genus and is known from only six sites in Cali-

fornia and Nevada. In 1986 only 603 individuals could be found. It is threatened by cattle trampling and proposed construction of power lines at two of its sites. In spite of all this, the commission denied it endangered status in California.

In a front page story in the *Sacramento Bee* (December 31, 1989), one of the commissioners who voted against the endangered status of this plant said, "Here's a very weedy looking plant. And what I'm really wondering is, why are we worrying about it?" Also, the protection of this species was opposed by the Los Angeles Department of Water and Power, which owned land on which this rare plant was located.

What the commissioner should have known was that this plant is in the same family as potatoes, tomatoes, tobacco, eggplants, and chili peppers, a very economically important group. The genetic potential of such a unique and rare plant, as a member of a family with agriculturally significant relatives, should have been a major consideration in the listing of this plant. Even if a state or federal agency has a conservation program that is well funded and offers strong regulations intended to protect rare species, without the proper consideration of all the biological facts, such a program will be incapable of making intelligent decisions. The biological features of a particular species should be more important than its aesthetic attributes.

1. K.E. Holsinger and L.D. Gottlieb, "Conservation of Rare and Endangered Plants: Principles and Prospects," in *Genetics and Conservation of Rare Plants*, eds. D.A. Falk and K.E. Holsinger (New York: Oxford University Press, 1991), 195–208.

The boundaries of communities and ecosystems are, again, largely human constructs. If an investigator is interested in the nutrient loss in a forest that has been clear-cut, then the ecosystem boundaries would likely include the land between the two ridges of a particular watershed down to a stream that is transporting the nutrients out of the system. Transitional zones between ecosystems are called **ecotones**, and these are ecologically important in that they may provide a habitat for some species that utilize both ecosystems (e.g., the northern flying squirrels in the southern Appalachian mountains use the ecotone between a high elevation spruce-fir forest and the northern hardwood community that is found adjacent to it at slightly lower elevations).

Ecosystem Function

Ecosystems, as indicated above, include both biotic (living) and abiotic (nonliving) components. Ecosystems are usually studied by ecologists concerned with some aspect of the environment affected by human activity. Abiotic components that are sometimes the subject of ecological investigation include the flow of energy and the cycling of matter.

The flow of energy is linear through ecosystems. Energy comes into photosynthetic systems as sunlight, then is converted by plants into various forms of chemical energy. Energy that comes in as sunlight often passes through one or more animals and decomposers and eventually leaves the system as radiant heat energy. Energy conversions are a good example of the **first law of thermodynamics**, which states that although energy may be converted from one form to another, it is neither lost from nor gained in a closed system. The **second law of thermodynamics** states that energy conversion will always be less than 100 percent efficient. In other words, there will always be some waste heat or **entropy** (energy "disorder") produced. For example, in converting the chemical energy in coal into electrical energy, only about 40 percent of the energy will become electricity; the remaining 60 percent will become waste heat. This waste heat is a potential source of thermal pollution. Note that the first law of thermodynamics still holds true—none of the energy actually disappears. Eventually all energy slowly leaks from our planetary system as low-level heat. For this reason, the flow of energy in the ecosystem is said to be linear.

Matter, however, is continuously cycled through ecosystems. Animals and other organisms ingest the carbon-based molecules made by plants to manufacture the chemical components needed for their own bodies (Figure 4–1). They also obtain the energy to sustain an appropriate level of metabolism by breaking down the carbon chemical bonds of the food they eat. Part

Invasive Exotics: The Invasion of the Alien Plant Species[1-3]

In southern Florida, the *melaleuca quinquinevia*, a relative of the Australian eucalyptus, is growing out of control. The plant was introduced in the 1920s, when the objective was to drain the Everglades and create valuable timber forests and more land for development. Today, more than 450,000 acres of the Everglades have been taken over by the melaleuca. Scientists estimate that the melaleuca forests are expanding their range by 50 acres a day.[4] Experts warn that continued growth could result in a transformation of the sawgrass prairies into forests.

At the present time, the growth is stressing the resources devoted to stopping the plant's expansion. The trees bloom three times a year, releasing thousands of seeds each time. Workers who chop down the trees, burn the trees, or inject them with chemicals cannot keep up. In an effort to help restore the Everglades, two tree-eating bugs, also from Australia, are being considered for introduction. Because the weevil is a natural enemy of the plant in Australia, scientists believe it will curb the growth of the trees in south Florida. An aquatic biologist for the South Florida Water Management district describes melaleuca as "rancid, oily, and volatile."[5] The weevils are "melaleuca addicts" and have not "taken to important south Florida plants like citrus trees, mango trees, or other vegetation."[6] Thus, the experts believe the Australian melaleuca weevil will eat the melaleucas but will not affect enough native vegetation to cause a problem.[7] The sawfly is another Australian insect being tested as a possible savior. Introduction of these pests, now under quarantine, awaits approval from state and federal officials.

The biggest problem is the absence of biological diversity. Melaleuca forests without insects become forests without insect-feeding reptiles, birds, and other predators. The end result is biological impoverishment.[8] But the melaleuca are not the only foreign plants introduced into the area. "Nonindigenous amphibians, reptiles and mammals in Florida are displacing native species—reducing the food supply for natural predators. Urban sprawl and farming have created loss of habitat. With all of this combined, we have a prescription for mass extinction of our native species."[9]

1. "A Stink of Eucalyptus: The Everglades," *The Economist*, 17 October 1992, 35, 36.
2. D.C. Schmitz, "Diversity Disappears in Florida: Our Native Plant Species Pushed out by Foreign Invaders," *Newsweek*, 13 March 1995, 14.
3. "Florida Tests Bug To Keep Imported Trees in Check," *St. Cloud Times*, 24 September 1996, 12A.
4. Schmitz, "Diversity Disappears in Florida."
5. M. Dillingham, "Will a Weevil from Down Under Find Melaleuca Finger-licking Good?" *Christian Science Monitor*, 29 October 1996, 13.
6. Dillingham, "Weevil from Down Under."
7. "Florida Tests Bug."
8. Schmitz, "Diversity Disappears in Florida."
9. Schmitz, "Diversity Disappears in Florida."

The Carbon Cycle

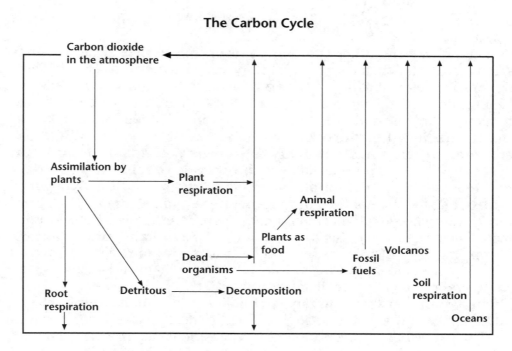

Figure 4–1 The carbon cycle.

of the energy released in this bond-breaking process provides energy for metabolism (e.g., synthesizing new molecules for growth and maintenance), part of it is expelled as heat energy, and the carbons are released back into the atmosphere as carbon dioxide gas. When an organism dies, organisms known as **decomposers**, such as fungi and bacteria, consume what chemical compounds are left in the dead organism to fuel their own metabolism. They also release carbon dioxide gas.

The whole process is referred to as the **carbon cycle**. Carbon atoms of humans and other organisms are recycled. We were all, for a large part, carbon dioxide gas blowing around in the earth's atmosphere until plants brought those molecules into the carbon cycle. We have all been a part of the ecosystem, sharing molecules with plants, herbivores, carnivores, and decomposers. This movement of elements, nutrients, and organic compounds from the abiotic environment into the biota and back into the nonliving environment is known as **nutrient cycling** or as a **biogeochemical cycle** (of which the carbon cycle is just one example). Nutrients such as nitrogen and phosphorus are likewise cycled through aquatic and terrestrial ecosystems.

Because plants and other photosynthetic organisms, like algae and some bacteria, can make their own food, they are called **autotrophs** (self-feeders). They are also referred to as **primary producers** when viewed in the context of energy flow through an ecosystem, because they are the first organisms to produce the organic molecules that travel through a biotic community. Organisms that ingest plant compounds to fuel their own metabolism (i.e., herbivores) are referred to as **primary consumers**. **Secondary consumers** in turn eat herbivores (and thus fall into the category of carnivores). **Tertiary consumers**, animals that eat other carnivores, are relatively infrequent in an ecosystem. Because of their dependence on several other levels in a community, carnivores (secondary and tertiary consumers) are often used as **indicator species** by ecologists to get an idea of the overall health of an ecosystem. Examples of these types of indicator species include wolves, bald eagles, and spotted owls. The various consumer organisms, including decomposers, are called **heterotrophs** (other eaters).

Primary producers and primary, secondary, and tertiary consumers are said to represent the different trophic levels, or feeding levels, of an ecosystem. The pattern of connections among the various organisms in different trophic levels is called a **food web**. Only about 5–20 percent of usable energy makes it from one trophic level to the next. This, in part, is because of the second law of thermodynamics. It takes a lot of producers to support the metabolic demands of a single consumer. Likewise, many herbivores are needed to support the life of a single carnivore. For this reason the movement of energy through an ecosystem is often represented by a pyramid of numbers of individuals, a pyramid of the mass of the biota (biomass), or a pyramid of energy flow, with high values at the lowest level of producers and subsequently smaller values further up the trophic hierarchy. Decomposers eat at all the consumer trophic levels. The energy relationships between the levels of a trophic pyramid illustrate why human populations in less developed countries can be supported by fewer resources per capita than human populations in developed countries, whose citizens eat more meat.

As has been discussed, energy and matter work their way from the bottom of a trophic pyramid up to the top. Other materials such as pesticide residues, radioactive materials from nuclear testing, and heavy metals from industrial pollution also move up through these various trophic levels. Often these pollutants become concentrated in the tissues of the organisms that ingest them (a process known as **bioaccumulation**).

Human Actions and Natural Systems

Essentially all of the ecosystems on the face of the earth have been altered by humankind. Some have been almost completely lost, such as the tall grass prairies. Others, such as the tropical forests, are predicted to diminish greatly before another generation of humans passes. While a background rate of species extinction is a normal part of evolution, the present whole-sale disappearance of species is argued to be, either in large part or solely, due to human actions. The present extinction rate in some ecosystems is estimated to be 1,000 to 10,000 times higher than normal. Deforestation and other kinds of habitat destruction are a primary cause of extinctions. Introduction of alien predators, such as the importation of rats to oceanic islands, is another major source of extinction. Biological diversity has steadily increased for billions of years, yet humans are reversing this trend in a matter of decades.

Contributing greatly to many of our environmental problems is the sheer number of humans inhabiting the earth. We are 5.5 billion strong and growing. Each day 260,000 more humans appear, for a total of 95 million per year. The growth in new scientific fields such as conservation biology and sustainable development is a measure of the attempt by the scientific community to find solutions to some of the problems caused by human population growth and the related problems. They are "crisis disciplines"[3] and are changing our attitude toward and approach to dealing with the earth's resources. Rather than looking at the earth as a means to achieve a given human or social end, as in past decades, these disciplines presume all the parts of natural ecosystems are essential for the efficient functioning of the earth's system as a whole.

THE SCIENTIFIC METHOD

The scientific method involves the construction of formalized, testable ideas (**hypotheses**) based on repeated observations. A hypothesis can never be proven; it can either be rejected or fail to be rejected. What separates the scientific method from other types of investigations is the emphasis on common perception. That is, if an observation leads to a question, the answer must be measurable or quantifiable. Say, for example, Nathan is a student of art, and he examines a work by Picasso. He may find it aesthetically pleasing. Lauren might view the same work of art and judge it to be highly overrated. In such a case, there is no way of determining which of the two assessments is correct, and it is tempting to say Nathan and Lauren just see things differently. On the other hand, a scientist would describe the red pigment used in the painting as having a precise, measurable chemical composition and as reflecting light within a precise range of wavelengths, and anyone who wondered whether the analysis of the pigment was right could use the same instruments to arrive at the same conclusions.

The objective of the scientific method is to convey reliable information. Such information can then be used as the basis for another, different analysis without having to begin with an exposition describing the characteristics of the color red, for example. Likewise, scientific writing is very formalized. Words like *proven* and *belief* are avoided. When asked by a student if he believed in evolution, a geologist friend of mine responded, "No, but I don't *believe* in electricity or gravity either!" What he meant was that all of these phenomena are described by theories that are accepted as the best explanations for what we can observe.

Existing theories may be subject to change upon the advent of new discoveries. The term *theory* has very different meanings in popular usage and among scientists. If a hypothesis is repeatedly tested and fails to be rejected, it is then presented to the rest of the scientific community. If others in the same field reproduce similar results, the idea will tend to become accepted. If the hypothesis is readily accepted, and it is of importance in describing other related phenomena, it may eventually be elevated to the position of a **theory**.

For example, biologists accept the **cell theory**, which states that all life is composed of one or more cells and that all cells come from preexisting cells. This hypothesis is considered theoretical because not all organisms have been looked at to see if they are composed of cells. As another example, nearly all biologists accept the theory of biological evolution. If a theory can be proven to have no possible exceptions, then it is elevated to the level of a *law*, such as the first law of thermodynamics.

As a result of the tentative nature of the scientific method, politicians, the press, and the public find it difficult to get simple yes-no answers from scientists. A good scientist will not claim factual status for an idea when it is still under study. The best explanation will be acknowledged, but the possibility that the explanation might change is never dismissed. As any student of ecology knows, things are always more complicated than they seem. Science is about unraveling the complexities of life to a point where they are quantifiably measurable. Once measurement takes place, the ideas that have not been disproven are incorporated into what might be called common knowledge.

THE LIMITATIONS OF SCIENTIFIC EXPERTISE

Scientists now realize that human disturbances are going to be a substantial element of the environment for the foreseeable future. No successful management plan or solution to an environmental problem can be achieved without taking into account this truth. One of the most recent contributions to environmental understanding emerging from scientific analysis is the attempt to integrate human influences into ecological systems. The knowledge of indigenous cultures is being incorporated into the design and use of nature reserves. The role of native human cultures in the maintenance of certain communities, such as those maintained by fire in prairies or the high-elevation grassy balds in the southern Appalachian mountains, must be understood in order to formulate management practices for such communities. Long-term management strategies have to deal with the global inequities of human utilization of natural resources. Such issues must be incorporated into all efforts to develop solutions to existing and future environmental problems, although assessing the impact of the disparate standards of living among human populations may be an uncomfortable focal point for some natural scientists.

It is a basic tenet of the scientific method that in most cases hypotheses and theories utilized in understanding environmental processes can never be proven. They can only be rejected or fail to be rejected. Most of the systems scientists explore are dynamic and subject to a myriad of unpredictable environmental influences. Further, the models that ecologists, climatologists, and other scientists develop are based on their observations, and data are constantly being refined and modified or outright debunked.

A classic example of a model that has been the subject of intense scientific study is the theory of island biogeography developed by MacArthur and Wilson.[4] Islands make great experimental sites. Their isolation reduces the number of outside influences that make understanding natural systems a complicated matter. One observed fact about islands is that if an island is stripped of its biota, the species will recover at a steady rate and then stabilize close to the number existing there prior to the disturbance (as occurred on the island of Krakatau after it was subjected to severe volcanic explosions a century ago). MacArthur and Wilson proposed that several factors contribute to this stabilization of species number, mainly colonization and extinction. When plenty of habitats are open, the colonization rate of new species is rapid. Once habitats become filled, competition among species increases, along with predation and disease. Species find more specialized niches or go extinct. As the island acquires more species, colonization slows and is balanced by extinctions. Eventually a theoretical equilibrium number of species is attained.

Other factors affecting equilibrium include the size of the island (the larger the island, the more species it can hold) and the distance of the island from a mainland (the closer to a mainland, the higher the rate of colonization of new species). This model has been tested and retested and most recently has been applied to the design of nature reserves. In our fragmented landscape, with isolated patches of wilderness surrounded by seas of agriculture and other human disturbances, our nature reserves can be viewed as habitat islands.

If the basic tenets of MacArthur and Wilson's model hold true, then the number of species that a reserve can maintain should be dependent on its size. Unfortunately, each reserve has special features, and while a reserve may be of suitable size to maintain the grazing herbivores it seeks to protect, it might not be of suitable size or composition to maintain an endangered predator.

Dan Simberloff has devoted much of his academic career to testing the island biogeography model. He argues that "the more realistically a model describes a given community, the less likely it is to describe realistically any other community, making a test of the model as an hypothesis difficult if not impossible. The model then ceases to be a generalized abstraction of elements common to all communities, but rather becomes just an increasingly elaborate narrative description."[5(p.78)]

The island biogeography model serves to illustrate the kinds of limitations faced by most theories and models dealing with ecological processes. They can lead scientists to new discoveries, but they themselves are not provable, or even falsifiable in some cases. What science provides is the degree of uncertainty of specific data, hypotheses, and theories. Science advances through controversy, but rather than this being a cause of dismay among ecologists, most see controversy as exciting and invigorating. It is not, however, viewed with the same excitement by the public and politicians. While the questions raised by scientific investigation are intriguing to the scientists, the public and policy makers want answers—which are often, scientists are forced to admit, in short supply.

CAN THE PUBLIC ACCESS EXPERT STUDIES?

Politicians and the public are often frustrated when trying to get a straight answer from a scientist about environmental issues. The cause of this frustration is that the hypotheses and theories derived from the scientific method, while they can be accepted as the best explanations at a given time,

INSIGHT

Krakatau: Island or Volcanic Remains?

In the morning of August 27, 1883, a series of intermittent volcanic explosions destroyed most of Krakatau, a small island in the Sunda Straits. Tidal waves set in motion by the eruption killed more than 30,000 people on the neighboring Indonesian islands of Java and Sumatra. The dust and gases injected into the atmosphere provided spectacular sunsets around the world for months after the eruption.[1]

For biogeographers, Krakatau provides a living laboratory. Sterilized in the huge volcanic explosion, the affected islands have seen rapid recolonization. The original island was tropical rainforest.[2] Nine months after the eruption, spiders were the only signs of life. Three years after the eruption, ferns had colonized the island. Ian Thornton, a zoologist, has been studying the recolonization of Krakatau by plants and animals since the mid-1980s. His book about the island, *Krakatau: The Destruction of an Island Ecosystem*,[3] describes the first trees, birds, and lizards to colonize the island and discusses the plant and animal life that exists there at present. It brings together over 100 years of research on the island's destruction and rebirth.

1. P. Francis and S. Self, "The Eruption of Krakatau," *Scientific American*, November 1983, 172–187.
2. T. Flannery, "Up from the Ashes," *Natural History*, March 1996, 6–7.
3. I. Thornton, *Krakatau: The Destruction of an Island Ecosystem* (Cambridge, MA: Harvard University Press, 1996).

are never viewed by scientists as "truth" or "fact." It is the very nature of science to look for alternative explanations and to talk about probability statistics, but this is generally not what the public wants. Often the public looks to science to provide indisputable evidence and clearly defined facts. The human understanding of the earth is simply not that sophisticated.

A well-known ecologist, M.E. Soulé, once stated, "Administrators, policy makers, and managers have a right to ask for the bottom line. . . . And biologists have the right and sometimes the obligation not to give an oversimplified, misleading answer to such a question. . . . Nevertheless, I think that scientists owe it to the rest of society to provide [a guideline], even when they know that sometimes the rules will be misunderstood and misused."[6(p.176)] In order to avoid misuse and misunderstandings, the public and politicians have to be educated in the fundamentals of scientific investigation. If the technical aspects of scientific publications are incomprehensible to policy makers, environmental groups, and the voting public, at least two courses of action can be taken to access expert studies.

For those interested in attaining a better understanding of scientific studies, the best strategy may be to seek relevant education so that they can correctly interpret these types of documents. Once a basic understanding of environmental biology and ecology is acquired, more detailed information within a specific discipline can be gained through reading and "translating" studies. This is a slow process at first, but the mastery of a certain amount of scientific terminology will foster a deeper understanding of scientific concepts. This also allows a better understanding of environmental issues.

Calvin and Hobbes   by Bill Watterson

Source: CALVIN AND HOBBES © 1993 Watterson. Dist. by UNIVERSAL PRESS SYNDICATE. Reprinted with permission. All rights reserved.

The second approach is to hire or contract with ecologists or environmental scientists and direct them to conduct literature searches and synthesize the present state of understanding of particular topics. This is typically the approach of federal policy makers, who often provide grants to generate technical reports with management implications. Often such reports indicate what is not known, identify problems, and suggest the direction of future investigations.

Popular Perceptions of Harm versus "Real" Harm

A group of young environmentalists recently asked that I conduct a vegetational survey of an area. They enjoyed "bouldering" in the area but discovered it had been slated for development. If a rare or endangered species was there, they reasoned, the land might be protected from development and perhaps even purchased to be "protected." I wondered how enthusiastic they would be if my efforts found a rare rock-community species that was worthy of protection. In this case the result of their endeavors would have been to exclude the activities they sought to protect. They probably view rock climbing as an environmentally friendly sport, but in fact it is capable of destroying some of the oldest and least disturbed plant communities in North America.

Or take the case of the organized boycott against the use of styrofoam hamburger containers in fast-food restaurants. Those containers no longer used chlorofluorocarbons, the chemical responsible in part for the depletion of the ozone layer. They also compress better than the cardboard containers that have replaced them. By advocating the abolition of the styrofoam containers, well-intentioned individuals may have created a need for more sanitary landfill space.

Conservation efforts involving rare or endangered species often center on what are called the **charismatic megafauna**. These are species that have features attractive to humans. A large-eyed, furry mammal will stir more conservation efforts than a nondescript lizard or toad. Likewise, a spectacularly beautiful rare wildflower with several closely related sister species that are not threatened may be given a higher protection status than a more nondescript species that is the last representation of an entire genus. Even though a certain species may not seem attractive to humans, it may play a critical role in the food web of a community or may have some important taxonomic or pharmaceutical attribute.

Such cases illustrate a couple of points. First, how deep does our environmental consciousness go? How much are we willing to alter our lifestyles to reduce our personal impact on the environment? Second, anyone involved with environmental concerns needs to educate him- or herself as to the relative impact of his or her conservation efforts. This is true of public and private agencies as well as individual citizens.

Science in Environmental Statutes

Most scientists feel uncomfortable with political involvement. Yet it is critical that scientists involved in environmental research projects participate in policy-making processes. Environmental research programs should be somewhat issue driven so that enacted legislation will have a chance of actually improving the environment. The sciences have contributed to environmental legislation in areas such as energy production, air and water quality, resource and solid waste management, toxic substance disposal, pesticide use, wildlife conservation, and land use conservation.

Most of this legislation was precipitated by scientific discoveries and the development of new technologies involved with the detection and estimation of the effects of pollutants in the latter half of the 1960s. These discoveries led to the formulation of environmental statutes addressing air and water quality and the use of certain pesticides. In 1960 only about 36 percent of Americans served by sewers had even primary wastewater treatment. New federal laws in 1961 and 1965 led to the construction of new wastewater treatment plants. The Clean Water Act of 1972 targeted the use of the best practicable technologies to clean up point and nonpoint pollution. The Safe Water Drinking Act followed in 1974. Water quality research has led to the increased detectability of the presence of more and more contaminants in smaller trace amounts. Further scientific advances allowing the detection of harder-to-find pollutants such as herbicides are anticipated.

CONCLUSION

This chapter was intended to highlight the interaction of scientific endeavors and social processes. Social scientists must work with natural scientists to better understand complex environmental questions. Natural scientists must work with social scientists to better understand why research findings that indicate an activity as having insignificant environmental effects may be interpreted as a potential threat. The few examples identified above illustrate the involvement of science in the development of environmental policy at many different levels and within the legal, social, cultural, and political arenas, among others.

Following the next chapter, a brief introduction to important federal environmental protection statutes, the book narrows its focus to discuss how the social structure developed so as to prevent and detect environmental crime. In reading about this topic, it will be important to remember the contributions of the natural science community to the development process. First, it is often a natural scientist who first observes the relationship between an environmental hazard and its effect on the biota. Second, studies in the natural sciences frequently result in technological developments that permit detection of an array of pollutants impacting a certain component of the ecosystem. Third, policy makers typically call on scientists to testify about the need to limit such pollutants or describe the likely long-term effects of unrestricted use. Science has provided the means by which to develop technologies to detoxify pollutants, clean up environmentally damaged areas, measure the "hole" in the ozone layer, and reduce pollution. Social science assessments of environmental issues would not be complete without specific acknowledgment of and frequent references to contributions from the natural sciences.

REVIEW QUESTIONS

1. What is the difference between biotic and abiotic components of an ecosystem?
2. Identify the five spheres affecting life on earth.
3. What is the carbon cycle? How is it related to the natural environment?
4. How is the earth's process of recycling different from human efforts to recycle?
5. What is the difference between a community and a population?
6. Why are indicator species important for assessing environmental degradation?

DISCUSSION QUESTIONS

1. Is scientific experimentation or social research more important for studying environmental issues?
2. How might a community seeking to consider both the scientific issues and the social concerns resolve a serious dispute about a controversial technology being introduced locally?
3. What might be the effects of inordinate attention to charismatic megafauna? What are the options for species preservation?
4. State the first and second laws of thermodynamics. How are they related to environmental studies?

5. What is bioaccumulation and why is it a cause for environmental concern?

6. Outline the objectives of the scientific method. Are hypotheses and theories discussed differently among natural scientists than among social scientists?

7. Does the finding that life has been regenerated on the island of Krakatau suggest that concern over environmental issues is in many cases premature? Be prepared to defend your response.

8. What are the difficulties average citizens might have if they were interested in gathering research data about specific actions occurring in their community?

REFERENCES

1. This level of organization is important for both applied and theoretical investigations. For example, an applied investigation might be the determination of the population growth patterns of catfish at a fish farm. The findings would enable fishery managers to harvest the specific proportion of a population that is most efficient for maximum productivity. A theoretical study might elucidate the genetic composition of a population of wildflowers (their gene pool) in order to gain insight about the natural history of the plants since the last glacial advance in the Pleistocene.

2. The 1988 fire in Yellowstone National Park sparked fires in five national forests surrounding the park. The fires affected approximately 793,880 of the 2,221,800 acres in the greater Yellowstone ecosystem. While many thought the fires were a tragic loss, biologists, ecologists, and others differed on the question of whether to intervene and attempt to stop them. Today, the Yellowstone ecosystem thrives, and many believe the money spent to extinguish the fires was wasted. As it was, the first snow of the season halted the progression of the wildfires. See J. Henry, *Wilderness* 57 (winter 1993): 24–30.

3. M.E. Soulé, "What Is Conservation Biology? A New Synthetic Discipline Addresses the Dynamics and Problems of Perturbed Species, Communities, and Ecosystems," *BioScience* 35 (1985): 727–735.

4. R.H. MacArthur and E.O. Wilson, *The Theory of Island Biogeography* (Princeton, NJ: Princeton University Press, 1967).

5. D.S. Simberloff, "Biogeographic Models, Species Distributions and Community Organization," in *Evolution, Time and Space: The Emergence of Biosphere*, ed. R.W. Sims et al. (London: Academic Press, 1983), 57–83.

6. M.E. Soulé, "Where Do We Go from Here?" in *Viable Populations for Conservation*, ed. M.E. Soulé (Cambridge: Cambridge University Press, 1987).

CHAPTER 5

A Review of Federal Environmental Legislation

Mary Clifford

TERMS	cradle-to-grave	national priority list (NPL)

cradle-to-grave
effluent standards
Emergency Planning and Community
   Right To Know Act
emission reduction credits
environmental impact statements
manifest system
National Ambient Air Quality
   Standards (NAAQS)
National Environmental Policy Act (NEPA)
National Pollution Discharge Elimination
   System (NPDES)

national priority list (NPL)
new source performance
   standards (NSPS)
nonattainment areas
nonpoint source
notification requirement
point source
potentially responsible party
small quantity generators
treatment, storage, and
   disposal facilities (TSDs)

The last 30 years has seen an unprecedented growth in environmental legislation (see Appendix B). Many environmental protection statutes were developed after specific incidents sparked local, national, or international attention. Examples include the toxic waste crisis at Love Canal, nuclear accidents at Three Mile Island and Chernobyl, and the lethal release of gas in Bhopal, India. In addition, various oil spills, including the Santa Barbara oil spill (1969), the Exxon Valdez spill (1989), and the Russian oil spill (1995), have captured international attention. Perhaps the biggest concern is that these are only a small sample of the kinds of incidents that have occurred over the last three decades.

Proposed legislative mandates to protect the natural environment are relatively new. Controversial language and ambiguous intent have resulted in numerous legal disputes surrounding existing environmental protection legislation. Corporations, governments, individuals, and their attorneys seek clarification in the courts. The controversies should not be surprising given the scope of the legislation. Previous notions of progress and technological development did not incorporate environmental effects. "The complex architecture of environmental law reflects not only the circumstances of its birth, but also the complexity of the problems it addresses and the

95

difficulty of reconciling the competing values environmental policy implicates."[1](p.72) In general, society had little regard for environmental concerns until very recently.

The statutory framework established to define and enforce environmental protection efforts continues to change. Enforcement agents are few in number, and at present, although the number of enforcement agents has increased, critics argue enforcement efforts are too few and far between to be an effective deterrent. The result has been an explosion of controversy. Further, justice is meted out on a case-by-case basis, and regulatory agencies, corporations, and individuals all see themselves as on the losing end of the conflict.

This chapter focuses on existing environmental protection legislation. First, attention is given to the National Environmental Policy Act (NEPA) and the Environmental Protection Agency (EPA). Second, particular elements of eight federal environmental protection statutes are presented (criminal provisions for their violation are outlined in Appendix C). Third, constitutional restrictions, common law doctrine, and common law remedies are outlined. Finally, criteria for establishing criminal intent are introduced, although they are discussed more fully in Part II.

Students in environmental studies and criminal justice must have a basic understanding of existing environmental laws. As we will see below, legislation drafted to protect the environment includes a wide range of provisions, and the legislative intent of these provisions is not always manifest. The information presented here provides a brief overview of the topic, but exhaustive coverage of environmental protection statutes is left to comprehensive legal texts.[2,3]

PROCEDURAL LAWS AND AGENCY DIRECTIVES

Environmental studies students would be wrong to assume all environmental protection legislation relates directly to plants, animals, and ecosystems. Some of the more prominent environmental protection statutes have a direct impact on public health and safety, workplace and worker safety, risk management, and scientific uncertainty.[4–8]

The **Safe Drinking Water Act** and the **Emergency Planning and Community Right To Know Act** are two examples of legislation enacted to guard against unnecessary threats to public health and safety. Passed in 1974, the Safe Drinking Water Act (42 U.S.C. §§300f–300j-26) requires the EPA to limit contaminants in public water systems. The EPA must set limits for maximum allowable levels of any contaminant in public drinking water systems, and the 1986 amendments to the act required more expeditious standard setting.[9]

The Emergency Planning and Community Right To Know Act (42 U.S.C. §§11001–11050), commonly referred to as the Community Right To Know Act, requires companies to disclose annually any releases of specific chemicals. With over 300 chemicals listed, companies must estimate how much of each chemical they released into the environment.[10] This information is used to prepare a toxics release inventory (TRI), which is available to the public. The first TRI results were published in April 1989. EPA officials were stunned. The 18,500 companies reporting estimated releases that totaled 10.4 billion pounds of toxic chemicals in 1987,[11] far more than EPA officials had expected.

Legislative action has increased information resources to help ensure better protection of public health and safety. The legal responsibilities for risk management and risk assessment decisions are increasingly being debated by scientists and legal scholars. Determining liability for individuals, corporations, and governing agencies is a daunting challenge for a society that values technological advancement. The issue of scientific uncertainty is currently one of the "hottest" issues in environmental law.[12] Significant concern is expressed about the ability of law to effectively address risk. The courts, at this time, remain the primary arbiters of environmental disputes.

Congress can pass legislation requiring the formation of agencies or administrative bodies to implement and oversee certain legislative or executive mandates. The **Occupational Safety and Health Administration** (OSHA), for example, has been established to protect workers from unsafe working conditions, and the EPA was created to administer legislation related to the environment. While OSHA is focused on worker safety issues, sometimes the agency confronts issues that have an environmental protection dimension. Therefore, interaction between the EPA and OSHA is not uncommon (see Figure 6–2 in Chapter 6). When workers handle hazardous chemicals, a potential environmental threat, both agencies may be involved.

A variety of laws have been developed to protect the public, both in and out of the workplace. While the EPA is responsible for enforcing environmental protection provisions, several other pieces of legislation, such as the National Environmental Policy Act, direct the *process* for implementing and overseeing policies to protect the environment.

The National Environmental Policy Act

The **National Environmental Policy Act** (NEPA) was enacted by Congress in 1969. NEPA requires all agencies of the federal government and related federal programs to identify and take into account environmental concerns as a part of any future project development. Section 101 of NEPA requires the use of all practicable or economically practical means to administer federal programs in the most environmentally sound manner.[13] The statute does not imply, however, that environmental concerns must be placed ahead of other national priorities; it requires instead that environmental objectives receive the same consideration as other federal government program objectives.

A second provision within NEPA established the **Council on Environmental Quality** (CEQ). This council is charged with advising the president about environmental issues. As part of the Executive Office of the President, the CEQ coordinates agency compliance with NEPA.[14]

Perhaps the most famous provision in NEPA is environmental impact statements (EIS). Section 102(2)(c), requires all agencies of the federal government to assess the environmental impact of any proposed federal action. The proposing agency is required to solicit from experts any information needed to adequately address questions about the project. **Environmental impact statements** are to be circulated to affected parties and must accompany the proposal through the agency review process. "In essence, the statute requires the agency to prepare a detailed explanation of the environmental consequences of this action, and to make that report available to high-level agency officials, other agencies, and the public."[15(p.26)]

No attention was given in NEPA to the enforcement of the provisions.[16] As a result, soon after the statute was passed it became clear that the courts would be involved in enforcing NEPA's provisions.[17] Since its inception, courts have argued that NEPA requires a strict standard of compliance and "mandates a particular sort of careful and informed decision-making process and creates judicially enforceable duties."[18]

The Environmental Protection Agency

The EPA is only one of several regulatory agencies focused on protecting health and the environment. A **regulatory agency** is charged with regulating and managing the policies outlined by Congress or other legislative bodies. Created by Richard M. Nixon in 1969 through an executive order, the EPA was given the responsibility to implement, and then oversee the progress of the 1970 Clean Air Act, and the 1972 Clean Water Act (known initially as the Federal Water Pollution Control Act). With this executive order, environmental protection responsibilities were consolidated into a single federal agency. Agency responsibilities were later expanded to include subsequent legislation directed at protecting the public from toxic chemicals and other environmental harms.

ENVIRONMENTAL PROTECTION AND THE NATURAL ENVIRONMENT

Although federal legislation to protect the environment existed long before the environmental activism of the late 1960s and early 1970s, the majority of environmental protection legislation has been passed since 1970. Because this text is ultimately concerned with the criminal enforcement of environmental offenses, attention is given here to eight federal statutes for which criminal penalties may be invoked. A review of the criminal penalties attached to each piece of legislation is provided in Appendix C.

The Federal Insecticide, Fungicide, and Rodenticide Act

The Federal Insecticide, Fungicide, and Rodenticide Act (FIFRA; 7 U.S.C.A §136) predates the EPA and NEPA. Enacted in 1947, FIFRA requires registration of pesticides used in interstate commerce.[19] The 1972 Federal Environmental Pesticide Control Act amended FIFRA to restrict pesticide use.[20] Presently, FIFRA requires all pesticides to be registered with the EPA. Manufacturers must provide information to demonstrate how the chemicals perform their intended function without having "unreasonable adverse effects on the environment."[21] With few exceptions, FIFRA prohibits the sale, distribution, and professional use of unregistered pesticides.[22]

As part of the registration process, the EPA must classify each pesticide as for either "general" or "restricted" use. This determination is made by considering the methods of application, the qualifications of the applicators, the amounts to be used, the geographic areas of use, and the species of pest targeted.[23] The registration of any pesticide will be discontinued after five years unless the registrant requests it be continued. Further, the EPA has the authority to cancel the registration of any pesticide if it has been determined to cause unreasonable adverse environmental effects.[24] Finally, the EPA may suspend registration of a pesticide if the pesticide poses "imminent hazard to human health."[25] In spite of efforts to amend FIFRA, the process for removing a registered pesticide is difficult.[26] Criminal penalties apply in the case of violations.

The Federal Water Pollution Control Act and the Clean Water Act

Attempts by Congress to deal with water pollution problems occurred as early as the Water Quality Act of 1948. Funding was provided for research and for helping states implement water pollution control programs.[27] Federal funding was expanded in 1956 with passage of the **Federal Water Pollution Control Act** (33 U.S.C. §§1251–1387). The Federal Water Pollution Control Administration was created to approve the water quality standards established by individual states.[28]

These early water quality laws were limited to state actions and achieved little. They did, however, increase the attention given to water pollution. In the 1960s, the "rediscovery" of the **Rivers and Harbors Act of 1899**, also known as the Refuse Act, aided in developing water quality protection. This legislation was originally drafted to bar unpermitted discharges of refuse into **navigable waterways**. Its purpose was to prevent interference with the navigation of national waterways, because of blockages created by excessive refuse dumping. Two subsequent Supreme Court decisions,[29,30] however, identified discharges of *industrial waste* into waterways as a violation of the statute whether or not navigation was threatened. Criminal provisions were outlined for its violation.

A comprehensive plan for federal regulation of water pollution did not emerge until passage of the Federal Water Pollution Control Act of 1972, which represented an entirely new approach to water pollution prevention. This legislation broke ground in three important areas. First, technology-based discharge limits were mandated. Second, Congress imposed a nation-wide permit system on **point source** discharges. A point source of pollution would be an industry or specific agent with an identifiable waste stream. The **National Pollution Discharge Elimination System (NPDES) Permit** program prohibits discharge of pollution into waterways unless the agent has been granted an NPDES permit. Third, Congress expanded the federal role in financing construction of municipal waste treatment facilities.[31]

The act was amended in 1977 and renamed the **Clean Water Act** (CWA), and its new goals included the achievement of fishable and swimmable waters by 1983 and the elimination of pollutant discharges into navigable waters by 1985.[32] The CWA distinguishes between two types of enforcement standards: those for point sources and those for nonpoint sources of water pollution. A **nonpoint source** of water pollution is an unconfined contamination of water from the land into a body of water. Runoff from city streets, parking lots, and agricultural fields and seepage from individual septic systems would be some examples. The primary difference between point and nonpoint sources is the overt production of waste. Pollution from point sources is easily identified. Nonpoint sources are less easy to identify and can include unknown releases. One of the act's provisions mandated the development of **new source performance standards (NSPS)**. NSPS required the EPA to develop and propose **effluent standards** (e.g., the maximum amount of pollutant allowed in wastewater discharge) for new technologies.

The established effluent limitations prohibited the discharge of any pollutant except those allowed by the permit process. This standard must reflect the best control technologies available. This type of provision is commonly referred to as a **technology-forcing provision**. Legislative efforts were taken to force industry to adopt the most advanced pollution control technology available at the time the new industry goes on line.

Further, the act created a management program for addressing problems of nonpoint source water pollution. It authorized citizen suits against violators and judicial review of EPA rule making in the U.S. Courts of Appeals. Finally, provisions within the act allow for compliance orders and administrative, civil, and criminal penalties for violations of the act. The 1987 amendments extended compliance deadlines and created a new program for controlling nonpoint source pollution.[33]

There have been several attempts to determine the direct impact the CWA has had on the level of pollution in our nation's waterways. In addition, several other federal statutes have been enacted to enhance federal efforts to deal with water pollution problems in the United States, including the Safe Drinking Water Act (1974), which was intended to supplement water quality standards; the Ocean Dumping Act (1972); the Coastal Zone Management Act (1972); and the Oil Pollution Act (1990).

The Clean Air Act

The federal government's first efforts to address air pollution problems in the United States passed with the Air Pollution Control Act of 1955.[34] The regulation of air pollution from the federal level began with the **Clean Air Act (CAA)** of 1963 (42 U.S.C. §§7401–7642). The latter act empowered the Secretary of Health, Education and Welfare to define air quality criteria based on scientific studies. The early efforts at pollution control proved to be a marked failure.[35] With several additional regulatory changes in the interim, the Clean Air Act of 1970 marked a major change in priorities and approach.[36] The EPA was required to identify air pollutants hazardous to human life, publish air quality criteria, and outline **National Ambient Air Quality Standards** (NAAQS).

NAAQS are categorized as primary or secondary standards. *Primary standards* are designed to protect the *public health*, while *secondary standards* are intended to protect *public welfare*. While public health refers to matters of human health and wellness, public welfare includes contamination of soils, water, crops, visibility, comfort, and human-made materials.[37] Each state was required to (1) develop a state implementation plan describing how that state intended to meet the NAAQS and (2) submit the plan for EPA approval. Few states were able to meet the deadlines imposed, and many areas have still not met the prescribed standards.

Areas that were unable to meet the NAAQS were designated **nonattainment areas**. Once an area was so designated, a plan was required from the area to ensure that significant deterioration of air quality was prevented. In addition, all new sources of air pollution were required to meet technology-based standards. Additional technological standards were imposed to reduce emissions from major sources in specific industrial categories. Also, emission standards for automobiles and light trucks were required, with a strict deadline identified. A final CAA provision outlined the need to control stratospheric ozone depletion.

The CAA was amended in 1990 to create new air quality standards. In addition, an acid rain control program was developed featuring **tradable emissions allowances**. The emission trading provision allows exchange or sale of air pollution **emission reduction credits**. These credits are gained when a permanent reduction in air pollutant emissions goes beyond the legally required limits. Such a provision is particularly useful when combined with the EPA's policy of allowing the creation of an imaginary bubble over several sources of air pollution, known as a **bubble policy**. Within this bubble, emissions of industries or other pollution sources are combined and treated as if they come from one emission point. Like the CAA, the 1990 amendments to the CAA required a national permit program to better track sources of pollution. Finally, controls on hazardous air pollutants were expanded.[38] Criminal provisions are outlined for violations of the CAA.

Resource Conservation and Recovery Act

Targeting those who generate, transport, treat, store, or dispose of hazardous solid waste, the **Resource Conservation and Recovery Act (RCRA)** (42 U.S.C. §6901) outlines goals for hazardous waste management. **Land disposal**, burying wastes in a local landfill, is stated to be the "least favored method for managing hazardous wastes."[39] The act identifies waste as hazardous based on characteristics of toxicity, reactivity, corrosivity, and flammability, and it gives the EPA power to regulate hazardous waste labeling, containment, transportation, and recordkeeping.[40] The EPA is responsible for developing a list of types of waste determined to be hazardous.[41]

The act requires EPA to establish a manifest recordkeeping system for hazardous waste. The **manifest system** is used to track hazardous waste from its point of generation to the place used for its disposal. RCRA also regulates transporters of hazardous waste and requires them to use the manifest system. Further, RCRA regulates facilities that treat, store, or dispose of hazardous waste. **Treatment, storage, and disposal facilities**, known as TSDs, are subject to a complicated permitting system. All TSDs must have appropriate permits. The permits, which are granted by the EPA, verify compliance with minimum standards to ensure safe handling. These permits also ensure that minimum technological requirements are met for certain facilities and that land disposal is avoided whenever possible. These standards are all mandated in RCRA, and established by the EPA.[42]

The act mandates accounting for all chemicals from their creation through subsequent transportation and disposal. For this reason, RCRA is said to provide **cradle-to-grave** coverage of hazardous waste. If documentation cannot be provided for wastes at any point in the life of the hazardous waste, penalties apply.[43]

Various elements of RCRA continue to be controversial. For example, RCRA exempted **small-quantity generators** from the reporting process. A small-quantity generator is defined by the EPA as one that produces 1,000 kilograms per month or less of hazardous waste. Although continued exclusion of these types of facilities has proven controversial,[44] provisions within the 1984 Hazardous and Solid Waste Amendments to RCRA acknowledged that municipal solid waste dumps not regulated by the act, could pose serious environmental hazards.[45] Facilities that accept waste from small-quantity generators and hazardous household waste must, at a minimum, perform groundwater monitoring and undertake corrective action when necessary.[46]

Like many of the other environmental statutes presented in this chapter, RCRA is more complex than presented here. Also like many of the federal environmental statutes, it includes provisions for citizen suits and judicial review. Criminal penalties may apply for violation.

Toxic Substances Control Act

Passed in 1976, the **Toxic Substances Control Act (TSCA)** (15 U.S.C. §§2601–2692) required premanufacture notification for all new chemicals. The EPA is authorized to require testing of any chemical substance (except those regulated under FIFRA or by the Food and Drug Administration [FDA]) or impose virtually any type of controls on those chemical substances. The controls could include a complete prohibition on the manufacture, processing, distribution, use, or disposal of a substance if it was found to present an unreasonable risk of injury to health or the environment.[47]

Three policies set forth in TSCA will be discussed. First, data collection is required for the development of a list identifying the environmental effects of chemicals. TSCA places primary responsibility for the development of this database on industry.[48] Second, the government is given adequate authority to prevent risks of injury and imminent hazards.[49] Third, the act states that "this authority should be exercised so as 'not to impede unduly or create unnecessary economic barriers to technological innovation while fulfilling the primary purpose of this Act to assure that . . . such chemical substances . . . do not present an unreasonable risk of injury.'"[50]

Because the statute attempting to offer protection from harmful chemicals, while at the same time attempting to prevent economic barriers to technological innovation, many argue it was written in such a way as to be totally ineffective. Others, while admitting it is not a masterpiece of insightful policy making, believe it was an important first step in regulating the creation and handling of toxic chemicals.[51] TSCA was amended in 1986 to address asbestos hazards, and amendments in 1988 were focused on indoor radon abatement.[52] The act contains the usual provisions on civil and criminal penalties, judicial enforcement, and judicial review.[53]

The Comprehensive Environmental Response, Compensation, and Liability Act

The **Comprehensive Environmental Response, Compensation, and Liability Act (CERCLA; 42 U.S.C. §9601)** is focused on repairing existing environmental damage. CERCLA has four basic elements.[54] First, it mandates the creation of an information-gathering and analysis system to allow federal agents to determine the amount of damage at a dump site and to develop priorities for response actions. This information is important for the EPA's development of a **national priority list (NPL)**, which ranks all sites identified for cleanup and is used to determine the priority for each site's cleanup.

Second, the act grants federal authority to respond to hazardous substance emergencies and to clean up leaking sites. The president can provide "removal" and "remedial" action. A **removal action** is a short-term emergency response, whereas a **remedial action** is intended to provide a long-term solution. The president is also required to employ a hazardous ranking system to determine the sites to be added to the NPL.

Third, the act creates a hazardous substances trust fund to pay for removal and remedial actions. Known as the Superfund, the fund received an initial $8.5 billion in allocations for the time period 1986–1991 with another $5.1 billion allocated in 1990 to extend the legislation through

1994. The term *Superfund* has become standard for referring to the CERCLA legislation.

Finally the fourth provision in CERCLA (§107) makes persons who are responsible for hazardous substance releases liable for cleanup and restitution costs.[55] Unlike other hazardous and toxic waste statutes, CERCLA imposes **joint and several liability** on those identified as responsible for creating a hazardous waste site. Joint liability is basically shared liability; several liability entails that each party held liable may be held responsible for the entire amount of the liability. In other words, the injured party, in this case the EPA, may sue all or any of the responsible parties, together or individually, and may collect (equal or unequal) amounts from each party until the injured party achieves satisfaction of damages.[56]

The courts have upheld that section 107 imposes **strict liability** on all participants, meaning each party is liable for all damages independent of fault or state of mind.[57] Any person or organization identified as a **potentially responsible party (PRP)** contributing to the resulting Superfund site may be liable for (1) the costs of removal and remediation, (2) any other necessary costs, and (3) damages to "natural resources" resulting from release of hazardous substances.[58]

CERCLA's **notification requirement** mandates reporting of releases of hazardous substances to the **National Response Center** (NRC). The NRC is a central U.S. clearinghouse for information about hazardous chemical spills and is responsible for notifying other agencies to develop a response to any release.[59] CERCLA also provides for the issuance of abatement actions, which are administrative orders requiring agents posing imminent and substantial endangerment to health, welfare, or the environment to cease the activities in question.

CERCLA has received considerable attention because of its strict liability and joint and several liability provisions. Violations of CERCLA provisions could result in criminal prosecution.

CONSTITUTIONAL LIMITATIONS, COMMON LAW DOCTRINES, AND COMMON LAW REMEDIES

Court action has had important results related to environmental protection. First, specific constitutional limitations have been identified. The **Commerce Clause**, which prohibits any actions that discriminate against interstate commerce,[60] has been applied to the out-of-state transportation of waste. Also, the **Supremacy Clause** allows federal law to preempt state regulation. Congress has preempted state regulation of pesticide labeling (under FIFRA, §24) and certain aspects of the TSCA (§18).[61] In addition, the **Takings**

Clause, under the Fifth Amendment, prohibits the taking of private property for public use without payment of just compensation.[62]

In addition to the constitutional issues, certain common-law doctrines can provide remedies for environmental protection issues where state and federal legislation cannot. The principal advantage of the common law is that it is decentralized and remedies can be tailored to individual circumstances (in the form of tort action), providing monetary damages to those directly injured, or injunctive relief.[63] Nuisance, for example, comes in two forms: private and public. A private nuisance is a nontrespassory invasion of another's interest in the private use and enjoyment of property. A public nuisance is an interference with a right common to the general public, and the government must initiate action unless private parties suffer injury different from that suffered by the general public.[64] A second common-law remedy is the doctrine of **trespass**, which protects against the invasion of personal interests caused by negligence or by abnormally dangerous activities (for which strict liability is imposed).[65]

Using common-law remedies, an aggrieved party may seek an injunction, or "injunctive relief." This requires an offending party to refrain from doing or continuing to do a particular act or activity.[66] If Halsey, a local landowner, believed ACME Chemical company was dumping chemicals upstream in a river that flowed through her property, and she had evidence to suggest these chemicals were causing damage to her property, then she could seek injunctive relief from the court. If the court granted her request, ACME Chemical would have to stop releasing the chemicals until conclusions could be made about whether the company was actually responsible for the damage. **Damages** may be awarded if Halsey can prove the harm to her property was caused by ACME Chemical. Damages can consist of monetary compensation awarded to the injured party—in this case, Halsey.[67]

CRIMINAL PROVISIONS IN ENVIRONMENTAL STATUTES

Most environmental statutes contain two separate categories of criminal provisions: strict liability and "knowing" violations.[68] First, strict liability does not require knowledge that an act constitutes a violation—all that is needed is to show that the violation occurred. This provision is reserved for flagrant acts. Second, **knowing violations** hold a greater degree of moral culpability. **Intent**, the state of mind in which a person knows and desires the consequences of his or her actions, is necessary for purposes of criminal liability. Because intent is difficult to determine, grounds for conviction include "inference" and a showing that the accused did not take adequate steps to prevent a violation.

Because several congressional or legislative ambiguities have been addressed in court cases, a list of related case law is provided in Appendix D. For additional information about the passage of significant legislation and other critical environmental activities, please reference the environmental timeline in Appendix B. Finally, Appendix C includes a summary of the criminal provisions attached to each of the federal environmental protection statutes discussed in this chapter.

REVIEW QUESTIONS

1. Be familiar with the primary provisions of the following statutes: the National Environmental Policy Act; Federal Insecticide, Fungicide, and Rodenticide Act; Safe Drinking Water Act; Clean Water Act; Clean Air Act; Resource Conservation and Recovery Act; Toxic Substances Control Act; and Comprehensive Environmental Response, Compensation, and Liability Act.
2. What do strict liability and joint and several liability entail?
3. What is the purpose of the Emergency Planning and Community Right To Know Act?
4. Review the provisions of the Rivers and Harbors Act of 1899 and the application of criminal sanctions to violators.
5. What redress does an individual have who cannot use his or her land because of existing environmental regulations?
6. What is the significance of calling a regulation that concerns hazardous materials handling a cradle-to-grave regulation?
7. What is the primary difference between CERCLA and other environmental statutes?
8. Outline the importance of the permit application under the Clean Air Act and the Clean Water Act.
9. How does NEPA differ from the other environmental protection statutes discussed in the chapter?

DISCUSSION QUESTIONS

1. Are criminal sanctions appropriate for continued violation of environmental protection statutes?
2. Should more environmental protection provisions exist? Fewer? Please explain your response.
3. Environmental regulations are complicated. Should more efforts be made to protect businesses? Why or why not?

REFERENCES

1. R.W. Findley and D.A. Farber, *Environmental Law in a Nutshell* (St. Paul, MN: West Publishing Co., 1992).
2. R. Percival et al., *Environmental Regulation: Law, Science and Policy* (Boston: Little, Brown, 1992).
3. Plater et al., *Environmental Law and Policy* (St. Paul, MN: West Publishing Co., 1992).
4. R. Percival, *Environmental Mate* (Boston: Little, Brown, 1995).
5. Percival et al., *Environmental Regulation.*
6. Plater et al., *Environmental Law and Policy.*
7. Findley and Farber, *Environmental Law in a Nutshell.*
8. R.W. Findley and D.A. Farber, *Environmental Law*, 3d ed. (St. Paul, MN: West Publishing Co., 1991).
9. Percival et al., *Environmental Regulation*, 108, 110.
10. Percival et al., *Environmental Regulation*, 431.
11. Percival et al., *Environmental Regulation*, 433.
12. Findley and Farber, *Environmental Law in a Nutshell*, 23.
13. Findley and Farber, *Environmental Law in a Nutshell*, xxiii–xxiv.
14. Percival, *Environmental Mate.*
15. Findley and Farber, *Environmental Law in a Nutshell*, 26.
16. Findley and Farber, *Environmental Law in a Nutshell.*
17. See decision written by Judge Skelly Wright, in *Calvert Cliffs' Coordinating Committee, Inc. v. U.S. Atomic Energy Commission*, at 449 F. 2d. 1109 (D.C. Cir. 1971).
18. Findley and Farber, *Environmental Law in a Nutshell*, 26.
19. Percival, *Environmental Mate.*
20. Percival, *Environmental Mate.*
21. Percival et al., *Environmental Regulation*, 489.
22. Findley and Farber, *Environmental Law in a Nutshell*, 212.
23. Findley and Farber, *Environmental Law in a Nutshell.*
24. Percival et al., *Environmental Regulation*, 489.
25. Percival et al., *Environmental Regulation*, 490.
26. Percival et al., *Environmental Regulation*, 490.
27. Percival et al., *Environmental Regulation*, 873.
28. Percival et al., *Environmental Regulation*, 873.
29. *United States v. Republic Steel Corp.*, 362 U.S. 482 (1960).
30. *United States v. Standard Oil Co.*, 384 U.S. 224 (1966).
31. Percival et al., *Environmental Regulation*, 875.
32. Percival et al., *Environmental Regulation*, 878.
33. Findley and Farber, *Environmental Law in a Nutshell*, 141.
34. Percival et al., *Environmental Regulation*, 761.

35. Percival et al., *Environmental Regulation*, 761.

36. Percival et al., *Environmental Regulation*, 763.

37. S. Ferrey, *Environmental Law: Examples and Explanations* (New York: Aspen Publishers, 1997), 142.

38. Percival, *Environmental Mate*.

39. Percival et al., *Environmental Regulation*, 220.

40. Findley and Farber, *Environmental Law in a Nutshell*, 232–233.

41. Percival et al., *Environmental Regulation*, 220.

42. Percival et al., *Environmental Regulation*, 220–221.

43. Findley and Farber, *Environmental Law*, 501.

44. Findley and Farber, *Environmental Law*, 498.

45. Percival et al., *Environmental Regulation*, 284.

46. Percival et al., *Environmental Regulation*, 284.

47. Percival, *Environmental Mate*.

48. Findley and Farber, *Environmental Law*, 481.

49. Findley and Farber, *Environmental Law*, 481.

50. Findley and Farber, *Environmental Law*, 481.

51. Findley and Farber, *Environmental Law*, 481.

52. Findley and Farber, *Environmental Law in a Nutshell*, 223.

53. Findley and Farber, *Environmental Law*, 482.

54. Findley and Farber, *Environmental Law in a Nutshell*, 240.

55. Findley and Farber, *Environmental Law in a Nutshell*, 242.

56. S.H. Gifis, ed., *Barron's Law Dictionary* (Hauppauge, NY: Barron's Educational Series, 1991), 255, 451.

57. T.M. Hammett and Joel Epstein, *Local Prosecution of Environmental Crime* (Washington, DC: National Institute of Justice, 1993), 6.

58. Hammett and Epstein, *Local Prosecution of Environmental Crime*, 6.

59. *Chemicals in Your Community: A Guide to Emergency Planning and Community Right-To-Know Act* (Washington, DC: U.S.E.P.A., September 1988), 1–36.

60. See *Philadelphia v. New Jersey*, 437 U.S. 617 (1978).

61. Percival, *Environmental Mate*.

62. Percival, *Environmental Mate*.

63. Ferrey, *Environmental Law*, 15–25.

64. Percival, *Environmental Mate*.

65. Percival, *Environmental Mate*.

66. Gifis, *Barron's Law Dictionary*, 238.

67. Gifis, *Barron's Law Dictionary*, 117.

68. V.J. Cass, "Toxic Tragedy: Illegal Hazardous Waste Dumping in Mexico," in *Environmental Crime and Criminality: Theoretical and Practical Issues*, ed. S. Edwards et al. (New York: Garland Publishing, 1996), 104.

PART I

Conclusion

Part I emphasized the importance of interdisciplinary studies when addressing environmental issues. Chapter 1 dealt with the difficulties associated with finding a useful definition of the term *environmental crime*. It suggested two frameworks for future definitions—one philosophical and one legal. Legal definitions will be useful for police officers and regulatory agents who must identify whether a violation of the law has occurred. Philosophical definitions can be used by those interested in expanding the concept of environmental crime to include issues of morality. Referencing the work of Ross and Sutherland, perhaps "environmental criminaloid" could be used to describe actions involving the environment that are seen to be immoral but are not illegal.

Chapter 2 provides a history of the environmental movement in the United States. The deep-seated ideological differences that existed early on can still be seen in the environmental groups of today. To understand the future, we must also look to the past.

Chapter 3 reviewed the economic and political issues linked to various aspects of current environmental conflicts. Technological innovation and extravagant lifestyles are being called into question. Much of the environmental controversy has been linked to the capitalist economic system and classical liberal political ideologies.

Chapter 4 advocated the integration of the natural sciences and the social sciences in the handling of ongoing environmental disputes. Collective efforts are needed to better understand human influences and scientific findings.

Chapter 5 introduced the reader to several of the most important environmental laws passed to date. These laws provide a foundation upon which U.S. citizens can structure their efforts to protect the environment. If the legislation is not enforced, the citizens do not feel protected, but neither do they feel protected if the laws are "overenforced." In other words, achieving the ostensible objective of environmental protection legislation is a monumental task.

Overall, Part I was intended to introduce the reader to several issues and disciplines that provide an important background for studying environmental crime. Students interested in environmental studies, criminal justice, and related fields must be clear about the fact that the information presented in Part I is only the tip of the iceberg. Much more difficult terrain exists below the surface. Those of us who have chosen to explore environmental crime further have a long way to go before we achieve full understanding. First, we must accept the interdisciplinary nature of the subject. We must strive to identify a viable definition (or definitions) of the concept that will be useful for future academic studies and for practitioners in the field. We must pay attention to the lessons history teaches us. We must understand the economic and political dynamics that directly affect the debate over the environment. We must acknowledge and understand the relevant scientific principles. Finally, we must follow the legislative activities intended to establish the parameters of behavior that public agencies and private companies display toward the natural environment. All of this must be done with an implicit understanding that the environmental protection laws mean little when they are not enforced.

Enforcing Environmental Protection Legislation: An Interagency Approach

It is sometimes necessary to remind students interested in criminal justice that the role of law enforcement changes over time, often in response to the emergence of new social issues. A review of the history of criminology reminds us that some the modern-day crimes were not previously viewed as crimes and did not fall within the ambit of law enforcement. Examples include crimes against children, domestic violence, white-collar crime, and computer crime, to name just a few.

Part II focuses on the efforts in the enforcement community to address environmental crime. When dealing with this type of crime, several issues must be weighed carefully. Part I provided a solid review of relevant issues for the student interested in better understanding environmental violations. By reviewing the definitional questions, the history of U.S. environmental movement, the politics and economics of environmental protection, the role of scientific expertise, and the major environmental protection statutes, the reader will undoubtedly have achieved a rough understanding of the complexities facing the enforcement community.

Chapter 6 describes the federal environmental regulatory structure, and Chapter 7 introduces state and local environmental enforcement objectives. Each individual city and each individual state has specific environmental protection needs. As a result, the environmental enforcement response must be developed in the community so that these specific needs are met.

Chapter 8 is an overview of the emerging role local law enforcement officers are playing in the fight against environmental crime. The role of the local police and the resources available to the environmental enforcement effort provided through the local police network will prove invaluable. Chapter 9 addresses the needs of the prosecutor by highlighting some of the common techniques for investigating and prosecuting environmental crimes. Chapter 10 reviews the action in the courtroom. The controversy surrounding criminal prosecution of environmental offenders and the role mandatory sentencing has played in issuing sentences for environmental offenders are discussed.

All of the chapters in Part II explore the role of local and state law enforcement agencies as "foot soldiers" in the war on environmental crime. Some argue that the police response is the only logical response, because police already provide a protection and investigation function in the community. Others argue that the police caseload is heavily burdened as it is and that the enforcement should come from the regulatory agencies. While the controversy remains, one thing is clear. A local law enforcement response would mean a ready response. Local law enforcement operations are already in place. Law enforcement officers have already worked in the criminal justice system and have assisted with investigations and prosecutions. The cost of training regulatory officials and placing the necessary number of officials in the field would be staggering. Local law enforcement agencies already have "officials" in the field. Yet police officers know that the process of identifying and enforcing environmental crimes has unique characteristics. If law enforcement officers are to become directly involved in environmental crime enforcement, the primary objective then will be to provide specific training so they can skillfully address the specific issues confronting this type of enforcement.

Part I advances the idea that an interdisciplinary approach to environmental protection is important. Traditionally, the study of the environment has been a responsibility primarily assumed by the natural sciences. Yet the studies of law and law enforcement practices have been exclusively linked to the social sciences. Noting once again an essential blending of natural sciences with the social sciences, researchers are beginning to acknowledge that the best strategy for investigating environmental crime and prosecuting environmental criminals is to combine the benefits of both branches of scientific study. Forensic science is only one example of scientific analysis used in police investigations. New technologies such as DNA testing, computer imaging techniques, and biometric devices are all examples of scientific technology used to catch criminals. With access to these specialized skills, local law enforcement officers could play a distinct role in the future of environmental crime investigation and prosecution. Just as academic interests must rely on many disciplines to develop a thorough understanding of environmental crime, practitioners in the field must rely on the expertise of many agencies concerned with environmental protection. Therefore, an interagency approach may meet with the most success when confronting environmental crime. Part II addresses many of these and related critical issues.

CHAPTER 6

The Federal Environmental Regulatory Structure

Bill Hyatt

TERMS	declaratory judgment	Office of Enforcement and
	enforcement agents	Compliance Assurance
	Freedom of Information	precedent
	Act	reckless act
	negligent act	voluntary compliance

Environmental protection encompasses a complex combination of legal, social, political, philosophical, economic, and scientific issues. The Environmental Protection Agency (EPA) is the regulatory agency charged with coordinating environmental protection efforts. The complexity of these interdependent efforts is evident immediately when you consider that enforcement requires action from people at all levels of government (federal, state, and local). Further, the EPA is not the only federal agency with a responsibility for protecting the natural environment. Ultimately, the effectiveness of environmental protection legislation depends, in large part, on the combined discretion of individuals involved in the enforcement process, including agency officials, corporate officials, members of the criminal justice system, and citizen activists, to name just a few.

When people examine environmental protection provisions, a thorough understanding is not afforded the faint of heart. Environmental statutes are constantly being added, updated, modified, and abandoned. Further, different states and local communities have dramatically different attitudes toward environmental protection. This difference is reflected in the local laws and enforcement efforts. Because environmental statutes, policies, and regulations exist at all levels of government, it is a full-time enterprise to keep up with current environmental protection provisions.

This chapter focuses on environmental enforcement at the federal level of government. Many state environmental protection agencies are modeled after the federal system. Therefore, a thorough review of the federal system provides a good starting place for learning about environmental protection and related regulatory structures at all levels of government. An introduction to the federal regulatory process is followed by an overview of the EPA. The history and current structure of the agency is outlined. Also included is a brief discussion of several other federal agencies that have jurisdiction over environmental matters. The enforcement options available to the federal enforcement agents are discussed in detail. From there, several procedural concerns attached to the environmental enforcement protocol are presented. These include a review of the permit process, search warrants, and privacy issues. A review of civil and criminal proceedings closes the chapter.

AN INTRODUCTION TO THE REGULATORY FUNCTION

Popular interest in maintaining the natural environment is reflected in the creation of laws to ensure it is protected and preserved. Yet, the natural environment is not protected by legal statutes alone. The environmental protection legislation passed by Congress would have little effect unless the laws and regulations were actually put into practice. A law, or even a series of laws, is intricately woven into interconnected activities by a regulatory agency. Regulatory policies are established to administer the provisions of the legislation passed by Congress. While Congress provides a general sense of what is intended by the legislation, specific regulations are needed to further describe *how* the enforcement of these laws is to be carried out.

To ensure that the statutory and regulatory provisions are followed, the agency may require **enforcement agents**. Enforcement agents are individuals charged with enforcing the statutes and regulatory agency provisions. Environmental enforcement agents, like many other law enforcement agents, exercise a significant amount of **discretion**. Regulatory agencies and their enforcement officers are often confronted with unprecedented or unanticipated situations. If the situations encountered are not adequately addressed in the legislation, the agency and its enforcement officers must outline a course of action they believe to be consistent with the legislative intent. Because this determination is subjective and open to question, an affected party might disagree with the agency actions.

If the actions taken by the regulatory agency or the enforcement agents are called into question, the parties might seek redress in the courts. The courts provide oversight of the regulatory agency's actions. As with any legal controversy, court action is sometimes necessary. When congressional intent is vague or when an alleged offender argues the regulatory agency has acted in contradiction to congressional intent, the facts of the case must be reviewed in the courts. When a court rules on a controversial element of a regulatory provision, the court's decision then becomes a **precedent**. A legal precedent acts as a model for directing future agency actions. In other words, the judicial interpretations form a part of the ongoing discussion about how environmental protection laws and regulations are to be administered. Lawmakers, laws, regulations, enforcement officials, and judicial interpretation are only a few of the elements needed to provide environmental protection. These agents and actions create a network of interdependent individuals and agencies. At the federal level, perhaps the most critical agency is the EPA.

A HISTORY OF THE ENVIRONMENTAL PROTECTION AGENCY

An enhanced understanding of federal environmental enforcement must begin with a discussion of the EPA. At present, regulatory responsibilities seem to have become hopelessly confusing. It seems environmental protection in the United States has come to resemble a jigsaw puzzle. Different environmental issues are like different pieces of that puzzle. Sometimes the pieces fit neatly, but most often they do not fit very well. Not only that, but a jigsaw puzzle comes with a picture of what the pieces are supposed to look like when they are placed correctly. Environmental protection lacks any such clear picture. In many cases environmental enforcement objectives have proven to be nearly incomprehensible for both the agents enforcing the law and the alleged violators.

The confusion is more easily understood if one considers the history of the agency (see Table 6–1). A significant attempt to coordinate environmental protection efforts did not happen in the United States until 1970, when President Nixon created the EPA by executive order.[1] Subsequently Congress approved the creation of the agency and outlined as its objective the enforcement of all environmental laws in the United States.[2] During the succeeding years, between 1972 and 1982, Congress passed and the president signed several major pieces of environmental protection legislation still in place today.

As is the case with many government actions, the creation of the EPA was argued to have been politically motivated. At the time, President Nixon was facing a presidential election. While some argued its creation represented a blatant political move to win favor in the upcoming election, others identified a clear purpose for the agency from the beginning. Creation of the EPA consolidated environmental enforcement responsibilities within one agency—something argued to be needed desperately. The early controversy over the creation of the EPA was only the first of a number of controversies that have confronted the agency during its brief existence.

Table 6–1 The Environmental Protection Leadership at the Federal Level

President	Interior Department Secretary	(Dates in Office)	EPA Administrator	(Dates in Office)
Nixon	Rogers Morton	(1971–1974)	William Ruckelshaus	(1970–1973)
Ford	Rogers Morton	(1974–1975)	Russell Train	(1973–1977)
	Stanley Hathaway	(1975)		
	Thomas Kleppe	(1975–1977)		
Carter	Cecil Andrus	(1977–1981)	Douglas Costle	(1977–1981)
Reagan	James Watt	(1981–1983)	Anne Burford	(1981–1983)
	William Clark	(1983–1985)	William Ruckelshaus	(1983–1985)
	Donald Hodel	(1985–1989)	Lee Thomas	(1985–1989)
Bush	Manuel Lujan	(1989–1992)	William Reilly	(1989–1992)
Clinton	Bruce Babbitt	(1993 to present)	Carol Browner	(1993 to present)

Source: Copyright © 1994. From *Environmental Politics*. By: Jacqueline Vaughn Switzer. Reprinted with permission of St. Martin's Press, Inc.

Since its inception, the EPA has become one of the largest and most controversial of the federal regulatory agencies. Certainly one of the factors contributing to the criticism is the broad spectrum of laws that it is required to enforce. The responsibilities identified for it to assume are seemingly limitless. The EPA has the authority to initiate control measures for new and existing chemicals that may pose a threat to human health and/or the environment. It has the authority to monitor water and air quality. It enforces laws that are intended to protect the health of society and the environment. Its mission is broadly defined, and efforts to identify the best means for accomplishing the agency's objectives have proven to be extremely controversial.

Substantial ambiguity exists in the current environmental protection legislation, particularly when it comes to determining how the case of an alleged violation should be handled. Although a significant player in pursuing enforcement action, the EPA does not have the authority to make a final determination on criminal enforcement. Russell Train, EPA Administrator from 1973 to 1977, attributed much of the agency's problem to the enormous amount of statutory responsibility assigned to the agency by Congress during the first years of its existence: "Many of the EPA's difficulties over the years can be traced to the fact that the Congress loaded the agency with far more statutory responsibilities, within a brief period of time, than perhaps any agency could effectively perform."[3(p.47)]

Another difficulty inherent in the organization of the EPA is the way in which its duties are delegated. Congress has never articulated a comprehensive environmental protection strategy but rather has passed separate laws as each perceived threat or need is identified. Following Congress's lead, the EPA has traditionally created a separate enforcement section within the agency to handle the administration of each new law (e.g., the Clean Air Act) rather than develop an overall strategy for environmental protection.[4]

Since the environmental laws and agency jurisdiction often overlap, both compliance and enforcement have become a regulator's nightmare. The procedures outlined to help achieve compliance or provide adequate enforcement have become cumbersome, confusing, and expensive. In many cases, different deadlines for compliance exist within a given statute,[5] which significantly complicates an already complex compliance and enforcement effort.

In its early days, the EPA had almost a missionary zeal. Enforcement was the objective. This enforcement effort was substantially slowed with the first oil embargo in the early 1970s. Believing the nation's economy in serious danger, the public became increasingly concerned about economic security. During the mid-1970s, by all appearances, the public interest in the environment had begun to wane.

Perhaps because of the battle over Watergate, President Nixon had little to say about the environment after his reelection, and President Ford, who completed Nixon's second term, is not known for promoting or supporting any environmental initiatives. Presidents Carter and Bush both expressed interest in protecting the environment, but the oil embargo during Carter's presidency and the Gulf War during Bush's term limited the time either devoted to environmental issues.

President Carter came to the office in 1977 and expanded EPA's jurisdiction with the signing of the Comprehensive Environmental Response, Compensation, and Liability Act in 1980. Also under the Carter administration, two concepts were proposed to help achieve compliance: the bubble concept and offset concept. The bubble concept, discussed in Chapter 5, sets allowable standards for an entire manufacturing operation rather than for each separate component. This allowed some aspects of a company's operations to be out of compliance with federal environmental laws as long as the company as a whole remained in compliance. The **offset rule** concept allowed polluting companies to go into a certain geographic area and continue to pollute so long as they could induce other industries in that area to reduce their pollution by an amount equal to the average of the polluting company.[6] This approach also allowed the polluting company to operate more than one plant in the same geographical area, because it could average the pollution of the two rather than have EPA judge each plant's compliance separately.

When President Reagan took office in 1981, political intrigue and infighting within the EPA seemed to take priority over environmental enforcement. At least 10 top aides in the agency either were fired or resigned during the early to middle 1980s.[7] Politicians during this period argued bitterly over the administration of the EPA. On the one hand, the Reagan administration subjected the agency to a series of debilitating budget reductions and changes in administrative procedures. On the other hand, critics claimed the agency needed to be "streamlined," having become bloated, top heavy, and confused about its mission. Cutting the funding and staffing of EPA was argued to be consistent with Reagan's promise to cut waste, fraud, and abuse in the federal government. Environmental advocates claimed, however, that Reagan was gutting environmental protection.

Under the Bush administration, the Clean Air Act was revised extensively. At the time of this writing, with President Clinton in his second term, it is still unclear how far-reaching Clinton's proposals for environmental protection will be. His major initiative, to elevate the EPA to a cabinet-level position, passed the Senate on May 4, 1993, but died in the House and has not been resurrected. The agenda of environmental protection was used extensively as a major theme during the Clinton reelection bid in 1996.

Throughout its contentious history, few of the agency's actions were as controversial as its decision, during the Reagan administration, to seek **voluntary compliance** (i.e., to encourage compliance with environmental regulations through cooperation with the businesses being regulated). Rather than using a consistently confrontational approach, EPA officials wanted companies to comply with environmental laws on a voluntary basis. Affected companies, or companies in violation of environmental protection provisions, were expected—whenever possible—to make efforts toward compliance.[8] The Reagan administration argued that this approach brought better compliance results than the policy followed under the Carter administration. One obvious result was a huge reduction in the number of enforcement actions.[9]

After five years of charges and countercharges regarding EPA operations, a degree of stability was brought to the agency with the appointment of William Ruckelshaus to the position of EPA administrator, for a second time, in 1983. Ruckelshaus's predecessor, Anne M. Burford, had developed a reputation as a critic of further environmental protection and was seen by some as trying to destroy the agency by reducing its budget. Although Burford argued that she was merely making the agency more efficient, a fight with Congress over agency records regarding the Superfund resulted in her resignation—and a loss of public confidence in the agency's objectives.

Ruckelshaus, a former Department of Justice senior official, made substantial gains on two fronts. First, the lead in gasoline was substantially reduced. Second, a major pesticide, ethylene dibromide, was removed from the market.[10] But even Ruckelshaus's tenure at the EPA was not without controversy. Acid rain became a divisive international issue. The Reagan administration, and EPA policy at the time, required more information on the problem of acid rain to be collected before any policy action would be taken. The administration supported research *only*. This created a substantial uproar among environmental groups—many on the Canadian side of the border—who insisted the administration had access to more than enough evidence to demand full-scale emission cuts by all of the offending industries within the United States.

Responding in some part to the political pressure, the EPA began a more active enforcement effort. Westinghouse Corporation, for example, was ordered to spend more than $100 million dollars on a cleanup operation in Indiana.[11] Shell Oil and the Department of Defense were to spend $1 billion on the cleanup and decontamination of a chemical weapons dump site at the Rocky Mountain Arsenal in Denver, Colorado.[12]

More important than this clear increase in enforcement was a decision made at about this time by Lee Thomas, who became EPA administrator following Ruckelshaus's second term. Thomas imposed large civil penalties that laid the groundwork for a major criminal enforcement effort, which began shortly thereafter. The purpose of this effort was to discourage the worst abusers of environmental policies. The enforcement agencies began to take strict action against companies releasing certain hazardous chemicals—chemicals that up to that time had been routinely leaked into the atmosphere. Some of the offending corporations were located in the United States, but others were located abroad. So again the federal agencies found themselves dealing with international environmental issues.

In response to the Bhopal, India, disaster on December 3, 1984, and to a congressional report that found that as many as 200 hazardous chemicals were being routinely discharged into the atmosphere in the United States, the EPA began developing emergency preparedness plans to address other environmental threats. The emergency preparedness plans were put into place in 1985. They described the EPA's primary responsibilities as including the following areas:

1) air quality
   a) set US air quality standards
   b) supervise states in development of air quality plans

2) water quality
   a) issue permits for discharge into any navigable waters
   b) coordinate the clean up of oil and chemical spills in US waterways
   c) regulate the disposal of waste material into the oceans
   d) issue, with the Army Corps of Engineers, permits for dredging and filling wetlands

3) the disposal of hazardous waste
   a) track more than 500 hazardous compounds from point of origin to final disposal sites
   b) set standards for the transportation and disposal of hazardous waste
   c) issue permits for treatment, storage and disposal facilities for hazardous waste
   d) maintain the Superfund multimillion dollar fund created from fees from industry and general tax revenues for emergency cleanup of hazardous dumps when responsibility for the dumping cannot be fixed at the time the cleanup is needed.
   e) investigate unauthorized dumping and seek reimbursement for the Superfund expenditures for the cleanup effort

4) regulation of chemicals, including pesticides and radioactive waste
   a) maintain a list of chemical substances now in commercial use
   b) regulate the use of chemicals that are dangerous to the environment or to individuals
   c) issue chemical testing procedures
   d) set use regulation for pesticides and can issue "stop sale use and removal orders" for pesticides in violation of the law which are already in circulation
   e) provide overall guidance to other federal agencies on radiation matters that affect personal health[13(p.45)]

While early EPA responsibilities covered all environmental protection issues, as the agency evolved its responsibilities became more focused. More recently, the EPA's enforcement efforts have been focused on air and water pollution, hazardous waste, and hazardous chemicals.

During the Clinton administration, the focus on environmental policies shifted from the EPA to Congress. Republican congressional leaders threatened to roll back a variety of environmental provisions. As the result of a landslide Republican victory in 1994, which overturned the Democratic majority in the House, the EPA's funding and several enforcement programs were in jeopardy of being cut.[14,15] Because of steady public support for the EPA and environmental issues, however, little action was taken. Environmental protection emerged as an important political issue for all political parties in the 1996 election.[16-22] While the popular mood seems to still indicate continued support for environmental protection, the long-term future of environmental protection remains controversial and uncertain.

EPA Regulatory and Enforcement Structure

The EPA is an independent agency within the executive branch of the federal government (Figure 6–1). It is headed by an administrator, who is assisted by a deputy administrator and nine assistant administrators. All parties are nominated by the president and are subject to Senate confirmation.

The EPA operates 10 offices of regional counsel throughout the United States (see Appendix 6–A). These offices review administrative enforcement efforts and forward problem cases to Washington for review. The regional offices also offer legal assistance to regional EPA administrators and work with state administrators whose agencies have primary jurisdiction for enforcement of environmental protection legislation. North Carolina and Texas are examples of states that exercise jurisdiction with the advice and

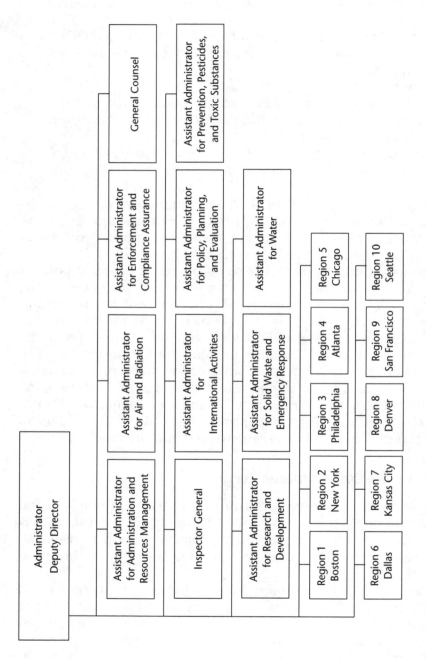

Figure 6–1 United States Environmental Protection Agency Organizational Chart. *Source:* Reprinted from United States Environmental Protection Agency, 1997.

oversight of EPA regional administrators. These state offices are organized along the lines of the EPA, and their statutes are either identical to or more strict than the federal environmental laws.

Jurisdiction of Other Agencies

Although overall responsibility for environmental compliance and enforcement rests with the EPA, several other federal agencies also have responsibility for protecting the natural environment or managing environmental resources. The EPA works in conjunction with federal, state, and local agencies to "minimize or eliminate adverse effects of exposure to toxic substances at spill and waste disposal sites."[23(p.629)] Although the EPA has been granted primary jurisdiction over environmental enforcement, many other agencies can become involved in environmental issues given the proper circumstances. Consider the following federal agencies and the role they play in ensuring environmental protection (Figure 6–2).

The degree of environmental contamination at U.S. military bases has been one of the more recent discoveries in dealing with hazardous waste cleanup.[24] The Department of Defense (DOD) has jurisdiction over what happens at a military installation, including disposition of military weapons that pose an environmental threat, such as chemical or nuclear weapons.

Besides having jurisdiction over military installations on U.S. soil, the DOD has jurisdiction within **foreign nations** and **global commons**. *Foreign nations* include "any geographical area (land, water, and airspace) that is under the jurisdiction of one or more foreign governments; any area under military occupation by the United States alone or jointly with any other foreign government."[25] The term *global commons* refers to any "geographical areas that are outside the jurisdiction of any nation, and includes the oceans outside territorial limits and Antarctica."[26] Therefore, any environmental concerns affecting foreign nations and global commons could fall under the DOD's jurisdiction. While the DOD does have jurisdiction under this treaty, our legal and constitutional restrictions would appear to prohibit it from taking any criminal or possibly civil action against foreign violators in the United States or in foreign courts. Likewise, it is questionable whether such a treaty would give the military jurisdiction over U.S. civilians for violations here, because the military would not have the authority to prosecute in the civilian courts. The Uniform Code of Military Justice, which governs all military prosecutions, makes no provisions for such jurisdictional problems.

The Department of Energy (DOE) and the Nuclear Regulatory Commission (NRC) have overlapping jurisdiction in many fields. Because of the history of nuclear weapon production in the United States, these agencies have

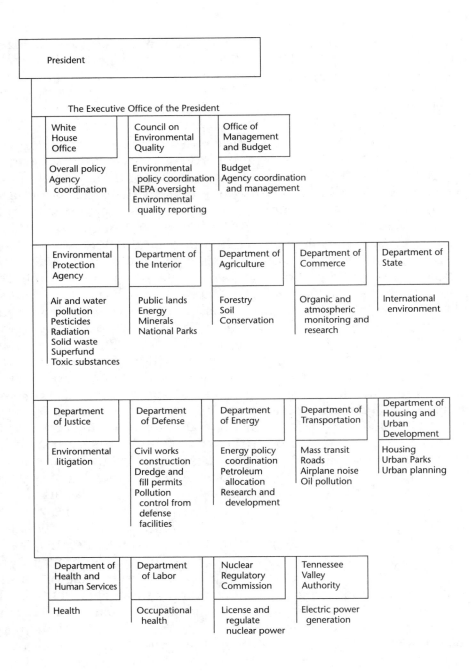

Figure 6–2 Executive Agencies with Environmental Responsibilities. *Source:* Reprinted from *Environmental Quality 1985, 1986,* Council on Environmental Quality.

close relationships with the DOD. Both are responsible for the permit process associated with the storage of spent nuclear fuel, the disposal of high-level radioactive waste, and the packaging and transportation of radioactive materials. Further, both have responsibilities that include the protection of plants and wildlife. The Nuclear Regulatory Commission is also responsible for the licensing requirements of special nuclear materials and the exportation and importation of nuclear equipment and materials.[27]

The Department of the Interior has authority over the National Parks, federal lands, and public lands. It provides for the development of fish, wildlife, water, and mineral resources; has jurisdiction over the national historic and scenic areas, including the Native American lands; and is responsible for the implementation of environmental policy and assessing the effects of that policy on the natural resources.[28] In effect, the Department of the Interior receives guidelines from the EPA regarding the statutory requirements for environmental protection enforcement and actually enforces the laws on lands under its jurisdiction according to the policies developed by the EPA. The department is also charged generally with protection of all lands under its supervision, including natural resources such as air and water, and thus it has indirect environmental protection responsibilities.

The Department of Agriculture has authority over the National Forest Service. It also has jurisdiction over the grasslands and their natural resources. The Department of Agriculture has a national soil and water conservation program as well as resource management programs.[29]

The Department of Justice (DOJ) is responsible for prosecuting all cases concerning the federal government. In the case of environmental protection, the DOJ is responsible for the criminal prosecution of individuals involved in hazardous waste violations or other violations of environmental law for which criminal provisions have been identified.[30]

The Department of Housing and Urban Development (HUD) has jurisdiction over land on which multifamily housing or facilities are under construction and it monitors the building of hospitals, nursing homes, and colleges. Applicants to HUD must comply with all statutes and provisions deemed necessary by HUD. Further, builders must be familiar with products, such as asbestos, that pose potential health risks.[31] The Endangered Species Act of 1973 is an example of environmental legislation that might affect HUD construction. If a permit application conflicts with federal environmental protection statutes, it is likely to be denied and further construction prohibited.[32]

Environmental issues may affect a variety of federal agencies. Any given situation involving environmental enforcement may require input from one or more federal agencies, or the issue may involve federal and local agencies. For instance, a discharge into a public sewage treatment system could involve both the EPA and the local municipal waste treatment agency. Transportation of hazardous chemicals spilled en route to a disposal facility would be under the jurisdiction of both the EPA and the state's department of transportation or highway patrol. Also, the federal Department of Highways would be involved if the spill occurred on a federal highway. Further, if the waste was being carried by a DOD vehicle and the spill crossed the highway onto federal or state park land, the Department of the Interior (or the state park authority) and the DOD would also have some jurisdiction. Thus, even though it is true that the EPA has the primary responsibility for enforcing the environmental laws, several agencies can have jurisdiction for initiating a response to a given environmental threat.

ENFORCEMENT OPTIONS FOR ENVIRONMENTAL VIOLATIONS

Environmental enforcement takes three basic forms: administrative enforcement (also commonly referred to as regulatory enforcement), civil enforcement, and criminal enforcement. In the administrative enforcement approach the agency notifies an alleged violator of the violation and orders the activity be stopped. If the violator complies, then the matter is ended. If the violator does not stop or does not agree the activity is in violation, the violator and the enforcement officials begin informal negotiations in an effort to reach a settlement.

If the informal negotiations do not achieve a resolution, an **administrative enforcement** action will be pursued. An administrative hearing is

Calvin and Hobbes   by Bill Watterson

Source: CALVIN AND HOBBES © 1991 Watterson. Dist. by UNIVERSAL PRESS SYNDICATE. Reprinted with permission. All rights reserved.

scheduled at which an administrative law judge hears the facts and the arguments of the parties and renders a decision. The decision can then be appealed to the EPA administrator, whose decision can in turn be appealed through the federal court system up to the level of the U.S. Court of Appeals. Ultimately, the case can go to the Supreme Court if the justices choose to grant **certiorari** (i.e., choose to hear the case).

If the EPA enforcement agents feel the matter cannot be resolved within the agency or if the violator refuses to participate in the administrative process, the EPA will refer the case to the DOJ for civil or criminal prosecution. The DOJ will review the request from the EPA and, based on the facts of the case, make a determination about how to proceed. If the case is minor or if the violator has few previous violations, chances are good the case will be handled through the **civil enforcement** process. In cases enforced civilly, the convicted offender is typically required to rectify the problem and may be fined. If the case is more serious or the violator has a long history of repeat violations, the agency may decide to pursue a **criminal enforcement** strategy. In this case, the accused offender will be prosecuted in the criminal courts and in addition to being fined, may serve time in jail or prison.

The range of options available to the environmental enforcement officials makes it particularly difficult to respond to cases of alleged environmental harm. These options increase the complexities attached to an already complex set of conditions. Because of the myriad choices involved in pursuing an environmental violation, many actors within the enforcement structure find themselves out of their realm of experience and expertise. For example, they may know that a chemical has been spilled but might not know the degree of harm associated with that particular chemical.

The variety of enforcement options also presents some difficulty for local law enforcement officers, who are in a position to assist regulatory enforcement officials on cases involving environmental crime. It is inherently difficult to deal with a set of laws and regulations when it is unclear where the boundaries between administrative, civil, and criminal violations lie.

Enforcement Powers

As mentioned above, the EPA's primary objective is to achieve voluntary compliance. Such compliance is sought from federal agencies, state and local agencies, private industry, and private citizens. If voluntary compliance cannot be achieved, then the EPA is authorized to enforce compliance, imposing penalties as outlined in the major environmental laws. The EPA either carries out enforcement functions or delegates enforcement authority to the states under appropriate agreements.

The EPA's **Office of Enforcement and Compliance Assurance** is responsible for overseeing all of the cases where voluntary compliance has not been obtained. The office gathers and prepares evidence of noncompliance, conducts civil enforcement proceedings, and when necessary assists the DOJ in criminal enforcement cases (most often cases involving water quality, air pollution, radiation, pesticides, solid waste, and noise pollution).

Because of the complexities of the enforcement and protection processes at the federal level, the EPA attempts to work with state environmental protection agencies through its regional offices. Although states are required to adopt the federal environmental protection standards, they have been given authority to enhance the federal standards if they so choose. In other words, a state may operate under environmental standards that are *more* stringent than those imposed at the federal level.

A variety of environmental protection and enforcement responsibilities exist at the state level. Some states only provide permit applications, while other states investigate, negotiate settlements, indict, or follow through with court action when necessary. The extent of state responsibility for enforcement of environmental law violations is pursuant to agreements between each state and the EPA. As might be expected, this varies from state to state, based on the local interest and the state's ability to effectively enforce the laws. More about state-level environmental enforcement is covered in the next chapter.

Federal Enforcement Priorities

While prosecutors have the discretion to bring (or not bring) cases, some basic criteria apply. These include the following:

- the degree of harm to the environment
- the degree of provable criminal intent
- the offending company's prior record
- the offending company's cooperation during the investigation and its willingness to pay to fix the problem
- media interest in the case
- the possibility of organized crime connections

The prosecutor's office must also take into consideration the cost of the prosecution and determine whether the investigative resources are available.[33]

In recent years organized crime figures have been linked to hazardous waste disposal. Many experts attribute their involvement to the fact that the severe penalties allowed by law are typically used as a last resort if at all. There is money to be made, with little chance of getting caught. It has been estimated that 14,000 regulated manufacturers in the United States create 150 metric tons of highly toxic hazardous waste each year,[34] and 90 percent of this waste is being dumped illegally.[35] The only thing needed to make large amounts of money in the illegal dumping of hazardous waste is "a truck and a lack of regard for public safety."[36(p.440)] Data are available from the *EPA's Accomplishment Reports* for the various fiscal years. While the degree to which organized crime has been involved in hazardous waste disposal is still in question, cases of alleged organized crime activity remain a priority for federal enforcement officials.[37]

Civil Proceedings

If the government decides to use a civil action, use of a **declaratory judgment** is standard practice. When this occurs, the court is asked to order the defendant in the case not to engage in the action in question. If, for instance, the defendant company wished to ship certain hazardous materials across the country in an open truck (a practice the EPA has determined not to be safe), the EPA could go to court for a declaratory judgment asking the court to find such a transportation method to be potentially dangerous. This action would seek to disallow, or prevent, this method. Rather than waiting until the material was transported and suing the company for any damages that resulted from its action, the declaratory judgment seeks to prevent damages. This action is most often used when the regulations do not specify which methods are considered "acceptable practice."

If the government has refused to issue a permit or if the defendant company is not abiding by the requirements of the permit, the government can bring a civil action against the company seeking money to repair the damages and to prevent the defendant from causing further damage. These actions can be heard before a judge or a jury, and the verdict may be appealed to the appellate court by either party if it feels the verdict was somehow made in error.

Criminal Prosecution

If the matter cannot be settled effectively using a civil proceeding or if evidence suggests the defendant company acted deliberately to cause damage to the environment, criminal proceedings offer the most severe remedy available. Although the EPA may be the investigating agency, it does not have the power to initiate a criminal action. Generally, enforcement agencies at the state level do not have such power, either. As stated earlier, the EPA refers these cases to the DOJ.

Before a criminal action may be initiated at the federal level, the DOJ, usually through a U.S. attorney, must either issue an **information** or convene a grand jury and seek a criminal indictment. An information states the existence of probable cause to suggest the defendant has committed a specifically described criminal act in violation of a specified criminal statute. Before an indictment can be made, a grand jury must hear evidence and make a determination as to whether probable cause exists.

Anything classified as a criminal violation could also be treated as a civil violation. In most cases, the criminal actions could be subject to a civil suit. For a variety of reasons, the burden of proof required is higher in a criminal case than a civil proceeding. In a criminal case, the government must prove its case **beyond a reasonable doubt**. This is an extremely high burden. In a civil case, the government must only prove its case by a **preponderance of the evidence**. Translated into percentages, a preponderance of the evidence would be 51 percent, while the criminal standard, beyond a reasonable doubt, would require proof in excess of 95 percent. Because such a high burden is difficult to prove in environmental cases, only a very small percentage of cases are prosecuted criminally.

Note that at the present time no common definition of what constitutes a criminal, as opposed to civil, violation of environmental law exists. The decision about which process to follow, criminal or civil, is left to the prosecutor and the investigating agency.

Also note that the prosecuting agency's decision to charge or not charge a violator criminally is, for practical purposes, unreviewable (i.e., the decision to proceed with a prosecution is not subject to appeal). A primary factor used to determine whether to proceed with the prosecution of an environmental offense civilly or criminally is the violator's intent. In order to be accused of a criminal offense, the accused offender must have intended to commit the act and must have known the act was wrong. Environmental enforcement maintains, to a similar degree, the importance of intent when identifying or classifying a criminal environmental offense.

To illustrate this in the case of an environmental violation, assume a company has dumped a highly toxic chemical into a local river. The result is damage to both the river system (the environment) and the human population along the river. In deciding whether the case should be prosecuted criminally, the prosecutor must have a clear understanding of the intent of the defendant company, including the company's officers and employees. If the defendant company, through its officers, knew the material was highly toxic and still elected to dump it in the river, criminal prosecution would be likely. If, on the other hand, it could be shown the defendant company knew the dumping of the material in the river was illegal but believed the material to be harmless, the case would likely be handled civilly.

If it could be shown the company knew or should have known the dumping could cause considerable damage but dumped the waste because legal disposal was extremely expensive, then criminal charges would be more likely. In this case, the conduct would be considered so reckless as to make the defendant criminally liable even though it did not have specific knowledge of the damage the chemical might cause.

If the company is criminally prosecuted, the criminal prosecution in no way replaces the civil suit as a vehicle for recovering damages. The criminal prosecution is for the purpose of punishing the defendant for wrongful actions. The purpose of a civil action is to require reimbursement to all injured parties affected by the damage caused by the defendant. Further, a prosector may wish to proceed with a criminal charge but because of lack of evidence be forced to pursue a civil conviction. The burden of proof is so high for a criminal conviction that the absence of critical pieces of evidence might necessitate instituting a civil action where the burden of proof is less stringent and more easily attainable.

An extremely controversial component of the criminal provisions of some environmental statutes allows prosecution of a company if that company violated an environmental protection regulation without knowledge that its actions would be harmful. Although the company did not know its actions could cause environmental damage, it can be considered to have acted in such a reckless (instead of negligent) manner as to pose serious danger to the environment. For example, if a company accidentally mislabeled certain hazardous chemicals and placed them with less dangerous chemicals that had been approved by permit to be dumped into a river system, its dumping of the hazardous chemicals would be considered a **negligent act**. If the company knew that the chemicals had lost their labels and did not know which chemicals were safe and which were hazardous but chose to dump them all without making any effort to determine the level of toxicity, the dumping would generally be considered a **reckless act**. The likely course for a reckless act is criminal prosecution.

One of the difficulties, as indicated in the discussion above, is how to determine when to use criminal, civil, or administrative actions to punish offenders. In more recent cases, particularly cases involving the Superfund, **strict liability** has often been used because it requires no proof of intent. Strict liability, remember, presumes any act that violates the statute is presumed to have been done willfully, knowingly, and intentionally. As a result, the violator is subject to criminal liability simply on proof that the act was committed by the defendant.

Using the example above, under a strict liability statute, the company responsible for dumping hazardous material into the river would be liable regardless of whether it intended to dump the materials. Even if it could be shown that the dumping was purely unintentional, criminal penalties could be applied. It is the opinion of many federal prosecutors, however, that strict liability cases carry with them unwelcome implications. As a result, these cases are not always treated as serious cases, particularly when it comes to punishment. Because the law is viewed by some as being too severe, the judicial system has been known to respond in kind.

Currently, virtually all of the environmental crimes in the United States require proof of intent to commit the crime, which makes their prosecution considerably more difficult. While the act itself, or the harm inflicted, can often be demonstrated relatively easily, determining responsibility for the specific decision to commit the act is often quite difficult. The result is that most prosecutors bring civil charges against the corporation rather than criminal charges against the officers of the corporation.

Even if criminal charges are brought in cases such as this, they are often brought against only the corporation, since it is nearly impossible to prove that a particular individual had the necessary criminal intent. Prosecuting only the corporation, however, is often thought to defeat the purpose of the criminal prosecution. Because a corporation cannot be jailed, the only remaining punishment is a fine, which is easily passed on to the public in the form of higher prices. Except for the possible adverse publicity attached to a criminal case, which might harm future sales, it is difficult to see how criminal proceedings differ from civil proceedings when the corporation rather than an individual within the corporation is prosecuted. Chapter 10 discusses a variety of punishment alternatives being developed in an effort to address this problem.

PROCEDURAL ISSUES FOR FEDERAL ENVIRONMENTAL ENFORCEMENT

Like other law enforcement officials, environmental enforcement officials must be concerned with due process rights, particularly in the areas of permits, search warrants, and privacy. One thing to note is that many environmental provisions allow an individual or company to produce some pollution. The pollution emitted, however, must be within the limits outlined in any permits directing that party's activities. Further, action cannot be taken in many cases without authorization granted through a search warrant. While some actions may allow for an immediate response, having search

INSIGHT

Poaching the Black Rhino in Africa May Be Deadly—for the Poachers[1]

Although controversy surrounds the question of how to punish environmental criminals in the United States, an interesting case involving poaching of the protected black rhino in Africa provides an example of the ultimate sanction for violators—death. In the early 1980s, Zimbabwe was home to Africa's largest concentration of black rhinos, about 3,000. In the past decade, however, poachers "armed with AK-47 machine guns and German assault rifles" turned the area into a "killing ground."[2(p.31)]

Rhino horns have been used in Chinese folk remedies for more than 2,000 years for "treating ailments from high fevers to convulsions to failing vision."[3(p.30)] Horns have also been used to make costly curved daggers that symbolize masculine power. The result has been a plummeting black rhino population that totals less than 315 today. The Zimbabwe government wasted little time in fighting back. In 1984, the Department of National Parks and Wildlife Management launched Operation Stronghold, a military style shoot-to-kill campaign aimed at rhino poachers. The game scouts hired to protect the animals trained for war. The scouts "killed about 178 poachers, arrested hundreds more and confiscated hundreds of guns and horns."[4(p.30)] Because the poachers were so well funded and the government scouts were lacking in rifles, radios, and transportation, the program ended in failure.

The government then responded to the threat of further depletion by moving the black rhinos to heavily guarded private conservancies. One conservancy's chief scout has an extensive history with the rhinos. He named one of the rhinos after his best friend, who was shot in the head by a poacher they were tracking. He has lost several of his scouts to poachers. Further, he works closely with the local people to educate them about the benefits the rhinos bring to their community. Because poachers typically come into the area from the outside, they usually attempt to enlist help from the locals in trying to locate the rhinos. The citizens are now being used to help turn the poachers in before they can get close to the rhinos.

Rhino conservationists are trying to develop additional methods for protecting the black rhino. Dehorning is one controversial method. Starting in 1991, scouts and veterinarians started sawing off the horns of the anesthetized rhinos. The theory is that the rhinos will no longer be attractive to poachers because they no longer have their horns. Others argue, however, that poachers will kill a hornless rhino they have tracked because they do not want to waste time tracking the rhino again. The dehorning program is also expensive for the scouts. Dehorning a rhino costs about $1,400 and must be repeated every two years because the horn grows back.[5]

Also controversial is the treaty that banned the rhino-horn trade in 1977. This treaty has not seemed to reduce the killing. Some argue if the rhino were extinct, the price of the horns would skyrocket. Following this logic, they argue that the answer is to allow trading of horns that have been cut off from animals legally. Supporters believe it will undercut the black market and reduce poaching. Only time will tell if the efforts taken on behalf of the black rhino will preserve this endangered population.

1. D. Rosenthal, "Showdown in Zimbabwe: In the Nation That Once Held Africa's Greatest Concentration of Black Rhinos, Private Citizens Struggle To Save the Last of the Animals," *International Wildlife*, December 1996, 28–36.
2. Rosenthal, "Showdown in Zimbabwe," 31.
3. Rosenthal, "Showdown in Zimbabwe," 30.
4. Rosenthal, "Showdown in Zimbabwe," 30.
5. Rosenthal, "Showdown in Zimbabwe," 35.

warrants always provides the officers with additional support for their actions. Finally, privacy concerns exist when dealing with "company secrets" or a citizen's right to know. The procedure used for protecting privacy rights and providing a means for public review of important documents is discussed below.

Permit Process

A permit process has been outlined in several pieces of environmental legislation. The permit process requires all parties affected by the law to identify themselves. Further, the affected companies provide information so that the regulatory agency can make a determination as to whether the actions contemplated meet the requirements of the statute. The agency establishes the permit guidelines, including the life of the permit, the scope of the authorized activity, and conditions for the addition or removal of particular materials under the permit. The law usually provides for the granting of general permits to be issued when a determination is made that only minimal damage will occur to the environment. In addition, most jurisdictions have provisions for emergency permits when the activity in question is necessary to prevent either loss of life or serious physical damage to the property and the potential for damage outweighs the possible damage of the activity for which the emergency permit is requested.

A company seeking a permit to engage in some activity regulated by an environmental law must submit an application providing relevant details about itself and its operations. Name and address, a description of the property where the proposed activity is to take place, and any other information determined by the permit-granting agency to be necessary is required. All information submitted must be accurate. Furnishing any false information is punishable under the criminal perjury or false statement provisions outlined in the legislation.

In effect, the permit process gives the compliance officers a blueprint to follow in determining whether or not the company's activity is in compliance with the law. Also, it gives the compliance officers a good idea of what they need to look for when checking to see if the provisions of the law have been followed. In theory, this process is argued to require a considerably smaller compliance staff for investigations. It also provides a negotiating tool when false or misleading information has been provided.

Once the permit has been granted, the EPA shifts its focus to making sure the requirements of the permit are followed. If the requirements of the permits are not followed, then the agency will seek one of the three remedies discussed earlier—an administrative, a civil, or a criminal enforcement action.

Administrative and Criminal Search Warrants

In order to adequately monitor compliance with established regulatory provisions, EPA investigators may need access to the company being monitored, which they can gain in three ways. First, they can ask the company officials for permission to enter the facility. Second, they can apply for an administrative search warrant. Finally, they can seek a criminal search warrant. Although the requirements for obtaining administrative and criminal search warrants are different, both types of warrants are issued by a court.

Criminal and administrative search warrants serve the same basic goal: to allow the investigators to come on the property of the potential defendant to conduct an inspection. The physical property and any relevant documents will be viewed to determine whether the company is in compliance with environmental regulations. The difference in the warrants lies in their enforcement objectives.

A criminal search warrant is issued to determine whether a criminal violation is occurring, and it can be obtained from a judicial officer only after the investigators have shown probable cause exists to suggest the defendant is committing a criminal act. Probable cause can be shown by an affidavit, sworn testimony, or physical evidence. The issuance of a criminal search warrant is intended to lead to the criminal prosecution of the defendant if the allegations are found to be true.

An administrative search warrant, on the other hand, is more routine in nature and is issued to determine whether the company in question is in compliance with government rules and regulations. Its primary purpose is to determine compliance, not to develop evidence to be used in a criminal case. If evidence indicating criminal conduct is uncovered in the course of the execution of an administrative search warrant, the information may be used in a criminal prosecution of the defendant.

Probable cause is not necessary for the issuance of an administrative search warrant. The affidavit offered in support of the warrant does not have to identify specific violations or particular conditions or actions. It only has to demonstrate a general and neutral enforcement plan. The warrant, however, cannot be for any arbitrary, capricious, or discriminatory purpose but must be part of a regulator inspection plan that covers all companies affected by specific environmental regulations. The purpose of administrative search warrants is to serve as a judicial check against selective enforcement, as outlined in *Marshall v. Barlow's Inc.*[38] An exception to the necessity for an administrative search warrant has been shown in the case of intensively regulated industries, such as mineral strip mining, auto salvage, and liquor distribution (see *New York v. Burger*).[39] Although some industries affected by environmental laws are considered to be closely regulated, the vast majority do not fall into this category and require an administrative search warrant. A search warrant, either criminal or administrative, is not required if the company in question consents to a search of its premises, although the search must be limited to the area for which the consent was given. A warrant is also not required in emergency situations, such as a fire, an explosion, or a leak of dangerous chemicals.

Privacy Concerns

The EPA and the states that enforce the laws under the direction of EPA are bound by the **Freedom of Information Act** (FOIA).[40] Basically the provisions of FOIA allow any person submitting required information to assert a claim of business confidentiality. If this claim is made, then the agency will treat the information as confidential, providing it has first determined the information to be properly claimed to be confidential.

If the EPA has an FOIA request for information that has no claim of confidentiality, the agency rules require notification of the submitting party to see if it wishes to assert such a claim. If an FOIA request is submitted and a claim of confidentiality has been made and upheld by the EPA, the party filing the request will be notified, and if it wishes to pursue the information, it can proceed to litigate the issue in court.

If a court orders the release of some or all of the information, the EPA will disclose it as ordered. Confidentiality does not apply to instances where the information provided discloses a need for further enforcement by another agency, such as a disclosure to the Federal Bureau of Investigation or the U.S. attorney in the areas of air pollution, water pollution, hazardous waste, toxic substances, medical waste, nuclear waste, accidental dumpings and spills, deliberate illegal acts that pollute in some way, and destruction of public lands or resources.[41]

CONCLUSION

In the fiscal year 1991, 81 federal criminal cases were brought against a total of 104 defendants, with 48 cases resulting in the conviction of 72 defendants.[42] At this time, EPA statistics indicate 258,851 companies of various sizes generate hazardous waste. During this same period, 393 civil cases were referred to the DOJ for commencement of a civil suit, and 3,925 administrative actions were handled by the EPA.[43] These cases were generated by 150 criminal investigators. If allocated proportionally, each investigator would have been responsible for monitoring compliance and investigating violations by 1,400 companies, clearly an enormous burden.

The following statement summarizes the philosophy behind environmental enforcement activities at the federal level. Despite the small numbers, felony prosecutions of environmental crimes stand out as the major change in environmental enforcement over the past 20 years. Civil judgments may carry little public stigma, but, in contrast, criminal sanctions can serve as effective deterrents. Incarceration is one of the costs of doing business that cannot be passed on to the consumer.[44] While efforts to criminalize environmental violations continue, the controversy surrounding these efforts remains as intense as ever.

REVIEW QUESTIONS

1. List two examples of regulatory agencies with environmental responsibilities.
2. Identify the regulatory agency or agencies exclusively responsible for environmental protection.
3. List and briefly describe the three enforcement options available to the EPA.
4. What role does the DOD play in environmental protection?
5. What attributes of a specific environmental infraction will help determine the EPA's response?
6. What standards of evidence differentiate civil from criminal proceedings?
7. What standards of evidence differentiate administrative from civil proceedings when an environmental crime is being prosecuted?

DISCUSSION QUESTIONS

1. What are the benefits and costs of voluntary compliance as an enforcement objective?
2. The Freedom of Information Act serves what purpose in environmental controversies?
3. What systematic difficulties with the environmental enforcement structure at the federal government level can you identify? What recommendations would you offer to address these structural concerns?
4. Several parties make up the system of environmental enforcement. If some do not do their job, the enforcement objectives will not be met. Identify and discuss some examples of potential enforcement difficulties within the current system.

REFERENCES

1. For a discussion of the function and history of the EPA, see T. Sullivan, ed., *Environmental Law Handbook*, 13th ed. (Rockville, MD: Government Institutes, Inc.,).
2. *Federal Regulatory Directory*, 7th ed. (Washington, DC: Congressional Quarterly, 1994).
3. *Federal Regulatory Directory*, 47.
4. *Federal Regulatory Directory.*
5. *Federal Regulatory Directory.*
6. *Federal Regulatory Directory.*
7. *Federal Regulatory Directory.*
8. *Federal Regulatory Directory.*
9. *Federal Regulatory Directory.*
10. *Federal Regulatory Directory.*
11. *Federal Regulatory Directory.*
12. *Federal Regulatory Directory.*
13. *Federal Regulatory Directory*, 45.
14. T. Delay, "The Environment: Democrats Seek More Wasteful Washington Spending To Protect Bureaucrats, Not the Environment," advertising supplement, *Washington Post National Weekly Edition*, 22–25 April 1996, E1–E2.
15. B. Babbitt, "The Environment: The GOP Seeks To Dismantle a Century of Bipartisan Environmental Laws," advertising supplement, *Washington Post National Weekly Edition*, 22–25 April 1996, E1–E2.
16. B. Knickerbocker, "The 1996 Election Could Be Green Party's Coming of Age," *Christian Science Monitor*, 7 August 1996, 3.
17. B. Knickerbocker, "Dole, Clinton Duel for Western Voters over Environment," *Christian Science Monitor*, 31 July 1996, 1, 4.
18. B. Turque and T. Rosensteil, "Turning Clinton Green: Inside an Obsessively Poll-driven Campaign Conversion," *Newsweek*, 15 July 1996, 26.
19. S. Begley and D. Glick, "The Eye of the Storm: In Today's Environmental Debates, the Moderate and Reasonable Center Has Become a Dangerous Place To Be," *Newsweek*, 1 July 1996, 59.
20. K. Shillinger, "Look for GOP Politicos To Start Hugging Trees," *Christian Science Monitor*, 19 April 1996, 1, 9.
21. R. Benedetto, "Clinton Hits GOP on the Environment," *USA Today*, 12 March 1996, 4A.
22. B. Knickerbocker, "Why the GOP Changed Little in Environment," *Christian Science Monitor*, 2 January 1996, 1, 11.
23. *Washington Information Directory*, 1996–1997 edition (Washington, DC: Congressional Quarterly, 1996), 629.
24. M. Renner, "Military Mop-up: The U.S. Military Doesn't Want Any More Rocky Flats or Cornhusker Coverups: It's Cleaning House and Claims To Have Undergone a 'Culture Change,'" *World Watch*, October 1994, 23–29.
25. CFR, 864.
26. CFR, 865.

27. *Washington Information Directory*, 194–199.

28. *Washington Information Directory*, 534.

29. CFR, 117.

30. CFR, 139.

31. CFR, 407.

32. CFR, 407.

33. D.J. Rebovich, "Prosecutorial Decision Making and the Environmental Prosecutor: Reaching a Crossroads for Public Protection," in *Environmental Crime and Criminality: Theoretical and Practical Issues*, ed. S. Edwards et al. (New York: Garland, 1996).

34. D.J. Rebovich, "Criminal Opportunity and the Hazardous Waste Offender: Confronting the Syndicate Control Mystique," *National Environmental Enforcement Journal*, December 1986, 3–7.

35. K. Krajick, "When Will Police Discover the Toxic Time Bomb?" *Police Magazine*, May 1981, 6–20.

36. S. Wolf, "Hazardous Waste Trials and Tribulations," *Environmental Law* 13 (1983): 376–491.

37. Broward County environmental crime training session, February 4, 1995.

38. 436 U.S. 307 (1978).

39. 482 U.S. 691 (1987).

40. 5 United States Code, §552.

41. 5 United States Code, §552.

42. D. Ross, "A Review of EPA Criminal, Civil, and Administrative Enforcement Data: Are the Efforts a Measurable Deterrent to Environmental Criminals?" in *Environmental Crime and Criminality: Theoretical and Practical Issues*, ed. S. Edwards et al. (New York: Garland, 1996).

43. Ross, "A Review of EPA Criminal, Civil, and Administrative Enforcement Data."

44. A. Szasz, "Organizations, Organized Crime and the Disposal of Hazardous Waste: An Examination of the Making of a Criminogenic Regulatory Structure," *Criminology* 24, no. 1 (1986): 1–27.

APPENDIX 6–A

EPA Regional Offices

Boston Area Office
EPA Region 1
1 Congress Street
DIC-B159
Boston, MA 02203
(617) 565-3636

New York Area Office
EPA Region 2
26 Federal Plaza
2nd Floor, Room 130
New York, NY 10278
(212) 264-8917

Philadelphia Area Office
EPA Region 3
841 Chestnut Street
Philadelphia, PA 19107
(215) 597-0122

Atlanta Area Office
EPA Region 4
345 Courtland Street NE
Atlanta, GA 30365
(215) 597-0122

Chicago Area Office
EPA Region 5
77 West Jackson N-4D
Chicago, IL 60604
(312) 886-9872

Dallas Area Office
EPA Region 6
First Interstate Bank Building
1445 Ross Avenue
Dallas, TX 75202-2733
(214) 655-6600

Note: This information comes from U.S. EPA Office of Criminal Enforcement, Criminal Investigation Division, September 1992 (EPA 300-S-92-002).

Kansas City Area Office
EPA Region 7
726 Minnesota Avenue
Kansas City, KS 66101
(913) 551-7060

Denver Area Office
EPA Region 8
Suite 500
999-19th Street (80CI)
Denver, CO 80202-2413
(303) 293-1427

San Francisco Area Office
EPA Region 9
75 Hawthorne Street, C-1
San Francisco, CA 94105
(415) 744-2485

Seattle Area Office
EPA Region 10
1200 Sixth Avenue (SO-074)
Seattle, WA 98101
(206) 553-8306

CHAPTER 7

State and Local Environmental Enforcement

Joel Epstein

TERMS	asbestosis	injunction
	C&D debris	midnight dumping
	clean waste	Pollution Prosecution Act
	Commerce Clause	Supremacy Clause
	cradle-to-grave	vegetative waste
	environmental media	waste tires
	hazardous waste	white goods

Environmental degradation has given rise to increased concern in communities throughout the United States. One of the consequences of this heightened concern is the development of departments of environmental regulation and control. Recent studies suggest over 100 specialized departments exist in the 50 states.[1,2] While several countries have displayed steady support for environmental agendas, the United States has shown waxing and waning interest in environmental issues. Environmental priorities are often determined by those in political office in any given year, and as a consequence change seems to be the only constant.

At both the federal and state levels, increased attention is being given to environmental enforcement. Recent public opinion polls suggest that the public is concerned about the potentially dangerous consequences of unregulated environmental violations. As early as 1984, findings from a Bureau of Justice Statistics survey suggested Americans believed environmental crimes were more serious than a number of "traditional crimes" such as burglary and bank robbery.[3] A 1991 survey found 84 percent of Americans believed that damaging the environment was a serious crime, and 75 percent believed that corporate officials should be held personally responsible for environmental offenses committed by their firm.[4]

The federal government sets standards for the industries argued to pose the most risk to the environment. Individuals in communities across the country argue that federal environmental policies do not respond to community-specific environmental needs. While the federal regulations provide a basic framework, some community issues are not adequately addressed by federal legislation. Federal monies, then, are being spent in certain communities to address environmental problems that are not a priority for them. Meanwhile, these same communities are forced to struggle with limited resources as they attempt to address their specific concerns.

Environmental protection efforts at the state and local level are the focus of this chapter. Attention will be given to the history of the federal enforcement structure as it has affected the evolution of state agencies. The state regulatory structure and area-specific environmental problems will be reviewed to allow exploration of the state response. Regulatory successes and difficulties with enforcement will also be considered. A review of the cooperative enforcement efforts developing within state agencies will close the chapter.

THE LEGAL CONTEXT OF ENVIRONMENTAL ENFORCEMENT

In Chapter 5, Halsey sought injunctive relief because a company was releasing harmful emissions into a river. The same actions could be used if Brian noticed unusual emissions from the stacks of a local factory. He could sue the company for injunctive relief, and if the court granted the **injunction**, the company would have to stop releasing the potentially harmful emissions until a determination could be reached regarding the degree to which the charges are justified. While this may be a successful short-term solution to a perceived air pollution problem, it can often have unexpected consequences. If Brian were successful in a civil proceeding, large fines would be imposed on the company. Although the company would have to pay the fine, these kinds of fines are easily passed on to the consumers as a "cost of doing business."[5] Increased cost for the company's product would be the result.

In all likelihood, administrative and regulatory procedures would be exhausted before court action is taken. The role of regulatory agencies is to ensure the regulations established are being followed. In the example presented above, Brian could seek support by reporting the factory's alleged infractions to the state regulatory agency. Agency staff are responsible for providing regular checks to determine if in fact the company is operating within the specifications outlined, and they can help to determine what the company is actually doing. If the regulatory agency could not attain a voluntary commitment by the company to comply with the relevant regulations, then more severe action would be the next step.

Regulators are constantly placed in a difficult political position when attempting to seek a resolution to an environmental conflict. They must proceed cautiously. Often they have to be sensitive to local political pressures.

Further, the agencies are often underfunded and therefore have significant resource constraints. The existing relationship between corporate interests and the government's interest in increasing compliance creates the need for a delicate balancing of issues. Brian simply may not want to wait until the government gets around to taking action, or he may not approve of the action the government is taking. Therefore, many environmental protection statutes have provisions for individuals to seek redress in the courts.

GENESIS OF THE LAW ENFORCEMENT RESPONSE

Local, county, and state law enforcement agencies create environmental crime investigation units for a variety of reasons. The particular geography or geology of a community may make it vulnerable to certain environmental crimes. Likewise, unusually fragile environmental conditions may demand meticulous protection of the ground water from improper waste disposal. Public or industry ignorance about the damaging effects of pollution may also drive law enforcement agencies to adopt a proactive environmental stance. The character of a community will often determine the numbers and types of environmental crimes and consequently the enforcement response.[6] By far, the majority of community concerns revolve around the issue of toxic or hazardous waste.[7]

The success of environmental enforcement efforts in any community is directly linked to the legal framework, the level of public support, the government, the press, and the local business community. In order to carry out a balanced response, agencies must have a firm grasp of relevant environmental laws and regulations and must work together to ensure they are enforced equitably within specified jurisdictional boundaries. Decisions regarding the appropriate use of criminal, civil, and regulatory processes depend not only upon overall knowledge of the legal framework but also upon the established decision rules in different situations. The EPA's Office of Criminal Enforcement has prepared guidelines in this area that state and local prosecution and investigative agencies may wish to consult.[8]

OVERVIEW OF THE LAW

A variety of federal and state laws, as well as county and local regulations, were developed to identify the parameters of environmental enforcement. Because of its complexity, however, much of this legislation is hard to understand and difficult to enforce.[9] State and federal court rulings have played a role in shaping enforcement efforts by interpreting statutes and regulations. State and local enforcement efforts have been strongly influenced by the federal environmental statutes. While state regulatory agencies can create stronger regulations, they must at a minimum maintain the federal standards.

A 1992 report by the American Prosecutors Research Institute's National Environmental Crime Prosecution Center explains that by virtue of the **Commerce Clause** and **Supremacy Clause** of the U.S. Constitution "states are preempted from legislating more lenient environmental standards than those that Congress has mandated" through federally enacted environmental statutes.[10] Therefore, if Oklahoma passed a law imposing more lenient fines or less stringent pollution standards in an area under the scope of a federal statute, the law would be unconstitutional and void. If more stringent standards were legislated in the state, however, the standards would not be preempted by federal environmental statutes, and businesses operating within the state would be expected to comply with the state standards.

Federal Legislation

Federal environmental statutes include minimum requirements for the handling and disposing of hazardous waste and for the assessing of criminal penalties for violations. Additionally, federal statutes (and thus their state equivalents) extend to such **environmental media** as air, land, and water and toxic substances, pesticides, and solid waste. The federal laws and regulations in these areas have varying applicability to the activities of local law enforcement.

Chapter 5 presented an overview of eight federal statutes that contain criminal provisions: the Clean Air Act (CAA); Comprehensive Environmental Response, Compensation, and Liability Act (CERCLA); Federal Insecticide, Fungicide, and Rodenticide Act (FIFRA); Clean Water Act (CWA); Resource Conservation and Recovery Act (RCRA); Rivers and Harbors Act of 1899 (RHA); Safe Drinking Water Act (SDWA); and Toxic Substances Control Act (TSCA). These separate pieces of legislation have a number of common characteristics useful for state agency officials to consider as they begin developing their own environmental enforcement agendas. Consider the following:

- Generally, both corporations and individuals are subject to either criminal or civil liability or both for violating provisions of one of these statutes.
- Federal environmental laws hold corporate officers and employees responsible if they knew or should have known that their acts violated a federal statute.
- Concerning the degree of knowledge that constitutes a violation, most courts require more than negligence but less than specific intent.

- The constitutionality of environmental protection legislation has been consistently upheld in the courts.[11]

Although the impact of the various shifts in the federal enforcement effort is not likely to be felt at the local level for some time, the EPA in recent years has demonstrated an increasingly strong commitment to criminal enforcement. One of the EPA's key objectives is to increase the capacity of state and local enforcement authorities.[12] In 1990, the **Pollution Prosecution Act** mandated, among other things, an increase in EPA criminal investigators. While the total budgeted was not allocated, enough funds were approved by Congress in 1992 to employ at least 200 criminal investigators.[13]

As indicated by congressional discussions and the 1996 presidential debates, the future of federal environmental protection efforts is, at best, uncertain. In July 1995, the narrow defeat of a bill to rein in the EPA was declared an unexpected victory for environmentalists.[14,15] While states continue to develop regulatory and enforcement programs, it is unclear how long the political climate will provide the economic support necessary to continue these programs. At present, the priority given environmental issues at the state level is dramatically different for each state.

Local Regulations and Ordinances

The federal statutory and regulatory framework remains the model for most state environmental agencies. Yet in spite of the enduring central importance of this framework, considerable state legislative activity in the environmental area has taken place since 1970. A recent National Institute of Justice report on local prosecution of environmental crime noted that state environmental laws and regulations reflect the complexities established at the federal level. Overall, many environmental violations do not constitute criminal offenses, yet others require criminal prosecution.[16]

A 1983 survey found that "between 1967 and 1983 the number of state environmental laws or amendments grew from 375 to 1,425."[17(p.3)]

> Concepts common to State environmental enforcement including prohibition and permitting of regulated activities, notice requirements (before a regulated act takes place as in the case of asbestos removal; during the regulated act, as in the case of discharge monitoring; and after the act, as in the case of a release of hazardous materials), cradle to grave regulation, and labelling and placarding requirements all attest to the prominent role the Federal approach has played in the shaping of State-level responses to environmental enforcement.[18(p.3)]

The most common environmental crimes that might be charged under recently enacted state laws include the following:

- *air pollution*—including open burning, catalyst removal, emissions inspection fraud, uncontrolled vehicle emissions, visible emissions violations, and illegal asbestos removal
- *water pollution*—including unpermitted discharges to surface water, sewers, or ground water; unpermitted filling of wetlands; and fraud in reporting discharge to publicly owned treatment works (POTWs)
- *pesticide distribution and use*—including sale, distribution, and use of unregistered pesticides; use of pesticides not in accordance with label instructions; and death or injury from illegal pesticide application and use
- *excessive noise*—operation of noise-producing equipment in excess of allowed decibel levels
- *possession or emission of chemicals* not reported on government inventories[19]

The environmental problems confronting state and local agencies are increasing the demands placed on these already overburdened agencies. Several tactics are being used to help address these and other types of environmental crimes. For example, state agencies are using forfeiture laws to seize equipment, making an effort to reduce legal complexities, and identifying the levels of severity associated with specific violations.

Forfeiture Laws

Many people are not aware that environmental enforcement officers have the authority to seize equipment if the equipment was used in an alleged illegal environmental activity. Seizure of equipment is becoming an important part of local law enforcement strategies focused on reducing environmental crime. For example, in New Jersey, state law permits the seizure of equipment owned by a company involved in illegal activity, including environmental offenses. In fact, the Middlesex County (New Jersey) Environmental Crimes/Arson Unit makes frequent use of the process. Under state law, a company is required to post a bond in order to reclaim seized equipment. The unit can then redeem the bond, and the monies raised are used for environmental investigation and prosecution efforts in the county. Middlesex County Sergeant Ken Huber notes that equipment seizure is often the most effective method of ending the illegal activity and preventing further damage.[20]

Also in New Jersey (under Title 13, Solid Waste Dumping), any cash settlement goes back to the municipality. This can increase a town's willingness to work with law enforcement agents and the county prosecutor's office on

INSIGHT

Citizens in Cairo Asked To "Hush up—or Else"[1]

With 13 million people, honking cars, screaming vendors, blaring loudspeakers, and roaring buses, the noise levels in Cairo have become unbearable. Environment and health specialists argue that productivity is lower and health problems are higher because of Cairo's noise. Noise levels in the loudest areas in the city are measured at 82 decibels. The FAA (Federal Aviation Administration) says noise reaching 80 decibels would sound like a diesel truck revving about 50 feet away.

The Egyptian government has responded to the rising noise levels by launching a massive antinoise campaign. For example, blaring horns will be banned, and violators will face a $150 fine and confiscation of their horns. If people honk their car horns excessively between midnight and 6 AM or in a hospital zone, they will face similar penalties. Mosques will be allowed to use their loudspeakers only to call people to services, not to project their sermons into the street.

In 1990 the Egyptian government started the Egyptian Environmental Affairs Agency. The antinoise campaign is part of a comprehensive program to stop all forms of pollution in Egypt, including air, water, and solid waste pollution. According to a 1995 law, the loudest areas and industries have three years to decrease the noise levels to 55 decibels. If the offenders do not comply by 1998, they will be "shut down, fined, and taken to court."

---

1.   S. Gauch, "Cairo's Noisy Citizens Asked To Hush-up or Else," *Christian Science Monitor*, 2 January 1997, 7.

environmental crimes. In a Middlesex County investigation of a wood recycler, investigators from the environmental crimes/arson unit seized $1.6 million in equipment.[21] Seizure of the wood recycler's trailers, tub grinders, bulldozers, and related heavy equipment effectively shut down the multi-million-dollar business. The company was charged both criminally and civilly when investigators discovered solid waste mixed in with its recycled products. When tested, some samples of the company's mulch were found to contain hazardous waste.[22]

Palm Beach County sheriff's deputies believe that law enforcement should make greater use of forfeiture provisions to seize equipment used in the commission of environmental crimes. Deputy Pearsall adds, "Certain individuals and businesses are reluctant to change operating procedures until it is demonstrated that their failure to comply directly affects the bottom line."[23] Palm Beach County also makes use of a Florida law allowing for the recovery of investigative costs. The recovered costs go into a line item in the budget and are used for future investigations, training, and equipment.[24]

Reducing Legal Complexities

The complexity of environmental laws and regulations is sometimes an obstacle to broader environmental enforcement. When this is seen as a problem, law enforcement and environmental agency leaders can call on legislatures to codify and simplify the law. County Investigator Steve Ogulin of the Sussex County (New Jersey) prosecutor's office feels that, while inadequate funding and staffing are a problem, "Simplifying the law [is where the real change needs to come]. Just the chemistry is hard enough. 'Is this a hazardous waste?' But some of the other stuff is impossible."[25(p.13)] For example, in one case, a decision about procedure hinged on the definition of a solid waste landfill in the city's Public Utilities Act.

Varying Levels of Severity

The fact that certain chemicals are defined as hazardous waste by the civil statutes but not by the criminal statutes also frustrates investigators. If an investigator makes an arrest, he or she wants the arrest to be legitimate; otherwise, it seems simply a waste of time. The absence of training for law enforcement officers on environmental crime issues makes it difficult for the officers to know how to proceed with an investigation and/or arrest. For this reason, the Broward County Sheriff's Office, working with the Department of Natural Resource Protection in Florida, has compiled a pamphlet for law enforcement officers, titled "Environmental Crimes Investigations for Law Enforcement Officers, Environmental Enforcement Officers and Code Enforcement Officers." (See Appendix E.) The pamphlet summarizes the state laws and outlines the levels of severity associated with specific environmental violations. It serves as a guideline for all enforcement agents who respond to environmental crimes and aids them in assessing the best way to proceed with each infraction.

Additionally, it must be noted that strict environmental enforcement is often seen as a threat to local business. According to Middlesex County's Sergeant Ken Huber, strict environmental enforcement in New Jersey is used by companies as an excuse to move businesses to Pennsylvania and elsewhere because environmental laws are either less strictly enforced or are considered lax.[26] In his recent book on hazardous waste crime, Donald Rebovich makes the same point: "Stricter state environmental laws, such as those in New Jersey, have prompted major corporations to relocate some of their facilities to Alabama and other states where environmental laws are still in the evolutionary stage."[27(p.25)] Although police are approached by local citizens concerned about environmental protection and seeking an officer's assistance, getting tough on environmental criminals can have significant economic implications for a community.

Estimating the Extent of Environmental Crime

Estimating the extent of environmental crime is both practically and conceptually very difficult. In general, offenses fall into one of three categories:

1. violations of permit conditions or other illegal acts already part of a state or federal regulatory scheme
2. acts committed by individuals or companies outside of the regulatory scheme
3. acts that would be illegal regardless of whether the actor was within the regulatory scheme.[28]

At the present time, little or no national research has been conducted to discover the numbers and types of environmental crime. As for the extent of illegal hazardous waste disposal, which makes up a large percentage of all environmental crime, no definitive studies document the scope of the problem. "The best estimate seems to place the total amount of hazardous waste generated between 247 million and 275 million metric tons per year."[29(p.5)] In any community, the victims can be individuals, the general public, and the environment, while the offenders can be individuals, domestic or foreign corporations, and even the government.

TYPES OF ENVIRONMENTAL CRIME

The environmental crime in a given community tends to reflect the industries and businesses in that community.[30] Certain problems, such as illegal waste tire disposal, improper disposal of furniture stripping and electroplating waste, used motor oil disposal, and hazardous waste dumped into streams and rivers, are found to some degree in all communities. Other environmental criminal activity is either unique or rare and closely tied to the special character of the city, county, or region where it occurs.[31]

The risks posed by environmental crime vary considerably. By far the most troubling crimes are those that pose a threat of serious bodily injury or death. Examples range from the dumping of illicit drug–manufacturing chemicals to the improper disposal of electroplating waste (both types of waste are highly toxic and can cause permanent soil and ground water contamination).[32]

Environmental offenders exploit lax enforcement to carry out their crimes. But the focus of a new local environmental crimes program—whether to stem the dumping of hazardous materials onto public lands or to stop illegal waste tire dumping—is entirely up to the locality. For example, Portland, Maine, and Palm Beach County, Florida, make an effort to identify discrepancies between solid waste generation estimates and the actual weight of solid waste crossing the scales at co-generation and solid waste facilities.[33] In some areas, however, where recycling and economic incentives have created markets for much of a community's solid waste and even used **white goods** (kitchen appliances), solid waste issues are of less concern.

Broward County, Florida, is not known for its heavy industry, but the county does handle a large quantity of industrial waste generated by light industry. Port Everglades, which once supplied fuel oil to the U.S. Air Force, is still home to a number of oil and propane gas companies and has been a source of past environmental problems. Broward County also has its share of **C&D debris** (construction and demolition debris, discussed in more detail below) from new construction and renovation, and it has many electroplaters, carpet cleaners, and furniture-refinishing businesses. Compliance with environmental and occupational safety regulations in these industries has long been acknowledged to be imperfect at best. Pollution from houseboats, including human wastes dumped directly into the intercoastal waterway, is another problem facing Broward County officials. Environmental law enforcement is limited by the fact that only the U.S. Coast Guard and U.S. Customs officers have jurisdiction to board boats on the waterway. Dredge and fill operations (which dredge or plow land to bury large quantities of waste) also plague the county.[34]

Although environmental crime varies from community to community, five offenses were targeted by the criminal enforcement agencies studied to date. Significant concern was expressed about the illegal transportation and disposal of

- hazardous wastes and hazardous materials
- waste tires
- construction and demolition debris
- white goods
- vegetative waste[35]

Hazardous Waste and Hazardous Materials

The two most important categories of toxicants involved in environmental crime are **hazardous materials** and **hazardous waste**.[36] Hazardous materials are substances identified by the EPA and U.S. Department of Transportation (DOT) as posing a high risk to health, safety, or property, especially when transported in commerce. Hazardous materials transportation is governed by the DOT.

Under the Resource Conservation and Recovery Act (RCRA) of 1976, the EPA may define hazardous waste as any solid waste, or combination of solid wastes, that, because of its quantity, concentration, or physical, chemical, or infectious characteristics, may

- cause, or significantly contribute to an increase in mortality or an increase in serious, irreversible, or incapacitating reversible illness; or
- pose a substantial present or potential hazard to human health or the environment when improperly treated, stored, transported or disposed of, or otherwise managed.[37]

Spills of hazardous materials often occur in highway or railroad accidents. The illegal disposal of hazardous waste includes a wide range of incidents and practices, from accidental spills to systematic efforts to profit by evading the expense of legal disposal. Agricultural runoff containing pesticides and other hazardous materials causes severe environmental damage in many areas of the country.

Perhaps the most common form of illegal disposal of hazardous waste is **midnight dumping**. In a typical midnight dumping scenario,

> Wastes are . . . disposed of in the nearest isolated area. Agents of generating companies can directly commit these offenses or criminally conspire with waste transporters or treaters who, for a percent-

Unscrupulous Waste Haulers Keep on Truckin'

Julienne Salzano describes the collapse of the Mianus River Bridge in Connecticut on June 28, 1983.[1] Many thought the bridge had collapsed due to years of heavy use. In reality, however, waste haulers would open the back drain on their storage tanks and "accidentally" release their loads onto the roadway as they drove across the bridge.[2] Committing this activity on rainy days made it more difficult for enforcement officers to detect. The corrosive liquid drained off the roadway, polluting the river and seriously weakening the metal support joints for the bridge. The result was the eventual destruction of the bridge.

Known as "sludge runners," these truckers disregard public safety in pursuit of larger profits and are believed to be linked to organized crime groups. "In 1993, investigators with the New Jersey attorney general's office executed 40 search warrants for offenders in New Jersey, New York, and Pennsylvania."[3(p.23)] Often sludge runners will offer to remove the waste product for half the market value of legal disposal. These unlawful truck operations often use other techniques to dispose of dangerous waste products. Their tactics include placing waste in 55-gallon drums and leaving the containers in vacant lots, along railroad lines, or across state lines. In other cases, the offenders will abandon dilapidated trucks containing the hazardous freight. The offenders do not reclaim the truck, because any penalty fee to reclaim the vehicle and pay for any cleanup would far surpass the value of the truck.[4]

Related to the illegal dumping of these wastes are businesses that sell diesel fuel mixed with corrosives, solvents, and other hazardous waste as home heating oil.[5] The adulterated fuel mixtures generate far more pollution than does virgin fuel. Because landlords can buy this "heating oil" at reduced prices, it is not uncommon to find certain areas of the city contaminated by airborne toxicants released when the contaminated fuel is burned. While some landlords may be aware of the nature of the product they are buying, others are unaware of what their furnaces are burning. It is interesting to note that many chemical recycling companies argue this to be a legitimate means of recycling these chemicals.

1. J. Salzano, "Sludge Runner: Keep on Trucking," *FBI Law Enforcement Bulletin*, May 1995, 22–26.
2. Salzano, "Sludge Runner," 22.
3. Salzano, "Sludge Runner," 23.
4. Salzano, "Sludge Runner," 24.
5. Salzano, "Sludge Runner," 23.

age of the legitimate treatment cost, will illegally dump the wastes. In some instances hazardous waste generators are the victims of fraud committed by midnight dumpers; payment is rendered by the generator to the treater for services that are never performed.[38(p.3–4)]

While the environmental crimes involving hazardous waste and hazardous materials vary according to local industry or population type, similar methods of operation are used regardless of the type of waste or material involved. One widespread practice involves criminal activity by a generator, transporter, broker, or treatment, storage, and disposal (TSD) facility. In an example of this activity, a generator may act alone or conspire with others to dispose illegally of hazardous waste, either by on-site disposal or by removal and disposal at unauthorized points. Often, an unlicensed transporter will contact unwitting (or uneducated) generators and convince them that a low-cost **cradle-to-grave** waste strategy is possible. The transporter may conspire with a known TSD or dispose of the wastes after falsifying the manifests. A less common practice, but one seen in several states, is to rent a truck, fill it with hazardous waste, and then abandon the vehicle.[39]

Illegal Disposal of Waste Tires

Waste tires, automobile tires discarded by car and truck owners or tire change businesses, were repeatedly identified by interviewees as a major focus of local environmental investigators. The practice of renting warehouses under fictitious names, filling them with waste tires and other wastes, and then abandoning them has become increasingly common in south Florida. In Saint Lucie County, a waste tire site regulators have been trying to clean up for years is now a mound of tires 2,000 feet long, 900 feet across, and 25 feet high.[40]

In New York City, environmental restrictions have raised the cost of disposing of tires. Discarded tires have increasingly become fixtures of the landscape in poorer neighborhoods in the South Bronx, Queens, and Brooklyn. In 1992, the Department of Sanitation collected roughly 200,000 illegally dumped tires. In New York City, illegal tire dumpers can be fined $1,000 to $7,500 and have their vehicles impounded by the city; the penalties reportedly deter few violators.[41] If the tires catch fire, a major toxic hazard is created. In Houston, Texas, a RAT hotline has been set up. Over the past two years, the city has given out $5,200 in rewards to people who turn in illegal dumpers. If someone gets caught dumping more than five pounds of trash in the city, he or she risks a year in jail and a $4,000 fine—in addition to the cleaning up of the garbage.[42]

Illegal Disposal of Construction and Demolition Debris

Once communities recognized the risks posed by the improper disposal of C&D debris containing hazardous wastes, legally disposing of debris from construction and renovation work became considerably more difficult and costly. Landfill space in many areas has grown limited, and many communities are deciding to preserve their landfill resources for the disposal of **clean waste**, such as household refuse. Additionally, the recognition of **asbestosis** and other industrial diseases has changed public attitudes toward the once routine discarding of waste such as asbestos insulation. Perhaps the greatest danger related to construction debris is the release of asbestos fibers during the demolition process.

The reluctance of landfill owners to accept commingled wastes has contributed to increased illegal dumping of C&D debris on private property. Middlesex County, New Jersey, located about halfway between New York City and Philadelphia, receives a disproportionately large share of illegally dumped C&D debris. An earlier National Institute of Justice report noted that "the Monmouth County [New Jersey] prosecutor's office identified the illegal disposal of construction and demolition debris, much of it trucked from New York City, as a growing problem."[43(p.7)]

Illegal Disposal of White Goods

White goods refers to common household kitchen appliances, such as refrigerators and ovens, that have entered the waste stream. If improperly disposed-of, white goods can pose a danger to the environment and the public. For example, refrigerators often contain freon, a combination of chlorine, fluorine, and carbon, used commercially as a coolant. If an improperly disposed-of refrigerator is punctured, the gas is released and can damage the ozone layer. The improper disposal of white goods not only is unsightly but also poses a severe threat to the environment. In addition, deputy sheriffs in Palm Beach County worry about ground water contamination from discarded appliances leaking mercury. This is a major hazard in south Florida, where the fragile water table is only three to five feet from the surface.[44]

Illegal Transportation and Storage of Vegetative Waste

Law enforcement investigators in some communities voice concern over the improper handling of **vegetative waste**, which includes tree stumps, branches, grass clippings, leaves, and other yard waste. While disposal of vegetative waste may not be regulated by environmental laws, some haulers

INSIGHT

Tire Fires: A Cause of Concern for All

Firefighters and police officers responding to the scene of an accident may find they are dealing with an even more hazardous situation than they thought.

Take, for example, the tire fire that occurred in Winston-Salem, North Carolina, in January 1996.[1,2] It began as a simple fire—a spark from a front-end loader ignited a stack of cardboard. The flames, however, quickly spread to pallets on the dock and then to rubber chips. The result was a massive blaze that sent thick plumes of black smoke into the air. The smoke from the fire could be seen for approximately 100 miles. What started as a small fire resulted in a roaring inferno that required nine fire engines and three aerial trucks to bring it under control.

Tire fires are particularly difficult for fire crews to handle for several reasons. First, they are hard to put out. Tires burn hotter than wood, and the fires do not respond well to water.

A second concern is the toxic smoke. Burning tires emit benzene, hydrochloric acid, and other dangerous, cancer-causing agents. These toxic chemicals are emitted into the air and carried by the wind. Officials in Winston-Salem advised the public in the path of the settling smoke to stay inside if possible and to be aware of the toxic chemicals in the smoke coming from the huge tire fire.

A third concern for the Forsyth County Environmental Affairs Department was the runoff from the fire hoses. The pollutants trapped in the water stream could drain into local streams and rivers. Local environmental officials were studying whether the runoff could harm the city's water supply. The petroleum byproducts "can kill everything from microbes to fish."[3]

1. L. Goldburg, "Burning Rubber: Big Fire at Recycler Began Small," *Winston-Salem Journal,* 26 January 1996, A1, A4.
2. S. Maxwell and C. Quinn, "Possibility of Toxic Air, Water Gets Agents From Environmental-Affairs Office Moving," *Winston-Salem Journal,* 26 January 1996, A4.
3. Maxwell and Quinn, "Possibility of Toxic Air, Water."

and disposal companies create illegal fire hazards on their property by storing large quantities of unprocessed vegetative waste. Because of the enormous amount that can easily be generated, such waste has recently been identified as an environmental management problem for many communities.[45]

ORGANIZATION OF THE LAW ENFORCEMENT RESPONSE

Sometimes it takes a company that brazenly flaunts environmental laws, coupled with strident community opposition, to push an environmental agency into action. In August 1993, years of lawsuits and community opposition to the illegal dumping of C&D debris on a privately owned two-acre lot in Bridgeport, Connecticut, finally resulted in jail terms and fines totalling $868,000 for the owners of a Connecticut demolition company. The area had come to be known as Mount Trashmore, and illegally dumped construction debris, including lead, asbestos, and creosote, once rose to a height of 35 feet.[46]

Policy makers in law enforcement and environmental agencies should be aware of the various organizational approaches that may be adopted to serve the enforcement needs of a community. For some communities, assigning county deputy sheriffs to the solid waste authority is the preferred strategy. Elsewhere, assigning criminal investigators to a specialized prosecutor's office environmental crimes unit may work better. The most traditional approach is to create law enforcement–based units and place responsibility for environmental crime investigation and enforcement on the shoulders of officers situated within the local police department.

A detailed description of the role of local police departments in investigation and enforcement efforts follows in the next chapter. Here are merely a few rules than can assist a department interested in developing a focused response to environmental crime. First, conduct an inventory of the department's resources. See what resources (e.g., lab technicians, existing departments dealing with similar issues) are already in place and provide a careful assessment of the needs of an environmental crime program. Second, review the department's strengths. It is conceivable that the personnel and the public support needed for an environmental crime program already exist. Third, establish interagency relationships. Like other police investigations, environmental crime investigations involve the collection and review of evidence by a diverse group of people. The more connections with specially trained individuals and outside agencies the department is able to maintain, the more likely it will have access to the things it needs to successfully complete environmental crime investigations. Finally, be sensitive to community concerns about the program. Businesses may be concerned about compliance issues. Take the time to show businesses you can support their efforts to achieve compliance without allowing exploitative environmental criminal activity to go unchecked. The ability to accurately assess local community support of or opposition toward environmental enforcement activity is critically important for any new program.

SITUATING THE ENVIRONMENTAL CRIMES RESPONSE

Paying attention to industrial and community concerns will help policy makers determine the best placement for their criminal investigation unit. The following issues should also be considered:

- Where are the greatest number of environmental problems located?
- What environmental media (air, land, water) are involved?
- What skills are required?
- What other agencies can and should contribute to the effort?
- Where will the resources needed for investigating cases be most available?[47]

A law enforcement response to environmental crime is also defined by the range of applicable laws and regulations. Federal environmental laws are enforced by federal authorities, while local ordinances are typically within the domain of local enforcement. Below is a description of existing state and local enforcement structures and several advantages and disadvantages.[48]

Law Enforcement Agencies

Local police are often viewed as a community's eyes and ears. Road and foot patrol officers know their beats and, if properly trained, can spot some types of environmental crime when they occur. Whether to designate a special investigator or create an environmental crimes unit will depend on the extent of local environmental problems and the fragility of the local environment. In some places, the county sheriff's office is the leading law enforcement agency, but elsewhere the police department has primary responsibility. Other agencies, such as drainage districts and fish and game departments, may also find it effective to employ criminal investigators and assign them to investigate illegal solid waste dumping. Programs in Broward County, Florida, and in Portland, Maine, described in more detail below, are possible models for cities and counties considering whether to place their own environmental enforcement efforts in the law enforcement realm.

Sheriff's Office

In 1990, the complexity of environmental cases prompted the Broward County Sheriff's Office to address the issue of enforcement from within the organization. Environmental enforcement cases in Broward County fall into two categories: regular solid waste cases (e.g., used tire dumping and C&D debris cases) are handled by community police; other cases (e.g., hazardous and biohazardous waste cases) are handled by the Organized Crime Division. The Community Oriented Police Enforcement (COPE) unit handles the first type, and a detective from the Organized Crime Division investigates cases that fall into the second category.

Police Department

Portland, Maine, has seen an unusually active local police response to environmental violations. Lieutenant Mark Dion of the Portland Police Department directs the department's effort to deal with the environmental crime problem. The effort began as a mini-investigation into the amount of waste being sent to a regional co-generation facility in Portland. It has since grown into a massive investigation of waste disposal practices in 40 communities in southern Maine. Initially, the Portland Police Department looked carefully at 11 companies involved in 15 different waste disposal schemes. Whereas elsewhere in the country the issue is usually illegal dumping and labor racketeering, the case in question involved an attempt to defraud the county and to engage in antitrust activity.

Tonnage at the co-generation facility was below that projected for participating towns. A preliminary investigation indicated that customers were being charged the legal disposal rate by haulers when in fact the waste was being disposed of illegally. To date Portland's investigation has led to *civil* indictments of 11 companies for the improper hauling of solid waste. As can be seen, involving local police does not necessarily mean that the result will be a criminal prosecution of violators.

Prosecutor's Office

An environmental law enforcement program based in a county prosecutor's office offers several advantages. The arrangement may lead to close cooperation between prosecutors and environmental crime investigators and will offer the opportunity for ongoing informal cross-training for both types of professionals. Sharing an office means there is always a prosecutor on hand to explain a point of law or an investigator to consult about anything unclear in the investigation report.

A potential disadvantage of the in-house relationship is that investigators may come to feel like less important players in case preparation. Situating the environmental investigators away from the local law enforcement agency may also have the unintended effect of reducing the number of informal leads derived from daily contact with fellow officers. These are potential disadvantages that by no means affect all prosecutor's office–based programs equally. Further, some such programs work very effectively with the investigators' offices located separately.

Sergeant Ken Huber, of the Middlesex County Prosecutor's Office Environmental Crimes/Arson Unit, directs the county's environmental crime effort. The specialized initiative team includes a sergeant, a detective, two investigators, and an assistant prosecutor who work as a joint environmental crimes/arson prosecution component within the office of Middlesex County Prosecutor Robert Gluck. Currently, about 70 percent of the unit's cases involve environmental crime, while the balance are arson investigations.

According to Sergeant Huber, smaller companies with no history of environmental wrongdoing have started to commit environmental crimes. Most of the investigations that are ultimately prosecuted involve first-time offenders who qualify for Middlesex County's Pretrial Intervention Program. Under the program, adjudication of an accused's civil violations precedes any criminal prosecution. In fact, case law in New Jersey holds that the imposition of civil fines against an environmental offender may preclude the bringing of criminal charges. Several Middlesex County cases involve individuals and companies charged with operating an unlicensed solid waste facility. An investigation of one local waste hauling company resulted in the sentencing of the firm's owner to Pretrial Intervention Program community service work at the Middlesex County Landfill.

State Environmental Management Agencies

In the late 1970s a number of environmental regulatory agencies, recognizing the effectiveness of criminal punishment for fighting environmental crime, began to develop environmental law enforcement responses. The two main types of environmental agency–based programs are described below.

Solid Waste Authority

Situating an environmental law enforcement program in a solid waste authority may give the investigators more independence than they would have if assigned to a law enforcement agency. The alternative siting also creates a forum for the open exchange of ideas and information between law enforcement agents and regulators.

The Palm Beach County Sheriff's Office Contract Service Division enables an outside organization to enter into a written agreement with the sheriff's office for "enhanced law enforcement." Deputies assigned to this unit communicate with a selected liaison within the outside agency, but they report to and are governed by sheriff's office supervisors.

Under a five-year-old contractual arrangement with the Palm Beach County Solid Waste Authority (SWA), the Palm Beach County Sheriff's Office provides environmental law enforcement services. Similar arrangements are also in place in some of the larger sheriff's departments in the state.

The SWA unit has a staff of two deputies located at the SWA site. The unit's annual budget of $105,000, which covers the two officers' salaries and benefits, vehicles, uniforms, and supervisory costs, is funded by the SWA. According to Deputy Sheriff Pearsall, "It is important for supervisory authority in criminal investigations to remain with the law enforcement agency and for both parties to understand that the agreement is for enhanced environmental enforcement, in order for the program really to work. This means all environmental laws, not just those governing solid waste."[49]

Although the SWA funds the unit, the sheriff's office absorbs additional costs, including costs for most training, specialized equipment costs, and investigative costs (e.g., it covers additional personnel and equipment, helicopter time, search warrant expenses, case-related travel, and photography expenses).

In addition, other members of the Palm Beach County Environmental Task Force, including the Florida Department of Environmental Protection and the Palm Beach County Public Health Unit, also supply personnel and resources. The two deputy sheriffs acknowledge that in an era of budget cuts, environmental law enforcement officers are tough to justify, and without the SWA's support this program might not have gotten off the ground. Nonetheless, Deputy Sheriff Pearsall feels that environmental enforcement must be proactive.

Deputy Sheriff Layne Schultetus reports that since the sheriff's office SWA program began, Palm Beach County has seen an increase in the solid waste flow across the county waste facility's scales and a reduction in the volume of illegal solid waste dumping in the county. While the bulk of Palm Beach County's cases involve solid waste, the two deputy sheriffs also handle C&D debris, wetlands, hazardous waste (including biohazardous waste), and waste oil investigations.

Increasingly, the Palm Beach County deputies assigned to the SWA are working to involve municipal law enforcement agencies in environmental investigations within the city limits because they are finding it difficult to keep up with the caseload.

State Department of Natural Resources

Captain William Murphy of the Environmental Investigations Section of the Law Enforcement Division of the Michigan Department of Natural Resources (DNR) directs the first criminal program of its kind. The section, established in 1978, a year before the New Jersey program, is staffed by 15 field investigators assigned around the state. The program began 15 years ago as an internal Michigan DNR initiative, created in response to several major environmental disasters that occurred in Michigan in the 1970s. There was no empowering legislation or statutory enactment of the program. Early in the 1970s Michigan suffered a frightening polybrominated biphenyl (PBB) accident: bags of PBBs were mistaken for cattle feed grain and mixed in with normal feed for cattle farms statewide. Studies continue to assess the health consequences of people eating beef raised on the PBB-contaminated feed. In response to another 1970s incident, in Montague, Michigan, a civil action was ultimately filed against Hooker chemical company for the improper and illegal dumping of massive amounts of hazardous chemicals into White Lake.

The Environmental Investigations Section conducts 130–150 investigations per year and handles cases involving all types of environmental media. As a result of good regulation and enforcement, hazardous waste cases represent a smaller share of the section's current workload. The section is seeing growth in the investigation of state CERCLA-type (Superfund) cases and in problems with oil and gas wells. According to Captain Murphy, oil wells cover much of the state's lower peninsula (roughly 85 percent), outside of the Lansing and Detroit areas. Many of the state's wells are old and have numerous problems, including leaking, spills, and abandonment, especially wells near Midland and Mount Pleasant. In Michigan, southern Florida, and many other farming communities, there is a growing focus on agricultural problems, including runoff; improper pesticide application; improper storage, especially at bulk storage facilities; and intentional improper dumping of excess, old, or unusable chemicals. In this new area of focus, the Environmental Investigations Section has met with some success; so far five chemical companies have been prosecuted.

CONCLUSION

State regulation and state enforcement of environmental crimes is increasing. In most state environmental enforcement agencies, the system reflects the model of enforcement established at the federal level. Little comprehensive research has been done to determine the most prevalent types of environmental offenses being committed. Further, most environmental crimes reflect the major industries within the community. Some initial indicators suggest that enforcement officers most commonly deal with hazardous waste and hazardous materials, waste tires, construction and demolition debris, white goods, and vegetative goods.

Hiring enough enforcement agents to ensure compliance and protection would require a daunting investment, especially since state resources for environmental protection efforts are underfunded as it is. The most logical enforcement strategy is to use mechanisms already in place—the state and local law enforcement agencies. The role of law enforcement officers in the enforcement of environmental protection statutes is discussed in the next two chapters. State and local police officers may provide the best means for increasing community awareness of environmental violations and for decreasing the number of violations people commit because they think no one is looking.

REVIEW QUESTIONS

1. Which regulatory structure has ultimate authority when it comes to environmental issues, the state agency or the federal agency? Explain.
2. What are the primary differences between state-level enforcement and federal-level enforcement of environmental violators?
3. What is the role of forfeiture laws in environmental enforcement efforts? How effective are these laws?
4. Identify the five most common types of environmental crimes found in communities across the country.
5. How is the Commerce Clause related to environmental enforcement issues?
6. What is the purpose of seeking an injunction against someone believed to be violating an environmental regulation?
7. What does it mean to say "environmental fines are just a cost of doing business"?

DISCUSSION QUESTIONS

1. What specific community issues are important for determining an appropriate environmental enforcement response?
2. What is the best location for environmental enforcement agencies? Explain.
3. Identify some of the liabilities for police and regulatory agencies when they establish environmental enforcement as a priority.

REFERENCES

1. D. Rebovich and R. Nixon, *Environmental Crime Prosecution: A Comprehensive Analysis of District Attorneys' Efforts in This Emerging Area of Criminal Enforcement* (Alexandria, VA: American Prosecutors Research Institute, 1993), 1.

2. "Environmental Crime Prosecution: Results of a National Survey," *Research in Brief* (Washington, DC: National Institute of Justice), December 1994.

3. Bureau of Justice Statistics, "The Severity of Crime," bulletin (Washington, DC: U.S. Department of Justice, 1984).

4. Arthur D. Little, Inc., "Environmental Damage Rated as Most Serious among Business Crimes: Corporate Executives Should Be Held Liable, Survey Shows," press release (Los Angeles County: National Institute of Justice, July 1991), 2.

5. J. DeCicco and E. Bonnano, "A Comparative Analysis of the Criminal Environmental Laws of the Fifty States: The Need for Statutory Uniformity as a Catalyst for Effective Enforcement of Existing and Proposed Laws," *Florida State University Journal of Land Use and Environmental Law* 5 (summer 1989).

6. S.M. Wolf, "Hazardous Waste Trials and Tribulations," *Environmental Law* 13 (winter 1983): 376–491.

7. S.M. Edwards, "Environmental Criminal Enforcement: Efforts by the States," in *Environmental Criminality: Theoretical and Practical Issues*, ed. S. Edwards et al. (New York: Garland Press, 1996), 233.

8. These guidelines can be obtained through the U.S. Environmental Protection Agency, Office of Enforcement and Compliance Assurance, Washington, DC 20460, (202) 260-9377.

9. Edwards, "Environmental Criminal Enforcement," 205.

10. Rebovich and Nixon, *Environmental Crime Prosecution*, 11.

11. R. Weiner, "Environmental Crimes," *American Criminal Law Review* 28 (1991): 427.

12. *History of the Criminal Enforcement Program* (Washington, DC: U.S. Environmental Protection Agency, 1995), 2.

13. D. Ross, "A Review of EPA Criminal, Civil, and Administrative Enforcement Data: Are the Efforts Measurable Deterrents to Environmental Criminals?" in *Environmental Criminality: Theoretical and Practical Issues*, ed. S. Edwards et al. (New York: Garland Press, 1996), 71.

14. M. Marks and J. DiPeso, "Eco-Gluttons? Not These Republicans," *Christian Science Monitor*, 1 October 1996, 19.

15. J. Hook, "House Upholds EPA's Powers in a Surprise Vote," *Christian Science Monitor*, 29 July 1995.

16. T.M. Hammett and J. Epstein, "Local Prosecution of Environmental Crime," in *Issues and Practices* (Washington, DC: National Institute of Justice, June 1993), 3.

17. R.D. Speer and G. Bulanowski, *Speer's Digest on Toxic Substances State Law*, 1983–1984 edition (Boulder, CO: Strategic Assessments), 3.

18. Hammett and Epstein, "Local Prosecution of Environmental Crime," 3.

19. J. Epstein and T. Hammett, "Law Enforcement Response to Environmental Crime," in *Issues and Practices* (Washington, DC: National Institute of Justice, January 1995), 1–78.

20. Epstein and Hammett, "Law Enforcement Response to Environmental Crime," 13.
21. Interview with Sergeant Ken Huber, Environmental Crimes/Arson Unit, Middlesex County Prosecutor's Office, Edison, New Jersey. The discussion is about the Dauman Pallet investigation.
22. Epstein and Hammett, "Law Enforcement Response to Environmental Crime," 13.
23. Interview with Deputy Sheriff James Pearsall, Palm Beach County Sheriff's Office, West Palm Beach, Florida, August 3, 1993.
24. Epstein and Hammett, "Law Enforcement Response to Environmental Crime," 13.
25. Epstein and Hammett, "Law Enforcement Response to Environmental Crime," 13.
26. Epstein and Hammett, "Law Enforcement Response to Environmental Crime," 14.
27. D. Rebovich, *Dangerous Ground: The World of Hazardous Waste Crime* (New Brunswick, NJ: Transaction Publishers, 1992), 125.
28. Hammett and Epstein, "Local Prosecution of Environmental Crime," 8.
29. J.E. McCarthy and M.E.A. Reisch, *Hazardous Waste Fact Book* (Washington, DC: Congressional Research Service, January 1987), 5–7.
30. Hammett and Epstein, "Local Prosecution of Environmental Crime," 7.
31. Epstein and Hammett, "Law Enforcement Response to Environmental Crime," 3.
32. Epstein and Hammett, "Law Enforcement Response to Environmental Crime."
33. Epstein and Hammett, "Law Enforcement Response to Environmental Crime."
34. Epstein and Hammett, "Law Enforcement Response to Environmental Crime," 4.
35. Epstein and Hammett, "Law Enforcement Response to Environmental Crime."
36. Epstein and Hammett, "Law Enforcement Response to Environmental Crime."
37. 42 U.S.C. §6903 (1983 ed., supp. 1991).
38. Rebovich, *Dangerous Ground*, 3–4.
39. T. Hammett and J. Epstein, "Prosecuting Environmental Crime: Los Angeles County," in *Program Focus* (Washington, DC: National Institute of Justice, August 1993), 1–16.
40. Epstein and Hammett, "Law Enforcement Response to Environmental Crime," 5.
41. M. Marricott, "Junked by Night: Dead Tires Haunt New York," *New York Times*, 17 May 1993, A1, B6.
42. R. Scherer, "On the Prowl with the Sanitation Police," *Christian Science Monitor*, 7 August 1995, 10–12.
43. Hammett and Epstein, "Local Prosecution of Environmental Crime," 7.
44. Epstein and Hammett, "Law Enforcement Response to Environmental Crime," 6.
45. Epstein and Hammett, "Law Enforcement Response to Environmental Crime."
46. Epstein and Hammett, "Law Enforcement Response to Environmental Crime."
47. Epstein and Hammett, "Law Enforcement Response to Environmental Crime," 22.
48. Epstein and Hammett, "Law Enforcement Response to Environmental Crime," 22–25.
49. Interview with Deputy Sheriff James Pearsall.

CHAPTER 8

Policing the Environment

Tim Carter

TERMS	advanced training	inservice training
	asset seizure and forfeiture	midnight dumping
	cocktailing	remediation
	commingling	tipping fees
	cross-training	whistleblower
	initial responders	

Love Canal and Times Beach are familiar symbols of America's failure to manage hazardous wastes. Media coverage of the dangers of asbestos, pesticides, radioactive materials, and other toxic wastes have sparked concern about threats to health and the environment. The technological growth of the United States has provided Americans with a comfortable lifestyle, but not one realized without costs. "Today, one hundred billion tons of hazardous waste are produced in the United States, ninety percent of which is disposed of in an environmentally unsound manner."[1] America's vast industrialization has resulted in enormous quantities of all sorts of waste, what some people have called "our gross national by-product."[2(p.44)]

The desire to control our nation's waste led to the creation of numerous environmental laws and regulations. Rules governing the generation, transportation, storage, treatment, and disposal of waste have proliferated in the last two decades and are now extensive in scope. Such laws exist at the federal, state, and local levels, but many environmental crimes continue to occur.[3-5] These crimes collectively represent an important and compelling criminal justice problem.

Just as federal legislation aimed at curbing environmental crime grew throughout the mid-1970s to the present, so have state and local efforts to regulate and control solid, hazardous, and toxic waste streams. Most state and local environmental crime control policies have been modeled after federal legislation. Nevertheless, the effectiveness of enforcement efforts at the state and local levels differs widely by jurisdiction.[6] Many local and state law enforcement agencies have become aware of the scope of the problem and are now taking proactive measures to prevent environmental crime.[7]

This chapter introduces the readers to some of those environmental criminals and the law enforcement agencies responsible for detecting their criminal activities. Several prominent environmental crime investigations serve as a backdrop for discussing the methods police can use to detect, investigate, and respond to environmental crimes. The chapter closes with a brief discussion of training techniques being developed to keep the law enforcement officers one step ahead of the environmental criminals.

PROACTIVE VERSUS REACTIVE ENFORCEMENT STRATEGIES

Many local and state agencies have yet to initiate proactive enforcement and have in place a reactive approach to addressing environmental crimes.[8] Shifting to proactive enforcement strategies and away from reactive enforcement has several advantages. First, actively looking for environmental crimes will provide sheriff's departments and local police agencies with the opportunity to catch some offenders in the act. This often makes subsequent prosecution much easier. Second, catching such criminals red-handed sends a message to other would-be offenders that law enforcement is aggressively seeking out such criminals. Creating a perception of omnipresent enforcement may increase general deterrence of environmental crime. Third, law enforcement intervention during the early stages of an environmental offense will also create a strong impression in the mind of the particular offender, thereby strengthening specific deterrence as well. Fourth, stopping environmental crimes in their early stages reduces the damage done to the environment and decreases the potential for serious health risks to members of the affected community. Where prevention fails, the effects on people and their environment may be irreversible.[9]

Remediation is the process of restoring a degraded site to some specified standard of cleanliness or a lower degree of potential harm.[10] Remediation, a reactive strategy, is simply not as good as prevention. Monetary penalties large enough to actually complete remediation of an area damaged by environmental crimes often are not or cannot be assessed by the regulatory agencies.[11] Remediation costs assessed against offenders, which are often civil rather than criminal sanctions, often fail to deter environmental crimes in the first place—potential profit simply outweighs the actual penalty. Furthermore, it is unlikely that these monetary penalties will ever be effective as a deterrent, because damage amounts "necessary to achieve a sufficient level of deterrence are probably beyond offenders' ability to pay."[12(p.324)] Therefore, it should be clear by now that proactive strategies are highly preferable to reactive ones wherever they are possible.

The need for proactive environmental law enforcement is critical and urgent, because current "resources devoted to inspection and enforcement seem modest in comparison with the likely extent of illegal disposal."[13(p.22)] Although it is almost impossible to use existing waste accountability methods to accurately gauge quantities of illegally disposed hazardous waste, it is likely that such disposal is increasing, just as the costs to dispose of waste properly are steadily rising. Hammit and Reuter studied the economic incentives to dispose illegally, and they explained the reasons for increasing costs:

> Largely as a result of the new statutes, the costs of hazardous waste disposal have increased manyfold since the 1970's and are likely to continue to increase. The causes include not only the increasingly stringent regulations themselves but also the difficulty of expanding treatment and disposal capacity by siting new treatment, storage, and disposal facilities (partly because of local opposition, wherever the proposed site), and industry and insurer fear of potential Superfund or other liability for cleanup or damages.[14(p.2)]

Economic incentives to dispose illegally have been discussed throughout this text. One hazardous waste hauler, forced to begin proper disposal, raised his rates from $600 per truckload to $10,000 after being informed his waste would no longer be accepted at the local landfill.[15] These two cases are also typical:

> When a firm that collected wastes from automobile repair shops raised its price from a flat $55/month to $88/month plus $2/gallon, it lost 40 to 50 of its 500 customers. A hauler that served dry cleaners found a similar response. One of his customers whose solvents recycling equipment routinely produced 42 spent filter cartridges per month surrendered only 21 per month thereafter; others were sometimes seen in his dumpster.[16(p.18)]

Dumping hazardous waste into regular solid waste for disposal is just one of the many illegal methods used. Liquid waste is often illegally poured into sewers and storm drains. Certain liquid hazardous and toxic waste can simply be evaporated, which damages the air quality. Waste of all types is buried or simply abandoned. Illegal burning of waste is another alternative, as is burial or dumping in bodies of water. The methods of illegal dumping are only limited by the perpetrator's imagination and the extreme to which he or she is willing to go to pollute the environment for a profit. Consequently, law enforcement officers must be aware of the illegal activity and constantly learn the new tactics of the perpetrators to ensure they are apprehended.

IDENTIFYING ENVIRONMENTAL CRIMINALS

There are different types of environmental criminals, and their methods of operation can be very different as well. There are also a variety of reasons why people commit environmental crime. Some people may accidentally, negligently, or unknowingly violate an environmental law. Others may face a financial crisis in their businesses and be motivated to reduce their operating costs by illegally disposing of waste. Basic greed is another motivator, and some may intentionally plan to pollute for profit. Some environmental criminals are even business associates or members of organized crime.[17,18] Environmental crimes can occur almost anywhere, and new criminal methods continue to evolve. Several standard environmental crime methods have now been well documented, and these are discussed briefly below.

Looking for Crimes Where They Happen

One type of environmental crime discussed briefly in Chapter 7 involves the illegal disposal of construction and demolition (C&D) materials, which many people mistakenly believe pose no threat to public health. Some components of C&D debris contain hazardous substances. For example, wallboard contains high levels of solvents and other chemicals. Wood debris torn out of older structures may carry lead-based paint. In some cases, wood used for structural support has been treated with arsenic.[19] Although many of these hazardous substances are present only in small amounts relative to the total waste volume, it is important to keep in mind the sheer volume of this type of waste, especially in some communities. For example, the C&D waste stream of Long Island, New York, represents almost one-fifth of all the solid waste generated on the island, a considerable quantity of materials.[20]

C&D debris is commonly used to fill large depressions and otherwise change contours of the landscape. Many property owners willingly accept such "clean fill," and construction companies are eager to dispose of materials from demolition projects in this manner, thereby circumventing the fees charged to dump at landfills (called **tipping fees**). Some businesses advocate the use of pulverized C&D debris as landfill cover. Landfill cover is usually dirt that is layered over solid waste to suppress garbage odors and to compact waste materials. Substituting crushed C&D for dirt, however, has some drawbacks. The physical act of crushing C&D debris accelerates the migration of the hazardous substances out of the solids, especially once the debris is exposed to rainfall. Furthermore, C&D debris, whether pulverized or not, provides an ideal medium for **cocktailing** (mixing together) liquid toxic waste. As an investigator with New York State's Bureau of Environmental

Crimes Investigations explained, the easiest way to dispose of hazardous waste is to cocktail a load of C&D. To get rid of a couple hundred gallons of PCB (polychlorinated biphenyl), for example, you "go to [a construction site] . . . and you just pour it over the top of the C&D material."[21(pp.74–75)]

During its investigations into environmental crime in the Empire State, the New York State Assembly Standing Committee on Environmental Conservation (NYSASCEC) found that an environmental criminal might "pick up a legitimate load of C&D material from a building contractor, for which he was paid a fair fee, adulterate it with a generous admixture of toxic, hazardous, industrial or medical waste which another customer was paying handsomely to dispose of, and finally cart it upstate to a landowner who was anxious to have an acre or two leveled off with what he thought was legitimate fill."[22(p.2)] This pattern of operating became widespread, resulting in an epidemic of illegal C&D dump sites throughout New York State.[23] Further inquiry revealed that some entrepreneurs were selling pulverized C&D, believed to be contaminated with liquid toxics, as topsoil to unsuspecting home owners.[24]

Probably more prevalent than pouring liquid toxicants over C&D is the practice of simply pouring the liquids over regular solid waste (garbage) already loaded onto trucks bound for landfills or solid waste transfer stations. Compared to landfills, transfer stations are relatively small operations that receive and hold solid waste for a short period of time while the waste is compacted and reloaded onto optimal-sized vehicles (e.g., 60-cubic-yard trailers) for transportation to licensed landfills. The absorbent nature of garbage would allow a large quantity of liquid waste to be concealed in just one average-sized garbage load. For example, one 20-cubic-yard container ("roll-off") of garbage can be saturated with approximately 60 drums of liquids.[25] After saturation, the load could be dumped as garbage at a landfill rather than at a licensed hazardous waste facility, and the hauler would pay only the tipping fee for regular solid waste, accruing enormous sums of money as the scam is repeated again and again.

Often enough, though, offenders simply dump anywhere that is convenient. Law enforcement personnel should be especially wary of **midnight dumping**. Some of these offenders will dump a single load quickly and never return, reducing the chance that law enforcement agents will apprehend them in the act. Others are more brazen and seek to operate an illegal site as long as possible, thereby increasing their profits from the continued dumping. In one case, a New York State Forest Ranger came upon an illegal dump-site that had obviously been operating for quite some time. The ranger noted in his patrol log the presence of white goods (i.e., junked refrigerators, ovens, etc.) on the site as well as solid, medical, and other hazardous waste materials: "I observed large amounts of paper, cardboard, some household garbage. I also found hospital refuse, EKG strips, Techs, orders from Lawrence Hospital. I also observed syringes or the catheters to the syringes and oxygen tubing, but by the time I got back to the location with the appropriate gloves, those items had been buried."[26] The ranger intended to bag some of the medical waste as evidence of hazardous waste dumping at the site, but when he went to get gloves, the site operator bulldozed over the evidence. It is noteworthy that some operators are willing to risk possible impoundment and seizure of very expensive heavy equipment by using it in an illegal long-term operation. Obviously, at least some of these environmental criminals fully expect not to be arrested.

The preceding example also reveals that medical waste has begun showing up in illegal dump sites. Medical waste is also easily mixed into regular garbage destined for licensed solid waste landfills. Some areas of the country now use medical waste combustion facilities as a better method of disposing of infectious waste. Local law enforcement officers should be aware, however, that "fly" or "bottom ash" (the byproduct of the combustion process) must still be disposed of somewhere. Depending upon the locality and on facility licensing, on-site disposal may or may not be allowed. Large commercial trucks departing from such facilities may be hauling fly ash to another disposal site, which may or may not be licensed to accept this waste byproduct. Additionally, if the combustion facility fails to achieve the optimal burning temperature to neutralize hazardous components in the medical waste (approximately 1400 degrees Fahrenheit), then the possibility exists that some hazardous chemicals will be emitted into the air or deposited in the landfill as bottom ash.[27–29]

By now it should be obvious that construction sites, landfills, and solid waste transfer stations represent potential hot spots for environmental crimes. Police officers and sheriff's deputies who are interested in catching environmental criminals in the act may want to consider making a special effort to observe activities at these sorts of businesses in their jurisdictions.

Lessons To Learn from the Careers of Two Convicted Environmental Criminals

Your local landfill may contain quite a bit more hazardous and toxic waste than it should. Consider the case of Russell Mahler, a convicted environmental criminal who operated for many years as a waste transporter and disposer. Some of Mahler's clients included industry leaders like Clairol, Corning, Exxon, Hitchcock Pollution Control Company, Koppers Company, Inc., and Pratt Whitney.[30–33] Mahler also served as the main oil re-

refiner for the U.S. Department of Defense. Mahler did so well collecting hazardous waste that he could not possibly treat or dispose of all of it properly. So he bribed New York City sanitation officials to allow millions of gallons of hazardous and toxic liquids to be poured onto the ground at various municipal landfills. Successful long-term investigations resulted in convictions for Mahler, several sanitation officials, and others who conspired in the plot.[34]

One of Mahler's techniques was to pour contaminated oils directly into sewers and rivers and onto the ground. One particularly imaginative method of disposing of contaminated waste (which companies had paid him to take off of their hands) was to dump toxic liquids into a bore hole leading into the abandoned Butler Tunnel mine shaft in Pittston, Pennsylvania. This operation (perpetrated by a Mahler company called Edgewater Terminals) might have avoided detection completely had the poisonous liquids not flowed into the Susquehanna River during a severe hurricane in July 1979, resulting in "a 35 mile long slick of oil and toxic wastes. . . . Pennsylvania authorities later learned that for a year and a half Mahler's company had been dumping nearly 65,000 gallons a month of substances known to cause cancer, birth defects and chromosomal damage into the Susquehanna River."[35(pp.7–8)] Cleanup and treatment of the Susquehanna and the Butler Tunnel mine were estimated to run nearly $10 million.

Another Mahler company, Quanta Resources Corporation, performed a hazardous waste cleanup operation in January 1981 at Chelsea Terminal (Staten Island, New York) under contract with Texaco, Inc.[36] Tests at Chelsea Terminal concluded that most of the waste oil at that location contained 600–700 parts per million (ppm) of PCB. Fifty parts per million of PCB is considered toxic. Also found on site was bromoform, a chemical known to cause cancer, liver disease, and death among humans. From January through March 1981, Quanta moved about 150,000 gallons of the poisonous waste from the Chelsea Terminal cleanup.[37] From April through June 1981, Quanta delivered what was purported to be fuel oil to apartment buildings in Brooklyn, Manhattan, and the Bronx. ABC-TV reporters happened to be following the story of "possibly contaminated fuel oils" being delivered by Quanta to various apartment buildings, and they commissioned independent tests of samples obtained from batches Quanta delivered. Laboratory test results obtained by ABC-TV indicated the presence of PCB in quantities as high as 3,000 ppm.[38]

In other violations of environmental law, Mahler's Northeast Oil Services of Syracuse, Anchor Oil, and Hudson Oil simply dumped toxic wastes into the sewer system of the city of Syracuse, New York. Acting on reports of suspicious discharges, the Syracuse Department of Drainage and Sanitation installed an automatic sampler in a manhole downstream of the Hudson Oil Corp. facility. Twice their sampling devices were tampered with and the samples spilled out. The department bolted down the manhole covers and monitored Hudson's discharge. No wastes were dumped for three weeks. When the monitoring stopped, reports came back that the company discharged 40,000 gallons of various liquid wastes over a weekend, including cyanide.[39(pp.2-3)]

Through further investigation, Onondaga County (New York) officials discovered that various trucks emptied their waste into large holding tanks on site. Supposedly, this was only a temporary containment method until the liquids could be transported to a permanent storage facility. Investigators found, however, that the storage tanks had been altered so their contents drained directly into the public sewage system.[40] Hudson's customers at this time included Carrier Air Conditioning Corporation and Carlisle Compressor Corporation. Included in their waste were oils, acids, and alkaline wastes (hazardous waste) as well as benzene, toluene, and xylene (toxic chemicals known to be carcinogenic). Also among the liquids poured into the Syracuse sewage system were "eight shipments of highly toxic nickel and copper plating wastes, chlorinated solvents with phenol derivatives and cyanide from Pratt and Whitney in Montreal."[41(p.6)]

Many environmental criminals are not as sophisticated or diversified as Russell Mahler was, but these crimes have all been duplicated by others since, and it is likely that others will continue to use these same techniques in the future. Meet William Carracino. Carracino, an illegal dumper turned informant, explained an easy way to get into the environmental crime business: "You can go out and rent a piece of property, don't buy it, rent it. Rent 10 acres, rent 20 acres. Start—get a permit—to handle [chemical waste] drums. Bring them onto the property and just store them. As soon as the heat gets too great just go bankrupt and get out."[42]

While Carracino had been the principal operator of Chemical Control Corporation in Elizabeth, New Jersey, he directed various illegal dumping operations.[43] He cocktailed dangerous chemicals with regular dirt for delivery as cover fill at municipal landfills. He dumped toxic chemicals directly into the adjacent Elizabeth River. Occasionally, when he had too much waste to get rid of using his usual methods, he sent tanker trucks to unmonitored construction sites and directed the drivers to drain the liquids into the excavations dug for building foundations. Carracino improperly and illegally stored over 50,000 barrels of hazardous liquid wastes on his 2.2-acre operation—licensed to contain a maximum 9,000 barrels.[44] Shortly after Chemical Control Corporation was ordered by state and local officials to remove the excess barrels and store the remaining waste properly, the facility exploded, causing devastating air, land, and water pollution.

Environmental crimes can be committed using far less sophisticated means. Smaller operators can simply rent a truck with phony identification or a stolen credit card, fill the truck with 55-gallon drums, and abandon it on the streets in practically any community. Environmental criminals have also been known to rent warehouses and self-storage units, fill them with whatever waste they want to dispose of, and leave town.[45] As industrialization and technology progress in the United States, so will the forms of environmental crime and the number of criminals, unless there is a substantial law enforcement response. Local law enforcement officers should be on the lookout for these known methods of operation, and others as well. Another important lesson to be learned from these examples is that the local law enforcement response is more likely to be successful if police and sheriff's deputies cooperate with other agencies that share responsibility for controlling environmental crime.

DETECTING ENVIRONMENTAL CRIME

Environmental crime programs evolve within law enforcement agencies for many reasons. Community concern about pollution may lead to greater sensitivity to environmental crime. An environmental catastrophe sometimes provides the impetus to act. In the past, these extra-organizational

Calvin and Hobbes   by Bill Watterson

Source: CALVIN AND HOBBES © 1987 Watterson. Dist. by UNIVERSAL PRESS SYNDICATE. Reprinted with permission. All rights reserved.

pressures have often been responsible for the creation of environmental crime units. In the recent past, however, local law enforcement agencies have become more aware of the extent and seriousness of environmental crime and have taken action to combat it.[46]

One of the first steps in developing an adequate law enforcement initiative is to decide how the initiative should be organized:

> Policymakers in law enforcement and environmental agencies should be aware of the various organizational approaches that may be adopted to serve the enforcement needs of a community. For some communities, assigning county deputy sheriffs to the solid waste authority is the preferred strategy; elsewhere, assigning criminal investigators to a specialized prosecutor's office environmental crime unit may work better. The most traditional approach remains law enforcement–based units in which responsibility for environmental crime investigation and enforcement rests with officers situated within the department.[47(p.18)]

When considering which organizational design is best for a community, it is important to identify the resource level and current missions of existing organizations. A successful response to environmental crime will require interagency coordination and cooperation. The law enforcement agency will find that positive relationships with the fire department, sanitation authority, health department, emergency response units, and other government agencies will greatly improve the environmental crime initiative.

At the same time, the law enforcement agency must give consideration to the local business and political climate. Environmental crime prosecution of a local enterprise that employs large numbers of community members could have political repercussions for the law enforcement agency. Fortunately, there are some methods to defuse a potential backlash. The local law enforcement agency should play a role in educating the community about environmental crime, especially the harms associated with these offenses. To do this, it should enlist the assistance of the media. It should also make a case that the business sector of any community is best served by ensuring that environmental criminals are identified and punished. Legitimate businesses invest a lot of money in ensuring compliance with environmental law. If their competitors are allowed to violate environmental laws, the offenders gain an economic advantage that harms law-abiding businesses. Additionally, some localities are highly dependent on tourism or on their unspoiled natural resources in general. Environmental crime can be especially harmful to the well-being of these communities.[48]

Detecting certain types of environmental crime can be very difficult without specialized equipment and training. However, sometimes environmental crime is easily detected. Persons residing close to the source of pollution often inform the sanitation, health, or enforcement authorities about noxious odors, suspicious occurrences, or unsightly operations. The ability of local law enforcement to develop a partnership with the community is just as important for preventing environmental crime as it is for preventing other types of crime. Sometimes employees of offending businesses may inform law enforcement or environmental regulatory agencies about violations. Additionally, inspections by regulatory or sanitation officials may result in the detection of crimes. Business competitors of polluting firms have also been known to notify authorities about environmental crimes. Local law enforcement officers can also detect environmental crimes directly if they know what to look for while patrolling their communities.

The biggest generators of problematic waste are large manufacturers of automobiles, furniture, clothing, and, of course, chemicals.[49] These manufacturers can be easily recognized and be put under observation by local law enforcement officers. However, there are an even greater number of smaller businesses that generate hazardous byproducts as well, and these companies may go unnoticed unless a conscious effort is made to enforce environmental laws.

According to the Midwest Environmental Enforcement Association, potential community offenders include "furniture builders or refinishers; electroplaters or metal stampers; automotive repair and body shops; gas stations; analytical laboratories; photo shops; funeral homes; dry cleaners; agricultural pesticide dealers; [and] hospitals."[50(pp.1-2)] Once sheriff's deputies and police officers are aware of the potential hot spots in their communities, they will be better prepared to detect environmental crimes before they occur or while they are occurring rather than merely react after the fact.

The EPA encourages local law enforcement officers and the general public to "keep their eyes and ears open" for environmental crimes.[51] Law enforcement officers should be on the lookout for unusual industrial operations or incidents, such as a sudden change in the quantity or density of smoke emitted from a smokestack or the appearance of suspicious waste coming out of a factory's discharge pipes. One unusual operation caught the eye of diligent law enforcement officers in New Jersey in the early 1990s. These officers became suspicious when they observed employees of General Marine, Inc., bringing different river barges alongside a larger barge loaded with sewage sludge. Although it initially appeared as though the sludge was being transferred from one barge to another for transport out to sea, subsequent observation revealed that the sludge was simply being dumped directly into the river, in violation of environmental law. The principal officers of the company were all convicted, and one received a prison term.[52]

Changes in odor should also act as a red flag, as should other sensory changes. Does whatever is in the air burn one's eyes? Has there been a change in the taste of the drinking water? Not all bad odors indicate violations of environmental law, but some do. One example of a community that experienced a noxious odor was the town of North Hempstead in New York in the late 1980s. The town had been operating the Port Washington landfill, and because it believed that crushed C&D debris would compress the existing mass of solid wastes, it agreed to accept, at no charge, 70,000 tons of pulverized C&D at the landfill. During and after the deposition of the C&D waste, the town and areas surrounding it were "plagued by hydrogen sulfide odors, which smell like rotten eggs."[53(p.443)]

Law enforcement officers should also investigate unsightly operations. Solid waste flowing out of a facility from its liquid waste discharge pipes should be considered suspicious. Are liquid discharges highly colored? Is a dumping area surrounded by dead vegetation or wildlife? In the late 1980s, at Tuxedo, New York, neighbors of an illegal dumpsite complained about medical wastes blowing across the street onto their lawns, and reports of dead pets and other animals were frequent. It was found that the gases and vapors emanating from the site were noxious.[54,55]

Local law enforcement officers should also be suspicious when they observe what they think are secretive operations. Are operations being conducted at unusual hours or in unlikely places? Bulldozers operating at night in a marsh area may indicate the illegal filling of a wetland. Is a tanker truck parked alongside or off of a roadway? If so, is anything draining out of the holding tank? Remember, though, tanker trucks do not have to be standing still to drain their contents onto the roadway. Veteran environmental crimes investigators in New Jersey in the early 1980s once encountered a suspicious vehicle that they followed through a rainstorm. The investigators' suspicions were confirmed when the waste liquids draining from the tanker truck literally melted their vehicle's windshield wipers.[56]

Another example of secretive and suspicious operations is that of the Penaluma Landfill near the town of Warwick, New York. Although the landfill was permitted to receive garbage and other solid debris, it was not allowed to take in hazardous or toxic waste. The operator of the landfill, who was himself also in the business of transporting solid and hazardous waste, conspired with other hazardous and toxic waste haulers to dump all sorts of materials illegally at Penaluma Landfill throughout the 1970s and into the 1980s. Collectively these waste haulers serviced some extremely large companies, such as Ford, International Paper Company, Reichhold Chemical, and Union Carbide, as well as numerous smaller firms and hospitals. Waste illegally dumped at Penaluma Landfill included radioactive P-32 compounds and other waste tagged "radioactive contaminated materials"; discarded medical waste such as "needles, syringes, organs and blood"; "paint and oil sludges"; and "powdered chemical dyes."[57(pp.77–80)]

Residents near Penaluma Landfill observed operations at the dump site. Believing that there might be a threat to their health, they reported that dumping began in the early morning hours and continued through the late night and that the truck drivers used flares to light their way. Trucks dumped 55-gallon drums of liquid waste, and bulldozer operators immediately covered the barrels. One resident observed that a bulldozer operator who had smashed a load of drums was burned by acid and was taken to the hospital. On other occasions, large tractor trailers dumped their loads into wetland areas beyond the boundary of the landfill. The material dumped (believed to be phosphorous) created an eerie orange-yellow glow.[58]

Operations that are extremely rapid may also be worthy of closer scrutiny. A police officer in Tuxedo, New York, became suspicious of the dumping operation when he observed that "75 to 80 truckloads were deposited each day between midnight and 8:00 a.m."[59(p.203)] One resident near the illegal dump reported the following:

> They would go in and dump and quite a few were dumping 35, 55 gallon drums and when they would dump there was a bulldozer there running over them to crush the drums or push them off the edge of the bank as soon as they dumped. Sometimes there were six or eight trucks dumping at the same time. By the time they got ready to leave what they had dumped was already pushed and covered over. It was a very rapid operation. They'd run over drums and all different kinds of liquids would come out.[60(pp.67–68)]

Others claimed that tanker trucks often drained their liquid contents into the site, and at least one automobile and a tanker truck "riddled with bullet holes" were reportedly buried at the bottom of the mass of materials dumped there.[61]

Law enforcement officers should carefully document their observations by making detailed written records of what they see, hear, and smell. Photographing or videotaping suspicious operations or incidents is even better. The officers should patrol their communities with an increased awareness of the various methods used by environmental criminals. Frequent contact with community members leads to rapport and cooperation and will increase the chance that the environmental crime initiative will succeed.

Another method of detecting environmental crime is for local law enforcement officers to become familiar with the commercial motor vehicle traffic that travels through their jurisdiction. As discussed in previous chapters, the federal Resource Conservation and Recovery Act of 1976 (RCRA) established a manifest system to track hazardous waste. Industries that generate waste are required to maintain manifests that show types of waste generated and the quantities turned over to haulers for disposal. Once the waste has been delivered to its destination, the receiving facility has the responsibility of returning the manifests to the generator so that accountability can be verified.[62]

There are many flaws in the manifest system, however, that affect its ability to track waste and effectively manage its disposal. One way to defeat the regulations is for the generator to legally dispose of part of the firm's hazardous waste. This provides the company with some documentation to show inspectors from a regulatory agency. The other portion of waste is simply dumped illegally.

Hazardous waste haulers themselves might attempt to increase profits by illegal dumping. "A hauler could forge the treatment, storage, disposal facility's signature on the manifest or the TSDF bill it shows the generator."[63(p.14)] By circumventing the waste facility altogether, the hauler increases his or her own profit margin by also pocketing the facility's fee. One way to reduce the incidence of this illegal technique would be for generators of waste to stop contracting with haulers for both transport and disposal services. Separate contracts with haulers and facilities and direct payments to each for services provided would eliminate some incentive for haulers to employ this scam.

In most jurisdictions, police officers or sheriff's deputies can stop and inspect commercial vehicles for possible violations of state laws and local ordinances. Their authority covers overloading, improper placarding for the type of cargo being hauled, loads not properly covered, unsafe operation, and other infractions of the state motor vehicle codes. Officers who have received proper training and are familiar with waste manifest documents will also be able to identify fictitious or otherwise suspicious-looking documents during vehicle inspections. Obvious indications of problems include missing documents and the carrying of heavier cargo, larger quantities of cargo, or different types of cargo than shown in the manifest documents. Law enforcement officers should become familiar with state laws and local ordinances governing transportation of waste in their jurisdictions. They should know the laws governing stops, inspections, and searches of commercial vehicles. Assuming adequate resources, formal spot-checks or crackdown operations could be employed on roadways with dense commercial truck traffic or where suspicious truck traffic has been spotted. Further information, assistance, and training should be available from the state department of transportation, the state police or highway patrol agency, and the regional environmental enforcement association.[64]

Responding to an Environmental Crime or Accident Scene

Local police officers or sheriff's deputies are usually the first personnel to respond at an environmental accident or crime scene. However, "the tools of the police officer's trade provide little or no protection from toxic, corrosive, reactive, flammable or other hazardous substances."[65(p.15)] Only specific knowledge and focused training can protect officers responding to a serious environmental incident.

Law enforcement officers know from their training and personal experience that swift arrival on the scene can prevent further injury, loss of life, and damage to property and may be a key determinant of success in the follow-up investigation. However, many environmental accidents and crime scenes present unique hazards and therefore require considerable self-restraint and caution. An officer who rushes into the scene to rescue a downed bystander may also become a victim. Some chemicals and hazardous products are odorless and invisible, so it is important to size up the situation before acting in haste. Patrol officers who know they are arriving at a site with environmental hazards should take several precautions.

Initial responders, those first to arrive on the scene, should never attempt to enter a site that is emitting suspected or known hazardous liquids or gases or that contains unconfined hazardous solids. Instead, the officers should determine the wind direction and direct all bystanders to move a safe distance upwind of the scene. Next, they should isolate exposed persons to prevent further contamination. Finally, they should secure the scene, request appropriate assistance, and wait for personnel properly trained in hazardous materials (HazMat) handling. Large spills or other situations may require evacuation procedures. The officers should never exceed the limits of their environmental incident training.[66]

Only officers and other personnel fully trained to respond to environmental crime scenes should enter the site, and entry should occur only after careful evaluation of the situation. If necessary, personnel should don the protective clothing and respiratory apparatus best suited for the particular known or suspected hazardous substance. Not all protective gear is alike; some types of protective clothing offer greater protection than other types. Respiratory protection depends on selection of the correct cartridge or filter that has the ability to remove the contaminants present in the air. For ex-

Police Are Vulnerable As First Responders

In the early 1980s, two New York state troopers responded to an accident involving an overturned truck.[1] The truck was spilling a thick liquid, and while investigating at the scene the troopers waded through the unknown substance. Once the truck had been removed from the scene, the troopers completed their paperwork and returned to patrol. Although the troopers did not touch the spilled liquid, their boots had become immersed in the toxic chemical. The chemical, toluenedisocyanite (known as TDI), was a solvent used in paint and tar removal. While the officers at the time were unaware of what was happening, the heater in their cruiser vaporized the TDI on their boots and created poisonous fumes. After finding themselves feeling weak, they pulled off the road and phoned for assistance. By the time the other officers arrived, the troopers were unconscious.

The troopers were discharged after a brief stay in the hospital, but neither was able to return to duty. They both retired on disability, and one died shortly thereafter.

---

1. J. Atkins, "Tragedy Stirs Action," *FBI Law Enforcement Bulletin*, May 1995, 24.

ample, gas masks issued by some police departments are designed to remove contaminants associated with crowd control agents. They are not effective, however, in most chemical environments."[67(p.4)]

Once all personnel are on the scene and prepared and an appropriate plan of action has been formulated, approach to the scene should be made from the upwind flank. Investigators and HazMat personnel should move cautiously toward the scene, watching where they step. They should look for the source of the hazardous waste threat and observe drums and containers for markings or labels. However, it is not necessarily safe to assume drums are correctly labeled, as some environmental criminals intentionally mislabel drums to conceal their crimes. Metal tanks, tanker trucks, and compressed air cylinders can also contain hazardous liquids. It is essential not to touch or move any containers or drums. Corrosive substances may be dissolving the drum from the inside out, and any attempt to move the container may cause it to crumble (additionally dangerous because some chemicals explode upon contact with oxygen in the air). Another good reason not to touch any suspected hazardous waste materials and containers is that corrosives may compromise the integrity of protective garments and some toxic substances can be absorbed directly through the skin.[68]

The investigators need to look for sources of danger, such as bulging or leaking drums, escaping vapors, and other unconfined waste. They should photograph the crime scene thoroughly (getting both establishing photos and evidentiary photos) and use standard investigative procedures. If the entire scene is to be videotaped, they must be careful what they record. According to Deputy Sheriff James Pearsall (Palm Beach County, Florida), "Panning from a bird chirping in a clean pristine field to the leaking drums can catch the jury's attention." But, he warned, "never photograph a bunch of people casually standing around a dangerous spill," because the defense attorney may be able to use such a photo to discount the seriousness of the crime.[69(p.30)]

The investigators should collect any evidence that exists at the scene, such as manifest documents, invoices, or other papers left among any solid waste on site. They should document license plate numbers on vehicles at the crime scene and record lot numbers on drums or containers. They should also look for tire tracks and footprints. According to the Midwest Environmental Enforcement Association, "Your best tool is standard investigative technique, with an environmental twist."[70(p.9)] All personnel who entered the crime scene should be thoroughly checked by medical professionals after exiting the site.

As with any investigation, all potential witnesses, victims, and suspects should be interviewed as soon as possible. The interview should be documented thoroughly, preferably recorded. The investigators should extend the investigation to the area around the scene (nearby residents often provide investigative leads). When they identify the site owner, they need to remember that he or she may be either a suspect or a victim.

INVESTIGATING ENVIRONMENTAL CRIME

Once suspects emerge in the investigation (either individuals or corporate entities), the investigators should learn as much as possible about them. To establish what crimes a company may have committed, it is first necessary to understand what the company is licensed and permitted to do. It is also necessary to determine what records the company is required to maintain so that the investigators will know what documentation to look for and what questions to ask when they confront the owners and operators of the business.[71]

The corporate records may reveal important information, such as the full range of hazardous waste handled by the company. An inability of the company records to identify where other waste has been legally disposed of may lead to spinoff investigations. Also, in an investigation where the exact nature of discovered pollutants or discharges is not yet fully known, the corporate records may provide the specifications. Getting access to the corporate records is therefore often a high priority for environmental crime investigators. Further, linking discovered waste to the corporate records is important for investigative and prosecutorial purposes. However, corporations know this as well, and many companies will not readily give up their records. Investigators must be prepared to obtain the legal warrants to search based upon probable cause, just as would be required in any other investigation. Although environmental regulation officials can often compel non-consensual inspection of certain records without a warrant, this authority does not extend to law enforcement personnel. Additionally, legal precedent in some jurisdictions forbids regulatory officials from inspecting such records without warrant if the regulators are cooperating in a criminal investigation.[72] For these reasons, it is crucial to establish a solid probable-cause basis for any warrants to search.

Many corporations understand the law better than law enforcement officers do. Although they often view environmental crime from a different perspective, both share a duty to know the law. Just as police and sheriff's deputies will work closely with their prosecutor counterparts, so will the corporate defendant depend upon its legal counsel. According to one corporate attorney, there are three main goals for the corporate manager who is served with notice of a search: "(1) assure that the warrant is honored and not exceeded by the agents; (2) establish and preserve a record upon which to challenge the use of evidence gathered in the search; and (3) get the evidence back."[73(p.4)]

The corporate attorney may advise the manager or owner of the business being searched to demand a copy of the warrant and read it carefully, noting the particular places to be searched and the things to be seized. He or she may also suggest that the operators, "to the extent that the warrant restricts the search to certain parts of the premises, deny the agents access to the remaining parts."[74(p.4)] At least one corporate attorney advises corporate managers to "direct the agents and supervise the search for those records [named in the warrant]. This is a rare instance where you want to volunteer help because it effectively limits the scope of the search."[75(p.5)] Additionally, the company's attorney will want employees to accompany the investigators during the execution of the warrant, noting where the law enforcement personnel go and what they search. The attorney will not want the company employees to be interviewed by the agents, however, or to provide any other assistance to the investigators conducting the search. Finally, the attorney will probably encourage the company to make specific demands of the government, including requests for written receipts for everything impounded, copies of all records seized, results of any tests conducted on samples taken, copies of any photographs or videos made, and an early return of original records and equipment that were seized.[76]

It is important to note that individuals or corporate entities subjected to searches of their records and premises are absolutely entitled to avail themselves of every legal protection described above. Therefore, in order to safeguard the rights of the accused and to reduce the risk of compromising subsequent prosecution, each member of the search team must understand what is within the scope of the warrant, which areas will be searched, and what is to be seized. While investigators are executing the search, it is permissible to question employees of the company, and a lot of useful information might be obtained from them. However, a search warrant does not provide a legal basis to compel employees to answer investigators' questions. On the other hand, corporate managers, owners, or legal counsel cannot legally prevent employees who volunteer information from doing so. An attempt to do so might expose employers to obstruction of justice charges.[77] An employee who cooperates in an investigation as a **whistleblower** may be the target of retaliatory action, such as termination of employment. A whistleblower is an insider of an organization implicated in wrongdoing who notifies authorities about the crimes and violations. In recent years, federal and state laws have evolved to protect whistleblowers because of the consequences many of them have experienced.[78] So, even though a terminated employee may later have legal recourse under civil remedies, investigators must remain extremely sensitive to a cooperative employee's position and conduct their interviews with the utmost discretion.

Employees who voluntarily provide information may reveal that their employers directed them to take actions the investigators know are illegal. Whistleblowers may also provide information that directly contradicts the records maintained by the company. It is also possible that different employees will provide conflicting accounts of operations or corporate documentation.[79] For all of these reasons, investigators should be ready to interview employees who may wish to voluntarily cooperate with them.

In the event that investigators have not yet developed sufficient probable cause to obtain a search warrant to enter a suspect place of business or site, other sources may provide useful information for developing the investigation. State (and some local) environmental regulators and licensing agencies maintain lists of known types of hazardous waste generated by companies. If the type of waste discovered has already been identified, cooperation with the regulatory agencies may yield a relatively short list of potentially responsible parties. In addition, environmental regulators, fire departments, and health officials may have already documented previous violations during routine inspections or service calls, and their documentation may support the need for a search.[80]

There are also useful techniques for less focused investigations. Observation of known illegal disposal sites can be conducted directly by officers using long-range photography or even aerial surveillance. It may be possible to trace abandoned drums or containerized waste by serial numbers or product markings. Once a suspect company emerges in the case, insider informants or disgruntled employees may be able to provide detailed information about or evidence of environmental crimes.[81]

It is also possible to conduct proactive investigations. Some sting operations are easy to set up. For example, in New York State in the early 1990s, investigators believed that there was a widespread problem with garbage transfer stations accepting hazardous wastes. An undercover informant (who was pretending to be a construction contractor seeking hazardous waste disposal) was sent to suspect transfer stations to see if his "hazardous waste" would be accepted. The specific sites were selected based on the operating backgrounds of the principal operators or owners of the stations. The investigation revealed that the informant was able to dump pickup truck loads of assorted wastes without any trouble at all. The informant reported the following transaction at one location:

I approached an employee named Bill, and I asked him if I could dispose of the contents of my truck. The pickup truck was fully loaded with a mixture of C&D, and old metal cans and plastic containers bearing the labels of various types of chemicals, including motor oil, paint, transmission fluid, and a few cleaning solvents. However, the cans actually contained water. . . . I handed Bill a twenty dollar U.S. currency bill, and he, in turn, gave me a receipt. He then directed me to dump the contents of my truck into the center of the pile.[82(pp.16–17)]

No one asked the informant about the contents of his load, and no one attempted to inspect the contents of the cans and plastic containers. The informant had been able to dump a similar load for $30 at another transfer station, and he successfully repeated his act at a third location, paying only $20 to dump the load of mixed waste. While at these sites and others, the informant also made note of numerous other violations, many of which he was able to videotape for later use.[83]

More elaborate undercover operations may be available to law enforcement organizations with greater resources or to those that happen to fortuitously develop the cooperation of waste-business insiders. In June 1995, Robert Morgenthau, Manhattan's district attorney, was able to initiate both civil and criminal RICO[84] actions against 17 individuals, 22 waste-handling companies, and 4 waste trade associations operating in and around New York City.[85]

Morgenthau got a break: a legitimate garbage hauler agreed to cooperate in the investigation, which was jointly conducted by the New York County District Attorney's Office and the New York City Police Department's Organized Crime Investigations Division. So the government not only had an insider informant but was able to place an undercover agent in the cooperating hauler's company. With the assistance of the waste-hauling-business informant and the undercover agent who had been placed in his company, the government was able to collect evidence of bid rigging, price fixing, restraint of trade, physical intimidation, and economic extortion within the garbage-hauling industry in and around the New York City area.[86] This investigation was the largest waste-related undercover operation District Attorney Morgenthau has yet conducted in his 21 years in office, and he put 10 assistant district attorneys on the case. More than 500 police officers participated at various times, and the government amassed 3,000 hours of electronic surveillance and executed 26 separate raids against the corporate defendants.[87]

But there are sometimes barriers to environmental crime investigations. Among these is the lack of ability to quickly and accurately determine the identities of individuals connected to waste-handling firms, their true extent of involvement, and their relationships with yet other corporate entities. In today's waste trades, a veritable potpourri of individual and corporate names are used by participants, and the result is a tangled web of complexity.[88]

The case of Russell Mahler, discussed at the beginning of the chapter, provides a good example of diversification of criminal enterprise across numerous corporate entities. Such diversification makes detection and investigation of the full scope of crimes exceedingly difficult. If nothing else, Mahler should be considered a brilliant strategist for conceiving the many chameleon-like re-creations and diversifications of his corporate entities and holdings. Not only did Mahler own Hudson Oil Refining Corporation, Northeast Oil Services, Polar Industries, Casco Equipment, Winslow Leasing, and Oil Transfer Corporation, but he

> was also a principal in Ag-Met Oil Service, Inc., which owned the waste oil re-refining plants in Syracuse, Long Island City, and Edgewater, New Jersey and owned the assets of the related re-refining companies, Newtown Refining Corporation, Anchor Oil Corporation, PSC Resources, Skies Oil Service, Inc., Tammy's Oil Service, Sea Lion Corporation, and Diamond Head Refining Corporation. Ag-Met later changed its name to Newtown Refining Corporation and in 1978 sold the re-refining plants to Portland Holding Company. The two New York State plants were then operated as Hudson Oil Refining Corporation and the New Jersey plant as Edgewater Terminal, Inc.[89(p.10)]

Complicating matters even further, Mahler was a multijurisdiction offender, operating businesses and facilities in New Jersey, New York, and Pennsylvania. Many of his enterprises would reincorporate, altering their names, shifting their assets, and sometimes changing locations. His numerous operations conducted their business across several regions of the United States.

New York State Assistant Attorney General James Sevinsky of the Environmental Protection Bureau complains that information about the principals of waste-related firms (i.e., the directors, main shareholders, and key employees) is often not available.[90] Currently, the only way to determine ownership interests and participation of individuals in such firms in many jurisdictions is by conventional investigative techniques. This entails running license checks of vehicles operating at a site, conducting physical surveil-lance to directly identify individuals and possibly following them over long periods of time, and interviewing insider informants. All of these tech-niques require a significant investment of time, effort, and resources.

Occasionally, other barriers to environmental crime investigations may be encountered. In communities where they operate, waste-related enter-prises often generate a lot of money, for either the owners of the business or the local government (e.g., taxes on tipping fees), or for both. Law enforce-ment officers seeking to shut down an illegal operation may face serious opposition to their efforts. Such was the case with the landfill at the town of Ramapo, New York, in the late 1970s.

Sheriff's deputies in the Rockland County Sheriff's Department initially became suspicious of operations at the landfill when they observed trucks owned by certain waste haulers bypassing the weigh scales at the Ramapo dumpsite. Weigh scales are typically used to determine the volume or weight of waste being dumped in order to set the tipping fee, or cost to dump. The deputies, who were working with a New York State Organized Crime Task Force (OCTF) investigator, believed that several carting compa-nies were disposing of liquid hazardous and toxic waste illegally at the land-fill. In testimony before the New York State Senate, former OCTF investiga-tor John Fine described some of the countermeasures used by landfill proponents to thwart law enforcement efforts to shut down the Ramapo dump:

> Deputies were run off the road. A police officer was threatened with a gun. City employees attempting to enforce a town environmental code were threatened. Their families were threatened. Political in-terference was rampant. Legislators threatened to cut off the sheriff's funds for his investigative staff. Town officials threatened the town chief of police and captain, withholding salary raises be-cause they helped with the investigation of the landfill. A candidate was run against the sheriff. Ninety percent of this man's campaign approximately was financed by [a principal of the] property which received the liquid waste.[91(p.4)]

The illegal dumping at Ramapo landfill continued much longer than it might have because of the complicity of some public officials, who not only disposed of the waste there but also controlled the operations at the site.[92] Fortunately, persistent and cooperative efforts by local and state law en-forcement agents finally brought an end to the illegal operation.[93–95]

TRAINING AND AGENCY RESOURCES

Law enforcement officers with backgrounds in chemistry or other hard sciences and those who already know arson and white-collar crime investigation techniques are often in demand when environmental crime units are staffed. Many environmental crimes investigators and supervisors have agreed that these backgrounds provide a useful foundation for further environmental crime training.[96] However, not all law enforcement officers selected to become environmental investigators will have the benefit of these backgrounds. Furthermore, even individuals with these backgrounds will need specific basic and inservice environmental crime training. In addition to investigative staff, line personnel like sheriff's deputies and police officers should receive appropriate environmental crime instruction. The training should reflect not only the education and experience level of the trainees but also their specific job functions.

Ideally, all local and state law enforcement officers should receive at least one course in environmental crime detection and response as a component of their basic training. Although local and state law enforcement training may be highly centralized in some jurisdictions,[97] in others it is very decentralized,[98] so it is difficult to make any definitive statement about the number of officers who have already received some environmental crime training or the specific content of such instruction. Nevertheless, many police training academies have already incorporated at least some environmental crime instruction in their basic peace officer certification programs.[99] Adequate basic training should at least cover the types of environmental crime; detection methods; first-responder actions; safety issues; appropriate evacuation and isolation distances; and agencies responsible for managing, regulating, and investigating hazardous wastes.[100]

In addition to basic training, contemporary law enforcement standards require all full-time state and local officers to complete a minimum of 40 hours of **inservice training** per year. Police officers and sheriff's deputies can often choose between a variety of inservice courses. Personnel without prior environmental crime training should give serious consideration to taking such a course. Those who have completed at least one course in the past may want to attend an advanced environmental crime course. Most local and state police academies now provide some inservice instruction in environmental crime. In addition, the four regional environmental enforcement associations offer training to local and state officers, prosecutors, and regulators.[101] The EPA also makes some of its basic safety, chemical, and investigation courses available to state and local officers at the federal facility in Edison, New Jersey. The Federal Law Enforcement Training Center

INSIGHT

A Minnesota Sting: But Who Got Burned?

Two Minnesota companies were charged December 14, 1992, with attempting to transport hazardous waste illegally in what officials called the first environmental crimes sting in the Midwest.[1(p.2105)]

The Minnesota Attorney General's Environmental Crimes Team (the "E-Team") organized a sting operation, under the name of "Red Lion Disposal," in order to determine "the extent of illegal transportation of wastes in the state and to obtain evidence to prosecute generators of waste who violated the state's hazardous waste transportation regulations."[2(p.2105)]

The sting organizers sent out approximately 600 fliers to businesses and manufacturers in four Minnesota counties. The businesses selected were those that had previously had problems with hazardous waste. The companies were asked to call the number on the flier for information about cheap disposal rates. After the Red Lion Disposal Company was contacted, its "staff" told the parties over the phone that they did not have the necessary permits and licenses to dispose of their hazardous wastes. If the parties wanted to continue with plans to set up a "collection" of waste, then Red Lion would oblige them. After the money changed hands, the law enforcement officers made their arrest. The parties arrested in the sting faced 18 months in prison, a $12,500 fine, or both.[3–7]

The Minnesota Pollution Control Agency (MPCA) Commissioner said the attorney general's office did not comply with the conditions of the sting established in his office. The sting was to make certain that the offending parties knew the waste would be dumped illegally, not just transported illegally. While the MPCA argued the sting was inappropriate, the attorney general's office argued it was "tragic" that the MPCA was backing away from aggressive environmental enforcement.

One of the alleged environmental offenders took some action of his own. In a letter to the state governor (one of the many fire extinguisher owners he serviced in his business), the man wrote about building his business from nothing to 12 employees; about his "beautiful and loving" wife and their four children; about his activities as a volunteer firefighter; about his regular church attendance; and so on. He said he was afraid that he would lose his business, that his legal expenses would be too much for him to pay, and that he would never recover from this ordeal.

The governor released his letter to the news media. Also, the media covered the fact that the secretary for the cabinet company, who actually wrote the check for the waste disposal, was a 61-year-old mother of 6 and a grandmother of 10. After writing the check, she was promptly arrested by law enforcement officers. The police took company records and even went through her purse.

1. "Two Minnesota Companies Charged in Sting for Illegal Transport of Hazardous Waste," *Environmental Reporter*, 0013-9211 (25 December 1992): 2105–2106.
2. "Two Minnesota Companies Charged."
3. J. Coffman, "Two Firms Charged in Waste Sting," *St. Paul Pioneer Press*, 15 December 1992, B1.
4. C. Laszewkski, "Pollution Control Chief Blasts Toxic Waste 'Sting,'" *St. Paul Pioneer Press*, 1C, 5C.
5. D. Rebuffoni, "Hazardous Waste 'Sting' Draws Legislator's Ire," *Minneapolis Star Tribune*, 17 December 1996, 2BW.
6. D. Grow, "Stung and Uncertain, He Got His Message to the Governor," *Minneapolis Star Tribune*, 26 December 1996, 1A.
7. "Putting a Sting into Minnesota Politics," *Minneapolis Star Tribune*, 6 January 1993 (editorial opinion).

(FLETC) in Brunswick, Georgia, likewise provides some opportunities for environmental crime training for state and local officers.

Less formal training can be developed by agencies themselves. The Broward County (Florida) Sheriff's Department, for example, combines regular inservice training with on-the-job training at roll call. Short blocks of instruction are efficiently delivered to uniformed officers using video-tapes, lectures, or handouts and bulletins immediately before the officers go on shift; the instruction covers topics like officer safety, report writing, and recognizing environmental crimes.[102] Training materials and aids are available through a variety of sources, including the Law Enforcement Television Network; the International Association of Chiefs of Police; and numerous local, state, and federal agencies.[103] Law enforcement agencies that are already responding to environmental crime problems can also use their experienced personnel as valuable on-the-job training resources. The use of field training officers is now a standard practice in police and sheriff's departments; inexperienced officers are paired with more experienced officers during tours of duty and thus are able to gain experience in natural, realistic situations from trainers who can provide hands-on instruction and supervision. This method of on-the-job training should be incorporated wherever environmental crimes expertise already exists within a law enforcement agency.

Depending on the particular needs of the law enforcement agency, one or more officers should possess **advanced training** in environmental crimes/incidents. Advanced training would likely include the following topics: types and uses of personal protective equipment, hazardous materials handling, decontamination procedures, environmental crime scene investigation and documentation, interagency liaison procedures, emergency command post operations and communication, basic site containment and remediation techniques, state and federal environmental incident–reporting requirements, and the legal aspects of environmental crime investigation and prosecution.[104]

Cross-training is another instructional method that not only provides personnel with specific relevant information but also allows them to better understand the roles of others involved in the environmental crime initiative. One excellent example of cross-training is the EPA/FLETC course. The course format brings environmental crimes investigators and environmental regulators together for training. For example, regulators learn the principles of securing a crime scene and collecting evidence and the chain of custody procedures. Criminal investigators learn about regulatory programs, administrative sanctions, and civil enforcement strategies. Past participants of this program have reported not only learning the basic job functions and challenges of their counterparts but also building working relationships with them during the cross-training experience.[105] In addition to the classes taken together, regulators and investigators also receive separate, advanced instruction in topics specific to their own job functions.

Although there are currently greater opportunities for environmental crime training than in the past, the need for such training often exceeds the availability of existing programs. However, it may be possible for local and state environmental crime units to create their own training programs or expand their current environmental enforcement efforts and to do so with minimal investment of their own resources. Virtually every state now operates its own **asset seizure and forfeiture** program for specific types of crime. The practice of seizing and selling the assets of people convicted of drug-related crimes has already attained widespread acceptance within law enforcement communities. In jurisdictions where the legal means exist, law enforcement agencies should work with prosecutors to convert convicted environmental offenders' assets into environmental crime training or enforcement resources. For example, the Middlesex County (New Jersey) Environmental Crimes/Arson Unit has made frequent use of the forfeiture program provided by state law to increase its resources. In addition, Middlesex County Sergeant Ken Huber notes that "equipment seizure is often the most effective method of ending the illegal activity and preventing further damage."[106(p.13)] One environmental crime investigation in that jurisdiction effectively shut down a hazardous waste cocktailing operation and resulted in the seizure of equipment valued at $1.6 million.[107]

Fines, fees, and restitution can also result in additional resources for environmental crime initiatives. For example, in just one California case

> Solano County recovered $250,000 in fines for its general fund, $75,000 for the Solano County Office of Emergency Services as a one-time equipment grant, $75,000 to the District Attorney Environmental Crime Unit (DAECU) as a one-time equipment grant, and $11.5 million for the purchase of land in both Solano and Contra Costa County to be [restored] to wetland habitat. The total cash value to the county from this settlement obviously covers the cost of the DAECU for a number of years.[108(p.1412)]

The DAECU used money recovered in other cases to acquire a "facsimile machine, video camera, all terrain vehicle, boat, lap-top computer, desk-top computer, cellular phones, and a $25,000 training grant."[109(p.1411)] All of this equipment is useful in combating environmental crime, and all of it was obtained at the expense of offenders, as a result of successful investigations and prosecutions.

An adequate laboratory facility is another invaluable resource for environmental crime investigations. Common problems with existing laboratories include understaffing, lengthy turnaround time, and misplacement of samples.[110] In some jurisdictions the situation is even worse. Some enforcement and many regulatory agencies rely on companies under investigation to conduct their own tests and report the results to the authorities.[111] A legislative inquiry into this practice in New York State in the early 1990s found that it was fairly widespread and that the main cause was the amount of money laboratory analysis costs the government. Speaking to environmental regulators and investigators, Maurice Hinchey, congressman from New York, said, "You ought not to have to rely upon the alleged goodwill and quality of information that is provided to you by the people you are investigating. It is an absurd situation. It is almost directly out of Alice in Wonderland."[112(p.214)] Unfortunately, the cost of laboratory analysis can sometimes be prohibitive, and meeting the cost remains a challenge for environmental crime units.

One possible solution is for a unit to fund laboratory analysis with resources available from asset forfeiture programs. However, because funding by forfeiture resources is usually unpredictable, a more realistic strategy would be for several law enforcement agencies to pool their resources to contract as-needed analyses from a reputable laboratory. Working together, environmental crime units could eventually raise enough capital to operate their own laboratories—or at least fund one shared laboratory facility.

Another factor critical to enforcement success is personnel retention. There simply are not enough people with experience in environmental enforcement. Turnover of personnel within environmental regulation agencies is high because industry often hires inspectors and investigators after they have been trained by the government. This **commingling** of personnel between regulatory agencies and the companies they are charged with regulating has had definite implications for environmental regulation and enforcement.[113] These turnover rates represent costs for the government agencies in terms of both budgets and efficiency; training of personnel is very expensive because it requires about a year and a half for an individual to become knowledgeable and proficient in this highly technical field.[114] Retention of experienced inspectors and investigators remains critical for any environmental enforcement program.

Environmental crime investigators with local and state law enforcement agencies have had less opportunity to leave their government positions and apply their acquired skills as private-sector employees. However, this could change in the future if environmental crime initiatives continue to increase. The more corporations become targets of environmental crime investigations, the more incentive they will have to hire experienced crime investigators to assist them during the investigation and prosecution stages.

CONCLUSION

Environmental crime is a serious contemporary problem that threatens the health and safety of millions of Americans.[115] The public attitude toward environmental crime has changed in recent years; whereas once environmental misdeeds were accepted as regulatory violations, the public is now more likely to view such offenses in the same way they view traditional crime.[116] Partly as a response to this change in the public's awareness of and attitude toward environmental crime, law enforcement agencies have become more committed to catching the perpetrators of this type of crime.

In the recent past, local law enforcement agencies have risen to the challenge posed by the many environmental criminals and their numerous methods of illegal operation. Just as environmental criminals find new ways to exploit the environment for profit, so have progressive law enforcement officers developed better strategies for responding to these crimes. Police officers and sheriff's deputies can play a vital, proactive role in any environmental crime initiative. Developing an awareness of the scope and magnitude of the problem is an important first step. The second step is to work with other agencies that share the responsibility of environmental enforcement in creating a structure for the initiative. The next logical step is to allocate appropriate resources and prepare enforcement personnel through proper training. Routine patrol activities and community-oriented policing can be used to detect environmental crimes. Investigative personnel can initiate proactive sting operations to reduce reliance upon less efficient reactive measures. With proper organization, resources, training, detection, and investigation initiatives, environmental law enforcement can live up to its motto of "protect and serve."

REVIEW QUESTIONS

1. Identify the benefits of proactive environmental enforcement when compared with reactive enforcement.
2. How is "remediation" a reactive enforcement policy?
3. Identify five common reasons why people commit environmental crimes.
4. Explain why dumping C&D debris is often not considered an environmental crime.

5. How does the economic base of a community help law enforcement determine what types of environmental crimes are likely to be committed in that community?
6. Identify the primary concerns law enforcement officers have when they approach an environmental crime scene.
7. Explain the importance of working with corporate attorneys when serving a warrant on a business suspected of committing environmental offenses.

DISCUSSION QUESTIONS

1. The chapter presented a good deal of information about Russell Mahler, a convicted environmental criminal. Would you decide to proceed with the prosecution of this offender? Why or why not? If yes, what elements of his activity would affect this decision most directly?
2. Discuss the impact that the local community would have on an environmental crime enforcement division. Would community support help or hinder the agency's objectives? Justify your response.
3. Explain the significance of law enforcement training specifically focused on environmental crime enforcement. Should such training be made a mandatory part of all local law enforcement training programs? Justify your response.

REFERENCES

1. S. Humphreys, "An Enemy of the People: Prosecuting the Corporate Polluter as a Common Law Criminal," *American University Law Review* 39 (1990): 311–354.
2. A. Block and F. Scarpitti, *Poisoning for Profit: The Mafia and Toxic Waste in America* (New York: William Morrow, 1985), 44.
3. A. Burns, "What Is the U.S. Justice Department Doing To Enforce Hazardous Waste Regulations?" *Organized Crime Digest* 8, no. 14 (1987): 4.
4. See also C. Cray, *Waste Management Inc.: An Encyclopedia of Environmental Crimes and Other Misdeeds* (Chicago: Greenpeace USA, 1991).
5. Humphreys, "An Enemy of the People."
6. Environmental Law Institute, *State Hazardous Waste Enforcement Study*, prepared for the Office of Waste Programs Enforcement, RCRA Enforcement Division, U.S. Environmental Protection Agency, 1987, 1–67.
7. J. Epstein and T. M. Hammett, "Law Enforcement Response to Environmental Crime," *Issues and Practices* (Washington, DC: National Institute of Justice, January 1995).
8. T. Carter, "Desperadoes, Dirt and Dustbins: The Regulation of Environmental and Organized Crime in New York State" (Ph.D. diss., Pennsylvania State University, 1996).

9. T. Carter, "Desperadoes, Dirt and Dustbins."

10. D. Mazmanian and D. Morell, *Beyond Superfailure: America's Toxics Policy for the 1990s* (Boulder, CO: Westview Press, 1992).

11. United States General Accounting Office, *EPA's Penalties May Not Recover Economic Benefits Gained by Violators*, report to Congress, GAO-GPO, 1991.

12. Humphreys, "An Enemy of the People," 324.

13. J. Hammit and P. Reuter, *Measuring and Deterring Illegal Disposal of Hazardous Waste: A Preliminary Assessment*, report prepared for the U.S. Environmental Protection Agency (Santa Monica, CA: The RAND Corporation, 1988), 1–85.

14. Hammit and Reuter, *Measuring and Deterring Illegal Disposal of Hazardous Waste*, 2.

15. Hammit and Reuter, *Measuring and Deterring Illegal Disposal of Hazardous Waste*.

16. Hammit and Reuter, *Measuring and Deterring Illegal Disposal of Hazardous Waste*, 18.

17. Block and Scarpitti, *Poisoning for Profit*.

18. Carter, "Desperadoes, Dirt and Dustbins."

19. Carter, "Desperadoes, Dirt and Dustbins."

20. New York State Assembly Standing Committee on Environmental Conservation, *Public Hearing on Illegal Dumping on Long Island: An Assessment of Solid Waste Disposal Practice on Long Island*, Hauppauge, NY, October 22, 1991.

21. New York State Assembly Standing Committee on Environmental Conservation, *In the Matter of a Private Hearing into the Involvement of Organized Crime in the Waste Disposal Industry*, testimony of William Farley, Kingston, NY, July 7, 1989, New York State Legislature, 74–75.

22. M. Hinchey, *Illegal Dumping in New York State: Who's Enforcing the Law?* (New York: New York State Assembly Standing Committee on Environmental Conservation, April 10, 1992), 1–83.

23. Hinchey, *Illegal Dumping in New York State*.

24. New York State Assembly Standing Committee on Environmental Conservation, *Public Hearing on Illegal Dumping on Long Island*.

25. New York State Assembly Standing Committee on Environmental Conservation, "Criminal Infiltration of the Toxic and Solid Waste Disposal Industries in New York State: Two Case Studies" in *The Business of Crime*, ed. A. Block (Boulder, CO: Westview Press), 175–196.

26. M. Hinchey, *The Tuxedo Story: A Report from Chairman Maurice D. Hinchey to the New York State Assembly Environmental Conservation Committee on Illegal Disposal of Wastes in the Hudson Valley*, pre-hearing report of August 30, 1989, 1–40.

27. W. Bunch, "Bronx Incinerator Has Locals Fuming," *New York Newsday*, 11 February 1994.

28. See also R. Sugarman, "Standards Go up in Smoke: 51 State Violations for Hospital Incinerator," *Bronx Daily News*, 7 November 1993.

29. For a case study of organized crime in the medical waste industry, see Carter, "Desperadoes, Dirt and Dustbins."

30. R. Marino, *Case History of a Toxic Waste Dumper* (New York: New York State Senate Select Committee on Crime, 1982).

31. R. Marino, *Hazardous Waste Landfill Dumping: The Consequences of Non-Enforcement of Environmental Conservation Law in New York State* (New York: New York State Senate Select Committee on Crime, 1982).

32. *U.S.A. v. John Cassiliano*, indictment filed in U.S. District Court, Southern District of New York, January 10, 1985. Indictment No. 85-CRIM.017.

33. *U.S.A. v. Russell Mahler*, sentencing hearing before the Honorable Herbert J. Stern, May 10, 1982, Newark, NJ. USDC Criminal No. 82-345.

34. *U.S.A. v. Russell Mahler*.

35. Marino, *Hazardous Waste Landfill Dumping*, 7–8.

36. *U.S.A. v. Russell Mahler*.

37. Marino, *Case History of a Toxic Waste Dumper*.

38. Marino, *Case History of a Toxic Waste Dumper*.

39. Marino, *Case History of a Toxic Waste Dumper*, 2–3.

40. New York State Assembly Standing Committee on Environmental Conservation, "Criminal Infiltration of the Toxic and Solid Waste Disposal Industries in New York State."

41. Marino, *Case History of a Toxic Waste Dumper*, 6.

42. Interview of William Carracino by Brit Humes, "The Killing Ground," ABC News, 1979.

43. Block and Scarpitti, *Poisoning for Profit*.

44. Block and Scarpitti, *Poisoning for Profit*.

45. E. Larson, "Chamber of Horrors: Self-Storage Lockers Often Harbor Secrets," *Wall Street Journal*, 5 January 1994, A1.

46. Epstein and Hammett, "Law Enforcement Response to Environmental Crime."

47. Epstein and Hammett, "Law Enforcement Response to Environmental Crime," 18.

48. Epstein and Hammett, "Law Enforcement Response to Environmental Crime."

49. Midwest Environmental Enforcement Association, "Introduction to Environmental Crime Enforcement: A Guide for Local Law Enforcement," Midwest Environmental Enforcement Association, Elgin, IL, undated, 1–19.

50. Midwest Environmental Enforcement Association, "Introduction to Environmental Crime Enforcement," 1–2.

51. U.S. Environmental Protection Agency, *Environmental Criminal Enforcement: A Law Enforcement Officer's Guide* (Washington, DC: U.S. Environmental Protection Agency, Office of Enforcement, September 1990), 1–15.

52. J. Fried, "Four in Prominent Harbor Family Are Charged with Polluting," *New York Times*, 2 July 1993, B7.

53. New York State Assembly Standing Committee on Environmental Conservation, *Public Hearing on Illegal Dumping on Long Island*, 443.

54. New York State Assembly Standing Committee on Environmental Conservation, *In the Matter of a Public Hearing into the Illegal Disposal of Wastes in the Hudson Valley*, New York State Legislature, September 14, 1989.

55. J. Rife, "Tuxedo Busts 6 at Dump," *Times Herald Record*, 17 October 1987, 3.

56. Block and Scarpitti, *Poisoning for Profit*.

57. M. Hinchey, *Organized Crime's Involvement in the Waste Hauling Industry* (New York: New York State Assembly Standing Committee on Environmental Conservation, July 24, 1986), 1–187.

58. Hinchey, *Organized Crime's Involvement in the Waste Hauling Industry*.

59. New York State Assembly Standing Committee on Environmental Conservation, *In the Matter of a Public Hearing into the Illegal Disposal of Wastes in the Hudson Valley*, New York State Legislature, September 19, 1989, 1–220.

60. New York State Assembly Standing Committee on Environmental Conservation, *In the Matter of a Public Hearing into the Illegal Disposal of Wastes in the Hudson Valley*, September 14, 1989, 67–68.

61. Hinchey, *Illegal Dumping in New York State*.

62. Hammit and Reuter, *Measuring and Deterring Illegal Disposal of Hazardous Waste*.

63. Hammit and Reuter, *Measuring and Deterring Illegal Disposal of Hazardous Waste*, 14.

64. Four associations serve the United States: the Midwest Environmental Enforcement Association, (847) 742–1249; the Northeast Environmental Enforcement Project, (609) 292–0987; the Southern Environmental Enforcement Network, (334) 242–7369; and the Western States Project, (602) 542–8514.

65. D. Gates and B. Pearson, "Hazardous Materials: Incident Response Training for Law Enforcement," *The Police Chief*, September 1991, 15–16.

66. Midwest Environmental Enforcement Association, "Introduction to Environmental Crime Enforcement."

67. Midwest Environmental Enforcement Association, "Introduction to Environmental Crime Enforcement," 12.

68. Midwest Environmental Enforcement Association, "Introduction to Environmental Crime Enforcement."

69. Epstein and Hammett, "Law Enforcement Response to Environmental Crime," 30.

70. Midwest Environmental Enforcement Association, "Introduction to Environmental Crime Enforcement," 9.

71. M. Wright and W. Imfeld, "Environmental Crimes: Investigative Basics," *FBI Law Enforcement Bulletin*, April 1991, 2–5.

72. Epstein and Hammett, "Law Enforcement Response to Environmental Crime."

73. D. Aufhauser, "Searches—What Do You Do When They Don't Bother To Knock?" *Sonreel News*, January–February 1993, 4–5.

74. Aufhauser, "Searches, "4

75. Aufhauser, "Searches," 5.

76. Aufhauser, "Searches."

77. Aufhauser, "Searches, "5.

78. G. Marx, *Undercover Police Surveillance in America* (Berkeley, CA: University of California Press, 1988).

79. U.S. Environmental Protection Agency, *Environmental Criminal Enforcement*.

80. Wright and Imfeld, "Environmental Crimes."

81. Wright and Imfeld, "Environmental Crimes."

82. New York State Assembly Standing Committee on Environmental Conservation, *Public Hearing on Illegal Dumping on Long Island*, 16–17.

83. New York State Assembly Standing Committee on Environmental Conservation, *Public Hearing on Illegal Dumping on Long Island*.

84. The federal Racketeer Influenced and Corrupt Organizations Act of 1970 has been used in recent years to prosecute crimes, including organized crimes, that are situated within legitimate industries or within ongoing criminal enterprises. Many states have also created statutes mimicking the federal legislation.

85. New York State Supreme Court Hearing, "Order To Show Cause with Temporary Restraining Order," filed by Robert Morgenthau on June 19, 1995, County of New York, NY, an unindexed order presented before Judge Walter Schackman.

86. For a full account of the government's case against the indicted principals, see Carter, "Desperadoes, Dirt and Dustbins."

87. R. Behar, "Talk about Tough Competition: How Bill Ruckleshaus Is Taking on the New York Mob," *Fortune*, 15 January 1996, 90–100.

88. A. Block, "Into the Abyss of Environmental Policy: The Battle over the World's Largest Hazardous Waste Incinerator in East Liverpool, Ohio," *Journal of Human Justice* 5 (fall 1993): 82–128.

89. Marino, *Case History of a Toxic Waste Dumper*, 10.

90. New York State Assembly Standing Committee on Environmental Conservation, *Public Hearing on Illegal Dumping on Long Island*, 290.

91. New York State Assembly Standing Committee on Environmental Conservation, New York State Assembly Standing Committee on Health, and New York State Assembly Standing Committee on Environmental Conservation Subcommittee on Toxic and Hazardous Substances, public hearing testimony of John C. Fine, OCTF Assistant Attorney General, New York, NY, March 14, 1980, 4.

92. New York State Assembly Standing Committee on Environmental Conservation, New York State Assembly Standing Committee on Health, and New York State Assembly Standing Committee on Environmental Conservation Subcommittee on Toxic and Hazardous Substances, public hearing testimony of John C. Fine, OCTF Assistant Attorney General, New York, NY, March 14, 1980, 4.

93. For a full account of governmental corruption at Ramapo landfill, see Block and Scarpitti, *Poisoning for Profit*.

94. Carter, "Desperadoes, Dirt and Dustbins."

95. Hinchey, *Organized Crime's Involvement in the Waste Hauling Industry*.

96. Epstein and Hammett, "Law Enforcement Response to Environmental Crime."

97. For example, the state of South Carolina maintains one central academy for certification of all state and the vast majority of local law enforcement officers, though two other police academies are accredited.

98. For example, the state of Texas is host to more than 100 police certification programs or centers.

99. Richard Hill, Director, University of Houston-Downtown Police Training Center, personal communication, February 29, 1997.

100. Gates and Pearson, "Hazardous Materials."

101. See reference 64 for contact information for the regional environmental enforcement associations.

102. Epstein and Hammett, "Law Enforcement Response to Environmental Crime."

103. For further information, contact the International Association of Chiefs of Police at (703) 836-6767.

104. Gates and Pearson, "Hazardous Materials."

105. Epstein and Hammett, "Law Enforcement Response to Environmental Crime."

106. Epstein and Hammett, "Law Enforcement Response to Environmental Crime," 13.

107. Epstein and Hammett, "Law Enforcement Response to Environmental Crime."

108. M. Pollack, "Local Prosecution of Environmental Crime," *Environmental Law* 22 (1992): 1405–1425.

109. Pollack, "Local Prosecution of Environmental Crime," 1411.

110. Epstein and Hammett, "Law Enforcement Response to Environmental Crime."

111. Carter, "Desperadoes, Dirt and Dustbins."

112. New York State Assembly Standing Committee on Environmental Conservation, *Public Hearing on Illegal Dumping on Long Island*, 214.

113. Carter, "Desperadoes, Dirt and Dustbins."

114. Hammit and Reuter, *Measuring and Deterring Illegal Disposal of Hazardous Waste.*

115. R. Nader et al., *Who's Poisoning America: Corporate Polluters and Their Victims in the Chemical Age* (San Francisco: Sierra Club Books, 1981).

116. Humphreys, "An Enemy of the People."

CHAPTER 9

Environmental Crime Prosecution at the County Level

Donald J. Rebovich

TERMS	culpability	intelligence exchange meetings
	disorderly persons statutes	triangulation

Focusing local prosecution efforts on distinct crime areas is not a new practice. In the last two decades, America's district attorneys—particularly in offices representing densely populated counties—have gravitated to specialized prosecutorial services to respond to crimes in areas such as drug abuse, domestic violence, child abuse, and, now, environmental crimes. To a large degree, such specialization efforts are in reaction to public concern. The general public has increasingly come to perceive environmentally destructive acts as "criminal." Laws are not enough; increased enforcement is part of the organizational answer to the burgeoning volume of such acts.

After years spent identifying critical needs, parameters of responsibility, and the best methods for prosecuting these types of cases, prosecutors have

---

Note: This research effort was conducted as the second half of a two-pronged study, conducted by the American Prosecutors Research Institute and supported by the National Institute of Justice, to explore the role of county prosecutors in the prosecution of environmental crime. The first half of the study involved a national mail survey of district attorneys on the extent of environmental crime prosecutions performed in their jurisdictions. Information gathered from this survey was used as a basis for selecting individual sites for personal interviews. Data on the level of environmental crime activity and the level of environmental crime prosecution were used to rank prosecutors' offices by extent of their environmental crime problem and control efforts, targeting the most active jurisdictions.

Source: Reprinted with permission from D. Rebovich and R.T. Nixon, Environmental Crime Prosecution: A Comprehensive Analysis of District Attorneys' Efforts in This Emerging Area of Criminal Enforcement, No. NCJ-150043, American Prosecutors Research Institute.

become practitioner specialists. While much has been said about the federal response to environmental crime, actions are also being taken at the local level. Such a specialization is essential for combating the increasing numbers of environmental crimes at all levels of government. This chapter presents excerpts from interviews conducted with prosecutors at the county level during a study of the role of county prosecutors in the prosecution of environmental crimes. The results help illustrate how county-level environmental crime prosecution is evolving into a recognized professional specialization.

THE STUDY

To have a demonstrable impact on offenses against the environment, the responsibilities of the prosecutor position must coincide with special relationships and conditions developed over time. This study was designed to bring the accumulated knowledge, experience, and expertise of the county prosecutorial community to the attention of the full range of major organizations, associations, and disciplines that share the responsibility for handling environmental crime prosecution. The responses of those interviewed at the study sites provide provocative insights into the unique world of the county environmental crime prosecutor. The hope is that when these various organizations make policy, develop programs, and devise strategies related to environmental crime, they will do so with a more complete understanding of the concerns, issues, and problems of the county prosecutors who handle these cases.

Site Selection

Seven county prosecutors' offices were selected for site visits for the purpose of conducting person-to-person interviews. These offices were located in Los Angeles County, California; Monmouth County, New Jersey; Suffolk County, New York; Pima County, Arizona; Richmond County, New York; Orange County, California; and San Diego County, California. County prosecutor offices in these sites were selected based upon the reported volume of environmental crime activity in their jurisdictions and the level of environmental crime unit sophistication.

Site visits were intended to examine critical dimensions of effective environmental crime prosecution units at the local level and to assess the influence organizational and systematic variables have upon the decision to pursue environmental crime prosecutions. These issues were explored using in-depth personal interviews with key program decision makers (e.g., environmental crime task force prosecutors, investigators, and health department inspectors), who produced detailed accounts of program operations and practices.

The Interviews

The focus of the in-depth interviews was on the overall composition and activities of those parts of the prosecutor offices responsible for environmental crime prosecution. Specifically, the interview items addressed (1) unit policies, (2) organizational structures, (3) communication networks, (4) leadership (e.g., delegation of authority and locus of control), (5) relationships with other criminal justice and regulatory organizations and participants, (6) decisions to prosecute, (7) plea negotiations, (8) trials, and (9) special problems influencing environmental crime prosecution effectiveness.

Following are summaries of the most common responses of those interviewed. Descriptive narratives have been condensed and synthesized to highlight major findings unearthed through the interview process. Using multiple informants of environmental prosecutors, investigators, and inspectors at each of the sites allowed researchers to triangulate the findings across information sources. **Triangulation** refers to the integration of different research data sources in an effort to establish a more thorough understanding of the topic of study. Consequently, triangulation allows a researcher to test levels of information reliability and validity by bringing more than one source of data to bear on individual issues.

Interview Results

The interview results presented here reinforce impressions provided by local environmental prosecutors in previous studies.[1-4] On an organizational level, they reveal how county prosecutors generate support for their emerging environmental prosecution programs and how they have come to rely, more than ever, on organizational task force structures to promote the interagency relationships necessary for successful prosecutions. On a case level, they describe meaningful factors that play a central role in determining the patterns and general characteristics of criminal and civil charging, plea negotiations, and case presentation at trial. Of special note is how those interviewed underscore potential pitfalls for county prosecutors in environmental cases and how the prosecutors strive to overcome them. Though sometimes constrained by limited funds and lack of expertise, these prosecutors are dedicated to controlling environmental crime at the local level, and they provide information that can help to guide other county prosecutors in the identification and implementation of improved policies, practices, and procedures in the prosecution of local environmental crime.

CREATING A PRESENCE: GOALS AND OBJECTIVES OF COUNTY TASK FORCES

Each of the county prosecutor offices visited was found to have been involved in or to have initiated operations that merged the efforts of a range of criminal justice and regulatory professionals responsible for environmental crime control throughout the county. The offices reflected what had been found in an earlier national mail survey conducted by the American Prosecutors Research Institute—that the presence of these task forces was becoming more common in suburban and urban counties. Those interviewed were asked about the current role of the task forces in their counties, how they are developed, and how they are organized.

Investigating and prosecuting environmental crimes throughout the county is the primary thrust of the environmental crime task force, according to the county prosecutors interviewed. Such crimes have been given a higher priority because of increasing concern expressed by the general public. The attitude that environmental offenses are serious and are criminal in nature is relatively new. For the task force, the toughest chore is to change the mindset of a general public that has not previously considered environmental offenses as being synonymous with crime. A chief objective of county environmental prosecutors is to make the public sensitive to the threat of environmental crime, including not only people who reside near areas where environmental offenses have been committed in the past but also people in areas where environmental crime might be perceived as only a distant threat.

The county environmental task force strives to make the community aware that a specialized unit has been organized to treat these offenses as serious crimes and prosecute them accordingly. The task force's presence is stressed not only to educate the general public but also to deter those who would consider committing this kind of offense. As one environmental prosecutor reported,

> I think, obviously, that the goal of the unit is to stop the crime. Some of the underlying goals are also obvious. This unit tries to maintain a very strong public presence and an obvious public presence because that will help you deter the crime—simply the fact of people being aware of your existence. People are becoming more

aware of the fact that this, which was once something in which authorities looked the other way, is now something criminal.

Prosecutors interviewed believed that an important vehicle for stressing the presence of a task force—and with it the potential for criminal prosecution and sanctioning—is the successful prosecution of a "high-profile" case. This type of case, pursued early in the evolution of the task force, not only will highlight the existence of the task force but will go far in building the credibility of the unit itself.

> When these organizations first get started, you look for a "big hit" or something that will draw public attention to it. Now that we've gotten public attention, what we look to do is maintain the awareness level to such that we can continue to be effective—sometimes with less resources. I would tend to think any special task force needs to have something that will bring attention, positive attention, to it— something to let people know that it's worthwhile to have limited resources channeled toward fighting the environmental problem. But I think it's especially important with the environmental situation because so many people are unaware of the fact that it is criminal. . . . Once you have people aware of the fact that you exist and believe that you can do the job, and that you will do the job, then you become almost a part of their consciousness. They know you're out there and they know you're working.

Prosecutors stressed, though, that this credibility is accompanied by the responsibility of maintaining the task force's reputation over time as the agency matures. When the public comes to view the task force as a cohesive organization rather than a loosely knit unit groping to find its way, higher expectations are likely to result. Considering the volatile nature of environmental crime offenses—and their prosecution—it is important to achieve a high level of productivity, or the credibility of the task force can be lost as quickly as it was gained.

TASK FORCE STRUCTURE AND ADMINISTRATION

The organizational makeup of the task force can be conceptualized easily if one thinks about assembling several distinct aspects of county government, representing, for example, such entities as the county prosecutor's office and the county health department. In one of the jurisdictions studied, the hazardous materials program was the program taking the lead when joint environmental crime investigations were conducted. The environ-

INSIGHT

If You Take Direct Action, You May Get SLAPPed.

By law, anyone "wrongly" brought to court can sue the accuser for punitive damages, or basically for the inconvenience of being brought to court.[1] One consequence is that strategic lawsuits against public participation (SLAPPs) are often brought by businesses or municipalities to prevent citizens from speaking out against specific development projects or in retaliation for such public opposition, and in many cases SLAPP lawsuits have been directed toward environmental activists who, in the form of an organized protest, interfere with business operations.[2]

SLAPP suits have common characteristics: they are civil complaints or counterclaims, filed against nongovernmental individuals or organizations because of their communications to government entities, officials, or the general population on a substantive issue of some public interest or concern.[3]

Some of the more common issues resulting in SLAPP suits include real estate development, zoning, environmental protection, wetlands and wildlife preservation efforts, and NIMBY ("not in my backyard") actions. The legal claims cited by those filing a SLAPP suit include defamation, business torts (interference with contract, business, restraint of trade), other torts (nuisance, invasion of privacy), and judi-cial or administrative torts (abuse of process).[4]

As the courts see more of these cases, they are also seeing more examples where a person named in a SLAPP lawsuit will SLAPP back. These countersuits are grounded in legal theories of malicious prosecution, abuse of process, violation of constitutional rights, violations of civil rights, defamation, and intentional or negligent infliction of emotional distress, for example.[5] Further, they are not filed to be won; they are filed to intimidate the person or group being SLAPPed.

Approximately 90 percent of SLAPP suits brought are identified as "legal harassment" and thrown out.[6] Nonetheless, these cases can be disastrous. Legal costs can devastate families, individuals, and volunteer groups. In West Contra Costa, California, the sewer district filed a $42-million lawsuit against one man and 490 unidentified John Does for opposing its plans to build an incinerator.[7] In another case, a woman who opposed a waste incinerator was SLAPPed and spent $50,000 of her own money defending her case. She SLAPPed back; after a long trial and much personal and professional hardship the jury awarded her $86.5 million in damages.[8]

The National Coalition against SLAPPs is located in Berkeley, California.

1. J. Viehman, "SLAPPed: Strategic Lawsuit against Public Participation," *Backpacker*, May 1994, 7.
2. C. Davis and D. White, "The Unslapped: A Primer for Protecting You and Your Affiliate against SLAPP Suits," National Wildlife Foundation, January 24, 1994 (Internet: cdavis@igs.apc.org).
3. Davis and White, "The Unslapped."
4. Davis and White, "The Unslapped."
5. J. Speart, "When Citizens SLAPP Back," *National Wildlife*, June–July 1994, 12–15.
6. Speart, "When Citizens SLAPP Back."
7. G. Pring and P. Canan, "Slapp-Happy Companies," *New York Times*, 29 March 1996, A15.
8. Speart, "When Citizens SLAPP Back," 12, 15.

mental health coordinator was described as being "on call"—prepared, in other words, to respond to everything from relatively minor regulatory violations to major offenses. The following example illustrates how the cooperative effort generated through the task force can be advantageous to public health on a county level:

> A task force detective helped us out a couple of weeks ago when we had a leaking underground storage tank for nine months. The [state environmental protection agency] wanted to process this guy as a routine thing even though there was a potential for ground water contamination . . . this guy had two underground storage tanks with four feet of water in them. The [state environmental protection agency] basically dropped the ball big time, so we asked the task force detective to help us out. The detective went out there with the health department and talked with this guy. We got his attention real quick. They pumped the tank out the next day. So, you got that end of the spectrum and the other end would be where there is a big area where there is a lot of solid waste and potentially hazardous waste dumping—like an illegal landfill. Here we have to put together maybe 10 people to write a health and safety plan and have to get together sample bottles, etcetera—a massive approach.

Many environmental crime task forces presently do not use "on loan" rotating investigative personnel. These task forces typically depend on the importation of personnel from outside agencies on an ad hoc basis, including municipal police departments and other local law enforcement agencies. Some county prosecutors interviewed expressed a great degree of satisfaction with their task force structure in that it fostered a sense of autonomy and did not overburden members with bureaucratic structure. From the perspective of health department participants, a symbiotic relationship within the task force permits them to take advantage of the criminal investigative expertise of the prosecutor's personnel. As one prosecutor put it, health department personnel are

> just as happy when they've got themselves in a situation where they have to confront a bad guy that they usually don't have to confront. If you're talking about something that is criminal, they can turn that over to us. They are usually welcome to be, and often are, with us when we go do this. At least they've got the protection of being with police officers when they are in a potentially confrontational situation. So the fact that we each have totally different responsibilities is a good one, I think.

THE IMPORTANCE OF VERTICAL AND HORIZONTAL COMMUNICATION

Interviewees reported that a critical feature enhancing the organizational effectiveness of a task force is the ability to freely communicate with professional colleagues from other disciplines and to communicate through the chain of command, starting from the district attorney down to the task force staff. Such open communication is important for the timely exchange of technical intelligence on the cases and for maintaining high morale in what may be viewed in some offices as a low-priority crime area. Prosecutors saw routine **intelligence exchange meetings** within the task force as being a superior means of keeping all task force personnel up-to-date on law enforcement *and* regulatory information. In these meetings, experts from the different areas of specialization come together to discuss issues relevant to environmental crime investigation and prosecution. The exchanges were seen as keeping task force personnel sensitized to the unique needs and problems of colleagues from other disciplines. These periodic meetings can also help make personnel more versatile in the role they play in successfully investigating environmental crime cases.

> We've started to do things where we can try to educate each other on different aspects of our field, so that even if we don't have anything "hot" to talk about, we'll get together. . . . One time this year, the health department taught some of our people a sampling technique. Even though the health department is most often going to be taking the sample, it was kind of a consensus that prosecutors would benefit from knowing how you were supposed to do it. We spent some time with them talking about courtroom testimony and how to handle cross-examination, [and] how to write a report with an eye toward the fact that you are going to be cross-examined about it. Those are the things which these people will not have special training in. This way, even though it's not ever going to be your full-time job, at least your awareness is elevated to such a point that you can't help but produce a better product.

The meetings were seen by task force staff as greatly enhancing the rapport between the health and law enforcement sides of the task force. As explained, they help create an open door policy between the two disciplines and are instrumental in reducing the tension that can occur in any group where specialists from a number of different disciplines come together to function as a "team." Prosecutor task force personnel viewed the meetings as an aid in mitigating some of the "turf battles" that can be common in crime control task forces. Creating an atmosphere conducive to open invitations for assistance from other disciplines is one of the greatest advantages of employing these intelligence exchange meetings, as is the assistance they provide in determining the most important factors in environmental crime cases (e.g., whether a particular case should be pursued civilly or criminally).

> As an environmental crime prosecutor, you often have to rely on the health department people to recognize what is criminal and what isn't. That's one of the areas where these guys are truly fantastic. I can get a lab report back and call them to find out what it means and how to deal with it. It is their expertise, combined with our ability to decide what we can prove, [that helps determine] if we can put together the elements of the offense.

Complementing the free lines of communication horizontally within the task force is the intimate contact and clear communication between the district attorney and those on the environmental crime task force. The close, active association with the environmental crime task force not only boosts the morale of task force members but also helps to ensure the task force is pursuing areas that reflect the appointed prosecutor's priorities.

> [The district attorney] stated from the very beginning that he was going to make prosecutions in environmental crime a priority. . . . [He] is briefed on every case that could be important in one way or another. He doesn't get a call every single time we open a file or every single time we close a file, but if there is anything with any significance—and that means anything that could lead to an indictable charge—we let him know right away. And if we close a case of any significance against a company or business in the area, or if we get a defendant that for one reason or another is noteworthy, he knows about it right away.

As explained by the interviewees, the significance of open lines of communication does not end with internal intelligence exchange and the leadership support of the district attorney or chief prosecutor. Open lines of communication are also essential for the effective referral of environmental violations to the task force. Some task force detectives believed that the primary source for discovering environmental violations is the local health department, and some interviewees identified the police department as an important secondary source. Environmental crime prosecution task forces have supported some police department efforts to develop environmental coordinators or liaisons to foster open lines of communication when an offense is discovered. In many cases, when police departments are interested in developing open lines of communication, they are prevented from doing so by financial constraints.

Lack of police initiative in this area is not always due to a lack of resources. Many times it is due to a deficiency of information on the seriousness of the offenses and a general lack of knowledge about the criminal law.

> Most of the environmental crimes are not contained in the state's criminal code; they are contained in different places. So as a result we found to our surprise that police officers of considerable experience and skill don't even know that these crimes exist. We've conducted some training sessions to make police aware, and we plan to conduct more in the future. The first step is to make them understand that [environmental crime] exists and then to teach them how to recognize it.

PROSECUTORIAL DECISION MAKING

One decision-making factor rises above the rest when considering whether to prosecute an environmental offense criminally: the level of harm or the level of threat of harm. County prosecutors equate this with the severity of the offense. As one prosecutor stated, "Before you can exercise your discretion in any meaningful way, you've got to understand what you're dealing with. We look primarily to what harm was caused." Prosecutors are often compelled to weigh the level of harm or the threat of harm against the potential cost of criminally prosecuting an environmental offense case. Therefore, in a situation where a relatively low level of harm or threat of harm exists, prosecutors may decide not to prosecute the case criminally. Because of the encouraging level of public support experienced by some interviewees with regard to environmental prosecutions, however, prosecutors were confident task force decisions would be supported and would not be considered overzealous. On occasion, prosecution task forces have found it more effective to use civil proceedings for some environmental violations (e.g., where criminal intent would be difficult to prove).

According to prosecutor respondents, the decision whether to prosecute an environmental violation as a civil or criminal offense depends on several factors. The old cliché "each case is different" applies here. Every fact pattern is different. The prosecutors are generally reluctant to put themselves in a position where only certain factors will be weighed to determine the sentencing recommendation given to the court. What is most important when filing criminal proceedings is the ensuing damage to the environment. One prosecutor reported that, while specific internal charging criteria may not be part of a formal charging protocol, the extent of public harm, the degree to which the act was performed intentionally, the history of the company in question, and the extent to which it has cooperated in the remediation process are all factored into the decision. Others agreed that a great amount of deference can be given to a defendant who actively participates in the remediation process.

> If you have done something wrong and you are willing to remediate your problem, then I would take that into consideration. I have a case where a defendant stored hazardous waste at various locations. He put the hazardous waste on a big truck and took it to an RV storage place. He transferred some across the street to another location and has yet to remediate the problem. . . . I went to court on the case and the corporation wanted to plead the case. I said no way. Number one, you have not remediated the wastes, and, besides, the defendant should serve some time in custody whether it is in county jail or whatever. Cooperation makes a big difference. When somebody has taken the effort to remediate the problem and to expend the money, I definitely look at that as [influencing] how serious a charge I am going to file and what I would expect in regard to a particular sentence.

The defendant's ability and willingness to clean up a polluted site plays an influential role in the charging and plea negotiation processes. As one respondent stated, "From the health department's standpoint, cleanup ultimately is the priority. Once it becomes a criminal case, we like to see the cleanup attached to it. That's another advantage of having the health department closely involved in the prosecution task force."

Culpability, or the degree of intentional behavior behind the offense, is another factor that determines the fate of the defendant. The line is drawn between the intentional disposal of hazardous waste and merely negligent disposal. Prosecution of corporations involves a separate guideline.

> If we are dealing with a corporation, one of the factors and one of the big break points on criminal versus civil prosecution is whether there are individuals whom we can demonstrate are responsible parties and whether they are criminally culpable or not. There are some instances where you have an historic pattern that the corporation engages in and it is very hard to attribute it to any individual. Perhaps the only directly involved individual is a low-level warehouse worker who actually engaged in the behavior. Generally speaking, we are not interested in targeting those kinds of people. On the other hand, if you have directors or managers of an enterprise who

we can demonstrate engaged in intentional or reckless behavior, it then becomes more likely to be a criminal case.

This requirement is a typical component of the approach to criminal proceedings used by environmental crime prosecutors at the county level.

> If I can prove that somebody was responsible within a corporation I don't see why I should take a plea from a corporation and let the individual defendants off. I know quite frequently attorneys representing corporations and defendants will say, "How about taking a plea from the corporation and letting my client walk out of the case?" I just don't feel that serves our community right. It doesn't send the right message. I think that the one message I like to send out is if you are the responsible person and involved in the acts, then you will be prosecuted. I believe that once this message gets out, fewer corporate executives or people in corporations will be inclined to violate hazardous waste control laws.

Individuals are targeted when it is their conduct that causes violations. Having individuals held responsible does not allow corporate officers to hide behind the corporation. It precludes the avoidance of liability resulting from a bankruptcy filing.

> Quite often when people do a criminal act, they look to the bankruptcy court as an escape hatch for them, where they can go in and file for bankruptcy and not have to pay their creditors. However, because of the fact that we expect to extract large penalties, we do obtain a certain priority in bankruptcy court for payment. If you fail to go to bankruptcy court and get on the list, then you could be shut out if something happens and then [be expected to] pay all the creditors.

Once the degree of harm and culpability of the defendant has been established, the prosecutor looks to other factors, such as the history of the individual offender or offending corporation. If the prosecutor is dealing with a recidivist, it is more likely that criminal prosecution will be pursued. Also, as one prosecutor maintained, "What is important is whether they had an environmental compliance program and whether that was, in our view, mere lip service or protective cover or it was really an effort to identify and remedy the environmental violations." Prosecutors acknowledged that a certain amount of "triaging" does occur. Lesser cases must sometimes be rejected or downgraded to office hearings when more serious cases are pending. Not being able to get to every case because of the need to deal with more serious violations is admittedly one the county prosecutor's frustrations.

As is the case with most prosecutor offices, a lack of resources becomes an issue when a county prosecutor's office confronts the option of parallel proceedings. Prosecutors emphasized that even in metropolitan jurisdictions, with added personnel available, it is a luxury that they cannot afford.

> If they handle a case criminally, the office generally tries to get a result that will deal with the defendant in that situation adequately so that they don't have to file a parallel civil suit, which will involve more resources being expended. Secondly, there is a complex discovery problem which the department needs to contend with. The county follows the federal department of justice model, which requires that they deal with the criminal case first before they address the civil, so there is no suggestion of leveraging a civil result with a criminal threat. If they choose to file a criminal case and then a civil case, they must either file them simultaneously and put the civil matter on hold (until the criminal matter is resolved) or in some cases not bring the civil suit (assuming the statute of limitations is not a problem) until the criminal is resolved but convey to the defendant that it is coming so there is no suggestion of sandbagging.

TRIAL ISSUES: JUDGE AND JURY CONCERNS

The degree to which judges and jurors perceive the environmental crime as crime was viewed by county prosecutors as a crucial determinant of success in environmental crime trials. For judges, part of the problem of accept-

Calvin and Hobbes

by Bill Watterson

ing environmental offenses as crimes can be traced to the contrast between environmental offenses and other offenses to which these judges are routinely exposed. These other offenses may entail elements of person-to-person violence and involve individual victims who have incurred injuries from the violent acts. In these cases, the cause and effect of injury will be clearer for the judges and will fall into the type of conventional crime these judges have become accustomed to over time. Environmental offenses may pale in comparison to traditional crime, and the rulings may reflect the judges' attitude. Some prosecutors interviewed contended that they proceed under the assumption that many judges are going to look at these cases as "major inconveniences" rather than serious crimes.

To neutralize the effects of ambivalent court judges, some of the environmental cases are being fought in municipal courts by county prosecutors. States with powerfully worded **disorderly persons statutes** make it possible for prosecutors to proceed with cases involving the disposal of solid waste. Because they are classified as a disorderly persons offense, they are handled in municipal courts instead of the criminal courts. Although disorderly persons offenses are technically not criminal offenses, they have "felony-type" punishments attached to them. For instance, penalties can include loss of driver's licenses for prescribed time periods, mandatory community service, serious fines that can exceed usual disorderly persons offense fines, and the forfeiture of conveyance if conveyance is instrumental in the offense commission. County prosecutors find that some municipal court judges react favorably to these laws and impose strict penalties on convicted offenders.

> It depends on the municipality—some judges are tough with the solid waste enforcement and others write it off. If it's politically correct in that community and there is a push in that community for cleanup, then you will find judges that will "slam the hammer" down on these guys and others who are more lenient. Minimum-mandatory for a first offense under this statute is something like $2,500 and a six-month loss of driver's license with no option by the judge.

Notwithstanding the support they get from municipal judges on disorderly persons offenses, county prosecution task force members still believe that a formidable obstacle to successful environmental crime trials is a general lack of appreciation for the danger of environmental offenses, coupled with the fact that the effects of an environmental crime are dispersed among many individuals. Prosecutors in an environmental crime trial are therefore obliged to skillfully present as much information as possible on the gravity of the offense and simplify that information to clarify the relationship between the offense and the harm it caused or will cause.

> We have a problem dealing with judges who just don't think it's their top priority, and we deal with juries who wonder why you're standing there saying the defendant didn't have a permit to do this. You're dealing with things which are not necessarily going to be terribly interesting. I think that's something where we need to develop a strategy to make people aware of the fact that these cases should be tried, and if they are tried, they should be treated the same way as any other crime.

PRESENTING EVIDENCE

County prosecutors agree that the road to success in environmental crime trials often is decided by how well prosecutors select tactics to present the evidence to judges and juries. The choice of whether to present the evidence in a scientific manner or opt for a circumstantial presentation depends on the ability of the prosecutor to convey the intricacies of environmental evidence. Prosecutors were surprised at the extent to which some juries seemed to grasp at least the broad outlines of the relevant scientific concepts. Prosecutors acknowledged that though jurors may not understand hydrocarbon rings or the atomic weights involved, they do understand what it means for a chemical to be toxic. Respondents stressed that a happy medium between the two approaches must be used if prosecutors are to succeed at trial.

> You have to bring in that technical guy to talk about the elements of the crime, because one of the things that the public wants to know if you go to trial, and probably a judge too, is what harm is it? It is important to bring in the scientific side of this to show that it is harmful. What you want to do is establish that this stuff is hazardous waste. Whatever it takes to keep it simple for the jury is what you want.

Despite having to dispel some of the preconceptions that jurors may have about the level of seriousness of environmental offenses, county prosecutors believed that they possessed a distinct advantage over their prosecutorial counterparts at the state and federal government levels when it comes to achieving a conviction. That advantage is the heightened chance that local jurors will be more inclined to identify with the circumstances of the case and the danger presented by the offense. In short, the jury is likely to be more involved and less detached than one assembled for a state or federal trial of environmental offenders.

> I have to believe that a local jury trial with people serving on the jury who live in the community where the event occurred is something that could have more impact. . . . Local jurors might be more concerned about the case because they know where the case comes from. If you take a case which comes from this county and you take it to a federal court in [an urban city], you'd be dealing with people who don't even know where our county is and don't even know that it's a waterfront community. They're likely to take the case less seriously.

In their quest to address nontraditional crime areas, county prosecutors throughout the country are increasingly responding to community demands to criminally prosecute what have been viewed historically as violations in legal gray areas—areas where there is uncertainty about how the justice system should process relevant violations. Until recently, many of these gray areas have been dealt with through state and federal law enforcement agencies and civil or regulatory means rather than through the county criminal justice system. As local community demands for protection against environmental violations have intensified, county prosecutors, particularly in densely populated jurisdictions, have become more inclined to assume prosecutorial responsibilities that previously have fallen outside of their domain and been left to agencies operating at other government levels.

THE ROLE OF EXPERTISE

Upon reviewing the remarks made by those interviewed for this study, it becomes plain how pivotal the task force unit is for the county environmental prosecutor, since it brings together the diverse entities necessary to help ensure effective prosecution. The chief prosecutor acts as the catalyst for consolidating these interdependent agencies into a functional, autonomous unit. In this role, the chief prosecutor must wear several hats—that of leader, manager, facilitator, and communicator. To make a difference in controlling environmental crime in the county, the chief prosecutor must keep the representatives of these various groups on track and working in concert to capitalize on each other's expertise through the structured exchange of information. This approach not only acts to build teamwork and a sense of mission within the task force but also strengthens the quality of the environmental crime control effort and helps facilitate the opening of routes of environmental case referral.

INSIGHT

Princess Cruises into Ocean Dumping Charge

Picture this: You are on vacation. You are taking that cruise you have always dreamed about. You brought along your video camera to capture . . . ocean dumping?

During the summer of 1993 a Michigan couple provided videotaped footage of crew members of the Regal Princess cruise ship throwing over 20 plastic bags of garbage into the ocean five miles off the Florida Keys. Encouraged by the federal government's reward system for environmental whistleblowers, the couple received $250,000, half of the record $500,000 fine paid by Princess Cruise Lines.[1]

In a one-week 1994 operation, affectionately titled "Operation Overboard," the FBI combined forces with the Coast Guard and state officials in Florida to put together a two-count federal indictment for ocean dumping involving another cruise ship.[2] Other allegations have affected Dolphin Cruise Lines and Regency Cruise Lines.[3]

As a part of its effort to increase enforcement of ocean dumping violations, the Coast Guard has set up a toll-free number for passengers who wish to report violations. The hotline refers these cases to the U.S. attorney's offices.[4] Given the huge amount of ocean to patrol, it has proven to be nearly impossible to determine the origin of garbage when it washes ashore on beaches up and down the coast. The 1987 Marine Plastic Pollution, Research, and Control Act established rules for disposing of all ship-generated garbage and flatly banned dumping of plastics, which take 400 years to decompose and kill an estimated 1 million birds and 100,000 sea mammals and turtles every year.[5]

Other seagoing vessels have also been suspect. Two businessmen who operated a cargo ship (the Khian Sea) and were responsible for dumping 11,000 tons of toxic incinerator ash into the Atlantic and Indian Oceans in 1988 were sentenced to jail and fined.[6] The president of the company was fined $20,000 and sentenced to 5 months in jail and 5 months' detention for lying to the grand jury. The company's vice-president was sentenced to 37 months in prison and fined $7,500.

In a more recent case, two members of a family-run marine transport company were convicted of federal fraud charges for the illegal dumping of sewage sludge in the waters off New York and New Jersey. The two sisters, along with their brother, were brought up on charges. The brother was acquitted, but the two sisters face up to five years in prison and a $250,000 fine.[7] The actions were allegedly carried out at the direction of their mother, who was not charged in this case because of illness but served 5 years' probation for a 1990 dumping violation. The companies involved in the 1990 case paid a $1 million fine. In 1995, all three siblings faced another federal charge alleging they conspired to hide 250,000 gallons of toxic oil sludge collected as a result of their ship-cleaning operations. The sludge was being held on a "rickety barge" rather than being treated or stored properly.[8] The three were acquitted in the 1995 case.

---

1. "Vacationers Go Undercover at Sea To Film Dumping," *New York Times*, 31 July 1993, A6.
2. State enforcement reports, Southern Environmental Enforcement Conference, December 1994, Sarasota, FL.
3. "Vacationers Go Undercover."
4. "Vacationers Go Undercover."
5. "Sleuths at Sea," *New York Times*, 6 August 1993, A14.
6. "Ship Operators Face Jail in Ocean Dumping," *New York Times*, 7 October 1993, B14.
7. J. Fried, "Two Convicted for Fraud over Dumping," *New York Times*, 2 April 1996, B5.
8. Fried, "Two Convicted for Fraud over Dumping."

The chief prosecutor's efforts to create a skilled task force will be enhanced enormously by the successful prosecution of a high-profile environmental case. Such a high-profile case can draw media attention to the task force objectives and can have a lasting impact on the impressions the general public forms about the task force's efforts. County prosecutors committed to making their mark in environmental crime control will find this to be a requisite first step toward creating a presence in the local battle against environmental crime, generating additional case referrals in the future, and establishing a track record that shows would-be polluters they stand a chance of getting caught and punished.

The county environmental prosecutor's policies on environmental crime prosecution charging and plea negotiations are, in some ways, no different from the policies in more traditional crime areas.[5–8] Integral to charging and plea negotiation decision making are such factors as criminal history, level of harm, and culpability. Specific to environmental cases, however, are the concern for the establishment of the degree of the threat of harm and the ability and willingness of defendants to remediate violated sites. To be a worthy match for private defense attorneys, many of whom will be able to avail themselves of an abundance of resources, county prosecutors must be quick studies in the skilled use of the expertise mustered through the county task force. The county prosecutor's bargaining power, then, becomes heavily reliant upon how well he or she has structured the task force to include those who can collect and present technical evidence persuasive enough to force the defense attorneys to question the client's chances were the case to go to trial.

PLAYING THE REMEDIATION CARD

Alleged environmental violators and their defense attorneys frequently take the position that charges, if they are to be filed at all, should be civil rather than criminal. Civil penalties and one-time cleanup costs are often viewed by corporate defendants as part of the cost of doing business.[9] A county prosecutor of environmental crime faces the challenge of accurately assessing and balancing the decision to move toward either a civil or criminal charge for a waste disposal violation, for example. First, the prosecutor must weigh the evidentiary component. Second, he or she must consider how important it is to ensure the safety of the local populace through immediate offender remediation of the site. A move to remediate is likely to be in exchange for a dropping, or lowering, of criminal charges. When the task force and the prosecutor's office have identified an obligation to seek strong criminal penalties in an effort to deter future environmental violations, such a quid pro quo will be viewed as less acceptable, and the county prosecutor must tread with care in making these decisions. Demonstrations of leniency intended to guarantee containment of the site's deleterious effects could be used by the press to portray the prosecutor's office as being soft on environmental criminals. On the other hand, too tough of a stance could result in an outpouring of empathy for the defendant, who might be viewed as a simple businessman unfairly victimized by an "overzealous" law enforcer.

The prospect of descending into a "no win" situation is enough to dissuade even the most courageous county prosecutor from assuming an active posture toward environmental crimes. Yet respondents at the study sites illustrate how a thorough understanding of the potential obstacles standing in the way of aggressive prosecution plus an openness to adapt to these obstacles can help pave the way toward responsible prosecution of environmental offenses. In some instances, such adaptation has taken the form of extraordinary dependence on municipal courts to fill gaps left by county criminal court systems. But adapting sensibly more often means (1) devoting forethought to the strategies used to gather convincing evidence for enhancing the office's position in plea negotiations and (2) crystallizing the cloudy legal concepts that play a role in environmental cases. These tasks must be completed to the satisfaction of judges and jurors when the cases reach the courtroom. Gaining the confidence to move forward with environmental cases at the county level clearly depends on the type of technical and strategic education that the county prosecutors and their task force members are able to obtain.

TRAINING AND TECHNICAL ASSISTANCE

One does not need to search far to identify some of the most important areas that demand training and technical assistance at the local level. Such areas include trial skills that incorporate the use of demonstrative evidence to simplify what can often be a collection of complex technical concepts and to dramatize the seriousness of the offenses committed. One example of such training would be instruction on the use of three-dimensional computer animation to reenact waste disposal scenes or trace criminal acts by replicating the flow of disposed waste. In addition, training should address the effective use of expert witnesses in the courtroom and the admissibility of scientific evidence.

A few less obvious training topics should also be considered if county prosecutors are to truly be well rounded in their approach to prosecuting environmental criminals. Criminal deterrence should emerge as a concern for county environmental prosecutors. Deterrence, as an objective, speaks to the need of county prosecutors to explore and become familiar with the efficacy of the full scope of sentencing options—options that offer differential treatment for situational and career environmental offenders. Training conducted by experienced prosecutors can acquaint environmental prosecutor novices with how to build professional relationships that will facilitate prudent sanctioning (e.g., local prosecutor–probation officer exchanges that achieve a reasonable penalty given the circumstances of the case). Education on the use of lesser sanctions, like public acknowledgment of wrongdoing in the local media and the occupational disqualification of offending corporate executives, can help steer less experienced prosecutors toward these options when more punitive sanctions are either inappropriate or unlikely to be imposed.

An additional area of needed training is the constructive use of the task force model itself to advance the interests of county environmental prosecutors. County environmental task force efforts are at a stage of development comparable to where the prosecutor-led narcotics task forces were in the mid-1980s. As the pace of environmental crime quickens in urban areas and spills over into suburban and rural regions, the call for effective crime control will intensify. Based on the best information to date, environmental prosecution task forces at the county level may be the most logical means of addressing public concern over the environment, and it is reasonable to expect the formation of more of these task forces in the near future.

The responses of the study interviewees can serve as a cautionary note. Their collective experience indicates the common problems that can befall a well-intentioned county environmental task force developer. Practical training programs on the stages of environmental task force development, thoughtful personnel selection practices, and trust-building policies can help overcome these problems and transform proponents of different regulatory and law enforcement ideologies into members of cooperative teams. Experienced task force managers from urban district attorney offices could act as facilitators of these programs and provide much-needed illumination for the new wave of aspiring county prosecutor task force leaders.

Finally, to make certain county task forces reach their full potential, they should create public awareness programs or continue existing ones. The American Prosecutors Research Institute's national mail survey of local environmental prosecutors[10] shows that only a minority of present environmental prosecution task forces have such programs, yet the interview results described in this chapter point out the important role that community support can play in making county environmental task force programs a success. County prosecutor offices that are weak in the area of public awareness will need to cultivate a wider base of influence through community interaction programs that teach the basics of environmental crime recognition and reporting. Further, they should announce the accomplishments of the county task forces to keep the public informed about their actions and successes. By reviewing the example set by those prosecutors who have established "community-oriented" environmental crime task forces, the county prosecutors of tomorrow will be better equipped to reassess the traditional boundaries of their role in addressing the problem of environmental crime.

CONCLUSION

County prosecutors have entered into new territory with the prosecution of environmental crimes. With broader responsibilities for protecting the public health, they must become intimately familiar with a variety of areas that require technical expertise. Environmental science, chemistry, waste-sampling techniques, and regulatory enforcement procedures are all integral to successful prosecution. This chapter, through the use of county prosecutors' own words, has indicated the difficulties inherent in developing expertise in this unique prosecution field—a field that mingles elements of law, public health, and science; that requires county prosecutors to nurture relationships with a host of government agencies; and that foists on them a seemingly endless struggle to rally support for the prosecution mission from a criminal justice system and a public that, at times, can show ambivalence toward the environmental protection cause.

The information provided through the county prosecutor task force interviews helps in understanding the processes and factors county prosecutors depend on to shape their crucial charging decisions in an arena where a fine line exists between the classification of a civil violation (where conviction leads to a monetary penalty) and a criminal offense (where conviction carries a potential prison term). Finally, it provides fresh insight into how task forces can be most effectively managed to stem the illegal disposal, transportation, storage, and treatment of wastes and to help reconcile the divergent interests of task force participants.

REVIEW QUESTIONS

1. What agencies are typically represented on an environmental crime task force?
2. What is the relationship between prosecutors in an environmental crime case and the enforcement agents? Be specific.

3. Explain the importance of "horizontal" and "vertical" communication in an environmental crime task force.
4. One of the most important decisions to be made by the prosecutor is whether to pursue a case civilly or criminally. What makes this decision so important?
5. How does a company benefit from filing bankruptcy when it is facing a stiff environmental crime penalty? What can the task force do to reduce the probability of such a company action?
6. What is meant by the suggestion that county prosecutors must perform triage?

DISCUSSION QUESTIONS

1. Chapters 6 and 7 outlined issues of importance for determining whether to pursue environmental crime cases at the federal and state level. How do the priorities for pursuing an environmental crime case differ for cases at the county level?
2. It becomes clear that each prosecutor's office has discretion about how to proceed with environmental crime cases. Would an established set of criteria for prosecution help or hinder the prosecutor's objective of convicting environmental criminals? Justify your response.
3. How and why are municipal courts (rather than the criminal courts) being used to fight environmental crime?

REFERENCES

1. A. Gunther, "Enforcement in Your Backyard: Implementation of California's Hazardous Waste Control Act by Local Prosecutors," *Ecology Law Quarterly* 17 (1990): 803–845.
2. T. Hammett and J. Epstein, "Local Prosecution of Environmental Crime," in *Issues and Practices* (Washington, DC: National Institute of Justice, 1993).
3. D. Rebovich, "Prosecutorial Decision Making and the Environmental Prosecutor: Reaching a Crossroads for Public Protection," in *Environmental Crime and Criminality: Theoretical and Practical Issues*, ed. S.M. Edwards et al. (New York: Garland Publishing, 1996).
4. D. Rebovich et al., *Environmental Crime Prosecution: A Comprehensive Analysis of District Attorneys' Efforts in this Emerging Area of Criminal Enforcement*, National Criminal Justice Reference Service no. NCJ-150043 (Washington, DC: National Institute of Justice, 1994).
5. S. Fisher, "In Search of the Virtuous Prosecutor: A Conceptual Framework," *American Journal of Criminal Law* 15 (1988): 197–261.
6. R. Flemming et al., *The Craft of Justice* (Philadelphia: University of Pennsylvania Press, 1992).
7. R. Frase, "The Decision To File Criminal Charges: A Quantitative Study of Prosecutorial Discretion," *University of Chicago Law Review* 47, no. 2 (1980): 247–329.

8. W. McDonald et al., "Prosecutorial Bluffing and the Case against Plea Bargaining," in *Plea Bargaining*, ed. W. McDonald and J. Cramer (Lexington, MA: D.C. Heath, 1980).

9. Hammett and Epstein, "Local Prosecution of Environmental Crime."

10. Rebovich et al., *Environmental Crime Prosecution*.

CHAPTER 10

Sentencing the Environmental Criminal

Mark A. Cohen

TERMS	compliance programs	remedial actions
	environmental audit	strict liability
	four goals of punishment	U.S. Sentencing
	knowing violation	Commission
	negligent	vicarious liability
	overdeterrence	willful

Although there is little disagreement that intentionally dumping hazardous wastes into a body of water should be considered a crime, there is much less agreement on the punishment that should be imposed on an "environmental criminal." To some, environmental crimes are as bad as violent physical assault; a public opinion survey found that knowingly polluting a city's water supply was viewed as just as serious a crime as rape, smuggling heroin, or assault with a gun.[1] Not all environmental crimes, however, are as egregious as intentionally dumping hazardous waste into a body of water. As we will see in this chapter, a company can be charged with an environmental crime when an illegal action is undertaken by one of its employees—even if the action was against company policy. Firms may also be charged with a crime even though an incident was purely accidental or caused by a negligent act (unintentional wrongdoing). Individuals may be sent to jail for filling in an area of land that had been classified as a wetland, even when no net harm to the environment is readily identifiable.

Concern has been expressed about the priority of imposing a substantial jail term for actions in violation of environmental regulations. This chapter reviews both the underlying theory and the practice of imposing penalties on environmental criminals. Before reviewing the actual punishment imposed, we look at the purpose of the criminal law. This will help us understand the type of sanctions used and how they affect the occurrence of environmental criminal behavior.

THE ROLE OF CRIMINAL SANCTIONS

Should criminal sanctions be used to enforce environmental laws that are now generally enforced by regulatory agencies? The traditional reasons for imposing the criminal law on convicted offenders is summarized in the **four goals of punishment**: deterrence, incapacitation, rehabilitation, and retribution. In addition, society might have a more basic reason for making an offense criminal—to impose a moral stigma on certain activities. Let us consider each of these as they apply to the commission of environmental offenses.

Deterrence

The first possible rationale for criminal enforcement of environmental laws is the failure of the regulatory agencies or of private citizens (through court actions) to adequately deter violators. For example, suppose a gas station operator faces the prospects of legally disposing hazardous waste at a cost of $10,000 or illegally disposing of the same waste for $500. Further, suppose the polluter knows she has only a 10 percent chance of being caught and punished for this law violation. Even if she is caught, the penalty for illegal disposal is $25,000. If the gas station operator chooses to illegally dump, it would amount to a savings of approximately $9,500 ($10,000 minus $500) in disposal costs, but the penalties (if caught) would be $25,000. The expected savings is reduced by $2,500 (10 percent [the chances of being caught] of $25,000). Thus, the gas station operator would expect to save $7,000 ($9,500 – $2,500) by dumping the waste illegally. This savings suggests the operator would not be deterred from continuing this illegal practice.[2] In theory, the government could raise the penalty to make sure that illegal dumping no longer "pays." For example, if the fine was increased to $100,000, the expected penalty would now be $10,000 (compared to $9,500 in lower disposal costs). This would make illegal disposal less attractive. Thus, the imposition of a fine is designed to deter individuals or firms from illegal behavior. Further, such a fine could be imposed by the U.S. Environmental Protection Agency (EPA) or civil courts without the need for criminal law at all.

In the above example, it took a fine of $100,000 to deter the gas station operator from illegal disposal. Suppose the owner is only able to pay a fine of $50,000. Anything beyond that amount would force the company into bankruptcy. In that case, the expected fine from dumping is only $5,000 (10 percent of $50,000), and illegal dumping once again looks attractive. Fines are no longer an adequate deterrence in this instance. Instead, jail or prison sentences might be needed to adequately deter the owner from dumping waste illegally. This suggests that the jail or prison sentences—and hence the threat of criminal law—might be needed for those offenses that cause very large harm or result in very large illegal gains to the offender.[3]

Incapacitation, Rehabilitation, and Retribution

In addition to deterrence, legal scholars traditionally distinguish three other goals of criminal punishment: incapacitation, rehabilitation, and retribution. Prison is an obvious means of incapacitation, because it takes criminals out of society and therefore prevents them from committing other violations. While an individual may be prevented from committing future criminal offenses, a corporation cannot be sent to prison. Although a corporation cannot be imprisoned, other incapacitative sanctions can be imposed. Examples of incapacitative sanctions that could prevent corporations from committing future crimes include debarment from future dealings with the government and revocation of a permit necessary for participating in a given activity.

At the present time, rehabilitation has fallen out of favor within the criminal justice system as a punishment philosophy because the system has failed to demonstrate an ability to reform repeat criminal offenders. Despite this, however, rehabilitation remains one of the objectives of criminal law. In the context of corporate crimes, considerable discussion has taken place about the possibility of "rehabilitating" a corporation. One method of rehabilitation would be to impose changes in the corporate management structure by instituting **compliance programs** (programs to induce compliance with the legal standards), for example.

The final punishment philosophy in criminal law is retribution. Criminal sanctions may also serve the goal of retribution. The idea behind retribution is that punishment is administered because the offender, as a result of his or her action, deserves to be punished.

It is important to note that except for the problem of bankruptcy, mentioned in the example above, all of these goals can just as easily be served through a combination of civil and administrative remedies. Thus, some commentators have questioned whether or not the criminal law is needed to enforce most regulatory offenses.[4] One reason to use the criminal law instead of relying on administrative or civil actions is that criminal sanctions might serve another purpose—to shape preferences and "educate" potential violators about the moral consequences of their actions.[5]

This moral component of the criminal law has traditionally been an important one. In order to be called a crime, an activity must generally involve an intentional act that causes or is intended to cause harm. Thus, if an automobile driver accidentally hits a pedestrian, it would be considered a tort, and the driver could be sued for damages. On the other hand, if the driver intentionally hit a pedestrian, a crime would have been committed. As we have seen in previous chapters, this traditional definition of a crime is not always followed in the case of environmental crimes. Instead, some environmental crimes can be committed without any intent on the part of the offender. In these cases, the moral component might be lacking, and the only question is whether noncriminal sanctions are adequate or if a more punitive criminal sanction is needed.

CAN ENVIRONMENTAL VIOLATIONS BE OVERCRIMINALIZED?

When a violent criminal mugs someone in the street, he or she is not engaging in any socially beneficial activity. Society would be better off if criminals never stalked innocent victims on the street. On the other hand, when a company pollutes in violation of its permitted levels or illegally dumps a hazardous waste, these activities are usually byproducts of socially beneficial activities. Although society might not want an automobile factory to emit pollution, it does not want to stop automobile production. So, while society has an important interest in reducing pollution and deterring illegal environmental activities, society also has an interest in ensuring that the requirements for complying and the penalties for not complying are not so severe that firms are inhibited from engaging in socially beneficial activities, such as the production of automobiles.

Recent trends in criminal law have caused many commentators to wonder if environmental violations have become overcriminalized. The concern is that high penalties will lead to **overdeterrence** for activities that society does not wish to prohibit entirely. For example, consider the case of oil spills. If the price of causing an oil spill is increased so high that firms do not engage in the shipping of oil, society is adversely affected. Further, it would not be advantageous for oil tankers to spend more than a socially desirable amount of their resources trying to ensure that adequate oil spill prevention safeguards exist. Finally, we do not want firms to spend an inordinate amount of their time and energy making sure they are not falsely accused of committing a crime. As discussed in the next section, environmental crimes have been defined so broadly that the risk of overdeterrence is a reality.

INSIGHT

Juvenile Treatment Goes Green

The Department of Justice (DOJ) and the Department of the Interior (DOI) have combined resources to create the Youth Environmental Service (YES) initiative. "The purpose of the YES initiative is to increase the capacity of states and communities to correct, treat, and rehabilitate adjudicated delinquents and to prevent at risk youth from entering the juvenile justice system by implementing environmental work and education programs on federally owned land."[1(p.1)]

Funding for YES programs is provided by the states and local communities. Partnerships are formed among federal, state, local, and private agencies to develop the work programs. The local communities are given wide latitude to develop programs that are catered to the specific community needs. Once the funding has been established, DOJ and DOI work with the communities to identify federal land and facilities that can support the programs.

By September 1994 six pilot programs had been established: two in Washington, D.C., two in Utah, and two in Florida.

---

1. R.C. Cronin, "Youth Environmental Service (YES) in Action: Program Summary," Office of Juvenile Justice and Delinquency Prevention (OJJDP), Office of Justice Programs, June 1996, 1.

CRIMINAL PROVISIONS FOR ENVIRONMENTAL OFFENSES

Virtually all environmental statutes include criminal provisions. They generally fall into two distinct categories: (1) "strict liability" or "public welfare" offenses and (2) offenses requiring some degree of knowing, willful, or negligent conduct. As has been discussed earlier, **strict liability** offenses do not require intent or even negligence to be shown. If an incident happens, the individuals or the company responsible can be held criminally liable regardless of their moral culpability. The original Refuse Act of 1899 made discharging refuse in navigable waters a public welfare offense, since it imposes criminal liability on a party who discharged refuse into navigable waters. Most of the subsequent environmental legislation, however, has failed to impose such a strict liability standard. Instead, the Clean Water Act provides for criminal sanctions when a discharge is willful or negligent.

Even though the terms **willful** or **negligent** might be used, the latter term is broad enough to allow prosecutors to charge firms with criminal negligence for failure to adequately prevent accidental oil discharges, as in the case of the Exxon Valdez oil spill. In contrast, the Clean Air Act does not contain a criminal negligence provision. Instead, the violation must involve a knowing conduct in order to be criminal. Not surprisingly, there have been fewer criminal prosecutions under the Clean Air Act than under the Clean Water Act.

Many of the other environmental laws (including RCRA, TSCA, the Safe Drinking Water Act, and FIFRA) impose a **knowing violation** standard, suggesting that some degree of intent or culpability must be present. However, case law now appears to define *knowing* broadly enough to include knowledge of the hazardous nature of the pollutant, not just knowledge of the actual violation. Thus, defendants can be charged with an environmental crime even if they do not know (or do not even have reason to know) the waste was being illegally disposed of after it left their hands.[6]

Under federal laws, corporations can be held criminally liable for virtually any illegal action by their agency or employees if the act takes place within their employment, even if the employees' actions were in direct conflict with company policy or management's orders. Some (but not all) state laws follow the federal law on the issue of **vicarious liability**.

Corporate officers may also incur criminal liability for the actions of their employees, even if they did not participate in the criminal activity themselves. For statutory violations requiring some degree of knowledge or willful conduct, individual liability will generally be applied to corporate officers who somehow failed to prevent, authorized, or tacitly acquiesced in a crime.[7] For public welfare (strict liability) or negligence statutes, individual criminal liability might be established solely on the basis that the offender was ultimately responsible for the activity, even if that responsibility was delegated.

SANCTIONS FOR ENVIRONMENTAL CRIMINALS

Environmental criminals are subject to many different types of sanctions and varying degrees of punishment. Not all sanctions imposed on environmental criminals are meted out by a criminal court. In fact, some of the largest penalties against environmental criminals may originate from actions taken by private parties, not by government prosecutors. This section reviews the types and magnitude of sanctions for environmental criminals.

The sentences handed down to environmental criminals have changed dramatically over time, and they continue to evolve as new crimes are defined and as public attitudes toward environmental offenses change. Although the Refuse Act of 1899 made it a criminal offense to discharge any refuse into navigable waters, few environmental offenses were prosecuted using that provision until the early 1970s.[8] Even then, in the decade of the 1970s, only 25 criminal environmental cases were prosecuted at the federal level.[9] The 1980s brought about significant changes in criminal enforcement of environmental offenses. The EPA established an Office of Criminal Enforcement, and the Justice Department established an Environmental Crimes Unit in the Land's Division in 1981. In the mid-1980s, Congress reclassified environmental crimes from misdemeanors to felonies.[10] The number of prosecutions has increased dramatically since that time, with the total reaching more than 250 in fiscal year 1995. Even more significant is the fact that more than 800 individuals and 350 corporations have been convicted, and a total of 350 years of actual jail time has been served since 1983.[11]

Types of Offenses and Offenders

Approximately 50 percent of federal prosecutions have involved violations of RCRA or CERCLA provisions. This indicates that most federal prosecutions are in response to the illegal disposal of hazardous waste. The second largest category (25 percent) comprises violations of the Clean Water Act. The remaining prosecutions are for false statements (12 percent) and TSCA (5 percent), Clean Air Act (4 percent), and FIFRA (3 percent) violations.[12] Although no comprehensive data are available outside the federal arena, a recent study of local prosecutors reported similar findings: that nearly half of the respondents reported that more than 50 percent of the prosecutions involved hazardous wastes.[13]

Most federal prosecutions of organizations for environmental crimes involve small, closely held corporations. Only about 40 percent of these companies are large enough to be listed in the Standard and Poor's Register, which requires annual sales of $1 million and 50 employees. Fewer had traded stock.[14] About half of all individuals indicted for environmental crimes are either owners, presidents, corporate officers, vice-presidents, or directors. Management and supervisory personnel constitute another 29 percent, and the remaining 19 percent were nonsupervisory personnel.[15]

Sentencing Guidelines

Until the passage of the Crime Control Act of 1984, judges had complete discretion over the sentences they imposed as long as they did not exceed the statutory maximum penalty. Thus, even if a violation called for a prison sentence of up to 10 years, a judge could decide to impose as little as six months or no jail time at all. There was no guarantee that similar offenses would be treated in a similar manner, and many judges were reluctant to send white-collar offenders to jail. This system led to a bipartisan call for an independent regulatory body. The **U.S. Sentencing Commission** was formed in 1986 to write guidelines for sentencing federal offenders. The commission published its first set of guidelines in November 1987. Since the law's basic purpose was to reduce judicial disparity, judges are required to apply the guideline sentence range for crimes committed after that date. Any departures from the guideline range must be explained in writing and are subject to appeal by either the government or the defendant.

Following a congressional mandate to increase sentences for white-collar offenders, the commission specifically set jail terms for individuals convicted of many white-collar offenses (including environmental crimes) at levels above past practice. In particular, the commission significantly increased both the probability of going to jail and the length of the jail term for most white-collar offenses.

Under the sentencing guidelines, the mandatory jail term for a person convicted of an "ongoing, continuous, or repetitive discharge, release or emission of a pollutant into the environment . . . without a permit or in violation of a permit" is 21–27 months. If the pollutant is hazardous, toxic, or a pesticide, this minimum is increased to 27–33 months. Further, if substantial cleanup expenditures are required, another 12–18 months is added to this range.[16] Other aggravating factors (such as prior criminal history) may also increase the sentence. In some cases, it is possible to reduce the sentence below the minimum levels mentioned above. If the defendant "clearly demonstrates a recognition and affirmative acceptance of personal responsibility for his criminal conduct," the guidelines sentence is reduced by about 6 months.[17] It is also possible to obtain a reduction of 6 months to 1 year if the person is only a minor or minimal participant in a larger group committing the criminal offense.[18] Finally, judges are permitted to depart from the guidelines if they desire for cases involving negligent conduct as opposed to knowing conduct.[19] Given the apparent broad interpretation of the knowing conduct standard, however, such departure rarely occurs.[20]

In 1991, the commission wrote guidelines for organizations convicted of federal crimes; the guidelines called for substantially increased penalties and higher reliance on terms of probation for corporations. Although the terms of probation applied to all crimes, the monetary fine provisions adopted in 1991 failed to include environmental crimes. At the time, the commission decided to study environmental crimes more thoroughly, as they were thought to be much different from other types of corporate crime, such as antitrust violations or fraud, which involve monetary harms only. Despite several attempts to arrive at a consensus, the commission has not yet adopted guidelines for monetary penalties for corporations convicted of environmental crimes.

Sentences for Environmental Criminals

Individuals and firms convicted of environmental crimes face various penalties, including (1) monetary criminal fines and other monetary payments to government agencies or others affected by the firm's actions, (2) nonmonetary penalties, and (3) jail sentences for individuals. Each is discussed in detail below.

Monetary Sanctions

Most individuals convicted of environmental crimes receive monetary penalties of $10,000 or less. The average fine is less than $15,000, and the maximum is reported to be $200,000.[21] Criminal fines for organizations convicted of environmental offenses are highest, with the median being about $50,000 and the mean fine being closer to $200,000 (the wide discrepancy is due to several recent cases in which the fines have exceeded $1 million). Multimillion-dollar fines appear to be reserved for large corporations, such as recent fines imposed on Exxon, International Paper, U.S. Sugar, and United Technologies. To date, the largest fine appears to have been levied against Exxon Corporation and its wholly owned Exxon Shipping Corporation after the Valdez oil spill. Exxon paid a total of $25 million

INSIGHT

Panda Pelts Can Bring Prison Time[1]

Giant pandas, currently numbering about 1,000 in the wild, are at risk of extinction. Chinese poachers may face the death penalty if they are caught poaching, but over 200 people have been arrested for illegal dealings in panda skins. *National Geographic* reported a prison sentence of 12 years for Wu Hui Yuan when he decided to buy and then resell a giant panda pelt. With the help of an associate, Wu Hui Yuan set up a meeting to sell the fur for approximately 200,000 yuan (about $37,000). When the money was exchanged, the police raided the room and arrested both men. For his assistance in the crime, Wu Hui Yuan's associate was sentenced to 8 years in prison.

---

1. "Sale of Panda's Pelt Brings Prison Term," *National Geographic*, October 1992.

in criminal fines plus $100 million in restitution to the federal government and Alaska.[22]

Firms convicted of corporate crimes are subject to penalties outside the criminal realm that may be just as punitive (if not more so). For example, in 1988 Ashland Oil accidentally discharged more than 500,000 gallons of oil into the Monongahela River near Pittsburgh. The firm was ordered to pay $2.25 million in federal criminal fines and agreed to pay $4.66 million to the state of Pennsylvania. The latter amount included reimbursement for state cleanup expenditures as well as civil penalties. Ashland also paid more than $44 million in civil settlements and $11 million in direct cleanup costs, and it reportedly spent more than $5.25 million in legal and administrative fees to handle the various class-action suits filed against the company.[23,24] Ashland's experience with the noncriminal side of monetary sanctions is typical.

Nonmonetary Criminal Sanctions for Organizations

Although monetary penalties may be substantial, in some cases they can be dwarfed by the effect of nonmonetary sanctions on organizations convicted of environmental crimes. Nonmonetary sanctions include corporate probation, suspension or debarment from government contracts, and other nontraditional forms of punishment. Probation may involve explicit requirements that a firm hire a compliance officer, institute new compliance procedures (including an **environmental audit**), and provide periodic reports to the sentencing court—all at the firm's expense. In some cases these provisions may last up to five years. In addition, firms may be temporarily suspended or permanently debarred from participation in government contracts under the Clean Water Act and Clean Air Act. Federal agencies are prohibited from entering into new contracts with convicted firms. Although these suspensions usually apply to the facilities that actually committed the crime, the EPA may apply a suspension to the entire company. Finally, judges may occasionally impose other nontraditional forms of sanctions, such as community service requirements, public apologies placed in newspapers, or sponsorship of various environmental programs.[25] For example, Transit Mix Concrete Company pleaded guilty to knowingly discharging pollutants into a tributary of the Arkansas River without a permit. The judge ordered the firm to spend $55,000 on a community service project and made the suggestion that the money be spent on improving hiking trails near the river.[26]

In some rare cases, the government may require forfeiture of assets or even the complete dissolution of a company. At least one state prosecutor has reportedly used forfeiture statutes to confiscate property such as garbage trucks and bulldozers used in illegal waste disposal operations.[27] The ultimate sanction of "capital punishment" (divestiture of all net assets) is mandated by the sentencing guidelines for organizations that "operated primarily for a criminal purpose or primarily by criminal means."[28(p.357)]

Prison Sentences for Convicted Environmental Criminals

As stated above, the federal sentencing guidelines went into effect for crimes committed after November 1, 1987. Prior to that time, only about 30 percent of convicted individuals received actual jail time. For those individuals receiving a jail sentence, the average length was about seven months. Under the new sentencing guidelines, virtually all persons convicted of knowing conduct violations under federal environmental statutes will spend time in jail or prison. As noted earlier, the legal standard for a knowing conduct violation is very broad. Thus, convicted individuals will be excepted from serving a term of imprisonment only in the case of negligence or strict liability violations that do not involve ongoing or repetitive problems or hazardous releases. "Minor participants" in a violation involving more senior corporate executives might also be spared jail time.

Despite the fact that individuals may be held liable for criminal offenses that are charged under theories of strict liability or negligence, few cases of nonintentional offenses result in imprisonment. For example, Pennwalt and its plant manager in Tacoma, Washington, notified the Coast Guard of a discharge of a hazardous substance. According to the prosecutor, "although a call was made the evening of the tank rupture to the local office of the U.S. Coast Guard, it transmitted to the government the information that there had been a spill of sodium chlorate solution but there was not mention of the fact that the material contained sodium dichromate, which was required by law to be reported."[29(p.14)] Although the plant manager faced up to nine years in jail and a fine of $650,000,[30] the judge fined him $5,000 and sentenced him to two years' probation.[31]

Noncriminal Sanctions for Corporate Crime

Individuals and organizations convicted of environmental crimes are subject to many sanctions outside the criminal law—both formal and informal. Examples of these sanctions include (1) noncriminal fines and court-awarded damages or settlement, (2) nonmonetary sanctions imposed by government agencies, (3) corporate or officer liability to shareholders, and (4) loss in reputation.

Aside from criminal fines, individuals and organizations may be fined by government regulatory agencies such as the EPA, often with enforcement through civil court actions. In a study of 84 companies sentenced for environmental crimes between 1985 and 1990, it was found that the noncriminal portion of the average fine exceeded the criminal fine ($182,000 in criminal fines and $261,000 in additional noncriminal penalties).[32]

Another source of monetary penalties consists of private tort actions taken on behalf of those who are injured as a result of an environmental offense. Unfortunately, it is extremely difficult to obtain reliable information on the frequency and magnitude of private tort cases related to corporate criminal offenses. One well-publicized case was against Orkin, a pesticide manufacturer found guilty of violating FIFRA following two deaths that resulted from the misuse of a pesticide. Orkin was fined $500,000 and ordered to perform 2,000 hours of community service. In addition, there was a significant private settlement awarded to the families of the victims.[33]

In many instances, a firm that is found guilty of a federal crime may be subject to ancillary nonmonetary sanctions imposed by other government agencies. For example, firms convicted of environmental crimes might be barred (temporarily or permanently) from bidding on government procurement programs. The debarment may apply to either the part of an organization involved in the offense or the entire company. In some cases, the Clean Air Act and the Clean Water Act actually prohibit federal government agencies from doing business with firms convicted of violations of those acts.

Although **remedial actions** and environmental audits are often part of a negotiated settlement arrangement between the guilty party and the EPA, sometimes other agencies, such as the Securities and Exchange Commission (SEC), may impose similar requirements on convicted offenders. In one well-publicized incident, the SEC issued a complaint against Allied Chemical Corporation for discharging toxic chemicals, including Kepone, into the environment from its own facilities and from the facilities of others. During the time that Allied was discharging toxic chemicals, it knew that tests showed animal and marine life was suffering from the adverse effects of Kepone. As a result, Allied was facing the possibility of substantial financial liabilities. Allied was found to have failed to disclose such potential financial exposure in its reports to shareholders and the investing public in violation of the antifraud and reporting provisions of the securities laws.[34] An injunction required Allied Chemical to undergo an independent environmental audit intended to inform the SEC on the state of its compliance programs and any other outstanding environmental risks. It also was slapped with a permanent injunction for failure to report to shareholders about future environmental risks.

A third sanction is corporate and officer liability to investors. Shareholders of companies may file derivative lawsuits seeking to recover the loss in

INSIGHT

The Kepone Disaster[1]

From 1966 until 1974, Allied Chemical manufactured Kepone in something called the Semi-Works, in Hopewell, Virginia. Beginning in 1974, Life Sciences Products manufactured Kepone for Allied. Allied bought the raw ingredients and shipped them to Life Sciences, and then Life Sciences would formulate the Kepone and sell the finished product to Allied.

In July 1975, the Virginia Department of Health closed the plant, and it closed the James River shortly after. At that time, Kepone was an active ingredient in roach bait and was used to kill roaches, potato beetles, and banana root borers, for example. It had an extraordinarily long life expectancy. Once the chemical got into an animal or fish, it would stay in the fatty tissue and just keep reprocessing. It would never flush out of the system.

An additional problem was the way the Life Sciences plant had been operating. The manager and the director of research had all of the information they needed to run a safe plant, but they engaged in unsafe practices. For example, if they had a bad batch of Kepone, they would take the hose from the batch and put it into the sanitary sewer. As a result, thousands and thousands of pounds of Kepone would hit the sewage treatment system at one time. The processing of the chemicals eventually destroyed the treatment plant.

Further, the company had passed memos back and forth that demonstrated knowledge of the regulations for hazardous chemicals and acknowledgment that compliance might cost the company a lot of money. Finally, the company decided the best thing to do was to do nothing. Four people were involved. Two pleaded guilty, and two were acquitted at trial. The counts against the two who pleaded guilty were dismissed. None of them ended up with convictions.

Three separate criminal proceedings came out of this case. The first was *United States v. Allied Chemical Corporation*, and the defendants included certain named Allied employees. There were 941 counts. Allied pleaded *nolo contendere* to 940 counts. The judge in the case explained that the *nolo* plea was tantamount to a guilty plea. The defendants were fined $13.24 million. Count 941 was a conspiracy charge, and it was dismissed.

The second was *United States v. Life Sciences Products*, and the defendants included company officers and the City of Hopewell. Allied was included as an aider and abettor, but it was acquitted. The city of Hopewell was fined $10,000 and placed on probation. Life Sciences was fined $3 million, and the Life Sciences officers (the plant manager and the director of research) were fined $25,000 each. The third criminal prosecution was *United States v. Life Sciences, Allied, and Life Sciences' Officers*. Allied was acquitted and Life Sciences was fined $10,000.

In addition to the criminal suits, several civil suits were filed. Two suits were from watermen and fishermen. Other suits came from employees at the facility. Many of these cases were settled out of court. The Commonwealth of Virginia sued Allied, Life Sciences, and Life Sciences' officers. That case was also settled.

---

1. W.W. Berryhill, moderator, "Allied Chemical, the Kepone Incident, and the Settlements: Twenty Years Later," *University of Richmond Law Review* 29 (1995): 493–520.

share values or recoup fines and other costs related to criminal prosecutions.[35] For example, a few years ago a group of investors filed a class-action suit claiming that "Waste Management, Inc. and several of its managing officers misrepresented or withheld information concerning the company's compliance with environmental regulations and disputes with regulatory authorities."[36(p.399)] The firm apparently settled the case for $11.4 million.[37] It is thought several such suits were filed in the Exxon Valdez case.[38]

The last noncriminal-law sanction is the loss of reputation. Firms convicted of crimes may suffer a loss in reputation and future business. There is growing evidence that the marketplace does indeed penalize firms for fraudulent activity.[39] Although this reputation loss is expected to be more prevalent where the victims of the crime were customers than in cases of regulatory violations such as pollution, it is possible that certain types of environmental offenses will result in marketplace penalty. For example, a firm convicted of falsifying documents might be viewed by customers as untrustworthy. Likewise, a firm convicted of negligently discharging hazardous wastes due to improper safety precautions may be viewed with some concern by customers who are in need of a high-quality product. Some major corporations have instituted "supplier policies" and choose suppliers partly on the basis of their environmental performance, including their use of recycled materials and their record of compliance with environmental laws. Thus, firms convicted of environmental crimes may lose large corporate customers. The growth in "green investing" and environmentally conscious mutual funds may also lead to reduced demand for a convicted firm's stock. There is even a possibility of consumer boycotts of companies with a bad environmental record.[40,41] All of these factors combined might lead to important marketplace penalties for companies convicted of committing an environmental crime. Although these potential marketplace penalties can be identified and some evidence suggests concern about the environment is having a significant effect on consumer attitudes, further studies are necessary to determine the magnitude and significance of this form of punishment.

IS THE UNITED STATES OVERCRIMINALIZING ENVIRONMENTAL VIOLATIONS?

Despite overwhelming public support for imposing criminal sanctions for environmental offenses, there is considerable concern that criminalization in this area has gone too far. Especially questionable is the use of imprisonment for individual offenders who violate strict liability or negligence standards or do not engage in egregious violations that cause significant environmental harms and the application of a vicarious liability standard in prosecuting corporations under federal criminal laws.

When considering imprisonment for strict liability, negligence, and nonharmful environmental offenses, one must consider the impact of the sentencing guidelines passed in 1987. Prosecutors began to bring cases against individuals who might never have gone to jail in the preguidelines era, and the higher incarceration rates and lengthy jail sentences have become extremely controversial. To see why incarceration for some environmental offenders is so controversial, consider one of the earliest environmental cases brought under the new guidelines. John Pozsgai "was charged with 41 counts of systematically filling a 14-acre tract of land, despite repeated warning by inspectors of the Corps of Engineers that such activity required a permit under the Clean Water Act."[42(p.146)] Following the sentencing guidelines, the judge sentenced him to 27 months in jail with no parole. According to one critic of this sentence, although Pozsgai did not obtain a permit despite repeated warnings, his offense was probably beneficial from an environmental standpoint. "The government does not dispute that the tiny stream adjacent to the property actually runs clearer due to Mr. Pozsgai's cleanup efforts."[43(p.146)] Further, "before the guidelines were promulgated, no person ever was imprisoned for discharging nontoxic, nonhazardous pollutants."[44(p.146)] This matter was appealed all the way to the U.S. Supreme Court, which refused to review the case.

In another case, Ocie and Carey Mills filled in a vacant lot with sand after having more than a year of discussions with the Army Corps of Engineers and the State of Florida's Department of Environmental Resources about whether or not their property was a wetland. Although the corps considered their property to be a wetland, Florida did not. The Mills were later sentenced to 21 months in jail for filling in a wetland.[45]

Wetlands prosecutions raise important questions about the appropriate use of criminal sanctions. Prosecutors tend to view these cases as straightforward violations of regulatory standards. According to one defense attorney, however, "The biggest problems with the definition of wetlands is that it is virtually impossible for an ordinary citizen to know whether property is wetland or not. Farmers face jail time and huge fines for plowing fields unless they first spend thousands of dollars on consultants to help determine what is and what is not a wetland. Even with the assurance of a consultant, there is no guarantee that the corps will agree."[46] The Pozsgai and Mills cases and others like them raise concerns about the fairness of environmental criminal law and the risk of overdeterrence by using the criminal law to enforce uncertain legal standards.

The second concern about using criminal law in certain environmental cases involves vicarious corporate liability. As noted earlier, under federal law (and under many state laws) a company is held strictly liable for a crime committed on its behalf by an employee—even if the action went against company policy or a supervisor's orders. Although few would argue against holding firms strictly liable for reasonable cleanup costs and third-party damages, punitive sanctions in such cases are another matter. To see why this is so controversial, consider the case of Eagle Picher, a company that was convicted of illegally disposing of hazardous waste. The hazardous waste was dumped by an employee against company policy, and the firm removed the barrels immediately upon learning of the violation. After the company pleaded guilty to a CERCLA violation for failure to notify, the judge fined the company $3,500.[47]

Prior to the advent of sentencing guidelines, judges had wide discretion in determining the sentence, as long as it was below the statutory maximum (or above the minimum in the few instances in which mandatory minimum sentences exist). Although one of the reasons for establishing the sentencing commission was to reduce unwarranted discretion and to ensure that similar crimes were treated in a similar manner, reducing discretion also eliminated a powerful check on prosecutorial discretion. For example, prosecuted in the preguideline era, Eagle Picher was given a slap on the wrist and fined after being charged with a crime for an employee's act that was clearly against company policy. The plant manager at Pennwalt who immediately notified the Coast Guard of an accidental spill (but unknowingly misreported the size and contents of the spill) was given a suspended sentence and a $5,000 fine by the sentencing judge. These sentences gave important signals to prosecutors about which cases they should pursue in the future. Under the current sentencing guidelines, however, the Pennwalt manager would likely have been sentenced to a term of about two years in jail. Eagle Picher might have paid hundreds of thousands of dollars in fines despite its good faith effort to discourage illegal activity among its employees. Unless sentencing guidelines provide for lenient treatment of individuals who act in good faith and significant reductions in fines are provided for companies held liable for employee actions despite their good faith effort to prevent those violations, overdeterrence is a real risk.

WHAT IS WRONG WITH OVERCRIMINALIZING ENVIRONMENTAL VIOLATIONS?

Two fundamental problems result from overcriminalizing environmental violations. First, as discussed above, imposing punitive criminal penalties might result in overdeterrence. In the case of Eagle Picher, for example, the company cannot guarantee an employee will never violate the law against company policy. To achieve that level of compliance would be too costly and in some cases might result in shutting down production facilities altogether. Second, by criminalizing minor infractions, criminal law risks becoming trivialized. If every action that harms society is a crime, criminal law loses its one distinguishing characteristic—the moral stigma attached to being labeled a criminal. Without that moral stigma, people might have much less respect for environmental laws and might be less apt to care about violations that are truly egregious.

The debate about the use of criminal sanctions in environmental enforcement actions is ongoing. Discussion of controversial issues is essential to ensure all the dimensions of each issue are covered. While many would argue the sentencing guidelines have accomplished their intended objective by increasing the number of people who receive jail time, others have been offended by the "silliness" of sending to prison someone who violated the Clean Water Act but in fact made a stream cleaner in the process. Strict standards provide a structure for making sanctions consistent for similar kinds of crimes. When environmental crimes are considered, however, violations can be difficult to classify effectively.

REVIEW QUESTIONS

1. Explain the purpose of an environmental audit.
2. How do the United States Sentencing Guidelines affect convicted environmental criminals?
3. How might criminalization of environmental violations result in overdeterrence, and why would that be a problem?
4. If an employee, without the knowledge of his or her employer, intentionally dumps hazardous chemicals into a waterway, could the employer be held responsible?

DISCUSSION QUESTIONS

1. Examine the four traditional goals of punishment and explain how they relate to the treatment of environmental criminals.
2. Many argue that the sentences given traditional criminals are not appropriate for environmental criminals. Do you agree or disagree? Justify your response.
3. If you agree that traditional sentences are inappropriate for environmental offenders, what alternatives would you recommend for sanctioning environmental offenders?
4. Should environmental criminals be sentenced to prison? Explain the dilemma faced by the criminal justice system.

REFERENCES

1. M.E. Wolfgang et al., "The National Survey of Crime Severity," NCJ-96017 (June 1985). The four scenarios alluded to are as follows: (1) a factory knowingly gets rids of its waste in a way that pollutes the water supply of a city. As a result, 20 people become ill but do not require medical treatment. (2) A man forcibly rapes a woman. She requires treatment by a doctor but not hospitalization. (3) A person smuggles heroin into the country. (4) A person intentionally shoots a victim with a gun. The victim requires treatment by a doctor but not hospitalization.

2. See G. Becker, "Crime and Punishment: An Economic Approach," *Journal of Political Economy* 76 (1968): 169–217, for a discussion of "optimal penalties" and deterrence.

3. S. Shavell, "Criminal Law and the Optimal Use of Non-monetary Sanctions as a Deterrent," *Columbia Law Review* 85 (1985): 1232, 1236–1237. This article discusses the factors that determine whether or not monetary fines alone will optimally deter individuals: (1) size of assets/wealth, (2) probability of detection and conviction, (3) size of private benefits from illegal activity, (4) probability that activity will cause harm, and (5) size distribution of the harm if it occurs.

4. J.C. Coffee, "Does 'Unlawful' Mean 'Criminal'?: Reflections on the Disappearing Tort/ Crime Distinction in American Law," *Boston University Law Review* 71 (1991): 193–246.

5. K.G. Dau-Schmidt, "An Economic Analysis of the Criminal Law as a Preference-shaping Policy," *Duke Law Journal* 1 (1990): 1–38.

6. J.F. Cooney et al., "Criminal Enforcement of Environmental Laws: Part II," *Environmental Law Reporter* 25 (1995): 10525, 19532. On the other hand, if an individual shows he or she has made a good faith effort to ensure the waste was properly disposed of, this might be an adequate defense.

7. "Individual Criminal Liability of Corporate Officers under Federal Environmental Laws," *Environment Reporter*, 9 June 1989, 340.

8. R.M. Carter, "Federal Enforcement of Individual and Corporate Criminal Liability for Water Pollution," *Memphis State University Law Review* 10 (1980): 576–611.

9. F.H. Habicht II, "The Federal Perspective on Environmental Criminal Enforcement: How To Remain on the Civil Side," *Environmental Law Reporter* 17 (1987): 10478. Although comparable estimates are not available for state criminal enforcement actions, they appear to have followed similar trends.

10. J.W. Starr and T.J. Kelly Jr., "Environmental Crimes and the Sentencing Guidelines: The Time Has Come . . . and It Is Hard Time," *Environmental Law Review* 20 (1990): 10096. These new felony provisions were part of the reauthorized Clean Water Act (1987) and the Resource Conservation and Recovery Act (1986).

11. P. Hutchins, "Environmental Criminal Statistics FY83 through FY95," Department of Justice, Environmental Crimes Section, memo, December 13, 1995.

12. M.A. Cohen, "Environmental Crime and Punishment: Legal/Economic Theory and Empirical Evidence on Enforcement of Federal Environmental Statutes," *Journal of Criminal Law and Criminology* 82 (1992): 1054–1108, 1073, Table 1.

13. National Institute of Justice, *Environmental Crime Prosecution: Results of a National Survey*, NCJ-150310 (Washington, DC: U.S. Government Printing Office, December 1994).

14. Cohen, "Environmental Crime and Punishment," 1074, note 12.

15. Cohen, "Environmental Crime and Punishment," 1075, Table 2.

16. U.S. Sentencing Commission, *Guidelines Manual* (2.139, 2.141, Washington, DC: U.S. Government Printing Office, 1994), 2Q1.2 and 2Q1.3.

17. U.S. Sentencing Commission, *Guidelines Manual*, 3E1.1 (Acceptance of Responsibility).

18. U.S. Sentencing Commission, *Guidelines Manual*, 3B1.2 (Mitigating Role).

19. U.S. Sentencing Commission, *Guidelines Manual*, 2Q1.2, comment, note 4.

20. According to U.S. Sentencing Commission, *Annual Report, 1993* (Washington, DC: U.S. Government Printing Office, 1994), downward departures were granted in about 6.3 percent of environmental and wildlife cases between October 1, 1992, and September 30, 1993.

21. The median and mean fine estimates are taken from Cohen, "Environmental Crime and Punishment," 1085, Table 5, note 12.

22. U.S. Environmental Protection Agency, Office of Criminal Enforcement, "Summary of Criminal Prosecutions Resulting from Enforcement Investigations: Fiscal Years 1983 through 1992," undated report.

23. "Ashland To Pay $4.7 Million in Spill," *Los Angeles Times*, 23 November 1989, D1.

24. "In Brief," *Corporate Crime Reporter*, 12 March 1990, 1082–1084.

25. See Cohen "Environmental Crime and Punishment," note 12, for examples of cases involving nontraditional criminal sanctions.

26. U.S. Environmental Protection Agency, Office of Criminal Enforcement, "Summary of Criminal Prosecutions Resulting from Enforcement Investigations," 99, note 22.

27. "EPA Enforcement Officials Outline Plans To Bolster against Corporate Polluters," *Environment Reporter*, 27 April 1990, 2012, citing John Kaye, prosecutor for Monmouth County, NJ.

28. U.S. Sentencing Commission, *Guidelines Manual* (Washington, DC: U.S. Government Printing Office, November 1991), 8C1.1, 357.

29. Interview with David Vance Marshall, *Corporate Crime Reporter*, 14 August 1989, 14.

30. J. Abramson, "Government Cracks Down on Environmental Crimes," *Wall Street Journal*, 16 February 1989, B1.

31. U.S. Environmental Protection Agency, Office of Criminal Enforcement, "Summary of Criminal Prosecutions Resulting from Enforcement Investigations," 85, note 22.

32. See Cohen, "Environmental Crime and Punishment," 1085, Table 5, note 12. Note, however, that since there were a few large noncriminal fines, the median was actually lower than the criminal fine ($13,859 versus $50,000).

33. "Pest Control Company Fined $500,00 in Death of Couple," *New York Times*, 18 November 1988, B7.

34. *SEC v. Allied Chemical Corporation*, SEC Civil No. 77-373, Litigation Release No. 7811 (March 4, 1977).

35. D.A. Bailey, "Legal Liabilities: The Director as Polluter," *Directors and Boards* 15 (Summer 1991): 40–42.

36. *Stanley V. Grossman et al. v. Waste Management, Inc., et al.* 589 F. Supp. 395 (June 14, 1984), 399.

37. "Waste Firm Settling Class Action," *Chicago Tribune*, 30 May 1985, C1.

38. "Getting Ready for Exxon vs. Practically Everybody," *Business Week*, 25 September 1989, 190.

39. For example, a study by Jonathan Karpoff and John R. Lott Jr. ["The Reputational Penalty Firms Bear from Committing Criminal Fraud," *Journal of Law and Economics* 36 (1993): 757] examined 71 firms that had been engaged in fraudulent activity and found a 3.5 percent loss in market share in 30 days following public announcements of investigations or prosecutions. However, the largest losses were suffered by firms who reported fraudulent financial statements. Losses for government and consumer fraud were smaller—although still significant.

40. According to an article in *Fortune*, "Not long after the March accident in Valdez, Alaska, 41 percent of Americans were angry enough to say they'd seriously consider boycotting the company" [D. Kirkpatrick, "Environmentalism: The New Crusade," *Fortune*, 12 February 1990, 44]. However, this apparently had little long-term effect on Exxon's sales. In contrast, the boycott of tuna due to concern for the safety of dolphins had an obvious effect on firms who did not want a tarnished reputation (see note 41).

41. J. Makower, *The E-Factor: The Bottom-Line Approach to Environmentally Responsible Business* (New York: Penguin, 1994), 103–106. Makower argues by way of examples that a relatively small number of individuals can generate a significant amount of media attention and publicity for a firm.

42. P.D. Kamenar, "Proposed Corporate Guidelines for Environmental Offenses," *Federal Sentencing Reporter* 3 (1990): 146.

43. Kamenar, "Proposed Corporate Guidelines for Environmental Offenses," 146.

44. Kamenar, "Proposed Corporate Guidelines for Environmental Offenses," 146.

45. J.S. Burling, "Prepared Statement of James S. Burling, Pacific Legal Foundation, before the Senate Environment and Public Works Committee Clean Air, Wetlands, Private Property and Nuclear Safety Subcommittee," November 1, 1995.

46. Burling, "Prepared Statement."

47. U.S. Environmental Protection Agency, Office of Criminal Enforcement, "Summary of Criminal Prosecutions Resulting from Enforcement Investigations," 38, note 22.

PART II

Conclusion

By considering federal, state, and local responses to environmental crime, we can begin to understand the complexities associated with the enforcement of environmental laws and the punishment of violators. For one thing, the environmental movement is still young and much is yet to be determined about how U.S. environmental policy will be shaped over time. Further, it is difficult to determine how much of the battle to protect the environment has been fought at the local level. Clearly, specific communities have confronted environmental tragedies and have implemented policies and enforcement strategies to protect the public. But questions still to be answered include the following: To what degree should environmental policy be enforced at the federal level, and how much authority should states and local communities have to enforce environmental laws as they deem appropriate? Too few studies have been done to draw any useful conclusions.

Law enforcement agencies across the country are showing increased support for the idea that environmental crimes can dramatically and negatively affect public health. Consequently, law enforcement training has been expanded to include environmental crime investigation, and local prosecutor offices have supported police efforts by developing their own techniques and strategies for ensuring the conviction of offenders.

While many are attempting to determine where the main environmental enforcement effort should be directed, others are focused on assessing the effects of the existing punishment structure. Should environmental criminals be treated as other criminals? Is prison time appropriate? Can the current criminal justice system absorb the effects of an all-out war on environmental crime similar to the "war on drugs"? Are there enough prison beds to allocate to environmental offenders? Are there other sanctions as severe as prison but that would allow for judicial discretion in determining the most appropriate placement?

When considering the idea of environmental crime, most people would probably agree that the environment needs to be treated with respect. People need clear air, good food, and clean water to drink. They may even agree that some aspects of the natural environment need to be protected. Yet a good way of protecting natural resources has evaded our understanding since the question of preservation versus conservation first emerged. Protecting the natural environment is a complicated task, and the issues associated with determining violations and imposing sanctions are controversial.

Part II was structured to provide the reader with a few ideas about how the U.S. system of environmental enforcement has developed. It stressed the importance of police and prosecutor support for the objective of convicting environmental criminals. Cooperation among agencies involved is key. Environmental enforcement policies mean little without enforcement agencies and agents who can punish offenders. Finally, Part II raised for consideration several issues unique to policing, prosecuting, and sentencing environmental criminals. Its overall purpose was to introduce the reader to the complexities associated with imposing the responsibility for environmental protection on the existing criminal justice system. At least one essential question was not introduced: Is the criminal justice system the best place to address environmental wrongdoing? Specific attention should be given to the question of whether the criminal justice system is the best place to address environmental violations.

Identifying Essential Connections

In Parts I and II, little attention was devoted to the social and cultural attitudes that underlie current views about environmental issues in general. The chapters in Part III remind us that the mainstream morality plays a large role in legislative and enforcement decisions, and they discuss in more detail some of the social and cultural ideologies presented in Part I.

Chapter 11 introduces the reader to several types of environmental criminals, including the government variety. For example, garbage disposal and waste water treatment are local government services that can negatively impact the environment if improperly managed. Of course, corporations can also be environmental offenders, but then we, too (either individually or collectively as a community), place stress on the natural environment by our irresponsible behavior.

Chapter 12 takes the reader on a challenging journey by posing for consideration the question of how we think about the natural environment. How should humans treat nonhumans? Should nonhuman animals be granted humanlike rights? Should humans be given the right to a healthy environment? Should all animals, human and nonhuman, be given the right to live out the life they were designed to live? The chapter also discusses several dilemmas that arise in current efforts to respect the inherent worth of individual animals or plants. It suggests that the efforts to enforce environmental laws must be considered in conjunction with current views regarding what constitutes acceptable behavior toward all inhabitants of the earth.

Chapter 13 asks the reader to think critically about the environmental messages found in the popular culture. Can environmental images be "mystified" and then used to sell products that are environmentally irresponsible? Could a conscientious consumer who is committed to buying environmentally responsible products be fooled into contributing to environmental harm? Does it matter if plastic bags are advertised as "degradable" or "biodegradable"? This chapter focuses on several ideas presented in political circles, in the marketplace, and in other arenas. The objective is to help the reader make sense of environmental rhetoric.

Chapter 14 stretches its focus beyond the borders of the United States. Much has been said about the irrelevance of political borders when it comes to migrating pollution. Several environmental controversies have sparked international incidents between neighboring nations. International agreements have been signed, and environmental advocates are concerned about how international environmental enforcement will develop in the future. This chapter identifies several of the primary issues and introduces the reader to the emerging global controversy over environmental protection.

The final chapter, Chapter 15, reviews specific research focused on environmental crime. To date, few studies and larger works have exclusively dealt with the topic of environmental crime. The chapter makes note of some key obstacles researchers interested in the area may find troubling.

Part III, in a sense, returns to the essential inquiries needed to further the study of environmental crime. Whereas Parts I and II provided insight into the current structure of environmental crime and environmental crime research, Part III invites critical assessment of the status quo. In order to evolve, environmental crime research will require scientific inquiry in all areas of environmental studies. As we have seen, the environment was traditionally studied in isolation from other disciplines. Direct links must now be forged to connect the social and cultural issues that influence scientific inquiry and the interpretation of natural science findings. Finally, innovation will be essential to combat the environmental ills of the present, and thus creative thinkers must be identified—and given an audience—in all areas of environmental studies.

CHAPTER 11

Five Types of Environmental Criminals

Mark Seis

TERMS	agency capture	Pollution Prosecution Act
	attainment area	of 1990
	cryptosporidium	promulgate
	eutrophication	state implementation
	midnight dumping	plan
	nonattainment area	

This chapter discusses various types of environmental law offenders. The inquiry begins at the federal level of government. The federal government has assumed responsibility to **promulgate**, or put forward, the majority of environmental laws and regulations in the United States. Federal environmental regulations require compliance on the part of federal agencies, state and local governments, corporations, and individuals. Some of the most significant violations of federal environmental regulations, however, have been committed by federal agencies.[1] This chapter also explores environmental offenses committed by state and local governments. State and local governments frequently violate federal environmental laws ranging from the Clean Air Act (CAA) to the Clean Water Act (CWA) to the Resource Conservation and Recovery Act (RCRA) to the Safe Drinking Water Act (SDWA). After examining government offenses, the chapter discusses corporate and individual environmental offenses.

FEDERAL ENVIRONMENTAL OFFENDERS

One of the more serious environmental threats facing the citizens of the United States is the environmental contamination caused by the U.S. nuclear weapons production complex.[2] Byproducts from plutonium and uranium used in the production of nuclear weapons add up to an enormous amount of radioactive and hazardous waste, which threatens to contaminate water, soil, and air. Kauzlarich and Kramer report numerous criminal, civil, and administrative environmental law violations that have occurred at the major U.S. nuclear weapons facilities. "The environmental crimes committed during the process of nuclear weapons production are the collective product of the interaction between a government agency [the EPA], the U.S. Department of Energy (DOE), and various private corporations."[3(p.5)]

President Carter created the DOE in 1977 as a cabinet-level department responsible for managing a diverse energy strategy that ranges from regulating fuel consumption to providing incentives for energy conservation, research, and development to the production of nuclear weapons.[4,5] Approximately one-third of the DOE budget is allocated for nuclear weapons production.[6] The DOE primarily oversees the production of nuclear weapons that are produced by DOE-contracted multinational corporations like DuPont, Westinghouse, General Electric, and Martin Marietta.[7] The DOE oversees 17 nuclear weapons facilities.[8]

Written into the contracts granted by the DOE to private corporations are requirements that obligate contractors to adhere to worker safety and environmental laws. Consider the following excerpt from a DOE and DuPont contract:

> The Contractor shall take all reasonable precautions in the performance of the work under this Contract to protect the safety of employees and of members of the public and to minimize dangers from all hazards to life and property, and shall comply with all health, safety, and fire protection regulations and requirements.[9(p.13)]

Primary responsibility for regulating private contractors lies with the DOE. The DOE is required by law to enforce compliance with three major pieces of environmental legislation: the RCRA, the CWA, and the CAA.[10]

RCRA requires as of 1984 that each DOE facility "identify its hazardous wastes; receive a permit in order to treat, store, or dispose of such wastes; monitor ground water at waste sites; close and care for sites that are taken out of operation; and undertake corrective action."[11(p.15)] Under RCRA statutes, "any person who knowingly . . . treats, stores, or disposes of hazardous wastes without a permit or in knowing violation of a material condition or requirement of a permit or interim status regulations or standards, may be guilty of a class D felony."[12(p.4)] Violation of any of these laws may result in up to five years in prison and a fine of $50,000 per day for individuals (not to exceed a maximum of $250,000) and $50,000 for corporations (not to exceed a maximum of $500,000).[13] Most DOE facilities were in clear violation of the RCRA because most did not even begin to apply for legal permits until 1986.[14]

The CWA of 1972 "regulates discharges from point sources including industrial discharges and municipal treatment plants, and provides for the issuance by the EPA of permits for pollutant discharges from point sources into any of the country's water."[15(p.5)] Most contamination around DOE facilities, however, is the result of illegally disposed waste that either leaches into local rivers and streams or sinks down through the soil into underground water aquifers. Most contaminated water around DOE facilities results from violations of the RCRA.[16]

Little is known about CAA violations because the private contractors are responsible for reporting violations to the DOE. The DOE is then responsible for reporting violations to the U.S. EPA.[17] Apparently the EPA has left the DOE to police itself with respect to CAA violations by its contractors.[18]

The DOE's regulation of itself and its contractors has been ethically and legally suspect. In fact, the DOE has attempted to undermine the applicability of many environmental laws under the banner of "national security."[19] As a result of the DOE's resistance to enforcing environmental laws regarding hazardous waste from nuclear weapons facilities, a U.S. General Accounting Office (GAO) report conducted in 1986 estimated that the total cost of bringing the industry into compliance with environmental laws would be around $250 billion.[20]

Violations of RCRA statutes have resulted in massive ground water and soil contamination in areas adjacent to many of the major DOE facilities. Out of seven facilities reviewed by the GAO, all were in violation of RCRA statutes.[21] A report conducted by Mobilization for Survival found that the Hanford nuclear facility, in violation of RCRA statutes, has contaminated

> 100 square miles of groundwater . . . with radioactive tritium, iodine, and toxic chemicals. Over a half million gallons of high level radioactive waste [have] leaked from underground tanks and more continues to leak into the soil. Billions of gallons of liquid wastes and waste water with radioactive chemical and radioactive elements have been dumped in Hanford soil, contaminating the Columbia River and its watershed.[22(p.14)]

The Savannah River Plant also has contaminated ground water around its facility "with nearly all forms of radioactive and hazardous waste, and over 51 million gallons of highly dangerous toxins are stored in leaking underground tanks beneath the facility."[23(p.14)] According to another GAO report, "Out of the nine facilities surveyed, all of the sites were in violation of the Clean Water Act."[24(p.15)]

One of the most compelling environmental crime cases in the United States involved the Rocky Flats DOE facility located just outside Denver, Colorado. The specific issues in this case are discussed in more detail in Case Study 3, "Rocky Flats: A Plea Bargain in Public View." In short, however, the

INSIGHT

Reproductive Problems Linked to Chemical Exposure?

In recent years, scientists and doctors have noticed a decrease in sperm counts. While the studies are considered to be controversial, many agree something disturbing is happening.[1] In addition to low sperm counts, the percentage of healthy sperm cells appears to be decreasing, and doctors have noticed an increase in testicular cancer and undescended testicles.[2] Chemical pollutants such as DDT, dioxins, PCBs, and other synthetic substances are blamed.[3]

Humans are not the only animals affected. Genital malformations in animals have been documented and attributed to chemical exposures. Alligators in southern Florida, for example, have been born with minuscule penises, making reproduction impossible. Researchers hypothesize that small amounts of industrial chemicals, delivered at just the right stage of fetal development, can "feminize" a male embryo, producing smaller testicles, low sperm output, and a miniaturized or missing penis.

Most recently, Minnesota officials reported sightings of deformed frogs with misshapen limbs, tails, missing or shrunken eyes, and small sex organs.[4] Similar reports have come in from Wisconsin, South Dakota, Vermont, and Quebec. Causes cited in explanation of the abnormalities include pesticides, parasites, or a combination of factors.

---

1. M.D. Lemonick, "What's Wrong with Our Sperm? Men's Reproductive Cells Seem To Be in Serious Decline Worldwide. One Possible Cause: Chemical Pollution," *Time*, 18 March 1996, 78, 79.
2. Lemonick, "What's Wrong with Our Sperm?" 78.
3. J.P. Myers et al., *Our Stolen Future* (New York: Dutton Press, 1996).
4. "Deformed Frogs Scare, Baffle State Scientists: Researchers Have Hard Time Finding Wetlands with No Deformed Frogs," *St. Cloud Times*, 2A.

DOE had contracted Rockwell International, which ran the facility from 1975 to 1989, to manufacture plutonium parts for nuclear warheads.[25] After two years of investigative work, 75 FBI and EPA agents raided the Rocky Flats facility for violations of the RCRA and the CWA.[26] The environmental crimes committed at Rocky Flats resulted in a plea bargain according to which "Rockwell pled guilty to ten criminal counts under two environmental laws: four felony counts under the Resources Conservation and Recovery Act; and one felony and five misdemeanors under the Clean Water Act."[27(p.33)] Comparing the crimes committed at Rocky Flats with the Exxon Valdez incident, a subcommittee report on the crimes committed at Rocky Flats noted

> The crimes at Rocky Flats were more egregious. The Rockwell officials responsible for the facility knowingly violated the law over prolonged periods of time and aggressively resisted all efforts to force them to comply with environmental standards. The environmental damage and effects on workers of the plant and citizens of the surrounding communities will not be made manifest for many years.[28(p.33)]

The total damage to Rockwell was a fine of $18.5 million; a sum that did not even match the profits Rockwell received from the government for operating the facility.[29]

THE PROBLEM OF PROSECUTING FEDERAL AGENCIES

Why was the DOE not charged with violating RCRA and CWA statutes? One reason is that Article 3 of the U.S. Constitution prohibits any federal agency from prosecuting another.[30] The EPA can, however, prosecute responsible *individuals* within the DOE for not executing the law when they are aware that violations are occurring. Since 1982, "the EPA has acted upon only three of 30 criminal complaints filed against a DOE employee."[31(p.17)] In the Rocky Flats case, no individual indictments of DOE employees were pursued. According to a House subcommittee report authored by Representative Howard Wolpe, the Department of Justice was willing to forgo prosecution of DOE officials because

> the prosecution pointed to a "DOE culture" that stressed weapons production over the environment and human health to rationalize and excuse the misconduct and possible criminal behavior of DOE officials. This created a situation in which no government official could be held culpable because the entire agency encouraged noncompliance with environmental laws. The result was a double stan-

dard in the administration of justice, where a government agency and its individual employees were allowed *lesser* standards of conduct than ordinary citizens.[32(pp.13–14)]

No DOE officials were ever charged with any crimes despite strong evidence that DOE personnel had knowledge of some of the crimes to which Rockwell pleaded guilty.[33]

The $18.5 million fine did not even amount to the bonuses paid to Rockwell by the DOE during the time the crimes were being committed.[34] A subcommittee report estimated that the real fine should have been somewhere "between $68.5 million and $78.5 million, depending on how many days Rockwell was deemed to have been in non-compliance with the ground water monitoring provisions."[35(p.34)] Ironically, the Justice Department was arguing for a "radically lower number throughout the period of negotiations."[36(p.106)] Further, the subcommittee report contends "that if this case had been in the hands of main Justice [the U.S. Department of Justice in Washington], the case would have been settled for a mere four or five million dollars."[37(p.107)]

STATE GOVERNMENT ENVIRONMENTAL OFFENDERS

Contemporary U.S. culture produces a large amount of waste that ends up in our air and waterways. Many federal environmental statutes, like the CAA and CWA, entrust the states with devising their own strategies to meet federal pollution safety standards. Local and state governments are responsible by federal law for bringing their political regions into compliance with federal pollution standards.

Section 107 of the CAA requires the EPA to divide the United States into air quality control regions (AQCRs). There are 247 AQCRs located throughout the country.[38] If needed, states can redefine the boundaries of AQCRs for the purpose of better air pollution control. Each state is responsible for the AQCRs that fall within its boundaries. Section 107(d)(1)(a) requires that the governor of each state submit to the EPA administrator an assessment that classifies each AQCR within the state's boundaries as a nonattainment area, an attainment area, or an unclassifiable area for each criteria pollutant.

A **nonattainment area** is one that does not meet or contributes to the failure of another AQCR's ability to meet primary National Ambient Air Quality Standards for criteria pollutants established by the EPA. There are six criteria pollutants: ozone, carbon monoxide, lead, sulfur dioxide, nitrogen dioxide, and particulate matter. Any AQCR that does not meet the primary standard for any of the six criteria pollutants is considered a nonattainment area. **Attainment areas** meet the primary air quality standards, and unclassifiable areas are usually rural areas that have no criteria pollution monitoring.[39]

Section 110 of the CAA requires that each state be responsible for devising **state implementation plans** (SIPs) for all AQCRs within its boundaries. SIPs are detailed control strategies designed to show how each air quality control region is going to maintain its air quality or bring into compliance a nonattainment air quality control region. Thus, for example, an AQCR that is in nonattainment for ozone may be required to provide many different SIPs detailing all the sources of ozone and how these sources are all going to be controlled to reduce ambient ozone levels to primary standards. Section 110 2(A) states that all SIPs shall "include enforceable emission limitations and other control measures, means, or techniques (including economic incentives such as fees, marketable permits, and auctions of emissions rights), as well as schedules and time tables for compliance." In addition, SIPs must provide methods, strategies, and predictive modeling for monitoring criteria pollutants within each AQCR.[40]

SIPs, then, constitute the primary tool for bringing nonattainment areas into compliance with National Ambient Air Quality Standards and for ensuring that attainment areas continue to meet national standards. Sanctions available to the EPA administrator for inadequate SIPs for nonattainment areas include limiting particular highway funds to projects designed to improve air quality (§179(b)(1)(A)). The EPA administrator may also impose a moratorium on new construction sites in a nonattainment area or force the entire AQCR to offset "the ratio of emission reductions to increased emissions . . . [by] at least 2 to 1" (§179(b)(2)).

Sanctions for inadequate SIPs do not have much bite, considering this is the main mechanism for controlling the majority of air pollution. A report by the U.S. Senate Committee on Environmental and Public Works titled *Three Years Later: Report Card on the 1990 Clean Air Act Amendments* gave the SIP strategy for reducing air pollution a C grade for several reasons. First, the SIP strategy has failed to meet primary air quality standards, so that 53.6 million U.S. citizens are breathing unhealthy air on a regular basis.[41]

Another reason given for the poor grade was the failure by the states to complete and implement the SIPs on time.[42] As of November 15, 1992, only 658 out of 1,061 SIPs required by the legislation (62 percent) were submitted on time.[43] Due to violations of these deadlines, the National Resources Defense Council has filed suit against the EPA for "improperly extending statutory deadlines."[44(p.7)]

By May 15, 1991, 35 states were required to submit SIPs for ozone, but 9 states and the District of Columbia did not meet the required deadline. At the end of 1993, the District of Columbia had still not submitted an SIP.[45] Sanctions for the 9 states and the District of Columbia were to be imposed in April 1993, but as of November 1993 no sanctions had been applied by the EPA.[46] By May 15, 1991, 23 states were required to submit SIPs for particulate matter. Eleven states failed to complete their SIPs by the deadline. Sanctions were to be imposed by the EPA in June 1993, but as of November 1993 no sanctions had been applied.[47] No sanctions means that air pollution reduction strategies are not being implemented and laws are not being enforced.

PROSECUTION OF STATE GOVERNMENT ENVIRONMENTAL OFFENDERS

As illustrated above, the EPA has been slow to demand compliance by the states. Sanctions for violations of specific deadlines in the 1990 amendments were not even imposed. Why? Because of the complexity of most environmental regulation, the EPA is forced to rely on the expertise of states in drafting legislation. Further, the EPA is also dependent in most situations on states for monitoring and prosecuting private sector violators of environmental regulations. EPA's reliance on state expertise, monitoring, and enforcement creates a forced working relationship between the EPA and the states.

Agency capture is the term used to describe the working relationship that occurs between regulatory agencies and the subjects of regulation.[48–51] Regulatory agencies like the EPA are forced to pursue policies "that generally coincide with preferences previously expressed by those being regulated."[52(p.484)] Although *agency capture* is usually used to describe the relationships between private companies and federal regulators, it is also appropriate for characterizing EPA's regulatory stance toward state and even municipal governments.

A good way to understand the nature of agency capture is to consider an example like the following:

> EPA's region V office has been working with Indiana regarding its required SIP submission for enhanced vehicle inspection and maintenance. Although the SIP was due by November 15, 1992, EPA agreed to accept a committal SIP, in which Indiana promised to submit its complete SIP revision by November 1993 and also promised

to obtain funding to implement the enhanced inspection and maintenance program during the 1993 State Legislative session. When the Indiana legislature adjourned its 1993 session without taking the necessary action outlined in the committal SIP, EPA sent a letter to the Governor of Indiana stating that the Agency intended to execute its discretionary authority to impose immediate sanctions. Although EPA has initiated the formal process for applying for sanctions, EPA does not intend to finalize the rule making until the legislature has a chance to reconvene in 1994 and consider the necessary legislation.[53(p.11)]

SIPs are the main means of controlling stationary pollution sources that emit criteria pollutants, but states have repeatedly failed to complete SIPs, provide realistic strategies, and implement them with success. The majority of states have failed to bring their AQCRs into compliance with primary air quality standards by the 1975 deadline promulgated in the 1970 legislation or the 1987 deadline promulgated in the 1977 amendment and will in all likelihood miss the 2010 deadline promulgated in the 1990 legislation.[54,55]

MUNICIPAL GOVERNMENT ENVIRONMENTAL OFFENDERS

Most municipal governments are entrusted with the responsibility of treating sewage, providing clean drinking water, and eliminating household and local industrial waste. All three of these tasks are regulated by federal environmental laws. These laws have become more stringent over the years and have placed municipalities between a rock and hard place. Municipalities are forced to juggle more with less. That is, municipal governments must deal with growing urban populations, which means more sewage, more solid and hazardous waste, and a greater demand for clean drinking water, but they must meet the increased need with less land for waste and less money to build better treatment facilities (mandated by federal law). Many municipal governments have not been able to keep up with the requirements of federal environmental laws, and frequent violations are the result.

Municipal treatment plants are required by the CWA to treat organic and inorganic pollutant byproducts before discharging them into waterways. A typical municipal treatment plant deals with sewage, industrial and household contaminants, and water from storm sewers, which contains a variety of organic and inorganic chemicals washed off the roads and lawns.[56] Municipal sewage treatment plants "reduce the flow of disease-carrying human waste into rivers and streams, where [it] could pose threats to human health

INSIGHT

The Village of Wilsonville et al.
v. SCA Services, Inc.

On April 18, 1977, the village of Wilsonville filed a complaint seeking injunctive relief in the circuit court of Macoupin County, Illinois. The village argued the chemical waste disposal site operated by SCA Services presented a public nuisance and a hazard to the community. The site was approximately 130 acres, with 90 of those acres within the village limits of the plaintiff and the remaining 40 acres adjacent to the village. On February 11, 1976, the defendant had applied to the Illinois Environmental Protection Agency (IEPA) for a permit to develop and operate the hazardous waste landfill. A developmental permit was issued by the IEPA on May 19, 1976. After a preoperation inspection was conducted by the IEPA, an operational permit was issued to the defendant on September 28, 1976.

Since the permit was granted, evidence had shown the substances deposited at the site were extremely toxic to humans. The court concluded that the case sufficiently established by a preponderance of the evidence that the chemical waste disposal site was a nuisance both presently and prospectively. It had to be shut down and cleaned up.

Even though SCA had been given a permit by the IEPA, the company was held responsible for the cleanup. The costs of cleaning up the Wilsonville site totaled about $50 million. In addition, the site owner settled a damage action brought by the village's 700 residents: $1 million was divided among those who were landowners, and $1.5 million was divided among all 700 residents.[1]

"The Illinois site was chosen by responsible people acting responsibly. Reliable generators performed accurately in consigning wastes, and suitable transporters brought it to a disposal site chosen by informed officials."[2(p.171)] So, who should be responsible for the cleanup?

---

1. *New York Times*, 26 June 1987, 14.
2. T.M. Hoban and R.O. Brooks, *Green Justice: The Environment and the Courts* (Boulder, CO: Westview Press, 1987), 171.

through contamination of drinking water, shellfish beds and other resources."[57(p.105)]

As discussed in Part I, the CWA requires that a point source cannot discharge any pollutant "into a navigable water without a permit."[58(p.275)] Any facility, public or private, is required to have a permit issued by the National Pollution Discharge Elimination System (NPDES) operated by its state (though approved by the EPA). Effluent limitation standards are established for each type of pollution based on the best technology to treat that particular type.[59]

Among the most frequent violators of the CWA are publicly owned municipal sewage treatment plants.[60] In a survey conducted by the GAO during an 18-month period in 1981–1982, 86 percent of 274 municipal sewage treatment plants reported that they were in noncompliance with federal effluent regulations, and 32 percent reported significant noncompliance.[61] Some of the reasons offered for violations included "operation and maintenance deficiencies, equipment deficiencies, and treatment plant overloading."[62(p.114)] A 1993 EPA report "found that more than two-thirds of the nation's wastewater treatment plants had serious lapses in water quality standards."[63(p.456)] Federal funds designed to help local municipalities update their equipment have been declining since the late 1980s.[64]

The dumping of illegally treated sewage in rivers and lakes has done serious damage to aquatic life and has in many cases prevented recreational use of major water resources. For example, in 1988 many beaches all along the East Coast were closed due to sewage debris.[65] The dumping of raw sewage into Boston Harbor became a hot political issue used by Bush to defeat Dukakis in the 1988 election.[66] In fact, the near death of Lake Erie, which was undergoing **eutrophication** in the late 1960s and early 1970s, was in large part due to the inadequate treatment of sewage.[67]

Municipalities also are mandated by the 1974 SDWA to provide drinking water that is free of microbiological contaminants and chemical contaminants. As of 1993, the EPA had established safe standards for 84 possible contaminants. Despite these regulations, "a 1993 report by the National Resources Defense Council . . . documented more than 250,000 violations within a two year period by 43 percent of U.S. public water systems, which collectively serve 123 million people."[68(p.306)] One only needs to remember the **cryptosporidium** (a microorganism) incident that caused 40 deaths in Milwaukee[69] and infected "more than 50 percent of the 800,000 individuals served by the city water system"[70(p.436)] to see the need for drinking water standards and strict enforcement of those standards. That same year, both New York City and Washington, D.C., had major drinking water scares, with fecal coliform bacteria being found in Washington's water supply.[71]

Municipalities also are faced with the onerous burden of disposing of relentless waves of trash. Owing to the variety of throwaway waste, landfills are a major environmental problem, because of the leaching of waste into water and soil as well as emission of toxic gases.[72] The Council on Environmental Quality reported the following regarding the landfill problem:

> In 1960 Americans generated municipal type solid waste at the rate of 2.65 pounds per person per day. By 1986 that figure climbed to 3.58 pounds, and the trend is up [to 4 pounds per person in 1988]. . . . In 1978, there were approximately 20,000 municipal landfills. . . . Today less than 6,000 are still in use. By 1993 about a third of these will be filled. Many more will be closed due to inadequate safety or environmental practices. . . . A large number of existing . . . landfills do not meet current . . . standards for safe design and operation. . . . More than half . . . make no attempt to control water pollution from the runoff of rain from their sites.[73(p.141)]

Commoner adds to the list of landfill problems that landfills are "often poorly controlled."[74(p.107)]

Incineration has been touted by many as the solution to the landfill crisis experienced by local governments, but incineration also creates many environmental hazards. The most salient are hazardous air pollutants and the remaining ash, which is often laced with toxins like lead, dioxin, chromium, and arsenic.[75] Under the RCRA, if ash is hazardous, then more stringent and expensive disposal methods must be used. The CAA also requires that expensive high-combustion incineration methods be used to ensure that levels of hazardous pollutants meet relevant emission standards.

Due to the high cost of meeting federal regulations regarding sewage treatment, landfill, and incineration operations, many local governments fail to comply with the regulations.[76–78] One can have sympathy for their plight because of the economic burden attached to disposing of waste properly, but their failure to comply means that our water, air, and land go unprotected.

PROSECUTION OF MUNICIPAL GOVERNMENT ENVIRONMENTAL OFFENDERS

State and EPA prosecutions of municipalities have been few in number. With respect to municipal sewage treatment violations, Russell notes that the GAO has criticized both the EPA and state environmental enforcement for allowing violations to continue uncorrected for long periods of time. It appears that any kind of formal enforcement action may be delayed for months or perhaps years, even after a significant violation is revealed by self-monitoring. This may be because taking the enforcement action far enough to assess a civil penalty adds substantially to the required time, since the Justice Department has to become involved.[79(p.258)]

In short, it is easier for the EPA to ignore violations because of the multitude of variables and legal considerations required of the EPA before pursuing simple civil charges, let alone criminal charges, in enforcing clean water legislation. The GAO has stated that "EPA's current enforcement philosophy for water pollution control still centers around voluntary compliance and the nonconfrontational approach established in 1982."[80(p.258)] The GAO has likewise "criticized the EPA for failing to administer the SDWA effectively."[81(p.306)]

Enforcement of standards for municipal landfills is also virtually nonexistent. In fact, owing to the cost involved in creating safe landfills, the EPA has provided some exemptions for small municipal landfills.[82] EPA's compromising position on enforcement standards toward municipalities has led one study cited in Valente and Valente (1995) to conclude that

> the purported aim of preventing ground water contamination has been diminished by the lengthy delay in promulgation of the [final implementation] rule and the absence of specific criteria for state implementation. . . . The new regulatory approach appears to rubber stamp the programs of a majority of states while granting exemptions and waivers for those unable to comply.[83(p.162)]

Granting exemptions and waivers to municipal violators is unequivocally the predominant mode of enforcement. In other words, there is no enforcement other than voluntary compliance by municipalities when it comes to meeting environmental standards.

Granted, the problems surrounding this lack of enforcement are complicated. Pollution treatment requires expensive equipment and lengthy procedures if federal requirements are to be met. For example, "upgrading all the nation's [waste treatment] facilities to consistently meet the EPA standards has been estimated at $83.5 billion, or more than 12 times the EPA's annual budget."[84(p.457)] These days municipal governments are under severe budgetary pressures just to maintain basic public services, let alone build new sewage and water treatment facilities and create safe landfills. Municipalities are now beginning to feel the brunt of excessive consumption. Strict

EPA and state enforcement would inevitably break the backs of many municipal governments and would bring heavy criticism from the federal legislators who control the EPA's purse strings. No enforcement, however, means unabated threats to our land, water, air, and health.

CORPORATE AND INDIVIDUAL ENVIRONMENTAL OFFENDERS

One type of environmental offender we are all familiar with is the corporate offender. The image of the greedy corporate CEO ordering some submissive employee to dump hazardous chemicals in the ocean, in a local creek, or down a sewer is commonly presented in movies and on the nightly news. There is little doubt corporate environmental crime is widespread, and its cost to the environment and human health is astounding.[85–91] Michael Edelstein notes that "this country generates between 255 million and 275 million metric tons of hazardous waste annually, of which 90 percent is improperly disposed."[92(p.3)]

Illegal disposal of hazardous waste poses a great danger to human health, and its consequences range from birth defects to sterility to breathing ailments to various types of cancer.[93] Because of the extreme dangers of hazardous waste, RCRA statutes involve criminal punishment. For instance, "under 42 U.S.C. 6928(d) of the RCRA, any person who knowingly transports or causes to be transported hazardous waste to an unpermitted facility or treats, stores or disposes of hazardous waste without a permit . . . may be guilty of a class D felony."[94(p.4)] Punishment for such violations includes up to five years' imprisonment and a maximum fine of up to $250,000 for an individual and $500,000 for a corporation.[95]

Some of the most notorious generators and illegal disposers of hazardous waste are chemical companies. Tallmer has documented numerous incidents of illegal dumping by Hooker Chemical company, including the famous case of Love Canal.[96] Hooker had dumped hundreds of tons of chemicals on a piece of land named Love Canal and then turned the land over to the local school board, which sold it to a private developer, which constructed a housing subdivision. A short time later, residents living over the dump site began to experience high rates of miscarriages, birth defects, and cancer.

One of the worst cases of illegal dumping documented by Tallmer involves a Hooker Chemical plant operating in White Lake, Michigan. Hooker was dumping barrels of hazardous chemicals on company property, which apparently leached into White Lake, killing scores of fish. When Hooker executives were asked to explain what had happened, they claimed they had "twenty or thirty" barrels behind the plant.[97] However, James Truchan,

East Liverpool Incinerator: A Burning Issue Still Unresolved

For over 15 years, a hazardous waste incinerator has been the center of a contentious community conflict in East Liverpool, Ohio. The facility was placed at the corner of Ohio, West Virginia, and Pennsylvania.

East Liverpool is a small industrial city of fewer than 14,000 people. The incinerator is situated approximately 400 vertical yards from an elementary school, 300 feet from the nearest house, and near the Ohio River—a major source of drinking water for the community. Additional concerns expressed by community activists include placement of the facility in a 100-year floodplain, atmospheric inversions, and a projected total of 5,000 truckloads of toxins annually.

Initial permits issued in 1980 are argued by community citizens to have prohibited the handling of toxic waste. Further, as plans changed, compliance with the legal regulations did not always follow. In 1984, the project was badly stalled because it was owned outright by Waste Management Inc. This company is a convicted felon. Under Ohio's "bad boy" law, convicted felons cannot get a license to handle hazardous wastes.[1] Four companies that signed the incinerator's original permit application changed their names at least nine times between 1981 and 1990.[2] At the present time, the incinerator is in "limited" commercial operation. Community opposition is as active as ever, and litigation is underway. But litigation never gets as much attention as the big demonstrations.[3]

****

Some critical points in the East Liverpool Ohio incinerator controversy include the following:[4–7]

- September 23, 1991: a consulting firm released a report saying the incinerator was safe.
- September 25, 1991: a group of nearly 400 citizens shut down a public meeting.
- October 13, 1991: 34 local citizens and two Greenpeace campaigners were held in three local jails, charged with civil disobedience, after a mass trespass on the property of the Waste Technologies, Inc. (WTI) incinerator. Actor Martin Sheen and chemist Paul Connett were both arrested. The project was said to be 80 percent completed.
- November 1992: a federal district judge in West Virginia refused to grant an injunction that would have stopped the initial tests of the incinerator but stated that the full operations could not move forward until the EPA affirmed the operation was safe.
- December 7, 1992: the *New York Times* ran an article stating the administration of president-elect Bill Clinton would request an investigation of the facility before it could begin operations. A spokesperson for the plant said the plant would begin limited burning of wastes, moving into full operations at the time of this writing.

- March 16, 1993: two companies, each originally contracted to send about a third of the hazardous waste supplied to the East Liverpool incinerator, reportedly renegotiated contracts with the company. The third firm, providing the final one-third of the waste to be shipped to the facility, was said to be monitoring the situation before making a decision.[8]

- December 1994: reports indicated criminal activities had been committed by at least four corporate executives of Von Roll (WTI's Swiss-based owner) in their home country. Other subsidiary companies are under investigation, and the company is said to be plagued with a staggering debt.

****

1. P. Montague, "The Governed Begin To Withhold Their Consent and 34 Are Arrested in Ohio," *Rachel's Hazardous Waste News*, 15 October 1991 (Internet: erf@igc.apc.org).
2. L.J. Davis, "Where Are You Al?" *Mother Jones*, November–December 1993, 44–49.
3. Interview with Alonzo Spencer, of Save Our Country, a local grassroots group in opposition to the facility, 24 October 1996.
4. Montague, "The Governed Begin To Withhold Their Consent."
5. Davis, "Where Are You Al?"
6. S. McMurray, "DuPont, BASF Plant To Cancel Incinerator Job," *Wall Street Journal*, 16 March 1996, A4.
7. Interview with Alonzo Spencer.
8. McMurray, "DuPont, BASF Plant To Cancel Incinerator Job."

an environmental enforcement agent, counted 20,000 barrels of toxic chemicals.[98] Michigan sued, and Hooker settled out of court for $1 million in penalties, agreeing to pay $20 million in cleanup costs. Three years later, White Lake was found so contaminated that residents were warned not to eat the fish or drink the water. In fact, many of the residents have suffered birth defects, sterility, and cancer. Federal charges asserting that Hooker officials covered up illegal dumping activities for over 20 years were dismissed by the Department of Justice.[99]

As noted in earlier chapters, one of the most common types of illegal hazardous waste disposal is called **midnight dumping**. Midnight dumping involves disposing of wastes "in the nearest isolated area. Agents of generating companies can directly commit these offenses or criminally conspire with waste transporters or treaters who, for a percentage of the legitimate treatment cost, will illegally dump the wastes."[100(pp.3–4)] While this is only one type of corporate environmental offense, it appears corporate criminals and their lawyers are getting more sophisticated in their illegal disposal techniques. As Hammett and Epstein explain,

> In recent years, hazardous waste violations have increasingly involved forging waste transportation manifests, mislabeling drums and waste shipments, disposing of waste on the generator's property (for example, pouring it down the drain or burying it), mixing hazardous waste with nonhazardous waste (sometimes called cocktailing), and shipping waste to neighboring states or nations with less stringent or effective regulation and enforcement.[101(p.5)]

Environmental crime research and prosecution rates suggest that illegal disposal of hazardous waste is probably the number one corporate offense.[102] Corporate methods of illegal disposal of hazardous waste include the dumping techniques noted above plus illegal incineration and effluent discharges.

Everyone has heard about safety shortcuts taken by corporations that have resulted in death and injury to consumers (e.g., the Ford Pinto case)[103] and employees (e.g., the Film Recovery System case).[104] Another type of environmental crime committed by corporations, one that does not involve waste disposal, is the manufacturing of products in violation of pollution standards. In November 1995, General Motors agreed to a $45 million settlement with the Department of Justice for CAA violations. The settlement required General Motors to pay an $11 million fine and spend more than $25 million to recall and retrofit vehicles and up to $8.75 million on projects to offset emissions from these vehicles.[105] GM apparently knew it was selling cars that violated the CAA.[106] It seems the 1991–1995 Cadillac models were equipped with a "defeat device" that allowed for more carbon monoxide pollution than is allowed by CAA standards. According to EPA Administrator Carol Browner, these illegal devices caused enough additional air pollution to blanket a major U.S. city, such as Washington, D.C., with a 10-foot layer of carbon monoxide.[107] Of course, carbon monoxide in high enough concentrations can be lethal, and in lesser concentrations it can create serious respiratory problems, especially for the elderly and young children.[108] The odd thing about this settlement was that the state department had no intention of pressing criminal charges despite what appeared to be overwhelming evidence that GM intentionally violated the carbon monoxide emission standard, which would have made it a good subject for criminal prosecution.[109]

Corporate environmental crimes vary from community to community. Chapter 7 outlined enforcement actions at the state level. The environmental crimes pursued by local law enforcement agencies include illegal disposal of waste tires, construction and demolition (C&D) debris, white goods, and vegetative waste.[110] Both corporations and individuals can be involved in the illegal disposal of waste whether hazardous or other. In fact, anyone owning a truck or for that matter a car can commit environmental crimes involving the illegal disposal of waste.[111]

A major environmental problem reported by Florida and New York law enforcement agencies is the illegal dumping of waste tires by individual automobile and truck owners and tire change businesses.[112] In addition to illegal waste tire disposal, Middlesex and Monmouth Counties in New Jersey have reported that many private property areas have been inundated with illegally dumped C&D debris apparently coming from New York City.[113] Such dumping may be the result of small businesses' trying to avoid the cost of legal disposal or individual entrepreneurs' seeking to enhance their well-being at the expense of public safety.

Palm Beach, Florida, has expressed major concern regarding the illegal disposal of kitchen appliances.[114] For example, refrigerator coolant systems contain chlorofluorocarbons (CFCs), which, if released into the atmosphere, cause damage to the ozone layer. Some kitchen appliances may also contain mercury, which is extremely hazardous to the environment.[115] Another major problem is the illegal disposal of vegetative waste by companies and individual home owners. Illegally dumped vegetation, especially if it accumulates, can create fire hazards.[116]

In sum, most corporate and individual environmental crime is committed in an effort to avoid costs of either implementing antipollution technology or avoiding the expenses of legal waste disposal. Because of their size, type of production, and volume of production, corporate environmental crimes have a much greater visibility and overall impact on our environment.[117–120] However, many individuals committing small environmental crimes can create serious environmental hazards. As discussed earlier, waste tires can become a significant community concern. For example, because of the cost of legal tire disposal, many residents in New York City have resorted to discarding their used tires in poor neighborhoods like the South Bronx, Queens, and Brooklyn.[121] Besides being aesthetically offensive, used tires create breeding grounds for disease[122] and if piled too high, fire hazards. In response to this illegal tire disposal, the city of New York has promulgated statutes that fine violators anywhere from $1,000 to $7,500 and require the impounding of their vehicles.[123]

PROSECUTION OF CORPORATE AND INDIVIDUAL OFFENDERS

While most major pieces of environmental legislation (e.g., the CWA, CAA, and RCRA) contain criminal sanctions, they are seldom used to enforce compliance of environmental laws.[124] For the most part, "the EPA and the States have taken an overwhelmingly administrative and civil approach to environmental enforcement."[125(p.13)] For each case in which a panoply of criminal charges are filed, there are hundreds, maybe even thousands, of violations that go completely undetected.[126] Part of the reason for the dearth of criminal charges is the lack of enforcement resources. Between 1982 and 1984, the EPA received 240 complaints about possible criminal violations of environmental laws but only had the resources to investigate 70.[127]

Despite the lack of investigators, criminal charges are being used in more cases.[128,129] For instance, "a total of 104 defendants were charged in federal criminal cases involving environmental violations in fiscal year 1991. . . . In fiscal year 1991, 72 defendants were convicted (45 individuals and 27 organizations) in 48 criminal cases. . . . A total of 14.1 million in fines was levied."[130(p.995)] The number of criminal prosecutions is expected to radically increase in the latter part of the 1990s owing to the passage of the **Pollution Prosecution Act of 1990**, which became effective in 1995.

Nevertheless, much more environmental crime exists than is detected and prosecuted. When environmental crime is detected, smaller companies and individual entrepreneurs are the ones more likely to receive criminal prosecution. For example, Yeager found that the larger the corporation, the more likely water pollution violations are to be overlooked by the EPA.[131,132] The smaller the business, however, the more likely water pollution violations are to be enforced. Yeager concluded one must be extremely cautious when relying on official sanctioning data of corporations, because it is systematically distorted in favor of larger corporations.[133] Hammett and

Epstein report that many local government prosecutors are reluctant to file charges for hazardous waste violations against major businesses because of economic and political pressure. Furthermore, they found that "juries often view indicted CEOs as upstanding community leaders and their companies as providing needed employment in the community."[134(p.15)]

Although it appears the trend toward increased criminal enforcement of environmental crimes is going to continue, the amount of arrests and prosecutions will still probably fall well below the amount needed to make a serious dent in environmental crime. As long as the basic strategy for enforcement remains *reactive*, individuals, corporations, and the various levels of government will undoubtedly continue to ignore the environmental statutes. Until environmental laws start prohibiting the generation of waste (i.e., taking a proactive approach), environmental crime is going to be rampant, especially in the wake of tougher laws requiring more expensive waste treatment facilities and procedures.

CONCLUSION

This chapter has explored a variety of different types of environmental crime committed by federal agencies, state and municipal governments, corporations, and individuals. Most environmental crime results from the problems of legally disposing of waste in a consumer-based society. We are a society that often forgets one of the most touted principles of ecology: there is no such thing as a free lunch.[135] Mass consumption means mass amounts of waste in need of disposal.[136–138] With waste accumulating in our water, in our air, and on our land, stiffer laws will be needed to prevent further degradation of our environment.

The United States has many tough environmental laws designed to mitigate pollution problems, but many of these laws are not being enforced with rigor. Until the various levels of government begin to take these laws seriously, environmental pollution is going to be an ever-growing threat, especially if we continue the economics of consumption. Although enforcement is improving, we still have a long way to go before enforcement acts as an effective deterrent and substantially reduces the number of violators of environmental laws.

REVIEW QUESTIONS

1. Are individual, corporate, and state violations handled differently? Which remedies (administrative, civil, or criminal) are most often pursued?

2. Can the federal government or an agent of the federal government be prosecuted for the violation of a federal law?
3. Why are sites where federal weapons programs are housed of specific interest to people who study environmental crime?
4. What is the difference between attainment areas and nonattainment areas? Please describe each.
5. Under the Clean Air Act, states are required to develop state implementation plans. What is involved in developing an SIP?
6. What makes municipal treatment plants sites where violations are likely to occur?

DISCUSSION QUESTIONS

1. Is the criminal justice system set up to handle violations of environmental law when the offender is a corporation or the government? How are such cases different from cases involving individuals?
2. Why is the federal government unlikely to prosecute a municipality for violations of federal environmental statutes?
3. What linkages, if any, exist between cases of corporate "short cuts" that result in death and injury to workers or consumers and cases involving environmental crime?
4. Discuss the specific issues associated with each type of environmental offender: federal violators, state violators, municipal violators, corporate violators, and individual violators.

REFERENCES

1. R.P. Percival et al., *Environmental Regulation: Law, Science and Policy* (Boston: Little, Brown, 1992).
2. D. Kauzlarich and R.C. Kramer, "State-Corporate Crime in the US Nuclear Weapons Production Complex," *Journal of Human Justice* 5, no. 1 (1993): 4–28.
3. Kauzlarich and Kramer, "State-Corporate Crime," 5.
4. J.V. Switzer, *Environmental Politics: Domestic and Global Dimensions* (New York: St. Martin's Press, 1994).
5. Kauzlarich and Kramer, "State-Corporate Crime."
6. J. Lamperti, "Government and the Atom," in *The Nuclear Almanac: Confronting the Atom in War and Peace*, ed. J. Dennis (Reading, MA: Addison-Wesley, 1991).
7. Kauzlarich and Kramer, "State-Corporate Crime."
8. Kauzlarich and Kramer, "State-Corporate Crime."
9. National Academy of Sciences, cited in Kauzlarich and Kramer, "State-Corporate Crime," 13.

10. Kauzlarich and Kramer, "State-Corporate Crime."
11. Reicher, cited in Kauzlarich and Kramer, "State-Corporate Crime," 15.
12. T.M. Hammett and J. Epstein, *Local Prosecution of Environmental Crime* (Washington, DC: National Institute of Justice, June 1993), 4.
13. Hammett and Epstein, *Local Prosecution of Environmental Crime.*
14. Kauzlarich and Kramer, "State-Corporate Crime."
15. Hammett and Epstein, *Local Prosecution of Environmental Crime*, 5.
16. Kauzlarich and Kramer, "State-Corporate Crime."
17. Kauzlarich and Kramer, "State-Corporate Crime."
18. Kauzlarich and Kramer, "State-Corporate Crime."
19. Kauzlarich and Kramer, "State-Corporate Crime."
20. Kauzlarich and Kramer, "State-Corporate Crime."
21. Kauzlarich and Kramer, "State-Corporate Crime," 15.
22. Cited in Kauzlarich and Kramer, "State-Corporate Crime," 14.
23. Kauzlarich and Kramer, "State-Corporate Crime," 14.
24. Cited in Kauzlarich and Kramer, "State-Corporate Crime," 15.
25. M.C. Seis and G.J. Howard, "Hegemony, Cooptation of Environmental Imagery, and the Social Control of Wayward Corporations," paper presented at the annual meeting of the American Society of Criminology, 9–12 November 1994, Miami, FL.
26. H. Wolpe, *The Prosecution of Environmental Crimes at the Department of Energy's Rocky Flats Facility*, Subcommittee on Investigations and Oversight of the House Committee on Science, Space, and Technology, Washington, DC, 4 January 1993.
27. Wolpe, *Prosecution of Environmental Crimes*, 33.
28. Wolpe, *Prosecution of Environmental Crimes*, 33.
29. Wolpe, *Prosecution of Environmental Crimes.*
30. Kauzlarich and Kramer, "State-Corporate Crime."
31. Kauzlarich and Kramer, "State-Corporate Crime," 17.
32. Wolpe, *Prosecution of Environmental Crimes*, 13–14.
33. Wolpe, *Prosecution of Environmental Crimes*, 14.
34. Wolpe, *Prosecution of Environmental Crimes.*
35. Wolpe, *Prosecution of Environmental Crimes*, 34.
36. Wolpe, *Prosecution of Environmental Crimes*, 106.
37. Wolpe, *Prosecution of Environmental Crimes*, 107.
38. R.A. Liroff, *Reforming Air Pollution Regulation: The Toil and Trouble of EPA's Bubble* (Washington, DC: Conservation Foundation, 1986).
39. M.C. Seis, "An Eco-critical Criminological Analysis of the 1990 Clean Air Act" (Ph.D. diss., Indiana University of Pennsylvania, 1996).
40. Seis, "An Eco-critical Criminological Analysis of the 1990 Clean Air Act."
41. U.S. Senate Committee on Environmental and Public Works, *Three Years Later: Report Card on the 1990 Clean Air Act Amendments* (Washington, DC: U.S. Government Printing Office, 1993).
42. Seis, "An Eco-critical Criminological Analysis of the 1990 Clean Air Act."

43. U.S. Senate Committee on Environmental and Public Works, *Three Years Later.*
44. U.S. Senate Committee on Environmental and Public Works, *Three Years Later*, 7.
45. U.S. Senate Committee on Environmental and Public Works, *Three Years Later*, 7.
46. U.S. Senate Committee on Environmental and Public Works, *Three Years Later.*
47. U.S. Senate Committee on Environmental and Public Works, *Three Years Later.*
48. H.C. Barnett, *Toxic Debts and the Superfund Dilemma* (Chapel Hill, NC: University of North Carolina Press, 1994).
49. M.H. Bernstein, *Regulating Business by Independent Commission* (Princeton, NJ: Princeton University Press, 1955).
50. N. Frank and M. Lombness, *Controlling Corporate Illegality: The Regulatory Justice System* (Cincinnati, OH: Anderson Publishing Co., 1988).
51. N. Frank and M. Lynch, *Corporate Crime and Corporate Violence: A Primer* (New York: Harrow and Heston, 1992).
52. J.E. Anderson, "The Public Utility Commission of Texas: A Case of Capture or Rapture?" *Policy Studies Review* 1 (1982): 484–490.
53. U.S. Senate Committee on Environmental and Public Works, *Three Years Later*, 11.
54. M.C. Seis, "Ecological Blunder in US Clean Air Legislation," *Journal of Human Justice* 5, no. 1 (1993): 58–81.
55. Seis, "An Eco-critical Criminological Analysis of the 1990 Clean Air Act."
56. M.C Valente and W.D. Valente, *Introduction to Environmental Law and Policy: Protecting the Environment through Law* (St. Paul, MN: West Publishing, 1995).
57. A.M. Freeman III, "Water Pollution Policy," in *Public Policies for Environmental Protection*, ed. P.R. Portney (Washington, DC: Resources for the Future, 1990), 105.
58. Valente and Valente, *Introduction to Environmental Law and Policy*, 275.
59. Valente and Valente, *Introduction to Environmental Law and Policy.*
60. Freeman, "Water Pollution Policy."
61. Freeman, "Water Pollution Policy," 113.
62. Freeman, "Water Pollution Policy," 114.
63. M.L. McKinney and R.M. Schoch, *Environmental Science: System and Solutions* (St. Paul, MN: West Publishing, 1996), 456.
64. B. Commoner, *Making Peace with the Planet* (New York: Pantheon Books, 1990).
65. Commoner, *Making Peace with the Planet.*
66. Commoner, *Making Peace with the Planet.*
67. Commoner, *Making Peace with the Planet.*
68. Valente and Valente, *Introduction to Environmental Law and Policy*, 306.
69. Valente and Valente, *Introduction to Environmental Law and Policy.*
70. McKinney and Schoch, *Environmental Science*, 436.
71. Valente and Valente, *Introduction to Environmental Law and Policy.*
72. Commoner, *Making Peace with the Planet.*
73. Cited in Valente and Valente, *Introduction to Environmental Law and Policy*, 141.
74. Commoner, *Making Peace with the Planet*, 107.
75. Valente and Valente, *Introduction to Environmental Law and Policy.*

76. Commoner, *Making Peace with the Planet*.
77. Freeman, "Water Pollution Policy."
78. P.R. Portney, ed., *Public Policies for Environmental Protection* (Washington, DC: Resources for the Future, 1990).
79. C.S. Russell, "Monitoring and Enforcement," in *Public Policies for Environmental Protection*, ed. P.R. Portney (Washington, DC: Resources for the Future, 1990), 258.
80. Cited in Russell, "Monitoring and Enforcement," 258.
81. Valente and Valente, *Introduction to Environmental Law and Policy*, 306.
82. Valente and Valente, *Introduction to Environmental Law and Policy*.
83. Valente and Valente, *Introduction to Environmental Law and Policy*, 162.
84. McKinney and Schoch, *Environmental Science*, 457.
85. J.S. Albanese and R.D. Pursley, *Crime in America: Some Existing and Emerging Issues* (Englewood Cliffs, NJ: Regents/Prentice Hall, 1993).
86. H.C. Barnett, "Crimes against the Environment: Superfund Enforcement at Last," in *White-Collar Crime: The Annals of the American Academy of Political and Social Science*, eds. G. Geis and P. Jesilow (London: Sage, 1993).
87. V.J. Cass, "Toxic Tragedy: Illegal Hazardous Waste Dumping in Mexico," in *Environmental Crime and Criminality: Theoretical and Practical Issues*, eds. S.M. Edwards et al. (New York: Garland Publishing, 1996).
88. S.M. Edwards et al., eds., *Environmental Crime and Criminality: Theoretical and Practical Issues* (New York: Garland Publishing, 1996).
89. Frank and Lynch, *Corporate Crime and Corporate Violence*.
90. S.L. Hill, ed., *Corporate Violence: Injury and Death for Profit* (Savage, MD: Rowman & Littlefield, 1987).
91. J. Reiman, *The Rich Get Richer and the Poor Get Prison: Ideology, Crime and Criminal Justice*, 4th ed. (Boston: Allyn & Bacon, 1995).
92. M. Edelstein, *Contaminated Communities: The Social and Psychological Impacts of Residential Toxic Exposure* (Boulder, CO: Westview Press, 1988), 3.
93. M. Tallmer, "Chemical Dumping as a Corporate Way of Life," in *Corporate Violence: Injury and Death for Profit*, ed. S.L. Hill (Savage, MD: Rowman & Littlefield, 1987).
94. Hammett and Epstein, *Local Prosecution of Environmental Crime*, 4.
95. Hammett and Epstein, *Local Prosecution of Environmental Crime*.
96. Tallmer, "Chemical Dumping as a Corporate Way of Life."
97. Tallmer, "Chemical Dumping as a Corporate Way of Life," 118.
98. Tallmer, "Chemical Dumping as a Corporate Way of Life."
99. Tallmer, "Chemical Dumping as a Corporate Way of Life."
100. D.J. Rebovich, *Dangerous Ground: The World of Hazardous Waste Crime* (New Brunswick, NJ: Transaction Publishers, 1992), 3–4.
101. Hammett and Epstein, *Local Prosecution of Environmental Crime*, 5.
102. Hammett and Epstein, *Local Prosecution of Environmental Crime*.
103. M. Dowie, "Pinto Madness," in *Corporate Violence: Injury and Death for Profit*, ed. S.L. Hill (Savage, MD: Rowman & Littlefield, 1987).
104. N. Frank, "Murder in the Workplace," in *Corporate Violence: Injury and Death for Profit*, ed. S.L. Hill (Savage, MD: Rowman & Littlefield, 1987).

105. Allen, "GM in $45 Million Settlement To Recall 470,000 Cars," *Reuters*, 30 November 1995.
106. Allen, "GM in $45 Million Settlement."
107. Cited in Allen, "GM in $45 Million Settlement."
108. McKinney and Schoch, *Environmental Science*.
109. Allen, "GM in $45 Million Settlement."
110. J. Epstein and T.M. Hammett, *Law Enforcement Response to Environmental Crime* (Washington, DC: National Institute of Justice, January 1995), 4.
111. Epstein and Hammett, *Law Enforcement Response to Environmental Crime*.
112. Epstein and Hammett, *Law Enforcement Response to Environmental Crime*, 5.
113. Epstein and Hammett, *Law Enforcement Response to Environmental Crime*.
114. Epstein and Hammett, *Law Enforcement Response to Environmental Crime*.
115. Epstein and Hammett, *Law Enforcement Response to Environmental Crime*, 6.
116. Epstein and Hammett, *Law Enforcement Response to Environmental Crime*, 7.
117. Albanese and Pursley, *Crime in America*.
118. Barnett, "Crimes against the Environment."
119. Frank and Lynch, *Corporate Crime and Corporate Violence*.
120. Reiman, *The Rich Get Richer and the Poor Get Prison*.
121. Epstein and Hammett, *Law Enforcement Response to Environmental Crime*.
122. McKinney and Schoch, *Environmental Science*.
123. Epstein and Hammett, *Law Enforcement Response to Environmental Crime*.
124. Hammett and Epstein, *Local Prosecution of Environmental Crime*.
125. Hammett and Epstein, *Local Prosecution of Environmental Crime*, 13.
126. J.W. Starr, "Environmental Enforcement Takes an Ominous New Turn: Managers and Officers Go Directly to Jail," *Environmental News* 2, no. 1 (1988): 1–3.
127. Hammett and Epstein, *Local Prosecution of Environmental Crime*.
128. Percival et al., *Environmental Regulation*.
129. Hammett and Epstein, *Local Prosecution of Environmental Crime*.
130. Percival et al., *Environmental Regulation*, 995.
131. P.C. Yeager, "Structural Bias in Regulatory Law Enforcement: The Case of the U.S. Environmental Protection Agency," *Social Problems* 34 (1987): 330–344.
132. P.C. Yeager, *The Limits of Law: The Public Regulation of Private Pollution* (Cambridge: Cambridge University Press, 1991).
133. Yeager, "Structural Bias in Regulatory Law Enforcement."
134. Hammett and Epstein, *Local Prosecution of Environmental Crime*, 15.
135. Commoner, *Making Peace with the Planet*, 14.
136. D.H. Meadows, *Beyond the Limits: Confronting Global Collapse, Envisioning a Sustainable Future* (Post Mills, VT: Chelsea Green Publishing Co., 1992).
137. R. Murphy, *Rationality and Nature: A Sociological Inquiry into a Changing Relationship* (Boulder, CO: Westview Press, 1994).
138. A. Schnaiberg and K.A. Gould, *Environment and Society: The Enduring Conflict* (New York: St. Martin's Press, 1994).

CHAPTER 12

Environmental Ethics, Criminal Law, and Environmental Crime

Nanci Koser Wilson

TERMS	land pyramid	procaryotes
	paradigm	transcendent self

Criminal law entered the environmental arena through the backdoor. For the most part, environmental law consists of "heavy administrative orders."[1(p.299)] When offenders are not in compliance with regulations, criminal law has been sought as a tool to force compliance. Although criminal prosecution of environmental crime cases is still used sparingly, many criminal justice experts argue that wrongful behavior "is generally deterred more by criminal prosecution than by civil or administrative action."[2(p.56)] Federal legislators added criminal sanctions to earlier administrative laws in an effort to force compliance. As discussed in earlier sections of the text, criminal penalties were included in the major federal environmental statutes enacted in the 1970s. As these acts have been reauthorized, Congress has expanded the range of violations for which criminal penalties apply while increasing substantially the size of the penalties.[3] States have followed suit. Edwards observes, "Any meaningful measure of whether or not a society is serious about the enforcement of environmental statutes has to include an assessment of states' efforts . . . with regards to the criminal prosecution of environmental violations."[4(p.205)] Law enforcement officials also put the case this way: "Criminal enforcement is an essential strategy for stemming environmental wrongdoing,"[5(p.1)] the effects of which cannot be replaced by regulatory activity. Prosecutors echo this sentiment, saying the response to environmental violations "rightly includes administrative, civil, and criminal remedies. Criminal penalties may, however, offer the most potent deterrent effect on potential violators."[6(p.xi)]

But effective criminal law requires more than the capacity to apply punitive sanctions; it requires an ethical base. Crime, after all, refers to those acts determined by society to be *morally* wrong. The criminal justice process serves not only to inflict punishment for actions already deemed immoral but to *create* moral outrage. This process, as Emile Durkheim noted,[7] affirms group sentiment and helps to create the "collective conscience" driving the determination of moral behavior.

In apparent agreement with Durkheim, the early shapers of American environmental law believed such law could aid in the formation of an ethical system oriented toward the environment. In establishing the EPA, Congress identified the need "to create and maintain conditions under which man and nature can exist in productive harmony."[8] The EPA's first director, William Ruckelshaus, saw the agency's mission as assisting in the "development of an environmental ethic."[9(p.6)]

But societies do not simply create ethical systems out of whole cloth; typically an ethical system evolves through practice. In finding the solution to problematic cases, laws emerge that govern the relations between parties to a dispute.[10] When Ruckelshaus identified his vision for the EPA, his problem was this. Although Americans have always possessed an ethical system, "our ethical heritage largely attaches values and rights to persons, and if nonpersonal realms enter, they enter only as tributary to the personal."[11(p.20)] To date, the process of developing our current ethical system has incorporated little discussion about the natural environment.

Our ethical system may be properly described as "humanistic" or "human centered." It focuses on the human species and on what is considered good for humans. Typical issues include how to distribute goods in an equitable

Calvin and Hobbes   by Bill Watterson

manner and how to restrain human wants that may interfere with the wants or goods of other humans. Because the system was created to deal with harms committed by humans against other humans, our current ethical **paradigm**—our model for thinking about ethical issues—does not provide a basis for considering crimes against the environment.

The preceding chapters have described the process of creating and enforcing environmental laws and prosecuting violations of these laws. A significant portion of the controversy associated with environmental laws and their enforcement has developed for two reasons. First, our current ethical system does not encompass the environment. As a result, early efforts to address environmental violations have been dealt with as if they fit neatly into the existing human-centered ethic. They do not. A second yet clearly related problem is that environmental laws and current attitudes toward the environment have been based primarily in reaction to problematic cases. Without an adequate ethical base, efforts to develop consistent legal responses continue to be unfocused, disorganized, and lacking in a common objective.

Controversy is inevitable when issues related to the environment are dealt with using our existing human-centered ethical system. Developing an environmental ethic—a system of ethical precepts that can be used to explain our treatment of the environment—could alleviate a significant portion of this conflict and provide guidance for assessing the merits of future environmental law cases. This chapter outlines three approaches to resolving the problem of creating an environmental ethic and identifies some of the logical and ethical problems associated with each.

MODEL 1: ENDOWING NONHUMANS WITH HUMANLIKE RIGHTS

One strategy for developing an environmental ethic is to extend our human-centered ethical system directly to nonhumans. Since our system is rights based, this solution simply endows nonhumans with rights similar to those reserved traditionally for humans. Animal rights advocates, as their name suggests, have articulated and acted on such a set of ideas. The Endangered Species Act implies that all species, not only humans, deserve protection. Although the act does not specifically mention natural or legal rights possessed by plants and animals, its framework acknowledges the importance of the species, both individually and as a part of the collective whole.

Ethicists who have proposed the existence of nonhuman rights have encountered strong opposition. To understand why, consider the following issues.

INSIGHT

Natural Toxins

Across the country people express concerns about hazardous chemicals and toxins in the environment. In many cases, however, those same people might be surprised to find out that some toxins are natural. Consider two well-known examples—the rattlesnake and the scorpion.

The scientific study of the chemicals produced by living plants and animals is called chemical ecology.[1] In some cases, scientists are learning how little they know about the animals they study. One example is a noisy jay-sized New Guinea bird called the pitohui, known to scientists since 1827. In 1989, chemical testing of this bird showed its skin and feathers contained poison. Extracts of pitohui skin and feathers were injected into mice, and the result was paralysis leading to convulsions and death in as little as 15 minutes. Further analysis showed the chemical to be the same found in poison dart frogs, so called because the Indians of South and Central America use the animal's skin to poison blowgun darts. The poison in the pitohui "is one of the most poisonous substances known, hundreds of times more powerful than strychnine."[2(p.12)]

Clearly, this animal, and others that are known to produce natural toxins, could be considered dangerous to humans. How should humans treat such species?

1. J. Diamond, "Stinking Birds and Burning Books: Want To Make New Discoveries in Chemical Ecology? Talk with a Tribal Hunter," *Natural History*, February 1994, 4–12.
2. Diamond, "Stinking Birds and Burning Books," 12.

First, human-centered ethics involve reciprocity. It is widely believed that each human actor is self-conscious and therefore capable of determining his or her own ethical behavior. But no reciprocal ethics can exist between humans and beings that do not or cannot act ethically. Does the sun have an obligation to rise each morning? Does your dog feel bad when he bites a neighbor's child? Ethical standards cannot be imposed unless the actor is capable of understanding that some acts are wrong and thus can make decisions that reflect this knowledge.

Consequently, whatever protections humans have from environmental harm are based on laws that require certain actions from other humans. If I have a right to clean air, it is a right that restricts someone else's right to pollute that air. If you have a right to be free from the threat of dog bites, it is the dog owners who must assume the responsibility for training their dogs or keeping them away from situations that could result in someone being bitten. For example, someone who was bitten by a stray dog is typically seen as being justified in retaliating—even killing the dog. However, someone who is taunting the dog will get little sympathy if the dog bites him or her as a result. It is assumed that taunting the dog is not a smart thing to do, and anyone who does so must assume responsibility for the consequences. On the other hand, different people attribute "rights" to both the human and the dog involved. Consistently poor treatment of dogs in all circumstances reinforces the idea that humans have the right to treat dogs poorly in any situation. An important question remains. What responsibility does each individual have to protect him- or herself from being bitten by a dog? Further, how are actions to be directed when such an act occurs? The answers to these questions all involve human action. While the actions displayed are not predetermined, the human rights are identified and reinforced based upon the human response.

Second, rights-based concepts of justice and crime are often absolutist. Criminal law in the United States is full of prohibitions and commands. One must not murder another human being. Parents must feed and take care of their children. Humans are viewed as having an absolute right to life. But the application of the justice process to the environment cannot be absolute. Life on earth is a series of food and service chains, as was discussed in Chapter 4. It includes predation and destruction in addition to the creation of new life and the sustenance of existing life. Aldo Leopold described the system of life as a **land pyramid**. Species on each layer are alike, not in where they come from or in what they look like but rather in what they eat.[12]

Thus, wolves and rivers simply cannot have an absolute right to existence. To claim such a right puts humans in an indefensible position. For example, suppose the AIDS virus had an absolute right to existence. HIV-positive humans would not be justified then in trying to fight the infection. This flies in the face of our view that humans have a right to live a life free from disease and be given adequate protection (often expected to come from the government) against unnecessary harm. Further, because of the interconnectedness of humans and nonhumans, humans would no longer be able to proclaim an absolute right to human welfare taking priority over the welfare of nonhumans.

A model 1 approach to environmental ethics must therefore stop short of bestowing nonhumans with absolute rights. Stone, for example, writes that "to say that the environment should have rights is not to say that it should have every right we can imagine, or even the same body of rights that human beings have established."[13(p.6)] But a weaker version of this approach would encounter similar difficulties, because many (if not all) Americans agree that human uses of nature take precedence over any rights held by nonhumans. Thus, in ardent opposition to the Endangered Species Act, some have suggested that even if species extinction is the result of human actions, and even if these actions are not essential to human existence, the human uses of nature should not be impeded. This would mean that humans could dam a river for recreational purposes, even if that action extinguished the snail darter, another species, or an entire riparian ecosystem.

Nash suggests that the problem is linked to the fact that throughout U.S. history certain groups of people have benefited from denying ethical treatment to other groups (or to nature).[14] Those who receive the benefits are often reluctant to relinquish them. Mies provides a harsh critique of the modern concept of rights, arguing that human rights are built upon the denial of rights to "nature" (or upon exploitation).[15] The logical flaw in the strategy of extending full human rights to nature is that, "in a contradictory and exploitative relationship, the privileges of the exploiters can never become the privileges of all" because such equal rights "would necessarily include the right to exploit others."[16(p.76)]

MODEL 2: ENDOWING HUMANS WITH THE RIGHT TO A HEALTHY ENVIRONMENT

Given the difficulties with granting rights to nonhuman species, we need another model for developing an environmental ethic. One possible strategy is to grant humans the right to a healthy environment. Several attempts have been made to give this concept legal force, but the U.S. justice system has consistently backed away from fully supporting such a right. Yet milder versions of such a right are the most consistent theme underlying current environmental law.

According to model 2, environmental law should regulate the competing rights of various human beings to use natural resources. One requirement, however, is that any use of natural resources must not endanger the health of other humans. This approach protects nonhumans only indirectly, insofar as the health of nonhumans is linked to human health. In addition, it encourages a balancing of perspectives regarding environmental safety. Questions like "how safe is safe?" and "can we afford clean air?" are asked and must be addressed.

Yet problems also plague this model. First, it fosters conflict, because it focuses solely on human health. It is not constructed to seek solutions that may benefit both humans and nonhumans. Such solutions—where both humans and nonhumans benefit—would reduce or eliminate conflict. Further, because nonhuman activity can affect human interests, the separation of interests is not clear. The lack of clearly identified boundaries also can create conflict.

Stone notes the following conflicts that occur in current environmental disputes:[17]

1. natural persons versus natural persons
2. natural persons versus corporations
3. corporations versus corporations
4. nation-states versus nation-states
5. natural persons versus animals
6. animals versus animals
7. right of a particular culture to survive versus various other interests
8. right of a species to survive versus various other interests
9. right of future generations versus rights of current generation
10. right of a habitat or the earth as a whole to exist versus various other interests

In a model 2 type approach, items 5, 6, 8, and 10 are secondary conflicts, which means they do not involve the opposition of humans against humans. The Clean Air Act makes a similar distinction—between primary and secondary standards. Primary standards directly concern human health. Secondary standards are protective of human needs, other than health, and are protective of "the environment." Given the traditional priority attached to human health, it is not surprising that no secondary standards have ever been promulgated.[18]

A second problem in model 2 is that human action is often too little, too late—even when the concern is human health. The focus on human welfare assumes that we know what is harmful. As discussed in Chapter 4, our scientific understanding has limits. Because environmental policy is largely based on our current scientific views, it also has limits. More and more often, concern is expressed about the interconnections within environmental systems. Because these systems are interconnected, it may be that any action that harms nonhumans has some potential to harm humans. For this reason, Aldo Leopold suggested that an environmental ethic should be used as a "mode of guidance for meeting ecological situations so new or intricate, or involving such deferred reaction"[19(p.203)] in cases when humans are unable to predict harm. For example, pesticides were added to crops and eventually moved up the food chain. One result was adverse health effects for humans. The composition of the atmosphere is believed to have been altered by human consumption of chlorofluorocarbons (CFCs). Again, humans had no knowledge that use of CFCs would have adverse, if not potentially devastating, effects. An environmental ethic that encompassed protections for nonhumans as well as humans might prevent such mistakes.

MODEL 3: THE LAND ETHIC OR THE ECOLOGICAL MODEL

This third approach was originally outlined in Aldo Leopold's 1949 book, *A Sand County Almanac*. He identifies the following components:

a. Humans are seen as plain members of (rather than rulers over) the natural community.
b. By implication, as a member of a community, the human has certain obligations to other members of the community.
c. These obligations are different from those one might have to other humans, and all are probably different from one another.
d. The general obligation would be to treat each member of the community according to its own nature. To treat a wolf as a mere resource, a means to another (usually human) end and not as an end in itself is wrong. But to treat a wolf like a man is also wrong. It is, *inter alia*, unfair to the wolf. The obligation is to the wolf *qua* wolf.[20]

The ecological model takes account of the differences between humans and nonhumans. Both are treated as worthy of moral consideration, although in different ways. A central feature is its focus on the interconnectedness of all forms of life, including the abiotic (nonliving) components of the environment, such as the land, the water, and the atmosphere. Leopold suggested that "a thing is right when it tends to preserve the integrity, stability and beauty of the biotic community. It is wrong when it tends otherwise."[21(p.225)]

To better understand this approach, consider Leopold's short essay "Thinking Like a Mountain." The author describes his youthful desire to kill wolves so that there will be more deer for him to hunt. "I was young then, and full of trigger-itch; I thought that because fewer wolves meant more deer, then no wolves would mean a hunter's paradise."[22(p.130)] Gradually he came to realize that when wolves no longer kill deer, deer overpopulate the mountain, eating all its brush. This in turn creates erosion, which eventually destroys the mountain. He wrote, "I now suspect that just as a deer herd lives in mortal fear of its wolves, so does a mountain live in mortal fear of its deer. And perhaps with better cause, for while a buck pulled down by wolves can be replaced in two or three years, a range pulled down by too many deer may fail of replacement in as many decades."[23(p.132)]

When Leopold suggests that one should "think like a mountain," he does not mean that the mountain has a right to be covered with trees. Nor is he saying that the trees have a right to be there or that the deer have a right to browse or that the wolf has a right to live by hunting deer. Instead, he is pointing out in simple terms nature's intricate interconnectedness. For humans to recognize this interconnectedness is essential. Simply stated, we are causally related to other creatures. We depend on them for a variety of "services" that are accomplished in complex ways. In Leopold's vision, harm to humans and harm to the environment amount to the same thing—at least in the long run. An environmental ethic based on this model would skirt the issue of separate or contradictory human and nonhuman interests by proposing the vision of a **transcendent self** that identifies with all of life. The transcendent self would take the emphasis off of individual humans and grant attention to the relationship between humans and ecosystems. "When we recall its diffusion of the boundary between the individual and the ecosystem, we cannot say whether value in the system or in the individual is logically prior."[24(p.25)]

Yet questions also arise for the ecological model. Identifying what is natural is not as easy as it may seem. What is the nature of the wolf? To which elements of the mountain do we owe respect? Other problems remain. First, our knowledge of such things is limited. We cannot always say with certainty what the essence of a thing is, whether that thing is human or nonhuman. Second, life on earth evolves. As a result, the nature of things changes, and something known to be true today may no longer be true tomorrow. Third, one could identify man's second nature to be culture. Culture is also natural. Consequently, some claim that our dominion over nonhuman nature is part of nature's plan—it is part of the natural order of things. Finally, contemporary humans are strikingly alienated from nature. Leopold wrote that humans are moving "away from rather than toward an intense consciousness of land."[25(p.223)]

While the ecological model provides an interesting variety of perspectives, it does not solve all of the problems that arise. It simply presents them in a different way. In short, even once it is learned (if it can be known) what is natural, then the ultimate ethical questions remain: What obligations do I owe to other members of the earth community? What obligation do I have to humans? What obligations do I have to plants and animals? What obligations do I owe to the biotic community in general?

Certainly, the ecological model will seem alien or even radical to some. People in the United States, however, already have much experience with this sort of ethical reasoning. Consider the following examples. First, owners of small animals are aware that they can be treated like humans only to a limited degree. Any successful owner of a pet (or a working animal like a guard or hunting dog) knows the animal's needs and nature must be considered. The pet owner knows he or she must work with that nature rather than against it. A dog's nature is to bond with the "pack," and a smart dog owner attempts to get the dog to view him or her as the pack leader. Further, a dog's nature, like that of a bear, is to chase objects that move. To expect a young dog not to chase young children, bicycles, or even cars is unrealistic. Through training, however, a dog can be taught to chase only specific items.

Similarly, the owner of a cat would be eternally frustrated if he or she expected the cat not to stalk and chase birds. Such behavior would be counter to the nature of the cat. But by belling the cat and perhaps keeping it indoors during the peak bird feeding hours, the cat owner can also be a successful birdwatcher. And while owners may realistically expect some rodent control, they must also expect cats to occasionally deliver a dead songbird (with pride) at their feet.

Such considerations do not completely solve the problem of what humans owe to a dog or a cat or a songbird. They do point, however, to the various forms of life and the necessity to respect the nature of each life form. They suggest minimally that obligations between humans and nonhumans begin with mutual respect.

A second example of the ethical reasoning outlined in the ecological model is provided by issues that arise in farming and gardening. Farmers who raise stock for the market help their situation by drawing a sharp distinction between pets and stock (a common rule taught to farm children is that you never name an animal that is bred for slaughter). Even so, ethical considerations of another sort apply to farm stock. Farmers must consider that they or their customers are going to eat the animals. Does this mean that a farmer's obligation is to the profit margin or to the consumer's health? Under models 1 and 2, conflicts often arise in answering this question. Under the ecological model, doing the "natural" thing will (in some cases) dissolve these conflicts. Because nature is a congruent whole, what is good for each constituent is good for the whole and vice versa. For example, raising organic dairy products can be good for humans, good for the farmer's profit margin, and good for the dairy cow. Again, the ecological model does not solve all problems. Where or how does a farmer draw the line between ethical and unethical treatment of stock? The underlying issue remains. Perhaps one believes bovine growth hormone regimens to be wrong,[26] but is dairying wrong in itself? The ultimate question under this model is how much of the cow's nature one can respect or foster while still owning it primarily to produce milk.

The gardener faces similar problems. Is it ethical to exterminate all forms of life that threaten the garden produce? Heavy use of chemical pesticides and fertilizers may threaten the community's drinking water supply. Shooting every rabbit that invades the broccoli patch may threaten not only the rabbit population but other components of the biotic community as well. How does a birdwatcher also protect the raspberry vines? Searching for a balanced approach that respects the variety of life in the garden is a difficult task. If the interconnectedness of life is the primary concern, this is probably the most successful approach to develop an environmental ethic.

To illustrate the very different forms of ethical reasoning, consider an apple from all three perspectives. Under model 1, which grants human rights to nonhumans, is it the objective, or right, of the apple to be eaten? Under model 2, which grants humans the right to a healthy environment, do humans have the right to eat good apples? In the case of models 1 and 2, an ethicist must focus on a way to measure the value of an apple and balance it against the rights of humans. Under these two models, the apple would have value only if eaten by humans. For those using such reasoning, the apple cannot realize its own value. If uneaten, it rots and is of no use to anyone. The eater's pleasure is genuine and thus remains the primary objective.[27]

For the advocates of natural rights (or the ecological model), the apple itself has intrinsic value—a value attaches to it that is not adequately measured by externally established assessments of worth. "The apple functions as a gamble in seed dispersal. Its value is realized when birds, deer, or humans take the bait."[28(p.117)] The apple takes care of animals by providing nourishment, and animals take care of the apple by providing seed disbursement.

A similar example involves the role of **procaryotes**. These are simple bacteria that ran a successful biosphere and represented life on earth for nearly two billion years. They are still today responsible for a great deal of the running of the present ecological systems. Lynn Margulis once remarked that the true function of mammals, including humans, might be to serve as ideal habitats for the few pounds of bacteria carried in the guts. They are kept warm and well-fed there, in what must seem their own private heaven.[29]

Humans and the apple (or humans and the procaryote) are not easily divisible into human assessments of value. Each type of organism is individually valuable and part of the same whole value. Neither can realize its own purpose without the other. This is the insight of ecology, and when using the ecological model one reaches different ethical conclusions than when using the other models. The others treat individual beings as separate or atomistic and possessed of degrees of importance, whereas the ecological model treats all things as interconnected and equally important.

GENERAL PROBLEMS WITH THE THREE MODELS

As noted at the outset, an environmental ethic could serve as a solid foundation for studying environmental criminal law more thoroughly. As discussed in the earlier chapters, the system of criminal justice acts on the assumption that harm has been caused by a particular individual who knew his or her actions were harmful.[30] Because attention to date has been limited to human-human interactions, little has been decided about how to deal with human-nonhuman interactions. Clearly, no matter which model is used, some problems remain.

One common feature of environmental harm is that it is cumulative—major harm often results from only minor actions that individually hardly seem worthy of concern. But to put the force of the criminal law behind environmental regulations requires that people see the harm caused by relatively minor infractions.

A second problem related to the cumulative nature of human environmental impact is that it is unclear who has the obligation to maintain common resources such as wetlands. *Just v. Marinette County*[31] dealt with this problem by describing it as a duty of the landowner to keep the land in a natural state. This has proven unworkable, and in *Lucas v. So. Carolina Coastal Council*[32] the court ruled that compensation must be provided to owners if they are required to maintain wetlands on their property. The ruling thus, "protects the right of property owners to engage in transformative activities which are wholly incompatible with the land's ecological functions."[33(p.198)] Given that a certain amount of wetlands is necessary to safeguard everyone's drinking water, how should the responsibility to maintain wetlands be allocated? American law has yet to find an adequate answer.

Whereas the equitable distribution of benefits and burdens is not a new problem for ethical theory, the equitable distribution of many environmental costs and benefits is. Many resources that have recently become scarce and therefore require distribution policies were formerly free and unre-

Modern Science Meets Native Tradition[1]

In Myanmar, formerly Burma, for more than 100 years men and elephants labored together to extract timber. The last country to use elephants for logging, Burma has a reverence for heritage that has allowed some of the largest tracts of forests on earth to flourish unspoiled.

The elephants offer several ecological benefits over machines. Consider the following:

- They enter and exit the forests on narrow paths, removing the need for an extensive network of logging roads.
- Whereas the elephants tread lightly, much of the vegetation destroyed in the construction of logging roads never recovers.
- Elephants run on renewable and cheap green fuel, whereas logging machinery requires expensive polluting petroleum.

Use of elephants, however, involves special difficulties:

- Currently, because of the demand for trees and the need to compete with foreign timber companies, 5,700 elephants are in use.

- To maintain the foresting herd, adolescent elephants (between the ages of 12 and 18 years) must be taken from wild herds.
- Too few elephants exist in the wild to maintain the large herds necessary to ensure enough timber can be extracted and the timber companies remain competitive.

In 1992, a veterinarian at the Myanmar Timber Enterprise contacted the Metro Washington Park Zoo in Portland, Oregon. The zoo has a 33-year-old program for breeding captive elephants, and because the Asian elephant is approaching extinction, the timber program desperately needs new elephants. Using the program's techniques for breeding elephants provides "a unique opportunity to conserve an endangered species. . . . If their numbers can be kept intact, there will always be a population of Asian elephants on the earth that is large enough and genetically diverse enough to yield many generations of healthy offspring."[2(p.83)]

---

1. M. Schmidt, "Working Elephants: They Earn Their Keep in Asia by Providing an Ecologically Benign Way To Harvest Forests," *Scientific American*, January 1996, 82–87.
2. Schmidt, "Working Elephants," 83.

stricted (drinking water is a good example). Reports suggest modern society "cannot afford" clean air. And while racism in modern American society is not new, the placement of toxic waste facilities in minority communities is a relatively new theme in academic discourse. These items taken together suggest there is a need to develop and adopt an environmental ethic for the purpose of ensuring equity and justice for humans and protection of the natural environment.

CONCLUSION

Stone suggests that there is currently a crisis in moral frameworks precisely because the old human-centered framework no longer fits our situation:

> Advances in technology, the bureaucratization, the scarcity of resources, the moral maturation of mankind forces our thought to run along radically different channels. . . . Today moral and legal conflicts [are] of a more complex and . . . multilayered kind than the traditional dilemmas. They are less satisfactorily modeled by the conventional person-oriented, or human-centered, frameworks.[34(p.36)]

As we have seen, contemporary humans are often baffled by attempts to move beyond conventional frameworks, to include nonhumans in their ethical systems. Yet, what is it that makes this such a difficult task? Even though nature is incredibly complex, our knowledge is incredibly limited. Many fail to take minimal actions that seem obvious. For example, air pollution could be reduced significantly through the use of mass transportation systems. Yet cities continue to reject plans for mass transportation systems. Another source of air pollution is charcoal lighter fluid. Metal lighter cones, which use discarded newspaper, are more cost efficient and less likely to taint the food being cooked, but Californians, when faced with this choice under new provisions of the Clean Air Act, protested with bumper stickers that read "Use a Barbecue, Go to Jail."[35]

Perhaps things are not as complex as Stone suggests. The first step is to admit that humans have ethical obligations to nonhumans. Once this step is taken, efforts to find appropriate human behaviors to meet these obligations can begin. Questions about the relationship between humans and other members of the biotic community cannot be ignored. Do humans have obligations to pets? Livestock? Plants? Water systems? Land?

Often these obligations coincide with one another. "This coincidence of human and ecosystemic interests, frequent in environmental thought, is ethically confusing but fertile."[36(p.22)] Many wonder why developing an environmental ethic is so confusing. It is complex, certainly, but humans have dealt with similar issues. A variety of different obligations to different members of the human community have been acknowledged. For example, it is generally accepted that people do not have the same obligations to a coworker or a stranger that they have to their children. Because all of the natural world is interconnected, often our obligations will coincide. For example, meeting the obligation to keep the soil healthy is one way of meeting the obligation to leave future generations of humans a decent environment.

In this process of developing an appropriate environmental ethic, environmental laws will play a vital role, since they will aid in the creation of an ecological collective conscience. Paradoxically, though, they will lack the force of "ordinary" criminal laws until such an ethic is well along the path of development. In the meantime, those who enact and enforce environmental statutes will continue to find themselves in morally confusing territory.

REVIEW QUESTIONS

1. Identify the pros and cons of model 1 (endowing nonhumans with humanlike rights).
2. Identify the pros and cons of model 2 (endowing humans with the right to a healthy environment).
3. Identify the pros and cons of model 3 (the land ethic).
4. Identify the model for environmental ethics that, in your opinion, is most sound, and justify your choice.

DISCUSSION QUESTIONS

1. Should plants and animals be accorded standing in a court of law?
2. What is the fundamental "paradigm shift" that would be involved in accepting any of the three models?
3. Is the United States ready for an environmental ethic? Discuss each side of this issue.
4. Are other countries in the world more prepared to address ethical issues involving the environment? What evidence can you offer to support your position?
5. Be creative and imagine a world where animals and humans have equal rights. What would be different about this world? What would be similar? Justify your response.

REFERENCES

1. F. Adler et al., *Criminology* (New York: McGraw-Hill, 1991), 299.
2. D. Ross, "A Review of EPA Criminal, Civil, and Administrative Enforcement Data: Are the Efforts Measurable Deterrents to Environmental Criminals?" in *Environmental Crime and Criminality: Theoretical and Practical Issues*, ed. S.M. Edwards et al. (New York: Garland, 1996), 56.
3. R. Percival et al., *Environmental Regulation: Law, Science, and Policy* (Boston: Little, Brown, 1992), 993.
4. S.M. Edwards, "Environmental Criminal Enforcement: Efforts by the States," in *Environmental Crime and Criminality: Theoretical and Practical Issues*, ed. S.M. Edwards et al. (New York: Garland, 1996), 205.
5. J. Epstein and T. Hammett, "Law Enforcement Response to Environmental Crime," *Issues and Practices* (Washington DC: National Institute of Justice, 1995), 1.
6. T. Hammett and J. Epstein, *Local Prosecution of Environmental Crime* (Washington, DC: National Institute of Justice, 1993), xi.
7. E. Durkheim, *Rules of Sociological Method* (New York: The Free Press, 1964).
8. Title I, sec. 101, NEPA.
9. J. Lewis, "The Birth of EPA," *EPA Journal* 11, no. 9 (1985): 6–9.
10. L. Pospisil, *Anthropology of Law* (New York: Harper and Row, 1961).
11. H. Rolston, *Philosophy Gone Wild* (New York: Prometheus, 1989), 20.
12. A. Leopold, *A Sand County Almanac* (Oxford: Oxford University Press, 1949), 215.
13. C. Stone, *Earth and Other Ethics* (New York: Harper and Row, 1987), 6.
14. R.F. Nash, *The Rights of Nature* (Madison, WI: University of Wisconsin Press, 1989), 8.
15. M. Mies, *Patriarchy and Accumulation on a World Scale* (London: Zed Books, 1986), 76.
16. Mies, *Patriarchy and Accumulation on a World Scale*, 76.
17. Stone, *Earth and Other Ethics*, 37.
18. M. Seis, "An Eco-critical Criminological Analysis of the 1990 Clean Air Act" (Ph.D. diss., Indiana University of Pennsylvania, 1996).
19. Leopold, *A Sand County Almanac*, 203.
20. Leopold, *A Sand County Almanac*.
21. Leopold, *A Sand County Almanac*, 225.
22. Leopold, *A Sand County Almanac*, 130.
23. Leopold, *A Sand County Almanac*, 132.
24. Rolston, *Philosophy Gone Wild*, 25.
25. Leopold, *A Sand County Almanac*, 223.
26. Bovine growth hormone (BGH) is the gene in a cow's cells that controls growth. Scientists have "transplanted the BGH gene into microbes which manufacture commercial quantities of the hormone. The synthesized hormone is injected on a daily basis into dairy cattle." As a result, the cow's appetite is boosted by "diverting more of the food from ordinary metabolism to milk production . . . the cows produce between 10 and 25% more milk during their peak milking period following calving." This increases profits for large dairy farmers, driving out the smaller ones, which cannot afford to absorb

the initial costs and losses. The effect on the animal is "to burn her out rapidly, so that within a few years she is exhausted from the speeding up of her biological processes." The cows live a shorter life, have more infections, and suffer more heat stress. See P. Hynes, *The Recurring Silent Spring* (New York: Pergamon Press, 1989), 185.

27. Rolston, *Philosophy Gone Wild*, 117.

28. Rolston, *Philosophy Gone Wild*, 117.

29. J. Lovelock, "Gaia: A Model for Planetary and Cellular Dynamics," in *Gaia: A Way of Knowing*, ed. W.I. Thompson (Great Barrington, MA: Lindisfarne Press, 1987), 95.

30. J. Hall and G.O.W. Mueller [*Criminal Law and Procedure: Cases and Readings*, 2nd ed. (Indianapolis, IN: Bobbs-Merrill, 1965), v] summarize the classical seven requirements as (1) legally proscribed (legality), (2) human conduct (conduct), (3) causative (causality), (4) of a given harm (harm), (5) which conduct coincides (concurrence), (6) with a blameworthy frame of mind (mens rea), (7) and which is subject to punishment (punishment).

31. 56 Wis 2cd 7, 201 N.W. 761 [WI 1972].

32. 112 S. Ct. 2886, 1992.

33. C. Valente and W.D. Valente, *Introduction to Environmental Law and Policy* (St. Paul, MN: West Publishing, 1995), 304.

34. Stone, *Earth and Other Ethics*, 36.

35. J.V. Switzer, *Environmental Politics: Domestic and Global Dimensions* (New York: St. Martin's Press, 1994), 198.

36. Rolston, *Philosophy Gone Wild*, 22.

CHAPTER 13

Mystification of Environmental Images: Identifying Environmental Crime

Dion Dennis

TERMS   bionomics
chaotics

1. The most beautiful thing about a tree is what you do with it after you cut it down.[1]
2. [Some] conservative Christians say that Congress has gone too far with threats to weaken the Endangered Species Act. . . . Some evangelicals urge their leaders to turn their churches into so-called Noah congregations, [arguing] that the biblical line that man has dominion over the earth does not permit man to allow species to grow extinct.[2]
3. To "Wise Users," environmentalists are "watermelons": green on the outside but "red" [communist] to the core.[3]
4. The idea [of pollution rights] is simple: EPA sets a nationwide "cap" on the total amount of a pollutant, such as sulfur dioxide, that can be released. Then EPA [dispenses] "pollution rights" permits to companies emitting sulfur dioxide. The amount of each permit is based on a company's past history of polluting; the biggest polluters are given [for free] the biggest "pollution rights." . . . If a polluter manages to reduce pollution below the amount allowed by the permit, then a portion of [this] "pollution right" can be sold for money to another polluter. . . . The concept is so popular that the Chicago Board of Trade now conducts a brisk business in "pollution rights." . . . The [vending] of "pollution rights" [transforms] the discussion from one of fairness and public health to one of economics and high finance.[4]

5. The Noah principle, [coined] by the biologist David Ehrenfeld, is shared by many scientists and conservationists [who believe] "that our fellow passengers on Spaceship Earth . . . have a right to exist."[5]

6. We believe that private property should not be taken without compensation and that environmental policies should use free-market forces, cost-benefit analysis and risk assessment and avoid unfunded mandates. These ideas are opposed by left-leaning environmentalists whose roots remain frozen in the era of wage and price controls.[6]

7. "What we're talking about is almost absolute laissez-faire economic theory, arguing that all regulation is theft," says Chip Berlet.[7]

8. "We are against environmentalists because we feel their whole approach . . . undermines this country's economic health," [says the] executive VP of the Center for the Defense of Free Enterprise (CDFE).[8]

9. The EDF (Environmental Defense Fund)–McDonald's arrangement is an example of "high-level capitulations" that "unfortunately allow companies to look a lot greener than they are." The corporate exploitation of "win/win" compromise has been relentless.[9]

10. In the perverse world of public relations, lobbying against environmental regulations is known as "environmental" or "green" PR. "Environmental PR people enjoy sweet dreams these days [1995] as visions of . . . chopping away at 'burdensome' green regulations dance in their heads."[10]

11. Frank Boren, a board member of ARCO Petroleum, [said], "While we're working with [mainstream environmental groups], they don't have time to sue us."[11]

12. The call to protect private property rights from "government land grabs" or "unconstitutional takings" appeals strongly to rural landowners and small businesspeople. . . . "As an organizing strategy, it is a kind of deviant genius . . . [that] puts environmentalists in the position of defending [an unpopular] federal government."[12]

13. So much of this movement [environmental backlash] is about manipulating language and manipulating people's understanding of concepts like environmentalism.[13]

14. Facts don't matter; in politics, perception is reality.[14]

15. Words mean things.[15]

INTRODUCTION

Environmental issues have never existed in an ideological vacuum. Depictions of desirable relationships between humans and the environment have been thoroughly if sometimes unpredictably mixed into preexisting and sometimes competing moral, political, spiritual, scientific, economic, and social worldviews. Review the quotations above. What worldviews are represented? Consider how unstated assumptions shape each claim.

Look at quotation 1. This statement reflects a utilitarian view that assumes human, commodity-based transformation of natural resources is inherently more "beautiful" than the natural resources themselves. Quotation 2 shows right-to-life evangelical discourse in the development of a "Noah" congregation. The right-to-life debate, usually part of the abortion or capital punishment debates, is extended to the Endangered Species Act. Quotation 3 reflects a bipolar Cold War worldview. This worldview is then superimposed upon a generation of environmental activists. Environmentalism is equated with communism, an ideology generally viewed negatively in the United States.

Quotation 4 returns to a utilitarian view but brings in the issue of ownership. It points out that the "right" to pollute public air and water, through enabling language in the 1990 Clean Air Act, has now become a commodity to be bought and sold at the Chicago Board of Trade. Quotation 5 makes mention of Noah, as in quotation 2, but the orientation is basically rooted in a humanistic, Star-Trek-like "prime directive" (Spaceship Earth) rather than the divine word of the Bible.

In quotations 6, 7, and 8, economic, regulatory, and environmental dangers are assumed to be the result of an unaccountable, overreaching federal government. At issue are proclaimed illegal "takings" under the Fifth Amendment to the U.S. Constitution. Such actions are argued to be promoted by left-leaning liberals who would destroy the fundamental wisdom of Adam Smith's "invisible hand." Smith thought the role of government should be limited to mitigating market folly.

Quotations 9, 10, and 11 refer to the cooptation of environmental organizations and agendas by clever corporate strategies. "Greenwashing" corporate images allows corporations to continue business as usual while giving the impression they are environmentally responsible. Quotation 12 points out the effectiveness of the Wise Use strategy of placing mainstream environmental groups in the position of defending unpopular federal regulations. Using the takings issue as a centerpiece, the emphasis is shifted from a "hate the interfering government" idea to a "hate the people who require or request such policies."

Finally, quotations 13, 14, and 15 refer to the struggle over symbolism. The main battle is over how environmentalism, as a concept, is represented in the public relations laboratory. Each side of the environmental debate, of course, wants to make sure the issues and images at the center of the debate reflect its concerns. In the words of quotation 14, "Facts don't matter; in politics, perception is reality."

In sum, environmentalism and its competing definitions are distributed in a variety of religious, humanistic, legal, bureaucratic, economic, political, scientific, and sociocultural venues. The selected definitions are often elaborations of professed fundamental views about the nature of reality. Therefore, they often take the form of statements about what is most threatening and dangerous (in an effort to focus society on the steps that *must* be taken to counter a perceived menace).

It follows, then, that the very definition of what constitutes a crime against the environment or what constitutes an appropriate civil remedy is the product of an agreed-upon set of assumptions. Decisions are made based on what is presumed by federal and state bureaucracies, transnational corporate interests, liberal environmentalists, rural crypto-militia types, and so on, to be the greatest current danger to social well-being. Ultimately, then, the collective perception of danger is the never-quite-stable result of the discourses or explanations of reality that are most available and seem most credible at the time.

What was recently popular (in the 1960s and 1970s), the view that government protection and regulation is essential, has been replaced by the contemporary idea that the effects of governmental regulation are at best problematic and at worst inherently obstructive and counterproductive. Consider the present controversy over dam construction and the recent effort, discussed in Chapter 3, to imitate a 100-year flood by releasing huge amounts of water from the Glen Canyon Dam.

It is the collective perception of environmental danger (which may change in concert with structural, economic, and demographic changes) that will ultimately shape the definition of environmental crime. Further, the depth of the perception may be measured by the establishment of enforceable sanctions for violators of environmental laws, since the perception, embodied in law and administrative policy, sets the parameters for such sanctions.

THE MYSTIFICATION OF ENVIRONMENTAL LANGUAGE

Below are brief sketches of several competing ideologies and practices. They provide an opportunity for the reader to think creatively about the

centripetal and centrifugal forces shaping the environmental debate. The presentation of these diverse (and in some cases opposing) ideologies is structured to stimulate thought on defining environmental crime as just another "construction" within the social construction of reality.

Ideology 1: The "Natural" Market and Unnatural Governmental Regulation: Toward Narrowing the Definition of Environmental Crime

For laissez-faire marketeers, the regulatory apparatuses of governance reflect inherently "bad" and "unnatural" governance. In other words, governments that regulate nonmilitary and nonsubsidy transactions, such as routine commercial exchanges, exist in an "unnatural" state. For these thinkers, "the genius of the free market" is itself the true expression of "the natural." Aided by a new wave of sociobiological ideologists, such as Michael Rothschild, they essentialize free-market, laissez-faire capitalism. In their view, capitalism is not the product of human social history but is genetically encoded into the constantly evolving DNA of successful animal and plant species. In a sense, capitalism and life are one and the same thing.

Rothschild and others argue that regulating capitalism's market processes is equivalent to acting against life itself. Popular on the corporate lecture circuit, Rothschild has described this ideology in a simple equation: **bionomics** is Adam Smith plus social Darwinism.[16] In other words, it is only when a natural law—in this case, the survival of the fittest—is allowed to operate maximally in an unregulated environment that the beneficial effects of Adam Smith's mysterious invisible hand can be seen. Anything other than minimal regulation is interference with life itself.

Widespread acceptance of this paradigm would inevitably narrow the range of actions considered environmental crimes. Bionomic approaches and their variants regard state regulation as an almost unmitigated evil, even in the realm of health and safety.

Ideology 2: On Private Property Rights, the Takings Clause of the Fifth Amendment, and State Sovereignty: Inverting the Definition of Environmental Criminality

A potent political force among landowners and small business owners in the rural West, the Wise Use Movement contends that regulations meant to safeguard environmentally sensitive zones on private property are unconstitutional "takings." Advocates cite the Takings Clause of the Fifth Amendment of the U.S. Constitution, which reads, in part, "nor shall private property be taken for public use without just compensation." Through proposed state referenda and legislation, complemented by the submission of federal legislation, supporters have fought to extend the legal notion of a government taking to include circumstances where the maximal potential reaping of profits from developing, mining, or logging private areas is constrained by federal environmental regulations. In effect, agencies that promulgate and then implement guidelines without first submitting an economic impact statement to the affected parties would be in violation of the Fifth Amendment.

Because of the expense of creating an assessment and compensation mechanism for potential (not actual) loss of profits, the effect of such legislation would stand the definition of culpability on its head. It might be likened to a doctor being sued by a terminally ill patient for using an experimental drug that had the potential for providing a cure but in actuality did not make a difference. The doctor took a risk in an effort to save the patient's life but for lack of success is held responsible for the patient's death.

In some cases, the agencies charged with implementing frameworks for defining and prosecuting environmental crimes would themselves be criminalized. In effect, the arrow of criminality would be inverted, to be pointed in the direction of the regulatory agencies. The result, intended or not, would be a general dismantling of environmental law enforcement.

Often private property rights claims are supplemented by the argument that the federal government consistently violates "state's rights" (state sovereignty). According to Mike Dowie, sparsely populated but geographically enormous Catron County, New Mexico, enacted, between 1989 and 1995, a series of county ordinances that

> told the U.S. government to shove it. Through a series of laws and an accompanying land-use plan that have made the county famous . . . the ordinances granted the commissioners unilateral power to veto federal endangered-species and wilderness regulations and to pass judgment on all timber and mining decisions . . . in a county where more than 65 percent of the land is owned by the federal government.
>
> More than 30 counties have passed measures that mimic Catron County's and at least 40 more are considering [it]. Nye County, Nevada, . . . has passed a symbolic ordinance that transfers full title to all federal land—93 percent of the county—directly to the state.[17]

In the sole case decided to date on the legality of such ordinances, *Boundary Backpackers v. Boundary County Commissioners* (Idaho), the plaintiffs won every round. And it is expected that federal and state courts in the West will continue to rule in favor of state and federal regulatory control.

Although the movement has found little support in the courts, the trend it represents is significant because it embodies the antigovernment sentiment so endemic across the western United States. Although that sentiment is not broadly radicalized enough to sustain the county movement, it may well be politically potent enough to weaken or deter prosecutions of potentially significant environmental crimes.

Ideology 3: Managing Perceptions, Manufacturing Public Images: Simulations of Environmentalism in the Corporate World

In his influential book *Moral Mazes*, ethnographer Robert Jackall draws a macabre portrait of the symbolic order of contemporary corporations. In a milieu where morality is defined by what the boss wants and where one's ability to interpret and reconstruct the highly ambiguous connotations of relevant symbols usually determines the success or failure of one's career,

Thoreau's Message Still Speaks to the Masses[1]

Just before Christmas 1996, David Shi contemplated one of life's little ironies. Shi was struck by the fact that one of the most popular books on tape is Henry David Thoreau's *Walden*. "Imagine commuters listening to Thoreau rhapsodize about life in the woods and the virtues of simplicity while they rush in quiet desperation through bumper-to-bumper traffic."[2(p.19)]

In *Walden*, Thoreau wrote about his "experiment in essential living." He intended to discover which cultural trappings could be discarded so he could more thoroughly enjoy the wonders of nature. The lesson Thoreau presented to observers at the time, and to commuters of today, is one of simplicity. "A person is rich," Thoreau noted, "in proportion to the number of things he can do without."[3(p.19)]

Second, Thoreau encouraged people to slow down and "take time to reflect on who we are, where we are, what we are doing, and what we value."[4(p.19)]

Thoreau's two-year venture into the woods reflected his interest in gaining perspective and was not intended as proof that people should live in exactly his manner of life during that period. His effort to attain a higher understanding of our place in the world was based in his rejection of the American dream of success.[5] It is truly ironic that Thoreau's message receives a sympathetic hearing from an audience that lives in an extremely technologically advanced society and commutes hours to the workplace to maintain or increase a very high standard of living.

1. D. Shi, "Thoreau Rides with Today's Commuters: The Author of 'Walden' Has Some Lessons for Harried Holiday Shoppers, Too." *Christian Science Monitor*, 13 December 1996, 19.
2. Shi, "Thoreau Rides with Today's Commuters."
3. H.D. Thoreau, *Walden, or Life in the Woods* (New York: The New American Library, 1960), 19.
4. Shi, "Thoreau Rides with Today's Commuters."
5. Thoreau, *Walden*, 251.

the meanings of words and deeds and symbols and causes often take on a disturbing elasticity. Consider the following:

> The February 1995 *O'Dwyer's PR Services* reports that "relief is on the way for PR clients on the environmental front. . . . Green PR people are advised to ride the Republican fueled anti-environmental backlash . . . but they should not be greedy."
>
> In the perverse world of public relations, lobbying against environmental regulations is known as "environmental" or "green" PR.
>
> In 1990 alone, U.S. businesses spent an estimated $500 million on hiring the services of anti-environmental PR professionals and on "greenwashing" their corporate image. . . . The object of this PR war is to change public perceptions about the environment and its despoilers.[18]

One tactic of these pseudo-green PR warriors is to sponsor groups and generate identifying logos and newsletters with proenvironmental monikers and symbols. In an October 4, 1995 article in the *Wall Street Journal*, reporter Tim Aeppel chronicled the multifaceted nature of the phenomenon. For example, Aeppel cautions readers to differentiate between a newly launched environmentalist organization, the Endangered Species Coalition (ESC), and the antienvironmental agendas of three groups whose names deliberately mimic the ESC's name: The National Endangered Species Act Reform Coalition, the Grassroots ESA Coalition, and the Endangered Species Coordinating Council. These three groups are lobbying for either a much watered-down reauthorization of the Endangered Species Act or for its outright repeal.

Use of questionable tactics by corporate PR departments, whose oft-proclaimed motto is "image is everything," is not unusual. If perception is reality and facts do not matter, then the battle is won when the general public comes to perceive, through the prolific production and aggressive circulation of symbols, antienvironmental organizations and practices as proenvironmental. Another effective strategy used by corporations over the last decade has been to resocialize environmentalist groups as institutional allies sharing common interests. This has been done in multiple ways, including the following.

First, during the 1980s, some of the largest mainstream environmentalist organizations acquired de facto status as "insider players." They began to deploy the usual armies of lawyers and lobbyists to negotiate and promulgate environmental policy and law and in effect were resocialized into Washington-based special interest groups. The consequence was sometimes a swift and profound redefinition of group identity and tactics (see Chapter 2).

Second, prominent corporations have injected substantial sums of cash into popular environmental groups, such as the Audubon Society, the Natural Resource Defense Council (NRDC), the Nature Conservancy, and the Environmental Defense Fund (EDF). Not surprisingly, with funding comes a new-found sensitivity to the concerns of corporate donors.

Third, Fortune 500 cash has apparently bought informational access to the practices and conceptual structure of some environmental groups. For example, in 1994, academic business researchers conducted an in-depth sampling of the operationally relevant cognitive habits of 34 active environmentalists from 21 organizations. Results from the study, published in a prominent management journal, have no doubt provided valuable profiling and demographic data on some varieties of environmental activists.[19]

It should be no surprise, then, that some groups have thoroughly adopted a commodity-based worldview. The best known example is the EDF. In the 1990s, the EDF's approach typifies what has come to be known as "third wave" environmentalism.[20] The organizing concept of this wave is the belief that negotiated market-based inducements, not government mandates, are the most effective devices for achieving pollution reduction. Chapter 5 discusses the creation of the emission reduction credits (so-called pollution rights) written into the 1990 Clean Air Act. The EDF has proposed other forms of pollution commodification, such as "the trading of lead rights among gasoline refiners" and "an allowance for the transfer of production entitlement of CFCs."[21] It is fair to say that the EDF is the inventor of this new type of commodity—the right to pollute.

From a bureaucratic and profit-making standpoint, pollution rights are a stroke of genius. Essentially they transform aspects of once undivided, uncommodified public goods, such as air, water, and soil, into tradable commodities that are bought and sold by a select group of polluters. As long as the players follow the generous rules developed under the 1990 Clean Air Act, generating predetermined levels of localized pollution, far from being a potentially criminal act, pollution reduction becomes a convertible private property right. Short of catastrophic mismanagement of these pollution rights, it is hard to see how the development and enforcement of a criminal code for environmental polluters will be allowed to occur.

ENABLING IDEOLOGIES AND PRACTICES

In this section, the ideologies of those opposed to the above-discussed limitations on the definition and enforcement of penalties for environmental crime are reviewed.

INSIGHT

Theology and Ideology: Where Less Is Actually More

American leaders in the colonial period argued against the seduction of material wealth and promoted the good of the public over private interests.[1] Claiming to have noticed a loss of the spiritual values that have directed human activity throughout history, some people currently are attempting to link spiritual issues with environmental issues. In 1992, citing recent scientific findings, prominent scientists, in a document entitled *An Open Letter to the Religious Community*, called on religious leaders to join the effort to build a sustainable world.

The scientists argued that humans are threatened by "self-inflicted, swiftly moving environmental alterations about whose long-term biological and ecological consequences we are still painfully ignorant."[2(p.42)] Changing public policy would not be enough; individual behavior must also change. The impact of religious teachings and church leadership has been documented throughout history, and so the authors of the open letter (including Nobel laureates) made an appeal to the religious community to aid them in effecting behavioral changes.

In response, American Christians and Jews combined forces and organized the National Religious Partnership on the Environment (NRPE). Representing over 100,000 congregations, the NRPE ultimately identified consumption as the "obvious but difficult choice" for focused consideration. Questions of social and environmental justice dovetail nicely into the search for a definition of meaning and self-worth outside the value structure of the marketplace.[3]

Smaller local groups have established programs that wrestle with similar issues. The question of meaning is central. "If you don't have an internal sense of your worth, you've got to be filled up by buying stuff. . . . If we can help people relearn their internal worth, then the need for stuff will, hopefully, go way down."[4(p.44)]

Consider these efforts to raise environmental consciousness:[5]

- Methodist churches in LA are bringing in leading scientists to lecture on environmental and related consumption issues.
- The New Roadmap Foundation has adapted a church-oriented version of *Your Money or Your Life*, a text organized around the idea of achieving financial independence in this age of consumerism.
- *Green Cross*, the magazine put out by a network of evangelical environmentalists, focused an issue on the topic of consumerism, calling it "a pernicious form of slavery."
- In Seattle, Earth Ministry, a nondenominational Christian group, is working on a curriculum that explores the connection between consumption and the global economy and that characterizes this economy as exploitive of people and land.

1. T. Furtwangler, "A Theology of Less: Christians and Jews Organize on Consumption," *YES! A Journal of Positive Futures*, Spring–Summer 1996, 42.
2. Furtwangler, "A Theology of Less," 42
3. Furtwangler, "A Theology of Less."
4. Furtwangler, "A Theology of Less," 44
5. Furtwangler, "A Theology of Less."

Ideology 4: The "Right-To-Life" Discourse Extended: An Emerging Christian Evangelical Environmentalism

> I'm appalled that people within the church world have taken an aggressive stand to destroy the Endangered Species Act. My premise is that this is a moral issue.[22]

In mid-1996, the National Coalition of Evangelicals launched a multifaceted, million-dollar campaign in support of the Endangered Species Act. Obviously, these fundamentalists do not take as their principal object of worship the capital accumulation process. If it is true that "morality is what the boss wants," that boss, for them, is not some institutionally savvy CEO. That boss is not thought to practice the ambiguous and contextually flexible morality often found in corporate hallways. In this case, a Divinity-based morality takes the form of a biblical exegesis of God's command to Noah.

In the Old Testament, God directed Noah to shepherd all forms of creation into the ark, not just the desirable, profitable, or convenient ones. Relating the meaning of this scriptural narrative to present-day circumstances, the coalition spearheaded a drive to persuade more than 30,000 affiliated church leaders to declare their churches to be "Noah congregations." For conservationists at the coalition, the Endangered Species Act is the contemporary equivalent of the ark.

Arguably, the coalition's efforts sparked a round of support and lobbying for the Endangered Species Act from many denominations and religions. Even more significantly, because such scriptural discourse is not based on utilitarian, econometric, or institutionally bound symbolic models and worldviews (typified by the "image is everything" ethos), it may have notable general appeal (beyond the Endangered Species Act) to an aging baby-boomer generation. The immutable facts of decline and death often trigger a search for enduring meanings. While walking down that inevitable road, members of that generation may yet discard some of the facile practices and discourses so fervently embraced during the 1980s and 1990s.

Ideology 5: The "Fourth Wave": Up from the Grassroots

In "The Fourth Wave," Mark Dowie divides the U.S. environmental movement into three periods. The periods he identifies consist of the initial efforts of the late nineteenth and early twentieth centuries; the period of protective legislation (1970–1980); and the season of "the suits" (the lobbyists and lawyers hired by environmental organizations in the process of transforming themselves into Washington insiders).[23]

But as the evolution of the Environmental Systems Company (ENSCO) conflict clearly shows (see Case Study 1), the story does not end with Armani suits negotiating emission reduction credit schemes over power lunches. For example, the heated conflict that surrounded the aborted construction of the ENSCO incinerator in Mobile, Arizona, represents what Dowie calls the Fourth Wave of environmental activism. The portrayal of the local ENSCO protestors in Case Study 1 is consistent with Dowie's characterization of Fourth Wave activists:

> Fourth wave leaders, in contrast to the well-bred, properly educated [professional bureaucrats] of mainstream environmentalism, are angry and impolite. They are blue-collar suburbanites like Lois Gibbs, the mad mother of Love Canal who has inspired thousands more to fight against the poisoning of their homes and neighborhoods.[24]

The potential of this type of movement is enormous. As shown in Case Study 1, successful opposition was based on the networking of local activists and national and transnational nongovernment organizations (like Greenpeace). At century's end, where political struggles are simultaneously more localized (ENSCO) and more totalizing (multiple sites across the planet face similar issues), a globally networked localism may prove an effective political model.

Finally, as faith in big government inexorably recedes, it may well be that what environmental activist Andy Mahler says is true: "What has become increasingly clear is that local people acting locally to protect local places represents the new civil and moral authority."[25]

Ideology 6: Changing Notions of Causality in Complex Systems

October 1987 provides a convenient symbol for the need to reimagine certain cause-and-effect relationships. For it was during the third week of October 1987 that stock prices took a brief but steep plunge. That plunge was not due to "real-world" conditions or even market perceptions of danger, instability, conflict, or shortages. Instead, the plunge was due to the iterative effect of "sell instructions" written into the code of computerized trading programs. The brief stock market crash of October 1987 was soon seen as an example of a nonlinear event. It focused much attention on the fact that small causes can lead, through iterations (repetitions with a difference), to large effects. In the explanations that followed in the weeks and months after the crash, the conventional notion that small causes produce small effects and large causes produce large effects gave way to newer models of causality. The initial scale of an event was no longer seen as necessarily determinative of the scale of its consequences.

The sensibility embodied in this new paradigm of causality, which theorist N. Katherine Hayles has dubbed **chaotics**, has now filtered down even into 30-second commercial TV spots. This new paradigm of causality may affect what is perceived as constituting an environmental risk or danger. Through the use of computer modeling and complex simulation programs, algorithms embodying this logic may soon be used to determine if a given initial event, such as a small spill in a remote location, could conceivably set in motion an iterative series that would produce large-scale effects. In essence, digital information processing and modeling, now extensively augmented by exponential increases in computer power and the routine availability of detailed satellite data, will soon form the basis for routine risk assessments. In the near future, environmentalists and business interests will increasingly rely on nonlinear, digitally produced models to make or buttress claims of guilt or innocence. The entrance of digital assessment technologies into environmental risk and damage assessment will no doubt produce some novel legal and scientific opportunities and obstacles, intended and unintended, as the years go by. The technologies are quite literally new means for the determination of truth. Whether these new modes will serve their intended end has yet to be decisively determined. However, it does free habits of thought and perceptions from older linear modes that incompletely focus on the symmetries of scale.

CONCLUSION

Limitations on the enforcement of criminal sanctions against environmental law breakers ultimately depend on a number of extralegal factors. As this chapter demonstrates, even the definition of an environmental crime involves complex and contingent social processes. In the mix are market and nonmarket ideologies, views on the scope and legitimacy of government regulation, notions of danger, general economic conditions, local and global political processes, public relations, networks of citizen groups and nongovernment organizations, bureaucratic definitions born from negotiations between agencies and interested parties, and novel forms of truth production. The most severe limitation for those who would define and enforce environmental crime is lack of awareness of this complex mix of factors.

REVIEW QUESTIONS

1. What does it mean to say that "relationships between humans and the environment have been thoroughly . . . mixed into preexisting and sometimes competing moral, political, spiritual, scientific, economic, and social world views"?

2. What is "unnatural governmental regulation"?
3. How is the constitutional Takings Clause used in an environmental context?
4. What is involved in "greenwashing" a company?

DISCUSSION QUESTIONS

1. Much of the discussion of environmental issues involves economics. How can economics be used to support and oppose environmental issues? Discuss different ways to frame critical environmental issues as they are discussed in conjunction with economics.
2. The chapter suggests that definitions of environmental crime are the product of an "agreed upon set of assumptions." How would you argue these assumptions are identified and then transferred to other groups or individuals in the society?
3. Several recent actions suggest that the Christian evangelical community is getting involved in the debate about environmental protection. What is the nature of the link between religion and the environment?
4. The last section of the chapter discusses a "new paradigm of causality" called chaotics. How is chaotics related to environmental issues in general and environmental crime in particular?

REFERENCES

1. R. Limbaugh, 1995, "Rush Limbaugh's Updated 35 Undeniable Truths of Life," truth number 8, electronic document available at http://key.cyberg8t.com/goscomm/r_ntruth.htm.
2. L. Hochberg, "All God's Creatures" *PBS News Hour*, 3 June 1996, electronic transcript available at http://www.pbs.org/newshour/bb/environment.html
3. W.K. Burke, "The Wise Use Movement: Right-Wing Anti-environmentalism," 1993, electronic document available at http://www.publiceye.org/wiseuse.html.
4. P. Montague, "The Right To Pollute," *Rachel's Environment and Health Weekly*, 18 May 1995, electronic document available at http://www.flora.ottawa.on.ca/afo/lists/h-info/month0595/0015.html.
5. C.C. Mann and M.L. Plummer, "The Butterfly Problem," *Atlantic Monthly*, January 1992, electronic document available at http://www.theatlantic.com/election/connection/environ/buttrfly.htm.
6. "Who's 'Truly Green'? And Who's Not?" *Environment Writer*, November–December 1995, electronic document available at http://www.sej.org/ewnov95.htm.
7. A. Pertman, "Wise Foot Soldiers on the March," *Boston Globe*, 3 October 1994, Health and Science sect., 25, electronic document available at http://www.cdfe.org/globe.htm.
8. Pertman, "Wise Foot Soldiers on the March."

9. J. Bleifuss, "Covering the Earth with 'Green PR,'" Issue 19, Summer 1995, electronic document available at http://www.pacific.net/~mec/news/ISS19/08GreenPR.html.

10. Bleifuss, "Covering the Earth with 'Green PR.'"

11. Bleifuss, "Covering the Earth with 'Green PR.'"

12. Burke, "The Wise Use Movement."

13. Burke, "The Wise Use Movement."

14. J. Krakauer, "Brown Fellas," *Outside Magazine*, December 1991, 72.

15. Limbaugh, "Rush Limbaugh's Updated 35 Undeniable Truths of Life," truth number 34.

16. "Adam Smith Meets Darwin: An Emerging Style of Business Combines Economics with Biology," *San Jose Mercury News*, 1336 words, 12 December 1994, electronic document available at http://newslibrary.infi.net/global/cgi-bin/sj/slwebcli_post.pl.

17. M. Dowie, "The Wayward West: With Liberty and Firepower for All," *Outside Magazine*, November 1995, electronic document available at http://outside.starwave.com/magzine/1195/11f_lib.html.

18. Bleifuss, "Covering the Earth with 'Green PR.'"

19. Bleifuss, "Covering the Earth with 'Green PR.'"

20. M. Dowie, "The Fourth Wave," *Mother Jones*, March–April 1995, electronic document available at http://www.mojones.com/mother_jones/MA95/dowie.html.

21. Montague, "The Right To Pollute."

22. Hochberg, "All God's Creatures."

23. Dowie, "The Fourth Wave."

24. Dowie, "The Fourth Wave."

25. Dowie, "The Fourth Wave."

CHAPTER 14

International Environmental Issues

Ray Michalowski

TERMS	Berne Accord of 1963	multilateral agreement
	bilateral agreement	neocolonialism
	biodiversity	nongovernmental organizations
	Earth Summit	pattern of flight
	global environmental accord	sustainable development
	global warming	transborder flow of toxic
	greenhouse gases	substances
	international law	transnational corporation
	Montreal Protocol	Vienna Accord

INTERNATIONAL ENVIRONMENTAL PROBLEMS

- *1991.* After years of debate and conflict, Canada and the United States sign the United States–Canada Air Quality Accord to limit the destructive impact of acid rain in Canada—50 percent of which is caused by smokestack emissions in the United States.[1]
- *1995.* Ken Saro-Wiwa, environmental and human rights activist, Nobel Peace Prize Nominee, and 1995 recipient of the Goldman Environmental Prize, is executed by the military government of Nigeria for charges related to his activities as the founder and leader of the Movement for the Survival of the Ogoni People (MOSOP). MOSOP sought to force Shell, Mobil, Texaco, and the other oil companies operating in the Niger river delta to repair the extensive environmental damage that years of oil spills, pipeline breaks, and toxic waste dumping had done to the rainforest and the river, the traditional sources of livelihood for the Ogoni people.[2]

These cases highlight the two key forces underlying the international dimensions of the environmental crime problems—transborder flows of toxic substances and transborder flows of economic decisions.

315

Transborder Flows of Toxic Substances

A **transborder flow of toxic substances** occurs when pollutants that originate within one nation-state spread to neighboring or even distant countries, through natural ecological processes such as the movement of streams, rivers, air currents, and living organisms or through the deliberate transportation of substances such as hazardous waste.

Most laws and legal systems stop at national borders. This means that one country cannot use its laws to control activities inside another country. The political boundaries around legal systems, however, do not correspond with the geography of environmental degradation. Environmental toxins spread through *ecosystems*, not legal systems. There are no political boundaries around ecosystems comparable to those around legal systems. Rivers and streams do not stop at borders, and even if they did, evaporation could still transfer toxins into the atmosphere, allowing them to drift to other places. The jet stream and other prevailing wind systems girdle the globe, spreading pollution from smokestacks, vehicles, and other sources well beyond the countries in which it originates. Migratory animals bearing environmentally caused diseases do not stop at border checkpoints. Meanwhile, the destruction of wildlife habitat and species extinction in one nation (or in international waters) can have destructive environmental, economic, and aesthetic impacts on places far removed from the source of the problem, much like a pebble dropped into the middle of a pond.

Ecosystems are just that—*systems*. This means that each part is connected, however distantly, to every other part.[3] "Spaceship Earth" is a single ecological system, and damage to any part of it will eventually harm the whole system. In recent years the scientific recognition of worldwide environmental threats such as ozone depletion and global warming have made the systemic and transborder nature of environmental problems increasingly apparent. The political boundaries around legal systems, however, have made it difficult to control free-flowing toxins and other far-reaching forms of environmental damage.

Transborder Flows of Economic Decisions

It is not only pollutants that move across borders. Like environmental toxins, economic decisions that originate in one country can have devastating human and environmental consequences in another. Since the late 1400s the pursuit of economic goals has increasingly bound the world into a single global economic system.[4] For 500 years powerful economic and military institutions from more developed nations have been able to make and implement economically motivated decisions affecting the lives, living conditions, and environments in less developed places throughout the world.

The colonization of Africa, India, and the Western Hemisphere by the powerful trading nations of Europe is a prime example of how economic interests and economic decisions flow across borders. From the fifteenth century through the mid-twentieth century, direct political and military control ensured that the land, resources, and people in less developed parts of the world would be used primarily to implement economic decisions originating in more developed nations. Nor was this transborder flow of economic decisions a gentle process. Over the centuries hundreds of millions of people in less developed parts of the world were killed or enslaved or had the environment on which they depended for their way of life destroyed to fulfill the economic desires of people in other parts of the world. In the late 1700s one observer of this global flow of economic interests described the process this way:

> I do not know if coffee and sugar are essential to the happiness of Europe, but I know well that these two products have accounted for the unhappiness of two great regions of the world: America [i.e., the Caribbean] has been depopulated so as to have land on which to plant them; Africa has been depopulated so as to have the people to cultivate them.[5]

Transborder flows of economic decisions by no means ceased with the end of formal colonization. As nations withdrew or lost political and military control over former colonies, a new engine of economic penetration—the **transnational corporation**—increasingly ensured that economic interests outside the borders of less developed nations would continue to shape economic development and resource use within them. This new form of economic control came to be known as neocolonialism.

The central feature of **neocolonialism** is that economic growth in less developed nations is shaped in very significant ways by investment decisions reflecting the interests of the managers and stockholders of transnational corporations. Historically, these corporations more often have promoted the exploitation rather than the preservation and development of the human and biological environments of their "host" nations. Part of the reason, as anthropologist John Bodley noted, is that when decisions are made by people who do not have to live with their consequences, far less care is taken to minimize their destructive impact on the natural and the cultural environment.[6] Unlike the Ogoni people, the oil industry executives whose decisions led to the cumulative ecological destruction of the Niger river delta do not depend on the waters and rainforest of the delta region for their livelihood and for the continuation of their culture. Nor does the environmental destruction of the Niger delta have any obvious consequences for the stockholders who benefit annually from oil industry profits generated from the exploitation of Nigerian oil.

Transborder flows of economic decisions accelerated rapidly in the years after World War II. Consumer economies expanded dramatically within much of the developed world, and manufacturing corporations initially rooted in the United States, Britain, Europe, and Japan increasingly sought cheaper labor and new markets in less developed nations. In the two decades between 1960 and 1980, the revenue of transnational corporations grew tenfold, from $199 billion to $2,155 billion.[7] A significant proportion of this growth resulted from increasing relocation of manufacturing facilities from developed nations, such as the United States, to less developed ones, such as Mexico, Guatemala, Malaysia, and Singapore. As early as 1975, over three-fourths of all U.S. corporations with sales of $100 million had manufacturing facilities in other countries.[8]

As transnational corporations expanded their industrial operations in developing nations, many of the environmental dangers associated with industrial production were relocated from developed nations, which were beginning to formulate environmental protection laws, to less developed ones, where the political leadership was unprepared, unwilling, or unable to address these new hazards. In some instances it was the very lack of environmental controls that made certain developing countries attractive sites for industrial relocation.

Corporate decision makers are well aware of how differences between nations' pollution control standards will affect operating costs and profits, and this awareness can influence decisions to relocate industries from developed to less developed countries. Recognizing this trend, Robert Strauss, the chief trade negotiator for President Carter, warned that there was an emerging **pattern of flight** as U.S. companies relocated in developing countries with less costly pollution control laws.[9] Another analyst of corporate relocation patterns noted that "hazard export is emerging as a driving force in new plant investment in many hazardous and polluting industries."[10] In some cases entire industries that depend on the use of highly toxic substances, such as asbestos, arsenic, mercury, and benzine dyes, have been exported to Korea, Mexico, Brazil, India, Ireland, and other developing nations.[11]

INSIGHT

A War on the Environment? American Troops in the Gulf War

Human history includes many wars and international conflicts. It is perhaps not surprising that wars can be extremely devastating to the natural environment. For this reason, among others, international laws of war have been outlined to identify specific actions disallowed during times of war.

In one of the most recent wars involving U.S. troops, traditional weapons were used—cruise missiles, stealth bombers, and smart bombs. The Iraqi response, however, was unprecedented. An estimated 1.5 to 11 million barrels of oil were released directly into the Persian Gulf.[1] Saddam Hussein set over 600 oil wells ablaze. The oil fires blackened the sky over Kuwait, and releases of sulfurous gases and toxic particles remained uncontained for almost a year. It took nearly 10,000 workers from 34 countries using 125,000 tons of equipment approximately eight months to extinguish all the fires.[2]

The intentional action in the Kuwaiti oil fields has resulted in questions about whether the Iraqi leadership should be charged with environmental war crimes.[3] "It is part of the purpose of the laws of war to place limits on environmental damage—to prohibit wanton environmental destruction with no legitimate military purpose."[4(p.310)]

A related environmental concern in the Gulf is that more than 60,000 veterans of the Gulf War have been plagued with mysterious illnesses, collectively referred to as the "Gulf War syndrome." While the facts thus far released to the public are sketchy, overwhelming evidence suggests that U.S. forces in Operation Desert Storm were exposed to a mix of potentially deadly toxins, including chemical nerve agents.[5]

Many agree on the need to call for environmental protection in war time, but others argue that international law should not constrict the use of modern weapons systems in response to violent aggression.[6] Despite the difference in opinions on the subject, a more important element remains: If international environmental protections for times of war are ratified, how are those provisions to be enforced?

1. M.J.T. Caggiano, "The Legitimacy of Environmental Destruction in Modern Warfare: Customary Substance over Conventional Form," *Environmental Affairs* 20 (1993): 479–506.
2. Caggiano, "The Legitimacy of Environmental Destruction in Modern Warfare," 481.
3. W.A. Wilcox, "Environmental Protection in Warfare," *Southern Illinois University Law Journal* 17 (1993): 299–315.
4. Wilcox, "Environmental Protection in Warfare," 310.
5. C. Shays, "On Gulf War Syndrome, Pentagon Still Retreats," *Christian Science Monitor*, 4 October 1996, 18.
6. Wilcox, "Environmental Protection in Warfare," 313.

INTERNATIONAL ENVIRONMENTAL PROBLEMS AND SOCIAL MOVEMENTS

A social problem is a harmful condition that people understand as both caused and correctable by human action. Harmful conditions do not become social problems until at least some people identify them as such. Social problems emerge when people create organized movements to bring the newly defined problems to the attention of the public and political decision makers. Consider, for instance, the matter of secondhand smoke. Although it was always considered to be a nuisance by some people, tobacco smoke did not always have the status of a social problem in the United States. Beginning in the 1970s, however, activist organizations such as GASP (Group against Smokers Pollution) stimulated public concern about second-hand smoke by publicizing data about the harmful health effects of second-hand smoke and by providing those who were bothered by tobacco smoke with a platform to speak out about the issue. Their efforts eventually led to the banning of tobacco smoke from a number of settings, such as airports, hospitals, public buildings, and university classrooms, and its restriction in many other settings, such as restaurants and workplaces.

Citizen groups that work to remediate some problem or condition are often termed **nongovernmental organizations** (NGOs). NGOs have played a central role in the environmental movement since its inception. Historically businesses and governments have had little inherent motivation to protect the environment. The accepted logic of economic competition and corporate profit making means that corporations must continually search for the least costly ways to extract raw materials from the environment, transform them into finished products, and create expanding consumer markets for their goods. Environmental protection is costly. It is far cheaper to ignore oil spills than to clean them up, and cleaning up oil spills after they have already caused environmental damage is cheaper than redesigning all the ships and pipelines that carry oil to ensure that spills are unlikely to occur. Dumping hazardous waste in rivers, in lakes, or on the land is far cheaper than rendering the waste safe or storing it in ways that will reduce the likelihood it will harm the biological environment. Similarly, it is far cheaper to release pollutants such as sulphur dioxide and nitrous oxide into the air than it is to clean up smokestack and vehicle emissions. While environmental damage is costly to everyone, corporations have typically been able to *externalize* these costs. That is, they have been able to avoid paying in any direct way for the environmental damage they cause.

Because there are relatively few incentives for profit-seeking institutions to protect the environment and many incentives to externalize the costs of environmental damage, the enactment of environmental protection laws in the United States and other nations has depended heavily on the actions of environmental NGOs. The same is true for international environmental problems. NGOs such as Greenpeace, Friends of the Earth, the Environmental Defense Fund, Physicians for Social Responsibility, Earth Council, the Rainforest Action Network, the Women's Environment and Development Organization, and thousands of other citizen action groups have played a crucial role in bringing the international dimensions of environmental protection to worldwide attention.

INTERNATIONAL MOVEMENTS TO PROTECT THE GLOBAL ENVIRONMENT

In the last half of the twentieth century a number of environmental issues emerged that highlighted both the global nature of many environmental problems and the need for international responses to pressing environmental issues. While some concern for global environmental problems existed prior to World War II, two events in 1946 helped galvanize movements for environmental protection at the international level.

The first event was the detonation of atomic bombs over the cities of Hiroshima and Nagasaki in the final days of World War II. The second was the establishment of the United Nations. The radioactive fallout from the atomic attacks on Japan, along with continued nuclear testing in the United States and later the Soviet Union, increased worldwide public awareness of how readily toxins dispersed into the atmosphere could spread around the globe. Fear of "radioactive fallout" become the most prominent international environmental issue of the early postwar period. Concern about the effects of radioactive fallout stimulated antinuclear sentiment in many nations and led both NGOs and many governments to work for international controls over atmospheric testing of nuclear weapons. Most of this activity was motivated by fear of the threat posed by radioactive fallout for human health rather than by a general concern for environmental protection. Nevertheless, the issues raised by atmospheric testing of nuclear weapons acted as powerful catalyst for the eventual development of movements for more broad-based protection of the global environment.

The establishment of the United Nations near the end of World War II also played an important role in the movement for international environmental controls. The United Nations provided a focus for the efforts of nations, scientists, and NGOs concerned about international environmental problems. In August 1963 the United Nations approved the multilateral Treaty Banning Nuclear Weapon Tests in the Atmosphere, in Outer Space, and under Water. This was not the first United Nations (U.N.) multilateral treaty dealing with environmental issues; there had been some earlier environmental treaties dealing primarily with marine issues. The ban on atmospheric testing of nuclear weapons, however, represented a major step toward addressing the global dimension of environmental problems and helped highlight the U.N. as a possible mechanism through which NGOs and other entities could begin to address these problems.[12]

From the 1960s onward, concern about the global dimensions of environmental damage and the movement for international environmental protection grew substantially. The earliest environmental issues addressed by the U.N. were fairly specific. Atmospheric nuclear testing, protection of particular bodies of water from oil spills, prevention of overfishing in particular areas, and environmental protection of Antarctica were typical objectives of the narrowly targeted treaties ratified by the U.N. from the late 1940s to the early 1970s. During the last quarter of the twentieth century, discussion of global environmental issues began to take on a different character. Increasing scientific documentation of global environmental problems, intensification of industrial assaults on the ecosystems of developing nations, acceleration of the rate of species loss, and emerging demands from poorer nations for a more equitable distribution of the earth's wealth led to the incorporation of many separate environmental issues under the umbrella of three major issue areas: (1) protecting **biodiversity**, (2) **global warming** and climate change, and (3) **sustainable development**. These three issue areas came to dominate the debate over international environmental protection in the 1990s.

Protecting Biodiversity

Biological diversity refers to the variability among and within species of plants, animals, microorganisms, marine life, and also the variability among entire ecosystems.[13] Biodiversity is threatened whenever a network of living organisms (and the nonliving environment that sustains them as a functional unit) is altered in ways that lead to extinction of one or more life forms in that network.

In recent years considerable energy has been focused on biodiversity issues by NGOs, governments, and businesses. The movement to protect biodiversity comes from a number of directions. One is individuals and groups who believe that biodiversity is intrinsically valuable. From this perspective, strategies to protect biodiversity and the overall ecological well-being of the planet must take precedence over any benefits that humans might derive from altering its ecological makeup. This planet-first approach is sometimes referred to as a deep ecology perspective.[14–16] For many other people, however, the reason to protect biodiversity is because it benefits human populations. The importance of biodiversity for human life has been framed in a number of ways:

- as necessary for the general preservation of the global biosphere and the evolutionary process that sustains human life
- as key to the preservation of the life ways of indigenous peoples and communities that depend upon biological resources for their subsistence
- as essential for providing stock for future development of medicines, crops, and other goods, including genetic engineering
- as a critical component of the aesthetic and recreational value people derive from natural settings

The most obvious example of human threats to biodiversity is the elimination of species of animals or fish from ecosystems through hunting, fishing, or destruction of habitat. Because ecosystems are systems, however, the consequences of these direct extinctions are often far more damaging than the loss of a single species. In the high desert of the southwestern United States, for instance, the virtual elimination of the mountain lion, one of the only predators that controlled the population of porcupine, resulted in widespread damage to piñon trees, whose bark happens to be a favorite porcupine food. As the trees are lost, so is habitat for many species of birds and nutrition for the many animals for whom the piñon nut is an important food source. Species extinction or damage to the species composition of an ecosystem also occurs in indirect ways. Dramatic changes or destruction of terrestrial or marine habitats through deforestation, damming of rivers, acidification of lakes and streams, or draining of wetlands can deprive whole species of sustaining environments. Similarly, the introduction of species of plants or animals not native to a given ecosystem can dramatically change species composition within an ecosystem by eliminating native plants or animals from that ecosystem. The introduction of kudzu in the southeastern United States and the salt cedar in southwestern riparian environments, for instance, has resulted in the disappearance or near-disappearance of many native plants.

Because the greatest current threats to biodiversity come from human activity, efforts to protect biodiversity must inevitably confront a complex web of social, economic, and political interests. The growing demand for more consumer goods, more crop land, more land for human settlement, more plastics and other petrochemical products, more electricity, more fuel for vehicles, and more electronic devices—not to mention the increased desire of economic institutions for more profits derived from stimulating and meeting greater consumer demands—represents a major threat to biodiversity. Thus, widespread acceptance of the general truth that we need to protect biodiversity often falters in the face of specific reasons to exploit the environment for human benefit. In the United States during the 1990s, for instance, conservative politicians mounted a powerful effort to weaken the Endangered Species Act on the grounds that protecting species such as birds and aquatic life by prohibiting or limiting exploitation of forests and wetlands was fundamentally misdirected because it put the needs of animals ahead of the needs of humans. A similar battle has been waged for years over the protection of rainforests in South America and elsewhere.[17] Thus, the international interest in creating legal structures that would protect biodiversity on a global basis must address a complex of local interests, including those of developing nations to use their resources for economic growth.

Global Warming and Climate Change

Concern about global warming and climate change emerged in the 1970s as a highly controversial part of the international environmental debate. By the mid-1980s, however, climatological data increasingly confirmed that the earth's temperature was in fact rising. Scientific data and computer modeling also pointed toward increases in the proportion of **greenhouse gases** in the earth's atmosphere as the most important human contribution to this warming trend. Greenhouse gases absorb higher levels of radiant energy than other components of the atmosphere. Thus, as the proportion of greenhouse gases in the atmosphere increases, so do planet temperatures. While natural biological processes can alter the level of greenhouse gases, evidence increasingly indicates that human activity is a significant contributor to the current trend in global warming. Activities such as the burning of fossil fuels and deforestation increase the levels of carbon dioxide, nitrous oxide, and methane in the atmosphere. Chlorofluorocarbons (CFCs) from manufacturing, refrigeration, and aerosol sprays have a double impact: they increase the greenhouse gases near the earth and reduce the stratospheric ozone layer that serves to block a portion of the sun's radiant energy from reaching the earth.

It has been estimated that the average surface temperature of the globe has increased between .6 and 1.3 degrees Fahrenheit over the last 100 years. While these numbers appear small at first glance, computer models indicate that this increase is both larger and faster than any change in the earth's temperature over the last 9,000 years.[18] A change of global temperature of this magnitude poses serious threats to ecosystems and human habitation. Rises in average sea levels due to increased melting of polar ice caps will lead to increased flooding of coastal communities and salinization of underground water supplies. Changes in patterns of rainfall and the moisture levels of soils will pose significant threats to agriculture. Entire ecosystems and entire human communities—particularly those dependent on subsistence agriculture—could be drastically and negatively affected if the current global warming trend continues.

Sustainable Development

The terms *sustainable development, sustainable use,* and *sustainable livelihoods* refer to production and consumption strategies that would promote a dignified continuation of human life on the planet while simultaneously minimizing practices that degrade the environment, consume nonrenewable resources, and threaten ecosystems. The central proposition of sustainable development is that current production and consumption practices cannot continue indefinitely and that the human future depends on developing alternative systems that (1) utilize renewable energy sources, (2) do not require extensive transportation of people between work and home and of goods between producers and consumers, (3) reduce overall levels of resource consumption, and (4) equalize disparities between rich and poor nations.

The movement for sustainability promotes two controversial ideas. The first is that global environmental problems can be solved only by radical restructuring of how people live, work, and consume at the local level. The second is that achieving sustainability will require drastic reductions in the current levels of economic and political inequality between social groups and nations. Despite the wide gap between the ideals of sustainability and actual systems of production and consumption, sustainability has become one of the most significant guiding principles of emerging efforts to achieve environmental protection at the international level.

LEGAL STRATEGIES FOR GLOBAL ENVIRONMENTAL PROTECTION

Specific environmental issues affect different countries in different ways. Some international issues, such as shared water resources distribution, must be dealt with between the parties involved. Other issues, such as ozone depletion, affect every nation and must be addressed globally. Several issues

INSIGHT

U.S. Nuclear Era: A Legacy of Secrets and Conspiracy

Radiation experimentation on humans? A series of investigative reports by Eileen Welsome, published between November 15 and 17, 1993, by the *Albuquerque Tribune*, named 5 of 18 people said to have been unknowingly injected with nuclear materials during the 1940s and 1950s.[1] Energy Secretary Hazel O'Leary appointed a panel of ethics experts to review whether researchers knowingly exposed people to dangerous levels of radiation and whether the test subjects were fully informed about the nature of the experiments.[2] Failure to obtain informed consent would have violated the 1947 Nuremburg Code and the medical profession's Hippocratic oath.[3]

In addition to the human experimentation, the Department of Energy (DOE) disclosed information confirming that 204 secret underground nuclear tests occurred during the past half century. The first nuclear test was said to have been held in 1963 and the last occurred in May 1990.[4]

O'Leary was "shocked and amazed" at the management shortcomings of the U.S. nuclear weapons complex during the Cold War.[5] The amount of environmental damage has been linked to severe health problems, including elevated levels of cancers. O'Leary presented a department finding that about 750,000 pounds of mercury (an element associated with birth defects and nervous system disorders) had been dumped into a tributary of the stream in Oak Ridge, Tennessee, by a nuclear facility that produced uranium components for nuclear weapons.[6] Additional concern was expressed because of an "environmental cleanup bill that may reach hundreds of billions of dollars."[7(p.1A)]

Others close to the controversy defend the plutonium tests. While agreeing such experiments would not be allowed today, they argue the standards were different then. Some argue the research done on humans decreased the overall threats posed to humans from radioactive dangers. Although the threats may have been reduced, reports continue to suggest even more information remains hidden. For example, a $26 million, seven-year study revealed many people were exposed to radiation released from the Hanford Nuclear Power Station in eastern Washington State.[8] More than 800,000 people lived in the region when the level of radiation released from Hanford was "enormous."[9]

Nuclear weapon facilities and nuclear power generation stations, because of the nuclear waste they create, have become the subject of intense controversy (Exhibit 14–1). The DOE released a report that estimates the cost of cleaning up federal nuclear sites at about $230 billion over 75 years. Significant attention will focus on five sites: plutonium-producing plants at Hanford, Washington, and Savannah River, South Carolina; and DOE facilities at Rocky Flats, Colorado, the Oak Ridge National Laboratory, and the Idaho National Engineering Laboratory.

Managing nuclear waste is becoming an multinational concern. Currently, the DOE has bilateral agreements with Belgium, Canada, France, Germany, Japan, Spain, Sweden, Switzerland, and the United Kingdom.[10] The DOE works with the Nuclear Regulatory Commission and the Environmental Protection Agency to address nuclear waste issues.

1. E. Welsome, "The Plutonium Experiment," *Albuquerque Tribune*, 15–17 November 1993, 1–47.
2. M. Puette, "Tough Legal Battle Looms for Radiation Victims," *USA Today*, 30 December 1993.
3. Puette, "Tough Legal Battle Looms for Radiation Victims."
4. "U.S. Hid 204 Nuclear Tests: Disclosure Is Attempt To Win Public's Trust," *Minneapolis Star Tribune*, 8 December 1993, 10A.
5. "U.S. Hid 204 Nuclear Tests," 1A, 10A.
6. "U.S. Hid 204 Nuclear Tests," 10A.
7. "U.S. Hid 204 Nuclear Tests," 1A.
8. "Wider Fallout from Nuclear Research Is Discovered," *New York Times* report, 11 April 1994, *Minneapolis Star Tribune*.
9. "Wider Fallout from Nuclear Research Is Discovered."
10. United States Department of Energy. "International Cooperation in Nuclear Waste Management," April 1990. (For more information, contact U.S. Department of Energy, Office of Civilian Radioactive Waste Management, Mail Stop Rw-43, Washington, DC 20585, tel.: 202-586-5722.)

Exhibit 14–1 Nuclear Facilities with a Controversial Past

- Fernald Nuclear Facility, northwest of Cincinnati, Ohio
- Hanford Nuclear Facility, Richland, Washington
- Idaho National Engineering Laboratory, Idaho Falls, Idaho
- Lawrence Livermore National Lab, east of San Francisco, California
- Los Alamos National Lab, Los Alamos, New Mexico
- Oak Ridge National Laboratory, Oak Ridge, Tennessee
- Pantex nuclear weapons plant in Amarillo, Texas
- Rocky Flats, outside of Denver, Colorado
- Savannah River, southeast of Aiken, South Carolina

that illustrate the difficulties associated with international environmental protection are presented below.

International Law versus National Sovereignty

Creating and enforcing national or international laws is a difficult process, particularly when dealing with environmental degradation. Modern history has produced a world that is divided into nation-states, each of which presumes to be a sovereign legal entity with the exclusive right to make and enforce laws governing what takes place within its borders. On the other hand, the desire for predictable and nonviolent ways of conducting international relationships has led to the development of "rules and principles . . . dealing with [the] conduct of states and international organizations."[19(p.)] These rules and principles are the basis of **international law**.

National sovereignty has posed and continues to pose barriers to establishing international rules to address global environmental threats. Serious ecological problems can create political pressure for environmental regulation within a particular nation-state. These kinds of political pressures, however, are far less effective beyond national boundaries. Corporations, politicians, and citizens residing within one nation-state are frequently reluctant to alter established patterns of producing and consuming simply because these activities are causing environmental harm somewhere else on the planet. Meanwhile, those who live with the environmental consequences of pollutants originating outside their nation frequently have little ability to pressure the government of the originating country, particularly if the originating country is a powerful developed nation and the affected nation is less developed and lacking in global power.

International Agreements of Limited Scope

Despite multiple sources of resistance to international environmental controls, at times national governments have also recognized that they share a mutual interest in minimizing or managing some environmental problems. This recognition can lead to the creation of international agreements to address the shared problem. The primary mechanism for establishing transborder environmental controls takes the form of international treaties or accords. These agreements may be bilateral, multilateral, or global in scope.

A **bilateral agreement** is a legal agreement between two neighboring nation-states that promise to undertake specified actions to reduce some transborder environmental problem. The problems most often addressed in this manner are the pollution of shared waters, transborder air pollution, and overfishing in common coastal waters. A typical example of a bilateral agreement is the United States–Canada Air Quality Accord of 1991. Through this accord the governments of the United States and Canada agreed to achieve specified reductions in their emission of sulfur dioxide and nitrous oxides from mobile and stationary sources, to share data about the sources of the atmospheric pollutants within their jurisdictions, and to regularly exchange information regarding emission levels, monitoring systems, and technologies for measuring and reducing the emission of pollutants. The Air Quality Accord also sets forth a system for settlement of disputes arising from implementation or nonimplementation of the various components of the treaty.

A **multilateral agreement** is an agreement among more than two nations seeking to alleviate some shared ecological problem. Like bilateral treaties, multilateral accords generally focus on a specific set of issues arising from some shared resource, most often water. The Berne (Rhine River) Accord of 1963, the Convention on the Protection of the Black Sea against Pollution, and the Regional Convention for the Conservation of the Red Sea and Gulf of Aden Environment are typical multilateral accords. Each of these treaties requires nations bordering on particular bodies of water to reduce the pollutants discharged into them and to take other specified actions to minimize future introduction of pollutants into the ecosystem in question.[20]

Bilateral and multilateral treaties are the most common form of legal instrument for addressing transborder environmental problems. There are over 300 bi- and multilateral treaties dealing with issues of transborder water issues alone.[21] The strength of bilateral and multilateral treaties and accords is that the nations entering into them frequently have a clear and immediate *common* interest in protecting some shared resource.

Calvin and Hobbes
by Bill Watterson

Source: CALVIN AND HOBBES © 1988 Watterson. Dist. by UNIVERSAL PRESS SYNDICATE. Reprinted with permission. All rights reserved.

Global Agreements

A **global environmental accord** or treaty is an agreement that binds all or nearly all the nations of the world to follow specific courses of actions in order to protect the environment. Because they lack the specific focus, limited scope, and immediate shared interests typical of bi- and multilateral treaties, global environmental accords are far more difficult to negotiate. Global environmental accords tend to be far broader in scope than bi- and multilateral environmental treaties in three important ways.

First, global environmental accords typically address problems from a systemwide and multidimensional perspective. For instance, protecting biodiversity globally means reducing *all* threats to all species in all ecosystems rather than addressing the specific problems posed by one or two pollutants in a single ecosystem or threats to a particular species.

Second, because global accords involve all the nations of the world, these agreements must accommodate many more conflicting and competing sets of interests than bi- or multilateral treaties. For example, the multilateral **Berne Accord of 1963** involves five nations: France, Germany, Luxembourg, the Netherlands, and Switzerland. While important differences exist between these nations, they also share many commonalities. All are developed European nations with high material standards of living, a common history, and relatively similar cultures. And, most important, they share an obvious common resource—the Rhine River. In contrast, global treaties must accommodate the interests of developed nations along with those of the least developed and must blend understandings arising from different cultures and political systems.

Third, global accords frequently address long-term problems in which the causes and effects are separated spatially or temporally. For instance, hazardous waste that is transported from an industrially developed nation to a poorer and less developed nation in another part of the globe will not appear as a problem to people living in the developed nation that generated the waste. The time lapse between a cause (e.g., pollutants in an ecosystem) and effect (e.g., increased cancer rates) may also make a problem difficult to recognize. Causal time lags can provide strong arguments for inaction or slow responses by those who benefit from the current ways of doing things. Finally, the effects of global environmental threats and the consequences of controlling them are not distributed equally. This often makes agreement on the importance of specific problems and the strategies for responding to them difficult to achieve. For instance, according to current estimates, global climate change is likely to have a more devastating effect on peoples and nations that depend on low-technology subsistence agriculture than on industrial nations, thus creating different levels of concern and urgency among different nations.[22] These kinds of conflicting interests make the negotiation of global environmental agreements, intended to be acceptable to over 150 sovereign nations, an exceptionally complex task.

Despite the impediments to global accords, recent developments in the international environmental arena suggest there is a growing worldwide recognition that many of the most serious environmental problems can be addressed only through world-scale agreements. In 1972 the United Nations held the first **Earth Summit**, formally known as the Stockholm Conference on the Human Environment. This conference revealed deep differences of opinion between developed and developing nations about who was responsibile for global environmental protection. Developed nations sought limitations on environmentally damaging development practices of the less developed nations such as clear-cutting of rainforests, overgrazing, unmanaged land clearing and farming, and lack of controls on mining and industrial waste disposal. In contrast, representatives of the less developed nations argued that it was the developed nations of the world, with their widespread industrialization, high levels of material consumption, and generation of hazardous waste, that posed the gravest threats to the global environment. Moreover, these representatives claimed that the costs of global environmental protection should be shouldered by the developed nations since it was these nations that had benefited the most from damaging the earth's environment. This conference, and the tensions within it, led to the establishment of a set of environmental principles that have shaped subsequent developments in the environmental arena. In an attempt to sidestep the tension between developing and developed nations, the conference agreed on the following:

- Nations have a responsibility to protect the ecosystems under their jurisdiction.
- Nations should pursue "sustainable development," that is, development plans should incorporate measures for preserving ecosystems, avoiding depleting nonrenewable resources, and preserving the earth's ability to reproduce other resources such as clean water, clear air, forests, and grasslands into their development plans.
- Every nation has a sovereign right to exploit its own resources, presumably in keeping with principles of environmental protection.
- Developed nations should offer financial and technological assistance to less developed nations to assist them in developing strategies for sustainable development.

These principles have served as a basis for negotiating agreements concerning transporting hazardous waste, protecting the earth's ozone layer, protecting biodiversity, and reducing global warming and climate change.

Hazardous Waste Transportation

In 1989 the United Nations Environmental Project convened the Basel Conference on the international transportation of hazardous wastes. The conference led to the Basel Convention on the Control of Transboundary Movements of Hazardous Wastes and Their Disposal. The process and problems leading to this convention exemplify four issues associated with the creation and enforcement of global environmental issues: the differing interests of developed and developing nations, the potential for corporate-state conflict, the potential for government support for environmentally destructive but lucrative activities, and the need for government ratification and enforcement of environmental treaties.

Historically, developed nations have been the primary producers of hazardous waste while developing nations have been the most common destinations for international shipments of these wastes.[23] (As a result, delegates to the Basel Conference from less developed nations supported a total ban on the transboundary shipment of hazardous waste, whereas representatives from developed nations sought an agreement that would not require that developed nations dispose of their waste entirely within their own borders.) This conflict of interest meant that any agreement would necessarily fall short of a complete ban on transboundary transportation of hazardous waste.

Another issue that surfaced at the conference was the relationship between international economic organizations and nation-states. Historically, hazardous waste from developed nations has entered less developed countries through business arrangements between waste-producing corporations or companies specializing in the transportation of hazardous waste and landholders or Third World business professionals who contracted to accept the waste. In fact, much of this international business was negotiated without any government involvement. Thus, one of the issues to be resolved was the relative autonomy of businesses. In the end, the agreement did not ban international traffic in hazardous waste, but it did limit it to shipments that had been agreed to by the government of the receiving nation after having been notified by the government of the originating nation.

The provision requiring government approval enables nations opposed to accepting hazardous waste from other countries to limit the ability of international corporations to enter into private hazardous waste agreements within their jurisdiction. On the other hand, under the Basel Convention, any nation willing to permit landholders or businesses within its boundaries to accept hazardous waste from other countries can do so. Given the long history of less developed nations permitting or even encouraging environmentally destructive activities by foreign corporations in order to generate foreign currency, some nations may simply agree to serve as international waste dumps for the developed world.

Finally, conventions such as the Basel agreement are applicable in only those countries that sign the agreement and *ratify* it through their own internal political process. By 1994, only 64 nations had ratified the Basel Convention, although 105 had initially signed it. Thus, while the Basel agreement was an important step toward addressing the problems of transboundary shipments of hazardous waste, there remain a number of loopholes through which international shipments of hazardous waste can still pass.

Protecting the Ozone Layer

Beginning in the 1970s scientists and climatologists began to speculate that the concentration of ozone in the higher reaches of the earth's atmosphere (15 to 30 miles above the surface) was being depleted by certain gases, particularly CFCs. Because stratospheric ozone is critical in shielding the earth from radiant energy, ozone depletion could contribute substantially to global warming and other climate changes.

In 1987 the **Vienna Accord** formally recognized the threat of ozone depletion and called upon signatory nations to engage in systematic research to identify the sources and consequences of ozone-depleting chemicals and to work to control, limit, reduce, or prevent ozone-depleting activities within their boundaries. Two years later, the Montreal Protocol on

Substances That Deplete the Ozone Layer extended the Vienna Accord by setting deadlines for specific actions to reduce ozone-depleting chemicals. The 81 nations that had signed the Vienna Accord ultimately agreed to phase out all production of CFCs by the year 2000. This agreement also provided a political context through which NGOs were able to effectively pressure DuPont, the largest U.S. producer of CFCs, to phase out all production of these chemicals by 1995.

The **Montreal Protocol** represents a concrete and potentially effective strategy to address a global environmental problem. However, because only slightly more than half of the world's nations are signatories to this agreement, there remains the possibility that some nations may seek to meet a continuing demand for CFCs. This may be particularly true in the case of Freon, which is needed to keep air conditioners and refrigeration units operating in less developed nations, many of whose citizens cannot readily afford newer non-Freon-based units or conversions of older Freon-based units.

Protecting Biodiversity

In 1992 a "Second Earth Summit" was held in Rio de Janeiro, Brazil. This conference, formally known as the 1992 United Nations Conference on the Environment and Development, resulted in two agreements: the Convention on Biological Diversity and the Framework Convention on Climate Change. These agreements are broader in scope than the hazardous waste and ozone conventions because the goals they set forth can be achieved only by simultaneously addressing multiple threats to the environment.

The Convention on Biological Diversity requires its signatories to take steps to limit activities that threaten species loss and ecosystem degradation within jurisdictions under their control *and* to ensure that activities within their jurisdiction "do not cause damage to the environment of other States or of areas beyond the limits of national jurisdiction."[24] These steps include rehabilitating and restoring degraded ecosystems, preventing introduction of foreign species that threaten ecosystems and eliminating those that have been introduced, creating and/or enforcing laws and regulations to protect threatened species, establishing special areas to protect threatened species or ecosystems, managing the risks associated with "the use and release of living modified organisms resulting from biotechnology," conducting environmental impact assessments of all proposed development projects, and in general regulating and managing biological resources "with a view to ensuring their conservation and sustainable use." The convention also addresses (1) the interest of Third World nations in having access to new biotechnology created in developing nations, often using genetic stock taken from species within developing nations, and (2) the interests of developed nations in having access to the genetic stock of plants and animals in the Third World nations. Thus, the convention grants the individual states the "authority to determine access to genetic resources" while requiring that countries "shall not impose restrictions" on access to genetic stock unless it violates other components of the treaty.

The Convention on Biological Diversity represents a significant step toward creating a worldwide commitment to defining the maximization of species as an important component of sustainable development. Like other international environmental treaties, however, it could be negotiated only by recognizing the sovereignty of nations. Thus, the convention affirms that "economic and social development and poverty eradication are the first and overriding priorities of developing countries" and that states have "the sovereign right to exploit their own resources [according to] their own environmental policies." These components of the treaty mean that steps to protect biodiversity will continue to be limited by other development priorities within the individual nations.

Framework Convention on Climate Change

The Framework Convention on Climate Change is designed to limit the emission of greenhouse gases worldwide. Because industrialized nations represent the largest source of greenhouse gas emission, the treaty established higher standards for these nations than for developing ones. During treaty negotiations the United States was the only industrialized nation that refused to accept binding rules for the reduction of greenhouse gases, and the U.S. delegation eventually succeeded in obtaining treaty language that made compliance with greenhouse gas reduction goals voluntary. In 1994, President Clinton reversed Bush administration policy and announced that the United States would comply with the treaty goals of reducing greenhouse gas emissions to 1990 levels.

DEVELOPMENT AND TRADE VERSUS ENVIRONMENTAL PROTECTION

During the last two decades of the twentieth century, recognition of the global nature of many environmental problems has promoted a search for international strategies for environmental protection. This has led to the negotiation of global conventions governing hazardous waste transportation, biodiversity, ozone depletion, and climate change, as well as numerous bi- and multilateral treaties of more limited scope. For the most part these treaties represent voluntary agreements with limited enforcement potential. Consequently, each nation's interest in protecting the biosphere and the pressure of world opinion remain the primary forces for ensuring compliance with international agreements to protect the global environment.

There are also powerful forces running counter to the protection of the global environment:

- the continued demand for increased standards of living
- the growth and expansion of transnational corporations
- the increased expansion of the free-trade movement

As citizens of both the developed world and the developing world struggle to consume more material goods, the strain on the world's resources, its biological diversity, and its atmosphere will intensify. It remains an open question as to how far nations will go to restrict the present growth of material consumption to ensure a healthy environment in the future.

Increased worldwide consumerism also has the consequence of expanding both the profitability and the power of transnational corporations. A number of transnational corporations already command greater wealth than many nations, giving them the ability to influence both the creation and enforcement of environmental laws within nation-states. Corporate promises of large-scale investments or fears that corporations will relocate to more hospitable countries remain important considerations when governments frame environmental and labor policies, especially governments of developing nations. The first and foremost goal of transnational corporations is to generate profits to be used internally and to be shared with their stockholders. As increasingly free-floating political entities, transnational corporations cannot be easily compelled to behave in socially and environmentally responsible ways.

For its part, the free-trade movement is designed to remove barriers to the worldwide movement of capital and goods by transnational corporations. The proponents of free trade argue that unless transnational corporations can invest where they deem it most profitable and can sell their products wherever there is a market for them, they will not be able to sustain the economic engine of world development, particularly development among the poorest nations. Environmental protection laws that slow the movement of goods and capital run counter to the goals of international free-trade agreements such as the General Agreement on Trade and Tariffs (GATT), the North American Free Trade Agreement (NAFTA), and agreements among the nations of the European Community.[25]

The tensions between free trade and environmental protection take several forms. First, there is a wide disparity among nations in the establish-

INSIGHT

Deadly Birth Defects on the Texas-Mexico Border Raise Concerns about Pollution

In the summer of 1992, U.S. headlines across the country reported higher than average instances of devastating birth defects in the Texas border town of Brownsville. Forty-two babies were born in a three-year period with neural-tube defect, for a rate three times the national average.[1] Typically, this type of birth defect comes in the form of anencephaly or spina bifida, and reports suggested the incidence of anencephaly in Brownsville was three times the national average for Hispanics and five times the national average for non-Hispanic whites.[2] When a baby is born with anencephaly, all or part of the brain or skull is missing or severely malformed, and it is usually stillborn or dies within several days of birth. Some neural-tube defect babies, however, are born with spina bifida. A baby with this type of birth defect has a deformity of the spinal cord that causes paralysis in the lower limbs or other neurological problems, but usually the baby will survive.

Across the border in Matamoros, Mexico, officials reported 42 cases of neural-tube defects over an 18-month period.[3] Matamoros is home to a variety of U.S. businesses, called maquiladoras (ma-kee-la-DO-ras), operating on the Mexican side of the border. The companies find the cheap labor, favorable tariffs, and lax enforcement of environmental laws attractive.

Many local health workers identify the toxic pollutants in the Rio Grande, the river that separates the two communities and from which Brownsville gets its water, as among the most likely causes for the outbreak. Although scientists suspect the culprit is environmental in nature, there is no scientific consensus as to the likelihood that these birth defects are the result of local pollution. Yet environmental groups have expressed concern for years that the toxic releases by the maquiladoras are contaminating the drinking water for the communities that lie all along the Rio Grande.

The national Toxics Campaign Fund found that 16 out of 22 factories along the border violated water quality standards.[4] Chemicals such as xylene, which can cause liver, lung, kidney, and brain damage, were found in some cases at levels 1,000 times higher than EPA limits allow.[5] Local groups and environmental groups argue that "since Mexico's environmental problems have increased in direct relation to the rise of the maquila industries, these industries should be made responsible for cleaning up the damage to the local areas."[6] However, the maquila industry officials and the Mexican government claim the pollution problem is being brought under control.

1. R. Suro, "Rash of Brain Defects in Newborns Disturbs Border City in Texas," *New York Times*, 31 May 1992, 18.
2. J. Hickson, "NAFTA Pollution Threat to U.S.-Mexican Border," *Green Left Weekly*, 6 December 1995.
3. Suro, "Rash of Brain Defects."
4. Suro, "Rash of Brain Defects."
5. Suro, "Rash of Brain Defects."
6. Hickson, "NAFTA Pollution."

ment and enforcement of environmental protection laws. If transnational corporations can easily and freely move goods from nations with lax environmental protection laws to those where such laws are more stringent, this can be a strong incentive to relocate industrial facilities to the former, since profits are likely to be higher. Thus, prohibiting the importation of goods produced in nations with lax environmental laws is a potential mechanism for enforcing international agreements regarding environmental protection. Free-trade agreements such as GATT, however, expressly prohibit the exclusion of products from one nation simply because they were manufactured elsewhere in an environmentally damaging manner. Similarly, the initial draft of NAFTA provided no guarantees that both environmental and labor standards in the United States would not be driven downward in order to ensure economic competitiveness with products produced under the less stringent laws of our NAFTA trading partners, particularly Mexico. In response to pressure by NGOs in the United States, several "side agreements" designed to protect against the erosion of environmental and labor laws in the United States were drafted as part of obtaining congressional approval for NAFTA. Both Canada and Mexico, however, are resistant to allowing the United States to encroach on their sovereignty by determining the content of Canadian or Mexican environment and labor laws. Thus, despite the side agreements, a substantial gap remains between environmental standards in the United States, Canada, and Mexico. This in turn means transnationals and other economic interests in the United States will continue to press for weaker environmental enforcement in order to ensure the U.S. economy remains competitive and that more U.S. jobs do not migrate elsewhere.

CONCLUSION

In the final analysis considerable progress has been made during the last quarter of the twentieth century in increasing awareness of the global nature of environmental problems and in developing international strategies to address these problems. However, the continued world dependency on fossil fuels and chemicals, the continued demand for expansion of material consumption, the desire for development within the Third World, and the expansion of transnational corporations that control most of the capital entail global environmental protection issues that will remain a source of conflict well into the foreseeable future.

REVIEW QUESTIONS

1. Discuss the difference between a bilateral and a multilateral treaty.
2. Define *nongovernmental organization* (NGO) and then provide three examples where NGOs have played an important role in the fight for increased environmental protection.
3. Can transborder flows of pollution occur between countries that are not contiguous? Please explain.
4. What effects does the global economy have on the negotiation and enforcement of environmental accords?
5. What are the three major environmental issues currently being addressed in the international arena?
6. What are the primary objectives of sustainable development?

DISCUSSION QUESTIONS

1. How would an international violation of environmental law be enforced?
2. What effect do global agreements have on domestic or international policy?
3. Are there other issues, such as the destruction of tropical rainforests, that should be addressed by global agreements? What are the difficulties associated with such action?
4. Some argue that the economic and cultural differences between countries make it difficult to address environmental issues collectively. Do you agree or disagree with their view? Please explain your position.
5. How would you assess the future of global environmental protection? Please justify your position.

REFERENCES

1. F. Mathys, "International Environmental Law: A Canadian Perspective," *Pace Yearbook of International Law* 3 (1992): 114–129.
2. A. Ferreria, *Econews*, 4, no. 20 (December 1995): http://www.edf.org.
3. B. Commoner, *The Closing Circle* (New York: Alfred A. Knopf, 1971).
4. A. Gunder-Frank, *World Accumulation 1492–1789* (New York: Monthly Review Press, 1978).
5. J.H. Bernardin de Saint Pierre, *Voyage from the Isle de France, Isle de Bourbon, The Cape of Good Hope with New Observations on Nature and Mankind by an Officer of the King* (1773), quoted in S.W. Mintz, *Sweetness and Power* (New York: Penguin, 1985), frontispiece.

6. J. Bodley, *Anthropology and Contemporary Human Problems* (Menlo Park, CA: Cummings Publishing Co., 1976).

7. J. Cavenaugh and F. Clairmonte, "From Corporations to Conglomerates," *Multinational–Monitor* 4 (January 1983): 16–20.

8. D. Blake and R. Walters, *The Politics of Global Economic Relations* (Englewood Cliffs, NJ: Prentice Hall, 1976).

9. R. Strauss, interview, *Environmental Reporter* 9 (July 1978): 451.

10. B. Castleman, "How We Export Dangerous Industries," *Business and Society Review* 27 (1978): 7–14

11. W. Leonard and C. Duerksen, "Environmental Regulation and the Location of Industry: An International Perspective," *Columbia Journal of World Business* 15 (1981): 55–68.

12. Multilateral Project, Tufts University Law School, at http://tufts.edu/fletcher/multilaterals.htm/MultlaProj.marine/html.

13. United Nations Convention on Biological Diversity, Rio de Janeiro, June 5, 1992, Article 2.

14. See, for instance, B. Devall and G. Sessions, *Deep Ecology: Living as If Nature Mattered* (Salt Lake City, UT: Peregrine Smith Books, 1985).

15. P. List, *Radical Environmentalism: Philosophy and Tactics* (Belmont, CA: Wadsworth, 1993).

16. C. Manes, *Green Rage: Radical Environmentalism and the Unmaking of Civilization* (Boston: Little, Brown, 1990).

17. G. Rehmke, "Eliminating Government Support for Deforestation Can Save Rain Forests," in *Global Resources*, ed. M. Polesetsky (San Diego, CA: Greenhaven Press, 1991), 150–157.

18. United Nations Environmental Project, Man Made Climate Change, Geneva, 1992.

19. American Law Institute, *Restatement of the Law: Foreign Relations Law of the United States* (St. Paul, MN: American Law Institute, 1986).

20. Multilateral Project, Tufts University Law School.

21. C. Valente and W. Valente, *Environmental Law and Policy* (St. Paul, MN: West Publishing, 1995), 411.

22. United Nations Environmental Project, fact sheet 4.

23. J. Vallette, *The International Trade in Wastes: A Greenpeace Inventory* (Washington, DC: Greenpeace, 1989).

24. United Nations Convention on Biological Diversity, *Basic Documents of International Environmental Law*, ed. H. Hoham.

25. J. Jackson, "World Trade Rules and Environmental Policies: Congruence or Conflict," *Washington and Lee Law Review* 49 (1992): 1227.

CHAPTER 15

Environmental Crime Research: Where We Have Been, Where We Should Go

Donald J. Rebovich

TERMS	environmental audit	occupational disqualification of
	environmental crime reduction	corporate executives
	equation	small quantity generators
	Environmental Crimes Project	(SQGs)

During the winter of 1995, the battle between the Clinton administration and the U.S. Congress over a balanced budget led to two separate shutdowns of the federal government. Countless U.S. employees were furloughed for periods that promised, at the time, to be fearfully protracted. During this time, television newscasters and local and national newspapers began listing the types of services the public would have to do without during the shutdowns. The delay of the delivery of Social Security checks and the closing of the Grand Canyon received the lion's share of attention by the media. The temporary termination of Superfund cleanup operations was relatively low on the list of suspended federal services being discussed, nevertheless cleanup was halted for many contaminated sites across the country.

Perhaps the lack of media attention reflected the perceived importance of environmental protection. Clearly, public attitudes about environmental issues have been difficult to follow. A January 1995 Times/CNN poll reported the American public was becoming increasingly skeptical about the cost-effectiveness of enforcing environmental regulations.[1] But while evidence has been offered to suggest public support for environmental protection efforts is lagging, other evidence contradicts this assessment. A May 1995 Roper Starch poll found that over 70 percent of Americans are sympathetic toward environmental concerns and oppose rollbacks of environmental protections.[2]

It may have been no wonder that a media occupied with America's grandest budgetary tug of war of the 1990s would pay scant notice to its impact on the environment. Over 15 years had passed since the birth of the Superfund.

It has been even longer since the threat of improperly disposed chemicals oozed into the American public's consciousness following Love Canal and Times Beach. The threat of toxic wastes was underscored in 1980 when the Surgeon General declared that the United States was on the edge of an environmental emergency created by unchecked illegal dumping of hazardous waste. The public was outraged, and public policy reflected popular concern.

Despite an apparent tempering of the public's past approval of environment protection efforts, evidence suggesting offenses against the environment are on the minds of citizens and politicians alike consistently emerges. Public support for environmental issues such as was reported in the Roper Starch poll is said to have prompted congressional Republicans in the 1995 session to abandon plans to revamp existing environmental regulatory laws.[3] As the twenty-first century approaches, the changing public climate concerning the importance of environmental crime has led to a reduction of funding support for research endeavors to study enforcement efforts of environmental statutes. As a result, the bulk of studies on environmental crime were conducted during the 1980s and early 1990s. This chapter provides a brief summary of several studies on environmental crime conducted in the United States. First, it reviews seven crucial projects on environmental crime. Next, it presents suggestions for future areas of environmental crime research. Finally, it discusses obstacles that future studies of environmental crime will need to overcome. It is clear much remains to be done by both academics and practitioners. Questions raised in the popular press about environmental crime are on the rise,[4] and efforts must be directed toward addressing the inquiries of an increasingly curious public. This chapter is an effort focusing in that direction.

ENVIRONMENTAL CRIME RESEARCH: WHAT HAS BEEN ACCOMPLISHED?

Until the mid-1980s, virtually no empirical research had been conducted on either the commission of environmental crime or enforcement efforts. By the mid-1990s, half a dozen studies had been completed, revealing information on environmental criminality from various perspectives.[5–10] Though not always similar in research approach, all attempted to understand and explain the nature of violations against the environment and how government enforcement agencies have addressed—or not addressed—these crimes.

Poisoning for Profit: The Mafia and Toxic Waste in America,[11] by Block and Scarpitti, was the first book on the subject of environmental crime. The authors asserted that hazardous waste crime, especially in highly industrialized states, was controlled and directed by organized crime syndicates, whose influence came via the solid waste industry. The hazardous waste industry, they claimed, was not just partly made up of career criminals but had largely been structured by organized crime syndicates. They dismissed the idea that hazardous waste crime was a variant of white-collar crime, arguing instead it was better understood as a type of organized crime.

Using investigative interviews to gather information, the authors concluded that the degree of organized crime infiltration into the hazardous waste treatment industry in the Northeast had been underestimated. In large part, Block and Scarpitti blamed enforcement ineffectiveness and public official malfeasance for the flourishing of organized crime in the hazardous waste industry. The book offered a number of provocative conclusions and sparked significant controversy. Ultimately, the authors came under attack over accusations made against certain public officials and a waste treatment corporation. In a settlement with the corporation, the book's publisher agreed to destroy the entire inventory of *Poisoning for Profit*.[12]

Hammitt and Reuter's *Measuring and Deterring Illegal Disposal of Hazardous Waste*,[13] published in 1988, contained interviews with local law enforcement personnel and industry representatives in Los Angeles County, Massachusetts, and Pennsylvania. The authors underscored the impact that **small quantity generators (SQGs)** can have on the environment. Although SQGs generate less than 1 percent of all hazardous waste in the United States, their share of illegal disposal is likely to be substantial due to high rates of noncompliance with environmental regulations. Hammitt and Reuter attributed this high rate of criminality to the high cost of legitimate treatment, storage, and disposal of waste. According to Hammitt and Reuter, SQG officials typically view the harm posed by the improper disposal of their waste as relatively minor in comparison with the harm caused by illegal disposals by larger corporations. This rationalization, combined with the belief that the dumping of small amounts of hazardous waste would go undetected, increased the chances that small business owners would violate environmental laws. In Massachusetts, the authors found several SQGs tended to legally dispose of a percentage of their waste and then falsify documents to hide the illegal disposal of other waste. Further, businesses resorted to increased illegal disposal when the cost of legally hauling hazardous waste was increased. As a result of their study, Hammitt and Reuter recommend prosecutors reach a maximum level of environmental enforcement efficiency through strategically targeting potential environmental criminals. Hammitt and Reuter's analysis of incentives for violations and possible deterrents to minimize illegal disposal suggests a profile of the kinds of businesses most likely to commit environmental crimes.

Gunther's 1990 study[14] of the implementation of California's hazardous waste control act by local prosecutors was an early attempt to glean valuable information from criminal justice professionals about the idiosyncrasies associated with controlling environmental crime. The study shows that local prosecutors have had to quickly acquire the qualities needed for successful decision making in the prosecution of environmental offenses. Survey data were used to point out how factors like the need to acquire sufficient evidence, the need to assess the gravity of violations committed, and the need to estimate the harm or potential harm posed by the offenses would become key determinants in the decision-making routes chosen by environmental prosecutors. The study also reveals how prosecutors view the ethical responsibility to withhold criminal charges in cases where there is serious doubt about the prosecutor's ability to prove guilt beyond a reasonable doubt.

Rebovich's 1992 *Dangerous Ground: The World of Hazardous Waste Crime*[15] describes the results of an eight-year, multistate study of state environmental crime cases and the control methods used in those cases. The offender profile developed from research results was found to be unlike the earlier findings of Block and Scarpitti, but it was consistent with some of Hammitt and Reuter's conclusions. The environmental offenders studied seemed, in most cases, to be ordinary, profit-motivated business owners who operated in a milieu where syndicate crime activity might be present but was by no means pervasive. According to Rebovich's study, the world of the environmental offender is one in which the intensity, duration, and methods of the criminal act are more likely to be determined by the opportunities available in the legitimate marketplace than by the orders of a controlling crime syndicate. Throughout the text, Rebovich argues that an individual's criminal activities are often the result of employee trust, antagonism, and specific requests made in the workplace. Criminal enforcement and prosecution agencies in the states studied were found to be dedicated but frequently handicapped by the failures of the regulatory enforcement agencies and a lack of adequate resources.

In 1993, Hammett and Epstein[16] published their findings on the prosecution of environmental crime at the local level of government. This study was more intensive than the earlier Gunther study. The authors described the experiences of five county prosecutors' offices that, by agency mandate, had made the prosecution of environmental crime a priority. The report clarifies how county prosecutors in some jurisdictions have taken on the responsibility of aggressively controlling environmental crime at the local government level. Although the study serves to dispel the myth that environmental crime control is beyond the capabilities of local government enforcement and prosecution agencies, it does confirm the obstacles that typically stand in the way of effective environmental crime control at the local level. Such obstacles were found to include lack of training, minimal access to adequate laboratory testing services, and difficulties with expert witness sources.

A 1994 empirical study of environmental crime also concentrated on the evaluation of the county prosecutors in the fight against environmental crime.[17] Rebovich and Nixon conducted a national mail survey of local prosecutors, asking them about subjects such as the most effective strategies in controlling environmental crime, the most serious obstacles they encounter, and how they overcome the obstacles. According to the findings, during the decision-making process leading to the assigning of charges, the average environmental prosecutor places the greatest weight on the offender's criminal intent and the degree of harm posed by the offense. In the mind of the average environmental prosecutor, pressures exerted by business or labor groups to withhold criminal prosecutions are generally outweighed by other pressures (from the public, for example) to follow through with criminal prosecutions. Rather than pursue a criminal conviction, the typical environmental prosecutor at the local level was apt to proceed with a civil case if the alleged offender was a business. According to the local prosecutors surveyed, one of the most effective strategies used to control environmental crime was to develop task forces that were multijurisdictional and multidisciplinary.

One of the most recent books published on environmental crime is *Environmental Crime and Criminality: Theoretical and Practical Issues*,[18] a collection of essays on ideas that have been or arguably should be applied to the fight against environmental crime. Due in large part to the interdisciplinary nature of the subject, much of the current research on environmental crime has been rather fragmented and has proven to be difficult to pursue. The collection of 11 research projects offers insights into theoretical, practical, philosophical, and future issues in the study of environmental crime.[19]

Finally, it is important to make note of the variety of articles on environmental crime published in newspapers, magazines, and journals. The tone of the articles is dramatically varied, depending upon the forum in which the article is presented. Business and trade journals tend to discuss the best methods for avoiding costly litigation and solving compliance problems. Environmental journals outline the best ways to catch environmental criminals. Law journals discuss recent court cases likely to impact social assessments of environmental harm. Technical journals outline new technologies for detecting harmful chemicals or for improving air quality. Discussions of environmental protection in the media are increasingly abundant and varied.

In short, several interesting studies have been authored with the specific intent of increasing understanding about environmental crime and its enforcement. While social and political attitudes about environmental protection seem to shift as often as the tides, the overall impression given by the studies mentioned above is that the interest in environmental crime shown by a variety of disciplines and industries is steadily increasing.

ENVIRONMENTAL CRIME RESEARCH: NEEDS FOR THE FUTURE

The research studies on environmental crime done to date have furnished the criminal justice community with some rich insights into the evolution of environmental criminality and the development of control efforts since the 1980s. While the authors draw different conclusions about the characteristics most representative of environmental criminals, they have taken the first authentic steps toward understanding environmental crime and how to deal with it. More information is needed, however, to help fill in the remaining gaps.

For example, the factors that influence environmental criminality include the following seven identified by Rebovich[20]:

1. the extent and duration of industrial growth
2. the availability of legal and illegal disposal outlets
3. the law enforcement response
4. the level of cooperation between regulators and those responsible for criminal prosecutions
5. the visibility of offenses
6. the maturity of the workplace criminal group
7. syndicate crime complicity

Exploratory research has been completed on how interaction among these factors can lead to fluctuations in the rate of environmental crime. The following has been proposed as the proper equation for reducing environmental crime: tighten environmental legislation + toughen enforcement + increase legitimate disposal alternatives = reduced rates of environmental offenses.[21] It is referred to here as the **environmental crime reduction equation**. Little has been done to determine if in fact this equation is correct. As time advances, the need for such research becomes more critical.

In the mid-1980s, amendments to the Resource Conservation and Recovery Act (RCRA) had been incorporated in response to a general concern that the environmental laws were not adequately addressing a large number of environmental violations.[22] These amendments include strict prohibitions on the land disposal of hazardous waste and tougher standards on the production, sale, and use of waste oil. In addition, the cutoff for low-level waste generators, previously exempt from EPA regulations, was significantly lowered. These amendments were in sharp contrast to congressional initiatives of the mid-1990s, which imposed deep cuts on environmental enforcement programs.[23,24] In the future, an obligation of environmental crime researchers will be to empirically examine the effects that variations in components of the environmental crime reduction equation have on environmental crime rates.

Environmental crime research should also focus on the potential new challenges that environmental law enforcement officers can expect to confront in the future. It is anticipated that the environmental crime enforcer of the 21st Century will have to adapt to changes driven by factors such as offender creativity in the execution of the offenses, similar creativity in the development of criminal conspiracies, and geographic dispersion of environmental crime.

Environmental law enforcement officers should expect environmental criminals to retool their criminal execution tactics to insulate them from an increasingly sophisticated enforcement community. Consider the current loosely structured federal definitions of recycling, for example. Efforts should be made to study the incidence and dynamics of offenses that involve the mixing of hazardous substances with nonhazardous substances to construct aggregates passed off as recycled products.

Research attention should also be paid to the changes in the characteristics of criminal conspiracies expected to take place in response to new enforcement programs. There is now a trend, for example, toward conspiracies designed to capitalize on Third World nations with relatively weak environmental laws. Wily offenders use these countries to launder waste by altering documents to falsely indicate the waste products are safe. Government studies have shown that Central and South America are prime locations for this type of illegal conduct. International studies of environmental crime are needed to help determine how prevalent these crimes are, identify the countries most vulnerable to these violations, and assess how waste importation laws and international enforcement might be revised to effectively deter these crimes.

As the general public becomes increasingly conscious of the cost of environmental enforcement efforts and as members of the U.S. Congress heighten their scrutiny of the overall effectiveness of environmental crime control, the empirical study of environmental enforcement at all government levels will gain importance. Comparative studies of charges successfully brought against environmental criminals versus charges dismissed will be needed to identify the significant factors leading to successful prosecution. Also, discerning the formal and informal procedures used by prosecutors to relegate criminal cases to civil proceedings is also becoming increasingly important. The success or failure of environmental cases prosecuted could be determined through discriminate analyses of environmental crime dispositions using characteristics of cases said by environmental enforcers to be instrumental in past qualitative studies (e.g., identifying the means by which the waste was discovered, the type and volume of the chemicals disposed, the proximity of the disposal to densely populated areas, and the degree of harm posed by the disposal). Hopefully, the results of such studies would set the foundation for a system that could statistically predict the chances for prosecutorial success and thus enhance prosecutorial decision making. In terms of sentencing effectiveness, recidivism research will be required to discover the effectiveness of the most punitive sanctions and of unconventional intermediate sanctions imposed in cases involving less serious violations. One such intermediate sanction is the **occupational disqualification of corporate executives**. This sanction disallows a corporate executive from working in the profession he or she was employed in when committing the relevant violation.

An area deserving of special research attention is the use of environmental audits. An **environmental audit** is an internal investigation of a company to determine if it is in compliance with all applicable environmental regulations. In many cases, audits are performed voluntarily by waste-generating corporations. Concerted attempts have recently been made by corporations to promote federal initiatives that would prevent enforcement agencies from using information obtained through a corporate self-audit. A 1995 Price Waterhouse survey of 369 businesses reported two-thirds of the manufacturing companies conduct voluntary environmental audits and would be encouraged to do more if penalties were eliminated for self-identified and corrected violations.

As would be expected, agencies like the EPA have been reluctant to provide immunity to regulated entities that report and correct environmental violations on their own. In the past, such information has been used as a "roadmap" in criminal enforcement and prosecution actions. Concern that self-auditing privileges will be used as a shield against prosecution of other environmental offenses remains.[25]

In spite of the concern expressed by the regulatory community, some state governments have moved toward legislatively approving self-auditing privileges. By mid-1996, coalitions of major companies had been successful in prompting 18 states to adopt legislation to protect companies from disclosure or punishment when they detect on-site environmental offenses. Some of the new state laws allow business officials to withhold the results of their audits from authorities and from the public.[26,27] While they have expressed little doubt of the importance of self-audits for confirming compliance with environmental regulations and minimizing waste in manufacturing, criminal justice officials have expressed great concern about the degree of control businesses are granted and the extent of protection they receive under these privileges. The general fear is that the new laws would simply be exploited by environmental offenders to avoid responsibility for their acts of pollution. A common misgiving mentioned by local prosecutors is that under such laws prosecutors would be prevented from seizing as evidence the types of documents routinely used in the investigations of illegal hazardous waste disposal.[28,29] Empirical research on corporate actions involving self-auditing privileges might help bring to a close the protracted national debate on what role, if any, self-auditing privileges have in environmental protection.

SOME KEY OBSTACLES TO OVERCOME

Media coverage and a number of scholarly works have helped spread information on the public health threat posed by environmental crime. Additional studies have focused on understanding the methods being used to control this type of crime. Since it is a relatively new type, scant information has been presented on the actual environmental law enforcement and prosecution experience. While criminologists are becoming generally better attuned to the theoretical and practical parameters of environmental crime and its control, they still confront important obstacles to environmental crime fighting. If these obstacles are left unaddressed by the research community, it is doubtful practitioners in the field will be able to overcome them.

A major barrier to the effective control of environmental crime is the absence of an effective, centralized information-sharing mechanism. Such a mechanism would allow federal, state, and local environmental law enforcers to assist each other in identifying environmental crime. Its absence is due, in large part, to the infancy of this area of crime. Also, traditional turf battles exist among competing agencies. Further, opening the books on environmental crime allows public scrutiny of official decision making in the charging and processing of politically sensitive criminal cases. Gunther[30] spotted the wide diversity of perspectives on environmental crime control held by assistant U.S. attorneys, deputy attorneys general, deputy state attorneys general, and deputy district attorneys. His study also illuminated the effect these conflicting perspectives have on one typical research problem—gaining access to relevant data. Access to data on environmental crime is essential for understanding key dimensions of environmental criminality and its control.

Though made in 1990, these observations reflect a situation that has remained largely unchanged. In some ways, the situation has become worse. Events that transpired from late 1992 through mid-1994 may lead to even more pronounced protection of environmental crime control data. In late 1992, two congressional committees and an academic group working for a third committee issued reports highly critical of the U.S. Department of Justice's Environmental Crimes Section. Through the use of interviews, case studies, and an analysis of aggregate criminal prosecution data, the **Environmental Crimes Project** concluded that the Environmental Crimes Section was lax in its prosecution of environmental offenders and persistently suffered from competency problems.[31] In "Congressional Oversight of Federal Environmental Prosecutions: The Trashing of Environmental Crimes,"[32] William Hassler claimed that the earlier report and its conclusions were methodologically flawed and replete with factual errors. Hassler took special exception to the biased characterization of prosecutors who supported the report's conclusions as "seasoned" and to the accusation that certain Environmental Crime Section prosecutors were "inexperienced" and disinclined to prosecute. Hassler also dismissed the research project's use of an estimate of the frequency of environmental crime prosecutions based on the U.S. gross domestic product as a benchmark for the number of cases actually prosecuted by the Environmental Crime Section.

A subsequent study[33] of Environmental Crime Section prosecutions conducted by the U.S. General Accounting Office in 1993 produced a more favorable assessment of the work of the Environmental Crimes Section. The impact of the controversy over the interpretation of the Environmental Crime Section data remains to be seen. Further, it remains an open question whether the controversy will affect the willingness of environmental crime officials to openly participate in future environmental crime research ventures. In this case, environmental crime control officials lined up publicly to either support or refute the Environmental Crime Project findings. The result was a political row, turning what might have been a credible research endeavor into another election year casualty. At the same time, the encounter increased the territorial gap between environmental control officials at local, state, and federal levels.

CONCLUSION

Studies on the prosecution and enforcement of environmental crime do exist, although they are sometimes difficult to find because of the interdisci-

Calvin and Hobbes

by Bill Watterson

plinary nature of the topic. Research in the area is in its infancy, and much work remains to be done. Thus far, attention has mainly been focused on characterizing typical offenders, delineating the methods for committing criminal acts, and determining how alleged offenders are handled in the criminal justice system. While this research provides a notable preliminary step, more specific attention is needed.

Research on the environmental crime reduction equation could prove useful for determining the importance of the relationship between legislation, its enforcement, and legal waste disposal alternatives. Efforts must be made to increase the size and availability of data on environmental crime. Attention must be focused on methods used to assess environmental crime data in order to minimize potential controversy. In addition, questions about the role of organized crime syndicates in hazardous waste disposal remain, and exploration of this issue would be useful for determining the best way to fight environmental crime.

For environmental crime enforcement to improve, control agents at all levels of government must agree to put aside traditional animosities and embrace the challenge of joint research and practice. Those interested in furthering the study of environmental crime must build systems to objectively document environmental crime and crime control efforts and effectively distribute pertinent information. Presently, law enforcement is hampered by a lack of training—and in some cases a reticence to classify violators of environmental statutes as criminals. Geographic factors may be equally influential and therefore need to be studied to achieve a greater understanding of the driving forces behind environmental crime. Attention must be given to the ways in which enforcement efforts might impede successful apprehension and prosecution. Also of great concern is the need for comprehensive and accurate data on the characteristics of offenders and offenses and the investigative, prosecutorial, and sentencing efforts focused on this crime area at multiple levels of government. Once collected and analyzed, the data could prove invaluable for deterring future violations and could enhance the investigation of environmental crimes that do occur.

Environmental audits and creative alternative sentencing practices are only two of the developing options intended to help decrease the occurrence of environmental crime. Research is necessary to follow up on these and other alternatives to determine their effectiveness. Offenses against the environment are a critical element of the culture emerging in the United States and across the globe at the turn of this century.

The areas of study mentioned above represent only the tip of the iceberg. So much has yet to be learned about our relationship with the natural environment that any individual effort to resolve the problem of environmental destruction can seem hopeless. Nonetheless, each research project provides a piece of the puzzle, and it is only by assembling the puzzle piece by piece that we will achieve a well-grounded view of our place in nature and of the best strategy for protecting the natural environment and the species that depend on it—including, of course, our own.

REVIEW QUESTIONS

1. In the first comprehensive study on environmental crime, the researchers linked hazardous waste dumping to organized crime. Have other studies of hazardous waste disposal confirmed or denied the initial link to organized crime?
2. What was the importance of identifying small quantity generators and assessing their impact on environmental crime?
3. One of the most recent books focused on environmental crime is entitled *Environmental Crime and Criminality: Theoretical and Practical Issues*. What are some examples of theoretical and practical issues in environmental crime research?
4. How might the environmental crime reduction equation be tested to determine if it was basically correct?

DISCUSSION QUESTIONS

1. What are the primary difficulties confronted by environmental crime researchers?

2. As indicated in the chapter, some research has linked environmental crime to organized crime. If a link between the two exists, should theories about organized crime be used to analyze environmental crime? Justify your position.
3. Consider the suggestions for future research presented at the close of the chapter. Do you have any additional suggestions to make?

REFERENCES

1. J. Adler, "The Greening of the Republican Platform," *Washington Post*, 4 January 1996, 24.
2. Adler, "Greening of the Republican Platform."
3. Adler, "Greening of the Republican Platform," endnote 2.
4. M. Clifford et al., "Defining Environmental Crime: Is the Genie out of the Bottle?" submitted for publication review.
5. A. Block and F. Scarpitti, *Poisoning for Profit: The Mafia and Toxic Waste in America* (New York: William Morrow, 1985).
6. J. Hammitt and P. Reuter, *Measuring and Deterring Illegal Disposal of Hazardous Waste* (Santa Monica, CA: Rand Corporation, 1988).
7. A. Gunther, "Enforcement in Your Backyard: Implementation of California's Hazardous Waste Control Act by Local Prosecutors," *Ecology Law Quarterly* 17 (1990): 803–845.
8. D. Rebovich, *Dangerous Ground: The World of Hazardous Waste Crime* (New Brunswick, NJ: Transaction Publishers, 1992).
9. T. Hammett and J. Epstein, "Local Prosecution of Environmental Crime," in *Issues and Practices* (Washington, DC: National Institute of Justice, 1993).
10. D. Rebovich and R. Nixon, "Environmental Crime Prosecution: Results of a National Survey," in *Research in Brief* (Washington, DC: National Institute of Justice, 1994).
11. Block and Scarpitti, *Poisoning for Profit*.
12. *Waste Management, Inc. v. William Morrow & Co., Inc., Alan Block and Frank Scarpitti* No. 85 L 0369, March 27, 1986.
13. Hammitt and Reuter, *Measuring and Deterring Illegal Disposal of Hazardous Waste*.
14. Gunther, "Enforcement in Your Backyard."
15. Rebovich, *Dangerous Ground*.
16. Hammett and Epstein, "Local Prosecution of Environmental Crime."
17. Rebovich and Nixon, "Environmental Crime Prosecution."
18. S.M. Edwards et al., eds., *Environmental Crime and Criminality: Theoretical and Practical Issues* (New York: Garland Press, 1996).
19. Edwards et al., *Environmental Crime and Criminality*, p. xii.
20. Rebovich, *Dangerous Ground*.
21. Rebovich and Nixon, "Environmental Crime Prosecution."
22. W. Mugdan and B. Adler, "The 1984 RCRA Amendments: Congress as a Regulatory Agent," *Columbia Journal of Environmental Law* 10 (1985): 215–254.

23. J. Cushman, "House G.O.P., Softening Stance, Issues Manifesto on the Environment," *New York Times*, 16 May 1996, 7.

24. J. Cushman, "Many States Give Polluting Firms New Protections," *New York Times*, 5 April 1996, 1.

25. A. Soden, "Regulatory Policy Discourages Voluntary Environmental Audits," *Corporate Legal Times*, August 1995.

26. Cushman, "House G.O.P."

27. Cushman, "Many States Give Polluting Firms New Protections."

28. Cushman, "House G.O.P."

29. Cushman, "Many States Give Polluting Firms New Protections."

30. Gunther, "Enforcement in Your Backyard."

31. J. Turley, "Preliminary Report on Criminal Environmental Prosecution by the U.S. Department of Justice," Environmental Crimes Project, National Law Center of George Washington University, 1992.

32. W. Hassler, "Congressional Oversight of Federal Environmental Prosecutions: The Trashing of Environmental Crimes," *Environmental Law Reporter*, February 1994, 10074–10087.

33. L. Stevens, "Environmental Crime: Issues Related to Justice's Criminal Prosecution of Environmental Offenses," testimony before the Subcommittee on Oversight and Investigations of the House Committee on Energy and Commerce, 103rd Cong., 2d sess., 1994.

PART III

Conclusion

As the interest in environmental crime increases, so will the importance of thorough and thoughtful research studies. Deliberate review of existing research provides an appropriate framework for determining the direction for future research. Part III offered a broad range of critical commentaries on the topic of environmental crime. Characterizing typical environmental criminals and identifying weaknesses in enforcement efforts will assist in ensuring that future efforts head in the right direction. Contemplating the philosophical foundations of the current attitude toward the natural environment should help everyone identify his or her responsibilities in the creation of clean communities that handle waste responsibly.

Part III invited a review of the role humans play, from within a consumer-based society, as producers and consumers of products that cannot be reabsorbed into the natural environmental cycles. This creates a number of dilemmas for increasing the effectiveness of environmental enforcement that mainstream America must attempt to resolve. Is it acceptable to say that municipalities in constant violation of water pollution guidelines should not be punished because they are providing a public good? Are we ready, on the other hand, to arrest the operators of a municipal treatment plant who fail to comply with such guidelines? If the municipal treatment plant did not meet the relevant standards because the city or county government did not fund the plant adequately, who would be responsible for noncompliance in that case? It should be clear by now that many critical environmental decisions must be made in tight economic times through an extremely political process. Perhaps culpability for environmental harm is assigned too quickly.

Would it be acceptable to look the other way when municipal facilities (providing public goods) are at fault but prosecute cases when private companies are the culprits? What if we prosecute only cases where people are injured? The answers to these questions are not easy. However, they need to be worked out. For one thing, the absence of equal treatment of offenders is as frustrating for environmental supporters as it is for the enforcement agencies. The path to a cleaner environment, based on responsible legislation and enforcement and punishments that fit the crimes, will require collective efforts from communities across the country and across the globe. Creative and critical discourse will prove essential.

PART IV

Case Studies

Community Opposition to Hazardous Waste Incineration: The Case of ENSCO

Mary Clifford

TERMS	best demonstrated available technology	solid waste
	capacity assurance plan	Superfund
	hazardous waste	Superfund remediation

Modern American society demands chemical production. People demand chemical solutions to rid their bathrooms of mold and mildew, to protect their home gardens and shrubbery from unwanted insects and other pests, and to fuel their transportation. Yet the scientific community continues to report that exposure to some of these chemicals is harmful to humans and to the earth's environment. In recent years, one of the most divisive issues communities have had to face concerns the handling of harmful chemicals and the disposal of the hazardous waste. Consider the following hazardous waste incinerator controversy confronting the Arizona community discussed below.

INTRODUCTION TO THE ISSUES

In modern society, people have been inundated with new technologies. The flood of new technologies means that many of these technologies are introduced without giving much attention to their unanticipated consequences. Further, when questions arise about the safety of any new technology, attention quickly shifts from the technology itself to the regulations governing the technology. Infinite numbers of new and controversial tech-

359

nologies exist. A number of communities within the last decade have been involved in controversies attributed to incineration technology.

The incineration of solid and hazardous waste in the United States has been surrounded in controversy. For example, in 1989 Craig Volland, a civil engineer, attacked the U.S. Environmental Protection Agency's (EPA's) plan to regulate garbage incinerators (used to dispose of solid waste), saying that the use of this technology would not protect the public health and that in fact this technology had already been abandoned in Europe for safety reasons.[1]

In 1991 Robert Collins and Henry S. Cole, of Clean Water Action's Research and Technical Center in Washington, D.C., claimed that incineration of municipal solid waste released mercury into the air.[2] **Solid waste** is any waste material not discarded into surface waters (via water treatment systems) or the atmosphere, such as household garbage.[3] Concern about the incineration of municipal solid waste was coupled with a question about the kinds of solid waste being incinerated. In this case the question involved mercury. Mercury, commonly known as the metal used in thermometers, has also used in batteries, paints, dyes, electronic devices, fluorescent lights, plastics, and other products.[4] When the productive life of such products has ended, people throw them in the trash. Now considered waste, they end up in a solid waste disposal stream. At low levels of exposure, mercury has been shown to damage the human central nervous system, impair mental development, and damage kidneys.[5] There is a legitimate concern, then, about what happens when solid waste is incinerated, and many believe incineration spreads mercury into the air, resulting in its eventual absorption into the food chain.

The incineration of **hazardous waste** is argued to be especially problematic.[6] Hazardous waste encompasses the byproducts of hazardous substances used in industrial production processes, for example, including many chemicals that pose a threat to human health or the environment. According to one definition, hazardous waste is solid waste that is "toxic, ignitable, corrosive, or reactive, as determined by specified tests."[7(p.118)]

Although the information describing incineration technology varies dramatically depending upon the source, a review of some numbers should prove insightful. An EPA publication states that over 57 billion pounds of hazardous waste are burned each year in U.S. incinerators, cement kilns, and industrial boilers.[8] According to *Rachel's Hazardous Waste News*, "less than 5 percent of this waste is burned in officially-licensed 'hazardous waste incinerators'—more than 95 percent is blended with fuel oil and burned as fuel in kilns and boilers where it is not being 'disposed of' but is being 'recycled' in the view of EPA."[9]

In the example just discussed, the definitions of *disposed of* and *recycled* are extremely controversial and extremely important. By law, the way waste oil is classified determines how industry must treat it. If the law defines the blending of waste oil as "recycling," then no action—short of changing the law—can be taken to prevent the practice. If the oil must be "disposed of," the law also has provisions for this process. Manufacturing companies might want the burning of waste oil to fall within the definition of *recycling*, but the local community would support the more rigid standard of disposal. With such controversies being related to the use of a single term—either *recycling* or *disposal*—legal definitions can become the cornerstone for environmental conflict.

It is amidst precisely this kind of definitional classification and conflict that local citizen concerns about business practices and related regulatory directives for that business emerge. For every report suggesting that incineration is the **best demonstrated available technology**,[10,11] another report outlines the dangers associated with incinerating solid or hazardous waste. Government and industry officials may argue that the blending of otherwise hazardous chemicals with fuel oil is acceptable. But people might wonder why such a chemical mixture can be burned when mixed with fuel oil but is classified as hazardous if burned in an incinerator. Because most people do not have a detailed understanding of chemistry or physics, they expect adequate answers from either the industry or the government regulatory agency involved. If questions are not answered to the satisfaction of concerned citizens and fears about the project are not allayed, the citizens may prevent the project from moving forward.[12]

To varying degrees, "environmental officials at the state and federal level encouraged an incinerator building binge during the 1980s, with 142 plants now burning about 30 million tons a year, or 16 percent of the nation's trash."[13(p.A1)] The EPA declared incineration to be one of the most effective means of dealing with hazardous wastes, suggesting that "a well-operated incinerator can destroy hazardous waste safely."[14(p.1)] Various groups continue to disagree with the EPA's position.

Communities across the country have mobilized to prevent the placement of hazardous waste incinerators near their homes.[15–19] Waste management industries and local government officials in search of responsible waste management technologies are faced with a difficult dilemma: How do they get rid of the waste generated by local citizens and simultaneously take into account public concern about health and safety?

Chapter 3 describes the potential conflict between the legitimization and accumulation functions of the state. Should the role of the government be limited to market regulation (accumulation function)? Or should the government protect citizens from potential harm (legitimzaation function)? This case study involves detailed analyses of the perceptions of local citizens, government officials, industry officials, and others who joined in or were thrust into one community's conflict about siting a hazardous waste incinerator in the community.

FUELING THE INCINERATION ARGUMENT

The **Superfund** legislation (the Comprehensive Environmental Response, Compensation, and Liability Act, discussed in Chapter 5) was intended to provide the means by which abandoned and/or potentially dangerous areas could be cleaned up. In the early 1980s, the Office of Technology Assessment estimated that total long-term national cleanup costs would exceed $100 billion and the task would likely be drawn out over several decades,[20] but a 1991 University of Tennessee study estimated public and private cleanup costs as high as $750 billion.[21]

Adding fuel to the fire, in 1988 the EPA mandated *permanent* remedies for **Superfund remediation**. Permanent remedies were to replace the traditional method of disposal in the landfill.

> Incineration, which is technology utilizing an integrated system of components for waste preparation, feeding, combustion and emissions control, has been proven to achieve acceptable levels of destruction of the organic portion of hazardous waste. Therefore, incineration is being proposed and adopted for remediation of several Superfund sites.[22(p.12)]

Local citizen groups, however, began expressing increased concern about the EPA solution. NIMBY activism (grassroots activism focused on a perceived community threat) has played a significant role in cases of community opposition to incinerator placements, and the use of incinerator technology as a means of dealing with hazardous waste has been curtailed at present in the United States, in large part because of the intense public opposition (NIMBY, remember, stands for "not in my backyard").

HISTORY OF THE ENSCO CASE IN ARIZONA[23]

In the case discussed here, a small community in Arizona was identified as the site for a proposed hazardous waste incinerator. The state of Arizona was under federal mandate to develop an adequate plan to meet the state's hazardous waste disposal needs (called a **capacity assurance plan**). In 1978, the state legislature approved a plan to develop a hazardous waste management facility. A land sale soon followed (in 1981), and bids were sought for a contractor. In 1983, the Environmental Systems Company (ENSCO) was selected by the state legislature and the Department of Environmental Quality to build an incinerator in Mobile, Arizona.

ENSCO began construction of the hazardous waste incinerator in 1988, with full government support. Once construction was underway, however, local citizens began to express concerns. National environmental groups became involved (see Exhibit 1), and media coverage of the protest increased public awareness and public opposition. This case study focuses on attitudes and perceptions of local community groups involved in the controversy. After listing the concerns expressed on each side of the conflict, the chapter concludes with a description of the conflict's resolution.

COMMUNITY GROUPS INVOLVED IN THE CONFLICT

The proposed hazardous waste incinerator gave rise to an intense public conflict. Members from several groups involved in the conflict were contacted to get their perception of the controversy. For the most part, the

Exhibit 1 Chronology of Events

1978	The Arizona state legislature approves plans to develop a hazardous waste management facility.
1981	A land sale is approved for the site of the hazardous waste facility near Mobile. Bids for a contractor are sought.
1983	The state of Arizona contracts with Environmental Systems Company, Inc., in El Dorado, Arkansas, to build the state's hazardous waste management facility. The plans include incineration technology as the primary method of disposal.
1988	Construction of the facility begins.
1989–90	Greenpeace and other citizen activist groups stage protests in opposition to the facility.
1990	Protestors are arrested and shot with stun guns at a public hearing in Mobile (May 7).
1991	The new governor of Arizona, Fife Symington, announces plans to buy out the ENSCO contract.
1991	Legislation proposed by the governor is approved by the legislature (July 3).
1992	ENSCO is paid approximately $44 million by the state of Arizona.

groups were either clear supporters of ENSCO or clear opponents of ENSCO. Groups on either side, however, gave different justifications for their position. Thus six groups identified as having played a significant role in both the conflict and its resolution are considered in this analysis: state officials, citizen activists, ENSCO officials, Mobile residents, the Arizona business lobby, and the media.

State Officials

In 1980, the Arizona state legislature passed A.R.S. 36-2801 (now A.R.S. 49-901–905). This piece of legislation authorized site acquisition, facility control, contract management, authority to promulgate rules and regulate transportation, and establishment of a trust fund for a hazardous waste management facility. Under the direction of Governor Bruce Babbitt (now U.S. Secretary of the Interior), the Hazardous Waste Siting Act was enacted into law.

In addition to their initial role in seeking out the ENSCO contract, state officials were responsible for negotiating a resolution to the conflict over the proposed siting of the hazardous waste management facility. The active role that state officials played in contracting with ENSCO and then arranging a buyout necessitates their inclusion as a key group involved in this conflict.

Citizen Activists

The citizens involved in organizing demonstrations and creating a very visible public outcry against the facility constitute the second group whose perspective is necessary for understanding the conflict. While some of the individuals involved in the citizen opposition were from outside the immediate area (Greenpeace had several representatives from its San Francisco office in Arizona to aid the organizational efforts of local groups), most of the activists lived in the Phoenix metropolitan area.

The activists' efforts were directed toward letting public officials know their views, staging events for media coverage (to increase public awareness), and debating those involved directly with the operation of the incinerator. Many citizens attended local public hearings, monitored public meetings on the incineration plan, and confronted incinerator operators with questions about the facility.

ENSCO Officials

The operators of the ENSCO facility assigned several people to work with public officials, citizen groups, and other public information sources to distribute information about the proposed incinerator. The EPA was recommending incineration as a permanent hazardous waste management option, and ENSCO was licensed to operate one of the most technologically advanced incinerators built to date. ENSCO's technology was selected because incineration would provide the community with a feasible means to deal with the state's solid and hazardous waste problem. ENSCO officials were invited into the community to provide a service, only to be identified later by citizens, grassroots groups, and government officials as a threat to the community.

Mobile Residents

The residents of Mobile, Arizona, were generally poor and uneducated and in many cases were unemployed. ENSCO officials held town meetings in Mobile and told the citizens that ENSCO would bring industry and jobs into their community. At first, by all reports, the interaction between Mobile residents and ENSCO officials was positive. Later, however, this attitude changed, and the people of Mobile became concerned about the effect the hazardous waste incinerator would have on their health.

Citizen activist groups from the Phoenix area eventually united with the residents of Mobile in opposition to the facility. Because early reports from Mobile suggested support for the facility, the small group of residents were treated separately from the activists and identified as a fourth group needing to be interviewed about the facility placement.

Local Media

Media stories about the ENSCO facility constituted a primary source of public information about the process of developing the hazardous waste facility. In fact, media coverage of the ENSCO story was identified as being a critical influence on public attitudes about the facility. Several reporters covering this story were interviewed and offered their own insights.

Arizona Business/Industry

The final group considered consists of representatives from the business community. The hazardous waste facility was advertised as being "good for business," because it would provide a cheap method of waste disposal. Throughout the interviews, it was clear citizens believed that business and industry would put profits before human health and safety.

CITIZEN QUESTIONS ABOUT THE HAZARDOUS WASTE FACILITY

Opposition to the ENSCO facility can be summed up in six areas of specific concern identified by the citizen groups. They argued that supporters of the facility would not or could not adequately address these issues. First, there were concerns about the impact the incinerator would have on community health and safety. Second, there were specific questions about the incineration technology. Third, state officials and ENSCO representatives were heavily criticized because of the way they handled the ENSCO contract. Concern was expressed about the site selection process, the selection of ENSCO as the contractor, and the location of the site—allegedly in a floodplain and on a fault line. The fourth concern was the lack of emergency response plans and the location of emergency crews. A fifth set of concerns erupted late in the conflict, because of confusion about the amount of hazardous waste to be imported to the ENSCO facility from other states. Finally, the role of the Arizona Department of Environmental Quality (DEQ) in managing the contract was identified as a "conflict of interest." Each of the concerns will be addressed below. Keep in mind that the federal guidelines for attaining a permit for operating a hazardous waste facility are extremely explicit and require extensive legal, financial, and technical resources. The permit process is not one to be embarked upon lightly.

Community Health and Safety

Citizens who lived in the Mobile area were split about their assessment of incineration as a potential threat to their health. While some Mobile residents argued that ENSCO selected their community because they were poor and because it thought members of the community could be easily pushed around, others disagreed with this assessment. One resident of Mobile, for example, did not understand the fuss, saying, "People in other communities with incinerators look healthy enough." While they were not sure what the effects would be, several Mobile residents interviewed did not seem overconcerned about harmful effects.

The same divisions, interestingly enough, were found in the interviews conducted with ENSCO supporters. While some supporters agreed that incinerators might be linked with illness, they disagreed that incineration presented a long-term threat to health. Overall, they agreed that the relationship between illness and incineration technology was unknown or nonexistent.

Members of the state government expressed concern that the threat to the human population would be greater without the incinerator. One state official suggested the facility would provide a means to reduce and perhaps prevent illegal dumping. The state has no way of knowing how much dumping goes on and where the dumping happens. Therefore, this facility would provide a cost-effective alternative to those who could not afford to ship their wastes out of state for disposal.

For the most part, members of the business community claimed not to believe that hazardous waste incinerators are harmful to human health. One businessperson expressed frustration at the extreme position taken by local activists. He argued that hazardous waste incinerators are operated by every American who drives a car. "If you want to talk about risk, then let's discuss the type of mobile incinerator that *you* operate. You take toxic chemicals and put them in the combustion engine and it emits hazardous gases."

Representatives from the business group saw consumers, particularly the environmentalists, as hypocritical. It was argued, for example, that each activist drove "mini toxic incinerators" to ENSCO opposition meetings. The argument that incinerators are dangerous flies in the face of the actions taken by each activist driving a car. Community groups do not organize against the use of cars because they pose a threat to human health and safety; yet cars require the use of toxic chemicals and emit hazardous gases. Gasoline contains benzene, a known carcinogen, and car emissions are believed to damage the earth's protective ozone layer. The point is that people drive cars because they represent the best transportation technology available. Incineration is used because it is currently the best available technology for waste disposal. One perception offered from business representatives was that illness in society is much more likely to manifest from the massive use of cars, rather than the organized and well-considered placement of hazardous waste treatment facilities.

Questions about Incineration Technology

Although all groups recognized there could be a link between incineration and health problems, ENSCO officials overwhelmingly argued that incineration was the technology of choice for hazardous waste disposal. Citizens, however, were equally convinced of the opposite. One state official noted the lack of information about the risks of incineration of hazardous waste for people's health and the environment: "Incineration may produce less risk than other technologies. Risk is probably low, but I guess there is a lot of uncertainty." All groups cited the degree of uncertainty as a critical factor in the public's perception of potential harm associated with the incineration technology.

The ENSCO Facility

A great deal of concern resulted from information about the ENSCO site and the actions taken by government officials to secure the ENSCO contract. While some argued that incineration was an unacceptable technology anywhere, other citizens were disturbed because they argued the state of Arizona had acted improperly in securing the ENSCO contract. Problems were identified, among other things, in the site selection process and placement of the facility in a floodplain.

Because of the long developmental history of the hazardous waste management plans, few if any people from the groups involved in the conflict had much information about the site selection process. The best sources of information were state documents and local media coverage. The decision to place the hazardous waste facility was made by the state legislature. Most accounts confirm that ENSCO was not involved in this siting decision. The decision was the result of a heated political debate, and members from all groups of the conflict agree that the site selection was not based on environmental considerations but rather involved the exchange of political favors among state officials.

Considerable concern was expressed about the placement of this proposed facility in a floodplain and on a fault line. The relevant facts, however, were unclear. Citizen groups claimed that both Tucson (which is south of Mobile) and Phoenix (which is north of Mobile) were regularly affected by severe flooding. Arizona's trademark monsoon rains and the related flooding, they argued, created a risk that the hazardous waste facility would be damaged— a risk simply too significant for state officials to ignore. Business representatives and ENSCO officials countered by citing the regulatory restrictions for building a hazardous waste incinerator. They argued ENSCO would not have received the permits necessary to build if the design was unsafe.

A state official agreed that some of the 640 acres set aside for the project were in a floodplain, but said that this area was part of the "buffer zone" between the facility and the local community. An ENSCO official agreed, saying, "The site where we were actually going to [build] was dyked way in excess of the 100-year flood. It was on the site at the highest spot. It was dyked because the regulations required it to be. Whether there were citizen activists or not, we would deal with those issues because to get permits we had to deal with those issues." Another ENSCO official wanted the record to show that the state of Arizona selected the site. He argued that the state must like building things in floodplains because "the city of Phoenix flood control maps show the state capital and much of Phoenix to be within the boundaries of a 100-year floodplain."

Emergency Response Crews

Citizen groups argued both the state and ENSCO had failed to provide adequate emergency response crews. ENSCO countered this claim by pointing to the permitting process: In order to receive the necessary permits for operation, ENSCO had been required to deal with the issue of emergency response capabilities. The citizen groups, however, noted that the closest emergency response crew was over 35 miles from the facility. ENSCO officials asserted that those making these claims simply had not reviewed the permit applications submitted by ENSCO and were "uninformed."

Importation and Transportation Issues

ENSCO officials and some state officials claimed that the need to import hazardous waste from other states (in order to make the facility profitable) had been discussed from the very beginning. The citizen groups felt they had been misled and stated they wanted a facility that would be used to dispose of waste produced in Arizona and nowhere else. They were not interested in becoming a dumping ground for the United States, or even the Southwest.

The citizen groups believed that the state and ENSCO knowingly downplayed the need to import waste because they knew opposition to the facility would have grown substantially. ENSCO officials said they had always been upfront about the need to import waste from other states, and state officials agreed that the issue of importing waste had been discussed openly by all parties from the beginning. The citizen groups' response was to suggest that the issue of importation simply reinforced their contention that the state agency dealing with ENSCO withheld necessary information from the public. ENSCO officials suggested that the need for imported waste *increased* during the construction phase of the project because of increased costs. One state official thought that the problem was not so much that there would be imported waste—that had always been understood—but that no one could specify how much would need to be imported to make the facility profitable.

The issue became more explosive when people began to ask questions about the roadways identified as transportation routes leading to the hazardous waste incinerator. Communities through which these roads traversed were outraged. They wanted confirmation that potential spills were considered, and they wanted to know that the local community emergency response crews were prepared to handle such spills. ENSCO, business representatives, and state officials defended the transportation routes, claiming that in general only 5 percent of the hazardous materials on the road were waste products and the other 95 percent were chemicals and other hazardous materials being transported to or from factories for use in manufacturing. Their frustration was clear: Why did people worry about a spill of hazardous waste when virgin hazardous chemicals were being transported through their communities every day? No one has rallied to oppose the transportation of "useful" hazardous chemicals. It seemed, in other words, that the issue was useful hazards versus nonuseful hazards, not the hazardous classification itself. Supporters of ENSCO again claimed to be confronted with "illogical" or "poorly considered" citizen complaints.

Conflict of Interest

From the beginning, concern was expressed about alleged improprieties on the part of the Arizona Department of Environmental Quality to secure the ENSCO contract. Another critique of state action was directed at the location of the regulatory responsibility. Citizen activists were concerned that the same state agency responsible for securing the ENSCO contract was responsible for overseeing the project. Several groups involved identified such action as clear conflict of interest.

Because the state of Arizona would receive money from the proceeds of the facility, the more money ENSCO was able to secure, the more money the state would receive. A state official who remained active in the ENSCO controversy argued that it was not wise to have the Department of Environmental Quality acting as both the permit-granting agency and the agency responsible for oversight and management. A state official concerned about the conflict of interest charges said, "If you have two offices in the same agency working on the same project, you have the fox guarding the chicken coop. If one of those agencies would have directly benefited, there is an inherent conflict of interest."

CRITICAL JUNCTURES IN THE CONFLICT

While the perceptions of the groups involved in the hazardous waste facility controversy provide some indication of the complexities of the issues, three events had an especially great impact on the outcome of the conflict. First, Greenpeace established a mammoth presence in the community. Greenpeace representatives from the San Francisco regional office were present and fully participating in the ENSCO controversy. Members of all of the groups involved agreed on one thing: When Greenpeace became involved with the incineration controversy, the tide began to shift in favor of the groups opposing the facility.

Greenpeace is known for staging media events to draw attention to environmental controversies. While some state and ENSCO officials and business representatives referred to Greenpeace as "an outside agitator," Greenpeace representative Bradley Angel and other local citizens asserted that local groups had invited Greenpeace into the community because they were having little success in trying to combat the "ENSCO monster" alone.

The second event occurred at a public hearing in Mobile, on May 7, 1990. Officers from the Maricopa County Sheriff's Department used stun guns to stun several protestors, including Greenpeace members and local citizens, and then arrested them.

While all agree those stunned and arrested were treated badly by the sheriff's department, some believe what happened at that public meeting was a tactic by Greenpeace to gain media attention. They suggest that Greenpeace went to that meeting to disrupt the proceedings and create a media frenzy. Greenpeace members and other citizen activists claim that high-profile members of the citizen groups were targeted by the sheriff's department and attacked without provocation.[24]

In any case, the stun gun incident mobilized the community against the ENSCO incinerator project. Several citizen activists openly admitted to becoming interested in the incinerator issue after reading about the use of stun guns at this public hearing. ENSCO officials said that the stun gun incident was the defeat of ENSCO handed to Greenpeace on a silver platter. An ENSCO official said, "The stun gun thing was 100 percent the downfall of the project. That was the end of the project. [The use of stun guns on local

Calvin and Hobbes   by Bill Watterson

Source: CALVIN AND HOBBES © 1986 Watterson. Dist. by UNIVERSAL PRESS SYNDICATE. Reprinted with permission. All rights reserved.

citizens] was such a harsh and horrible thing; by inference whatever it was about had to be harsh and horrible too."

Finally, the media coverage of the ENSCO story increased dramatically after the protestors were stunned at the public hearing. One representative from the local media said, "Technical stories [about ENSCO] were not popular. . . . They didn't get good play. After the stun gun hearing, [those stories] got 1-A." A content analysis of three local newsprint sources confirms that assessment.

RESOLUTION OF THE ARIZONA CONTROVERSY

The resolution to the hazardous waste incinerator controversy in Arizona was finalized on July 3, 1991, with the passage of HB2121. The state of Arizona sold two buildings at the prison in Florence to raise the initial capital needed to pay ENSCO for the contract buyout. The initial price of the buyout was $44 million.[25] Arrangements to pay for these prison buildings involved a lease-to-purchase agreement between the state and a private company, payable over the next 20 years.

The reaction to the approval of the contract buyout was nearly complete elation. Citizens "won" because the facility would not be built. ENSCO "won" because it would be amply compensated for the work it had done. Arizona businesses were perhaps the biggest losers, since they would have to continue transporting waste outside of the state or find some other method of disposal. Finally, state officials had reason to be ambivalent: while it was nice to be able to support the people of Arizona in their opposition to the facility, the state still had to find a solution to its hazardous waste problem. Indeed, Arizona was no longer in compliance with federal environmental laws, which require states to have a plan for managing their hazardous waste.[26] The state officials found themselves back at the same place they were 11 years before, when the legislature had first voted to pursue plans to build a hazardous waste management facility.

CONCLUSION

This case study analyzes one community's struggle to develop a state hazardous waste disposal plan. Collective activism defeated an attempt by the state of Arizona to build a hazardous waste incinerator near the town of Mobile. For the most part, the involved state agencies and business groups were less than pleased with the outcome of the ENSCO buyout. Supporters of ENSCO were unclear about why the local citizens became so vocal in their opposition to the project in the last year of a planning process that took over 10 years.

This group identified Arizona officials as being "extremely forward think-ing" and thorough in their quest for a model hazardous waste facility. The people of Mobile had seemed enthusiastic about the benefits the facility would bring to their community, at least until Greenpeace became involved and the media coverage became intense and highly critical.

The final message from representatives of the ENSCO facility was directed to the citizen groups that opposed the ENSCO facility. They wanted to make it clear that in the end the groups had not hurt ENSCO at all. First, ENSCO "was more than amply compensated" for the work done in Arizona, and its Arkansas facility was still in operation. Indeed, because the citizens of Ari-zona had moved this country one step closer to never having another haz-ardous waste incinerator, its Arkansas facility would do even more business. More communities would have to ship more hazardous waste for further distances because the Arizona facility did not get built.

The long-term consequences of the conflict in Arizona are unknown. No one can say whether increases in midnight dumping have occurred or illegal handling of wastes has increased because waste producers cannot afford to dispose of hazardous waste legally. The people of Arizona saw derailment of the plan as a great victory, but the supporters of ENSCO saw those same people as the big losers. The taxpayers of Arizona will be paying off the debt incurred to buy out ENSCO's contract, and they were at least temporarily left without a plan to meet their hazardous waste management needs.

REVIEW QUESTIONS

1. Is this case study a good example of the NIMBY syndrome? Explain.
2. What is the primary difference between hazardous waste and hazard-ous materials?
3. Are hazardous waste and hazardous materials treated differently?
4. What does it mean to say that incineration was determined by the EPA to be the best demonstrated available technology?
5. After reading the information presented, do you think you would have offered support for the ENSCO facility or the local community mem-bers? Be prepared to justify your position.

DISCUSSION QUESTIONS

1. What is the relationship between legislative efforts to ban land dis-posal and attempts to place incinerators?
2. If you were a member of the Arizona State Department of Environmen-tal Quality, would you be happy with the resolution to the conflict?

3. If you were a citizen concerned about the health and safety of the local community, would you be pleased with the actions taken by the state in this case?

REFERENCES

1. C. Volland, "A Critical Review of EPA's Plan To Establish a Dry Scrubber Technology Standard for Municipal Solid Waste Incinerators," 1989. Volland is President of Spectrum Technologies. For a copy of the paper, send $3 to: 616 E. 63rd St., Kansas City, MO 64110; (816) 523-2525.

2. R. Collins and H.S. Cole, *Mercury Rising: Government Ignores the Threat of Mercury from Municipal Waste Incinerators* (Washington, DC: Clean Water Action Research and Technical Center, 1990).

3. See H. Stevenson and B. Wyman, *The Facts on File Dictionary of Environmental Science* (New York: Facts on File, 1991), 230.

4. Stevenson and Wyman, *Facts on File Dictionary of Environmental Science*.

5. P. Montague, "Scientists Suspect Poisoning of Fish by Mercury Emissions from Incinerators," *Rachel's Hazardous Waste News*, 12 September 1990 (Internet: erf@igc.apc.org).

6. A hazardous waste is defined in the RCRA as "a solid waste or combination of solid wastes which because of its quantity, concentration, physical, chemical, or infectious attributes may a) cause or significantly contribute to an increase in mortality or an increase in serious irreversible or incapacitating reversible illness; or b) pose a substantial present or potential hazard to human health or the environment when improperly treated, stored, transported or disposed of, or otherwise managed." The criteria for identifying a hazardous substance under RCRA include measures of toxicity, persistence, and degradability in nature; potential for accumulation in tissue; and other related factors, such as flammability and corrosiveness [U.S. Office of Technology Assessment (Washington, DC: U.S. Government Printing Office, 1983), 271].

7. Stevenson and Wyman, *Facts on File Dictionary of Environmental Science*, 118.

8. U.S. Environmental Protection Agency, *Permitting Hazardous Waste Incinerators*, EPA/530-sw-88-024 (Washington, DC: U.S. Environmental Protection Agency, Office of Solid Waste, April 1988), 1.

9. P. Montague, "Emissions into the Local Environment from a Hazardous Waste Incinerator," *Rachel's Hazardous Waste News*, 5 June 1991 (Internet: erf@igc.apc.org).

10. *The best demonstrated available technology* is a term used to describe the treatment standard for hazardous waste that avoids land disposal. As for EPA's use of incineration, see W. Reilly, "Aiming before We Shoot: The Quiet Revolution in Environmental Policy," speech delivered at the National Press Club, 26 September 1990 (available through the EPA's Public Affairs Office, as well as reference 11).

11. R. Loehr et al., "Reducing Risk: Setting Priorities and Strategies for Environmental Protection," pub. no. SAB-EC-90-021 (Washington, DC: U.S. Science Advisory Board and U.S. Environmental Protection Agency, 1990).

12. C. Piller, *The Fail-safe Society: Community Defiance and the End of American Technological Optimism* (New York: Basic Books, 1991).

13. J. Baily, "Up in Smoke: Fading Garbage Crisis Leaves Incinerators Competing for Trash," *Wall Street Journal*, 11 August 1993, A1, A2.
14. U.S. Environmental Protection Agency, *Permitting Hazardous Waste Incinerators*, 1.
15. Piller, *The Fail-safe Society*.
16. P. Montague, "The Governed Begin To Withhold Their Consent and 34 Are Arrested in Ohio," *Rachel's Hazardous Waste News*, 16 October 1991 (Internet: erf:@igx.apc.org).
17. S. Yozwiak, "$44 Million ENSCO Deal: State Plan Would Buy out Waste Plant," *The Arizona Republic*, 4 May 1991, A1, A2.
18. B. Ridlehoover and D. Johnson, "El Dorado Residents' Opinions Change, Fade with Time," *Arkansas Democrat*, 16 December 1990, K2.
19. B. Ridlehoover, "Hindsight Would Mean 'No' for ENSCO: Former EPA Official Cites Environmental History," *Arkansas Democrat*, 16 December 1990, K1, K4.
20. D. Mazmanian and D. Morell, *Beyond Superfailure: America's Toxics Policy for the 1990s* (Boulder, CO: Westview Press, 1992), 13.
21. R. Abramson, "U.S. Waste Cleanup Bill Put at $750 Billion," *Los Angeles Times*, 10 December 1991, 1, A 29.
22. In 1988, EPA published documentation emphasizing the EPA mandate for permanent remedies in Superfund site remediation or cleanups. See Environmental Protection Agency, *Experience in Incineration Applicable to Superfund Site Remediation* (Cincinnati, OH: Center for Environmental Research Information, December 1988).
23. This case study of the ENSCO case is based on M. Clifford, "Environmental Systems Company, Inc. in Arizona: Implications for the Social Constructionist Theory and Methodology" (Ph.D. diss., Arizona State University, 1993).
24. The citizens who were stunned sued the Maricopa County Sheriff's Department.
25. The $44 million buyout price has been identified as misleading, because estimated costs to the state over the 20 years are projected to be between $88 and $121 million.
26. The Capacity Assurance Plan (CAP), was a provision added to the Superfund legislation. Under this plan, states were to prove to the EPA that they had sufficient waste management capacity to handle all the hazardous waste that would be created within the state in the next 20 years. When ENSCO's contract was bought out, the state had no CAP.

Hazardous Waste Regulation: Legacies of the Past and Projections for the Future

Harold Barnett

TERMS	common law	petrochemicals
	deregulation movement	proactive liability
	enforcement first	retroactive liability
	strategy	Sewergate
	fund first strategy	transaction costs

One of the most watched environmental protection efforts is the Superfund program. Brought into existence by the Comprehensive Environmental Response, Compensation, and Liability Act (CERCLA), the legislation was intended to fund the cleanup of areas contaminated with hazardous waste. This case study critiques the Superfund as a solution to the hazardous waste disposal problem in the United States. It describes the implementation of the Superfund legislation, explains how it is determined who pays, and presents a profile of common violators. It then considers a set of critical questions, including "How clean is clean?" and "Why are communities opposed to hazardous waste facilities?" At the close of the case study, some insights are offered as to the future of Superfund.

HAZARDOUS WASTE REGULATION IN THE UNITED STATES: A BRIEF HISTORY

The ancient Greeks knew that lead was toxic. Early stories in literature reflect exposures to toxic substances. Lewis Carroll's Mad Hatter, for example, suffered from the effects of mercury poisoning, common among those in the hatters trade. Application of hazardous materials, however, was minimal until the Industrial Revolution of the late eighteenth century. The increase in production and economic growth resulting from the use of natural resources to drive mechanized equipment in industry was unprecedented. While the harnessing of these natural resources—water (hydroelectric dams) and coal (steam engines), for example—brought about huge industrial expansion, it also brought about an unprecedented increase in use of and human exposure to hazardous materials.

Sulfur dioxide, eventually linked to acid rain, spewed from factory smokestacks early in the Industrial Revolution. Toxic metals used to dye cloth flowed freely from the waste streams of textile mills. The post-1930s **chemical revolution** allowed another quantum increase in production of goods and production of hazardous waste. Building on a petroleum foundation, modern industry replaced natural materials such as cotton, wool, rubber, metals, soap, manure, and natural solvents with products derived from the **petrochemical** industry. Today organic chemicals are in the waste streams of most manufacturing industries. All primary petrochemicals, as well as many petrochemical derivatives, are highly toxic.[1]

Prior to the 1970s, control of pollution was often a private affair and relied on **common law** remedies.[2] In the late 1960s, as a result of a burgeoning environmental movement, highly publicized examples of damage to the environment, and presumed threats to public health, the problem of industrial hazardous waste increasingly became a focus of public concern. As discussed in Part I of this text, several pieces of environmental protection legislation were passed after 1970. And with the passage of RCRA, Congress believed that the last remaining loophole in environmental law, the unregulated land disposal of discarded material and hazardous waste, was now closed. Then Congress and the American public heard about Love Canal.

Superfund and Environmental Crime

Two important points should be noted before we examine the Superfund hazardous waste site cleanup program. First, Superfund involves issues of environmental crime as they are broadly defined. As Chapter 1 showed, there is a need for a "legal definition" of environmental crime, but exclusive use of such a definition means that only those behaviors identified in criminal statutes will be classified as environmental crime. As a result, hazardous waste crime would generally be limited to failure to report spills or other uncontrolled releases into the environment. Midnight dumping, for example, is considered a crime because it is illegal to dispose of hazardous waste in this fashion. The vast majority of toxic waste found at Superfund sites, however, was deposited in a manner *that was legal at the time of disposal*. Most hazardous waste disposal and the consequences of that disposal

at a Superfund site would not constitute a crime using a narrow legal definition.

Following suggestions by E.A. Ross and Edwin Sutherland, many contemporary theorists and writers studying corporate and white-collar violations
have adopted a broader definition of criminality. Crime is defined by them
to include not only behaviors prohibited by the law but also "morally offensive" or "inappropriate" actions that should be illegal.[3,4] Environmental
crime would thus include violations addressed through civil and administrative proceedings.

Because many Superfund sites are the product of actions that were legal at
the time, these actions can be considered criminal only if the broader
(philosophical) definition is used. Superfund assesses threats to public
health and the environment, leaves disposers retroactively liable for their
actions, and gives the U.S. Environmental Protection Agency (EPA) the legal
power to demand that the disposers help pay for cleanup. Little attention is
paid to the intent of the actor or the type of action: if an individual placed
chemicals now known to be hazardous in a place now needing remediation,
he or she can be held responsible for the cost of cleanup.

Superfund and Political Economy

While it is important to understand the difference between the legal definition of an environmental crime and the broader definition, one other
point is critical for introducing the Superfund program: the history of
Superfund can be understood only if the program is viewed in its proper
politicoeconomic context. As has been discussed throughout this text, conflict over environmental and economic values has been played out in the
political arena. The political and economic strength of those who advocate
environmental cleanup programs and the strength of those who are expected to pay for that cleanup often determine the legislative outcome.
Superfund legislation determines who is responsible for hazardous waste
site conditions and who will pay for site cleanup. The intensity of the debate
over these issues is ultimately driven by estimates that cleanup could cost as
much as $100 billion and that over 25 million people are at risk from expo-
sure.

All environmental issues create, to some degree, economic and political
conflict. Superfund is uniquely divisive, however, because of the high costs
involved and because it has bipartisan legislative support. The passage of
CERCLA in 1980 put it at the close of "the environmental decade."
Throughout the 1970s the environmental movement had gathered political
strength fed by heightened awareness of environmental degradation and

mounting popular support for government control over industrial pollution. Its collective force helps explain the outpouring of legislation during that decade.

The history of Superfund would have been different if another political economic movement had not emerged in the mid-1970s. The **deregulation movement** was fed by the perception that government regulation was a major cause of the economic malaise of the 1970s—a combination of high unemployment and spiraling inflation. This perception resulted in legislation to deregulate banking, airlines, telecommunications, and railroads. By the end of the 1970s, the foes of regulation were attacking environmental and worker safety legislation as posing a substantial threat not only to corporate profitability but also to the nation's economic health.

Passage of CERCLA in 1980 placed its implementation in the hands of the avowedly antiregulation Reagan administration. The Superfund was passed by a lame duck Congress on the eve of Ronald Reagan's presidency. It created a $1.6 billion fund financed by taxes on the petroleum and chemical industries (collectively, the petrochemical industry). The fund was to be used when those responsible for Superfund site conditions could not be identified. When responsible parties could be identified, the EPA was granted strong enforcement powers to induce them to pay for cleanup.

Superfund was reauthorized by the **Superfund Amendments and Reauthorization Act** of 1986 (SARA). SARA increased the cleanup fund to $8.6 billion and clarified the EPA's enforcement powers. In response to inaction on the part of the Reagan administration and distrust of its commitment to environmental progress, Congress imposed specific cleanup schedules on the EPA.

SARA taxing powers were reauthorized in 1990, to expire in 1995. The Clinton administration proposed changes to Superfund in 1994, after more than a decade of controversy over cleanup progress and EPA enforcement actions. At the time of this writing, summer 1997, revisions are still being debated by a Republican-dominated Congress.

WHO PAYS FOR THE SUPERFUND?

Images of Love Canal horrified the nation. In 1978, Michael Brown published a series of articles in the *Niagara Gazette* and wrote a book entitled *Laying Waste*. Brown described John Love's failed vision of an industrial city served by a navigable power canal and the eventual use of the abandoned canal by Hooker Chemical Company to dispose of "a veritable witch's brew of chemistry, compounds of truly remarkable toxicity. There were solvents that attacked the heart and liver, and residues from pesticides so dangerous that their commercial sale had subsequently been restricted or banned outright by the government."[5(p.9)]

By the 1960s, a school, playground, and homes sat atop the closed dump site. Brown's reporting of the chemicals dumped by Hooker (e.g., mercury, benzene, chlorinated compounds, dioxins), the contamination of aquifers and drinking water supplies, and the likely injuries from exposure provided a picture of environmental disaster. His images of life in Love Canal made an abstract threat palpable: children coming home from the playground with hard pimples on their bodies, women giving birth to deformed and mentally retarded children, a strange black sludge seeping through basement walls, chemical water flooding yards, and families torn between abandoning homes and protecting their children's health.[6]

Environmentalists and many congressional leaders saw Love Canal as the tip of the iceberg. Data provided by the EPA suggested that the nation was dotted with similar toxic time bombs.[7] The EPA and the **Council on Environmental Quality** provided evidence of contamination of ground water by toxic chemicals—a water source once thought pure—and estimates of health risks to people who depended on ground water for their drinking water supply. For the majority in Congress who accepted this evidence, the first condition was met for defining past hazardous waste disposal in uncontrolled sites as environmental crime: Uncontrolled hazardous waste sites caused harm to public health.

Government attempts to halt actions causing harm to the public traditionally rely on legal remedies. Regulatory agencies identify corporate behavior that threatens public welfare and then use legal powers to persuade the violating corporations to change their behavior and/or to rectify the damage. This course of action was considered inappropriate for hazardous waste sites for at least two reasons. First, many sites were abandoned, and it was difficult, if not impossible, to identify the party or parties responsible for site conditions. Second, at many sites where responsible parties could be identified, protection of public health and the environment required a rapid response. It was not possible to wait several years for the EPA to induce a private party to undertake cleanup. The solution was to establish a fund to finance government-initiated cleanup.

The debate over financing the Superfund helped to set the second condition for classifying hazardous waste disposal as environmental crime: the imposition of sanctions. The EPA had examined abandoned hazardous waste sites and concluded that their toxic contents could be traced back to a limited number of chemical feedstocks. Chemical feedstocks are the basic building blocks for all inorganic and organic chemical products. These feedstocks could in turn be linked to a set of powerful industries—the chemical, petroleum-refining, primary metals, fabricated metals, electric and electronic, and transportation equipment industries. Environmentalists and congressional supporters argued that the Superfund should be financed by a tax on these chemical feedstocks. Since the industries that produced and utilized the feedstocks had profited from pollution, it was appropriate to make the polluters pay.

In opposition, the petrochemical and manufacturing industries contended that the country as a whole had benefited from the fruits of the chemical revolution. Since all of us had experienced a vast improvement in our standard of living, it was only fair that we all share in the cost of cleanup. Industry officials argued that the Superfund should be financed by general government revenues. They argued these waste processes should be handled like society handles monies for other common services, such as local, state, and federal highways. In other words, since everyone benefits from the products, everyone should pay for the costs of cleanup.

The environmentalists' argument prevailed. With the increasing federal deficits of the 1970s, Congress needed to find a new source of revenues to finance cleanup. CERCLA mandated a $1.6 billion cleanup fund, to be raised over five years, financed primarily through a feedstock tax on the petrochemical industry. It was expected that the feedstock tax would be passed forward through the chain of commerce to the users of chemical products. Many also expected, but few emphasized, that a portion of the tax would be passed backward to the Internal Revenue Service as a corporate profit tax deduction. While the philosophy of "make the polluters pay" seemed to prevail, the reality was that consumers and taxpayers would share in the cost of cleanup.

While clearly a tax is not a legal sanction, imposing a cleanup tax on industrial polluters was a first step in establishing the "make the polluters pay" philosophy that is the foundation of the Superfund enforcement program. Had the argument of the industrialists prevailed, hazardous waste cleanup might have become a public works project like highway construction. There might have been no enforcement program and no sanctioning of disposers. Superfund would not meet the definition of environmental crime, and this chapter would not have been included in a text for students studying environmental crime.

By the mid-1980s, it was clear that $1.6 billion would not be enough to deal with the more than 500 Superfund sites that had been added to the federal cleanup program. Further, it had become apparent that the Reagan administration could not be trusted to spend money on cleanup. The **Sewergate** scandal of 1981–1982 highlighted the illegal means pursued by some high-ranking EPA administrators to use Superfund for political ends and to short-circuit enforcement.[8]

The underlying fact was that the EPA had established a cleanup strategy intended to minimize the use of Superfund resources. The Reagan administration thought that it could conserve the fund and avoid a "Son of Superfund." Part of the strategy to limit expenditures on cleanup was to choose temporary remedies. At many sites, this required the EPA to return to the site and perform another stopgap cleanup at a later time.

Congress attempted to rectify these problems by enacting SARA. SARA mandated cleanup schedules that the EPA would have to meet. SARA also acknowledged congressional dissatisfaction with the temporary cleanups executed or planned at many sites and required that more permanent cleanups be chosen when feasible (as discussed in more detail below). This would raise the average cost of cleanup from around $8 million to perhaps $25 to $30 million and would require an increase of the Superfund. The chemical industry argued that a higher tax would damage its competitiveness in international markets and that the tax base should be expanded. Congress, facing an even larger federal deficit than in 1980, chose to raise $8.6 billion for cleanup by increasing the tax on petroleum refiners and establishing a corporate environmental tax. Superfund taxing authority was renewed in 1990. President Clinton's 1994 proposal to increase the size of the cleanup fund died in Congress. As of late 1997, Superfund was refunded at its 1986 level, but no further action has been taken.

WHO PAYS FOR CLEANUP?

Enforcement is the bottom line of the "make the polluters pay" philosophy. Superfund enforcement combines congressional mandate, agency strategy, and court interpretation to determine who is responsible for cleanup. Defining liability for cleanup was the major enforcement issue for the initial Superfund legislation. Should liability be retroactive or proactive? Should negligence be taken into account? Should a polluter be liable for more than a proportionate share of cleanup costs?

Strong advocates of Superfund—President Carter, House and Senate environmental committee members, state representatives, and environmentalists—supported retroactive liability as a minimum condition for Superfund enforcement. Since disposal at Superfund sites had already occurred, those who were responsible for disposal would not have to pay for cleanup if liability were proactive (**proactive liability** would apply only to disposal that occurred *after* the passage of Superfund). The petrochemical and manufacturing industries, voicing a position they would take throughout the debate over liability, argued that it was unfair, if not unconstitutional, to hold industry liable for actions that were legal at the time they were done.

Industrial testimony did not emphasize that under the permissive environmental regulations that prevailed up until the 1970s, almost all forms of hazardous waste disposal were legal. Supporters of **retroactive liability** argued that liability must be strict, joint, and several. For example, if ACME Farm and Feed Corporation sent hazardous waste to a landfill believing the waste was safe, any subsequent problems could not be attributed to negligence. Under a **strict liability** standard, the corporation would be responsible for cleanup.

Joint and several liability means a corporation's responsibility for cleanup costs can exceed its proportionate share of the hazardous waste involved when responsibility is not divisible. For example, if ACE Chemical Corporation was responsible for 30 percent of the hazardous waste at a dump site, Triple A Roofing Company was responsible for 20 percent, and no other responsible corporations could be identified, a joint and several liability standard could result in ACE and Triple A being liable for 100 percent of cleanup costs. It must be stressed that the business owners of both companies may have complied with existing environmental regulations at the time they dumped their waste. Under a strict, joint, and several standard, however, the only information relevant for prosecution is whether they were in fact responsible for the waste being dumped in the area now determined to be a Superfund site.

Strict, joint, and several liability is necessary for retroactive liability and provides the teeth of the Superfund program. The typical abandoned hazardous waste site has poor records or no records from which to identify the hundreds of companies that dumped their waste over many decades. In most cases, it is impossible to determine whether the disposer had exercised due care or was negligent. Further, it is extremely difficult, if not impossible, to prove that a specific volume of waste had been disposed of by a specific corporation and to relate that volume of waste to the cost of site cleanup. If liability is not strict, joint, and several, the EPA would face a near insurmountable enforcement task. Since it would be able to prove neither negligence nor responsibility for specific hazardous wastes, it would seldom be able to establish responsibility, which means that many polluters, because their role in the disposal of toxic waste could not be proved, would avoid contributing to cleanup costs. The solution to this problem was to use a strict standard of enforcement that requires any polluter identified as having disposed of waste in a given Superfund site to pay for the site's cleanup.

The petrochemical and manufacturing industries were adamant in their opposition to the liability standards. They argued the standards were dangerous and precedent setting, resulted in a denial of due process, and violated the principle of constitutional rules against ex post facto laws. Industrial interests also feared that these liability standards could be applied to personal injury cases involving Superfund sites. To allay these fears, the law allowed a responsible party held liable for more than its proportionate share of cleanup costs to sue other responsible parties so that parties could be attached to the specific cleanup action and would have to contribute to the cleanup.

In the rush to pass cleanup legislation before the inauguration of President Reagan, advocates of Superfund agreed to delete provisions for strict, joint, and several liability. Federal courts, after much litigation, eventually confirmed that strong liability provisions were consistent with congressional intent. Congress finally codified these standards in the Superfund Amendments and Reauthorization Act of 1986.

The EPA was mandated to carry out Superfund's enforcement provisions. An active EPA stance was essential to meet the expectation that 40 to 60 percent of site cleanups would be performed by **potentially responsible parties**. The EPA could issue administrative orders or pursue civil action to induce private party cleanup. It could hold recalcitrant parties liable for an amount equal to three times the cleanup expense resulting from their refusal to act. The EPA could also sue private parties to recover cleanup costs financed from the Superfund.

Over the 15-year history of Superfund, the EPA adopted three distinct strategies to carry out its enforcement responsibilities. First, nonconfrontational voluntary compliance was the strategy chosen by EPA Administrator **Anne Gorsuch Burford**. Administrator Burford, a Reagan nominee and an advocate of deregulation, believed that incentives were more effective than threats in inducing corporate compliance. During her two-year reign, the EPA provided responsible parties every opportunity to negotiate settlements and seldom used expenditures from the cleanup fund to leverage its position. If the EPA did not move forward on cleanup, it could not threaten responsible parties with treble damage suits. Responsible parties had scant incentive to settle with the EPA if the agency was not going to punish them for their recalcitrance. By late 1982, the EPA's slow progress on implementation, combined with public revelations of sweetheart settlements and cleanup expenditures tied to political goals, forced the resignation of Administrator Burford and other top EPA officials. **Rita Lavelle**, the head of the Superfund program, went to jail for perjury before Congress.[9]

To reestablish the legitimacy of the EPA, William Ruckelshaus, the EPA's first administrator, was again chosen to head the agency. Ruckelshaus and his successor Lee Thomas pursued a **fund first strategy**. Under fund first, the EPA used fund-financed cleanup as a bargaining tool to induce defendant corporations to settle. The idea was that corporations would expect that a cleanup conducted by EPA would be especially expensive and would be willing to settle to avoid the added expense. The agency was far more aggressive than under Administrator Burford and achieved a substantial increase in both settlements for private party cleanup and cost recoveries for fund-financed cleanup.

The EPA's new aggressiveness created animosity in the business community. Industrial targets of EPA enforcement protested the agency's take-it-or-leave-it approach. The agency would typically target a small number of major responsible parties so as to keep negotiations manageable. These targets would in turn bring **contribution suits**[10] against remaining responsible parties, which sometimes numbered in the hundreds. The issues to be resolved by the courts grew exponentially. Progress on settlement and cleanup suffered substantial delay. Corporations would also sue their insurers to have cleanup costs covered under policies that the insurers claimed did not apply. By 1985, one study found that the transaction costs associated with litigation amounted to 55 percent of cleanup costs.[11]

The **transaction costs** are the legal and related expenses involved in settling a dispute, not including monies spent on the cleanup itself. The high transaction costs of EPA's enforcement program were a major issue during the debate over SARA. Congress could not both provide relief to industry and have enforcement's contribution to cleanup grow in proportion to a Superfund that had expanded more than fivefold, from $1.6 to $8.6 billion. Congress chose to strengthen enforcement. Among other changes desired by the EPA, SARA disallowed the merging of contribution suits into the agency's legal action. Industry could draw some solace from provisions that encouraged the EPA to place greater reliance on negotiations and to more fully utilize incentives for settlement.

After the passage of SARA, the EPA had to meet the new cleanup schedules imposed by a distrusting Congress. It also had to conserve the Superfund so that a growing number of sites could receive **permanent remedies** when feasible. Accordingly, the EPA placed renewed emphasis on enforcement. The agency continued to secure settlements but was soon criticized for their terms. There was a broad consensus that the EPA was achieving these settlements by negotiating less effective, less costly remedies with responsible parties. The EPA protested that it made no sense to choose a cleanup remedy that a responsible party would not agree to undertake. Further, resource limitations restricted the EPA's ability to threaten recalcitrant parties with legal action and to then carry through with these threats. By 1988, congressional oversight committees believed that the enforcement program was not meeting expectations and feared that a continuation of the current strategy would lead to a premature depletion of the fund.

The fund first strategy was terminated soon after the election of President George Bush. The new EPA administrator, William Reilly, immediately performed a management review of Superfund. The review concluded that an aggressive **enforcement first strategy** could both conserve the fund and encourage corporate contributions to cleanup. Congress acknowledged the new strategy by increasing EPA staff to support a greater enforcement effort. EPA regional offices were instructed to issue unilateral orders (with treble damage penalties for noncompliance) to compel corporate settlement and to initiate cost recovery and treble damage actions against those who would not settle. Evidence available for the early 1990s demonstrates that this tougher stance compelled responsible parties to increasingly enter into settlements for expensive phases of the cleanup process.

As settlements have increased, so too has dissatisfaction on the part of enforcement targets. Current major targets claim that EPA has failed to negotiate settlements or to offer inducements for compliance, contrary to the intent of SARA. Corporations held liable for more than their proportionate share see their only viable option as compliance with EPA orders, followed by legal action against third parties. Since a substantial percentage of Superfund sites are municipal landfills, municipalities have become prime targets in these contribution suits, as have a diverse set of minor disposers who historically used landfills.

Financial institutions that foreclosed on property in the wake of the real estate market collapse of the late 1980s are also fearful of EPA enforcement. Providers of environmental damage insurance are among the most vocal critics of Superfund liability standards. Insurance companies have indemnified polluting corporations for cleanup costs and legal expenses and have suffered legal expense in disputing their obligation to make these payments. A recent Rand Corporation study found that the nation's insurers spent $480 million in 1989 for indemnification and transaction costs, with some 88 percent of this expenditure representing transaction costs.[12]

Superfund liability standards have never been sacrosanct. Industry opposed them from the outset on grounds of fairness. Since the mid-1980s, these standards have been increasingly criticized for their high transaction costs and for being little more than an extremely costly funding mechanism.[13]

Driven by a "make the polluters pay" philosophy, EPA attempts to sanction major responsible corporate parties, who in turn attempt to pass a high percentage of their cleanup costs onto third parties and insurers. The trans-action costs generated by this redistribution absorb substantial amounts of money that might otherwise be directed toward the financing of cleanup. Some possible solutions to this problem are discussed below.

WHO ARE THE VIOLATORS?

The list of corporations targeted by the EPA as bearing responsibility for hazardous waste site conditions reads like a sample of *Fortune* 500 firms. The corporations that share responsibility for the largest number of sites include major petrochemical producers (DuPont, Monsanto, Union Carbide, Rohm and Haas, Mobil Chemical, Allied, Ashland Chemical, and Exxon) as well as leaders in manufacturing industries (General Electric, Westinghouse, Ford, and General Motors).[14] These corporations have the legal resources to effec-tively challenge the EPA in court and the political power to receive a sympa-thetic hearing from members of Congress.

Since a large percentage of Superfund sites are municipal landfills, the hundreds of disposers at a typical site include municipalities, universities, hospitals, and a diverse group of small contributors ranging from pizza par-lors to the Boy Scouts. The EPA has argued that almost all of the waste com-ing from municipalities is solid, as opposed to hazardous, waste and has attempted to limit the share of cleanup costs these municipalities must bear. It has also issued regulations to allow small contributors to pay up front for a share of cleanup costs and thereby minimize transaction costs.

Currently about 1,300 nonfederal Superfund sites exist across the coun-try.[15] In addition, over 140 priority hazardous waste sites are owned by the federal government, in particular the Department of Defense and the De-partment of Energy (DOE). These latter sites were often operated by a private company under contract to a federal agency. They are listed along with other Superfund sites but are not eligible for Superfund-financed cleanup. The EPA does have the authority to negotiate cleanup with other federal agencies. At the Rocky Mountain Arsenal site near Denver (commonly known as Rocky Flats), soil and ground water were polluted by the army and its lessee (see Case Study 3). A projected $2 billion cleanup is to be shared by that company and the army. DOE operations at its nuclear weapons plants involved practices that were prohibited private concerns. At DOE sites, in-cluding the notorious Hanford Reserve in Washington State, soil and ground water were contaminated through the disposal of toxic solvents, asbestos, insecticides, herbicides, dioxins, and heavy metals into unlined pits, lagoons, and ditches.

WHY IS THERE NO VICTIM COMPENSATION?

Victims of exposure to toxic substances released from hazardous waste sites can seek compensation under state law. Academic research and studies conducted by the Library of Congress and a Superfund task force all conclude that the likelihood of compensation is extremely low. The victim faces at least three substantial barriers. The first barrier to compensation for victims is the statute of limitations. Some states require the victim to act well before he or she is likely to be aware of an injury. Second, the victim must prove by a preponderance of evidence that the defendant's actions caused the victim's injury. This is usually a very demanding burden of proof. State courts often exclude scientific evidence as a basis for presuming such a link exists and for allowing a case to go forward. Finally, the cost of satisfying legal burdens of proof can be extraordinarily high. The cost can be shared through a class-action suit, but a court might not allow a class-action suit when the injuries associated with a single hazardous waste site are diverse in type and timing.

Remedies to rectify this situation and to ease the burden on victims were proposed for inclusion in the Superfund acts of 1980 and 1986. Advocates of change proposed that victims be allowed a hearing in federal court (a **federal cause of action**). In contrast to state court procedures, medical and scientific studies would be admissible to establish the likelihood that an injury resulted from the release of a toxic substance. If this likelihood is established, a presumption of causation would be created in the plaintiff's favor and a hearing could commence. The plaintiff would still need to satisfy the traditional causal burden of proof to receive compensation. Legislation to allow a **compensation fund** to compensate victims also was proposed. When unable to obtain satisfaction in a state court, the victim could pursue a claim against the compensation fund. If honored, the victim would receive payment from the fund, which would in turn seek cost recovery from responsible parties.

Industrial and insurance industry representatives were vehemently opposed to these changes. They argued that with a presumption of causation, the 97 to 98 percent of cancers they believed were due to sources other than exposure to toxic substances would now be attributed to hazardous waste sites.[16] They claimed that the burden of proof would shift from the plaintiff to the defendant and that the courts would be flooded with waves of spurious litigation. In the SARA debate, the Reagan administration supported industrial claims that a federal compensation fund would be open ended and potentially enormous and that the resulting litigation would further cripple an already overburdened federal court system. Opposition was ultimately driven by fear of the unknown—and fear of the presumably substantial cost of victim compensation awards. Personal injury claims of $2 billion had been filed by Love Canal residents. Congressional conservatives raised the prospect of economic disaster if corporations were required to satisfy such claims for even a handful of Superfund sites.

The political strength of the opposition and the fear of economic chaos killed any meaningful victim compensation reform. SARA did set a uniform state limitations period starting when the victim knew that damage was caused by hazardous waste exposure. A federal agency was directed to prepare toxicological profiles of the 275 hazardous substances most commonly found at Superfund sites and to perform health assessments at each Superfund site in order to help the EPA make appropriate cleanup decisions.

STATE EFFORTS TO ADDRESS CLEANUP ISSUES

Only a fraction of uncontrolled hazardous waste sites qualify for the federal Superfund program. Those that do not qualify but still pose serious risks must be dealt with through state programs. As of 1988, the states had identified nearly 29,000 sites requiring cleanup.

The states vary greatly in their capacity and willingness to promote cleanup through public funding or enforcement programs. Some states with major hazardous waste–generating industries and their toxic legacies—such as New Jersey, California, and Massachusetts—have active programs. The size of a state's budget is the major barrier to its cleanup efforts. Opponents of Superfund often have attempted to increase state financial obligations as a strategy for slowing down the cleanup process.

Superfund imposes obligations on states for sites included in the federal program. The states must pay 10–50 percent of the remedial cleanup costs, depending on whether the site is privately or publicly owned. No cost is shared for limited, short-term removal actions. But the Superfund program can also afford benefits to states with sites designated on the federal Superfund **National Priorities List**. The more demanding cleanup standards and costs often associated with the federal program provide a viable threat for the states to levy in their enforcement negotiations. If the parties responsible for creating a hazardous waste site will not settle, the state can recommend the site for listing as a Superfund site. SARA requires that states provide hazardous waste disposal capacity as a condition for participation in Superfund.

An ongoing tension exists between the federal and state cleanup programs. The states have criticized the federal program for its bureaucratic delays and have proposed that they be given greater discretion over Superfund financed cleanups. The EPA has in turn criticized the cleanups initiated at the state level as inadequate.

HAZARDOUS WASTE SITE ISSUES

How Clean Is Clean?

The extent and cost of cleanup are driven by perceptions of risk to public health and the environment. The "how clean is clean?" debate centers on whether protection of public health should be based on cleanup standards regardless of cost or on risk assessment and cost-benefit analysis. The case for standards rests on scientific findings of minimal safe exposure levels for toxic substances and the belief that protection should be uniform for all Superfund sites. In theory, toxic threats should be removed regardless of the likelihood of exposure. Citizens should not be denied protection at sites where necessary remedial cleanups are more expensive. Evidence that the EPA placed substantial weight on cost in its pre-1985 cleanup classification decisions resulted in SARA's mandating the use of standards to make such decisions.

In contrast to a **standards-based system**, **risk assessment** involves asking whether a substance is toxic and then applying a set of techniques to determine the incidence of exposure and injury likely to result from its release. Cost-benefit analysis compares the estimates of exposure and injury with expected cleanup costs to determine the number or value of statistical lives saved per dollar spent at each site. Advocates of risk assessment and cost-benefit analysis argue that both techniques are essential for an efficient and fair allocation of cleanup resources. They point to research findings that the cost of cleanup at many Superfund sites is not justified in terms of likely public health benefits.[17]

Opponents of these techniques question the objectivity of risk assessment and argue that cost-benefit analysis can be and has been used as a rationale for not taking action when people are in fact exposed to risk of serious injury. Disagreements over the application of standards versus risk assessment and cost-benefit analysis were among the highly divisive issues that stalled passage of the Superfund Reform Act of 1994.

A closely related problem is the choice between temporary and permanent cleanup remedies. Temporary remedies involve containment of waste rather than removal of the sources of contamination. Permanent remedies are intended to destroy the hazardous waste or permanently turn it into nonhazardous waste through chemical, biological, thermal, or physical means.[18]

Permanent remedies are substantially more expensive, whereas containment or other temporary remedies have significant risks of failure and renewed exposure.

The preference for temporary remedies during the first half of the 1980s—primarily to hold down cleanup costs—was criticized by environmentalists and congressional oversight committees, especially when use of stop-gap remedies required the EPA to return to the site for a subsequent cleanup. SARA mandated a preference for permanent cleanups where feasible. The higher Superfund tax levels after 1986 were necessary to pay for this preference. The average cost of cleanup increased from around $8 million to the $25 to $30 million range.[19]

Why Are Communities Opposed to Hazardous Waste Facilities?

As shown by Case Study 1, the siting of new hazardous waste facilities sometimes faces effective local community opposition. Such opposition stems in large part from public perceptions of the risks involved and of the inadequacy of government efforts to address these risks.

Since the late 1970s, the public has been sensitized by media reports of leaking hazardous waste sites and of communities living in fear of injury and death. Hostility to siting proposals has been fed by the expectation that all land-based storage facilities will eventually fail. The construction and operation of new hazardous waste facilities is subject to the demanding standards set down in the RCRA. Local communities receive little comfort from the fact that some 20 percent of Superfund sites had previously been regulated under the RCRA. Their discomfort is increased each time the federal government wavers on its commitment to strong disposal standards and to adequate Superfund cleanups.

Experts argue that many Superfund sites pose little risk to public health, where risk is defined in terms of the likelihood of an excess incidence of cancer. Local communities respond to a much broader set of risks associated with hazardous waste site exposure, from severe undiagnosed headaches and dizziness to deformed babies. Efforts by the EPA and state officials to downplay these fears and to impose sites on suspicious communities generate backlash and strong opposition. The history of Superfund and the RCRA provides scant basis for trust in the EPA or the experts. Whereas communities once had to rely solely on their own resources to fight new facility sitings, they can now draw on the expertise of those who have previously been involved in hazardous waste siting battles. Andrew Szasz argues that the growth in the ecopopulist movement has changed the battle cry from "not in my backyard" (NIMBY) to "not in anyone's backyard."[20]

RESOLUTION OF SUPERFUND ISSUES

Superfund supporters and opponents agree that the program has not lived up to expectations. They disagree on solutions. The short-term removal program is generally acknowledged to provide a rapid and effective response to imminent hazards. In contrast, the remedial cleanup program is generally criticized for its expensive and protracted studies of site conditions and cleanup remedies, its delay in executing cleanups, and its high cleanup costs. Superfund enforcement has resulted in contributions by responsible parties of billions of dollars to cleanup efforts but is criticized for its substantial transaction costs. Legal disputes among the EPA, responsible parties, third parties involved in contribution suits, and insurance companies absorb additional billions that could be better directed to the cleanup effort.

Congress has attempted to legislate solutions to these problems. Often unable to reach a consensus, it has allowed contradictory and vague elements to remain in the Superfund program. Left to solve the problems itself, the EPA either cannot find solutions or chooses solutions that prove unacceptable to Congress. Attempting to learn from this experience, the Clinton administration created a task force comprising experts and representatives of the diverse groups with interest in Superfund to craft a workable compromise program prior to congressional debate. The recommendations of the task force were embodied in the Superfund Reform Act of 1994. The act proposed an increase in five-year appropriations to the cleanup fund from $8.6 billion to $9.6 billion. The current emphasis on standards would be replaced by a set of national cleanup goals. The EPA would establish cost-effective generic remedies to reduce the time and expense currently involved in examining many alternative remedies at each site. The preference for permanent remedies would apply only to hot spots within a site. The EPA would develop guidelines for conducting risk assessments based on realistic assumptions. While the application of cost-benefit analysis was not explicitly called for, the EPA would continue to choose remedies that had reasonable cost in relation to other factors. The future use of sites would be considered in choosing remedies so as to avoid the application of expensive remedies in situations where the risk of exposure was small. EPA administrator Carol Browner expected that these changes would reduce cleanup costs by upwards of 20 percent. The proposal would allow more site contamination problems to be addressed at greater speed and lower cost.

To reduce transaction costs, the act would create an environmental insurance resolution fund by taxing past and future environmental damage insurance premiums. Parties held liable for disposal at Superfund sites prior to 1985 could choose to have a portion of their cleanup costs reimbursed from this fund. The act contained incentives for responsible parties to choose this option rather than engaging in costly litigation with their insurers. Money previously absorbed by transaction costs would now be directed to cleanup.

The act would also establish a procedure for a nonbinding allocation of responsibility among all liable parties at a site. Responsible parties that accepted this procedure could avoid the cost of third-party contribution suits. Additional reductions in transaction costs would be achieved. The proposed legislation died in committee prior to the November 1994 elections, with several central issues unresolved. Two examples are the allocation of the tax among various components of the insurance industry and the importance the EPA would assign to risk assessment versus cleanup standards.

THE FUTURE OF SUPERFUND

The history of Superfund demonstrates that it is extremely difficult to find solutions to the complex problems posed by decades of hazardous waste disposal. Underlying the disagreement is the reality that tens of billions of dollars are at stake and tens of millions of lives are affected. A viable Superfund can emerge only through consensus on the issues of harm and sanctions, the two considerations that define environmental crime.

In survey rankings of environmental threats, the public places hazardous waste near the top and experts place it near the bottom, but both cannot be correct. So long as the experts discount the noncancer health fears of the public and so long as the public remains distrustful of the methods applied by the experts, we cannot reach consensus on the harm posed by Superfund sites. With no consensus, Superfund will continue to waste valuable resources in studies of site conditions and remedies. The EPA will have little guidance in deciding which hazardous waste sites pose the greatest threat.

Regarding sanctions, it must be determined whether a retroactive "make the polluters pay" philosophy should be maintained, leaving Superfund within the realm of environmental crime, or whether Superfund sites should be viewed as the unintended consequences of productive activity, their cleanup to be treated as public works projects. Making polluters pay satisfies the public's sense of fairness. It comes, however, with high transaction costs and a degree of official dishonesty. It is an unfortunate truism that we can legislate a tax but not its incidence. Just as we all pay a portion of the Superfund taxes levied on corporations, we all share in the cleanup costs imposed on these same corporations through enforcement. Congress, when voicing its commitment to make polluters pay, seldom emphasizes these realities. Unfortunately, the choice between these options has been blocked by self-interest and national politics, preventing the development of a program. A movement toward consensus initiated by the Clinton administration and supported by major environmental and corporate interests failed. As in the past, failure turned on issues of who would pay and the extent of the threat posed. The 105th Congress is again debating Superfund. Some commentators believe that the chances for reform are better now than in any of the past three years. The Clinton administration still advocates the maintenance of strong liability standards and the reinstatement of Superfund taxes. In contrast, some well-placed conservative Republicans are opposed to both strong liability and sufficient funding; they essentially wish to reject both the "make the polluters pay" and the public works approach. Despite optimism in some quarters, the future of Superfund remains uncertain. Perhaps a characteristic irony of environmental politics is that conservative efforts to virtually eliminate Superfund may result in legislation that once again fails to meet the needs of the public and industry by providing an efficient cleanup program while substantially reducing enforcement-related conflict and transaction costs. As in the past, an inability to resolve basic areas of disagreement up front will leave society at undue risk and fated to bear the ongoing costs of conflict.

REFERENCES

1. H.C. Barnett, *Toxic Debts and the Superfund Dilemma* (Chapel Hill, NC: University of North Carolina Press, 1994), 11–16.

2. For discussion of early hazardous waste regulation, see S.S. Epstein et al., *Hazardous Waste in America* (San Francisco: Sierra Club Books, 1982).

3. The broad definition is introduced in E.H. Sutherland, *White Collar Crime* (New Haven, CT: Yale University Press, 1983), chap. 4.

4. For contemporary application of the term, see M.B. Clinard and P.C. Yeager, *Corporate Crime* (New York: The Free Press, 1980).

5. M. Brown, *Laying Waste: The Poisoning of America by Toxic Chemicals* (New York: Washington Square Press, 1981), 9.

6. Barnett, *Toxic Debts and the Superfund Dilemma*, 57.

7. Barnett, *Toxic Debts and the Superfund Dilemma*.

8. The name "Sewergate" derives from the comparison of this scandal to Watergate. For an excellent analysis of Sewergate, see Andrew Szasz, "The Process and Significance of Political Scandals: A Comparison of Watergate and the 'Sewergate' Episode at the Environmental Protection Agency," *Social Problems* 33 (1986): 202–217.

9. Barnett, *Toxic Debts and the Superfund Dilemma*, 80.

10. Recall that under CERCLA, a corporation sued by the EPA for more than its proportionate share of cleanup costs can in turn bring suit against other responsible parties for their proportionate shares.

11. See J.C. Butler, III, "Costs of Superfund Litigation," in U.S. Congress, House of Representatives, *Reauthorization of Superfund* (Washington, DC: U.S. Government Printing Office, 1985), 1300–1321.

12. See J.P. Acton and L.S. Dixon, *Superfund and Transactions Costs: The Experience of Insurers and Very Large Industrial Firms* (Santa Monica, CA: Rand Corporation, 1992).

13. See, for example, P.S. Menell, "The Limitations of Legal Institutions for Addressing Environmental Risks," *Journal of Economic Perspectives* 5 (summer 1991): 93–114.

14. Barnett, *Toxic Debts and the Superfund Dilemma,*

15. Barnett, *Toxic Debts and the Superfund Dilemma,*

16. This statistic came from a study by R. Doll and R. Peto, "The Causes of Cancer," *Journal of the National Cancer Institute* 66 (1981): 1191–1308. Academic experts questioned the interpretation of their findings offered by opponents of victim compensation.

17. For discussion of the pros and cons of risk assessment, see J.A. Hird, *Superfund: The Political Economy of Environmental Risk* (Baltimore, MD: The Johns Hopkins University Press, 1994), especially chaps. 2 and 3.

18. For discussion of alternative remedies, see U.S. Office of Technology Assessment, *Superfund Strategy* (Washington, DC: U.S. Government Printing Office, 1985), chap. 6.

19. Barnett, *Toxic Debts and the Superfund Dilemma.*

20. For an excellent discussion of the populist environmental movement, see A. Szasz, *EcoPopulism: Toxic Waste and the Movement for Environmental Justice* (Minneapolis, MN: University of Minnesota Press, 1994).

Rocky Flats: A Plea Bargain in Public View

Brian Lipsett

TERMS   Atomic Energy Commission   nolo contendere
              Department of Energy

This case study examines an "environmental crime" involving both private industry and the federal government. A major defense contractor, Rockwell International, was prosecuted and convicted for violations of environmental laws at the government-owned Rocky Flats nuclear weapons defense facility in Colorado. The analysis of this case is based on books, articles, news media accounts, and congressional investigations.

BACKGROUND

Rockwell International is "a diversified corporation engaged in research, development, and manufacture of many products for commercial and government markets."[1(p.1)] The company is primarily involved in the design and manufacture of electronic, aerospace, and automotive equipment. Rockwell does a considerable amount of its business with the federal government. In 1992, for example, 43 percent of the company's entire sales went to NASA and the Department of Defense, although that percentage has decreased in recent years due to federal defense spending cutbacks.[2,3]

The Rocky Flats defense facility, located outside of Denver, Colorado, was built in 1951 by the **Atomic Energy Commission** (AEC) and was operated by Dow Chemical under contract with the AEC until 1975, when Rockwell International took over operations. From 1951 until the facility was shut down in January 1992, workers at the plant designed, built, modified, or retired approximately 4,000 nuclear warheads each year.[4]

Over time, the population of the nearby Denver metropolitan area increased. The growth, slow at first, became quite rapid in the mid-1970s. This meant that more and more people came to live in close proximity to the facility. As the population around the Rocky Flats plant grew, accidents, leaks, explosions, fires, and releases of plutonium became an increasing concern to the people in the surrounding area. In 1975, for example, nearby residents filed several lawsuits against the AEC (which became the **Department of Energy** [DOE] in 1977), Dow Chemical, and Rockwell International, alleging property damage. That litigation was settled out of court in 1985 for $10 million.[5]

A number of organizations, ranging from disarmament and environmental groups like Greenpeace to local grassroots environmental groups, continued raising safety and utility issues. In February 1989, the Sierra Club filed suit against the DOE and Rockwell, charging that they were burning plutonium in an incinerator without federal permits.[6] Under a discovery order, the DOE and Rockwell were required to release internal documents to Sierra Club lawyers on Monday, June 12, 1989.[7]

THE RAID

On Tuesday, June 6, 1989, between 75 and 120 Federal Bureau of Investigation (FBI) agents, Environmental Protection Agency (EPA) investigators, and DOE inspectors raided the plant.[8,9] The agents seized over 180 boxes of documents in search of evidence that might prove that DOE and Rockwell had violated environmental laws while operating the plant.[10] An FBI affidavit released to the media alleged the defense plant's operations had violated several environmental laws. A United Press International story described the raid and the accompanying search warrant affidavit on June 10, 1989:

> A search warrant affidavit accuses operators of the Rocky Flats nuclear weapons plant of contaminating air and drinking water near the facility, which is the subject of three separate investigations. A U.S. magistrate Friday unsealed the 116-page FBI affidavit that was used to obtain a search warrant for the plant northwest of Denver. The affidavit says aerial infrared pictures taken last year show radioactivity in the air above the plant. The Justice Department claims plant operators illegally burned plutonium at night during a time when its incinerator was supposed to have been shut down for safety reasons. The affidavit also accuses the Department of Energy and Rockwell International, which operates Rocky Flats

under contract to the DOE, of illegally dumping chemicals into two creeks that flow into two nearby reservoirs that supply drinking water to some northwest Denver suburbs.[11]

So, at the outset of this case, an FBI affidavit was released to the public through the news media. The affidavit charged the operator, Rockwell International, with certain criminal acts. Charges were also directed at the facility owner, which was the DOE. The charges included alleged illegal burning of radioactive materials and the dumping of toxic waste into the tributary of a public drinking water supply, both extremely serious allegations.

Several months later, in October 1989, DOE released a report on the Rocky Flats situation that served as its official account of environmental problems at the Rocky Flats plant. According to an Associated Press story published in the *Los Angeles Times* on October 6, 1989, "The Rocky Flats nuclear arms plant, which is under investigation by the FBI for possible criminal violation of environmental laws, poses no imminent threat to public health, the Energy Department concluded in a study released Thursday."[12(p.26)] Although the report attempted to resolve a key issue—the threat to human safety posed by the operation at Rocky Flats—it did so rather awkwardly. After dismissing any possible imminent threat, the DOE report admitted that radiation measurement devices at the site were in such poor condition it was impossible to tell how much plutonium might have escaped into the environment. Indeed, the report documented a number of serious problems (which the news article points out), but the meaning of "imminent threat" was left for the public to interpret.

THE SETTLEMENT

After the 1989 press release, the situation remained relatively quiet until March 1992, when Rockwell pleaded guilty to five felony violations of environmental law and agreed to pay an $18.5 million fine to settle the case. At the time, this was the second largest criminal penalty for environmental violations, second only to the Exxon Valdez penalty of $125 million.

> Michael J. Norton, U.S. Attorney for the District of Colorado, said the hazardous waste fine against Rockwell is the largest in U.S. history. The Rockwell fine is the second largest environmental fine ever assessed, behind the $125 million Exxon Valdez oil spill penalty. . . .
> . . . Norton said the government did not prove other allegations raised against Rockwell during an investigation of the plant, including charges of midnight incinerations and willful dumping of chemicals into creeks.

Barry M. Hartman, acting assistant attorney general for the Justice Department's environment and natural resources division, said the investigation of Rocky Flats was the most complex and difficult environmental case ever investigated by the Department of Justice.[13(p.A33)]

The charges leveled at the time of the raid, alleging illegal burning of radioactive waste and contaminating a drinking water tributary with toxic chemicals, were replaced with a guilty plea by Rockwell and a statement by the prosecutors that the evidence did not bear out the charges in the original investigation, upon which the raid was based. The Department of Justice (DOJ) heralded its own efforts by claiming a record fine, with the caveat that the case was the most "complex and difficult" ever. Equally, Colorado law enforcement received a boost: "$2 million of the fine will be remitted to the state of Colorado, to settle the state's claims against the contractor. State Attorney General Gale Norton said the fine is the largest for an environmental crime in Colorado history."[14(p.A33)]

The settlement of the case follows a familiar pattern well documented by the research of such organizations as Citizen's Clearinghouse for Hazardous Waste, Greenpeace, and other groups.[15,16] It suggests a kind of ritual involving various organizational actors (i.e., the FBI, EPA, state of Colorado, DOJ, DOE, and Rockwell International). The news media provided a kind of stage on which the drama played itself out. A number of serious charges were leveled by law enforcement officials as a means of justifying an extraordinary raid on a federal nuclear weapons facility. These charges were reported almost word for word by the print news media. Later, the charges were mitigated—first in a report from one of the parties involved in the raid, DOE (remember, DOE also owned the plant), and finally through a settlement that exonerated Rockwell and its employees (and DOE and its employees) from the most serious and compelling charges.

THE SETTLEMENT TURNS SOUR

In the Rocky Flats case, as in most high-profile cases of this nature, the settlement caused people to expect the situation to wind down. This is not, however, what happened here. Following the sentencing of Rockwell, in late summer of 1992, a U.S. Representative from Colorado began charging a coverup. In September 1992, the House Committee on Science, Space, and Technology opened an investigation of the DOJ's prosecution effort against Rockwell, while another committee held hearings on the DOJ's handling of a number of other unrelated environmental prosecutions. In late September, FBI agent Jon Lipsky informed the House Committee on Science, Space, and Technology's investigative subcommittee, chaired by Howard Wolpe (D-MI), that he had pertinent information the committee wanted, but because it would violate grand jury secrecy laws, he could not reveal why DOJ had convicted Rockwell but not individuals at Rockwell or the DOE who may have ordered or allowed violations of environmental law.[17]

Also in September 1992, members of the special citizen grand jury empaneled in 1989 to review the evidence and issue indictments in the Rocky Flats case began talking to the press. An article entitled "The Secret Story of the Rocky Flats Grand Jury" appeared in the free alternative Denver newspaper *Westword*.[18] Within weeks stories about a renegade grand jury and behind-closed-doors plea bargain negotiations began spreading through the news media. The Justice Department's lead attorney in Colorado, Michael Norton, denounced the "run away" grand jury as a bunch of environmentalists and nuclear disarmers.[19] In October 1992, Sherman Finesilver, the judge in the Rockwell case, asked the Justice Department to investigate the grand jury secrecy laws. The call for an investigation by Finesilver apparently caused the grand jurors to meet together to plan a strategy. In November, the members of the grand jury held a press conference on the steps of the Denver courthouse and issued a statement calling on President-elect Bill Clinton, upon inauguration, to launch an investigation into the government's prosecution of Rockwell and the DOE.[20]

A media circus was underway, and grand jury foreman Wes McKinley became an overnight celebrity.

> McKinley was quite a sight on the steps of the federal courthouse in downtown Denver on the following Wednesday morning, what with his boots and jeans and kerchief and big white cowboy hat. They'd expected half a dozen reporters, but 30 showed up, along with about 200 spectators. . . . For the national news media, the story line now was irresistible: A runaway grand jury led by a cowboy foreman, fighting to uncover a sinister cover-up. Most of the big national newspapers and news weeklies ran stories and editorials.[21(p.23)]

The interest value of a "runaway grand jury led by a cowboy foreman" undoubtedly pushed the media to go to great lengths to scoop the story, and "six days after the press conference, the syndicated TV tabloid show 'Inside Edition' beat out a gaggle of other television programs by chartering a plane and flying through a blizzard to drop a crew near McKinley's ranch."[22(p.23)]

So, by the winter of 1992, the tidy settlement of the environmental crime case reached in March had turned rather messy. The news media played an important role. The 23 members of the special grand jury, a group of ordinary citizens, were the crucial element. They refused to back down in the face of what they perceived to be an unjust resolution of the case, and they went down in history for their defiance.

> On November 20, 1992, a federal grand jury . . . decided to take historic action. After listening to almost three years of testimony, members of Special Grand Jury 89-2 stood outside the Denver courthouse to complain that their efforts to investigate and punish criminal conduct at a federal facility were actively hampered by the Justice Department.[23(p.23)]

At this point, we can take note of another "record." For the first time in U.S. history, a citizen grand jury came forward with information indicating that the federal government had failed to enforce the law fairly and evenly. This historic action by a citizen grand jury invited a storm of media coverage and served to justify congressional intervention and investigation. The resulting hearings and reports indeed suggested malfeasance on the part of the Justice Department's Washington-based Environmental Crimes Section in handling environmental crime prosecutions. This development invited further scrutiny from the media and the public.

THE INVESTIGATION OF THE PROSECUTION OF ROCKWELL

Two congressional subcommittees were, by September 1992, investigating the manner in which the DOJ handled cases of environmental crime.[24,25] One of these, the Subcommittee on Investigations and Oversight for the House Committee on Science, Space, and Technology, issued a report on its investigation in January 1993. The report, entitled "The Prosecution of Environmental Crimes at the Department of Energy's Rocky Flats Facility," put into the public record a considerable amount of otherwise confidential documentation and testimony concerning the plea bargaining that had gone on.

In his letter of transmittal to the chair of the Committee on Science, Space, and Technology, Howard Wolpe, chair of that committee's investigation and oversight subcommittee, offered the following observations regarding the findings of the subcommittee's investigation:

> First, our investigation revealed a very troubling lack of public accountability in the Federal Government. Serious environmental crimes are committed, but no individuals were held responsible. The crimes were attributed to a "culture" at DOE—not the actions of

responsible individuals. This is the white collar equivalent of blaming an armed robbery on "society"—not the individual holding the gun.

Second, it should be noted that the most important thing that Federal prosecutors bargained away in negotiations with Rockwell was the truth. By entering into this plea agreement, the prosecutors bargained away the right to fully and accurately inform the American people and the Congress about the conditions, activities, and crimes at the Rocky Flats facility. Conditions that, I might add, continue to this day even though Rockwell has been replaced as the facility's contractor. And these conditions are not unique to Rocky Flats; they can be found throughout the DOE complex. . . .

Third, I would like to indicate my sympathy for the courageous individuals who served on the Rocky Flats grand jury. . . . These citizens were so offended by the plea agreement with Rockwell that they have placed themselves in legal jeopardy by publicly discussing the settlement. . . . In my view, it would be both ironic and outrageous if the Department of Justice prosecutes the grand jurors themselves with more vigor than they demonstrated in prosecuting Rockwell for serious environmental crimes.[26]

THE CULTURE OF THE DEPARTMENT OF ENERGY

At his confirmation hearing before the U.S. Senate, in February 1989, President Bush's choice to run the Department of Energy, Admiral James D. Watkins, made his first public statement concerning what he would do if he was confirmed as energy secretary. In his opening remarks, Admiral Watkins noted DOE's culture of secrecy and suggested that the culture had evolved out of years of operating without public scrutiny and in response to weapons production goals. He stated that there was "an urgent need to effect a significant change in [DOE's] deeply embedded 35-year culture. By use of the word 'culture' I mean that set of values that permeates the work atmosphere within which operations take place."[27] Watkins acknowledged a number of serious problems, many having to do with environmental contamination, and promised that if he was confirmed, he would work to change the DOE's culture to one focused on environmental compliance.

Roughly four months later, and 11 days after the raid on Rocky Flats, Watkins was quoted in the news media stating that he was fully intent on changing the DOE's culture to "a new culture of professionalism."[28(p.A1)] It is likely Watkins was briefed prior to the raid, although he later asserted that his knowledge of the situation arose out of his own internal review and not out of any information coming from law enforcement.[29] In any event, it is apparent from the record that Watkins's expressed mission of cultural change at DOE had become a central theme of his administration.

The culture at DOE also appears to have weighed heavily on the minds of the DOJ line attorneys in Denver and their supervisors in Washington, D.C. In closed hearings before the Wolpe investigative subcommittee, several individuals from the investigation and prosecution team testified that the existence of a DOE culture that allowed violations to occur was central to the decision not to prosecute individual offenders within DOE. In essence, the new DOE administrator, Admiral Watkins, who had come to the job with the expressed intent of reforming the organization, claimed to discover that the organization's operating culture was deficient and needed to be changed. As a result, the prosecution of the case focused on the culture of the DOE as its rationale for not prosecuting any individuals at DOE. The decision to rule out any prosecution of DOE employees seems to have been the main reason why charges against Rockwell alleging illegal incineration of hazardous and radioactive waste were dropped, despite the existence of substantial evidence.

The Wolpe subcommittee took a very dim view of this matter:

> In the Plaintiff's Sentencing Memorandum prepared for this settlement, great emphasis is placed on what the Justice Department refers to as the "DOE culture" as an explanation of the criminal activity that occurred at Rocky Flats, and as a rationale for not indicting DOE personnel. What has emerged in the course of this investigation is that in the eyes of the Justice decision-makers this "cultural" factor mitigated against indictment of DOE or Rockwell personnel who in their view were simply products of the bureaucratic "culture" in which they were operating. . . . This signals a troubling double standard in the administration of justice. An agency and its individual employees are placed above the law. Unlike ordinary citizens who will be held accountable for their infractions, government personnel are apparently immune from prosecution if their conduct—no matter how egregious—has been sanctioned by the agencies.[30(pp.108–109)]

An additional item that reflects on the significance of culture is found in a letter to Attorney General William P. Barr from Barry Hartman, Assistant Attorney General for Environment and Natural Resources. The letter illustrates the role that main justice played in directing the handling of the case, and demonstrates that the whole issue of cultural reform orchestrated by

Calvin and Hobbes

by Bill Watterson

Energy Secretary Watkins was central to the settlement of the case and the rehabilitation of the DOE.

> We have tried to convince the [U.S. Attorney in Colorado] to accurately reflect the fact that DOE failures were the results of attitudes prior to Admiral Watkins becoming Secretary.[31]

In short, DOE officials were not prosecuted because DOJ attorneys had determined that it would not be possible to hold individuals accountable for an organizational culture that sanctioned violations of the law. Also, according to then-operating internal directives and official pronouncements, DOE had been reformed by the new administrator through his efforts to change the DOE's organizational culture. Prosecutors in the U.S. Attorney's Office in Colorado were required by their superiors to observe this myth.

THE PLEA BARGAIN

The term *plea bargain* can be broadly defined as "'every form of discussion between the prosecution and defense' that might lead to disposition without trial."[32(p.351)] In general, plea bargains are useful for several reasons. First of all, a plea bargain can allow the defendant in a case the opportunity to avoid a lengthy trial and sentence through negotiating down the crime charged, the penalty sought, and so on. A plea bargain also can lessen the amount of time that defense attorneys, prosecutors, and the judge must spend on a given case. Finally, a plea bargain can permit prosecutors to get something out of what would otherwise prove to be a difficult case to try in court because of a lack of evidence, procedural problems, and so on.

In the Rocky Flats case, the plea bargain process was lengthy and exhaustive. It lasted for nearly the entire period of time the citizen grand jury sat hearing evidence (nearly three years). It also appears that the plea bargaining proceeded without any input from the grand jury. In the end, the prosecutors met just about every demand put on the table by Rockwell's lawyers.

> In their negotiations with the prosecutors, Rockwell's attorneys made it clear that there were certain "core interests" that had to be met before settlement could be agreed to. These included no individual indictments, no fraud, false statement or conspiracy charges; incinerations, worker health/safety violations which alleged off-site release; indemnification by DOE for some or all of the costs of defending the criminal and related civil litigation; and a "global settlement" of related enforcement actions including civil penalties and a pending qui tam suit; no debarment; and public statements that there were no "midnight" burnings or substantial off-site health or environmental consequences from the charged conduct.[33(p.37)]

According to the Wolpe subcommittee investigation, the prosecutors maintained two core bargaining chips: no U.S. taxpayer reimbursement for fines paid by Rockwell and a large enough fine to justify the settlement. The prosecutors evidently felt that the case would be difficult and time consuming to bring to trial, and so they settled for an $18.5 million fine, guilty pleas on four felony counts under the RCRA, and one felony and four misdemeanors under the Clean Water Act. Interestingly, the line attorneys in Colorado were forced to argue with their D.C. superiors for a higher penalty, up from the $15.5 million proposed by Main Justice (the Washington-based part of the Justice Department).

> The point is not that the government probably could have won a few million dollars more from Rockwell—though it probably could—the point is that main Justice was consistently pushing for a radically lower number throughout the period of negotiations. . . . It appears that main Justice never did view Rockwell's criminal behavior as particularly noxious. . . . While we may never know how much more the government could have won if they had pushed Rockwell harder, the truth is that if this case had been in the hands of main Justice, the case would have been settled for a mere four or five million dollars.[34(pp.106–107)]

The issue of off-site environmental harm was a particularly important matter. If the court settlement required Rockwell to admit to off-site harm and/or worker health and safety violations, neighbors of the plant and workers at the plant could use that fact in civil cases. It would have exposed the company to increased civil liability and, due to an indemnification clause in Rockwell's contract with DOE (which meant that the federal government would ultimately have to pay any fine), might have caused additional losses for U.S. taxpayers.

> DOE's contractual obligation to indemnify Rockwell for civil liabilities meant that it would be the federal government who would actually suffer the potentially large monetary exposure. Consequently, DOE took the wholly inappropriate action of injecting itself into the criminal plea bargain negotiations on behalf of the defendant in an attempt to influence the prosecutors to accept a plea that would minimize the civil exposure of the defendant, and ultimately itself.[35(p.116)]

DOE in fact made an attempt (in addition to similar attempts by Rockwell's lawyers) to win a **nolo contendere** plea for Rockwell in order to settle the case and avoid civil liability (evidence from a nolo contendere case is more difficult to use in civil proceedings than evidence from cases involving guilty pleas). In the event of a guilty plea, substantiation of off-site contamination would have increased civil liability exposure for both Rockwell and the DOE.

> Over time and in the interest of settlement, allegations that involved the off-site release of chemicals—and radio-nuclides—were either dropped or rewritten into a format that implied they were mere "technical" violations of permit and other regulatory requirements. . . . Rockwell expressed great reluctance to pleading to Clean Water Act (CWA) violations with its implications of off-site effects.[36(p.67)]

In summary, it appears that the resolution of the case required that the federal government's own lawyers commit themselves to a settlement that protected the federal government and U.S. taxpayers from liability. In order to do this effectively, the prosecution agreed to make certain statements (approved by Rockwell's attorneys) that denied any off-site consequences for the crimes to which Rockwell pleaded guilty. It was these and other matters (such as a lack of individual indictments, particularly of DOE officials, and obstruction by the prosecution team of the grand jury's interest in issuing a report) that rankled the grand jury and caused them to go public.

THE CITIZEN GRAND JURY

Special Citizen Grand Jury 89-2 was convened on August 1, 1989. In his charge of duties and responsibilities to the grand jury, Judge Finesilver reiterated the reasoning behind the Colorado U.S. Attorney's Office request to Main Justice that it authorize the empanelment of a special grand jury, a request that was obviously approved. The judge told the grand jury that they were needed because the case would involve a lengthy investigation and the possible need for a report from the jury on their findings.[37]

He also argued very strongly for the grand jury to accept and assert their own independence. According to the Wolpe subcommittee, Finesilver told the jurors to neither "yield your powers nor forgo your independence of spirit . . . because you may tend to expect such high quality from the government's agents that there is a potentially grave risk to your independence of thought and action, which may cause you to lapse into reliance when you should be dubious and questioning."[38(p.134)] Rather than yield their independence to the prosecutors, the grand jury members should "exercise your own judgement, and if the facts suggest a different balance than that advocated by the government attorneys, then you must achieve the appropriate balance even in the face of their opposition or criticism."[39(p.134)]

In the end, it appears that the grand jurors took this advice seriously. They asserted a strong interest in indicting individuals and issuing a report. Rockwell's lawyers, however, continued to maintain objections to the possibility that there be any individual indictments or a report by the grand jury. This matter caused considerable dissension within the prosecution team. Prosecutors in the U.S. Attorney's Office in Colorado insisted on the need for a grand jury report for a number of reasons. Their Washington, D.C.–based supervisors wanted to go along with Rockwell for a different set of reasons.

> Rockwell lawyers first proposed that there be no grand jury report in a letter to U.S. Atty. Norton on June 27, 1991. [Assistant U.S. Attorney] Ken Fimberg, scrambling to nip the notion in the bud, advised Norton that the grand jury "would lynch us if we agreed to this."[40(p.22)]

Assistant U.S. Attorney Fimberg's warnings proved to be quite accurate, but they had no impact on the ultimate decision by DOJ officials to block any effort by the grand jury to issue a report.

> By then, Fimberg had come to realize his most ominous foe in the fight over a grand jury report was going to be the Justice Department, not Rockwell. For once, he wasn't isolated. The entire prosecution team wanted a grand jury report. But Barry Hartman, then head of the Environment and Natural Resources Division in Washington, did not.[41(p.22)]

Ultimately, the argument that held force in these internal deliberations came from Hartman in Washington, D.C. From his perspective, there was no statutory authority for the grand jury to write a report because there were no ongoing violations (i.e., the situation at Rocky Flats did not constitute an ongoing criminal conspiracy). Here it seems appropriate to point out that one of the likely premises guiding Hartman's reasoning was that the culture at DOE was being or had been reformed and that there was thus no need to remove (i.e., debar) Rockwell from a list of eligible contractors that DOE could hire to do its bidding. Put differently, the decision by DOJ to bargain away a report by the grand jury serviced a myth of cultural reform at DOE and allowed Rockwell to continue to receive lucrative government contracts. In all probability, the absence of a grand jury report also lessened civil liabilities for both Rockwell and DOE.

These developments apparently so angered the grand jury members that they took historic action. In the view of the Rocky Flats grand jury, there was ongoing, organized criminal activity involving government collusion. The grand jury's self-fashioned report, first leaked to *Westword*, opens as follows:

> The Department of Energy ("DOE"), its contractors—Rockwell International, Inc. ("Rockwell") . . . and many of their respective employees have engaged in an ongoing criminal enterprise at the Rocky Flats Plant ("the Plant"), which has violated Federal environmental laws. This criminal enterprise continues to operate today at the Rocky Flats Plant, and it promises to continue operating into the future unless our government, its contractors and their respective employees are made subject to the law.[42(p.2)]

The report of Special Citizen Grand Jury 89-2 was finally released in January 1993. It was redated by DOJ prosecutors, and all references to individuals the grand jury wanted to indict were deleted. Annotated commentary that poked holes in the report was included by DOJ prosecutors. While both Judge Finesilver and DOJ found the grand jury's report deficient in many ways, the force of their objections is tempered by the observations of Wolpe's subcommittee investigation. In essence, the subcommittee report placed the blame for deficiencies in the grand jury report on the shoulders of the prosecution team, which tried to disband the grand jury. The report also placed some of the blame on Judge Finesilver, who withheld professional support from the grand jury when it became apparent that it was going to write a report regardless of what Rockwell and DOJ had agreed to in the plea bargain.

Eventually, the FBI criminal investigation into whether the grand jury members had violated secrecy laws was dropped and news media interest faded. In 1994, the House and Senate changed hands, and a new set of representatives and senators with other interests took control of the congressional committees and investigative subcommittees. The congressional focus on DOJ shifted to that agency's handling of the standoffs in Waco, Texas, and Ruby Ridge, Idaho, and efforts were made by some members of Congress to gut environmental laws. The story of Special Citizen Grand Jury 89-2 has been relegated to history, and its potential impact on the criminal justice system may never be fully realized.

POSTSCRIPT

In 1996, the Justice Department announced that Rockwell International had pleaded guilty to three felony charges and agreed to pay a $6.5 million fine for illegally storing and disposing of hazardous waste at a weapons laboratory in Simi Hills, California. The charges arose in the wake of a 1994 explosion that killed two laboratory scientists as they were attempting to dispose of explosive hazardous waste by burning it.[43] Also in 1994, DOE began releasing information indicating that it and its predecessor, the Atomic Energy Commission, had engaged in radiation experiments on unsuspecting human subjects for several decades. Whether reform of the culture of DOE has been successful remains an open question.

REVIEW QUESTIONS

1. Whom would you identify as the "environmental criminal" in the case of Rocky Flats?
2. Who called the special grand jury and why?
3. What is the relationship between the AEC and DOE?
4. What is the relationship between DOE and Rockwell International?

DISCUSSION QUESTIONS

1. Would you argue that government agencies, such as the military, should be exempted from compliance with environmental regulations that interfere with the maintenance of national security?
2. What about the case of Rocky Flats makes this an unusual case for enforcement divisions?
3. How does the "culture at DOE" (as it was described above) compare with typical explanations for criminal activity? Would you agree that the "cleanup" at DOE should be seen as a sign of corporate rehabilitation?
4. What are some of the similarities between the actions committed by DOE and more traditional criminal activity? Consider street gangs, inner city crimes, robbery, burglary, and violent crimes, for example.

5. What recourse did the citizens of Denver have as concern mounted about the weapons manufacturing plant? What rights should citizens have to question the government when they are concerned about possible injury from operations at a government facility?

6. Chemical and nuclear weapons are extremely hazardous to humans (that is why they are weapons). As we saw recently in the Gulf War, dramatic environmental damage can be the result of war. Should guidelines be established for war to ensure environmental protection? If the answer is yes, how would these guidelines be enforced?

REFERENCES

1. Rockwell International Annual Report on form 10K for fiscal year 1995, 1.
2. *Overview—Rockwell International*, Multimedia Business 500 CD-ROM, Allegro, 1994.
3. Rockwell International Annual Report on form 10k from fiscal year 1995.
4. C. Piller, *The Fail-safe Society: Community Defiance and the End of American Technological Optimism* (New York: Basic Books, 1991), 40.
5. Piller, *Fail-safe Society*, 44–45.
6. "Rocky Flats Charges Detailed in Search Warrant Affidavit," United Press International, 10 June, 1989.
7. "Rocky Flats Charges Detailed in Search Warrant Affidavit."
8. "Rocky Flats Charges Detailed in Search Warrant Affidavit."
9. "Rockwell Pleads Guilty to Violations at Rocky Flats, Will Pay $18.5 Million," Federal Contracts Report, Bureau of National Affairs, 27 March, 1992.
10. "Rockwell Pleads Guilty to Violations at Rocky Flats."
11. "Rocky Flats Charges Detailed in Search Warrant Affidavit."
12. "No Imminent Threat Found at Rocky Flats: But Energy Department Study Raises Doubts on Plant's Nuclear Waste Disposal," *Los Angeles Times*, 6 October, 1989, 26.
13. "Rockwell Pleads Guilty to Violations at Rocky Flats."
14. "Rockwell Pleads Guilty to Violations at Rocky Flats."
15. S. Lester, "CDC: Coverup, Deceit, and Confusion," *Everyone's Backyard* (1983): V1–V14.
16. "WMX: Trash into Cash," Greenpeace, 1993.
17. *The Prosecution of Environmental Crimes at the Department of Energy's Rocky Flats Facility*, report of the Subcommittee on Investigations and Oversight of the House Committee on Science, Space and Technology, 4 January 1993, 92–93.
18. B. Seigal, "Showdown at Rocky Flats," *Los Angeles Times Magazine*, 15 August 1993, 22.
19. J. Turley, "The Government versus the Grand Jury," *Chicago Tribune*, 23 September, 1993, 23.
20. Seigal, "Showdown at Rocky Flats."
21. Seigal, "Showdown at Rocky Flats," 23.
22. Seigal, "Showdown at Rocky Flats," 23.
23. Turley, "The Government versus the Grand Jury," 23.

24. U.S. Environmental Protection Agency, Criminal Enforcement Program, *Hearing before the Subcommittee on Oversight and Investigation of the Committee on Energy and Commerce*, House of Representatives, 10 September 1992.

25. *Prosecution of Environmental Crimes at the Department of Energy's Rocky Flats Facility.*

26. Letter of transmittal from Howard Wolpe, Chair, Subcommittee on Oversight and Investigation of the House Committee on Science, Space and Technology, to George E. Brown Jr., Chair of the House Committee on Science, Space and Technology, 4 January 1993.

27. "Confirmation Hearing for Adm. James Watkins as Energy Secretary," Federal News Service, 22 February 1989.

28. T.R. Reid, "Health Safety Given Priority at Arms Plants; DOE Puts Production 2nd," *Washington Post*, 16 June 1989, A1.

29. "Press Conference with Energy Secretary James Watkins," Federal News Service, 27 June 1989.

30. *Prosecution of Environmental Crimes at the Department of Energy's Rocky Flats Facility*, 108–109.

31. *Prosecution of Environmental Crimes at the Department of Energy's Rocky Flats Facility*, 108–109.

32. J. Somehow, *Criminal Justice* (St. Paul, MN: West Publishing, 1988), 351.

33. *Prosecution of Environmental Crimes at the Department of Energy's Rocky Flats Facility*, 37. Note: A "qui tam" suit is a lawsuit under a statute that gives a part of the penalty to the plaintiff and the balance to the state.

34. *Prosecution of Environmental Crimes at the Department of Energy's Rocky Flats Facility*, 106–107.

35. *Prosecution of Environmental Crimes at the Department of Energy's Rocky Flats Facility*, 116.

36. *Prosecution of Environmental Crimes at the Department of Energy's Rocky Flats Facility*, 67.

37. *Prosecution of Environmental Crimes at the Department of Energy's Rocky Flats Facility*, 122–123.

38. *Prosecution of Environmental Crimes at the Department of Energy's Rocky Flats Facility*, 134.

39. *Prosecution of Environmental Crimes at the Department of Energy's Rocky Flats Facility*, 134.

40. Seigal, "Showdown at Rocky Flats," 22.

41. Seigal, "Showdown at Rocky Flats," 22

42. "Report of the Special Grand Jury 89-2," Colorado Federal District Court, 19 February 1992, 2.

43. R. Mokhiber, "Rockwell Pleads Guilty to Environmental Crimes, Will Pay $6.5 Million Fine," *Corporate Crime Reporter*, 15 April 1996, 4.

Controversy amid Controversy: Reauthorizing the Endangered Species Act

Mary Clifford

TERMS	clear-cutting	Lacey Act
	Endangered Species Act	Migratory Bird Act
	Habitat-Conservation Plan	species recovery plan
	incidental take permit	Tellico Dam

Aldo Leopold once noted the first rule of intelligent tinkering is to save all of the pieces.[1] Many argue this is what the U.S. Congress had in mind 24 years ago when it passed a tough version of the **Endangered Species Act** (ESA). On the assumption that "each life-form may prove valuable in ways we cannot yet measure, and that each is entitled to exist for its own sake,"[2(p.7)] legislative action was taken to protect threatened species. Passed in its original form in 1973, the ESA was intended to give the federal government the authority to protect any species threatened with extinction. Responding to increases in public concern about species extinction, the ESA has been hailed by supporters as the most important piece of legislation in the twentieth century, certainly "the single strongest piece of environmental legislation ever fashioned."[3(p.46)] Douglas Chadwick, a field biologist and author, describes the ESA as "our compact with other living things—a guarantee that we will not knowingly end their existence and that we will actively work to prevent their extinction from non-natural causes. An enlightened expression of our finest values, it represents a stride forward in the moral progress of humankind."[4(p.46)]

The 1973 list of threatened and endangered U.S. species included 109 names. As of April 30, 1995, the total was 956 U.S. species and 560 foreign species.[5] In addition, over 3,700 species await the full review necessary to qualify for inclusion on the list of threatened or endangered species.[6,7] Of the 956 U.S. species listed as endangered or threatened in 1995, the U.S. Fish and Wildlife Service reports that nearly 40 percent are stable or improving and 54 percent are covered by approved recovery plans (in addition, draft recovery plans exist for 24 percent of the species).[8,9]

Yet not everyone is happy with the impact of the ESA. In its relatively short life, the ESA has been the centerpiece of controversy. A multitude of unforeseen and unintended consequences have developed, prompting even supporters of the act to argue the need for reform. Immediately below is a review of the central elements of the initial legislation, followed by outlines of several current controversies. The case study closes with a presentation of various suggestions for developing solutions to the problems that continue to plague the ESA.

A BRIEF HISTORY OF THE ENDANGERED SPECIES ACT

Many Americans have heard about the dodo bird and the passenger pigeon. The dodo was a large flightless bird that went extinct in the late seventeenth century. The passenger pigeon, during the last century, thrived in large numbers. Flocks of the pigeons were said to darken the sky when they flew overhead. In 1914, the last bird died in the aviary at the Cincinnati Zoological Gardens. The story made national headlines.[10]

Many have wondered what role humans should play in species protection. Several different pieces of legislation have been passed to protect specific animal populations. The **Lacey Act**, for example, passed in 1900, prohibited interstate commerce of fish or wildlife taken in violation of federal, state, or foreign law,[11] and the **Migratory Bird Act** of 1918 limited hunting

Calvin and Hobbes   **by Bill Watterson**

Source: CALVIN AND HOBBES © 1988 Watterson. Dist. by UNIVERSAL PRESS SYNDICATE. Reprinted with permission. All rights reserved.

and prohibited the taking of nests or eggs of specific migratory birds.[12] Overall, these early efforts at species protection focused on specific members of a protected class of species, and their results were consequently unpredictable and inconsistent.

The most comprehensive legislation focused on species protection has been enacted within the past 30 years. In particular, three separate statutes have provided a foundation for endangered species protection. The first of the three enacted was the **Endangered Species Preservation Act of 1966 (ESPA)**. The Secretary of the Interior was charged with developing a program "to conserve, protect, restore, and propagate selected species of native fish and wildlife."[13] The provisions of the legislation were designed to protect habitat through land acquisitions. At this point, no procedures were outlined for identifying a species as threatened or endangered.

The **Endangered Species Conservation Act of 1969 (ESCA)** was an attempt to remedy the limitations of the earlier statute. It included more specific definitions of types of protected wildlife and covered wildlife threatened with worldwide extinction.[14] "Instead of using the broad term 'fish and wildlife' (which was interpreted as only vertebrates) the 1969 law included any wild mammal, fish, wild bird, amphibian, reptile, mollusk, or crustacean."[15(p.300)] Further, procedures for identifying and listing animals as endangered were more fully developed, and the government's land acquisition authority was expanded. The ESCA resulted in the Convention on International Trade in Endangered Species of Wild Fauna and Flora, which was responsible for treaties banning the international trade in endangered species.[16–18]

The further refined **Endangered Species Act of 1973 (ESA)** is perhaps the most comprehensive environmental protection legislation in the world. Section 4 of the ESA directs the Fish and Wildlife Service (FWS) and the National Marine Fisheries Service (NMFS) to develop recovery plans for any listed species.[19] Section 7 of the legislation applies the provisions of the act to federal government agencies, and section 9 applies them to individuals and private landowners. Section 11 contains the ESA's enforcement provisions, including provisions for both civil and criminal penalties if any part of the ESA is violated. The law allows for forfeiture of any item used to aid in the commission of a violation of the act.[20]

The Secretary of the Interior, through the FWS, and the Secretary of Commerce, through the NMFS, are responsible, under section 4 of the ESA, "for listing any species, subspecies, or 'distinct population' that is endangered or threatened."[21(p.322)] The FWS (or the NMFS for marine animals) must publish "notices of review" that identify species being considered as candidates. The notice for a given species seeks biological information to complete the status review for that species.[22] The listing is to be based on scientific information and is intended to be unaffected by economic or political considerations. No limitations or timelines were imposed on decisions to list a species.[23]

Once a species has been chosen for listing, the FWS publishes a proposed rule in the *Federal Register*. At this stage, any interested parties are encouraged to comment and submit additional information. All information received in the form of public comments is considered in the final rule-making process.

> Within one year of when a listing proposal is published, one of three possible courses of action must be taken:
> 1. A final listing is published (as proposed or revised);
> 2. If the biological information then on hand does not support the listing, the proposal is withdrawn; or
> 3. If, at the end of one year, there is substantial disagreement within the scientific community concerning the biological appropriateness of the listing, the proposal may be extended, but only for an additional six months. After that, a decision must be made on the basis of the best scientific information available.[24(p.70)]

Emergency provisions exist, which allow an immediate listing of a species for up to 240 days while the normal process is taking place. Once a species is listed, prohibitions against harming the species are imposed on both the federal government (via section 7) and any person subject to U.S. jurisdiction (via section 9).[25]

The FWS has the responsibility to develop **species recovery plans** for endangered and threatened species. The intent of the ESA is to protect species until their numbers grow large enough that they can maintain themselves without the aid of the ESA provisions.

MIXED REVIEWS FOR THE ESA

The ESA and other laws like it have met with mixed acceptance, and in some cases have sparked heated conflicts. Some increases in the numbers of endangered or threatened populations are attributable to the environmental protection legislation. The California condor,[26] the bald eagle,[27] the timber wolf,[28] and the American alligator[29] are only a few of the species whose numbers have increased largely because of the ESA. When the ESA works, people are generally pleased. But when the ESA interferes with land use and individual rights, it makes headline news.

Certain Problems with the Endangered Species Act

The controversy over the northern spotted owl received national attention after a 1986 Audubon report documented decreasing numbers.[30] Soon after, the spotted owl was "listed" as endangered under the Endangered Species Act. In 1991 U.S. District Court Judge William Dwyer banned most logging in Oregon and Washington to ensure survival of the estimated 3,000 owl pairs. Protecting its habitat meant the owl had a better chance for survival; it also meant disaster for the timber industry.[31] The controversy in the Pacific Northwest over the northern spotted owl, with environmentalists pitted against loggers, has been in the news for several years, but it is not the only dispute that has erupted as a result of species protection legislation. Consider some of these less familiar cases.

In 1991, the Mountain Lion Protection Act was passed in California. Opponents of the act claim that California's lion population has since exploded from about 2,500 to between 6,000 and 8,000.[32] Prior to passage, the only known attack on humans happened in 1911, but encounters between humans and mountain lions, some of which have proven fatal for the humans, are now on the increase.[33] In large part owing to lawsuits pending against the state (and an award of $2 million to the parents of a five-year-old girl mauled in a public park), a bill to overturn the Mountain Lion Preservation Act was introduced into California's legislature.[34] Although the repeal of the legislation did not pass, animal rights groups were outraged. Currently, public education programs are being developed to educate people about how to live safely with the mountain lion.

In another example, sea lions, a protected species since 1972, are eating the seriously endangered steelhead trout.[35] Despite its best efforts (e.g., shooting the sea lions with rubber-tipped arrows and feeding them bad-tasting fish), the state has been unable to protect the steelhead, whose numbers have decreased significantly since the mid-1980s. As a result, a team of veterinarians, marine mammal caretakers, and federal and state marine mammal biologists have developed guidelines to solve the problem. The NMFS has given the state permission to target predatory sea lions for execution if they have a demonstrated history of eating steelhead.[36] The sea lion generally wait for the fish as they pass through the fish ladder at the Ballard locks in Puget Sound on their way to Lake Washington, where they go to spawn. Because the numbers of steelhead trout have fallen so drastically, federal officials have said they cannot continue to experiment with possible solutions; they must take action. Some argue that the steelhead are easy prey because they have difficulty finding the fish ladder at the locks. Opponents of the NMFS response identify the poorly engineered fish ladder as the primary problem, not the sea lions. They argue the state must find another alternative for protecting the endangered fish.[37]

In other parts of the West, the prairie dog has been getting attention. While some argue these animals are integral to the ecosystem of the prairie, others think they are a pest. Ecologists, aware that the prairie dog has never been extremely popular, are warning that prairie dog colonies and the ecosystems they support may be at risk.[38] It appears that those leading protection efforts will have their work cut out for them. In Wyoming, landowners are free to "shoot, poison, or firebomb prairie dogs at will," according to Bob Luce, a biologist at the Wyoming Game and Fish Department.[39] In fact, some ranchers invite gun enthusiasts onto their land to shoot prairie dogs. The activities are so popular, ranchers can charge up to $160 for the opportunity to shoot. Called "prairie dog derbies," they are day-long shooting competitions intended to boost tourism and attract revenue.[40] With losses sometimes amounting to nearly 1,000 animals per derby, the reaction to these events is mixed. In some circles, people express dismay or alarm; in others, people celebrate the "catch of the day."

Beware: Civil and Criminal Penalties May Apply

In some cases, endangered species protection is aggressively enforced. As has been discussed throughout this text, many factors will determine the course of an enforcement action. Take the example of the bald eagle. The fine for the illegal killing, possession, or sale of a bald eagle can run as high as $500,000, and the accused violator can be sentenced for up to five years in prison for each offense. Enforcement agents have used section 11 of the Endangered Species Act to prosecute violators to the fullest extent allowed by law. Consider some of the following examples of individual criminal charges assigned for ESA violations.[41]

A newly introduced participant in the Yellowstone wolf restoration project was killed in April 1995. Known to the researchers who studied him as Arnold, he was an alpha male, or leader of his wolf pack. Arnold's killer decapitated and skinned him, hid his carcass, and threw his radio collar into a creek. Surprisingly, a hunter who witnessed the killing contacted local officials. Upon receiving the name of the perpetrator, the federal authorities searched the home of the accused and found Arnold's head and pelt. The man confessed to shooting the wolf but pled not guilty to violating the Endangered Species Act. A federal court jury in Billings, Montana, disagreed, finding the man guilty of killing, possessing, and transporting a wolf. He faced a maximum penalty of $150,000 fine and two years in jail.

In another case involving an endangered species, an immigrant to America was charged with killing Tipton kangaroo rats and destroying 330 acres of their habitat. The story got huge press coverage, much of which is argued to be false or exaggerated, and many people rallied to the man's defense. The media reports suggested this man was new to this country, barely spoke English, and had no idea his property was listed as a natural habitat for the Tipton kangaroo rat. Conservative political commentator Rush Limbaugh even entered the conflict, demanding support for humans and jobs over animals.

But according to court documents the reality was quite different. The accused immigrant was far from poor and had bank accounts totaling more than $2 million. Further, he was reported to be a fugitive from his native land who had fled outstanding indictments of fraud and inflicting bodily injury. Finally, on at least four separate occasions over a period of more than two years, federal officials documented encounters in which they told him he needed to file incidental-take permits for the three endangered species living on his property before proceeding with plans for the property's development. After wildlife enforcement officers observed continued plowing of the critical habitat, a search warrant was obtained, the man was arrested, and his tractor was seized in a final effort to enforce the ESA mandates. In this case, the charges were dropped, on the condition the man get the proper permits and donate $5,000 to habitat protection in the country.

In Nebraska, wildlife service special agents report lots of support for protection efforts. One story reflects this support. An all-terrain vehicle (ATV) operator destroyed nesting colonies of endangered least terns and threatened piping plover colonies near Columbus. The nesting colonies were well posted, and local residents who had adopted the birds were watching them with spotting scopes at the time. Approximately 15 people volunteered to testify for the prosecution. A description of the driver and the vehicle was given to local officials. Under Nebraska's new nongame and endangered species law, the offender was fined $500 and was made to relinquish his ATV to the Nebraska Game and Parks Commission.

As indicated earlier, ESA sanctions apply not only to private citizens but also to government employees. The U.S. Department of Defense (DOD) manages more than 25 million acres of land nationwide.[42] DOD is thought to have "more endangered species per acre than any other federal land management agency."[43(p.11)] Recently, three civilian Army employees at Fort Benning were charged with conspiracy to violate the Endangered Species Act—a felony. They had designated for clear-cut logging pine forests that included habitat for the endangered red-cockaded woodpecker.[44] In a 1994 case in Hampton, Virginia, a commander and another officer at Fort Monroe were officially reprimanded. They had ordered base workers to destroy yellow-crowned night heron nests. While the birds are not endangered, they are protected under the Migratory Bird Treaty Act.[45]

These formal sanctions have outraged many. Senator Jesse Helms (R-NC) and others argue that military bases should not be held to the requirements of the ESA—matters of national security should supersede such a law. Others suggest that the amount of DOD land and the number of species on DOD land make military installations the perfect place for research and conservation efforts.

Public Use of Private Land

The examples presented above are only a few of the controversies caused by the ESA. Should anyone be upset by entrepreneurs who make money on their own land by hosting prairie dog derbies? What about (nonhuman) animal rights? Protected plants? The impact of the ESA—on both intentional and unintentional violators—seems to be too much for many to accept, and while some people have expressed concern about the actions taken to protect animals, others are concerned about the designations of land as critical habitat.

The main question concerns the right of individuals to do whatever they choose with the property they own. A growing number of property rights activists argue that private landowners face unjust government regulation as a result of the ESA. Two integral terms lie at the core of this conflict: *takings* and *harm*.

Takings

Section 9 of the ESA prohibits any person from importing, exporting, *taking*, possessing, selling, delivering, carrying, transporting, or receiving any endangered species of fish or wildlife.[46] The legislation further states that to *commit a taking* is to "harass, harm, pursue, hunt, shoot, wound, kill, trap, capture or collect" a species.[47] The ESA expressly prohibits any actions covered by the term *taking* as defined above. Therefore, by law landowners cannot take an endangered species. This means they cannot harass, harm, pursue, capture, or collect an endangered species, or they would be guilty of committing a violation of federal law—the ESA. Consequently, if a landowner finds an endangered species on part of his or her property, he or she cannot proceed with plans for the land inconsistent with the regulations outlined in section 9 of the ESA. In short, the land cannot be used for any commercial purposes, because it must remain intact to preserve the endangered species.

Be advised, the taking of an endangered species should not be confused with the Takings Clause of the U.S. Constitution. The Takings Clause says private property cannot be taken for public use without just compensation to the owner of that property. Opponents of the designation of land as critical habitat argue that in fact this is what is happening under the ESA. They claim the federal government is using their land without offering adequate (or any) compensation. Further, landowners have suggested that they be allowed to do what they want to with their land as long as they do not seek to *harm* any endangered species. So, the definitional question has shifted from discussions about what constitutes a taking, to discussions about what constitutes harm inflicted on an endangered species population. Legal controversy ensued.

Harm and the 1995 U.S. Supreme Court Decision

On June 29, 1995, the U.S. Supreme Court ruled on the use of the term *harm*. Property owners suggested that Congress's intent in framing the ESA was misinterpreted by the Department of the Interior when Secretary Babbitt argued habitat destruction would constitute a harm. Timber officials, for example, claimed that, while the law clearly prohibits them from killing protected species, it does not prevent them from pursuing activities, like logging, that would only indirectly inflict harm on creatures living in the forest, endangered or not. The question revolved around habitat destruction. They argued if a company harvested timber, but left species living in those trees untouched, then there could be no commission of harm.

The Secretary of the Interior, through the director of FWS, disagreed: "Harm in the definition of 'take' in the Act means an act which actually kills or injures wildlife. Such an act may include significant habitat modification or degradation where it actually kills or injures wildlife by impairing essential behavioral patterns, including breeding, feeding, or shelter."[48(p.72)]

The Court supported the interpretation of the Interior Department. In a six-to-three ruling, it "found that the plain meaning of the act's words and its ambitious goal of preventing extinctions justified the regulations that the Interior Department issued to enforce it."[49(p.A14)] The Court also stated that "the Secretary of the Interior reasonably construed Congress' intent when he defined 'harm' under the Endangered Species Act to include habitat modification."[50(p.1)]

Babbitt v. Sweet Home Chapter of Communities for a Great Oregon[51] was identified as a win for environmentalists. *Harm* was not to be limited to direct action against a species but rather would include actions that indirectly reduce its chance of survival. Many hoped the Court's decision would resolve much of the existing controversy surrounding the 23-year-old ESA. Yet some of the biggest problems remain.

ECONOMIC CONFLICT RESULTS IN POLITICAL FIRESTORM

Given the intent and scope of the ESA, much has been accomplished, and several influential groups of scientists have come out in support of the act. The National Academy of Sciences, for example, issued a report in May 1995 giving the act "high marks."[52] Many agree, however, that elements of the ESA need attention. If certain individuals are bearing an unjust burden, something must change. Not allowing someone to fully explore potential property uses might result in a significant economic loss.

No dispute reflects the core of the ESA controversy like the conflict in the Pacific Northwest over the northern spotted owl. Yet the history of this dispute is full of surprises. Because of the restrictions placed on logging, economic devastation was predicted for the Northwest. But recent news reports suggest the forecasted devastation simply did not occur.[53] Local economies that once relied exclusively on timber have diversified and become stronger as a result. Further, some economists suggest the recent economic boom in the Northwest is partly due to the environmental regulations.[54] Adding to the surprises were the findings of a study designed to measure the economic impact of the ESA. Conducted by a political science professor at the Massachusetts Institute of Technology (MIT), the study's "premise was that if the act hampers growth, then the economies of states with the largest share of the country's 955 species listed as endangered or threatened should have fared the worst."[55(p.13)] In short, the findings "strongly contradict" the idea that the ESA has a harmful effect on state economies, even at the county level.

Yet the surprises do not stop there. Recent research has suggested the spotted owl might not be endangered after all.[56] Population estimates for the species have more than doubled from the initial estimates.[57] Further, preliminary genetic tests suggest no significant differences exist between the genetic composition of the California spotted owl and Mexican spotted owl and the northern spotted owl. The number of spotted owls in total exceeds the number necessary for the birds to thrive.[58]

Critics argue the owl, endangered or not, has come to represent the need for preserving "old-growth" forests, not the spotted owl,[59,60] because much of the conflict is related to the destruction of critical habitat. Due to concern over the owl, strict limits were placed on the amount of timber that could be harvested from public lands. Much of the land involved in the spotted owl dispute is federally owned land. Sources suggest "the federal government will lose $20 billion in timber sales, and home buyers will lose billions more because the resulting timber shortage helped to double raw timber prices."[61(p.82)]

At the onset of the controversy, many timber companies hired wildlife biologists to carry out their own studies of the spotted owl. In some cases, these studies turned up several sightings of the spotted owl in regions where the birds were not expected. Contrary to their initial objective, to find enough spotted owls to prove the species did not need protection, their efforts had the opposite effect. Gregg Easterbrook relates the story of one wildlife biologist who found so many owls that his employer had to "file plans that placed about 50,000 additional acres into pure preservation status, and further restricted company logging since tree harvests that might 'take' a spotted owl are essentially forbidden even on private land."[62](p.211)

ESA restrictions on what people can do with their own land have created a backlash. Robert H. Nelson argues the backlash is "becoming as dangerous to endangered species as any amount of tree-cutting."[63](p.82) Nelson describes farmers and other landowners stripping out every trace of wildlife habitat to prevent finding an endangered species and consequently reducing their land use options. The phenomenon he describes as "shoot, shovel, and shutup" is destroying both species and habitat.[64]

The critical issues in the spotted owl debate, as with all other environmental issues, are more complicated than can be represented in a 60-second sound bite. Other explanations have been offered for the measured decline of spotted owls in the Northwest. For example, **clear-cutting** was legalized for use on Forest Service land in 1976. Referring to an Oregon State University Master's thesis that identified a decline in spotted owls due to habitat loss, some have argued that the forest harvesting practice of clear-cutting could account for the noted decline in Northwest owl populations. Clear-cutting is the removal of all trees in a tract of land, with no consideration given to size or species. Because this practice leaves the land without any vegetation, the risk of erosion becomes greater. "Though clear-cutting can be defended in a few circumstances, selection logging and the related shelter-cutting, in which trees are removed in clumps so the forest canopy remains, are generally superior both for the habitat preservation and sustained timber income."[65](p.26) One issue that needs to be decided soon is which objective is at the heart of the conflict—the protection of the owls or the old-growth forest.

The controversy surrounding the northern spotted owl reflects a fundamental difference separating ESA supporters and opponents: the relative importance of short-term economic gain versus long-term protection of an endangered ecosystem. Traditionally, blatant economic interests have rarely found a foothold in species protection debates. One of the first cases was in 1978, when a nearly completed **Tellico Dam** project was halted by a Supreme Court order because of concern about the impact of the dam on the tiny snail darter fish.[66] Commercial fishing on the Snake and Columbia Rivers has been virtually destroyed as a result of dam construction (for hydroelectric power).[67] The salmon fishing industry used to see annual profits greater than $60 million, but since the first major hydroelectric dam was built more than 50 years ago, the annual run of salmon has declined from more than 10 million fish to around 2.5 million,[68] and the salmon populations are endangered.[69]

Is the ESA about economics or politics? The MIT professor discussed earlier who conducted a scientific study to determine the economic impact of the ESA argued the conflict is entirely political. The strongest scientific data, he asserted, could not persuade some policy makers of the merits of the ESA.[70] Public policy is ruled by anecdotes, stories of individual experiences—the flashier the better.

In fact, politics at the federal level in 1995 looked more like a collage of environmental and antienvironmental activity. After the Republicans emerged victorious in the 1994 elections and assumed power in the House and Senate, concern about the future of environmental protection legislation mounted. Yet party lines were not so clearly drawn. In September 1995, legislation was introduced to overhaul the ESA.[71,72] In March 1995, the Senate passed an amendment suspending funding for any prospective or new listing under the ESA.[73] For 13 months the mandatory moratorium was in effect. Senator Kay Bailey Hutchinson (R-TX), sponsor of the moratorium amendment, suggested the action was necessary to "strike a balance between the need to preserve species, and to protect private property rights of private land owners."[74(p.12)] In April 1996, Congress lifted the ban, but the EPA's operating budget had been reduced.[75,76] Legislative efforts to retract the ESA were met with a degree of opposition that surprised many—especially the authors of the legislation.[77]

THE FUTURE OF ENDANGERED SPECIES PROTECTION EFFORTS

In the final analysis, total agreement can be reached on one thing: the ESA has had a colorful history. Yet most believe the ESA is in need of revision. Unfortunately, the current political climate has increased the uncertainty of future outcomes of any legislative revision. When revisions are suggested, significant conflicts erupt. A middle ground seems nonexistent. Despite this, I conclude with a presentation of various recommendations for the improvement of the ESA.

"Sensible species protection" should include three elements.[78] First, the problem of endangered species protection should be treated as a federal problem (state boundaries and endangered ecosystem boundaries do not often coincide). Second, because not every species can be saved, a system of priorities must be developed to determine which ecosystems are most important to humans and what the cost will be for their protection. Third, the ESA should include ways of compensating landowners who find endangered species on their land (e.g., tax breaks or land swaps).

In fact, the Clinton administration is exploring more creative interpretations of the ESA and attempting to discover viable compromises for owners of private land who support endangered populations. By preparing a **Habitat-Conservation Plan (HCP)**, a landowner agrees to undertake or underwrite habitat restoration elsewhere. An **incidental take permit** provision, added in the 1982 revisions to the ESA, allows a landowner to pursue a proposed course of action if the secretary finds that the take will be incidental and will not appreciably reduce the species' chances for survival and recovery in the wild.[79] Further, the secretary has been employing the "threatened" classification more than the "endangered" classification because the former allows more managerial discretion. Finally, the Department of the Interior is exploring federal-state cooperative agreements outlined in section 6(c).[80] An example is the "Safe Harbor" program. If a landowner agrees to create a new habitat for an endangered species, the landowner can do anything he or she chooses with the new habitat created.[81] The landowner's only obligation is to maintain the original habitat for the original species. The purpose of such programs is to provide landowners options when it comes to addressing the endangered species occupying their land. Safe Harbor seeks voluntary cooperation from private landowners in improving the habitats of endangered species. In return, landowners are protected from any additional legal liability in the future.

Another recommendation is to ensure the separation of science and politics. Because the ESA involves a two-step process (a scientific assessment to determine the status of a species and the development of a plan for recovery), the scientific assessment must take priority over political bickering.[82] In addition, the federal funds needed to ensure the ESA is administered as it was intended must be allocated. The legislation cannot be as effective as intended if it is not fully funded.[83] Finally, it may be worthwhile to revisit and improve the regulations governing the law's implementation procedures.[84]

The National Research Council of the National Academy of Science offered an overall positive review of the legislation, arguing it to be "well founded in science."[85(p.1124)] The council, however, suggested the process for designating land as a critical habitat is simply too long. It called for "immediate establishment of smaller, interim habitats until larger areas can be secured."[86(p.1124)] It also advised the use of models of ecosystem dynamics that have been developed since passage of the original ESA. Models of ecosystem dynamics are used to predict risks of extinction under a variety of conditions.[87] Finally, it recommended that additional biodiversity management programs be created. Species protection would be "more efficient" if entire ecosystems were protected rather than focusing efforts on the saving of individual species.[88]

The controversy over the ESA has reached an all-time high. The recommendations for revision presented above are based on the assumption that it would be better to tinker with rather than completely overhaul the existing legislation. As Leopold might have suggested, intelligent tinkering is the first step toward ensuring the preservation of many endangered species well into the future.

REVIEW QUESTIONS

1. Identify the three primary statutes directed toward species protection.
2. What is the process of identifying and classifying an endangered species?
3. What is a recovery plan? Who authorizes a recovery plan and how is the plan's success or failure measured?
4. Many are familiar with the controversy surrounding efforts to protect the northern spotted owl. Identify at least three problems associated with endangered species protection.
5. Many arguments have been presented to show that environmental protection legislation can negatively affect the economy of a particular area. What is one argument that environmental regulations generally benefit the economy of a region?
6. What is the difference between a constitutional taking and a taking under the Endangered Species Act?
7. Identify the central issue in the spotted owl controversy. Does it matter whether the controversy is focused on owls or old-growth forests? Please explain your response.

DISCUSSION QUESTIONS

1. Directly involved in the ESA conflict is a debate about jobs versus the environment. What position do you take in this debate? Please explain your position.
2. What arguments can be made for imposing criminal sanctions for violations of the Endangered Species Act? Do you agree or disagree with the application of criminal penalties for such violations? Justify your response.
3. Should military bases and other Department of Defense property be exempt from compliance with environmental protection legislation? Outline each side of this controversy.

4. Should the constitutional takings provision be applied to private land that harbors an endangered species? Explain.
5. Has the time for endangered species protection passed? What evidence would you use to support each side of this question?

REFERENCES

1. "An Issue That Deserves Special Notice," *National Wildlife* 30, no. 3 (1992): 3.
2. D. Chadwick, "Dead or Alive: The Endangered Species Act," *National Geographic*, March 1995, 7–9.
3. D. Chadwick, "Strength in Humility: The Endangered Species Act Calls upon Us To Grow up and Share the Neighborhood," *Sierra*, January-February 1996, 46.
4. Chadwick, "Strength in Humility," 46.
5. Fish and Wildlife Service of the U.S. Department of the Interior, "The Endangered Species Program," *Congressional Digest* 54, no. 1 (1996): 69–71.
6. Fish and Wildlife Service of the U.S. Department of the Interior, "The Endangered Species Program," 71.
7. Chadwick, "Dead or Alive," 9.
8. Fish and Wildlife Service of the U.S. Department of the Interior, "The Endangered Species Program," 71.
9. T.H. Watkins, "What Is Wrong with the Endangered Species Act?" *Audubon*, January-February 1996, 36–41.
10. W.E. Scott, *Silent Wings: A Memorial to the Passenger Pigeon* (Madison, WI: Wisconsin Society for Ornithology, 1947), 39.
11. A. Gidari, "Endangered Species Act: Impact of Section 9 on Private Landowners," *Environmental Law* 24 (1994): 444–453.
12. J.V. Switzer, *Environmental Politics: Domestic and Global Dimensions* (New York: St. Martin's Press, 1994), 300.
13. Endangered Species Protection Act of 1966, Pub. L. No. 89-669, 80 Stat. 926 (repealed 1973), §1(b).
14. Switzer, *Environmental Politics*, 300.
15. Switzer, *Environmental Politics*, 300.
16. The Endangered Species Conservation Act of 1969, Pub. L. No. 91-135, 83 Stat. 275 (repealed by ESA of 1973, §14, 87 Stat. 884, 903).
17. The Convention on International Trade in Endangered Species of Wild Fauna and Flora, March 3, 1973, 27 U.S.T. 1087, 993 U.N.T.S. 243. The United States ratified the convention on September 13, 1973.
18. Gidari, "Endangered Species Act," 448.
19. Endangered Species Act of 1973, 16 U.S.C. §1533(f)(1988).
20. Gidari, "Endangered Species Act," 453.
21. W.W. Stelle, "Major Issues in Reauthorization of the Endangered Species Act," *Environmental Law* 24 (1994): 321–328.
22. "The Endangered Species Program: Implementation of the ESA," *Congressional Digest*, March 1996, 69–71.

23. Switzer, *Environmental Politics*, 302.
24. "The Endangered Species Program: Implementation of the ESA," 70.
25. Endangered Species Act of 1973, 16 U.S.C. §1538(a).
26. T. Wilkinson, "Homecoming," *National Parks*, May-June 1996, 40–45.
27. L.S. Walters, "Bald Eagles Soar Again over Mighty Mississippi," *Christian Science Monitor*, 28 February 1996, 3.
28. L. Line, "The Endangered Timber Wolf Makes a Surprising Comeback: Left To Help Itself to a Natural Habitat, a Species Flourishes," *New York Times*, 25 December 1995, C4.
29. S. Milius and D. Johnson, "Where Would They Be without the Law?" *National Wildlife*, April-May 1992, 50–59.
30. "Report on the Advising Panel on the Spotted Owl," National Audubon Society, 1986. Cited in Easterbrook, G., *A Moment on the Earth: The Coming Age of Environmental Optimism*, (New York: Viking Penguin, 1995), 212.
31. G. Easterbrook, "The Birds," *The New Republic*, 28 March 1994, 27.
32. T. Sanders, "California's Lion-Protection Law Ought To Be Caged," *Christian Science Monitor*, 7 August 1995, 19.
33. Sanders, "California's Lion-Protection Law Ought To Be Caged."
34. Sanders, "California's Lion-Protection Law Ought To Be Caged."
35. B. Fisher, "Get Tough Tactics for Saving Trout," *Christian Science Monitor*, 22 March 1996, 3.
36. Fisher, "Get Tough Tactics for Saving Trout."
37. Fisher, "Get Tough Tactics for Saving Trout."
38. J. Lloyd, "The Prairie-Dog Divide: To Reduce or Protect?" *Christian Science Monitor*, 8 May 1996, 3.
39. Lloyd, "Prairie-Dog Divide."
40. Lloyd, "Prairie-Dog Divide."
41. The stories about Arnold, the Tipton kangaroo rats, and the nesting colonies in Nebraska are included in T. Williams, "Defense of the Realm: Is the Endangered Species Act Really Working? Ask the Public Servants Trying To Enforce It in the Cantankerous West," *Sierra*, January-February, 34–39, 121–122.
42. J. Cohn, "New Defenders of Wildlife," *BioScience* 46, no. 1 (1996): 11–14.
43. Cohn, "New Defenders of Wildlife," 11.
44. Cohn, "New Defenders of Wildlife," 12.
45. Cohn, "New Defenders of Wildlife."
46. Gidari, "Endangered Species Act," 452.
47. Endangered Species Act Amendments of 1978, Pub. L. No. 95-632, 92 Stat. 3751 (1978) (codified at 16 U.S.C. §1532(5)(A)(i) (1988)), §3(14), 1973 U.S.C.C.A.N. at 982.
48. "Habitat Modification and the Endangered Species Act: The *Sweet Home* Decision," Congressional Research Service report, *Congressional Digest* 75, no. 3 (1996): 72, 96.
49. J.H. Cushman, "Endangered Species: Environmentalists Win Victory, but Action by Congress May Interrupt the Celebration," *New York Times*, 30 June 1995, A14.
50. *Babbitt v. Sweet Home Chapter of Communities for a Greater Oregon*, No. 94-859, argued 4/17/95, decided 6/29/95.

51. 1995 West Law 382088 (U.S.), p. 1.

52. E. Pennisi, "Report Backs Endangered Species Act," *Science* 286 (1995): 1124.

53. D. Lick, "Having Owls and Jobs Too: In the State Where Protection of the Northern Spotted Owl Was Supposed To Destroy Jobs, a Booming Economy Debunks the 'Owl-vs-Jobs' Premise," *National Wildlife*, August-September 1995, 8–13.

54. Lick, "Having Owls and Jobs Too."

55. D. Brittan, "Defending an Endangered Act," *Technology Review*, August-September 1995, 13–15.

56. Easterbrook, "The Birds," 22.

57. R.H. Nelson, "Shoot, Shovel, and Shut Up," *Forbes*, 4 December 1995, 82.

58. Nelson, "Shoot, Shovel, and Shut Up."

59. Easterbrook, "The Birds," 22–29.

60. Nelson, "Shoot, Shovel, and Shut Up."

61. Nelson, "Shoot, Shovel and Shut Up," 82.

62. G. Easterbrook, *A Moment on the Earth*, 211–227.

63. Nelson, "Shoot, Shovel and Shut Up," 82.

64. Nelson, "Shoot, Shovel and Shut Up."

65. Easterbrook, "The Birds," 26. Easterbrook refers to Eric Forsman, an Oregon State graduate student who wrote his Master's thesis on spotted owls and made the claim that the owls were declining because of habitat loss. Easterbrook revisits several elements of Forsman's work in his article.

66. *Tennessee Valley Authority v. Hill*, 437 U.S. 153 (1978).

67. J. Ogan, "The Need for a Smolt Travel Time Objective in the Columbia Basin Fish and Wildlife Program To Protect and Restore the Northwest's Imperiled Salmon Runs," *Environmental Law* 24 (1994): 673–716.

68. J. Adler and Mary Hager, "How Much Is a Species Worth?" *National Wildlife*, April-May 1992, 8–10.

69. Adler and Hager, "How Much Is a Species Worth?"

70. Brittan, "Defending an Endangered Act," 14.

71. "Watch on Congress: Species Act's Provisions Endangered?" *Charlotte Observer*, 8 September 1995.

72. W. Kosova, "Ways To Skin the Act," *Audubon*, January-February 1996, 43–45.

73. A. Cockburn, "End of an Environmental Era," *The Nation*, 17 April 1995, 516.

74. E. Stern, "Endangered Species List: Extinct?" *Mother Earth News*, August-September, 12–13.

75. " . . . and an Endangered Species List," *Science News*, 11 May 1996, 297.

76. "The Government Ended a 13-Month Congressional Moratorium," *Christian Science Monitor*, 22 May 1996, 2.

77. Kosova, "Ways To Skin the Act," 45.

78. "Sensible Species Protection," *Christian Science Monitor*, 6 July 1995, 20.

79. R. Meltz, "Where the Wild Things Are: The Endangered Species Act and Private Property," *Environmental Law* 24 (1994): 369–417.

80. Meltz, "Where the Wild Things Are."
81. T. Williams, "Finding Safe Harbor," *Audubon*, January-February, 26–27.
82. C.C. Mann and M.L. Plummer, "Endangered Species Act: Finding a Better Balance," *Christian Science Monitor*, 31 July 1995, 19.
83. Mann and Plummer, "Endangered Species Act."
84. A. Easter-Pilcher, "Implementing the Endangered Species Act," *BioScience* 46 (1996): 355–363.
85. Pennisi, "Report Backs Endangered Species Act," 1124.
86. Pennisi, "Report Backs Endangered Species Act," 1124.
87. Pennisi, "Report Backs Endangered Species Act."
88. Pennisi, "Report Backs Endangered Species Act."

Environmental Crimes at the U.S.-Mexico Border

Mark J. Spalding and Richard G. Opper

TERMS   anencephaly
Border Environment Cooperation Commission
Commission for Environmental Cooperation
environmental media
ISO 14000
La Paz Agreement

Law of Ecological Equilibrium
Mutual Legal Assistance Treaty
NADBank
nongovernmental organizations
PROFEPA
SEDESOL
SEMARNAP

Crimes against the environment know no borders. Chemical spills or unregulated emissions are subject to the laws of nature, not of man. While this is true of environmental crimes everywhere, criminal enforcement is essentially an extension of the sovereign authority (also called police power) of states and nations. This case study focuses on environmental crimes as seen through the eyes of two prosecuting authorities based in southern California. Its purpose is to illustrate how U.S. statutes are used in criminal enforcement proceedings for environmental crimes along the 2,000-mile U.S.-Mexico border and how the statutory and border realities affect that enterprise.

THE ENVIRONMENTAL CONTEXT OF THE BORDER

Historically, many diverse interactions between Mexico and the United States have established the tone for relations between the two countries. An agreement in the 1960s resulted in an integrated work program shared across the border. As recently as 1983, an agreement between the presidents of both countries, the La Paz Agreement, attempted to establish guidelines for binational cooperation between the United States and Mexico. In 1988, increasing numbers of environmental issues prompted Mexico to adopt the Law of Ecological Equilibrium. Finally, when Mexico and the United States were negotiating the conditions for NAFTA, three new international bodies were created to address the environmental issues. These issues will be discussed in more specific detail below.

The North American Free Trade Agreement (The Maquiladora Industry)

Any discussion of environmental crime at the border has to begin with an understanding of environmental conditions generally. The border region of both countries was initially an arid, sparsely populated area poor in critical water resources. The border began on its present course with the creation of the maquiladora (or twin plant) program first adopted by Mexico in the mid-1960s. The theory behind the maquiladora program was to afford an opportunity for foreign manufacturers to import raw materials into Mexico "in bond" free from customs, duties, or tariffs. The raw materials were then transformed through manufacturing operations, which historically were labor intensive. Finished products were then shipped back to the twin plant on the other side of the border for packaging, distribution, and sale. The entire process took place without customs, duties, or taxes being imposed by either country. Eventually the program became so successful that over 2,000 maquiladora operations existed by the 1990s.

This growth created an economic incentive for workers looking for steady wages from the interior and southern areas of Mexico to move to the border. Tens of thousands of people came to the northern border area in search of economic advancement. Unfortunately, the communities to which they migrated became crowded before they had an opportunity to develop the necessary infrastructure to support the population growth. In addition, the industrialization of the border region created pollution problems. Industrial activity produced substantial industrial waste, and the new inhabitants required additional resources and created additional human waste. Solid and liquid waste disposal, sanitation, and industrial discharge became important issues and attracted the attention of both national governments. As a result, in 1983, President Reagan met with President De La Madrid in La Paz, a town in Baja California, to execute what has become the historic **La Paz Agreement**. The La Paz Agreement was essentially a framework for binational cooperation. It provided a protocol for solving problems as they emerged through the adoption of what were known as "annexes" dealing with specific environmental problems related to the border area.

The 1983 La Paz Agreement

There is a question whether the La Paz Agreement qualifies as a treaty. Essentially an agreement between the presidents of the two nations, it has never been ratified by the U.S. Congress, as provided for in the Constitution. Nonetheless, both nations have observed its provisions, and it has provided a framework for binational cooperation for almost 15 years. With the growth of the maquiladora industry, questions arose about how to properly handle the waste products that were created by the manufacturing processes. Mexican law (not the La Paz Agreement) requires that waste products created from the maquiladora operations be repatriated back to the United States. Annex III of the La Paz Agreement now requires that the exporting nation notify the receiving nation of any transboundary shipments of hazardous waste. These requirements are implemented by regulations promulgated by the U.S. Environmental Protection Agency (EPA). Failure to notify the receiving nation with appropriate documentation of the repatriated waste can constitute a federal or state crime, depending on the type of waste materials and the amount being repatriated.

As a consequence of the adoption of these importation rules, a variety of practical considerations evolved in a short period of time. The need for binational forms and manifests persists through the present. Documents that in Mexico are called *guía ecológica* have different names and contain different information north of the border. Facilities to act as hazardous waste transfer stations, trucks designed for specific transportation needs, and people trained to handle hazardous waste are needed as new challenges for businesses working in the border region are introduced.

The 1988 Law of Ecological Equilibrium

Environmental issues continue to expand in importance in Mexico as well as in the United States. In 1988, Mexico adopted a national law called the **Law of Ecological Equilibrium**. Reflecting Mexico's increasing concern with environmental matters within its borders, this law was intended to have a comprehensive impact on all **environmental media**—air, water, and land—and led to the adoption of environmental regulations that, while sporadic at first, now fill volumes. The law also provided for the potential criminalization of environmental activities in Mexico.

Because of the Mexican legal system, where due process regulations are quite different from those in the United States, the law also provided for immediate administrative sanctions against companies that violate Mexican law within Mexican territory. It is possible for a Mexican regulator to visit a facility, find an infraction, and immediately close the facility for an indefinite period of time. Reopening the facility would depend on the facility's ability to correct the problem or enter into a contract with regulatory authorities for a plan to correct the problem.

NAFTA

Despite the many legislative enactments that occurred on both sides of the border, the need for trained regulators, enforcement agents, and a better understanding and communication of regulations was readily apparent to those who trafficked the border on a daily basis. Environmental issues were not declining but gaining in importance. The problems on the border were gaining recognition in both nations as constituting a significant challenge, for which Band-Aid solutions would be ineffective. Further, it did not appear the economic growth in the area resulted in any additional financial resources to be used in addressing the problems. Within this context, the proposal by the two nations to enter into a free-trade agreement sparked heated debate on environmental matters as they related to border activities and business.

When the countries began to negotiate the agreement that is now known as NAFTA, environmental concerns were driving the debate about the agreement and impacting the possibility of its very existence. In addition, the phenomenon of **nongovernmental organizations** (NGOs), which had long been an important aspect of U.S. environmental policy development, was readily transplanted to Mexico. The growth of NGOs was unprecedented and remarkable. It has often been remarked that NGOs led to the increasing use of criminal remedies for environmental violations within the United States, and the same has been true on the border. NGO reaction to tragedies such as the discovery of clusters of babies with **anencephaly** resulted in an outcry that caused investigations and ultimately the inception of civil and criminal litigation.

The environmental concerns were articulated so forcefully that in order to adopt the trade agreement, the nations accepted the creation of three new international bodies specifically dedicated to the enforcement of environmental law: the trilateral commission, called the **Commission for Environmental Cooperation** (CEC); the **Border Environment Cooperation Commission** (BECC); and its sibling organization, the **NADBank**, a development bank designed to provide funding for acute environmental infrastructure needs along the U.S.-Mexico border.

Interestingly enough, neither the development of new criminal law nor the application of criminal sanctions to environmental problems along the border ever became part of the NAFTA debate. The NAFTA debate did not highlight the need for any new criminalization of environmentally destructive conduct by people or companies, and so the essential statutes that are used in the prosecution of environmental crimes are the same statutes that are found and used by prosecutors throughout the United States.

U.S. LAWS: IMPACT ON BORDER ENVIRONMENTAL CRIME

Several pieces of environmental legislation created in the United States have affected interaction on the U.S.-Mexico border. Several of the more important environmental regulations affecting the border region are discussed below in conjunction with the customs regulations. Constitutional protections may prevent searches without cause in the United States, but at the border warrantless searches are as elaborate as the custom officials deem necessary.

The Clean Air and Clean Water Acts

In the United States, criminal remedies are available to enforce all the major environmental statutes. On the Mexican side of the border, facilities may exist whose emission levels are unacceptable by American standards but permitted under Mexican standards. Cross-border prosecution for smokestack violations would infringe Mexico's sovereignty. Speculation that the Clean Water Act may have application beyond the jurisdictional boundaries of the United States has been offered, but so far these waters—in the form of prosecutions proceeding to the District Court level—have not been tested.

It should be noted that the Clean Water Act was passed with specific attention to the possibility of transborder pollution (see 33 U.S.C. §1320 or the Federal Water Pollution Control Act §310). Section 310 of the act expressly recognizes the possibility that pollution originating in the United States may endanger the health or welfare of persons in a foreign country. When the Secretary of State advises the EPA administrator of the existence of such pollution and requests that it be abated, the EPA administrator may convene a hearing that could result in the institution of enforcement proceedings (including criminal enforcement proceedings) against any person causing the pollution. Interestingly enough, in order for this section to be utilized for the benefit of foreign nationals, it requires the foreign country suffering the pollution to have granted rights (to the United States) to call for the abatement of pollution that might be impacting interests in the United States. As of this writing, the authors know of no instance in which this unusual section of the Clean Water Act has been used to justify either civil or criminal enforcement proceedings.

The Toxic Substances Control Act

A somewhat unusual statute, the Toxic Substances Control Act, did provide the basis for some testing of the extrajurisdictional authority of the EPA in conjunction with the Department of Justice. In the summer of 1993, almost 100 maquiladora operations received administrative subpoenas demanding that they report on chemical substances used, stored, and discharged in Mexican facilities. The initial reaction of many of these maquiladoras, which, although Mexican corporations, have business relationships with U.S. parent or affiliate corporations, was to question the authority of the EPA to demand such information. The fundamental concept of the corporate identity was to separate and isolate the liabilities of the company, and these were companies located in Mexico, theoretically beyond the jurisdiction of the U.S. government. Eventually, many of these administrative subpoenas resulted in negotiated agreements to provide information to the U.S. government in return for the withdrawal of the subpoenas and the avoidance of the precedent-setting litigation that would have followed enforcement.

The Resource Conservation and Recovery Act

The law that provides the greatest opportunity for prosecutions related to border environmental crime is the Resource Conservation and Recovery Act (RCRA). The RCRA has often been referred to as a "cradle to grave" scheme for the regulation of hazardous substances (including hazardous waste). The statute covers the use, generation, transportation, storage, and disposal of all such materials. The overlay of border law as it applies to RCRA is best illustrated by the simple realization that such materials, when transported between countries, pass through separate jurisdictions that implicate customs laws, tax laws, and a variety of other regulatory schemes that are not triggered by transportation within the United States.

The La Paz Agreement of 1983, which provided the need for the EPA's adoption of regulations for the transboundary transportation of these materials, used the RCRA as the legal foundation for regulations in the border context. When the U.S. and Mexican presidents met in La Paz and agreed to coordinate on how hazardous waste will travel between the two countries, requirements such as those calling for a 60-day advance notice prior to shipment acquired a criminal enforcement mechanism by virtue of having been adopted under the regulatory authority accorded EPA by the RCRA.

Customs

In addition, the U.S. laws, as they relate to the customs jurisdiction, provide another critical overlay to environmental crimes on the border. Constitutional requirements for a search warrant or probable cause simply do not apply at border crossings. Vehicles and their cargo, passengers, and drivers are all subject to warrantless searches as invasive and intrusive as customs agents may believe appropriate. Further, the customs agents provide an added resource to law enforcement by having the personnel located on the border with the sole directive of examining and inspecting vehicles, cargo, and passengers. Unlike shipments of cargo within the United States, which are seldom subject to such intense scrutiny, cargo passing from nation to nation may have to run a battery of inspectors and inspections. Today's border reality includes sophisticated high-technology equipment that can X-ray an entire truck to determine whether there are hidden cavities of contraband. The same technology is also used to determine whether manifests accurately reflect what is actually being carried.

RCRA CRIMES AND EXAMPLES OF CRIMINAL CHARGES

Some patterns are beginning to emerge with regard to the types of crimes and criminals found at the border. Given the widespread use of the RCRA as the basis for criminal prosecution for import or export of hazardous waste (the single most defining "border environmental crime"), it is not surprising that businesses, as opposed to individuals, bear the brunt of prosecutorial efforts.

Southbound Hazardous Materials

The businesses that violate environmental law by bringing hazardous waste from the United States southbound to Mexico tend to be small, marginally profitable operations trying to avoid the expense of proper disposal. Typical of prosecutions of such businesses was one brought in the Southern District of California against Ignacio Lopez, operator of Mexican Parking and Warehouse, Inc., a trucking and transportation firm in Calexico that allegedly transported hazardous waste from the United States to Mexico between September 1991 and January 1992. True to kind, the prosecution against Lopez was founded upon his failure to have an appropriate hazardous waste manifest, required under the RCRA, and his further failure to have the documents required by Annex III of the La Paz Agreement, which calls for notification to the receiving nation and documentation of its acceptance of the hazardous waste prior to shipment.

Another example was a prosecution brought against an El Monte, California, corporation and three of its employees on three felony counts in connection with an alleged attempt to illegally export hazardous waste to Mexico on March 22, 1992. SBICCA of California, Inc., and the three employees were charged with "Conspiracy To Transport Hazardous Waste without a Manifest to Illegally Export Hazardous Waste" (an RCRA violation). SBICCA is a shoe manufacturing company that made polyurethane shoe soles using an injection mold system that utilizes solvents to clean the shoe mold. The hazardous waste in question was alleged to be spent solvents, including 1,1,1 trichloromethane.

Some interesting aspects of the SBICCA prosecution derived from the way in which this case came to the attention of U.S. authorities. It was alleged that one of the employees drove a truck containing the hazardous waste from El Monte to Tijuana, Mexico, and there the driver offered $200 to a Mexican customs official to admit the truck containing the hazardous waste to Mexico. The customs official refused the proffered bribe and reported the truck to the U.S. customs officials, who determined that the truck did not have the manifest required by law to accompany all shipments of hazardous waste. In all, twenty-four 55-gallon drums of the spent solvent waste were shipped to Mexico. In December 1992, three officers of the corporation pled guilty to federal misdemeanor charges of accessory after the act, and the SBICCA company pled guilty to one federal felony count of illegal exportation of hazardous waste, for which it was sentenced to a $50,000 criminal fine.

Northbound Hazardous Materials

A different pattern is emerging with regard to the illegal shipment of hazardous waste generated in Mexico and heading northbound to the United States, in part because of the very nature of the maquiladora industry, where large corporate interests are responsible for developing twin plants for the construction and manufacture of goods. Large, well-financed companies tend to be the ones apprehended and prosecuted for violation of hazardous waste importation laws when materials are headed back to the United

States. It is possible that this phenomenon occurs because the maquiladora plants located in Mexico are generally "cost centers" for the corporation. As manufacturing units that do not actively participate in sales and distribution of goods (although it is expected this may change as a result of agreements reached under NAFTA), these manufacturing units are often given strict budgets from home offices. Often, compensation and bonuses for the managers who run these cost centers are based upon their satisfactory performance in meeting these budgets.

Whether the waste transport violations are driven by the demands of budgets made by others or are the result of the inadequate training or inexperience of the employees charged with handling hazardous waste in the Mexican facilities, or are due to simple neglect or error, the RCRA has proved to be a powerful tool for prosecutors. One case, again from the Southern District of California, which has been one of the most active offices for the federal prosecution of environmental crimes along the entire U.S.-Mexico border, was brought against Fisher Price, the well-known toy manufacturer. The waste in question was solder waste, contaminated with lead. The solder was generated in making circuit boards at the Fisher Price facility in Tijuana. Fisher Price had imported solder waste from its facility for approximately a year, storing the waste at a facility in Chula Vista, California, until the amount was sufficient to be transported, with a manifest, for recycling at various facilities on the East Coast. Failure to have used the manifest to transport the materials from the maquiladora facility to Chula Vista, however, resulted in the prosecution and the imposition of a $25,000 penalty, the maximum amount then allowable for the charges.

BINATIONAL COOPERATION

Cooperation between Mexico and the United States in the criminal prosecution of environmental violators has been the result of a combination of factors. Below, attention is given to the formal and informal agreements and protocols for cooperation, the resources and training shared between the two countries, and the possibility for simultaneous prosecution. While interactions between the two countries are limited, some indications of the potential that exists for effective environmental enforcement are provided here.

Formal versus Informal

Various interesting observations can be made about the nature of prosecutorial cooperation at the U.S.-Mexico border. First, it must be recognized that there are formal agreements and protocols for cooperation at different levels. Not only did the 1983 La Paz Agreement provide the framework for cooperation on environmental issues, but separate treaties exist between the United States and various countries that formalize agreements for cooperation.

Mutual Legal Assistance Treaty

Among these agreements is the **Mutual Legal Assistance Treaty**, which provides, among other things, for procedures for obtaining certified copies of legal documents or the service of subpoenas in foreign countries. Certified documents from Mexico are recognizable for the gold seal and ribbons attached when an official notary public has reviewed and approved them as authentic. In order to request such documents, however, local prosecutors are required to use the Department of Justice's Office of International Affairs in Washington, D.C., where special assistants who have specific background and experience with different countries assist in making sure documents are appropriately requested through formal channels.

Personal Relationships

Many prosecutors have noted one of the most effective forms of binational cooperation consists of the personal relationships that exist between people and agencies of both countries. In a way, this reflects the nature of doing business in Mexico generally. Contrasts between authority and power, closely held by the federal government in Mexico City, and personal relationships are at the heart of business dealings at all levels. Business professionals often note that transactions in Mexico require time to establish an understanding of the people with whom they are working. Spending social time together to develop personal relationships helps build the trust fundamental to business success in that country.

Local versus Federal

The importance of establishing trust between business partners is obvious in the official relationships maintained between local and federal prosecutors on both sides of the border. While power and authority flow from the central organs of government in Washington, D.C., and Mexico City, the real work gets done as a result of personal relationships built up over the years between people who have worked together in similar situations and have begun to have a measure of each other as human beings. This informal protocol of coordination is reputed to be highly effective and efficient. One well-known prosecutor of environmental crime on the border has reported to the authors that every case brought on this side of the border is coordinated with Mexican authorities on a local level. That is to say, while it may be federal prosecution authorities on both sides of the border who are over-seeing a particular case, the oversight is maintained by direct connections between the prosecutors and not as a result of formal protocols requiring the involvement of high-level officials from each nation's capital.

Examples of coordinated prosecutions involving high-level enforcement officials of both countries do exist. One of the best known is the prosecution of the Alco Pacifico Company, which had transported used car batteries from Texas through California and eventually to a maquiladora facility lo-cated in a small community just outside of Tijuana for the purpose of recy-cling the lead into usable products. The Tijuana maquiladora facility even-tually went bankrupt and was unable to pay its workers. A huge amount of lead dust was left abandoned on the facility grounds. Criminal prosecution for this highly visible case was not begun by federal prosecution authorities in the United States but rather by the Los Angeles District Attorney's Office, which had a long-established special environmental crimes unit.

Analysis of the material indicated that because of the type of concentra-tion of this particular lead, the RCRA, the statute regulating disposal of wastes, was not implicated. California, however, had listed hazardous sub-stances that were more numerous and of lower concentration than those listed for the federal act. The federal authorities were therefore constrained from prosecuting, but the L.A. District Attorney, in consultation with repre-sentatives of the government of Mexico, began a series of prosecutions against American nationals and American companies. While prosecutors and policy makers on both sides of the border believed that coordination and cooperation between the DA's office and **SEDESOL** (then the Mexican version of the EPA) was good, cooperation between the DA's office and the EPA was strained. (The strain was perhaps exacerbated by indecision on na-tional policy as a result of the NAFTA debates.)

Sensitive to the binational aspects of this prosecution, however, the Dis-trict Attorney's Office coordinated all actions closely with the newly cre-ated enforcement arm of Mexico's environmental ministry, then called SEDESOL. The enforcement arm is known by the acronym **PROFEPA** and is essentially the Attorney General for enforcement of environmental laws. Then headed by Dr. Santiago Oñate, PROFEPA worked closely with Mr. Eng of the Los Angeles District Attorney's Office over a period of months as the prosecution was planned and then implemented. It resulted first in the Alco Pacifico Company of California pleading guilty to a felony viola-tion and agreeing to pay a penalty of $2.5 million, and later to a guilty plea by its president, who at one time was rumored to be considered for extradition to Mexico for prosecution and internment in that nation for the crime.

Sampling Protocols

Binational cooperation on environmental crime has several practical aspects as well. For example, if the crime involves hazardous waste, part of the proof involves evidence regarding the nature of that waste. Usually, samples are taken from materials that are later sent to laboratories for analysis. If these samples have to be taken in Mexico, it requires close coordination between U.S. and Mexican authorities. The standard operating procedure provides for Mexican regulatory authorities to actually take the samples while U.S. investigators stand by as witnesses. The U.S. investigators then receive the samples and begin the chain of custody receipt to ensure that all materials are later admissible as evidence in a court of law.

Resources and Training Cooperation

The lack of certified laboratories in Mexico qualified to undertake the chemical analysis of hazardous waste samples is another problem that besets binational coordination. There are efforts to address the need to enhance regulatory capacity and analytic (or laboratory) capacity on both sides of the border, and particularly in Mexico, at both the national level (through grants by the EPA) and at the local level. In one such effort, San Diego sent trainers to assist Mexican regulatory officials in establishing the highest level of competence for all evidence-gathering procedures. Binational training cooperation and opportunities for environmental consultants and laboratories to develop offices in Mexico have contributed substantially toward achieving binational technological parity.

Prosecutors in San Diego recently agreed to the establishment of a binational laboratory, where federal experts from the United States will work with federal experts from Mexico. Chemists will be trained, and federal experts will learn from these chemists each country's protocols for sampling and testing hazardous waste. As this work proceeds, it is anticipated that a conformed set of testing protocols will be developed as another tool for enhanced cooperation and coordination in the prosecution of binational environmental crimes.

Personal Jurisdiction

Lastly, it should be obvious that one important factor influencing the criminal prosecution of environmental criminals in the border area is the availability of personal jurisdiction over the defendants. If U.S. prosecution authorities want to take action against a company that has improperly manifested hazardous waste sent to the United States, they may find the target defendant to be a Mexican national outside of their prosecutorial jurisdiction. Close cooperation between U.S. and Mexican authorities has allowed U.S. prosecution efforts against companies involved in transborder shipments of hazardous materials to lead to prosecutions in Mexico. No known credible record of the number of such prosecutions or the result of such simultaneous prosecutorial activities exists at the present time. Further, no known tracking of environmental prosecutions in Mexico is being conducted. Although prosecutors on the U.S. side of the border believe Mexican authorities are active in prosecuting environmental crimes in Mexico, no one knows the degree or number of such prosecutions or the resulting sentences or fines.

Because Mexican law allows regulatory officials, as an administrative measure, to close down a plant for an environmental violation, this provision is widely used by Mexican enforcement authorities. As a result, most environmental offenses in Mexico are handled at the administrative level, and plants are closed and not allowed to reopen doors until discharges are eliminated or spills are cleaned up. It is not believed that a great number of environmental offenses lead to criminal prosecution. Nonetheless, Mexican law offers a very broad criminal overlay to environmental conduct should PROFEPA or Mexican state enforcement authorities find an appropriate matter to handle on that basis. This overlay may provide a healthy incentive for cooperation by companies involved in administrative proceedings.

THE FUTURE OF ENVIRONMENTAL CRIMES ALONG THE U.S.-MEXICO BORDER

No one's crystal ball is better (or worse) than ours, so we feel entirely comfortable in predicting what will occur in the coming years. A variety of trends suggest several initiatives the future might bring.

ISO 14000

For example, enthusiasm (on the part of businesses) for acceptance of the newest international environmental management standards promoted by the International Organization for Standardization (ISO) is increasing. These standards, which will direct environmental management issues within businesses or other organizations, have come to be known as the **ISO 14000** series of guidelines. Discussion of these guidelines and the different approach they recommend for companies when it comes to accommodating a more sensitive environmental policy has been widespread. Environmental NGOs are worried, however, that the ISO 14000 process will result in lowest common denominator standards by agreement among the polluters who are participating in the process.

In essence, the guidelines are reflective of the principles of "total quality management" but are oriented toward environmental friendliness and not production efficiency. The guidelines call for increased sensitivity to all phases of industrial production, and there are even special guidelines dealing with environmental labeling of products and life cycle analysis that will try to trace the impact particular products or processes have from the time raw materials are purchased to the time the products are used and then discarded. Other discussions focus on whether or not adoption of ISO 14000 standards (which are nongovernmental and would be voluntary in nature) will create a "safe haven" that will protect a company from criminal prosecution. We do not yet know whether adoption of these standards will have such an effect, as the standards themselves are still in draft form. Since they have not yet been internationally adopted, full acceptance by multinational industrial companies has not been achieved. The current widespread acceptance of ISO 9000 standards, which govern quality control (outside of the United States), indicate ISO 14000 may have a significant impact on the maquiladora manufacturing plants. On the other hand, if the United States eschews ISO 14000, the maquiladoras focused on the U.S. market will too.

Self-Auditing

An approach similar to the ISO 14000 approach has already found some support in the Mexican government. Recent publicity given to a self-auditing initiative heralded by PROFEPA and **SEMARNAP** (the agency that has succeeded SEDESOL as Mexico's chief environmental protection agency) suggests that the devaluation of the peso and the resulting economic difficulties have forced the country to look for new regulatory approaches. Initiatives include the development of a Mexican equivalent to the EPA's Toxic Release Inventory (self-reporting of toxic releases) as a result of the NAFTA agreements. While many are skeptical that self-auditing will result in increased environmental compliance and sensitivity, the practice is gaining wider acceptance among governments looking for ways to stretch thinner budgets over a wider territory.

Audit Privilege

In addition, increased use of self-audits or neutral third-party registration and certification has led to an increasingly heated dialogue over whether the results of such audits should be confidential or available to prosecuting authorities (so they can use that information when considering an indictment). The controversy has been most acute in the United States, where a new policy by the EPA on self-audit privilege has raised a host of questions yet to be satisfactorily resolved.

Economics and Enforcement

As discussed earlier in the text, a link exists between economics, the environment, and the type and number of criminal enforcement activities initiated. While the link is obvious, what it entails is considerably less so. The optimists like to argue that a rising tide lifts all boats and that prosperity will provide enhanced resources for poor communities to deal with environmental difficulties. This view is difficult to refute theoretically but much harder to verify in practice. The extremely difficult economic times Mexico endured through 1995 as a result of the devaluation of the peso leave little doubt about the impact of an economic slump on environmental enforcement. The difficulty the EPA has had receiving approval for its budget requests will also have a significant impact on environmental enforcement in the United States. And just as Congress has slashed EPA's budget, several important states, such as California, have also slashed resources devoted to monitoring and regulating the use of hazardous substances. The result, as one might expect, is less enforcement. In the future, however, this may not always be the case. Environmental enforcement may be pursued to generate revenue from fines, for example.

Several questions remain regarding the potential impact of the economy on environmental enforcement. Does the future hold the promise of economic prosperity? If it does, will this prosperity result in more resources being devoted to environmental regulation? And if more resources are focused on environmental regulation and compliance, will there be more criminal prosecutions? Or, as one might hope, will more successful efforts to maintain compliance result in less of a need for criminal prosecutions?

The Future of the Border Itself

It seems most likely that environmental criminal prosecution on the border will be linked directly to the future of the border itself. It is not likely that the rapid rate of industrialization will diminish soon, partly because of the viability of border locations for certain types of business operations. The border is, after all, close to U.S. markets, allows the possibility of overnight delivery of goods, and has a ready supply of relatively inexpensive labor.

These factors suggest that whether the maquiladora industry continues to thrive or becomes obsolete as a result of NAFTA, manufacturing in the border area is here to stay—and likely to grow. The nature of the businesses, their success at achieving compliance with regulations, and our national talent for enhancing resources to support manufacturing with appropriate water distribution systems and wastewater collection and treatment systems may play a large role in determining the future of criminal enforcement of environmental laws in this sensitive area.

REVIEW QUESTIONS

1. Many people accept the La Paz Agreement as an international treaty. Is it in fact a treaty? Explain your response.
2. Is failure to notify a receiving nation of repatriated waste through proper documentation a federal or a state violation? How is this determination made?
3. What are the differences between a typical illegal shipment of hazardous waste heading south and a typical illegal shipment heading north?
4. Which of the environmental protection statutes outlined in Chapter 5 is used most often in the prosecution of violations at the border?
5. In the United States, the EPA has an enforcement division. The Mexican enforcement structure is similar. What are the names of the regulatory agency and its enforcement division?

DISCUSSION QUESTIONS

1. What differences can be identified to help understand U.S. and Mexico and environmental enforcement issues?
2. Do you think the information presented here adequately reflects the experience of other cities along the U.S.-Mexico border? Please explain.
3. What do the actions along the U.S.-Mexico border suggest for other international environmental treaties? Please explain.

Comments in Closing

Mary Clifford

This text is structured to help readers identify, isolate, integrate, and explore specific issues related to environmental crime enforcement. The very first chapter was a review of the concept of environmental crime. Popular culture, in many cases via the press, has adopted the term *environmental crime*, but questions remain as to whether the term captures the essence of the concept as it is used by academics, practitioners, politicians, journalists, and environmentalists, among others. It appears, however, the term is here to stay, and therefore those interested in studying environmental crime may have to work around the potential definitional limitations.

It is clear that environmental protection laws have been written and punishments have been identified for individuals (or groups) who violate these laws. It is not clear, however, if these are good laws, or adequate punishments. The history of the environmental movement and of the political and economic climate in the United States was reviewed in Chapter 2 as the foundation for discussing current environmental protection efforts. Proponents and opponents of environmental protection seem to agree that current efforts are not working. Solutions, however, are more difficult to find than are comments critical of actions being taken by "the other side."

One special target of criticism has been the natural sciences. If only scientific inquiry could answer the questions that plague the environmental controversies, then we could find the right answer. Scientists are accused of being bought off by big companies or of playing politics and breaking their commitment to objectivity. While everyone is likely to agree that the role of science is central to environmental studies in general—and environmental crime specifically—questions about how science should best be used remain controversial.

How do we begin to identify the intricacies involved in determining why society's best efforts at environmental protection have fallen short? Parts II and III addressed that question. Part II reviewed recent developments (and problems) in the federal environmental enforcement structure. Attention was also focused on efforts at state and local levels of government to better address community-specific environmental concerns. Communities that were dissatisfied with the guidelines outlined by the federal government began developing their own protocols for addressing the environmental issues that affected them most. In fact, the local push for environmental protection exposed more problems than were initially anticipated.

The strategies for fighting environmental crime being developed in local communities often involve local law enforcement. Thus the role of local police and eventually local prosecution teams in dealing with environmental crime was also explored in Part II. There is controversy associated with involving local law enforcement, however. Some argue police have enough to do without being bothered with environmental crime enforcement, whereas others point out that the police are the eyes and the ears of the community and can detect potential environmental hazards better than anyone else.

The punishment of environmental offenders also gives rise to controversy. Many argue that jail or prison should be reserved for serious violent offenders, and they do not agree that environmental criminals fall into that category. Supporters of harsh penalties for environmental offenders, however, argue that deliberate or reckless destruction of air, land, and water resources may have more damaging long-term effects on large masses of people than violent crime and that the sanctions should be comparable.

Part III invited readers to review how they think about environmental issues in general. First, it discussed unlikely types of environmental offenders, including municipal governments and government agencies. Government agencies are supposed to serve the public, but sometimes their public responsibilities lead to commission of an environmental crime. Part III then presented a brief discussion of ethics and posed the question of whether integrating different ethical models might help direct popular attitudes about environmental protection and reduce the need for criminal enforcement. Linked closely to this discussion was a review of "greenwashing" techniques and a reminder to readers to be critical thinkers and listeners when evaluating those who espouse an environmental agenda.

The last two chapters of the book illustrated the point that the topic of environmental crime is expanding. For example, as discussed in Chapter 14, a variety of critical environmental issues already confront the global community. Therefore, the environmental controversies confronting the international arena are reminiscent of many of the issues raised in the opening chapters of Part I: definition of terms; assessment of the history; and an understanding of the local politics and economic structure. It should be clear, however, that the scope of the issues being studied has expanded tremendously. It is not enough to understand the U.S. definition of environmental crime, the U.S. history of environmental protection, or the U.S. political and economic structure. Definitional, historical, political, and economic issues play a role in the way each country is affected by internal and international environmental problems. The United States and other "throw-away" societies are believed by members of the developing world to be a significant cause of environmental *problems* rather than the main champions of environmental solutions.

The final chapter reviewed several important pieces of research on the topic of environmental crime. The student of environmental crime must remember to consider the other countries that have confronted similar environmental problems and have developed cultural and political solutions to their environmental dilemmas. The research done in the United States presented here is intended to provide only a brief introduction to a body of research that is continually growing.

The chapters in this book represent only one editor's vision of several critical areas that need further study. Because environmental crime research is in its infancy, it is still possible to make a significant impact on its direction. As air and water resources decline in quality, communities across the globe will confront a harsh reality: Humans need clean air and water to survive. The emergence of international communications, multinational corporations, and transportation technologies has bestowed on everyone the ability to travel anyplace in the world. Pollution can travel as well. Pollution problems come from many sources; consequently, solutions offered must be considered from all angles. Technology, for example, has been argued to be at the root of many environmental problems; however, one must remember that it was technology that allowed humans to detect the hole in the ozone layer. Humans responded with global action, and some believe the biggest threat to the ozone layer has been identified and addressed. Perhaps solar technologies or hydropower will eventually be able to power our cars and help reduce air pollution. Reduced air pollution will help reduce acid rain and will reduce to some degree contamination of water bodies. This is just one example of how technological solutions may help aid in protecting environmental controversy. But remember the intricacies associated with scientific inquiry also apply to technological inquiry. Human attitudes dictate what technologies or ideologies will sell. In the final analysis, giving attention to existing ethical attitudes—assessing both the hidden meaning and the covert action—may provide the most useful research of all.

Glossary

abatement. The process of reducing the intensity of or eliminating pollution completely in a given area.

abiotic. Nonliving components of the environment (e.g., the water, soil, and atmosphere).

accumulation. Refers to the government's obligation to create and maintain conditions under which profitable capital accumulation is possible.

administrative penalties. Also referred to as regulatory enforcement, one of the three basic environmental enforcement options. *See also* **civil enforcement** and **criminal penalties**.

advanced training. A type of specialized training that provides the officers with an even more specialized understanding of a particular law enforcement issue. In the case of environmental crimes, advanced training might include training in the use of personal protective equipment, environmental crime scene investigation and documentation, and basic site containment and remediation techniques, for example.

agency capture. Describes the working relationship that occurs between regulatory agencies and the subjects of regulations. The concern is that no real enforcement happens if the regulators become too amiable with the companies being regulated.

anencephaly. A birth defect, linked to chemical exposures. A cluster of cases in Brownsville, Texas, was attributed to the maquilla industry. Thought to be related to chemical exposure at a specific stage of fetal development, the result is either anencephaly, a malformed brain and skull, or spina bifida, paralysis in the lower extremities.

451

asbestosis. A chronic lung disease produced by excessive inhalation of asbestos.

asset seizure and forfeiture. Enforcement agents have the authority to impound, or seize, equipment if it is being used in the commission of certain environmental crimes. Those accused of environmental crimes must, by law, relinquish their equipment to authorities.

atmosphere. The gaseous layer covering the earth. The atmospheric regions are the troposphere, stratosphere, mesosphere, chemosphere, thermosphere, ionosphere, and exosphere. The atmosphere and the lithosphere, hydrosphere, and biosphere make up the earth's ecosystem.

Atomic Energy Commission. The agency that preceded the Nuclear Regulatory Commission (NRC). The NRC is a five-member government commission responsible for issuing licenses for the construction and operation of nuclear power plants; it succeeded the AEC in January 1975.

attainment area. An area that is in compliance with federal standards.

autotrophs. Plants and other photosynthetic organisms, like algae and some bacteria, that can make their own food (self-feeders).

Ballinger, Richard. Appointed as Secretary of the Interior under President Taft; known for his policy conflicts with Chief Forester Gifford Pinchot.

Basel Convention of 1989. Convened by the U.N. Environmental Project in 1989, the Basel Convention on the Control of Transboundary Movements of Hazardous Wastes and Their Disposal attempted to establish a collective understanding regarding the international transportation of hazardous waste.

Berne Accord of 1963. A multilateral environmental agreement involving France, Germany, Luxembourg, the Netherlands, and Switzerland.

best demonstrated available technology. Treatment standard for hazardous waste; if met, prevents waste from being disposed of in landfills.

beyond a reasonable doubt. High burden of proof for proving guilt or innocence. Associated with criminal cases, this standard requires proof of more than 95 percent certainty.

bilateral agreement. A legal agreement between two neighboring nation-states.

bioaccumulation. The process of accumulating concentrations of a chemical in an organism. Examples of these include the pesticide DDT, strontium 90 from nuclear weapons testing, and the heavy metal pollutant, cadmium.

biodiversity. Variability among and within species of plants, animals, microorganisms, and marine life and also among entire ecosystems. Biodiversity is threatened whenever a network of living organisms and the nonliving environment that sustains them as a functional unit is altered in ways that lead to the extinction of one or more life forms in that network.

biogeochemical cycles. The movement of elements, nutrients, and organic compounds from the abiotic environment into the biota and back into the nonliving environment. The nutrient cycle is one example.

biomass. Any biological material; all the plants and animals in a given area.

bionomics. A theory that holds that anything other than minimal regulation is interference with life itself. Bionomic approaches regard state regulation as an almost unmitigated evil, even in the realm of health and safety.

biosphere. The entire planetary ecosystem. It includes all living (biotic) and nonliving (abiotic) parts of the earth. *See also* **atmosphere**, **hydrosphere**, and **lithosphere**.

biotic. The types of plants and animals found in an area.

Border Environment Cooperation Commission (BECC). One party of the trilateral commission designed to oversee environmental protection on the U.S.-Mexico border. *See also* **Commission for Environmental Cooperation** and **NADBank**.

bubble policy. The EPA policy of allowing the creation of an imaginary bubble over several sources of air pollution. Within this bubble, emissions of the industries or other pollution sources are treated as if they come from one emission point. Some aspects of a company's operation can be out of compliance with federal environmental laws as long as the company as a whole remains in compliance.

Burford, Anne Gorsuch. Director of the EPA during the Reagan administration. Advocated voluntary compliance. Resigned in a time of conflict, when EPA officials were accused of dealing lightly with businesses that violated EPA regulations.

C&D debris. Construction and demolition debris; a common problem facing state enforcement officers.

Capacity Assurance Plan. Requirement that all states have a hazardous waste disposal plan to adequately address their hazardous waste disposal needs.

capital. Property, machines, buildings, tools, and money used to produce goods and services.

capitalism. An economic system characterized by freedom of the marketplace.

carbon cycle. Process in which decomposers, such as fungi and bacteria, consume chemical compounds left in dead organisms to fuel their own metabolism and then release carbon dioxide gas. This whole process is referred to as the carbon cycle.

carcinogen. A cancer-causing substance.

Catlin, George. Famous artist who traveled extensively in the western United States and painted pictures depicting Native American life. He kept a journal of his thoughts, and in published articles made an appeal for a national park to preserve the American wilderness before it vanished.

cell theory. Theory that all life is composed of one or more cells and that all cells come from preexisting cells.

Cerrell Report. In 1984, the California Waste Management Board hired Cerrell and Associates to conduct a study (known as the Cerrell report) identifying the demographic characteristics of the neighborhoods most and least resistant to local placement of hazardous waste facilities. The report suggested the easiest communities in which to site hazardous waste facilities were poor, economically vulnerable communities. Because these are often minority communities, many argue that the report is an example of environmental racism.

certiorari. A writ from a higher court requesting the record of a case for review.

chaotics. A new paradigm of causality. Chaotics denounces the linear notion that small causes produce small effects and large causes produce large effects. This ideology suggests that a small action, as identified initially, may have catastrophic effects.

charismatic megafauna. Species that tend to be especially interesting to humans.

chemical revolution. The economic transformation caused by the increased use of chemicals in manufacturing.

Chicago School of Human Ecology. School of thought that used ecological principles to explain the emergence of certain social conditions, particularly deviance and criminal behavior.

civil enforcement. Enforcement of a violation through the imposition of civil penalties.

civil penalties. Noncriminal sanctions, such as fines.

classical liberalism. A politicoeconomic philosophy that views government's proper role as protection of freedoms.

Clean Air Act. The Clean Air Act of 1970, replacing the Clean Air Act of 1963 and the Air Quality Act of 1967 established the current basic framework for the federal regulation of air pollution. The act was amended in 1977 and 1990.

clean waste. Waste that contains no hazardous materials.

Clean Water Act. Replacement of the Federal Water Pollution Control Act. Required a national permit program to better track sources of pollution.

clear-cutting. A method of tree harvesting that takes out all the trees in a specific acreage at the same time.

cocktailing. The mixing together of wastes. Usually done to hide hazardous liquid wastes among legitimate solid waste materials.

Commerce Clause. Clause of the U.S. Constitution (Article I, Section 8) that prohibits any actions that discriminate against interstate commerce.

commingling. See "cocktailing."

Commission for Environmental Cooperation (CEC). One party of the trilateral commission designed to oversee environmental protection on the U.S.-Mexico border. *See also* **Border Environment Cooperation Commission** and **NADBank**.

commodities. Articles of trade or commerce, traditionally agricultural and mining products.

common law. System of jurisprudence used in the United States. Originating in England, it is based on precedence rather than statutory law.

compensation fund. A fund to allow compensation to victims. If a claim is honored, the victim would receive payment from the fund, which would in turn seek cost recovery from potentially responsible parties.

compliance. The act of meeting regulatory or statutory requirements.

compliance program. Program whose purpose is to induce compliance.

Comprehensive Environmental Response, Compensation and Liability Act (CERCLA). The full title of the Superfund legislation.

conservation, "human centered." A position held by those interested in protecting nature to preserve human civilization and civilized people.

containment remedies. Also known as temporary remedies, these remedies are intended to seal hazardous waste on-site or off-site, restrict the movement of contaminants, and prevent further groundwater contamination.

contribution suits. Lawsuits targeted at parties known to be partly responsible for hazardous waste dumping at a given site. These parties would then have the option of tracking down and suing other responsible parties, and indeed the total number of contribution suits could number in the hundreds.

cost-benefit analysis. Use of an economic model to assess the costs of a particular action and balance them against the benefits received by that same action.

Council on Environmental Quality. Council charged with advising the president about environmental issues.

cradle-to-grave mandate. Requirement covering a substance from creation to annihilation, such as the RCRA mandate requiring an accounting for all chemicals from their creation through subsequent transportation and ending with their disposal.

crimes against nature. Acts that offend the moral sensibilities of society.

criminal enforcement. Enforcement directed toward violations to which criminal sanctions apply.

criminaloid. E.A. Ross's term for those individuals who committed acts that were viewed as fundamentally immoral but were not illegal and therefore not classified as criminal.

criminal penalties. Criminal sanctions, such as a jail sentences.

cross-training. A form of officer training that brings together various individuals and agencies involved in environmental crime enforcement. The effort is intended to familiarize all parties involved about the responsibilities of each separate agency, to produce better overall results.

cryptosporidium. A type of microorganism. It infected the water system in Milwaukee and caused 40 deaths.

culpability. The degree of intentional behavior behind a specific environmental offense.

damages. Monetary compensation that the law awards to someone who has been injured.

declaratory judgment. Order from a judge requiring a defendant not to engage in a given activity. Standard practice when the government decides to use a civil action.

decomposers. Organisms, including bacteria and fungi, that break down complex organic matter into simpler materials. Decomposers eat at all the trophic levels.

deep ecology. An environmental philosophy that holds that consideration must be given to the planet first.

Delaney Amendment. Legislation that allowed the federal Food and Drug Administration (FDA) to ban any suspected carcinogen.

Department of Energy. The federal executive department, created in 1977, with responsibility for energy policy in the United States.

deregulation movement. A political movement to deregulate banking, airlines, telecommunications, and railroad industries, for example, based on the assumption that government regulation was a major cause of the economic malaise of the 1970s.

discretion. The freedom or authority to make decisions, such as an enforcement officer's freedom to assess a specific situation and decide how or whether to proceed with an arrest.

disorderly person statute. A statute used as a prosecutorial tactic when environmental enforcement/prosecution is questioned. The statute allows the solid waste disposal cases to be tried in a municipal court by county prosecutors. Although not technically felony offenses, the use of this statute allows for "felony-type" punishments when such prosecution at the federal level seems unlikely to result in conviction.

dominance. After a species moves into an area, the process whereby it comes to dominate other species.

Earth Day. An annual celebration of environmental issues and awareness. First held on April 22, 1970.

Earth Summit. The Stockholm Conference on the Human Environment.

economic growth. An increase in the capacity of the economy to provide goods and services for final use.

economics. The science dealing with the production, distribution, and consumption of commodities.

economic system. A society's system for producing, distributing, and consuming commodities.

ecosystem. A community of living organisms and the abiotic substances. A level of organization within the living world that includes both the total array of biological organisms and the chemical-physical factors that influence the organisms.

ecotone. A zone of transition between two well-defined vegetative areas.

Edwards, Edwards, and Fields. Editors of a 1996 collection of articles titled *Environmental Crime and Criminality: Theoretical and Practical Issues*. Their collection of 11 research projects offers insights into theoretical, practical, philosophical, and future issues in the study of environmental crime.

efficiency. Providing the maximum satisfaction of consumer preferences revealed by the market.

effluent standard. The determined acceptable limit of effluent a company can discharge into a waterway.

Emergency Planning and Community Right To Know Act. Requires companies to disclose annually any releases of specific chemicals (over 300 listed). Companies must estimate how much of each chemical they released into the environment, and this information is used to prepare toxic release inventories, which are available to the public.

emission reduction credit. A credit gained when a permanent reduction in air pollutant emissions goes beyond the legally required limits.

Endangered Species Act. Federal legislation in the United States that is intended to give the federal government the authority to protect any species considered to be threatened with extinction.

enforcement agent. An individual whose primary responsibility is to ensure specific statutory provisions are upheld.

enforcement first strategy. EPA regional officers were instructed to issue unilateral orders to compel corporate settlements and to initiate cost recovery. Treble damages were imposed on those who did not agree to settle.

entropy. The disorder in a closed system that results from the second law of thermodynamics (energy in its initial state is always higher than in its final state).

environmental audit. An internal investigation of a company to determine if it is in compliance with the required environmental regulations.

environmental crime reduction equation. The theory that the ideal equation for the reduction of environmental crime is tightened environmental legislation plus toughened enforcement plus increases in legitimate disposal alternatives equals reduced rates of environmental offenses.

Environmental Crimes Project. A pro bono project of the National Law Center of the George Washington University. Created by law professor Jonathan Turley, the project has assisted government, industry, and academic groups in the development of environmental criminal law. The project works exclusively on environmental crime research and legislation.

environmental criminology. An established discipline that focuses on social ecology or structural (environmental) factors and their relationship to criminal activity.

environmental damage insurance. Insurance that indemnifies polluting corporations for cleanup costs and legal expenses.

environmental impact statement (EIS). A report required by the National Environmental Policy Act that details the anticipated consequences of a proposed federal action in an effort to determine how that action will affect the natural environment.

environmental justice. The equitable distribution of socially useful but environmentally destructive activities and operations. It is thought that because minority communities have fewer resources, unwanted waste facilities are often located in poor areas, putting these communities at greater risk. Citizen groups have been organizing in an effort to protect these communities.

environmental media. The substances (air, land, and water) through which environmental contaminants travel. Water, for example, is the primary medium addressed by the Clean Water Act.

environmental racism. The overly frequent placement of environmentally hazardous operations and activities in minority communities.

eutrophication. The addition of excessive plant nutrients to a water system. The process leads to prolific growth of aquatic plants.

externalities. Effects the production process has on those not a party to the process.

federal cause of action. A hearing in federal court.

Federal Insecticide, Fungicide, and Rodenticide Act. An amendment to 1947 legislation that established the basic framework for pesticide regulation. It was amended in 1988 to require more expeditious review of pesticides for registration with EPA.

Federal Water Pollution Control Act (FWPCA). The predecessor of the Clean Water Act. Enacted in 1972, the FWPCA banned unpermitted discharge of pollution into surface waters and established a national permit program. *See* **NPDES permit program.**

first law of thermodynamics. Energy is neither lost nor gained from a closed system but is converted from one form to another.

food web. The pattern of connections among the various organisms in different trophic levels.

foreign nation. Any geographical area (land, water, and airspace) that is under the jurisdiction of one or more foreign governments; any area under military occupation by the United States alone or jointly with any other foreign government.

four goals of punishment. Deterrence, incapacitation, rehabilitation, retribution.

Freedom of Information Act (FOIA). Statute allowing for public review of private information. If the EPA has an FOIA request for information, efforts must be made to acquire the requested information. If an FOIA request is submitted and a claim of confidentiality has been made and upheld by the EPA, the person filing the request will be notified and can proceed to litigate the issue in court if he or she wants to pursue getting the information.

fund first strategy. EPA emphasized Superfund-financed cleanup as a bargaining tool to induce defendant corporations to settle. Corporations would be willing to settle to avoid the extra cost they expected from EPA cleanup.

global commons. Refers to any geographical areas that are outside the jurisdiction of any nation, such as the oceans outside territorial limits and Antarctica.

global environmental accord. Agreement that binds all or nearly all the nations of the world to follow a specific course of actions to protect the environment.

global warming. The increase in the earth's temperatures allegedly being caused by, among other things, the release of certain gases into the atmosphere and the mass destruction of tropical rainforests.

grassroots groups. Local groups usually focused on combatting an unwanted action in their community.

green crime. Term used in analyzing how political and economic factors are tied to the occurrence of corporate violence against the environment.

greenhouse gases. Atmospheric gases that absorb outgoing infrared energy emitted from the earth, contributing to the greenhouse effect. The more important greenhouse gases are carbon dioxide, water vapor, methane, nitrous oxide, and the chlorofluorocarbons.

Gunther. Author of a 1990 study of the implementation of California's hazardous waste control act by local prosecutors titled "Enforcement in Your Backyard: Implementation of California's Hazardous Waste Control Act by Local Prosecutors." Gunther's results illustrate how local prosecutors have had to become quick studies in the qualities needed to practice successful decision making in the prosecution of environmental offenses.

Habitat-Conservation Plan. A strategy proposed by a landowner to underwrite habitat restoration elsewhere.

Hammett and Epstein. "Local Prosecution of Environmental Crime" (in *Issues and Practices*, Washington, DC: National Institute of Justice, 1993) describes the experiences of five county prosecutors' offices which, by agency mandate, had made the prosecution of environmental crime a priority. Although the work serves to dispel the myth that environmental crime control is beyond the capabilities of local governmental enforcement and prosecution agencies, it does confirm the obstacles that can typically stand in the way of effective environmental crime control on the local level.

Hammitt and Reuter. *Measuring and Deterring Illegal Disposal of Hazardous Waste* (1988) provided interviews with local law enforcement personnel and industry representatives in Los Angeles County, Massachusetts, and Pennsylvania. Through their research, the authors underscored the impact small quantity generators (SQGs) have on environmental crime.

hazardous materials. Any substance that poses a threat to human health or the environment if released in significant amounts.

hazardous waste. Any solid waste listed as hazardous under the Resource Conservation and Recovery Act. Toxicity, corrosivity, ignitability, and reactivity are typical characteristics of hazardous materials.

heterotrophs. Organisms that ingest plant compounds to fuel their own metabolism.

human-centered conservationism. The position taken by those whose main goal is to protect nature in order to preserve human civilization.

hydrosphere. The part of our planetary surface where the various forms of water are found. It includes liquid water at the surface and underground, polar ice caps, and water vapor in the lower atmosphere.

hypotheses. Formalized, testable ideas based on repeated observations.

incidental take permit. The application for this permit seeks to allow land use activity to continue in places where endangered species may exist. The incidental take permit, if granted, suggests that the impact of the action will not impact the overall numbers of a given species.

indicator species. Species used by ecologists to get an idea of the overall health of an ecosystem. Top-level carnivores (secondary and tertiary consumers) depend on several other levels in a community, and a decrease in carnivore populations signals problems with the rest of the ecosystem.

individual rights. One of the fundamental principles of the United States system of governance. Refers to the idea that protection of the rights granted individuals in the United States is one responsibility of federal government.

information. A written accusation charging a person with a crime. An alternative to an indictment as a means of beginning a prosecution. The purpose is to inform the defendant of the charges and the court of the facts in the case.

initial responders. Those individuals who first arrive on an accident or crime scene.

injunction. Legal ruling requiring an offending party to refrain from doing or to discontinue a particular act or activity.

inservice training. Specialized training offered to law enforcement officers. Most departments require officers to take a specific number of training hours per year.

intelligence exchange meetings. Meetings of task force members intended to keep personnel up to date on relevant law enforcement activities and regulatory information. The objective is to keep parties at all levels of environmental enforcement informed about the needs of other agency representatives.

intent. The state of being aware of the consequences of one's actions. Intent is required for criminal liability.

international law. Law governing the relations between nations; rules and principles that govern questions of right between nations.

invasion. The process by which a new species invades an area.

ISO 14000. A proposal from the International Organization for Standards that will direct environmental management issues within businesses and other organizations.

joint and several liability. The sharing of rights and liabilities among a group of people collectively and/or individually. The injured party may sue some or all of the defendants together or each one separately. The injured party may collect equal or unequal amounts from the defendants.

knowing violation. A violation where there exists a general intent to do the prohibited act.

Lacey Act. Passed in 1900, prohibited the interstate commerce of fish or wildlife taken in violation of federal, state, or foreign law.

land ban provision. Provision of the RCRA requiring alternatives to disposal of hazardous waste in landfills.

land disposal. Dumping of wastes in local land fills.

land pyramid. "Pyramid" consisting of "layers" of species that are alike, not in where they come from or how they look, but rather in what they eat. It includes predation and destruction in addition to the creation of new life and the sustenance of existing life. Aldo Leopold described this system as a land pyramid.

La Paz Agreement. A framework for binational cooperation between the United States and Mexico. It outlines a protocol for solving environmental problems related to the border regions.

Lavelle, Rita. Former head of the Superfund program in the Reagan administration. She went to jail for perjury before Congress.

Law of Ecological Equilibrium. Mexican law, passed in 1988, having a comprehensive impact on all environmental media. The legislation led to the adoption of subsequent environmental regulations.

legal standard. Use of the law as the sole factor for determining right and wrong.

legitimization. The second function of the state. (See **accumulation.**) Dictates the state's responsibility to create and maintain social harmony.

Leopold, Aldo. Considered by some to be the father of modern preservationism. Author of *A Sand County Almanac*, which suggests humans should be viewed as only one among numerous members of the biological community.

lithosphere. The earth's outer crust and upper mantle.

LULUs. Locally unwanted land uses.

mala in se. Evil in itself. The term is used to refer to acts that are wrong irrespective of whether there is an enacted law that prohibits them.

mala prohibita. Acts that are illegal merely because they are prohibited by an enacted law are said to be mala prohibita.

manifest system. Documentation that identifies cargo being transported. Transporters of hazardous waste are required by the RCRA to use a set of shipment forms to track wastes in transit from their origin to their final site for disposal.

maquiladora industry. The "twin plant" program adopted by Mexico in the 1960s. The program was structured to place foreign manufacturers in Mexico and allow them to import raw materials into Mexico free from customs, duties, and tariffs. Finished products were then shipped to a twin plant on the U.S. side for packaging and distribution. Over 2,000 maquiladora operations existed by the 1990s.

Marsh, George Perkins. Wrote *Man and Nature* in 1864. Marsh highlighted the demise of earlier civilizations because they had destroyed their natural environment. For Marsh, humans had a responsibility to conserve and use resources wisely to preserve them for future generations.

midnight dumping. The unpermitted disposal of hazardous chemicals in an unauthorized area.

Migratory Bird Act. 1918 legislation that limited hunting and prohibited the taking of nests or eggs of specific migratory birds.

Montreal Protocol. The Montreal Protocol on Substances That Deplete the Ozone Layer is a global environmental accord to phase out all production of chlorofluorocarbons by the year 2000. It was agreed to by the 81 member countries that signed the Vienna Accord.

morphology. The branch of biology that deals with the structure of plants and animals.

Muir, John. Cofounder and first president of the Sierra Club. Author of several books on nature and wilderness and a primary figure in the development of the national park system.

multilateral agreement. Legal agreement between a group of nations seeking to alleviate some shared ecological problem.

Mutual Legal Assistance Treaty. One of many agreements focused on achieving cooperation between the United States and Mexico. This treaty provides procedures to obtain certified copies of legal documents or the service of subpoenas in foreign countries. In the United States, requests for such documents are processed through the Justice Department's Office of International Affairs.

NADBank. A development bank designed to provide funding for the environmental infrastructure acutely needed along the U.S.-Mexico border. *See also* **Commis-**

sion for Environmental Cooperation and Border Environment Cooperation Commission.

National Ambient Air Quality Standards (NAAQS). Primary air quality standards that are intended to allow an adequate margin of safety in banning pollutants to protect the public health. Unlike the primary standards, which directly relate to human health, the secondary standards are not intended to address health concerns but rather deal with air color and odor.

National Conservation Commission. Commission appointed by President Theodore Roosevelt in 1908 to inventory natural resources.

National Environmental Policy Act (NEPA). A 1969 statute that requires federal agencies to consider environmental factors in decision-making processes.

National Priority List (NPL). A national listing of hazardous waste disposal sites most in need of remediation. The list is updated annually by the EPA.

National Response Center (NRC). CERCLA's notification requirement mandates reporting of releases of hazardous substances to the NRC. The NRC is a central U.S. clearinghouse for information involving hazardous chemical spills and is responsible for notifying other agencies so they can develop a response.

natural law. Refers to the "immutable moral principles" associated with the natural order, including ideas promoted by the Church and later directing the development of English common law.

natural order. Moral assessment and reference to the natural social order.

natural resources. Items found in nature that can be used to produce goods.

nature centered. Oriented toward protecting the environment as an end in itself rather than as a means of human survival or prosperity.

navigable waterways. Waters that are suitable for boat traffic.

negligent. Failing to exercise a degree of care that a person of ordinary prudence would exercise under the same circumstances. Legal standard used in assessing liability.

neocolonialism. Form of economic control in which outside economic interests shape economic development and resource usage within a less developed nation.

new source performance standards. Effluent standards to be proposed for new technologies.

NIMBY (not in my backyard). A grassroots philosophy driving activism against controversial practices in a specific locale.

nolo contendere. A plea by a defendant that eschews the opportunity to present a defense but does not admit guilt.

nonattainment area. An area unable to meet the National Ambient Air Quality Standards.

noncompliance. Not meeting regulatory or statutory requirements.

nongovernmental organization (NGO). An organization outside the government focused on addressing a specific social issue. Greenpeace, which lobbies for environmental protection legislation, is a prime example.

nonpoint source. A nonlocalized source of pollutants, such as street runoff.

notification requirement. A requirement that information concerning a fact or an action be communicated to a person (or entity) by an authorized person. Notification of a potentially responsible party about a cleanup action is required under CERCLA. Also, CERCLA has a requirement that releases of hazardous substances be reported to the National Response Center.

NPDES permit program. Under the Clean Water Act, an individual must be granted a permit to release effluent into a specific waterway. The National Pollution Discharge Elimination System was put in place to assist with monitoring the release of effluent and the types of chemicals being released.

nuisance. A private nuisance is a nontrespassory invasion of another's interest in the private use and enjoyment of property. A public nuisance is an interference with a right common to the general public.

nutrient cycle. *See* **biogeochemical cycles.**

occupational disqualification of a corporate executive. The dismissal from a profession of a corporate executive who has committed an environmental violation.

Occupational Safety and Health Administration (OSHA). A federal agency established to protect workers from unsafe working conditions.

Office of Enforcement and Compliance Assurance. EPA division responsible for overseeing all cases where voluntary compliance has not been obtained.

offset rule. Rule allowing a polluting company to go into a geographic area and continue to generate a certain amount of pollution so long as it could induce other companies in that geographic area to reduce their pollution by an equal amount.

Olmsted, Frederick Law. Active in establishing urban parks. Was responsible for the design of Central Park in New York City.

organisms. Living species.

overdeterrence. Establishment of a standard so high that it prohibits any form of the action. For example, if the price of causing an oil spill was increased to the point that firms no longer engaged in the shipping of oil, society would be adversely affected.

paradigm. A way of thinking about things that is longstanding. In this case, the presently constructed set of ethics used to assess human relations with the natural environment.

pattern of flight. Referred to early concerns that U.S. companies were leaving the United States and being drawn toward developing countries with less costly pollution controls.

permanent remedies. In the context of hazardous waste disposal, technologies intended to permanently change or destroy the hazardous composition of waste through chemical, biological, thermal, or physical means.

personal injury action. Action to protect against invasion of personal interests caused by negligence or by abnormally dangerous activities for which strict liability is imposed.

petrochemical industry. The petroleum and chemical industries combined.

photosynthesis. A process in green plants and some bacteria in which light energy is absorbed by chlorophyll-containing molecules and converted to chemical energy.

Pinchot, Gifford. In 1898 Pinchot took over as head of the Division of Forestry in the Department of Agriculture. After working under several presidents, Pinchot was eventually fired because of his critique of the Department of Interior during the Taft administration.

poaching. Taking of a game animal out of season or through an illegal means.

point source. A localized source of pollution, such as a factory or an oil refinery.

Pollution Prosecution Act of 1990. Act mandating the federal government to have 200 investigators working on environmental crime by October 1, 1990, in addition to 35 FBI agents. Funding for this legislation was not approved by Congress. In 1992, the funds were approved and the mandate required 200 officers by 1994.

population. The individuals in a given species.

potentially responsible parties. Those individuals identified as being responsible or at fault for a hazardous waste dumping site.

Powell, John Wesley. Powell and a team of men were the first nonindigenous people to explore the Colorado River through the Grand Canyon. He explored the Rocky Mountains and various regions of the arid West.

precedent. A model for directing future official actions. For example, judicial interpretations become part of the ongoing discussion about how laws and regulations are to be used to administer environmental protection legislation.

preponderance of the evidence. Burden of proof necessary in a civil proceeding (51 percent certainty).

preservationism. "Nature-centered" doctrine that wilderness should be preserved irrespective of human needs.

primary consumers. Organisms that ingest plant compounds to fuel their own metabolism. *See* **heterotrophs.**

primary producers. The organisms that produce the organic molecules that travel throughout a biotic community. *See* **autotrophs**.

proactive liability. The type of liability applied to individuals for illegally dumping hazardous waste after the passage of Superfund.

procaryotes. Simple bacteria that were the predominate life form on earth for nearly two aeons. They still make up a large part of present ecological systems.

PROFEPA. The enforcement arm of the federal agency in Mexico responsible for environmental oversight.

Progressive Conservation Movement. Political movement in the early 1900s that advocated the federal government play a role in protecting the natural environment.

promulgate. To make known; to put into effect by legal decree.

public goods. Goods that cannot be efficiently supplied to one person without also enabling many other persons to enjoy them. The national parks are a public good.

public land. Land owned by the federal government.

radical environmental group. Group willing to use "extreme" tactics or direct action in opposing environmental degradation.

RCRA (Resource Conservation and Recovery Act). Legislation that outlines goals for hazardous waste management.

Rebovich, D.J. Author of *Dangerous Ground: The World of Hazardous Waste Crime* (1992). The book describes the results of an eight-year, multistate study of state environmental crime cases. The offender profile developed from research results was found to be unlike the findings of the earlier Block and Scarpitti work.

reckless. Legal standard used for assessing liability. A reckless act is an act that is more than careless and approaches willful conduct.

Reclamation Act of 1902. Act providing for government construction of irrigation projects to be paid for by water users.

regulatory agency. A government body responsible for the control and operation of a specific area of public interest.

regulatory enforcement. Actions designed to compel compliance with regulations.

remedial action. An action intended to correct a situation.

remediation. The process of restoring a degraded site to some specified standard of cleanliness.

removal action. A short-term response to a hazardous substance emergency.

retroactive liability. Liability that applies to actions that were legal at the time they occurred but have since become illegal.

risk assessment. EPA uses a risk assessment to determine the cleanup classification of a dumpsite based on whether the substances are toxic, the likelihood of exposure, and the likelihood of injury if exposure occurs.

Rivers and Harbors Act of 1899. Also known as the Refuse Act, this legislation was originally drafted to ban unpermitted discharge of refuse into navigable waterways and thus prevent blockages created by excessive refuse dumping.

Ross, E.A. Coiner of the term *criminaloid*, which refers to individuals who behave immorally but cannot be classified as criminal because no law exists that prohibits their behavior.

Safe Drinking Water Act. Enacted in 1974, this statute requires the EPA to set maximum allowable levels of contamination in public drinking water systems. Amended in 1986.

Sagebrush Rebellion. An anticonservation political movement in the late 1970s. Several states passed legislation that assumed ownership of the federal lands held within their state boundaries in response to unwelcome government action regarding those lands.

scientific method. A research method used in most of the sciences and some of the humanities. It involves the construction of testable formalized ideas, called hypotheses, based on repeated observations. The scientific method is characterized by systematic observation and analysis.

secondary consumers. Animals that derive their nutrition by eating herbivores and other carnivores.

second law of thermodynamics. Principle that energy in its initial state is always higher than its final state.

SEDESOL. Predecessor of SEMARNAP. SEDESOL was designed to provide oversight of environmental matters within the Mexican federal government.

SEMARNAP. Agency that currently provides oversight of environmental matters within the Mexican federal government.

Sewergate. "Scandal" involving the bungling of EPA procedures and regulatory authority during the Reagan administration.

small quantity generator (SQG). Facility that produces only a small amount of hazardous wastes and is therefore subject to less strict federal standards.

social transformation. A period of tremendous social change.

solid waste. Waste materials not discarded into surface waters via water treatment systems or emitted directly into the air.

species. A group of organisms that can successfully interbreed with each other under natural conditions.

species recovery plan. A projected plan of recovery for a listed endangered species. The recovery process includes an outline of specific methods for species recovery, survival, and declassification.

standard-based system. System based on specific standards or criteria, such as the system for determining the cleanup classification of hazardous waste sites.

state implementation plan. A federally required state plan, such as the plan each state must devise to show how it intends to meet air quality standards.

stratosphere. The second layer of the atmosphere above the earth; it begins at about 7 miles and extends to about 30 miles above sea level.

strict liability. Liability without fault. This liability standard does not require negligence for an individual to be convicted.

succession. The orderly and sometimes predictable changes in a biological community over time. Growth of new species can drive out other life forms.

Superfund. A fund set up under the Comprehensive Environmental Response, Compensation, and Liability Act (CERCLA) to help pay for the cleanup of hazardous waste sites and to force, through legal action, those responsible for creating the sites to clean them up.

Superfund Amendments and Reauthorization Act (SARA). Act passed in 1986 to revise the Superfund program.

Superfund remediation. Cleanup at hazardous waste sites on the National Priority List.

Supremacy Clause. Clause in Article 6 of the U.S. Constitution that outlines the federal government's power over the states. Federal law is the "supreme law" in the United States.

sustainable development. Economic growth that occurs in an environmentally sound manner and does not result in the depletion of natural resources.

Sutherland, Edwin. One of the first criminologists to call into question the traditional theories of criminology.

symbiosis. The living together of different species to their mutual benefit.

synthetic chemicals. Chemicals that do not occur in nature but are engineered and produced by humans.

synthetic materials. Materials produced by humans.

Takings Clause. Provision in the Fifth Amendment of the U.S. Constitution that prohibits the taking of private property for public use without payment of just compensation.

Taylor Grazing Act. The 1934 statute that established federal regulatory control of public lands in the West.

technology-forcing provision. A legislative provision intended to compel advances in pollution prevention technologies.

Tellico Dam. A large dam construction project, which was halted by a Supreme Court ruling after concern was raised about the impact the dam would have on the tiny snail darter fish.

tertiary consumers. Carnivores that eat other carnivores. Tertiary consumers in an ecosystem are much rarer than primary and secondary consumers.

theory. An accepted explanation for what is observed.

Thoreau, Henry David. A prominent author who wrote about the importance of wilderness for human spirituality.

tipping fees. Fees charged to dump wastes at landfills.

tradable emissions allowance. *See* **emission reduction credit**.

transaction costs. All legal and related expenses involved in settling a dispute.

transborder flow of toxic substances. Transfer of pollutants originating within one nation-state to neighboring or even distant countries through natural ecological processes.

transcendent self. A self that has knowledge that is beyond the limits of experience.

transnational corporation (TNC). A company with divisions in two or more countries.

treatment, storage, and disposal facility (TSD). A facility where hazardous waste is treated, stored, and/or disposed of.

trespass. The physical invasion of property.

triangulation. A research methodology that refers to the integration of different research data sources in an effort to establish a more thorough understanding of the topic of study.

troposphere. The layer of the atmosphere closest to the surface of the earth; it begins around seven miles above sea level.

TSCA (Toxic Substances Control Act). Legislation that requires premanufacture notification of all new chemicals.

TSD. *See* **treatment, storage, and disposal facility**.

U.S. Bureau of Reclamation. Bureau responsible for overseeing the hydroelectric dam construction projects in the arid West.

U.S. Environmental Protection Agency. The U.S. federal agency in charge of environmental compliance and protection.

U.S. Sentencing Commission. Formed in 1986 to write guidelines for sentencing offenders and thus reduce judicial disparity. The first set of guidelines from the commission was published in November 1987.

vegetative waste. Organic waste consisting of tree stumps, branches, grass clippings, leaves, and other yard waste.

vicarious liability. Liability that falls on one person for the actions of another. In many cases, an employer may be held liable for the actions of an employee.

Vienna Accord. An international convention that formally recognized the threat of ozone depletion and called upon nations to engage in systematic research to identify the sources and consequences of ozone depletion. The countries party to the convention agreed to work to "control, limit, reduce, or prevent" ozone-depleting activities within their boundaries.

voluntary compliance policy. Policy enacted by the EPA during the Reagan administration to encourage compliance through cooperation with regulated businesses. Little emphasis is placed on sanctions.

waste tires. Automobile tires discarded after they are no longer useful.

wetlands. Land areas that are covered with water for a large portion of the year.

whistleblower. An employee, or insider, who notifies or cooperates with enforcement authorities investigating alleged illegal activity.

white goods. Large kitchen appliances once they have entered the waste stream.

wildlife crime. A violation of a criminal law designed to protect wildlife.

willful. Voluntary; done deliberately. An action is willful if it is intentional, knowing, or voluntary and thus not accidental.

Wise Use Movement. A political movement advocating individual and group action (in some cases violent action) against the federal government or agents of the federal government. The movement advocates removal of federal officials from management of government-owned lands, primarily in the West.

Wolpe, Howard. Chair of the Science, Space, and Technology's investigative subcommittee.

Important Environmental Activities

1681—William Penn issues ordinance that for every five acres cleared one acre must be left forested.

1710—Massachusetts Colony enacts laws to protect waterfowl in the coastal areas.

1849—U.S. Department of the Interior established.

1871—U.S. Fish Commission established.

1872—Yellowstone National Park established.

1875—American Forestry Association established.

1879—U.S. Geological Survey established.

1881—Division of Forestry established.

1885—Niagara Falls is protected by law.

1891—Forest Reserve Act passed; Yosemite National Park established.

1892—Sierra Club established.

1897—Forest Management Act passed.

1899—Rivers and Harbors Act passed.

1902—Bureau of Reclamation established.

1905—National Audubon Society established.

1906—Antiquities Act passed.

1908—Grand Canyon declared a national monument.

1916—National Park Service Act passed.

1920—Mineral Leasing Act and Federal Water Power Act passed.

1924—Oil Pollution Control Act passed.

Source: Data from S. Cable and C. Cable, *Environmental Problems: Grassroots Solutions*, pp. xvii–xxii, © 1995, St. Martin's Press and J.P. Lester, *Environmental Politics and Policy*, p. 2, © 1991, Duke University Press.

1933—Civilian Conservation Corps and Tennessee Valley Authority established.

1935—Wilderness Society established.

1936—National Wildlife Federation established.

1940—U.S. Fish and Wildlife Service established.

1946—Atomic Energy Act passed.

1948—Federal Water Pollution Control Law passed.

1952—Air pollution reported to have killed 4,000 in London.

1956—Water Pollution Control Act amendments passed.

1960—Multiple Use-Sustained Yield Act and Air Quality Act passed.

1962—Rachel Carson publishes *Silent Spring*.

1963—Clean Air Act passed.

1964—Wilderness Act passed.

1965—Water Quality Act and Solid Waste Disposal Act passed.

1966—Endangered Species Act and Clean Water Restoration Act passed.

1967—Environmental Defense Fund established; Air Quality Act passed.

1968—National Wild and Scenic Rivers Act and National Trails System Act passed.

1969—Cuyahoga River in Cleveland catches fire; Santa Barbara suffers serious oil spill.

1970—National Environmental Protection Act, Clean Air Act amendments, Water Quality Improvement Act, and Resource Recovery Act passed; National Resource Defense Council established.

1971—Alaska Native Claims Settlement Act passed.

1972—Noise Control Act; Clean Water Act; Federal Environmental Pesticide Control Act; Ocean Dumping Act; Marine Protection, Research and Sanctuaries Act; and Coastal Zone Management Act passed. U.N. Conference on the Human Environment held in Sweden.

1973—Endangered Species Act.

1974—Safe Drinking Water Act, Strip Mining Act, and Land Use Policy Act passed.

1976—Federal Land Policy and Management Act, Resource Conservation and Recovery Act, and Toxic Substances Control Act passed.

1977—Clean Air Act amendments, Clean Water Act amendments, Surface Mining Control and Reclamation Act, and Federal Pollution Control Act amendments passed.

1978—National Energy Act, National Parks and Recreation Act, Environmental Pesticide Control Act, and Quiet Communities Act passed; President Carter issues executive order for military to comply with environmental legislation; Love Canal becomes headline news.

1979—Nuclear accident at Three Mile Island occurs.

1980—Comprehensive Environmental Response, Compensation, and Liability Act and National Energy Act passed.

1981—Citizen's Clearinghouse for Hazardous Waste founded; Earth First! established.

1983—Times Beach becomes headline news.

1984—Hazardous and Solid Waste amendments and Safe Drinking Water Act passed; numerous deaths occur due to accidental toxic gas release in Bhopal, India; Cerrell Report issued.

1986—Chernobyl nuclear accident occurs; Superfund amendments and Reauthorization Act passed.

1987—Clean Water Act passed; Commission for Racial Justice established.

1988—DOE releases plan for rebuilding and cleaning up military's weapons complex.

1989—Exxon Valdez responsible for large oil spill off Alaskan coast.

1990—Clean Air Act reauthorized.

1992—U.N. Rio de Janeiro Conference and First World Conference on Environmental Problems held; Federal Facilities Act passed.

1994—DOE began releasing information about radiation experiments on humans.

1995—The Supreme Court ruled on *Babbitt v. Sweet Home* question regarding the definition of "harm" under ESA.

1995–1996—Republican-dominated Congress attempted to reduce the impact of environmental protection legislation.

1996—Rockwell pleaded guilty to three felony charges for illegal storage and disposal of hazardous wastes. The result was a $6.5 million fine after two workers were killed trying to dispose of the material.

1997—31 groups filed a formal legal petition to the EPA over its approval of genetically engineered plants.

APPENDIX C

Criminal Sanctions Outlined in Federal Environmental Legislation

As discussed throughout this text, environmental violations are sometimes punished using criminal sanctions. This section is organized to help describe the extent of those penalties available to judges and juries who handle environmental crimes. Please note, however, that federal legislation is like the wind; it changes all of the time. This section should serve as a model for those interested. A more thorough legal response should be left to environmental law textbooks and environmental litigators.

FEDERAL INSECTICIDE, FUNGICIDE, AND RODENTICIDE ACT

Under the Federal Insecticide, Fungicide, and Rodenticide Act (FIFRA), criminal penalties apply to anyone who knowingly violates any provision of the statute. For FIFRA, the mens rea requirement is satisfied if the prosecution shows that the defendant knew of the "registered" status of a particular poison at the time of the misuse.[1] Further, "the act of 'any officer, agent or other person acting for or employed by any person shall in every case be deemed to be the act, omission, or failure of such person as well as of the person employed.'"[2(p.272)] In practice, liability is determined by the degree of involvement, either in recommendation or supervision of that employee.[3]

The penalties for FIFRA vary. Commercial applicators, wholesalers, dealers, retailers, or other distributors who violate FIFRA may receive a maximum fine of $25,000 per violation, imprisonment of up to one year, or both. Registrants or producers who violate the act face stiffer penalties: a maximum fine of $50,000 per violation, imprisonment of up to one year, or both. Private applicators receive lesser penalties: a $1,000 fine per violation, imprisonment for up to 30 days, or both.[4]

FEDERAL WATER POLLUTION CONTROL ACT

Section 309(c) of the Clean Water Act (CWA) established four different levels of criminal penalties.[5] The penalties differ in severity depending on whether the violations are negligent, are knowing, involve knowing endangerment, or involve knowing falsification of information or tampering with monitoring equipment. Each level has two different penalty ranges: one for first-time offenders and a second for people who have previously been convicted of a CWA violation.[6]

For example, Section 309(c)(1) requires the criminal penalties for a negligent violation to include a fine, imprisonment, or both. If a fine is imposed, it must fall within a range between $2,500 and $25,000 per day of violation for a first-time conviction. A prison term of up to one year may also be assessed.[7] Knowing violations require higher penalties: Fines must fall between $5,000 and $50,000 per day of violation, and prison terms of up to three years may be awarded. Subsequent offenses carry double penalties. Finally, under Section 508, criminal conviction will result in excision from the list of those who may provide contract services to the government.[8] (See also the Coastal Zone Management Act, the Oil Pollution Act, and the Ocean Dumping Act.)

CLEAN AIR ACT

Criminal violations can occur under several sections of the Clean Air Act (CAA). Violation of the National Ambient Air Quality Standards (NAAQS) can result in a criminal fine, up to five years in prison, or both. Knowingly making false statements, failing to report as required, or tampering with EPA monitoring devices can lead to criminal fines, up to two years in prison, or both.

If a violator negligently releases hazardous air pollution or knowingly releases hazardous air pollutants and understands the release will place another person in danger of death or serious bodily harm,[9] the violation may result in a criminal fine of up to $1,000,000 for each violation, up to 15 years in prison, or both. For a second violation, the penalties may be doubled.[10]

RESOURCE CONSERVATION AND RECOVERY ACT

A criminal violation of the Resource Conservation and Recovery Act (RCRA) is committed if one:

1. knowingly transports or causes transportation of RCRA regulation waste to a TSD facility not possessing interim status or a permit for that waste;
2. treats, stores, or disposes of an RCRA regulated waste without a permit or in knowing violation of a material condition of a permit or interim status regulation or standard;
3. dumps an RCRA regulated waste into the ocean without a permit issued under the Marine Protection Research and Sanctuaries Act;
4. makes a false material statement or representation, or omits material information in documents filed, maintained, or used for the purpose of complying with EPA or state RCRA regulations;
5. destroys, alters, conceals, or fails to file a document or record required under the EPA or state RCRA programs;
6. transports or causes the transportation of hazardous waste without a manifest;
7. exports hazardous waste to a foreign country without consent of the recipient government, or in the absence of a treaty allowing export.[11(p.289)]

RCRA criminal violations are outlined in Section 3008(d)(1)-(2). Knowing violations carry a fine of not more than $50,000 per day per violation, imprisonment for not more than 5 years, or both, for the first offense. Additional criminal penalties can be imposed for various other acts and omissions of parties involved, as outlined in the statute.

The EPA is argued to be pursuing an aggressive approach to secure criminal convictions under the RCRA.[12] Corporate officers are especially vulnerable when pursued under the "responsible corporate officer doctrine." This imposes sanctions similar to the strict liability doctrine. The Supreme Court has recently declined to address the legality of imposing this kind of standard, and therefore it is not uncommon for corporate officers to be faced with criminal sanctions under RCRA when the company is in violation.[13]

Finally, government agencies are not exempt from RCRA compliance. Consequently, the EPA and state environmental enforcement agencies have the authority to impose fines and other penalties against federal agencies (see also the Federal Facilities Compliance Act of 1992).[14]

TOXIC SUBSTANCES CONTROL ACT

Section 16(b) of the Toxic Substances Control Act (TSCA) authorizes criminal penalties against anyone "who knowingly or willfully violates" the statute.[15] Some argue few criminal proceedings have been pursued for violations of TSCA, with the exception of illegal disposal of PCBs.[16] In the PCB cases, a felony conviction was supported when the prosecution could prove (1) the defendant intentionally caused the disposal (2) of a PCB mixture containing an unauthorized amount of PCB (3) in a manner inconsistent with federal regulations.[17]

The criminal provisions of TSCA are considered to be less stringent than the criminal provisions found in other environmental statutes.[18] Under TSCA, violators are subject to a fine of not more than $25,000 per day of violation, imprisonment of up to one year, or both.

COMPREHENSIVE ENVIRONMENTAL RESPONSE, COMPENSATION, AND LIABILITY ACT

The plaintiff in a Comprehensive Environmental Response, Compensation, and Liability Act (CERCLA) action is required to show the following:

1. the site involved is a facility as defined in 42 U.S.C. §9607(9);
2. the defendant is a responsible person under 42 U.S.C. §9607(a);
3. a release of a hazardous substance occurred; and
4. the release caused the plaintiff to incur response costs.[19(p.278)]

If the above criteria are met, criminal penalties may apply. Criminal sanctions can be imposed upon any person in charge of a facility who fails to report a release of a hazardous substance to the appropriate federal authority. Section 109 of CERCLA was amended in 1986 to add criminal sanctions and more specific information on the civil penalties.[20] The 1986 revisions of Superfund (known as SARA, or the Superfund Amendments and Reauthorization Act) now impose felony penalties of up to three years' imprisonment for the first offense, up to five years for subsequent offenses, and/or a fine of $250,000 for organizations submitting false claims for reimbursement from Superfund or for failing to notify the EPA of a hazardous waste release.[21] The knowing destruction or falsification of records carries the same penalties as failure to notify of a hazardous waste release. Failure to notify EPA of an unpermitted hazardous waste disposal site results in a fine of no more than $10,000 and/or up to one year imprisonment.[22]

SARA also provided a bounty provision. Section 109(d) states that the government can pay out of the Superfund an award of up to $10,000 for information leading to the arrest and conviction of persons responsible for a criminal CERCLA offense.[23]

While some federal environmental statutes identify defenses for involved parties, the only way to avoid liability in CERCLA is to show the alleged violation was "an act of God, an act of War, or an unforeseeable act or omission of a third person."[24(p.280)] Just a reminder: the Superfund legislation is one of the most controversial and complicated pieces of environmental protection legislation. Consequently, the information presented here is extremely brief. Please see works specifically focused on the Superfund for more explicit information about both criminal and civil sanctions.

REFERENCES

1. S. Ferrey, *Environmental Law: Examples and Explanations* (New York: Aspen Law and Business, 1997), 272.
2. Ferrey, *Environmental Law.*
3. Ferrey, *Environmental Law.*
4. Ferrey, *Environmental Law.*
5. Curran et al., "Environmental Crime," *American Criminal Law Review* 32 (1995): 245–308.
6. Curran et al., "Environmental Crime."
7. Curran et al., "Environmental Crime."
8. Curran et al., "Environmental Crime."
9. Curran et al., "Environmental Crime," 285.
10. Curran et al., "Environmental Crime."
11. Ferrey, *Environmental Law*, 289.
12. Curran et al., "Environmental Crime," 266.
13. Curran et al., "Environmental Crime."
14. Ferrey, *Environmental Law*, 289.
15. Curran et al., "Environmental Crime," 270.
16. C. Hathaway et al., "A Practitioner's Guide to the Toxic Substance Control Act: Part 3," *Environmental Law Reporter* 24 (1994): 10379.
17. Curran et al., "Environmental Crime," 270.
18. Curran et al., "Environmental Crime."
19. Curran et al., "Environmental Crime," 278.
20. Ferrey, *Environmental Law*, 371.
21. Curran et al., "Environmental Crime," 281.
22. Curran et al., "Environmental Crime."
23. Ferrey, *Environmental Law*, 371–372.
24. Ferrey, *Environmental Law*, 280.

APPENDIX D

Environmental Legal Cases

Aberdeen & Rockfish Railroad Co. v. Students Challenging Regulatory Agency Procedures S.C.R.A.P. II), 422 U.S. 289, 95 S.Ct. 2336, 45 L.Ed.2d 191 (1975).

Abramowitz v. U.S. EPA, 832 F.2d 1071 (9th Cir. 1987).

Aceto Agricultural Chemicals Corp. v. U.S., 1373 (8th Cir. 1989).

Adams v. Vance, 570 F.2d 950 (1978).

Agent Orange Product Liability Litigation, In re, 597 F. Supp. 740 (D.C.N.Y. 1984).

Alabama Power Co. v. Costle, 636 F.2d 323 (1979).

Allen v. the U.S., 588 F. Supp. 247 (D.Utah) revd. on other grounds, 816 F.2d 1417 (10th Cir. 1987).

Alyeska Pipeline Service Co. v. Wilderness Society, 421 U.S. 240, 95 S.Ct. 1612, 44 L.Ed.2d 141 (1975).

American Meat Institute v. EPA, 526 F.2d 442 (7th Cir. 1975).

American Mining Congress v. EPA, 842 F.2d 1177 1189 (D.C. Cir. 1987).

American Paper Institute v. U.S. EPA, 660 F.2d 954 (4th Cir. 1981).

American Petroleum Institute v. U.S. EPA, 906 F.2d 729, 285 U.S. App. D.C. 35 (D.C. Cir. 1990).

American Textile Manufacturers Institute, Inc. v. Donovan, 452 U.S. 490, 101 S.Ct. 2478, 69 L.Ed.2d 185 (1981).

Amlon Metals, Inc. v. FMC Corp., 775 F. Supp. 668 (S.D.N.Y. 1991).

Amoco Production Co. v. Village of Gambell, AK, 480 U.S. 531, 107 S.Ct. 1396, 94 L.Ed.2d 542 (1987).

Andrus v. Allard, 444 U.S. 51, 100 S.Ct. 318, 62 L.Ed.2d 210 (1979).

Andrus v. Sierra Club, 442 U.S. 347, 99 S.Ct. 2335, 60 L.Ed.2d 943 (1979).

Angel v. United States, 469 U.S. 1208, 105 S.Ct. 1171, 84 L.Ed.2d 321 (1985).

Appalachian Power Company v. Train, 620 F.2d 1040 (4th Cir. 1980).

Arkansas v. Oklahoma, 112 S.Ct. 1046 (1992).

Baltimore Gas and Electric Company v. Natural Resources Defense Council, Inc., 462 U.S. 87, 103 S.Ct. 2246, 76 L.Ed.2d 437 (1983).

Bergsoe Metal Corp., In re, 910 F.2d 668 (9th Cir. 1990).

Bersani v. Robichaud, 850 F.2d 36 (2d Cir. 1988).

Boomer v. Atlantic Cement Co., 26 N.Y.2d 219, 309 N.Y.S.2d 312, 257 N.E.2d 870 (1970).

Boone v. Kingsbury, 206 Cal. 148, 273 P. 797 (Cal. 1928).

Branch v. Western Petroleum, Inc., 657 P.2d 267 (Utah 1982).

British Airways Bd. v. Port Authority of NY and NJ, 564 F.2d 1002 (1977).

Brown v. United States, 552 F.2d 817 (8th Cir. 1977).

Burbank, City of v. Lockheed Air Terminal Inc., 411 U.S. 624, 93 S.Ct. 1854, 36 L.Ed.2d 547 (1973).

California Coastal Com'n v. Granite Rock Co., 480 U.S. 572, 107 S.Ct. 1419, 94 L.Ed.2d 577 (1987).

California, State of v. Watt, 712 F.2d 584, 229 U.S.App. D.C. 270 (D.C. Cir. 1983).

California, State of v. Watt, 668 F.2d 1290, 215 U.S.App. D.C. 258 (D.C. Cir. 1981).

Calvert Cliffs Coordinating Committee v. United States Atomic Energy Commission, 449 F.2d 1109 (D.C. Cir. 1971).

Camfield v. United States, 167 U.S. 518, 17 S.Ct. 864, 42 L.Ed. 260 (1897).

Cannons Engineering Corp. v. United States, 899 F.2d 79 (1st Cir. 1990).

Cappaert v. United States, 426 U.S. 128, 96 S.Ct. 2062, 48 L.Ed.2d 523 (1976).

Carolina Environmental Study Group v. United States, 510 F.2d 796 (D.C. Cir. 1975).

Carson-Truckee Water Conservancy District v. Clark, 741 F.2d 257 (9th Cir. 1984).

Chem-Dyne Corp. v. United States, 572 F. Supp. 802 (D.C.Ohio 1983).

Chemical Manufacturers Association v. EPA, 899 F.2d 344 (5th Cir. 1990).

Chemical Manufacturers Association v. EPA, 870 F.2d 177 (5th Cir. 1989).

Chemical Manufacturers Association v. NRDC, 470 U.S. 116 (1985).

Chevron, U.S.A. v. Natural Resources Defense Council, 467 U.S. 837 (1984).

Citizens To Preserve Overton Park, Inc. v. Volpe, 401 U.S. 402, 91 S.Ct. 814, 28 L.Ed.2d 136.

Colorado, State of v. United States Department of the Interior, 880 F.2d 481, 279 U.S. App.D.C. 158 (D.C. Cir. 1989).

Commonwealth Edison Co. v. Pollution Control Bd., 62 Ill.2d 494, 343 N.E.2d 459 (Ill. 1976).

Corrosion Proof Fittings v. EPA, 947 F.2d 1201 (5th Cir. 1991).

Darby v. United States, 312 U.S. 100, 312 U.S. 657, 61 S.Ct. 451, 85 L.Ed. 609 (1941).

Delaney v. EPA, 898 F.2d 687 (9th Cir. 1990).

Deltona Corp. v. United States, 657 F.2d 1184 (1981).

Dow Chemical, Inc. v. Alfaro, 786 S.W.2d 674 (Tex. 1990), cert. denied, 111 S.Ct. 671 (1991).

Duke Power Co. v. Carolina Environmental Study Group, Inc., 438 U.S. 59, 98 S.Ct. 2620, 57 L.Ed.2d 595 (1978).

Eagle-Pricher Industries v. EPA, 759 F.2d 922 (D.C. Cir. 1985).

E.I. duPont de Nemours & Co. v. Train, 430 U.S. 112, 97 S.Ct 965, 51 L.Ed.2d 204 (1977).

Environmental Defense Fund, Inc. v. EPA, 548 F.2d 998 (1976).

Environmental Defense Fund, Inc. v. EPA, 465 F.2d 528 (1972).

EPA v. National Crushed Stone Association, 449 U.S. 64, S.Ct. 295, 66 L.Ed. 268.

Ethyl Corp. v. EPA, 541 F.2d 1 (D.C. Cir. 1976) (en banc).

FERC v. Mississippi, 456 U.S. 742, 102 S.Ct. 2126, 72 L.Ed.2d 532 (1982).

Ferebee v. Chevron Chemical Co., 736 F.2d 1529, 237 U.S. App. D.C. 164 (D.C. Cir. 1984).

First English Evangelical Lutheran Church of Glendale v. County of Los Angeles, 482 U.S. 304, 107 S.Ct. 2378, 96 L.Ed.2d 250 (1987).

Fleet Factors Corp. v. United States of America, 901 F.2d 1550 (11th Cir. 1990).

Flint Ridge Development v. Scenic Rivers Ass'n of Oklahoma, 426 U.S. 776, 96 S.Ct. 2430, 49 L.Ed.2d 205 (1976).

Ford Motor Company v. United States, 814 F.2d 1099 (1987).

Garcia v. San Antonio Metropolitan Transit Authority, 469 U.S. 528, 105 S.Ct. 1005, 83 L.Ed.2d 1016 (1985).

General Electric Co. v. Litton Industries Automation Systems, Inc., 920 F.2d 1415 (8th Cir. 1990).

General Motors Corp. v. United States, 496 U.S. 530, 110 S.Ct. 2528, 110 L.Ed.2d 480 (1990).

Georgia v. Tennessee Copper Co., 206 U.S. 230 (1907).

Geo-Tech Reclamation Industries, Inc. v. Hamrick, 886 F.2d 662 (4th Cir. 1989).

Getty Oil Company (Eastern Operations), Inc. v. Ruckelshaus, 467 F.2d 349, cert. denied 409 U.S. 1125, 93 S.Ct. 937, 35 L.Ed.2d 256 (1973).

Greater Westchester Homeowners Association v. City of Los Angeles, 26 Cal.3d 86, 160 Cal.Rptr. 733, 603P.2d 1329, cert. denied 449 U.S. 820, 101 S.Ct. 77, 66 L.Ed.2d 22 (1980).

Gwaltney of Smithfield v. Chesapeake Bay Foundation, 484 U.S. 49 (1987).

Hadacheck v. Sebastian, 239 U.S. 394, 36 S.Ct. 143, 60 L.Ed. 348 (1915).

Hagerty v. L&L Marine Services, 788 F.2d 315 (5th Cir. 1986).

Hanly v. Kleindienst [Hanly II], 471 F.2d 823 (2d Cir. 1972) cert. denied 412 U.S. 908, 93 S.Ct. 2290, 36 L.Ed.2d 974 (1973).

Hanly v. Mitchell [Hanly I], 460 F.2d 640 (2d Cir. 1972), cert. denied 409 U.S. 990, 93 S.Ct. 313, 34 L.Ed.2d 256.

Hayes Intern. Corp. v. United States, 786 F.2d 1499 (11th Cir. 1986).

Hazardous Waste Treatment Council v. EPA, 886 F.2d 355 (D.C. Cir. 1989).

Hercules, Inc. v. EPA, 598 F.2d 91 (1978).

Hodel v. Indiana, 452 U.S. 314, 101 S.Ct. 2376, 69 L.Ed.2d 40 (1981).

Hodel v. Virginia Surface Mining and Reclamation Ass'n, Inc., 452 U.S. 264, 101 S.Ct. 2352, 69 L.Ed.2d 1 (1981).

Hoflin v. United States, 880 F.2d 1033 (9th Cir. 1989).

Holland v. United States, 373 F.Supp. 665 (D.C. Fla. 1974).

Hughes v. Alexandria Scrap Corp., 426 U.S. 794, 96 S.Ct. 2488, 49 L.Ed.2d 220 (1976).

Hughes v. Oklahoma, 441 U.S. 322, 99 S.Ct. 1727, 60 L.Ed.2d 250 (1979).

Hunt v. Chemical Waste Management, Inc., 584 So. 2d 1367 (1991), cert. granted, 60 U.S.L.W. 3208 (1992).

Huron Portland Cement Co. v. City of Detroit, Mich., 362 U.S. 440, 80 S.Ct. 813, 4 L.Ed.2d 852 (1960).

Illinois Central Railroad Co. v. Illinois, 146 U.S. 387, 13 S.Ct. 110, 36 L.Ed. 1018.

Illinois v. General Electric Co., 683 F.2d 206 (7th Cir. 1982).

Industrial Union Department, AFL-CIO v. American Petroleum Institute, 448 U.S. 607 (1980).

International Harvester Co. v. Ruckelshaus, 478 F.2d 615 (1973).

International Paper Co. v. Ouellette, 479 U.S. 481, 107 S.Ct. 805, 93 L.Ed.2d 883.

International Union, UAW v. OSHA, 938 F.2d 1310 (D.C. Cir. 1991).

Izaak Walton League of America v. St. Clair, 353 F. Supp. 698, reversed 497 F.2d 849 (8th Cir. 1974).

Johnson & Towers, Inc. v. United States, 741 F.2d 662 (3rd Cir. 1984).

Joslyn Mfg. Co. v. T.L. James & Co. Inc., F.2d 80 (5th Cir. 1990).

Just v. Marinette County, 56 Wis.2d 7, 201 N.W.2d 761 (1972).

Kaiser Aetna v. United States, 444 U.S. 164, 100 S.Ct. 383, 62 L.Ed.2d 332 (1979).

Kayser-Roth Corp., Inc. v. United States 910 F.2d 24 (1st Cir. 1990).

Kennecott Copper Corp. v. Train, 526 F.2d 1149 (9th Cir. 1975), cert. denied 425 U.S. 935, 96 S.Ct. 1665, 48 L.Ed.2d 176 (1976).

Keystone Bituminous Coal Association v. DeBenedictis, 480 U.S. 470, 107 S.Ct. 1232, 94 L.Ed.2d 472 (1987).

Kleppe v. New Mexico, 426 U.S. 529, 96 S.Ct. 2285, 49 L.Ed.2d 34 (1976).

Kleppe v. Sierra Club, 427 U.S. 390 (1976).

Lead Industries Ass'n, Inc. v. EPA, 647 F.2d 1130, 208 U.S. App. D.C. 1 (D.C. Cir. 1980).

Lone Pine Steering Committee v. United States EPA, 777 F.2d 882 (3rd Cir. 1985).

Lujan v. National Wildlife Federation, 110 S.Ct. 3177 (1990).

Madison v. Ducktown Sulphur, Copper & Iron Company, 113 Tenn. 331, 83 S.W. 658 (1904).

Maine v. United States, 420 U.S. 515, 95 S.Ct. 1155, 43 L.Ed.2d 363 (1975).

Marks v. Whitney, 6 Cal.3d 251, 98 Cal.Rptr. 790, 491 P.2d 374 (1971).

Marsh v. Oregon Natural Resources Council, 490 U.S. 360 (1989).

Maryland Bank & Trust Co. v. United States, 632 F.Supp. 573 (D.Md. 1986).

Massachusetts, Commonwealth of v. United States, 856 F.2d 378 (1st Cir. 1988).

Metropolitan Edison Co. v. People against Nuclear Energy, 460 U.S. 766, 103 S.Ct. 1556, 75 L.Ed.2d 534 (1983).

Midatlantic National Bank v. NJ Dept. of Environmental Protection, 474 U.S. 494, 106 S.Ct. 755, 88 L.Ed.2d 859 (1986).

Midwest Oil Co. v. United States, 236 U.S. 459, 35 S.Ct. 309, 59 L.Ed. 673 (1915).

Miller v. Schoene, 276 U.S. 272, 48 S.Ct. 246, 72 L.Ed. 568 (1928).

Milwaukee, City of v. Illinois and Michigan [Milwaukee IL], 451 U.S. 304, 101 S.Ct. 1784, 68 L.Ed.2d 114 (1981).

Minnesota by Alexander, State of v. Block, 660 F.2d 1240 (8th Cir. 1981), cert. denied 455 U.S. 1007, 102 S.Ct. 1645, 71 L.Ed.2d 876 (1982).

Minnesota Public Interest Research Group v. Butz, 541 F.2d 1292 (8th Cir. 1976), cert. denied 430 U.S. 922, 97 S.Ct. 1340, 51 L.Ed.2d 601 (1977).

Minnesota v. Block, 660 F.2d 1240 (8th Cir. 1981).

Minnesota v. Clover Leaf Creamery Co., 449 U.S. 456, 101 S.Ct. 715, 66 L.Ed.2d 659 (1981).

Mississippi Commission on Natural Resources v. Costle, 625 F.2d 1269 (5th Cir. 1980).

Missouri v. Holland, 252 U.S. 416, 40 S.Ct. 382, 64 L.Ed. 641 (1920).

Missouri v. Illinois, 200 U.S. 496 (1906).

Monsanto Co. v. United States, 858 F.2d 160 (4th Cir. 1988), cert. denied 490 U.S. 1106, 109 S.Ct. 3156, 104 L.Ed.2d 1019 (1989).

Mountain States Legal Foundation v. Andrus, 499 F.Supp. 383 (1980).

National Audubon Society v. Superior Court of Alpine County, 189 Cal.Rptr. 346, 658 P.2d 709 (Cal. 1983).

National League of Cities v. Usery, 426 U.S. 833, 96 S.Ct. 2465, 49 L.Ed.2d 245 (1976).

National Solid Wastes Management Association v. Alabama, 910 F.2d 713 (11th Cir. 1990).

Natural Resources Defense Council, Inc. v. Costle, 564 F.2d 573 (D.C. Cir. 1977).

Natural Resources Defense Council, Inc. v. Morton, 458 F.2d 827 (D.C. Cir. 1972).

Natural Resources Defense Council, Inc. v. US EPA, 683 F.2d 752 (3rd. Cir. 1982).

Natural Resources Defense Council, Inc. v. US EPA, 595 F.Supp. 1255 (S.D.N.Y. 1984).

Natural Resources Defense Council, Inc. v. US EPA, 824 F.2d 1146 (D.C. Cir. 1987).

Rands v. U.S., 389 U.S. 121, 88 S.Ct. 265, 19 L.Ed.2d 329 (1967).

Reeves, Inc. v. Stake, 447 U.S. 429, 100 S.Ct. 2271, 65 L.Ed.2d 244 (1980).

Reserve Mining Company v. EPA, 514 F.2d 492 (8th Cir. 1975).

Riverside Bayview Homes, Inc. v. United States, 474 U.S. 121 (1985).

Robertson v. Methow Valley Citizens Council, 490 U.S. 332, 109 S.Ct. 1835, 104 L.Ed.2d 351 (1989).

Rocky Mountain Oil and Gas Association v. Watt, 696 F.2d 734 (10th Cir. 1982).

Roosevelt Campobello International Park Community v. EPA, 684 F.2d 1041 (1st Cir. 1982).

Ruckelshaus v. Sierra Club, 463 U.S. 680, 103 S.Ct. 3274, 77 L.Ed.2d 938 (1983).

Scientists' Institute for Public Information v. Atomic Energy Commission, 481 F.2d 1079 (D.C. Cir. 1973).

Seattle Audubon Society v. Evans, 771 F. Supp. 1081 (W.D. Wash. 1991), affd., 952 F.2d 297 (9th Cir. 1991).

Secretary of the Interior v. California, 464 U.S. 312, 104 S. Ct. 656, 78 L.Ed.2d 496 (1984).

Sierra Club v. Army Corps of Engineers, 701 F.2d 1011 (2nd Cir. 1983).

Sierra Club v. Costle, 657 F.2d 298 (D.C. Cir. 1981).

Sierra Club v. Morton, 405 U.S. 727 (1972).

Sierra Club v. Peterson, 717 F.2d 1409 (D.C. Cir. 1983).

Silkwood v. Kerr-McGee Corp., 464 U.S. 238, 104 S.Ct. 615, 78 L.Ed.2d 443 (1984).

Sindell v. Abbott Laboratories, 163 Cal.Rptr. 132, 607 P.2d 924 (Cal. 1980).

Spurr Industries, Inc. v. Del E. Webb Development Co., 108 Ariz. 178, 494 P.2d 700 (1972).

State Department of Environmental Protection v. Ventron Corp., 94 N.J. 473, 468 P.2d 700 (Ariz. 1972).

Sterling v. Velsicol Chemical Corp., 855 F.2d 1188 (6th Cir. 1988).

Stryker's Bay Neighborhood Council, Inc. v. Karlen, 444 U.S. 223 (1980).

Students Challenging Regulatory Agency Procedures (SCRAP I) v. United States, 412 U.S. 669, 93 S.Ct. 2405, 37 L.Ed.2d 254 (1973).

Suffolk Country v. Secretary of Interior, 562 F.2d 1368 (1978), cert. denied 434 U.S. 1064, 98 S.Ct. 1238, 55 L.Ed.2d 764 (2nd Cir. 1977).

Sylvester v. United States Army Corps of Engineers, 882 F.2d 407 (1989).

Tennessee Valley Authority v. Hill, 437 U.S. 153 (1978).

Thomas v. Peterson, 753 F.2d 754 (9th Cir. 1985).

Thornton, State ex rel. v. Hay, 254 Or. 584, 462 P.2d 671 (1969).

Train v. Natural Resources Defense Council, Inc., 421 U.S. 60, 95 S.Ct. 1470, 43 L.Ed.2d 731 (1975).

Union Electric Co. v. EPA, 427 U.S. 246, 96 S.Ct. 2518, 49 L.Ed.2d 474 (1976).

Union Oil Co. of California v. Morton, 512 F.2d 743 (9th Cir. 1975).

United Steelworkers of America v. Marshall, 647 F.2d 1189 (D.C. Cir. 1980).

Ventron Corp. v. State, 94 N.J. 473, 468 A.2d 150 (1983).

Vermont Yankee Nuclear Power Corporation v. NRDC, 435 U.S. 519 (1978).

Wall Tube & Metal Products Col., In re, 831 F.2d 118 (6th Cir. 1987).

Waste Industries, Inc. v. United States, 734 F.2d 159 (1984).

Weinberger v. Catholic Action of Hawaii/Peace Education Project, 454 U.S. 139, 102 S.Ct. 197, 70 L.Ed.2d 298 (1981).

Weinberger v. Romero-Barcelo, 456 U.S. 305, 102 S.Ct. 1798, 72 L.Ed.2d 91 (1982).

Wells, Mfg. Co. v. Pollution Control Bd., 73 Ill.2d 226, 22 Ill.Dec. 672, 383 N.E.2d 148 (Ill. 1978).

Weuerhaeuser Co. v. Costle, 590 F.2d 1011 (D.C. Cir. 1978).

Wheeling-Pittsburgh Steel Corp. v. United States, 818 F.2d 1077 (3rd Cir. 1987).

Whitmore v. Arkansas, 495 U.S. 149, 110 S.Ct. 1717, 109 L.Ed.2d 153 (1990).

Wickland Oil Terminals v. Asarco, Inc., 792 F.2d 887 (9th Cir. 1986).

Wilsonville, Village of v. SCA Services, 86 Ill.2d 1, 55 Ill.Dec. 499, 426 N.E.2d 824 (1981).

Environmental Crimes Investigations for Law Enforcement Officers

**BROWARD COUNTY
SHERIFF'S OFFICE**
2601 West Broward Blvd.
Fort Lauderdale, Florida 33311
(305) 321-5000

**BROWARD COUNTY
DEPARTMENT OF
NATURAL RESOURCE PROTECTION**
500 East Broward Blvd., Suite 104
Fort Lauderdale, Florida 33394
(305) 765-5181

Courtesy of Detective Michael Szish and the Broward County Sheriff's Office, Fort Lauderdale, Florida.

Table of Contents

Environmental Crime State Statutes
(at a glance)

Introduction

In order to ensure that the citizens of Broward County have a clean and healthy place to live and work, it is the responsibility of all sworn law enforcement personnel and environmental regulatory agents to detect and apprehend those persons suspected of violating the statutes, rules, and codes that were designed to protect our environment.

One agency that is on the forefront in the enforcement of environmental rules and regulations in our county is The Broward County Department of Natural Resource Protection. D.N.R.P. is a regulatory and enforcement agency designed to protect, restore and enhance the County's natural resources and quality of life. The Agency's four priorities are to anticipate future environmental problems, develop projects for pollution prevention, enforce rule violations, and the issuance and tracking of permits. The structure of the D.N.R.P. administration is designed to direct six of its divisions, two considered "service divisions": the Monitoring Division and Permit Division, and four "technical divisions": the Biological Resource Division, Air Quality Division, Water Quality Division, and Hazardous Materials/Solid Waste Division.

In 1991, the Broward County Department of Natural Resource Protection, the Broward County Sheriff's Office, and other law enforcement entities joined resources in order to more effectively combat the illegal disposal of wastes and enforce environmental regulations. This booklet has been designed, printed, and circulated by the Broward County Sheriff's Office with the intention of giving Law Enforcement Officers and Environmental Compliance Officers a comprehensive look at some of the most frequently violated State Statutes, Florida Administrative Code rules, and County Ordinances.

WARNING

This booklet was designed as a quick reference guide so field personnel could readily classify an incident that is impacting the environment. In addition, a phone list has been included so field personnel can make contact with the appropriate agency for investigation of an environmental incident.

Changes in Florida State Statutes and Florida Administrative Code occur frequently. Statutes and Code should be verified prior to taking action.

THIS BOOKLET SHOULD NOT BE USED AS A TRAINING GUIDE. UNTRAINED PERSONS SHOULD NOT ATTEMPT TO HANDLE, TRANSPORT, OR DISPOSE OF HAZARDOUS OR BIO-HAZARDOUS WASTE. IT IS A VIOLATION OF FEDERAL LAW (29-CFR-1910.120 (3)(i) FOR ANY PERSON TO ENGAGE IN HAZARDOUS WASTE REMOVAL OR OTHER ACTIVITIES WHICH EXPOSES OR COULD EXPOSE A PERSON TO THE HAZARDOUS SUBSTANCE. IF YOUR AGENCY DOES NOT HAVE O.S.H.A. CERTIFIED PERSONNEL TO HANDLE THE INVESTIGATION OF ILLEGALLY DUMPED HAZARDOUS OR BIOHAZARDOUS WASTE, CONTACT THE BROWARD COUNTY SHERIFF'S OFFICE'S, ORGANIZED CRIME DIVISION.

403.413 FLORIDA LITTER LAW

(1) SHORT TITLE — This section may be cited as the "Florida Litter Law."

2) DEFINITIONS — As used in this section:

a) "Litter" means any garbage; rubbish; trash; refuse; can; bottle; box; container; paper; tobacco product; tire; appliance; mechanical equipment or part; building or construction material; tool; machinery; wood; motor vehicle or motor vehicle part; vessel; aircraft; farm machinery or equipment; sludge from a waste treatment facility; water supply treatment plan, or air pollution control facility; or substance in any form resulting from domestic, industrial, commercial, mining, agricultural or governmental operations.

b) "Person" means any individual, firm, sole proprietorship, partnership, corporation, or unincorporated association.

c) "Law enforcement officer" means any officer of the Florida Highway Patrol, a county sheriff's department, a municipal law enforcement department, a law enforcement department of any other political subdivision, the Department of Natural Resources, or the Game and Fresh Water Fish Commission. In addition, and solely for the purposes of this section, "law enforcement officer" means any employee of a county or municipal park or recreation department designated by the department head as a litter enforcement officer.

d) "Aircraft" means a motor vehicle or other vehicle that is used or designed to fly but does not include a parachute or any other device used primarily as safety equipment.

e) "Commercial purpose" means for the purpose of economic gain.

f) "Commercial vehicle" means a vehicle that is owned or used by a business for a commercial purpose.

g) "Dump" means to dump, throw, discard, place, deposit, or dispose of.

h) "Motor Vehicle" means an automobile, motorcycle, truck, trailer, semitrailer, truck tractor, or semitrailer combination or any other vehicle that is powered by a motor.

i) "Vessel" means a boat, barge, or airboat or any other vehicle that i powered by a motor.

3) RESPONSIBILITY OF LOCAL GOVERNING BODY OF A COUNTY OR MUNICIPALITY —

The local governing body of a county or a municipality shall determine the training and qualifications of any employee of the county or municipality or any employee of the county or municipal park or recreation department designated to enforce the provisions of this section if the designated employee is not a regular law enforcement officer.

4) DUMPING LITTER PROHIBITED — Unless otherwise authorized by law or permit, it is unlawful for any person to dump litter in any manner or amount:

a) In or on any public highway, road, street, alley, or thoroughfare, including any portion of the right-of-way therefor, or any other public lands, except in containers or areas lawfully provided therefor. When any litter is thrown or discarded from a motor vehicle, the operator or owner of the motor vehicle, or both, shall be deemed in violation of this section;

b) In or on any freshwater lake, river, canal, or stream or tidal or coastal water of the state, including canals. When any litter is thrown or discarded from a boat, the operator or owner of the boat, or both, shall be deemed in violation of this section; or,

c) In or on any private property, unless prior consent of the owner has been given and unless such litter will not cause a public nuisance or be in violation of any other state or local law, rule, or regulation.

5) PENALTIES; ENFORCEMENT —

a) Any person who dumps litter in violation of subsection (4) in an amount not exceeding 15 pounds in weight or 27 cubic feet in volume and not for commercial purposes is guilty of a noncriminal infraction, punishable by a civil penalty of $50. In addition, the court may require the violator to pick up litter or perform other labor commensurate with the offense committed.

b) Any person who dumps litter in violation of subsection (4) in an amount exceeding 15 pounds in weight or 27 cubic feet in volume, but not exceeding 500 pounds in weight or 100 cubic feet in volume and not for commercial purposes is guilty of a misdemeanor of the first degree, punishable as provided in S.775.082 or S.775.083. In addition, the court shall require the violator to pick up letter or perform other community service commensurate with the offense committed. Further if the violation involves the use of a motor vehicle, upon a finding of guilt, whether or not adjudication is withheld or whether imposition of sentence is withheld, deferred, or suspended, the court shall forward a record of the finding to the Department of Highway Safety and Motor Vehicles, which shall record a penalty of three points on the violator's driver's license pursuant to the point system established by S. 322.27.

c) Any person who dumps litter in violation of subsection (4) in an amount exceeding 500 pounds in weight or 100 cubic feet in volume or in any quantity for commercial purposes, or dumps litter which is a hazardous waste as defined in S. 403.703, is guilty of a felony of the third degree, punishable as provided in S.775.082 or S.775.083. In addition, the court may order the person

1: Remove or render harmless the litter that he dumped in violation of this section;

2: Repair or restore property damaged by, or pay damages for any damage arising out of, his dumping litter in violation of this section; or

3: Perform public service relating to the removal of litter dumped in violation of this section or to the restoration of an area polluted by litter dumped in violation of this section.

d) A court may enjoin a violation of this section.

e) A motor vehicle, vessel, aircraft, container, crane, winch, or machine used to dump litter that exceeds 500 pounds in weight or 100 cubic feet in volume is declared contraband and is subject to forfeiture in the same manner as provided in SS. 932.703 and 932.704.

f) If a person sustains damages arising out of a violation of this section that is punishable as a felony, a court, in a civil action for such damages, shall order the person to pay the injured party threefold the actual damages or $200, whichever amount is greater. In addition, the court shall order the person to pay the injured party's court costs and attorney's fees. A final judgment rendered in a criminal proceeding against a defendant under this section stops the defendant from asserting any issue in a subsequent civil action under this paragraph which he would be estopped from asserting if such judgment were rendered in the civil action unless the criminal judgment was based upon a plea of no contest.

FELONY ELEMENTS
OF THE
FLORIDA LITTER LAW
FSS 403.413 (5)(c)

As in any felony investigation, there are elements of the Florida Litter Law which must be detailed in a probable cause affidavit by the investigating officer in order to prove a violation of this statute. Those elements which require some type of documentation are: the **WEIGHT** of the material, the **VOLUME** of the material, the act of dumping was for a **COMMERCIAL PURPOSE**, or the substance dumped was **HAZARDOUS MATERIAL/WASTE**.

WEIGHT
Any amount of litter/debris over 500 pounds

In order to prove this element of the Florida Litter Law, the litter/debris which is dumped by the suspect must be weighed at a certified scale. The litter/debris should be collected and then transported to the Broward County land fill on U.S. 27 and weighed. If the amount is found to be over 500 lbs., a scale receipt and copy of the scale's most recent calibration certificate should be obtained and attached to the case filing packet. The name of the scale operator should also be obtained and listed as a witness in the police report. Be sure to pick up and weigh only the debris resulting from the violation being investigated. If only a portion of the debris was dumped at the time of arrest, the entire content of the vehicle should be weighed. Photograph the debris if possible.

VOLUME
Any amount of litter/debris over 100 cubic feet

In order to prove this element, the pile of debris must be measured. Document the **length** in feet, multiplied by the **width** in feet, multiplied by the **height** in feet. This will give you the total cubic feet of the debris. Document the implement used to measure the debris and photograph the debris if possible.

COMMERCIAL PURPOSES
Any amount of litter/debris dumped for financial gain of the suspect

In order to prove this element, the fact that the suspect violated the statute for financial gain must be substantiated by showing the suspect was paid to remove and/or dispose of the litter/debris which was illegally dumped.

Documentation obtained from the suspect's possessions and/or a search of the suspects vehicle, subsequent to arrest, may provide the evidence needed. Items such as receipts made out by the suspect for work contracted, contracts, permits, checks payable to the defendant that are connected to the removal or disposal of the debris, or cash paid for contracted work should be seized as evidence.

In addition, a business owner who conducts illegal dumping activities in order to avoid paying for proper disposal of litter/debris generated by the business is dumping for commercial purposes. In this type of case, your investigation should show how much the defendant is saving in business costs by illegally dumping material generated by the business.

HAZARDOUS WASTE
Any amount of hazardous waste

If a uniformed officer on-views an incident or responds to a complaint involving any type of hazardous material, secure the area. The Broward County or Municipal Fire Department's Hazardous Materials Team and the Sheriff's Office or Municipal Police Agency should be contacted during the first stages of a hazardous materials incident. The Broward Sheriff's Office has established liaison with local, state, and federal regulatory agencies and will conduct a joint investigation with those entities.

The definition of hazardous waste is found in FSS 403.703 (23), which states "Hazardous waste" means solid waste (solid waste can be a liquid), or a combination of solid waste, which, because of its quantity, concentration, or physical, chemical, or infectious characteristics, may cause, or significantly contribute to, an increase in mortality or an increase in serious irreversible or incapacitating reversible illness or may pose a substantial or potential hazard to human health or the environment when improperly transported, disposed of, stored, treated, or otherwise managed.

ENVIRONMENTAL CONTROL FSS 403.161

Section 403.161 of the Florida State Statutes allows a law enforcement officer to initiate criminal prosecution against a violator who fails to comply with certain sections of state environmental regulations or causes pollution. In order to determine which violations are addressed in this statute and which violation is a misdemeanor or felony, the entire statute must be read carefully.

"POLLUTION" is the presence in the outdoor atmosphere or waters of the state of any substances, contaminants, noise, or manmade or man-induced impairment of air or waters or alterations of the chemical, physical, biological, or radiological integrity of air or water in quantities or levels which are or may be potentially harmful or injurious to human health or welfare, animal or plant life, or property or which unreasonably interfere with the enjoyment of life and property, including outdoor recreation unless authorized by applicable law.

"THE DEPARTMENT" refers to the Florida Department of Environmental Regulation.

"WILLFUL" refers to the fact that the caused pollution was done willfully. It is not necessary for the suspects to have knowledge that their actions would result in pollution.

F.S. 403.161 Prohibitions, violation, penalty, intent —

1) It shall be a violation of this chapter and it shall be prohibited for any person:

    a) To cause pollution, except as otherwise provided in this chapter, so as to harm or injure human health or welfare, animal, plant, or aquatic life or property.

    b) To fail to obtain any permit required by this chapter or by rule or regulation, or to violate or fail to comply with any rule, regulation, order, permit or certification adopted or issued by the department pursuant to its lawful authority.

    c) To knowingly make any false statement, representation, or certification in any application, record, report, plan, or other document filed or required to be maintained under this chapter, or to falsify, tamper with, or knowingly render inaccurate any monitoring device or method required to be maintained under this chapter or by any permit, rule, regulation, or order issued under this chapter.

    d) For any person who owns or operates a facility to fail to report to the representative of the department, as established by department rule, within one working day or discovery of a release of hazardous substances from the facility if the owner or operator is required to report the release to the United States Environmental Protection Agency in accordance with 4. U.S.C. s.90603.

2) Whoever commits a violation specified in subsection (1) is liable to the state for any damage caused and for civil penalties as provided in s.403.141.

3) Any person who willfully commits a violation specified in paragraph (1)(a) is guilty of a felony of the third degree punishable as provided in ss. 775.082(3)(d) and 775.083(1)(g) by a fine of not more than $50,000 or by imprisonment for 5 years, or by both, for each offense. Each day during any portion of which such violation occurs constitutes a separate offense.

(4) Any person who willfully commits a violation specified in paragraph (1)(a) due to reckless indifference or gross careless disregard is guilty of a misdemeanor of the second degree, punishable as provided in ss. 775.082(4)(b) and 775.083(1)(g) by a fine of not more than $5,000 or by 60 days in jail, or by both, for each offense.

5) Any person who willfully commits a violation specified in paragraph (1)(b) or paragraph (1)(c) is guilty of a misdemeanor of the first degree punishable as provided in ss. 775.082(4)(a) and 775.083(1)(g) by a fine of not more than $10,000 or by 6 months in jail, or by both for each offense.

6) it is the legislative intent that the civil penalties and criminal fines imposed by the court be of such amount as to ensure immediate and continued compliance with this section.

WASTE TIRES

Regulations regarding the handling, transportation, storage, and disposal of waste tires is detailed in section 17-711, titled "Waste Tire Rules", of the Florida Administrative Codes.

Waste tire collectors are required to register with the Florida Department of Environmental Regulations and obtain a permit prior to transporting waste tires. Once obtained, a Waste Tire Collector decal is issued to the hauler and should be displayed on the drivers door of the vehicle while tires are being transported. A sample of a Waste Tire Collector decal is shown below. If a vehicle is observed hauling what appears to be 25 or more waste tires and no decal is visible, probable cause exists to stop the vehicle for further investigation. In addition, it is a violation to contract an unregistered tire hauler to haul waste tires. Persons who violate these two regulations can be charged with a first degree misdemeanor.

Prior to making an arrest for the above violations, contact the F.D.E.P. in Tallahassee at (904) 922-6104, and verify if the person being investigated is registered. Document the date and time you make the verification and request the name and address of the person who verified the information. An affidavit should be sent to that person, verifying the information obtained, for court purposes. If no verification can be made at the time of the stop, the case should be filed with the State Attorneys Office once the documents are obtained. Of course, if the suspect gives a statement such as "what permit" or "I have no permit", during an investigative interview, then the arrest can be made on probable cause if the hauler is carrying more than 25 waste tires. (See definition of "Waste Tire Collector")

The portions of F.A.C. 17-711 provided in this booklet can be used as a reference in order to assist in making a probable cause arrest. Copies of section 17-711 and FSS 403.161(5) should be presented with your event report and probable cause affidavit for quick reference by the State Attorney during case filing.

Decal should be displayed on drivers door when transporting 25 or more waste tires.

17-711.100 INTENT.

It is the purpose of this rule to protect the public health, welfare and the environment by providing for the regulation of waste tire storage, collection, transport, processing and disposal.

17-711.200 DEFINITIONS

2) "Department" means any and all persons, natural or artificial, including any individual, firm or association; any municipal or private corporation organized or existing under the laws of this state or any other; any county of this state; and any governmental agency of this state or the Federal government.

5) "Processed tire" means a waste tire that has been cut, shredded, burned or otherwise altered so that it is no longer whole.

8) "Tire" means a continuous solid or pneumatic rubber covering encircling the wheel of a motor vehicle.

9) "Tire disposal" means to deposit, dump, spill or place any waste tire, processed tire, or residuals into or upon any land or water.

11) "Waste tire" means a whole tire that is no longer suitable for its originally intended purpose because of wear, damage, or defect.

13) "Waste tire collector" means a person who removes and transports more than 25 waste tires or processed tires at any one time from one place to another over public highways.

17-711.300 WASTE TIRE PERMIT REQUIREMENTS

3) After July 1, 1989, waste tire collectors shall register with the Department and shall meet the requirements for waste tire collectors in Rule 17-711.520, F.A.C.

17-711.400 WASTE TIRE PROHIBITIONS

2) After July 1, 1989, no person shall dispose of waste tires or processed tires except at a permitted solid waste management facility. Collection or storage of waste tires at a permitted waste tire processing facility or waste tire collection center prior to processing or use does not constitute disposal, provided that the collection and storage complies with Rule 17-711.540, F.A.C. The

illegal disposal of waste tires or processed tires may be considered a violation of section 403.413.F.S., as well as other provisions of the law.

5) No person may contract with a waste tire collector for the transportation, disposal, or processing of waste tires unless the collector is registered with the Department or exempt from registration requirements.

17-711.520   WASTE TIRE COLLECTOR REQUIREMENTS

1) The requirements of this section apply to collectors of waste tires and processed tires.

2) Persons who use company-owned or company-leased vehicles to transport tire casings for the purposes of retreading between company-owned or company-franchised retail tire outlets and retread facilities owned or franchised by the same company are not considered waste tire collectors unless they also transport waste tires.

3) After July 1, 1989, any person engaged in collecting or transporting waste tires for the purpose of storage, disposal, or processing shall display a current decal with their waste tire collector registration number obtained from the Department. The decal shall be displayed on the outside of the driver's front door of each truck used to transport tires. Common carriers may display decals on removable marking panels.

8) Any person who fails to comply with this rule is subject to having their waste tire collector registration number revoked, as well as other penalties provided by law.

9) When a waste tire collector registration number expires or is revoked, the applicant shall immediately remove all registration decals from all vehicles.

10) A waste tire collector shall leave waste tires and processed tires for storage or disposal only in a permitted waste tire processing or collection facility, at a permitted solid waste management facility, or at another site approved by the Department.

USED OIL

The transportation, storage, and disposal of used oil is addressed in the Florida Administrative Codes, Chapter 17-710, titled Used Oil Management. Also included in the chapter are permit requirements for used oil transporters. However, the most common area the road patrol officer faces is disposal.

As with waste tires, failing to comply with any rule, regulation, order, permit, or certification adopted or issued by the F.D.E.R. with regards to used oil management is a violation of FSS 403.161(5). If used oil is dumped along with its container, such as a 55 gallon drum, the drums and oil can be either weighed or measured in order to fit the statute requirements for a felony under 403.413. In addition, if it can documented that the dumping of the oil is causing environmental harm, felony charges outlined in 403.161 may apply. In this case a thorough crime scene investigation must be conducted.

The portions of the Used Oil Management section provided on the following page can be used to assist in completing a probable cause affidavit; however, the complete section should be reviewed prior to taking action. The sections of the Florida State Statute and Florida Administrative Codes addressed in an arrest should be copied and submitted with your case filing package.

F.A.C. 17-710
USED OIL MANAGEMENT

17-710.200 DEFINITIONS:

2) "Collection" means the accumulation of used oil from one's own operations or from other persons.

3) "Used oil" means any oil which has been refined from crude oil or synthetic oil and, as a result of use, storage, or handling has become unsuitable for its original purpose due to the presence of impurities or loss of its original properties, but which may be suitable for further use and is economically recyclable.

17-710.400 PROHIBITIONS:

1) No person may collect, transport, store, recycle, use, or dispose of used oil or oily wastes in any manner which endangers the public health or welfare or the environment.

2) No person may discharge used oil into soils, sewers, drainage systems, septic tanks, surface or ground waters, watercourses, or marine waters.

3) [a] Except as provided in [b], no person may mix or commingle used oil with solid waste that is to be disposed of in landfills or directly dispose of used oil in landfills.

[b] The Department shall allow disposal of used oil commingled with solid waste if it determines that it is not practicable to separate the used oil from the solid waste, and if such disposal will pose no significant threat to public health or the environment.

4) Any person who unknowingly disposes into a landfill any properly segregated from other solid wastes by the generator is not guilty of a violation under this rule.

5) No person may mix or commingle used oil with hazardous substances that make the used oil unsuitable for recycling or beneficial use.

6) Used oil shall not be used for road oiling, dust control, weed abatement or other similar uses that may release used oil into the environment.

BIOHAZARDOUS WASTE

The investigation of crimes involving hazardous and biohazardous incidents are mentioned in this booklet solely for the safety of the road patrol officer and first line supervisor. **NO** untrained personnel should enter a scene or attempt to investigate any incident involving hazardous and biohazardous materials.

Biohazardous waste is packaged for disposal in several types of containers; however, the most common container is a red plastic bag labeled with the universal symbol for biohazardous waste, shown below. In most cases, there is information either on the bag or on its container identifying the generator of the waste.

Any incident involving illegal disposal, accidents, or spills, should be handled as an immediate health threat. The area should be secured and detectives from Broward Sheriff's Office, or Municipal Police Agency, should be contacted. The detective can then assist the on-scene supervisor in reference to the proper environmental or public health agencies which should be contacted. In Broward County, incidents involving biohazardous materials are handled by HRS, who can be contacted at 467-4935.

Biohazardous waste symbol

F.A.C. 17-712.200

BIOHAZARDOUS WASTE, as defined means any solid waste or liquid waste which may present a threat of infection to humans. The terms includes, but is not limited to, nonliquid human tissue and body parts; laboratory and veterinary waste which contains human disease-causing agents; discarded sharps; human blood, human blood products, and body fluids. The following are also included:

a) Used, absorbent materials such as bandages, gauze, or sponges supersaturated, having the potential to drip or splash, with blood or body fluids from areas such as operating rooms, delivery rooms, trauma centers, emergency rooms, or autopsy rooms.

b) Devices which retain visible blood adhering to inner surfaces after use and rinsing such as intravenous tubing, hemodialysis filters and catheters; and

c) Other contaminated solid waste materials which represent a significant risk of infection because they are generated in medical facilities with care for persons suffering from diseases requiring strict isolation criteria and listed by the U.S. Department of Health and Human Services, Centers for Disease Control, "CDC Guideline for Isolation Precautions In Hospitals," July/August, 1983.

STATE OF FLORIDA
ENVIRONMENTAL CRIMINAL
ENFORCEMENT STATUTES

HAZARDOUS WASTE

Prohibited Act	Criminal Violation
SS. 316.302(4) As motor carrier, transports without proper placarding or shipping papers or in violation of other rules and regulations.	1st Degree Misdemeanor
SS. 403.161 Willfully: Fails to obtain any permit required by Chapter, rule or regulation, or violates or fails to comply with any rule, regulation, order, permit or certification. Knowingly makes false statement, representation or certification in any document filed or required, or falsifies, tampers with or knowingly renders inaccurate any monitoring device or method.	1st Degree Misdemeanor
With reckless indifference or gross careless disregard except as provided, causes pollution so as to harm or injure human health or welfare, animal, plant, or aquatic life or property.	2nd Degree Misdemeanor
Willfully, except as provided, causes pollution so as to harm or injure human health or welfare, animal, plant, or aquatic life or property.	3rd Degree Felony
SS. 403.413(5) Dumps in violation of subsection litter which is hazardous waste.	3rd Degree Felony

STATE OF FLORIDA
ENVIRONMENTAL CRIMINAL
ENFORCEMENT STATUTES

HAZARDOUS WASTE

Prohibited Act	Criminal Violation
SS. 403.727(3)(b)	
Knowingly or exhibiting reckless in-difference or gross disregard for human health, with respect to biohazardous or hazardous waste.	
Transports or causes to be transported to facility which does not have a required permit.	
Disposes, treats or stores at any place but permitted facility, or in knowing violation of material permit condition, requirement, rule or standard, if has substantial likelihood of endangering human health, animal or plant life or property.	3rd Degree Felony
Makes any false statement or representation or knowingly omits material information in document required.	
Generates, stores, treats, transports, disposes of, or otherwise handles and knowingly destroys, alters, conceals or fails to file document required.	
Transports or causes to be transported without manifest.	
SS. 895.01.08	
From pattern of racketeering activity (including transporting, treating, storing, or disposing of hazardous waste without permit):	
Uses or invests proceeds in real property or operation or enterprise;	1st Degree Felony
Acquires or maintains interest in real property or enterprise;	
Conducts or participates in enterprise through such pattern.	

STATE OF FLORIDA
ENVIRONMENTAL CRIMINAL
ENFORCEMENT STATUTES

WATER POLLUTION

Prohibited Act	Criminal Violation
SS. 298.66	
Willfully or otherwise obstructs any canal, drain, ditch or watercourse, or damages or destroys any drainage works.	3rd Degree Felony
SS. 373.123	
Constructs, or enlarges, or causes to be constructed or enlarged, canal, or enlarges or deepens natural stream in such a manner as to permit salt water to move inland of established saltwater barrier line.	2nd Degree Misdemeanor
SS. 373.336	
Violates part regarding regulation of wells, or regulation or order.	2nd Degree Misdemeanor
SS. 387.06	
Discharges sewage or surface drainage, or permits same to flow into underground waters.	Misdemeanor
SS. 387.07	
Willfully or maliciously defiles, corrupts, or makes impure any spring or other source of water reservoir, or destroys or injures any pipe, conductor of water, or other property pertaining to aqueduct, or aids or or abets in any such trespass.	1st Degree Misdemeanor
SS. 387.08	
Deposits, or permits or allows any person to deposit, in any waters of lakes, rivers, streams, and ditches, any rubbish, filth, or poisonous or deleterious substance liable to affect health of persons, fish, or livestock, or places or deposits any such deleterious substance in any place where it may be washed or infiltrated into such waters.	2nd Degree Misdemeanor

STATE OF FLORIDA
ENVIRONMENTAL CRIMINAL
ENFORCEMENT STATUTES

WATER POLLUTION

Prohibited Act	Criminal Violation
SS. 403.161	
Willfully: Fails to obtain any permit required by chapter, rule or regulation, or violates or fails to comply with any rule, regulation, order, permit or certification.	1st Degree Misdemeanor
Willfully: Knowingly makes false statement, representation, or certification in any document filed or required, or falsifies, tampers with, or knowingly renders inaccurate any monitoring device or method.	1st Degree Misdemeanor
With reckless indifference or gross careless disregard, except as provided, causes pollution so as to harm or injure human health or welfare, animal, plant, or aquatic life or property.	2nd Degree Misdemeanor
Willfully, except as provided, causes pollution so as to harm or injure human health or welfare, animal, plant, or aquatic life or property.	3rd Degree Felony

STATE OF FLORIDA
ENVIRONMENTAL CRIMINAL
ENFORCEMENT STATUTES

AIR POLLUTION

Prohibited Act	Criminal Violation
SS. 316.2935 Knowingly and willfully violates subsection regarding tampering with air pollution control equipment on motor vehicle.	2nd Degree Misdemeanor 1st Degree Misdemeanor for Dealer
SS. 403.161 Willfully: Fails to obtain any permit required by chapter, rule or regulation, or violates or fails to comply with any rule, regulation, order, permit, or certification. Knowingly makes false statement, representation or certification in any document filed or required, or falsifies, tampers with, or knowingly renders inaccurate any monitoring device or method.	1st Degree Misdemeanor
With reckless indifference or gross careless disregard, except as provided, causes pollution so as to harm or injure human health or welfare, animal, plant, or aquatic life or property.	2nd Degree Misdemeanor
Willfully, except as provided, causes pollution so as to harm or injure human health or welfare, animal, plant, or aquatic life or property.	3rd Degree Felony

STATE OF FLORIDA
ENVIRONMENTAL CRIMINAL
ENFORCEMENT STATUTES

OTHER

Prohibited Act	Criminal Violation
SS. 376.3071(10) **STORAGE STANKS**	
Falsifies inventory or reconciliation records with willful intent to conceal existence of serious leak, or intentionally damages petroleum storage system.	3rd Degree Felony
SS. 381.0098(5) **BIOHAZARDOUS WASTE**	
Violates section or rules	2nd Degree Misdemeanor
SS. 403.413(5) **LITTER**	
Dumps litter in violation of subsection in amount exceeding 15 pounds or 27 cubic feet.	1st Degree Misdemeanor
Dumps litter in violation of subsection in amount exceeding 500 pounds or 100 cubic feet or any quantity for commercial purposes.	3rd Degree Felony

BROWARD COUNTY
CODE VIOLATIONS
PROHIBITED ACTS

Pollution Control Violations	Prohibitions
AIR POLLUTION	27-173
DREDGE AND FILL	27-333
EROSION PREVENTION	27-269
HAZARDOUS MATERIALS	27-367
INDUSTRIAL	27-358
WELLFIELD PROTECTION	27-379
STORM WATER SYSTEMS	27-403
NOISE POLLUTION	27-233
OPEN BURNING	27-283
SOLID WASTES	27-214
SPECIAL WASTES	27-220
STORAGE TANKS	27-303
TREE ABUSE	27-423
WATER POLLUTION	27-193

CONTACT NUMBERS

Broward County Sheriff's Office 305-321-5000

Broward County Department of
    Natural Resource Protection 305-519-1400

Broward County Fire Department (Emergency) 911
    Haz-Mat Station 32 305-985-1918

Broward County Code Enforcement 305-765-5030

Broward County Solid Waste Authority 305-978-1150

Broward County Property Appraisers Office 305-357-6857

Florida Health and Rehabilitative Services
    (H.R.S.) 305-467-4935

Florida Department of Environmental Protection (D.E.P.)
    State Warning Point 904-488-1320
    Permit Information 904-922-6104
    West Palm Beach Office 407-433-2650

Florida Game and Fresh Water
    Fish Commission 305-523-7711

Florida Marine Patrol 305-325-3346

OTHER NUMBERS

U.S. Coast Guard 305-927-1611

Community Policing
    (B.S.O. Code Enforcement) 305-321-4100

E.P.A./Atlanta 404-347-4885
E.P.A./Miami 305-536-3047

Index

Page numbers in *italics* denote figures and exhibits;
those followed by "t" denote tables.

505

About the Contributors

Harold Barnett, PhD, is a professor in the Department of Economics, University of Rhode Island. In addition to his work on environmental policy, he has written extensively on corporate and white-collar crime in the United States and Sweden. Author of *Toxic Debts and the Superfund Dilemma*, a study of the political and economic forces that have shaped U.S. hazardous waste policy, his current research is focused on exploring how we do and should define environmental crime.

Tim Carter, PhD, is an assistant professor of criminal justice at the University of Houston—Downtown. In addition to his extensive academic training, he has also worked in several positions in the field of criminal justice, including correctional officer, probation and parole officer, and U.S. Army Police Investigator. His most recent papers have focused on the topics of environmental regulations and organized crime, environmental regulatory failure, and government corruption.

Mary Clifford, PhD, is an assistant professor of criminal justice at St. Cloud State University and director of the Private Security Minor. She has been teaching environmental crime courses in criminal justice programs for over six years. She has authored articles and book chapters on environmental crime, comparative criminology, and private security.

Mark A. Cohen, PhD, is an associate professor of management in the Owen Graduate School of Management at Vanderbilt University and the Director of the Vanderbilt Center for Environmental Management Studies. He has worked as a staff economist for the U.S. Environmental Protection Agency and with both the Federal Trade Commission and the U.S. Sentencing Commission. He has authored many articles published in journals such as the *American Criminal Law Review, Journal of Criminal Law and Criminology, Journal of Environmental Economics and Management*, and the *Journal of Law and Economics*, and his book *Debating Corporate Crime* was recently published by Anderson Publishing Company.

Dion Dennis, PhD, is an assistant professor in the Department of Criminal Justice, History, and Political Science, Texas A&M International University. Dr. Dennis has published in peer-reviewed, abstracted, and indexed electronic and print journals. His research interests are eclectic and have most recently included work on AIDS, the "information oligarchy," and twentieth-century popular culture.

Sally M. Edwards, PhD, is an assistant professor in the Department of Political Science, University of Louisville. Dr. Edwards coauthored *Environmental Crime and Criminality: Practical and Theoretical Issues* and has received several "outstanding faculty of the year," adult education, and departmental teaching and service awards.

Terry D. Edwards, JD, is an associate professor in the Administration of Justice Program, University of Louisville. Coauthor of *Environmental Crime and Criminality: Practical and Theoretical Issues*, he is involved in the IACP's Environmental Crime Task Force, has participated in Southern Environmental Enforcement Network conferences, and has presented extensively on the subject of environmental crime at national criminal justice meetings.

Joel Epstein, JD, is a senior associate and consulting attorney with Education Development Center, Inc. in Newton, Massachusetts. The author of several reports on environmental crime for the National Institute of Justice, Mr. Epstein has presented his research findings at professional conferences across the United States. He also served as an invited Environmental Crime Expert at the 9th United Nations Congress on Crime and the Treatment of the Offender held in Cairo, Egypt.

Bill Hyatt, JD, is a professor of criminal justice at Western Carolina University. He was an attorney in the U.S. Department of Justice for 15 years, as the Chief of the Organized Crime Strike Force in Washington, D.C. In addition to having written various book chapters and articles published in criminal justice journals, he has been acknowledged for his classroom performance as the 1992 recipient of his university's outstanding teaching award.

Brian Lipsett is a doctoral candidate at Pennsylvania State University Administration of Justice Program and executive director of a private nonprofit organization. He was a research analyst for Citizen's Clearinghouse for Hazardous Wastes, served as editor of its newsletter, and published two books with that organization: *Drinking Water: An Endangered Resource* (with Stephen Lester) and *Medical Waste: Public Health vs. Private Profit.*

Ray Michalowski, PhD, is a professor of criminal justice at Northern Arizona University. His published works span a variety of topics including criminological theory, the practice of law and justice in Cuba, the political economy of crime and punishment, environmental crime, corporate crime, and computer crime. You can visit the syllabus for his course on environmental crime on line.

Richard G. Opper, MPA, JD, is a partner at McKenna and Cuneo and works in its environmental department. He served as the attorney general for the territory of Guam and was asked to join the U.S. State Department's delegation to the 1994 World Conservation Union in Buenos Aires and act as a private-sector advisor on international environmental law. Representing both private and public entities, he focuses on complicated environmental and natural resource litigation matters.

Donald J. Rebovich, PhD, is an associate professor at San Diego State University in the Department of Public Administration and Urban Studies and the Department of Criminal Justice Administration. He has worked as a private consultant in criminal justice management and authored the 1992 book *Dangerous Ground: The World of Hazardous Waste Crime* (Transaction Publishers). His research experience includes 10 years in the New Jersey State Division of Criminal Justice on the Drug Program Evaluation, and 6 years as research director at the American Prosecutors Research Institute. His research has been published in professional criminal justice journals and by the National Institute of Justice.

Mark Seis, PhD, is professor of sociology at Ft. Lewis College. He is coauthor of *A Primer in the Psychology of Crime* (1993) published by Harrow and Heston. Dr. Seis has published articles in various criminal justice and related journals and has presented on environmental philosophy. His current research interest is environment and society.

Mark J. Spalding, JD, MPIA, is an international environmental policy and law consultant and attorney in Del Mar, California. He has a national and international reputation as one of the foremost experts on NAFTA's environmental components and institutions, and actively participated in the negotiations and drafting of the Environmental Side Agreements to the NAFTA. As a guest scholar at the University of California—San Diego Center for U.S.-Mexican Studies, his research focuses on the implementation of these side agreements. He is the Chair of the California State Bar, Environmental Law Section's International Environmental Law Committee. Mark is an adjunct professor at the University of San Diego's School of Law and a guest lecturer at University of California—San Diego's Graduate School of International Relations and Pacific Studies. He is the Executive Editor of the *Journal of Environment and Development* at UCSD.

Gary Walker, PhD, is an associate professor of biology at Appalachian State University. His research interests include forest ecology, conservation genetics, and cliff-face ecology in the southern Appalachian Mountains. He worked as a collaborator with Chinese forest ecologists in mountain reserves in eastern and central China in 1989. In 1994, he served as a consultant for the Environmental Services Group for the Armenian Relief Fund in Khosrov Preserve of Armenia, and in 1995, he worked as a consultant for a private reserve in Costa Rica.

Nanci Koser Wilson, PhD, is an associate professor in criminology and women's studies at Indiana University of Pennsylvania. She has contributed chapters for several books and written articles for various journals in women's studies, criminal justice, and victimology. She is active in the American Society of Criminologists, the Academy of Criminal Justice Sciences, and several other academic organizations.